Numerical and Statistical Methods with SCILAB
for Science and Engineering

Numerical and Statistical Methods with SCILAB for Science and Engineering

Gilberto E. Urroz

greatunpublished.com
Title No. 304
2001

Numerical and Statistical Methods with SCILAB
for Science and Engineering

Numerical and Statistical Methods with
SCILAB
for Science and Engineering

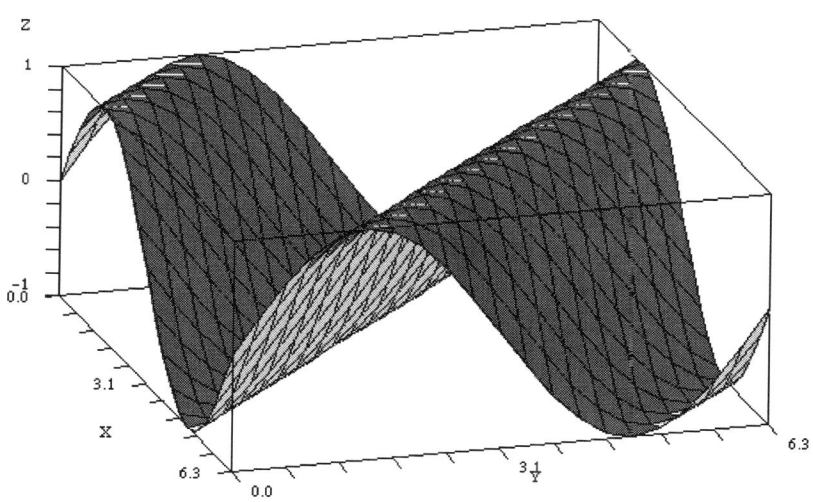

Volume I
Introduction• Programming• Graphics• Vectors• Matrices • Linear algebra• Solution to non-linear equations• Data fitting and interpolation• Ordinary Differential Equations

By

Gilberto E. Urroz, Ph.D., P.E.

© 2001 Gilberto E. Urroz
All rights reserved

Table of Contents

PREFACE XIV

1 INTRODUCTION TO SCILAB 1

GETTING STARTED WITH SCILAB 2
MENUS IN THE SCILAB WORKSHEET 4
SIMPLE OPERATIONS WITH SCILAB 5
SIMPLE SCILAB INPUT AND OUTPUT 7
SCILAB COMMAND HISTORY 7
SELECTIVE WORKSHEET OUTPUT 8
THE PFE SOFTWARE 11
CURRENT DIRECTORY / CREATING A WORK DIRECTORY 11
A PREVIEW OF SCILAB FUNCTIONS 12
EXERCISES 12

2 SCILAB PROGRAMMING, IO, AND STRINGS 14

SCILAB PROGRAMMING CONSTRUCTS 14
Comparison and Logical Operators 14
Loops in SCILAB 15
Conditional constructs in SCILAB 15
FUNCTIONS IN SCILAB 17
Global and local variables 18
Special function commands 18
Debugging 19
An example of a function - Calculation of Frobenius norm of a matrix. 20
INPUT/OUTPUT IN SCILAB 20
- *Saving and loading variables.* 21
- *Unformatted output to the screen.* 21
- *Unformatted output to a file.* 21
- *Working with files.* 22
- *Writing to files.* 22
- *Reading from the keyboard* 23
- *Reading from files* 24
MANIPULATING STRINGS IN SCILAB 24
String concatenation 24
String functions 25
Converting numerical values to strings 26
String catenation for a vector of strings 27
Converting strings to numbers 27
Executing SCILAB statements represented by strings 28
Producing labeled output in SCILAB 29
Using the function disp 30
The variable ans 30
EXERCISES 31

3 GRAPHICS WITH SCILAB 34

TWO-DIMENSIONAL GRAPHICS 34
The plot command: simple x-y plots 34
The SCILAB Graphic window 35
Creating a plot with error bars 36
Adding a simple grid to the plot 36
Other on-line commands for managing graphics 37
Changing global parameters of a plot 37
The plot2d command 37
Defining the grid 44
Other two-dimensional plot commands 48
Histograms 50
Creating sub windows with the command xsetech 51
Modifying plot properties 52
Storing a plot as a pixmap – an example of animation 53
The colormap 53
Density plots 55
Color map of a matrix 59
Plotting a function of the form $y = f(x)$ 60
Plotting a function of two variables using grayscale 60
Plotting a vector field in the plane 61
Direction field vector plot for an ordinary differential equation 62

THREE DIMENSIONAL GRAPHICS 62
Plotting data in 3D 63
Three-dimensional surface plot with color or gray scales 63
Plotting functions in 3D 68
Grayscale or colorscale three-dimensional plot for functions 69
Parametric curves in space 69
Contour plots in the plane and in space 69
Three dimensional histograms 70
Animation of three-dimensional graphs 72
Combination of two-dimensional and three-dimensional plots 73

OVERVIEW OF SCILAB GRAPHICS FUNCTIONS 73
EXERCISES 74
.... 77

4 VECTORS 79

- OPERATIONS WITH VECTORS 79
- VECTORS IN CARTESIAN COORDINATES 82
- VECTOR OPERATIONS IN SCILAB 83
- CALCULATING 2×2 AND 3×3 DETERMINANTS 87
- CROSS PRODUCT AS A DETERMINANT 89
- POLYNOMIALS AS VECTOR COMPONENTS 91
- APPLICATIONS OF VECTOR ALGEBRA USING SCILAB 94
  - *Example 1 - Position vector* 94
  - *Example 2 - Center of mass of a system of discrete particles* 95
  - *Example 3 - Resultant of forces* 97
  - *Example 4 – Equation of a plane in space* 101
  - *Example 5 – Moment of a force* 103
  - *Example 6 – Cartesian and polar representations of vectors in the x-y plane* 104
  - *Example 7 – Planar motion of a rigid body* 105
- EXERCISES 111

5 MATRICES AND LINEAR ALGEBRA ... 113

DEFINITIONS ... 114
Matrices as tensors and the Kronecker's delta function ... 115
MATRIX OPERATIONS ... 115
Einstein's summation convention for tensor algebra ... 117
Addition and subtraction ... 119
Multiplication by a scalar ... 124
Matrix multiplication ... 124
Inverse matrices ... 126
Verifying properties of inverse matrices ... 127
Creating identity matrices in SCILAB ... 129
The Vandermonde matrix ... 130
The Hilbert matrix ... 131
Magic squares ... 132
SYMMETRIC AND ANTI-SYMMETRIC MATRICES ... 133
MANIPULATING ELEMENTS OF VECTORS AND MATRICES ... 135
Determining the size of vectors and matrices ... 135
Extracting elements of vectors and matrices ... 136
Generating vectors and matrices containing random numbers ... 136
Extracting rows and columns with the colon operator ... 137
Programming constructs with matrix elements ... 137
Composing matrices by adding vectors ... 138
Composing a matrix by adding vectors one at a time ... 139
Replacing elements of vectors or matrices ... 140
Sum and product of matrix elements ... 142
MATRICES AND SOLUTION OF LINEAR EQUATION SYSTEMS ... 143
Solution to a system of linear equations using linsolve ... 143
Solution to an under-determined system of linear equations using the least-square method ... 148
Solution of a system of linear equations using the left-division operator ... 150
Solution using the inverse matrix ... 151
CHARACTERIZING A MATRIX ... 152
Matrix decomposition - a brief introduction ... 152
Singular value decomposition and rank of a matrix ... 156
Norms of a matrix or vector ... 159
Determinants, singular matrices, and conditions numbers ... 162
The determinant of a matrix ... 163
Properties of determinants ... 164
Cramer's rule for solving systems of linear equations ... 167
The function TRACE ... 168

- GAUSSIAN AND GAUSS-JORDAN ELIMINATION 169
  - *Gaussian elimination using a system of equations* 169
  - *Gaussian elimination using matrices* 170
  - *Gaussian elimination algorithm* 171
  - *Pivoting* 178
  - *Gaussian elimination with partial pivoting* 181
  - *Solving multiple set of equations with the same coefficient matrix* 182
  - *Calculating an inverse matrix using Gaussian elimination* 184
  - *Calculating the determinant with Gaussian elimination* 185
  - *Gauss-Jordan elimination* 188
  - *Calculating the inverse through Gauss-Jordan elimination* 189
- EIGENVALUES AND EIGENVECTORS 190
  - *Calculating the first eigenvector* 191
  - *Calculating eigenvectors with a user-defined function* 193
  - *Generating the characteristic equation for a matrix* 195
  - *Generalized eigenvalue problem* 196
- SPARSE MATRICES 199
  - *Creating sparse matrices* 199
  - *Getting information about a sparse matrix* 201
  - *Sparse matrix with unit entries* 202
  - *Sparse identity matrices* 202
  - *Sparse matrix with random entries* 203
  - *Sparse matrices with zero entries* 203
  - *Visualizing sparse matrices* 204
  - *Factorization of sparse matrices* 205
  - *Solution to system of linear equations involving sparse matrices* 207
  - *Solution to system of linear equations using the inverse of a sparse matrix* 208
- SOLUTION TO A SYSTEM OF LINEAR EQUATIONS WITH A TRI-DIAGONAL MATRIX OF COEFFICIENTS 209
  - *Solution to tri-diagonal systems of linear equations using sparse matrices* 211
- ITERATIVE SOLUTIONS TO SYSTEMS OF LINEAR EQUATIONS 213
  - *Jacobi iterative method* 214
- MATRIX APPLICATIONS 216
  - *Electric circuits* 216
  - *Structural mechanics* 218
  - *Dimensionless numbers in fluid mechanics* 221
  - *Stress at a point in a solid in equilibrium* 225
  - *Principal stresses at a point* 230
  - *Multiple linear fitting* 232
  - *Polynomial fitting* 234
  - *Selecting the best fitting* 239
- EXERCISES 241

6 SOLUTION TO NON-LINEAR EQUATIONS 248

INTRODUCTION TO COMPLEX NUMBERS 248
   Examples of basic complex number operations in SCILAB 249
   Complex number calculations 251
SOLUTION TO QUADRATIC AND CUBIC EQUATIONS 254
   Quadratic equations 254
   Cubic equations 256
THE MANY ROOTS OF A REAL OR COMPLEX NUMBER 258
   Principal values of a cubic root 260
POLYNOMIALS AND SOLUTIONS TO POLYNOMIAL EQUATIONS 261
SOLUTION OF A SINGLE NON-LINEAR EQUATION 263
   Interval-halving or bisection method 264
   The Newton-Raphson method 267
   The Secant Method 271
   Fixed-point iteration 274
SOLVING SYSTEMS OF NON-LINEAR EQUATIONS 276
   SCILAB function for Newton-Raphson method for a system of non-linear equations 278
   Illustrating the Newton-Raphson algorithm for a system of two non-linear equations 279
   Solution using function newtonm 281
   "Secant" method to solve systems of non-linear equations 281
   Illustrating the "secant" algorithm for a system of two non-linear equations 282
SOLVING NON-LINEAR EQUATIONS WITH THE *FSOLVE* FUNCTION 285
   Solving single non-linear equations with fsolve 286
   Solving a system of non-linear equations with fsolve 287
APPLICATIONS OF NON-LINEAR EQUATIONS 289
   Projectile motion 289
   Analysis of a simple three-bar mechanism 293
   Solving the Darcy-Weisbach and Coolebrook-White equations for pipeline flow 296
   Solving pipe flow with the Swamee-Jain equation 300
   Solving for discharge and head for a pipe-pump system 303
   Graphical solution to the pump-pipeline system 304
   A function to solve a pipe-pump system 305
EXERCISES 306

7 NUMERICAL INTEGRATION USING SCILAB 312

INTEGRALS CALCULATED THROUGH SUMMATION OF RECTANGLES 312
   Applications of function Sumint for calculating integrals 315
TRAPEZOID RULE FOR NUMERICAL INTEGRATION 319
   Trapezoid rule calculation using SCILAB function inttrap 321
   Additional examples for function inttrap 322
   Plotting the trapezoidal approximation 323
SIMPSON'S 1/3 RULE 324
SIMPSON'S 3/8 RULE 328
NEWTON-COTES FORMULAS 330
ROMBERG INTEGRATION 332
OTHER INTEGRATING FUNCTIONS PROVIDED BY SCILAB 334
   Integration by quadrature 334
   Integration by spline interpolation 335
   Calculation of definite integrals 335
INTEGRALS OF FUNCTIONS OF A COMPLEX VARIABLE 336
   Functions of a complex variable 336
   Derivative of a complex function 337
   Integrals of complex functions 339
APPLICATIONS OF INTEGRALS OF ONE VARIABLE 342
   Areas under curves 342
   Area between curves 343
   Center of mass of an area 344
   Volume of a solid of revolution 346
   Moment of inertia of an area 347
   Area enclosed by a curve in polar coordinates 351
   Fluid dynamics: calculating discharge in pipe for laminar flow 352
LINE INTEGRALS 353
   Evaluation of line integrals 354
   Line integrals independent of path 357
   Work of a force as a line integral 358
DOUBLE INTEGRAL IN A RECTANGULAR DOMAIN 359
   User-defined function for calculating double integrals 361
   Applications of function DoubleIntegral 362
   Double integrals transforming integration region into a rectangle 364
   Simpson's 1/9 rule for double integrals 366
APPLICATION OF DOUBLE INTEGRALS 371
   Area properties with double integrals 371
   Calculation of areal properties in Cartesian coordinates 373
   Change of variables in double integrals 375
   Area calculation using double integrals with polar coordinates 375
   Double integral applications in polar coordinates 376
A FINAL NOTE ON THE NUMERICAL CALCULATION OF DOUBLE INTEGRALS 379
EXERCISES 380

8 DATA FITTING AND INTERPOLATION 386

SIMPLE LINEAR INTERPOLATION 386
POLYNOMIALS IN SCILAB 388
   Defining a polynomial variable 388
   Identifying the polynomial variable, degree, and coefficients 389
   Some operations with polynomials 389
   Polynomial division 390
   Polynomial long division 390
   Polynomial fractions 391
   Matrices with polynomial elements 392
   Evaluating a polynomial or polynomial matrix 394
   Characteristic matrix and characteristic equations 394
   Polynomial functions applied to polynomial matrices 395
   Derivatives of polynomials 395
   Generating a polynomial given its coefficients 397
   Generating a polynomial given its roots 397
   Obtaining the roots of a polynomial 398
   Indefinite integrals for polynomials 398
NUMERICAL METHODS WITH POLYNOMIALS 399
   Polynomial deflation 399
   Direct fitting of a polynomial 401
   Lagrange polynomials 402
   SCILAB function mtlb_diff 405
   Difference Tables 407
   Newton Forward-Difference Polynomial 411
   Newton Backward-Difference Polynomial 413
   Stirling centered-difference polynomial 415
   Bessel centered-difference polynomial 418
   Least Squares Polynomial Approximation 420

Interpolation with splines 425

MULTI-VARIATE DATA FITTING 435
   Successive univariate polynomial interpolation 436
   Direct multivariate polynomial fitting 439
   Least-square multivariate polynomial fitting 440
EXERCISES 452

9 ORDINARY DIFFERENTIAL EQUATIONS 458

INTRODUCTION TO DIFFERENTIAL EQUATIONS 458
DEFINITIONS 459
    Ordinary and partial differential equations 459
    Order and degree of an equation 459
    Linear and non-linear equations 459
    Constant or variable coefficients 460
    Homogeneous and non-homogeneous equations 460
SOLUTIONS 461
    General and particular solutions 461
    Verifying solutions using SCILAB 462
    Initial conditions and boundary conditions 462
SYMBOLIC SOLUTIONS TO ORDINARY DIFFERENTIAL EQUATIONS 463
    Solution techniques for first-order, linear ODEs with constant coefficients 463
    Integrating factors for first-order, linear ODEs with variable coefficients 466
    Exact differential equations 466
    Solutions of homogeneous linear equations of any order with constant coefficients 467
    Obtaining the particular solution for a second-order, linear ODE with constant coefficients 469
APPLICATIONS OF ODES I : ANALYSIS OF DAMPED AND UNDAMPED FREE OSCILLATIONS 472
    Undamped motion 472
    Damped motion 473
    Creating phase portraits of oscillatory motion 477
APPLICATIONS OF ODES II : ANALYSIS OF DAMPED AND UNDAMPED FORCED OSCILLATIONS 479
APPLICATIONS OF ODES III: OSCILLATIONS IN ELECTRIC CIRCUITS 483
FINITE DIFFERENCES AND NUMERICAL SOLUTIONS 484
    Finite differences 485
    Finite difference formulas based on Taylor series expansions 487
    Forward, backward and centered finite difference approximations to the first derivative 487
    Forward, backward and centered finite difference approximations to the second derivative 488
    Solution of a first-order ODE using finite differences - Euler forward method 489
    Finite difference formulas using indexed variables 494
    Solution of a first-order ODE using finite differences - an implicit method 495
    Explicit versus implicit methods 498
    Outline of explicit solution for a second-order ODE 498
    Outline of the implicit solution for a second-order ODE 499
SYSTEMS OF ORDINARY DIFFERENTIAL EQUATIONS 500
    Systems of ordinary differential equations using matrices 500
    Systems of linear homogeneous ODEs - solution using matrices 501
    Systems of linear nonhomogeneous ODEs - solution using matrices 505
    Converting second-order linear equations to a system of equations 506

SCILAB FUNCTIONS FOR THE NUMERICAL SOLUTIONS OF INITIAL VALUE PROBLEMS (IVP) 509
APPLICATIONS OF NUMERICAL SOLUTIONS TO IVPS 522
   Systems of ODEs from mechanical systems 522
   System of ODEs from Electric Circuits 526
   Solving a fourth-order equation 530
   The Van der Pol equation 532
   The Rössler flow 535
SOLUTIONS TO BOUNDARY VALUE PROBLEMS (BVPS) 538
   The shooting method 538
   Outline of the implicit solution for a second-order BVP 542
   Function bvode for the solution of boundary value problems 542
   Function bvode applied to a third-order boundary value problem 547
   Application of bvode to a third-order problem with one interior fixed point 548
   Application of bvode to a fourth-order problem with two interior fixed points 550
BOUNDARY VALUE PROBLEMS WITH EIGENVALUES 552
   Numerical solution to a boundary value problem with eigenvalues 552
   A function for calculating eigenvalues for a boundary value problem 554
EXERCISES 556

APPENDIX A - REFERENCES A-1

APPENDIX B – INDEX A-4

PREFACE

The present book on numerical and statistical methods using SCILAB started as a collection of computer laboratory guides for the class *ENG 2200 - Numerical Methods in Engineering I* in the College of Engineering at Utah State University during the Fall Semester 1998. The original material was enhanced by additional documents produced for the class *CEE 6510 - Numerical and Statistical Methods in Civil Engineering*, taught during the Fall Semester 2000.

The book consists of two volumes. Volume I includes chapters 1 through 9, while Volume II includes chapters 10 through 18. A description of the chapters for both volumes follows.

The book is intended to teach the use of SCILAB as well as the development of solutions in mathematics and statistics for engineering and scientific applications. The first three chapters aimed for the beginning SCILAB user. Chapter 1 is a brief introduction to the software, Chapter 2 presents the basic programming constructs, and Chapter 3 presents the variety of two- and three-dimensional graphics that can be produced with SCILAB.

Chapter 4 deals with vectors as physical quantities utilizing SCILAB. The chapter includes operations with vectors, such as dot and cross products, and applications of vectors to specific problems in science and engineering. Chapter 5 covers matrix operations and their applications in linear algebra. Included in this chapter are matrix decomposition, eigenvalues and eigenvectors, and a number of matrix applications to problems from the physical sciences.

Chapter 6 is dedicated to the solution of single or systems of non-linear equations, using SCILAB's own functions as well as by the implementation of numerical methods. Chapter 7 presents a variety of methods for numerical integration of single and double integrals including user-defined and pre-defined SCILAB functions. Chapter 7 includes a variety of applications of integrals, including line and double integrals, in the physical sciences.

Chapter 8 introduces the concepts of SCILAB polynomials and discusses a number of method for polynomial interpolation and approximation. Chapter 8 also includes data fitting by functions other than polynomials. Chapter 9 discusses ordinary differential equations and presents a number of numerical solutions to initial and boundary value problems, using both SCILAB functions as well as user-defined functions. Both Chapters 8 and 9 are complemented with a number of examples and problems from different physical sciences.

Chapter 10 introduces orthogonal functions (e.g., Bessel, Lagrange, Laguerre, etc.), and applies orthogonal functions to problems of the quadrature of integrals and Fourier analysis. The latter subject includes not only Fourier series, but also Fourier transforms and their applications to discrete data. Applications of Fourier analysis to the solution of ordinary differential equations are also presented in Chapter 10. Chapter 11 presents analytical solutions to typical second-order partial differential equations through the use of Fourier series. Numerical solutions to partial differential equations are also presented in Chapter 11.

Chapter 12 is a brief presentation on optimization problems using SCILAB. This chapter presents the use of linear programming, quadratic programming, and general non-linear optimization.

Chapter 13 introduces the use of SCILAB to the statistical analysis of sample data, including measures of central tendency and spreading, frequency distributions, histograms, etc. This chapter also introduces basic concepts of probability to be used in subsequent chapters.

Chapter 14 discusses discrete and continuous random variables, probability distributions, moments, mean, variances, and standard deviations. It also discusses the analysis of bivariate probability distributions. Chapter 15 introduces a variety of discrete and continuous probability distributions (Binomial, Poisson, Beta, Gamma, etc.), and discusses the application of the normal distribution to the analysis of sample data. This Chapter also includes the principles of synthetic data generation and statistical simulation. Chapter 15 includes also a brief introduction to the SCILAB statistical toolbox *Stixbox*. Both Chapters 14 and 15 include a variety of problems on random variables and probability distributions.

Chapter 16 presents the techniques of statistical inference for the generation of confidence intervals and hypothesis testing on one and two means, one and two proportions, and one and two variances. The chapter includes also chi-square applications in RxC tables and goodness-of-fitting of probability data.

Chapter 17 presents the concepts and applications of simple linear regression, multiple linear regression, residual analysis, polynomial and other non-linear data fittings. Chapter 18 presents the analysis of simple time series and spatially-distributed data. Concepts such as de-trending, autocovariance, and removal of seasonal components are presented for time series analysis, while the concepts of contouring, semivariograms, and kriging are used in the analysis of geostatistical data. Chapter 17 ends with examples of generation of one- and two-dimensional signals using inverse Fourier transforms.

1 Introduction to SCILAB

This chapter is intended to get the user started using SCILAB through simple exercises in numerical calculations. The chapter starts by describing how to download and install SCILAB in a Windows environment. Installation of the software in other operating systems is very similar and is explained in detail in the SCILAB website.

What is SCILAB?
SCILAB is a numerical, programming and graphics environment available for free from the French *Government's "Institut Nationale de Recherche en Informatique et en Automatique - INRIA* (National Institute for Informatics and Automation Research)." It is similar in operation to MATLAB and other existing numerical/graphic environments, and it can be run using a variety of operating systems including UNIX, Windows, Linux, etc.

SCILAB is a self-contained package including a large number of intrinsic numeric, programming and graphics functions. Once unpacked and installed in your computer it will consume about 40MB of RAM. Make sure you have at least that much memory in your hard disk before downloading and installing SCILAB.

Where to find SCILAB
SCILAB is available for free from the SCILAB web page: http://www-rocq.inria.fr/SCILAB/
Once, you have accessed this web page, follow the procedure described below to download and install SCILAB in your computer.

How to download the software
Scroll down in the SCILAB main web page and click on the button labeled *Getting SCILAB*. Next, click on the highlighted text *ftp.inria.fr* in the new web page. This will take you to their ftp directory. From that directory you need to click on the file *SCILAB25.exe*. Then save it in the directory of your choice. This file has a size of 12,962 Kbytes, therefore, it may take a few minutes to download even through a high-speed internet connection.

How to install SCILAB
Run the program *SCILAB25.exe*, press *Install* and select the name of the target directory (i.e., where you want to store SCILAB and its associated files), and wait for the installation to finish. If you don't have enough space in your hard disk to store all SCILAB files the installation will be interrupted and an error message shown.

How to get documentation for SCILAB
To get documentation on SCILAB scroll down the SCILAB main web page and click on the *documentation* button. This will take you to their documentation page, showing the following options:

- *Introduction to SCILAB*
- *Communication Toolbox Documentation*
- *Lmitool: Linear Matrix Inequalities Optimization Toolbox Documentation*
- *Metanet User's Guide and Tutorial*

■ *Scicos: a Dynamic System Builder and Simulator*
■ *SCILAB's Internals Documentation*

The documentation is available in *html* format, which you can access by clicking in any of the options shown above. If you want to have your own copy of the documentation *PostScript* or *PDF* format, press the appropriate option in the web page.

Things that SCILAB lets you do
SCILAB can be used for simple arithmetic operations as well as for some algebraic operations, to generate graphics, to program functions, and to solve linear algebra problems and ordinary differential equations, among other things.

Getting started with SCILAB

■ To *get started*, launch the SCILAB application.

■ To *load a value into a variable* use an assignment statement (one that includes the equal sign), e.g., a = 3.2. Try the following exercises for simple arithmetic operations:
a = 3.2 <return>
b = 6.4 <return>
a+b <return>
a-b <return>
a*b <return>
a/b <return>
a^b <return>
who <return>
The last command will return a list of the active variables in your worksheet. Many of them are system variables that cannot be modified by the user.

■ SCILAB has a number of *special constants*, such as *%i, %pi,* and *%e*, corresponding to the unit imaginary number, π = ratio of circumference to diameter, and e = the base of the natural logarithms, respectively. The value *%eps* is another special constant corresponding to the maximum value for which *1 + %eps = 1.* Other important constants are *%inf* = infinity, and *%nan* = not-a-number. Boolean (i.e., logical) constants are *%t* = true and *%f* = false.

Try the following exercises to see what values are returned by SCILAB:
%e <return>
%i <return>
%pi <return>
%eps <return>
%inf <return>
%nan <return>
%t <return>
%f <return>

■ *Comments* in SCILAB are represented by the double forward slash (//). Anything in front of // is taken as a comment. For example, enter:

```
a = 4.5 // redefining a <return>
```
SCILAB will return the value of 4.5 for a and ignore the comment after the //

■ *Scalars*: real, logical, string, polynomial, rational, and basically any object that is not between brackets in SCILAB is referred to as a scalar. Examples are:
```
a = 1 // real constant <return>
2>1 // Boolean constant (i.e., logical) <return>
'my name' // character string or constant <return>
r = poly(1.,'x')   // polynomial with variable 'x' and root at 1.0 <return>
q = y/r   // rational expression <return>
```

■ *Using the "Introduction to SCILAB" demo*: SCILAB is provided with a number of demos to show the software abilities. To access the demos select the *File* menu, then the *Demos* option. This will provide a dialogue window (*SCILAB Choose*) with a list of subjects, such as *Introduction to SCILAB*, *Graphics*, etc. Select the *Introduction to SCILAB*, and press OK. A file with SCILAB commands is loaded in memory. To see each line press <return>. The lines are shown and executed (if executable). Comments have been added to each line to explain the operation shown. (The entire demo session is listed in pages 118 to 137 of the documentation file *Introduction to SCILAB*.) Keep pressing the <return> key to observe a good summary of SCILAB abilities. In particular, pay special attention to item 2 (MATRICES) since SCILAB is a matrix-based system. Also of interest are the items labeled OPERATIONS and SOME NUMERICAL PRIMITIVES. (The term *primitives* is used to refer to simple numerical operations pre-programmed in SCILAB or any other numerical environment).

■ *Using other demos*: To see any of the other demos provided with SCILAB select the option *Demos* from the *File* menu, then select the Demo subject you want (e.g. *Graphics: Introduction*), and select a particular demo (e.g., *plot2d3* in *Graphics: Introduction*). Notice that, when using graphics in SCILAB, the program generates a window called *SCILABGraphic0*.

■ *Getting help*: In the *Help* menu there are three options that you can use to get help from SCILAB:

- *Help Dialogue:* provides a list of help items classified by chapters. There will be two windows available using this option, the lower window shows the chapter titles while the upper window shows the subjects in the chapter currently selected. Select the item you want to display and press the Show button located to the left side of the help window.
- *Topic:* enter a topic you want help with in the window shown when using this option and press the OK button. If no help is available you will get a message indicating so in the main SCILAB window. If help is available, SCILAB will show you the corresponding instructions. For example, use this option and request information on the keyword *inv*. It will give you information on the inverse operation for matrices.
- *Apropos:* enter a keyword related to the topic that you are looking for (e.g., *inverse*) and press the OK button. You will see a window with topics including the keyword you selected. Scroll through the list and find that topic closer to your interest (e.g., *inv - matrix inverse*), and press OK to get information on that particular topic.

Menus in the SCILAB worksheet

■ *The "Functions" menu*: There are three options available in this menu, these are:
- *Define User Function:* allows the user to define a function to be used in the current SCILAB worksheet. For example, suppose that you want to define the function *llama(x,y) = x + y*. Select this option and enter the following (your reply is shown in italics): (1) Name of output variable? *z* [OK]; (2) Name for function? *llama* [OK]; (3) Variable/s? *x,y* [OK]; (4) Code? *'z = x+y'* [OK]. SCILAB's response is: → deff('[z]=llama(x,y)',['z = x+y']). (To see more information on the *deff* command use the help options as shown above.)
- *Show Commands*: provides you with a list of SCILAB commands (e.g. *quit, exit*). To find more information about any of the commands use the Help menu as described above, or simply type *help* followed by the command name, e.g., *help exit*. You can see a list of commands also by typing the SCILAB command *what*.
- *Show Variables*: shows variables currently in use. It is the same as typing *who* in the SCILAB prompt.

■ *Pause mode*: when entering Pause mode, SCILAB creates a new (numbered) prompt. In this mode you can enter SCILAB commands without affecting the main line of calculation (represented by the main SCILAB prompt →). To get into the pause mode you can type *pause* at the main prompt or click on the *Pause* option in the upper menu bar of the main SCILAB window. (The option *Interupt* [sic] in the upper menu bar also allows you to enter into pause mode, however, it will interrupt any operation currently being executed by SCILAB).. You can have several levels of pause, one for every time you enter *pause* command. To leave the current pause level and move the upper one type *return*. To move up two levels use the command *quit*. (Note, when used in the main SCILAB prompt, *quit* will terminate your SCILAB session). For more information on the pause mode use the help feature as described above, or simple type *help pause*.

■ *Other options in the upper menu bar*: the options *Restart*, *Resume*, *Abort* and *Interupt* [sic] are available to recover initial SCILAB environment, resume, and abort or interrupt any operation, respectively. Help is available on the *Resume* and *Abort* options.

■ *The "File" menu*: The following options are available in the *File* menu:
- *Getf*: use it to load a function. (Type *help getf* for additional information).
- *Exec*: to execute a script file. (Type *help exec* for additional information).
- *Save*: to save variables (Type *help save* for additional information).
- *Load*: to load a saved variable (Type *help load* for additional information).
- *Change Directory*: self-explanatory.
- *Get Current Directory*: self-explanatory.
- *Demos*: see above.
- *History*: allows you to repeat or modify the most recent operations in SCILAB.
- *Run bash command*: Related to UNIX bash shell.
- *Exit*: ends current SCILAB session.

Simple operations with SCILAB

■ *Simple scalar operations*: the following exercises will get you acquainted with a few of SCILAB's abilities for operating with scalar values.
```
a = 2 <return>
b = 3 <return>
Save a <return>
clear a <return>
a <return>
b <return>
load a <return>
a <return>
exp(a) + exp(b) <return>
sin(a*%pi/b) <return>
```
(*Note*: the clear command is used to eliminate variables, as in *clear a*, as shown above. By itself, clear deletes all variables recently defined. Therefore, be very careful when using this command).

■ *Vectors*:
- To enter vectors use the square brackets and separate the elements with commas or blanks for a row vector, e.g.: v = [-1. , 2., %pi].
- The transpose of a vector (or matrix) is expressed using the apostrophe, for example, type: v'
- To enter a column vector, use any of the following procedures: w = [3; -2; 5] <return> or
  r = [6 <return>
  -2 <return>
  10] <return>
- You can create a row vector by indicating a starting value, an increment (or decrement), and an ending value, all separated by the colon (:) operator as follows

    vector_name = starting_value : increment : ending value

  for example: x = -10.0 : 0.5 : 10.0 <return>
- If you prefer to store it as a column vector, try the following: `xt = x'` <return>
- Let's apply a function to the vector x, try `y = sin(x*%pi/10)` <return>
- We can plot the vectors *x,y* using: `plot(x,y,'x','y','first plot')` <return>
- [Type `help plot` <return> for more information]
- Let's restart SCILAB and operate with other vectors: Press the *Restart* option in the upper bar menu.
- Enter the row vectors, u = [-1. 2. 3.] and v = [6. -10. 0.]
- Perform the following operations:
  u + v <return>
  u - v <return>
  u*v <return>
  u*v' <return>
  u'*v <return>

© 2001 - Gilberto E. Urroz
All rights reserved

- To extract elements of the vectors, try:
  u(3) <return>
  u(2) + v(1) <return>
- Try the following exercise: a = 1; b = 2; c = 3; r = [a, b, c] <return>
- To suppress SCILAB responses use the semi-colon after entering a command. For example, try: s = [-1., 2.]; <return>
- Vectors can also contain characters as their elements, e.g., letters = ['a', 'b', 'c', 'd'] <return>

Note: Expressions such as 'a', 'b', etc., are referred to as strings. Therefore, only those string operations such as *concatenation*, *part*, etc. are allowed for vectors with character elements. SCILAB strings and string operations are presented in a subsequent chapter.

Matrices:
- Here are several ways to enter matrices: (press Restart)
  A = [1. 2. 3.; 4. 5. 6.; 1. -1. 0.] <return>
  B = [1. 1. 1. <return>
  2. 3. -1. <return>
  5. 7. -2.] <return>
  u = [1. 3. -5.]; v = [4. 2. 3.]; w = [-1. 0. 1.]; <return>
  C = [u; v; w] <return>
  r = [u, v, w] <return>
  D = [u' v' w'] <return>
- *Matrix operations*: try the following operations:
  A + B <return>
  C - D <return>
  A*B <return>
  B*A <return>
  C*u <return>
  D*v' <return>
  rank (A) <return>
  inv(A) <return>
  cond(B) <return>
  det(C) <return>
  A*inv(A) <return>
  inv(B)*B <return>
  spec(A) <return> (calculates eigenvalues)
  trace(C) <return>
  (Note: to find out more about any of the commands listed here type *help* followed by the command name, e.g., *help spec*).

Solution of linear systems: two possibilities are:
(Press *Restart*)
A = [1. 3. 2.; 2. 1. -1.; 5. 2. 1.]; b = [2; 3; 4]; <return>
xa = inv(A)*b <return>
xb = linsolve(A,b) <return>
(Note: type *help linsolve* to learn more about this command).

Simple SCILAB Input and Output

■ _Output_: To get a list of your current session use the function _diary_. The format is as follows: _diary (output_filename)_, where the filename is written within quotes. To end collecting output in the current diary output file use _diary(0)_. For example, try the following session:

(Press _Restart_)
```
diary ('session1.txt') <return>
A = [1. 2. 3.; 2. 3. 1.; 3. 2. 1.];b=[5; 4; -1.];<return>
A <return>
b <return>
x = linsolve(A,b) <return>
diary(0) <return>
```

Next, use NOTEPAD, or other text editor, to open the file _session1.txt_ to see the contents of the file. The default directory for storing a _diary_ file is the _bin_ subdirectory within the SCILAB directory.

Note: The SCILAB worksheet does not allow cutting and pasting. Therefore, the use of the _diary_ function with a filename is the only way to copy SCILAB output into a text file.

■ _Command Input_: you can read SCILAB commands from a script file, which is basically a text file listing all the commands you want to use. As an example, create the following text file in the _bin_ subdirectory of the SCILAB directory using NOTEPAD, and call it _session2.txt_:

```
//-----------------------------------------------------------------------
clear
A = [1. 2. -3.           // entering
     3. 4. 5.            // elements of
     7. 8. 9.]           // matrix A
b = [1.; 2.; 3.]         // enter vector b
xa = inv(A)*b            // calculate x using matrix inverse
xb = linsolve(A,b)       // calculate x using SCILAB's own linsolve function
//-----------------------------------------------------------------------
```

Then, press _Restart_ in SCILAB, and type: _exec('session2.txt')_
You will see SCILAB execute all the commands in your file, stopping at the end of the file.

SCILAB command history

All commands entered in a given SCILAB session get stored into a SCILAB command history buffer. The commands are thus accessible for re-use or edition. All the command history functions are available through the option _History_ under the _File_ menu in the SCILAB worksheet. The most useful commands are _cntl-P_ and _cntl-N_, which lets you access the previous command or the next command, respectively, in the command history buffer. Once a command is recalled from the command history buffer it can be edited by using the backspace or delete keys, or by inserting new characters by simply typing at the proper location.

For example, try the following SCILAB session:

1 - Press the *Restart* option in the menu bar to clear the SCILAB environment.
2 - Enter the following commands (you don't need to enter the comments):

```
-->x = [0:%pi/20:2*%pi];
```

```
-->y = sin(x) + sin(2*x);
```

3 - Use *cntl-P* and edit the previous command (`y = sin(x) + sin(2*x);`) to read:

```
-->z = sin(x) + cos(x);
```

4 - Use *cntl-P* once more to edit the previous command (`z = sin(x) + cos(x);`) to read:

```
-->p = cos(x) + cos(2*x);
```

5 - So far you have created vectors *x*, *y*, *z*, and *p*. Next, we use the function *xset* with the option *'window'*, and the function *plot* to produce a plot of *y*-vs.-*x*:

```
-->xset('window',0); plot(x,y)
```

6 - Use *cntl-P* to edit the previous command to read:

```
-->xset('window',1); plot(x,z)
```

7 - Continue using *cntl-P* to edit the last commands and produce the following plots:

```
-->xset('window',2); plot(x,p)
```
```
-->xset('window',3); plot(y,z)
```
```
-->xset('window',4); plot(y,p)
```
```
-->xset('window',5); plot(z,p)
```

Selective worksheet output

Suppose you have been working on a lengthy SCILAB session whose command history buffer contains some results that produced errors as well as some intermediary results that are not of interest to you for output. For your output, you can select only those commands relevant to your final results by using *Cntl-P* and *Cntl-N*. Try the following SCILAB session that explores some basic vector operations using vectors x and y:

1 - Press the *Restart* option in the menu bar.
2 - Enter the following SCILAB commands:

```
-->x = [1, 2, 5, -4]
```

```
 x  =

!  1.    2.    5.   - 4. !

-->y = [0, 2, 3,-5]
 y  =

!  0.    2.    3.   - 5. !

-->x*y
     !--error    10
inconsistent multiplication


-->x.*y
 ans  =

!  0.    4.    15.    20. !

-->sum(ans)
 ans  =

     39.

-->sum(x.*y)
 ans  =

     39.

-->x*y'
 ans  =

     39.

-->x'*y
 ans  =

!  0.    2.      3.   - 5.  !
!  0.    4.      6.   - 10. !
!  0.    10.    15.   - 25. !
!  0.  - 8.   - 12.     20. !

-->y'*x
 ans  =

!   0.     0.      0.     0.  !
!   2.     4.     10.   - 8.  !
!   3.     6.     15.   - 12. !
! - 5.  - 10.   - 25.    20.  !

-->x*y' + y'*x
 ans  =

!  39.    39.    39.    39. !
!  41.    43.    49.    31. !
!  42.    45.    54.    27. !
!  34.    29.    14.    59. !

-->b = x*y' + y'*x
```

```
 b  =

!   39.    39.    39.    39.  !
!   41.    43.    49.    31.  !
!   42.    45.    54.    27.  !
!   34.    29.    14.    59.  !
```

Note: These commands and their corresponding results represent an exploratory session for vector operations.

3 - Suppose that you are only interested in the commands defining vectors x and y, in the operations that produce the dot product of the vectors (i.e., sum(x.*y) and x*y'), and in the very last command (b = x*y' + y'*x). Using the *diary* command create the file *c:\myVectors.txt* and collect only the commands of interest out of the command history buffer by using *cntl-P* and *cntl-N* as needed.   The resulting SCILAB session should look like this:

```
--> diary('c:\myVectors')

-->x = [1, 2, 5, -4]
 x  =

!   1.    2.    5.   - 4. !

-->y = [0, 2, 3,-5]
 y  =

!   0.    2.    3.   - 5. !

-->sum(x.*y)
 ans  =

    39.

-->x*y'
 ans  =

    39.

-->b = x*y' + y'*x
 b  =

!   39.    39.    39.    39.  !
!   41.    43.    49.    31.  !
!   42.    45.    54.    27.  !
!   34.    29.    14.    59.  !

-->diary(0)
```

The session, except for the very first command () is stored in file *\myVectors.txt*. This file can be edited or printed from a text editor such as NOTEPAD, or my favorite, PFE (*Programmer's File Editor*) available for free from:

http://www.lancs.ac.uk/people/cpaap/pfe

The PFE software

> PFE is a text editor designed for text-based programming in languages such as FORTRAN, JAVA, C++, etc. PFE allows the user direct access to DOS windows for compilation and testing of programs, runs DOS commands from the PFE interface, allows recording and playing of Macro commands, and permits easy navigation of files by allowing line numbering for easy debugging of programs.
>
> PFE can be used in combination with SCILAB to type scripts and function files or to edit *diary* files produced from within SCILAB.

Current directory / creating a work directory

SCILAB uses a current directory where files are saved by default, for example when using the function *diary*. To see the current directory use:

```
-->pwd
```

Under a Windows operating system, the default current directory is typically \

The command *pwd* stands for *print working directory*.

I recommend that you create a sub-directory, or folder, called *work* and locate it under the SCILAB main directory. For example, under a Windows operating system, the SCILAB main directory will typically be

c:\Program Files\SCILAB2.5

Thus, your *work* directory would correspond to:

c:\Program Files\SCILAB2.5\work

At the beginning of a SCILAB session, you can change the current directory to the *work* directory by using the function *chdir*:

```
--> chdir('c:\Program Files\SCILAB2.5\work')
```

You can use your *work* directory to store scripts and functions that you create. For example, if you create a script called *script1* in the *work* directory, once you change the current directory to the work directory, you can simply use:

```
-->exec('script1')
```

to run your script.

If you type a function called *function1* in the *work* directory, with the work directory selected as the current directory, you can load the function by simply using:

```
-->getf('function1')
```

Scripts and function files can be created using NOTEPAD, PDE, or any other text editor.

A preview of SCILAB functions

Here are some *useful functions* in SCILAB that we will explore in more details in subsequent chapters:
- Elementary functions: `sum, prod, sqrt, diag, cos, max, round, sign, fft`
- Sorting: `sort, sortup, gsort, find`
- Specific matrices: `zeros, eye, ones, matrix, empty`
- Linear algebra: `det, inv, qr, svd, bdiag, spec, schur, trace`
- Polynomials: `poly, roots, coeff, horner, clean, freq`
- Random numbers: `rand`
- Programming: `function, deff, argn, for, if, end, while, select, warning, error, break, return`
- Comparison symbols: `==, >=, >, <=, <, =, &` (and), `|` (or)
- Execution of a file: `exec`
- Debugging: `pause, return, abort`
- Spline functions, interpolation: `splin, interp, interpln`
- Character strings: `string, part, evstr, execstr`
- Graphics: `plot, xset, driver, plot2d, xgrid, locate, plot3d, Graphics`
- Ordinary differential equation solvers: `ode, dassl, dassrt, odedc`

To find out more about these functions use the help command. For example, try:

```
-->help roots
```

```
-->help eye
```

```
-->help trace
```

Exercises

Determine the result of the following calculations using SCILAB if $a = 2.3$, $b = -2.3$, $c = \pi/2$, $x = 2/\pi$, and $y = \sqrt{3}$:

[1]. $(a^2 + bc + x)$
[2]. $sin(c) + y/c$
[3]. $(a+c)/(x+y)$
[4]. $1/(cos(c) + ln(x))$
[5]. $(a+c)^3/b$

Check if the following Boolean statements are true or false based on the values of b, c, x, and y given above.

[6]. $a > c$
[7]. $a = b$
[8]. $(2a+b)/x^2 < 1$
[9]. $x + 2ab + b^2 \leq 23$
[10]. $2ac = 2cb$

[11]. Use SCILAB's help facility to find out information about function *deff* and use it to define a function $y = f(x) = x^2 + 1$.

Using the vectors $u = [3, 2, -1]$, and $v = [4, -6, 2]$, calculate the following operations:

[12]. $w = u+v$
[13]. $r = u./v$
[14]. $z = v*u$
[15]. $t = v.*u$

Using the matrices A, B, and C, shown below, perform the following operations:

$$A = \begin{bmatrix} 5 & 5 & -2 \\ 1 & -2 & 0 \\ 4 & -1 & -2 \end{bmatrix}, \quad B = \begin{bmatrix} -5 & 4 & -\pi \\ -1 & -1 & 10 \\ 0 & 4 & -2 \end{bmatrix}, \quad C = \begin{bmatrix} 2 & 5 \\ 1 & -3 \\ 4 & 2 \end{bmatrix}$$

[16]. $A + B$
[17]. $A \cdot B$
[18]. $B \cdot A$
[19]. $B \cdot C$
[20]. $A \cdot B \cdot C$

2 SCILAB Programming, IO, and strings

Programming is the basic skill for implementing numerical methods. In this chapter we describe the fundamental programming constructs used in SCILAB and present examples of their applications to some elementary numerical methods. The second part of this chapter is dedicated at exploring input/output functions provided by SCILAB including operations with files. Finally, manipulation of strings in SCILAB is presented.

SCILAB programming constructs

SCILAB provides the user with a number of programming constructs very similar to those available in FORTRAN and other high-level languages. We present some of the constructs below:

Comparison and Logical Operators

SCILAB comparison operators are

==	equal to
<	less than
>	greater than
<=	less than or equal to
>=	greater than or equal to
<> or ~=	not equal to

SCILAB logical operators are

&	and
|	or
~	not

As an example, try the following commands in SCILAB:
3 <> 2   <enter>
3 == 3   <enter>
(2>1)&(3>1) <enter>
(2>1)&(3>5) <enter>
(2<1)&(3>1) <enter>
(2<1)&(3>5) <enter>
(2>1) | (3>1) <enter>
(2>1) | (3>5) <enter>
(2<1) | (3>1) <enter>
(2<1) | (3>5) <enter>
~(2<1) <enter>
~(2>1) <enter>
~(2>1) | (3>5) <enter>

Loops in SCILAB

SCILAB includes *For* and *While* loops. The *For* loop is similar to the DO loop in FORTRAN or the FOR..NEXT loop in Visual Basic. The basic construct for the *For loop* is:

```
for index = starting_value : increment : end_value, ...statements..., end
for index = starting_value : end_value, ...statements..., end
```

If no increment is included it is supposed to be equal to 1.
For example, enter the following For loops in SCILAB:

```
r = 1; for k = 1:0.5:4, r = r+k, end <enter>
xs = -1.0; dx = 0.25; n = 10; for j = 1:n, x = xs + (j-1)*dx, end <enter>
for m = 1:10, a(m) = m^2, end <enter>
a <enter>
```

The basic construct for the <u>While loop</u> is:

```
while condition, ...statements..., end
```

For example, try the following *while* loop:

```
s = 100; while s>50, disp(s^2), s = s - 5, end <enter>
```

For and *while* loops can be terminated with the command *break*, for example, try the following:

```
for j = 1:10, disp(j), if j>5 then break, end, end <enter>
```

Conditional constructs in SCILAB

In the example above we used an *if... then...end* construct. There are two type of conditional constructs in SCILAB, one is the *if-then-else-end* construct (as in the example above) and the second one is *the select-case* conditional construct. Different forms of the *if-then-else* construct are:

if *condition* then *statement*, end
if *condition* then *statement*, else *statement*, end
if *condition* then *statement*, elseif *condition* then *statement*, else *statement*, end

Try the following examples:

x = 10; y = 5; if x> 5 then disp(y), end <enter>
x = 3 ; y = 5; if x>5 then disp(y), else disp(x), end <enter>
x = 3; y = 5; z = 4; if x>5 then disp(x), elseif x>6 then disp(y), else disp(z), end <enter>

The general form of the *select-case* construct is:

select *variable*, case *n1*, *statement*, case *n2*, *statement*, ..., end

Try the following examples:

```
x = -1; select x, case 1, y = x+5, case -1, y = sqrt(x), end <enter>
r = 7; select r, case 1, disp( r), case 2, disp(r^2), case 7, disp(r^3), end <enter>
```

All these constructs can be programmed in files following a structure similar to FORTRAN or Visual Basic programs, and then executed from within SCILAB. Such files are referred to as *scripts*. For example, type the following SCILAB script into a file called *program1.txt*:

```
clear      //erase all variables
x = [10. -1. 3. 5. -7. 4. 2.];
suma = 0;
[n,m] = size(x);
for j = 1:m
      suma = suma + x(j);
end
xbar = suma/m;
xbar
```

Save it into the bin subdirectory. Within SCILAB type:

```
exec('program1.txt') <enter>
```

Note that since x is a row vector (actually a matrix with $n = 1$ row and $m = 7$ columns), the *size* function provides you with an array of two values in the statement `[n,m] = size(x)`. Then, m is used in the *for* loop and in the calculation of *xbar*.

As an alternative to using a row (or column) vector is the use of lists. A list is a collection of data objects not necessarily of the same type. In the following example we limit ourselves to using lists of numbers. To define a list we use the list command, for example, try:

```
y = list(0., 1., 2., 3., 4., 6.) <enter>
size(y) <enter>
```

In this case, the size of the list, unlike that of a vector or matrix, is provided as a single number. A modified version of the script in *program1.txt* is shown below. Type this file into *program2.txt* and save it in the *bin* sub-directory under the SCILAB directory:

```
//Same as program1.txt, but using lists
clear      //erase all variables
x = list(10., -1., 3., 5., -7., 4., 2.);
suma = 0;
n = size(x);
for j = 1:n
      suma = suma + x(j);
end
xbar = suma/n;
n
xbar
```

To run the script, from within SCILAB type:

```
exec('program2.txt')<enter>
```

Functions in SCILAB

Functions are procedures that may take input arguments and return zero, one or more values. Functions are defined either *on line*, using the *deff* command, or as a *separate file* that needs to be loaded using the *getf* command. Following some examples of *on-line* functions are presented:

deff('[z]=Euler(r,theta)','z=r*exp(%i*theta)') <enter>
Euler(1.0,-%pi/2) <enter>

deff('[r,theta]=cartpol(x,y)','r=sqrt(x^2+y^2)'; 'theta=atan(y,x)']) <enter>
[radius,angle] = cartpol(3., 4.) <enter>

These functions could have been defined by using the *Define User Function...* option in SCILAB's *Functions* menu. For example, select this option and enter the following (your reply is shown in italics):

   (1) Name of output variable? *x,y* [OK];
   (2) Name for function? *polcart* [OK];
   (3) Variable/s? *r, theta* [OK];
   (4) Code? *['x=r*cos(theta)','y=r*sin(theta)']* [OK].

SCILAB's response is:

→ `deff('[x,y]=polcart(r,theta)',['x=r*cos(theta)';'y=r*sin(theta)]).`

Try the following application:

[h,v] = polcart(10.0,%pi/6) <enter>
polcart(100.0,%pi/3) <enter>

The last command will give you only the result for y since the function call was not assigned to an array as in the first case.

Functions defined in files must start with the command

```
Function [y1,...,yn] = fname(x1,...,xm)
```

Where *fname* is the function name, [y1,...,yn] is an array of output values, and x1,...,xm are the input values. Type in the following function into a file called sphecart.txt using a text editor (e.g., NOTEPAD, or PDE):

```
function [x,y,z] = sphecart(r,theta,rho)
//conversion from spherical to Cartesian coordinates
x = r*cos(rho)*cos(theta)
y = r*cos(rho)*sin(theta)
z = r*sin(rho)
```

In SCILAB load the function using:

getf('sphercart.txt') <enter>
[x1,y1,z1]=sphercart(10.0, %pi/3, %pi/6) <enter>

Notice that SCILAB on-line functions are similar to FORTRAN function declarations, while SCILAB functions defined in files are similar to FORTRAN or Visual Basic function sub-programs or subroutines. The main difference is that FORTRAN and Visual Basic functions can only return one value, while SCILAB functions can return zero, one or more values.

Global and local variables

A global variable is one define in the main SCILAB environment, while a local variable is one defined within a function. If a variable in a function is not defined, or is not among the input parameters, then it takes the value of a variable of the same name that exist in the calling environment. This variable remains local in the sense that modifying it within the function does not alter its value in the calling environment unless the command *resume* is used.
For example, using the function *sphercart*, try the following:

```
clear
getf('sphercart.txt') <enter>
theta = %pi/3 <enter>
rho = %pi/6 <enter>
[x,y,z] = sphercart(10.0,theta)<enter>
```

Since *rho* is defined in the calling environment, even though that value is missing in the calling sequence to the function *sphercart*, it takes the value of *rho* in the calling environment.

Note that it is not possible to call a function if one of the parameters in the calling sequence is not defined. Try the following:

clear
getf('sphercart.txt') <enter>
theta = %pi/3 <enter>
[x,y,z]=sphercart(10.0,%pi/3,rho) <enter>

Because *rho* is not defined in this case, the function can not be evaluated.

Special function commands

These are SCILAB command used almost exclusively in functions:

`argn`: returns the number of input and output arguments of the function
`error`: suspends a function's operation, prints an error message, and returns to previous environment level if an error is detected
`warning`: prints a warning message
`pause`: temporarily suspends the operation of a function
`break`: forces the end of a loop
`return` or `resume`: use to return to the calling environment and to pass local variables from the function environment to the calling environment.

For additional information use the help feature in SCILAB with these functions. The following example illustrate the use of some of these special function commands. Enter the function in a file called func1.txt, and save it in the bin sub-directory of SCILAB:

```
function [z] = func1(x,y)
[out,in]=argn(0)
if x == 0 then
      error('division by zero');
end,
slope = y/x;
pause,
z = sqrt(slope);
s = resume(slope);
```

Then, within SCILAB enter the following:

clear <enter>
getf('func1.txt') <enter>
z = func1(0,1) <enter>
z = func1(2,1) <enter>

In the second call to *func1*, the -1-> prompt indicates a *pause* mode. The function operation is temporarily suspended. The user can, at this point, examine values calculated inside the function, plot data, or perform any SCILAB operation. Control is returned to the function by typing the command *return* <enter> (*resume* can also be used here). Operation of the function can be stopped by using *quit* or *abort*. When *return* (or *resume*) is used, the function calculates and reports the value of *z*. Also available in the environment is the local variable *s* which is passed to the global environment by the resume command within the function. Type <enter> to see the value of *s*.

Debugging

The simplest way to debug a SCILAB function is to use *pause* command in the function. When this command is encountered the function stops and the prompt -> is shown. This indicates a different "level" of calculation that can be used to recall variable values including global variables from the calling environment, experiment with operations, produce a graph if needed, etc. Using a second pause will produce a new level characterized by the prompt ->, and so on. The function resumes execution by typing the command *return* or *resume*, at which point the variables used at the higher level prompts are cleared. Execution of the function can be interrupted with the command *abort*.

An additional feature for debugging that is available in SCILAB is the insertion of breakpoints in the function. These are pre-identified points in the function to which you can access during the function execution to check the values of the variables or perform other operations. Check the commands *setbpt*, *delbpt*, and *disbpt*.

You can also trap errors during the function execution by using the commands *errclear* and *errcatch*. Check these commands using SCILAB help. At a higher level of expertise in SCILAB debugging the user can try the function *debug(i)* where i = 0, 1, 2, 3, 4, denotes a debugging level. Check out the *debug* function using help.

An example of a function - Calculation of Frobenius norm of a matrix.

This function is to be stored in file *AbsM.txt* within subdirectory *bin* in the SCILAB directory. (Note: While the name of the file containing a function does not have to be the same as the name of the function, it is recommended that they be the same to facilitate loading and operation of the function).

The Frobenius norm of a matrix $A = [a_{ij}]$ with n rows and m columns is defined as the square root of the sum of the squares of each of the elements of the matrix, i.e.,

$$\|A\|_F = \sqrt{\sum_{i=1}^{n}\sum_{j=1}^{m} a_{ij}}.$$

The function AbsM(A), listed below, calculates the Frobenius norm of a matrix:

```
function [v]=AbsM(A)
// This function calculates the Frobenius norm of a matrix
// First obtain the matrix size
[n m] = size(A);
// Then initialize suma and add terms a(i,j)^2
suma = 0;
for i = 1:n
        for j = 1:m
                suma = suma + A(i,j)^2;
        end
end;
// take square root and show result
v = sqrt(suma);
// end of the function
```

Within SCILAB try the following commands to load and run the function for a particular case:

```
clear <enter>
getf('AbsM.txt') <enter>
R = [1. 3. 4. 2. <enter>
3. -2. 5. -7. <enter>
1. 3. 4. 5. ] <enter>
AbsM(R) <enter>
```

Functions are defined throughout the book in relation to different mathematical subjects, i.e., vectors, matrices, integrals, differential equations, etc. The following sections of this chapter deal with the subjects of input/output and string manipulation in SCILAB.

Input/Output in SCILAB

Saving and loading variables.

To save variables in a file use the command *save*. Let's try some examples:
A = [1. 2. 3.; -3. 4. 5.; 2. 4. 5.; 1. 3. 2.]; b = 1:10; <enter>
A <enter>
b <enter>
save('DataAb.dat', A,b)<enter>

Next, using NOTEPAD or PDE, open the file *DataAB.dat* in sub-directory *bin* of SCILAB. You will notice that you cannot see the numbers in the file. That is because they have been saved in a binary format. Let's clear the variables in SCILAB and re-load the values of A and b using the command *load*:

clear <enter>
load('DataAb.dat') <enter>
A <enter>
b <enter>

Unformatted output to the screen

To print strings and variables without a format you can use the *print* function. The general form of the function is: *print (unit or filename, x1, x2, (y1, ..,))*. The unit value for the screen is either 6 or %io(2). Try the following examples:

x = 5; y = sin(%pi*x/10); r = 1:2:25; A = rand(5,3); <enter>
%io(2) <enter>
print(6,x,y) <enter>
print (6,A,r)<enter>
print(%io(2),x,y,r)<enter>
print(%io(2),A) <enter>

Notice that the function *print*, as with the function *disp* used earlier, prints the last variable in the list first. Try some more examples:

Print(6,x,'x value =') <enter>

Notice that, in this case, the string 'x value =' is printed together with the string 'x = ', which is a default from the print command. Therefore, it is not a good idea to include an identifying string when using the *print* function to print to the screen.

Unformatted output to a file

You can use the print function to print to a filename, for example, try:

print('data1.txt',A,r)<enter>
print ('data2.txt',x,y)<enter>

Next, using NOTEPAD open the files data1.txt and data2.txt. Notice that the output includes all the identifiers and brackets (!) provided by SCILAB.

■ *Working with files.*

The following command allows you to open a file:

[unit [,err]]=file('open', file-name [,status] [,access [,recl]] [,format])

file-name: string, file name of the file to be opened

status: string, The status of the file to be opened
- "new"   : file must not exist new file (default)
- "old"   : file must already exists.
- "unknown"   : unknown status
- "scratch"   : file is to be deleted at end of session

access: string, The type of access to the file
- "sequential" : sequential access (default)
- "direct"   : direct access.

format: string,
- "formatted" : for a formatted file (default)
- "unformatted" : binary record.

recl: integer, is the size of records in bytes when access="direct"

unit: integer, logical unit descriptor of the opened file

err: integer, error message number (see error), if open fails. If err is omitted an error message is issued.

You can also use the command *file(action,unit)*

where *action* is one of the following strings:
- "close":   closes the file.
- "rewind":   puts the pointer at beginning of file.
- "backspace":   puts the pointer at beginning of last record.
- "last":   puts the pointer after last record.

Once a file is open it can be used for input (read function) or output (write function). Some examples of file opening, input and output are shown below.

■ *Writing to files.*

The following programs use the values of x, y, A, and r defined above. In these examples we open and write to files, and close them. Notice that this command is oriented towards printing matrices -- one at a time -- therefore, as shown in Example 2, it is better if you put together your data into a matrix before printing it. Notice also that the format part, which is enclosed between quotes, is basically a FORTRAN format.

- Example 1.
    ```
    u = file('open','data3.txt','new')<enter>
    write(u,A,'(3f10.6)')<enter>
    ```

```
file('close',u)<enter>
```

- Example 2.
    ```
    x1 = 0:0.5:10 <enter>
    x2 = x1^2 <enter>
    B = [x1',x2'] <enter>
    m = file('open','data4.txt','new')<enter>
    write(m,B,'(2(f10.6,2x))') <enter>
    file('close',m)<enter>
    ```

- Example 3. Including labels. Note: labels are written separated from the variables
    ```
    A = rand(2,3); B = rand(2,3); C = A + B <enter>
    u = file('open','data5.txt','new') <enter>
    write(u,'this is matrix A','(a)') <enter>
    write(u,A,'(3(f10.6,2x)') <enter>
    write(u,'this is matrix B','(a)') <enter>
    write(u,B,'(3(f10.6,2x)') <enter>
    write(u,'this is matrix C = A + B','(a)') <enter>
    write(u,C,'(3(f10.6,2x)') <enter>
    file('close',u) <enter>
    ```

Reading from the keyboard

Reading from the keyboard can be accomplished by using the *read* function with unit %io(1) or 5. The general form of the read function is:

[x]=read(file-description,n,m,[format]),

i.e., a variable must be assigned a value (could be a matrix of size n,m) during the operation of *read*. The file description can be a unit or number assigned to a file or to the keyboard. The format is not necessary. Also, to read a single value use m = 1, n= 1, as shown below.
For example, type the following function into a file called *inout.txt*:

```
function inout()
//this script illustrates using read and write
write(%io(2),'Enter a real variable x:','(a)');
x = read (%io(1),1,1);
write(%io(2),'Enter a real variable y:','(a)');
y = read (%io(1),1,1);
z = x+y;
write(%io(2),'the sum of x and y is:','(a)')
write(%io(2),z,'(10x,e13.7)')
//end of function
```

Within SCILAB, type the following commands, and responses to prompts:
```
Getf('inout.txt') <enter>
inout( ) <enter>
1.2 <enter>
```

```
2.4 <enter>
```

Notice that the function *inout* has no arguments. Still, in the function definition as well as in the function call it has to have a pair of parentheses.

■ *Reading from files*

Use the same read command as used while reading from the keyboard, but using an open file unit to read. For example, suppose that you have a file called *signal.txt*, containing the following values:

```
1.0    2.0    4.0
2.0    3.0    9.0
3.0    4.0    16.0
4.0    5.0    25.0
5.0    6.0    36.0
6.0    7.0    49.0
```

If you know the number of rows (n=6, in this case). To read the matrix of values, use:

```
u=file('open','signal.txt','old')  <enter>
A=read(u,6,3);  <enter>
A <enter>
```

If the number of rows is unknown using $=-1$ will ensure that the entire file is read. It is assumed that the file contains only the matrix of interest. For example,

```
file('rewind',u)  <enter>
B = read(u,-1,3);  <enter>
B  <enter>
file('close',u)  <enter>
```

Manipulating strings in SCILAB

A string is basically text that can be manipulated through SCILAB commands. Strings in SCILAB are written between single or double quotes. The following are examples of strings:

```
'myFile'   'The result is: '   'a b c'  'abc'  'a'  'b'  'c'
"Text to be included"   "Please enter the graphic window number"   "1" "3" "5"
```

String concatenation

The joining of two or more strings is called *concatenation*. The *plus* symbol (+), when placed between two strings concatenates the strings into a single one. In the next example variables s1, s2, and s3 are defined and concatenated:

```
-->s1 = 'The result from '
 s1  =

 The result from
-->s2 = 'multiplication '
 s2  =

 multiplication
-->s3 = 'is given below.'
 s3  =

 is given below.
-->sOut = s1 + s2 + s3
 sOut  =

 The result from multiplication is given below.
```

String functions

The function *length* determines the number of characters in a given string, for example:

```
-->length(sOut)
 ans  =

    46.
```

The function *part* allows the extraction of characters from a given string. For example, to extract the first character of a string use:

```
-->part('abcd',1)
 ans  =

 a
```

The next command extracts the first and second character of a string:

```
-->part('abcd',[1,2])
 ans  =

 ab
```

In the next example, characters 1 and 3 of the string are extracted:

```
-->part('abcd',[1,3])
 ans  =

 ac
```

To extract a series of character, the characters' positions in the string are indicated as a sequence of values in the vector representing the second argument to function *part*:

```
-->part(sOut,[4:1:15])
 ans  =

  result from
```

The function _strindex (string index)_, with a typical call of the form _strindex(string1,string2)_ determines the position of the first occurrence of sub-string _string2_ within _string1_. For example,

```
-->strindex(sOut,'mult')
 ans  =

    17.
```

Once the position of a sub-string has been determined you can use the function _part_ to extract that sub-string or other sub-string starting at that position. For example, this function call extracts characters 17 to 24 of string _sOut_:

```
-->part(sOut,[17:24])
 ans  =

 multipli
```

The function _strsubst (string subst_itution), with a typical call of the form

$$strsubst(string1, string2, string3)$$

replaces sub-string _string2_ with sub-string _string3_ within string _string1_. For example, the next call to function _strsubst_ replaces the sub-string 'multiplication' with 'division' within string _sOut_:

```
-->strsubst(sOut,'multiplication','division')
 ans  =

 The result from division is given below.
```

Converting numerical values to strings

The function _string_ is used to convert a numerical result into a string. This operation is useful when showing output from numerical calculations. For example, the next SCILAB input line performs a numerical calculation, whose immediate output is suppressed by the semi-colon, and then produces an output string showing the result. The output string produced consists of the sub-string "The sum is" concatenated to the numerical result that has been converted to a string with string(s).

```
-->s = 5+2; "The sum is " + string(s)
```

```
ans  =

The sum is 7
```

The following command produces an array or vector of strings. The strings in the vector represent the numbers from 1 to 5.

```
-->sNum = string(1:5)
 sNum  =

!1   2   3   4   5  !
```

An attempt to add the first two elements of vector *sNum* produces instead their concatenation, verifying that the elements are indeed strings, and not numbers:

```
-->sNum(1)+sNum(2)
 ans  =

 12
```

String catenation for a vector of strings

To generate a string consisting in inserting a particular sub-string between the characters of a vector or array of strings use the function *strcat* (*string catenation*). The next example produces a string resulting from inserting the character ' - ' between the elements of *sNum*:

```
-->strcat(sNum,' - ')
 ans  =
 1 - 2 - 3 - 4 - 5
```

Converting strings to numbers

To convert a string representing numbers into their numerical equivalent you can use function *evstr* (*evaluate string*). The next command, for example, converts the string elements of vector *sNum*, defined earlier, into their numerical equivalents:

```
-->nNum = evstr(sNum)
 nNum  =

!   1.    2.    3.    4.    5. !
```

The plus sign (+) applied to the two first elements of *nNum* would add, rather than concatenate, those elements:

```
-->nNum(1) + nNum(2)
 ans  =

    3.
```

The function *evstr* can be used to evaluate numerically any string representing number operations. Some examples are shown below:

```
-->evstr('2+2')
 ans  =

    4.
-->evstr('sin(%pi/6) + 1/3')
 ans  =

    .8333333
```

The following example uses function *evstr* to evaluate the numerical values defined in the elements of a vector. This particular example uses the values of a couple of variables *s* and *m*, which must be defined before attempting the evaluation of the strings.

```
-->s = 2, m = 3
 s  =

    2.
 m  =

    3.
-->evstr(['2' 'sqrt(s)' 'm + s'])
 ans  =

!   2.    1.4142136    5. !
```

Executing SCILAB statements represented by strings

To evaluate assignment statements or SCILAB commands defined by strings we use function *execstr (execute string)*. For example,

```
-->execstr('a=1')
```

Although the statement *a=1* is executed through the use of *execstr*, no output is produced. To check that the statement was indeed executed, request that SCILAB show the value of a:

```
-->a
 a  =

    1.
```

You can use *execstr* to evaluate a series of commands by placing the commands in an array or vector:

```
-->execstr(['a=1','b=2','a+b'])
```

Once again, no output is shown, so the result from the last element in the vector is lost, but variable b (from the second element in the vector) was indeed stored:

```
-->b
 b  =

    2.
```

A second example of multiple statements executed through *execstr* follows:

```
-->execstr(['s=2' 'm=3' 'r=sqrt(s)' 'q=m+s'])
```

Check the results of the statements by using:

```
-->[s m r q]
 ans  =

!   2.    3.    1.4142136    5. !
```

The following example shows the execution of a small program whose lines are presented as string elements of a vector:

```
-->execstr(['a=2' 'x=[]' 'for j = 1:4' 'x = [x a^j]' 'end'])
```

The result from the last command can be seen by entering:

```
-->x
 x  =

!   2.    4.    8.    16. !
```

Producing labeled output in SCILAB

The following example shows a way to produce labeled output in SCILAB. The data for the output is contained in vector *d* of dimensions 1×m:

```
-->d = [0.5:0.25:1.5];

-->[n m] = size(d);          // m is the list of the

-->for j = 1:m, 'distance no. ' + string(j) + ' is ' + string(d(j)) + '.', end
 ans  =

 distance no. 1 is .5.
 ans  =

 distance no. 2 is .75.
 ans  =

 distance no. 3 is 1.
 ans  =

 distance no. 4 is 1.25.
 ans  =

 distance no. 5 is 1.5.
```

Using the function *disp*

The previous result uses the variable *ans* to show each line of output. This is the standard way that SCILAB uses to show the current output. The result shown above can be simplified even further by using the function *disp* (*disp*lay), as follows:

```
-->for j=1:m, disp('distance no. '+ string(j) + ' is ' + string(d(j)) + '.'),
end

 distance no. 1 is  .5.

 distance no. 2 is  .75.

 distance no. 3 is 1.

 distance no. 4 is 1.25.

 distance no. 5 is 1.5.
```

The function *disp* can be used to display any result, not only strings. The following example shows the function *disp* used with string as well as numerical output:

```
-->a = 2; A = [2,3;-1,4]; B = a*A;

-->disp('Matrix B is:'), disp(B)

 Matrix B is:
!   4.    6. !
! - 2.    8. !
```

The variable *ans*

The variable *ans* (*ans*wer) contains SCILAB's current output. You can refer to the last SCILAB output by using the variable name *ans*. For example, the following commands uses the contents of *ans* to operate on the most recent SCILAB output:

```
-->3+2
 ans  =
    5.

-->exp(ans)
 ans  =
    148.41316
```

To verify that the result obtained is correct use:

```
-->exp(5)
 ans  =
    148.41316
```

Exercises

[1]. Write a SCILAB function to calculate the factorial of an integer number:

$$n! = n \cdot (n-1) \cdot (n-2) \ldots 3 \cdot 2 \cdot 1$$

[2]. Write a SCILAB function to calculate the standard deviation of the data contained in a vector $x = [x_1 \, x_2 \ldots x_3]$.

$$s = \sqrt{\frac{1}{n-1} \sum_{k=1}^{n} (x_k - \bar{x})^2},$$

where $\bar{x}$ is the mean value of the data,

$$s = \frac{1}{n} \sum_{k=1}^{n} x_k.$$

[3]. Write a SCILAB function to calculate the function defined by

$$h(\xi) = \begin{cases} \ln(\xi + 1), & 0 < \xi \leq 1 \\ \ln(2) + \exp(-\frac{\xi}{2}), & 1 < \xi \leq 4 \\ 0, & elsewhere \end{cases}$$

[4]. Plot the function $h(\xi)$ in the interval $-1 < \xi < 10$.

[5]. Save the data used in exercise [4] into a text file, then, retrieve the data into vectors and y and calculate the mean and standard deviation of and y using the function developed in exercise [2].

[6]. Write a SCILAB function that finds the median of a data sample. The median is defined as that value located exactly in the middle of the data sample once it has been sorted in increasing order. The algorithm to find such value is given by:

$$x_m = x_{(n+1)/2}, \text{ if } n \text{ is even}$$

$$x_m = (x_{n/2} + x_{(n+2)/2}), \text{ if } n \text{ is odd}$$

where n is the sample size. To order the data sample you can use the SCILAB function *sortup* (use `-->help sort` to find more about this function).

[7]. The coefficients of the binomial expansion

$$(a+b)^n = C(n,0)a^n + C(n,1)a^{n-1}b + C(n,2)a^{n-2}b^2 + \ldots + C(n,n-1)ab^{n-1} + C(n,n)b^n,$$

are given by

$$C(n,k) = \frac{n!}{k!(n-k)!}.$$

Write a SCILAB function that produces a table of binomial coefficients for n = 1, 2, ..., 5. Use the function developed in exercise [1] to calculate factorials of integer numbers.

[8]. Write a Maple procedure to define a function given by

$$f(x) = \begin{cases} x^2 - \sin(x), 0 < x \le 1 \\ 1/(1+x^2), 1 < x \le 2 \\ \sqrt{x^2+1}, 2 < x \le 3 \end{cases}$$

Plot the function for 0 < x < 3.

[9]. Write a SCILAB function that request from the user the values of the bottom width (b) and water depth (y) for a rectangular cross-section open channel (see figure below) and prints the area ($A = bh$), wetted perimeter ($P = b+2h$), and hydraulic radius ($R = A/P$) properly labeled. Try the function for values of b = 3.5 and y = 1.2.

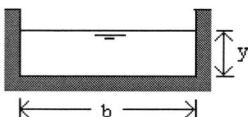

[10]. Write a SCILAB function that request from the user the values of the initial position (x_0, y_0) of a projectile, the initial velocity given as a magnitude v_0 and an angle θ_0, and the acceleration of gravity g (see figure below). The function also requests from the user an initial time t_0, a time increment Δt, and an ending time t_f. The function produces a table of values of the velocity components $v_x = v_0 \cos(\theta_0)$, $v_y = v_0 \cos(\theta_0)$, the magnitude of the velocity, $v = (v_x^2 + v_y^2)^{1/2}$, the position of the projectile $x = x_0 + v_0 \cos(\theta_0)t$, $y = y_0 + v_0 \sin(\theta_0)t - gt^2/2$, and the distance of the projectile from the launching point, $r_0 = ((x-x_0)^2+(y-y_0)^2)^{1/2}$. The function also produces plots of x - vs. - t, y - vs. - t, r_0 - vs. - t, and y - vs. -x in different graphic windows. [Note: to generate a new graphics window use the SCILAB command
>xset('window',j) where j is the window number.]

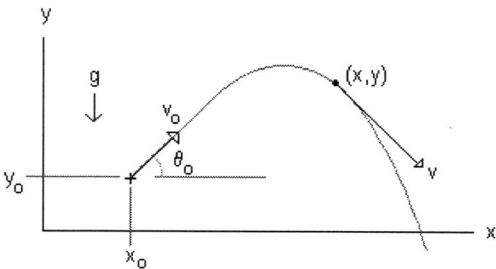

[11]. Suppose you want to plot the function $r(\theta) = 3.5(1 - \cos(2\theta))$. Write a SCILAB function that generates values of θ from 0 to 2π, calculates the values of r, and the Cartesian coordinates $x = r\cos(\theta)$, $y = r\sin(\theta)$, and prints a table showing those values, i.e. θ, r, x, and y. The function also produces a plot of y-vs.-x.

3 Graphics with SCILAB

SCILAB provides a number of functions for producing a variety of two- and three-dimensional graphics. Some examples of graphics and their applications using SCILAB are provided in this chapter. The chapter includes description of two- and three-dimensional graphics, as well as some examples of graphics animation.

TWO-DIMENSIONAL GRAPHICS

The *plot* command: simple x-y plots

In the solution of non-linear equations of the form $f(x) = 0$, it is often convenient to be able to plot the function $y = f(x)$ to visualize the location of the roots of the function. SCILAB offers the command *plot* to obtain such graphics. The general form of the command is:

plot(x,y,[xcap,ycap,caption])
plot(y,[xcap,ycap,caption])

where *x* and *y* are column vectors (of the same length), *xcap* is the x-axis label, *ycap* is the y-axis label, and *caption* is the plot title.

In the following example, we first generate a column vector t with the values (0.00, 0.25,...,10.0) using the command

```
t = (0:0.25:10)';
```

Next, we generate a vector $s = 2t^2 - 2t + 1$, by using:

```
s = 2*t^2-2*t+1;
```

Finally, we use the *plot* command to plot s vs. t, as follows:

```
plot(t,s,'time(s)','position(ft)','linear motion')
```

SCILAB will generate a graphics window called *SCILABGraphic0* showing the plot (see figure below).

The SCILAB Graphic window

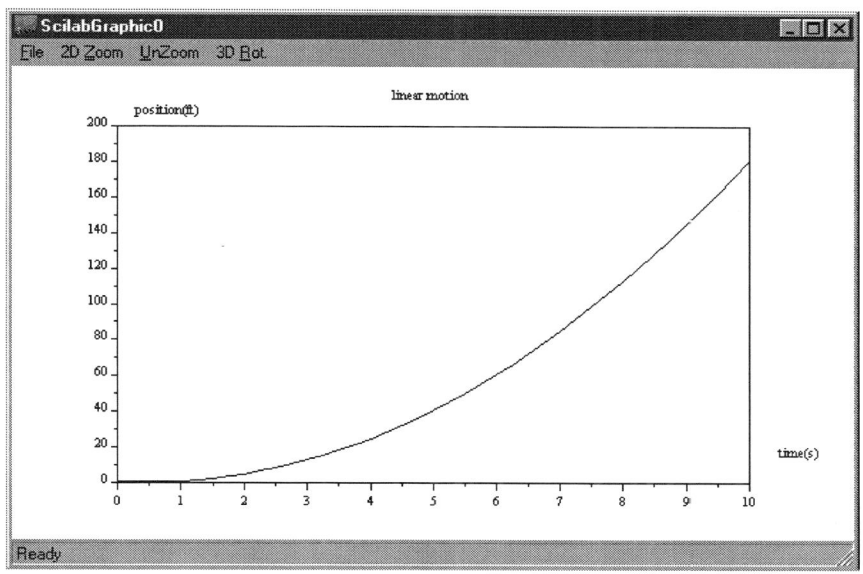

The following menus are available in the SCILAB Graphic window:
- *File*
- *2D Zoom*
- *UnZoom*
- *3D Rot*

Within the *File* menu you will find the options:

- *Clear*: erases current graph
- *Select*: (operation not clear)
- *Print(SCILAB)*: prints current graph.
- *Export*: allows you to save the plot in formats such as Postscript, GIF, etc.
- *Save*: allows you to save the plot in SCILAB format, the default fi ename has the suffix *scg*. (e.g., *plot1.scg*)
- *Load*: allows you to read in a plot saved in SCILAB format.
- *Close*: to close the current SCILAB graphics window.
- *Print(Windows)*: prints graph to Windows default printer
- *Copy to clipboard(EnhMetafile)*: copies graph to clipboard as an enhanced metafile that can be pasted into other documents, such as a MSWord file.
- *Copy to clipboard(Metafile+DIB)*: similar to the previous option. (Note: when pasting to MSWord, for example, the previous option seems to produce a better quality graph.)
- *Redraw*: to redraw graph if manipulation of the same has diminished its quality.
- *Update Ini*: (operation not clear)

Clicking on the *2D Zoom* menu option allows you to select an area for zooming by dragging the cursor through the area of interest. When you release the mouse's left button the selected area will be zoomed in the graphics window. Click on the *UnZoom* menu option to recover the original graph.

The *3D Rot* menu option is used with three-dimensional graphics to rotate the point of view. It will not work with two-dimensional graphics such as the present one.

Creating a plot with error bars

The command *errbar* lets you add error bars to plots of functions. The call to the command has the form

```
errbar(x,y,em,ep)
```

where x, y, em, and ep are four matrices of the same size. These matrices contain the values of the plot coordinates (x,y) and the values that determine the error bars according to the formula:

$[y(i,j)-em(i,j), y(i,j)+ep(i,j)]$.

As an example, try the following commands:

```
x = (-%pi:%pi/50:%pi); y = sin(x);        // Calculate vectors x and y
em = 0.05.*rand(x); ep = 0.1*rand(x);     // Generate random errors
plot(x,y)                                  // Plot y vs. x
errbar(x,y,em,ep)                          // Add error bars
```

Adding a simple grid to the plot

To add a grid to the plot use the command:

```
xgrid()
```

With this call, grid properties are chosen by SCILAB. The function xgrid( ) can use an integer value as argument that determine the color of the gridlines. For example, try the following SCILAB commands to see the different grid types:

```
x = (-%pi:%pi/50:%pi); y = sin(x);
plot(x,y,"x","y","a plot")
xgrid()
xgrid(1)
xgrid(2)
xgrid(3)
xgrid(4)
xgrid(15)
xgrid(21)
```

Other on-line commands for managing graphics

These are generic graphic commands that can be used from the SCILAB command window to manipulate the current graph window.

xbasc(): clears the current graphics window

xclear(*i*): clears one or more graphic windows without affection the contents of the graphs.

xdel(*i*): deletes a graphic window

xselect(): brings up the current graphic window

xsave(*'filename', i*): saves the graph of window *i* in the file designated by the string 'filename'

xload(*'filename',[i]*): loads the graph the file designated by the string 'filename'. The window number, *i*, is optional.

winsid(): returns the number of the current graphics window.

Changing global parameters of a plot

Global parameters of a plot refers to settings to be used in the plot such as the type and size of font used in labels, the type and size of the marks for plotting points, the colormap (a matrix of color definitions for filling areas in the plt), the window number to be open or created, the position of the graphic window, etc. Many of these properties can be changed by using the function *xset*:

  xset(*choice-name,x1,x2,x3,x4,x5*)
  xset( )

The parameter of this function are a string *choice-name*, and five numbers, *x1,x2,x3,x4,x5*, which depend on the value of the string *choice-name*.

Some calls for the function *xset* are shown below:

   xset(*"alufunction",number*): Used to set the logical function for drawing. It works only under X11

NOTE: X11 is the driver for X-Windows environments in UNIX and LINUX operating systems. Most graphical functions that start with x act on the X11 driver, however, some can also be used to control the SCILAB graphics window in Windows or other operating systems

The logical function used (*alufunction*) is set by *x1*. *src* is the source, i.e., what we want to draw. *dst* is the destination, i.e., what is already drawn where we want to draw.

Usual values of *x1* are: 3 for copying (default), 6 for animation and 0 for clearing.

0: clear,	i.e.,	"0"
1: and ,	i.e.,	"src AND dst"
2: and reverse,	i.e.,	"src AND NOT dst"
3: copy,	i.e.,	"src"
4: and inverted ,	i.e.,	"(NOT src) AND dst"
5: noop ,	i.e.,	"dst"
6: xor,	i.e.,	"src XOR dst"
7: or,	i.e.,	"src OR dst"
8: nor,	i.e.,	"(NOT src) AND (NOT dst)"
9: equiv,	i.e.,	"(NOT src) XOR dst"
10: invert,	i.e.,	"NOT dst"
11: or reverse,	i.e.,	"src OR (NOT dst)"
12: copy inverted ,	i.e.,	"NOT src"
13: or inverted ,	i.e.,	"(NOT src) OR dst"
14: nand ,	i.e.,	"(NOT src) OR (NOT dst)"
15: set ,	i.e.,	"1"

xset(*"auto clear","on"/"off"*): Switch "on" or "off" the auto clear mode for graphics. When the auto clear mode is "on", successive plots are not super-posed, i.e., a xbasc() operation (the graphics window is cleared and the associated recorded graphics is erased) is performed before each high level graphics function. Default value is "off".

xset(*"background",color*) : Set the background color of the current graphics window.

xset(*"clipping",x,y,w,h*) : Set the clipping zone (the zone of the graphics window where plots can be drawn) to the rectangle (x,y,w,h) (Upper-Left point Width Height). This function uses the current coordinates of the plot.

xset(*"colormap",cmap*): Set the colormap as a m x 3 matrix. m is the number of colors. Color number *i* is given as a 3-uple cmap(i,1), cmap(i,2), cmap(i,3) corresponding respectively to red, green and blue intensity between 0 and 1.

xset(*"dashes",i*): Set the dash style to style i (0 for solid line). This is used only when in black and white mode:*xset("use color",0)*. Use *xset()* to see the styles.

xset(*"default"*): Reset the graphics context to default values.

xset(*"font",fontid,fontsize*): Set the current font and its current size.

xset(*"foreground",color*): Set the foreground color of the current graphics window.

xset(*"fpf",string*): Set the floating point format for number display in contour functions. string is a string giving the format in C format syntax (for example string="%.3f"). Use string="" to switch back to default format.

xset(*"hidden3d",colorid*): Set the color number for hidden faces in plot3d.

xset(*"line mode",type*): This function is used to set the line drawing mode. Absolute mode is set with type=1 and relative mode with type=0. (Warning: the mode type=0 has bugs)

xset(*"mark",markid,marksize*): Set the current mark and the current mark size. Use *xset()* to see the marks.

xset("*pattern*",*value*): Set the current pattern for fillingfunctions. value is an integer projected in the interval [0,whiteid]. 0 is used for black filling and whiteid for white. The value of *whiteid* can be obtained with xget("white").

xset("*pixmap*",*flag*)

>If flag=0 the graphics are directly displayed on the screen.
>If flag=1 the graphics are done on a pixmap and are sent to
>the graphics window with the command xset("wshow"). The pixmap
>is cleared with the command xset("wwpc"). Note that the usual
>command xbasc() also clears the pixmap.

xset("*thickness*",*value*): Set the thickness of lines in pixel (0 and 1 represent 1 pixel thick).

xset("*use color*",*flag*)

>If flag=1 then xset("pattern",..) or xset("dashes",..) will be
>used so as to change the default color for drawing or for
>filling patterns.
>If flag=0 then we switch back to the gray and dashes mode.

xset("*viewport*",*x*,y): Set the position of the panner.

xset("*wdim*",*width*,*height*): Set the width and the height of the current graphics window. This option is not used by the postscript driver.

xset("*window*",*window-number*): Set the current window to the window window-number and creates the window if it does not exist.

xset("*wpos*",*x,y*): Set the position of the upper left point of the graphics window.

xset("*wresize*",*flag*)

>If flag=1 then the graphic is automatically resized to fill
>the graphics window.
>xdel();xset("wresize",1);plot2d;xset("wdim",1000,500)

>If flag=0 the scale of the graphic is left unchanged when the
>graphics window is resized. Top left panner or keyboard arrows
>may be used to scroll over the graphic.
>xdel();plot2d();xset("wresize",0);xset("wdim",1000,500)

xset("*wshow*"): See xset("*pixmap*",*1*) above.

xset("wwpc") : See xset("*pixmap*",*1*) above.

Changing parameters with *xset()* or *xsetm()*:

The command *xset()*, or the command *xsetm()*, both without arguments, can be used to set some of the graph properties through a series of input boxes provided by SCILAB. For example, if you use:

```
xset()
```

You can change the following properties (see Figure below):

fontID gets changed to times italic
fontsize gets changed to 14
markID gets changed to "+"

Press the *"Next>"* button so that you can change the next set of properties (see second Figure below):

marksize gets changed to 10
Thickness gets changed to 4
pixmap/flag gets changed to "On"

Press the *"Next>"* button so that you can verify the third set of properties (see third Figure below):

use colors will be kept as *"Yes"*
colors will be kept as 33
alufunction will be kept as scr (see options for *alufunction* above)

Press the *"Finished"* button when done modifying properties.

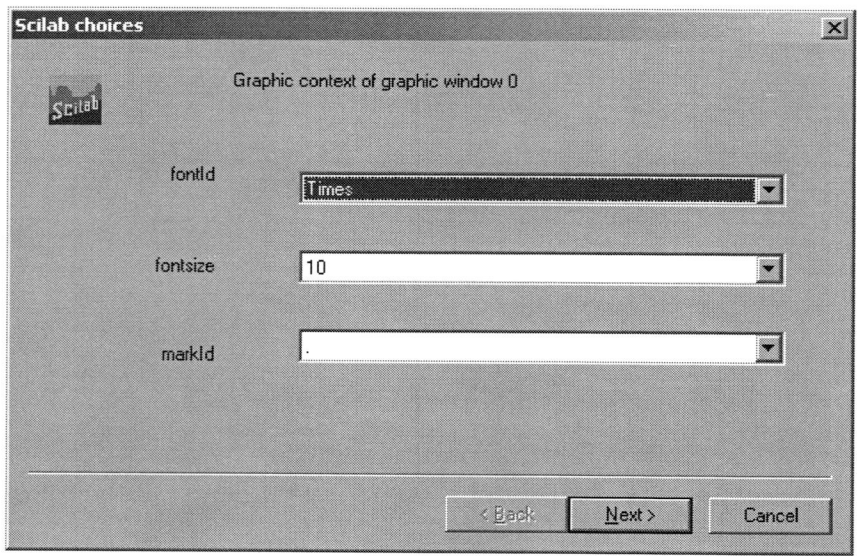

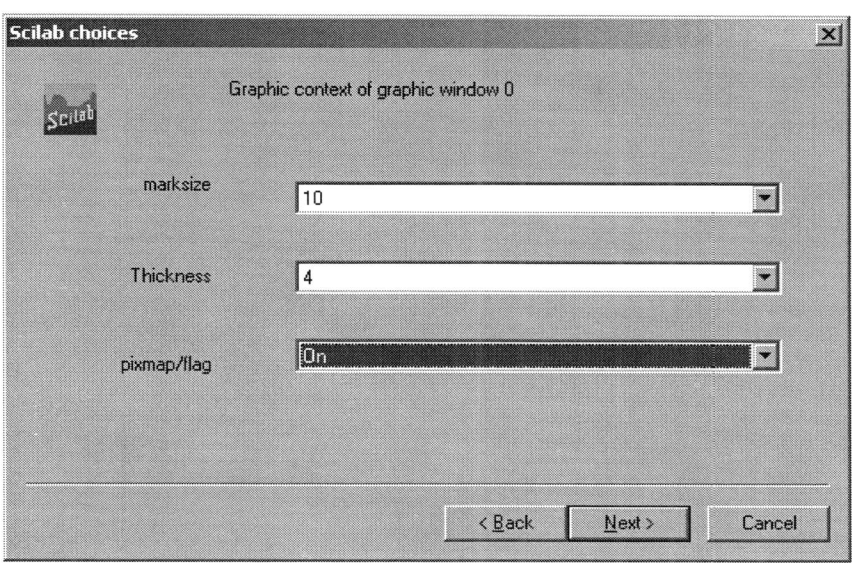

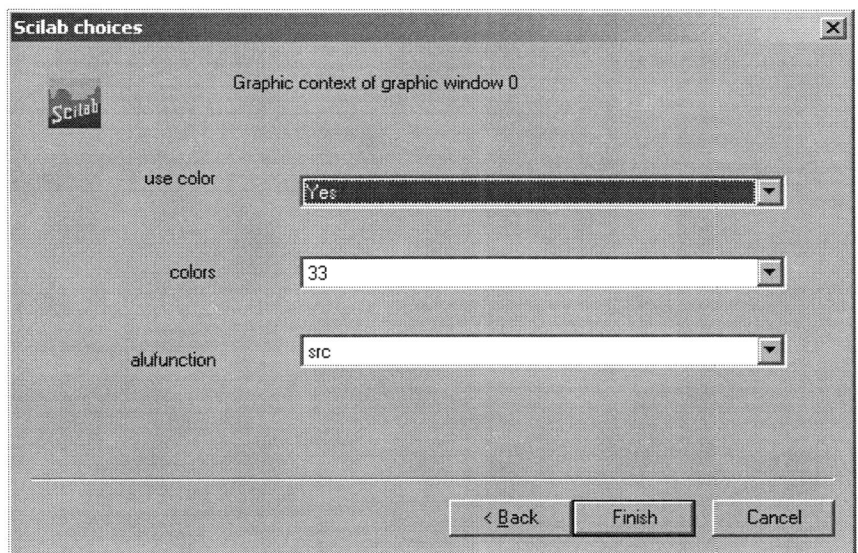

Create the following plot:

```
t = (-10:0.1:10); s = 3.2.*(1 - exp(-0.2*t));
```

```
plot(t,s,"time(hrs)","position of asteroid(10000 km)","Astronomy Plot")
```

To reset the graphical properties use:

```
xset('default')
```

This will clear out the current graphics window. Try the plot again, using:

```
plot(t,s,"time(hrs)","position of asteroid(10000 km)","Astronomy Plot")
```

This time you will get the default settings for the graph.

Changing the font style and size with xset('font', fontId, fontSize)

You can use the function *xset* to change the font size. The *fontSize* corresponds to typical font sizes used in texts, while *fontId* refers to the following font styles:

0	Courier
1	Symbol
2	Times
3	Times Italic
4	Times Bold
5	Times Bold Italic

Try the following exercise to see the different font options:

```
x = (0.1:0.1:20); y = sqrt(1+x^2);
for j = 0:5, xset('window',j), xset('font',j,4), plot(x,y,"x","y","title"), end
```

Generating new graphics windows

The command

xset('window', window_number)

generates a new graphics window. The window_number must be a nonnegative integer. The default value is SCILABGraphic0, corresponding to window_number = 0.

This exercise shows how to produce four different graphs in four different windows:

```
x = (-10:0.1:10); y = sin(2.*x);
z = cos(2.*x) - 1; w = 1./(x+1); t = abs(x);
xset('window',1); plot(x,y,'x','y','First Plot')
xset('window',2); plot(x,z,'x','z','Second Plot')
xset('window',3); plot(x,w,'x','w','Third Plot')
xset('window',4); plot(x,t,'x','t','Fourth Plot')
```

Changing the background color

The background color of the graphics window is by default white. You can change that background color using the call

xset('background', color)

where the parameter *color* must be a nonnegative number. The available colors, for color values from zero to 20, in a Windows 98 environment, are:

0	black	1	black	2	dark blue
3	bright green	4	sky blue	5	bright red
6	purple	7	bright red	8	white
9	light blue	10	blue	11	dark blue
12	sky blue	13	dark green	14	dark green
15	bright green	16	dark green	17	dark greenish blue
18	greenish blue	19	dark red	20	dark red
21	red	22	dark purple	23	bright purple
24	dark reddish brown	25	dark reddish brown	26	reddish brown
27	dark orange	28	pink	29	pink
30	pink	31	pink	32	dark yellow

There are slight differences between colors 4 and 12, and between colors 13, 14, and 17.

The user is encouraged to try the following exercises to check the different background colors:

```
for j = 1:20, xset('window',j), xset('background',j), end
```

Changing the foreground color

The foreground of a graph corresponds to those lines such as the frame of a plot, the labels, the grid marks, etc. The foreground color can be changed by using

xset('foreground', color)

where the parameter *color* was defined above for background color changes.

To see changing of foreground and background colors simultaneously, try the following exercise:

```
x = (-%pi:%pi/100:%pi); y = sin(x);
xset('background',32);   // background = yellow,
xset('foreground', 13);  // foreground = green
plot(x,y,"x","y","sine")
```

To find current settings use

```
xget( )
```

This is similar to the function xsetm( ).

The *plot2d* command

This command can be used if you want to plot more than one two-dimensional plot. The *plot2d* command has the general form:

plot2d(x,y,[style,strf,leg,rect,nax])
plot2d(y);

where
x,y are two matrices of the same size *(nl,nc)*, *nc* = number of curves, and *nl* = number of points for each curve (if *nl=1*, it is assumed that there is only one curve of *nc* points);
style is a real vector of size *(1,nc)*. The style to use for curve j is defined by *style(j)*. For the *plot2d* function the value of style represents the color of the curve used for the plot.
strf is a string of length 3, written as "*xyz*", where if x=1 captions are displayed (Captions are given by the string leg1@leg2@..., corresponding to legends for the different curves being plotted);
    y controls the computation of the frame,
        if y=0 the current boundaries, set by a previous call to an other high level plotting function, are used;
        if y=1, the argument *rect* is used to specify the boundaries of the plot. `rect=[xmin,ymin,xmax,ymax];`
        if y=2 the boundaries of the plot are computed using *max* and *min* values of x and y.,
        if y=3, it is similar to y=1 but produces *isoview* scaling;
        if y=4, it is like y=2 but produces *isoview* scaling;
        if y=5, it is like y=1 but the boundaries and *ax* can be changed to produce nice-looking graduations (this mode is used when the zoom button is activated);
        if y=6, it is like y=2 but the boundaries and *ax* can be changed to produce nice-looking graduations (this mode is used when the zoom button is activated);

    z controls the display of information on the frame around the plot;
        if z=1, an axis is drawn the number of tics can be specified by the *nax* argument. *nax* is a vector with four entries [nx,Nx,ny,Ny] where nx (ny) is the number of sub-graduations on the x (y) axis and Nx (Ny) is the number of graduations on the x (y) axis;
        if z=2, the plot is framed but no grid is shown;
        if z takes any other values no frame is produced.

Simple examples of *plot2d( )*

Some examples of simple applications of the command *plot2d* follows:

First, we create the following (row) vectors:

```
x = (-2*%pi:%pi/100:2*%pi);
y = sin(2.*x);
z = cos(x);
w = exp(-abs(0.1*x)).*sin(x);
```

Next, we will use a simple call to the function *plot2d* to see what results:

```
plot2d(x,y)
plot2d(x,z)
plot2d(x,w)
```

The default graphic window is *SCILABGraphic0*. The function *plot2d* places one plot on top of the other in the default graphic window. This graphic output is not very useful because the vertical scales get recalculated with every new graph added. We will show later how to place more than one plot in a single graph with a common vertical scale.

The next exercises show calls to the function *plot2d* using the transpose of the (row) vectors created earlier. Close the graphic window before running these exercises:

```
plot2d(x',y')p
plot2d(x',w)
plot2d(x',z')
```

As with the three previous examples, the graphic output is messy as the vertical scales for each individual plot are different.

Creating multiple plots with plot2d( )

One can create individual plots in different graphic windows by using, for example, the following commands:

```
xset('window',1); plot2d(x',y'); xtitle('Plot 1')
xset('window',2); plot2d(x',z'); xtitle('Plot 2')
xset('window',3); plot2d(x',w'); xtitle('Plot 3')
```

You can combine the three graphs into a single set of axes by using the following form of the plot2d command:

```
xset('window',4); plot2d([x',x',x'],[y',z',w']); xtitle('Combined plot 1')
```

The command `plot2d([x',x',x'],[y',z',w'])` indicates to SCILAB that three graphs will be created together with the abscissa values (x-values) of the plots given by the set `x'`, `x'`, `x'`, and the ordinate values (y-values) given by `[y', z', w']`. When producing a multiple-plot with this form of the command, the vectors that describe the plots must be passed as column vectors. Because we defined the vectors `x`, `y`, `z`, and `w`, as row vectors, we need to add the apostrophe (i.e., `x'`, `y'`, `z'`, `w'`) in the function call. Alternatively, you can create the vectors as column vectors from the very beginning, e.g.,

```
x = (-2*%pi:%pi/100:2*%pi);
y = sin(2.*x); z = cos(x); w = exp(-abs(0.1*x)).*sin(x);
```

and produce the combined plot as:

```
xset('window',5); plot2d([x,x,x],[y,z,w]); xtitle('Combined plot 2')
```

Notice that each of the three plots is shown with a different color in the two examples shown above. Also, we have used the command *xtitle* to add a title to the plot. This command can be used with any two or three-dimensional plots in SCILAB.

The following example shows another way of plotting more than one function of the same independent variable:

```
x = (0:0.1:10)';
xset('window',0);
plot2d([x,x,x], [ sin(x) cos(x) abs(sin(x) - cos(x))])
```

In this case, rather than creating vectors (such as vectors y, z, and w, used earlier), we define the functions to be plotted (`sin(x) cos(x) abs(sin(x) - cos(x))]`) within the call of the function *plot2d*.

Changing the line styles in multiple plots

So far we have used the *plot2d* command with only two arguments, namely the vectors of abscissa and ordinate values of the plots. We can use additional arguments in the call of this function that lets us have more control on the output. For example, the following call to *plot2d* is used to plot three curves simultaneously.

`plot2d([x,x,x],[sin(x) cos(x) sin(x)+cos(x)],[10 20 30])`

This call to *plot2d* includes a third argument, besides those describing the vectors that produce the plots. The vector, namely [10 20 30], represents *style* or *color* vector. We are assigning the colors identified as 10, 20, and 30, respectively, to the three plots in question. (See the section before that describes changing the foreground and background colors in a SCILAB plot). Try the command described in your SCILAB command window to see the result.

Adding a caption to the plots

The following call to *plot2d* plots the same functions as before, but it adds captions to the plot that identify the three different curves:

`plot2d([x,x,x],[sin(x) cos(x) sin(x)+cos(x)],[10 20 30],'100',...`
`    'position@velocity@acceleration')`

The command includes the vector [10 20 30] representing styles for the three curves, and the string '100' which is to be interpreted as follows:

1   Captions for the curves, given by the string *position@velocity@acceleration*, are to be displayed
0   Do not change the current graph boundary setting (i.e. use current setting)
0   Do not produce a frame in the plot

The command also includes the particle .. which is used in SCILAB to indicate continuation of a command in the next line. Try this command to see the results.

NOTE: if you experience difficulties using the last command, try this command first:

`plot(x,sin(x)+cos(x))`

This command sets up the proper scale for the plot before you try the more complicated *plot2d*.

Changing the command window limits

If you want to determine the plot window dimensions in the call to the function plot2d, you need to change the 0 in the middle position of the control string '100' to 1. For example, if you want to set your plot window to cover the ranges $-\pi < x < \pi$, and $0 < y < 1$, try the following command call:

```
plot2d([x,x,x]',[sin(x) cos(x)sin(x)+cos(x)]',[10 20 30],'110',...
   'position@velocity@acceleration', [0 0 %pi 1])
```

The last argument in the call to *plot2d* shown above includes the window dimensions as [*xmin ymin xmax ymax*] = [0 0 %pi 1], i.e., the plot window extends from point (0,0) to point (π,1). Try this command to see the result. Because the control string '110' includes a zero in the last position, the command, as shown, will not produce a frame for the plot.

Showing the frame in the plot

If you want to show the frame in the plot, you need to change the string '110' to '111' in the command above. The 1 in the third position of this control string allows the user to define the grid in the plot by adding a vector [*nx,Nx,ny,Ny*] to the function call. In this vector *nx* and *ny* are the number of sub-graduations on the x and y axes, respectively, and *Nx* and *Ny* are the number of graduations on the x and y axes, respectively. Try the following command:

```
plot2d([x,x,x]',[sin(x) cos(x) sin(x)+cos(x)]',[5,10,15],'101',...
   'position@velocity@acceleration', [0 0 %pi 1], [10 5 10 5])
```

Additional examples of *plot2d( )*

Additional examples of use of the *plot2d* command follow:

```
xset('window',1);
x=-2*%pi:%pi/100:2*%pi; plot2d(sin(x));    //simple plot

xset('window',2);
plot2d([x;x;x]',[sin(x);sin(2*x);sin(3*x)]');//multiple plot

xset('window',3);  //multiple plot with captions
  plot2d([x;x;x]',[sin(x);sin(2*x);sin(3*x)]',...
   [1,2,3],"111","s(m)@v(m/s)@a(m/s^2)",[0,-2,2*%pi,2],[2,10,2,10]);

xset('window',4); plot2d(x',sin(x)',1,'041')   //isoview plot

xset('window',5); plot2d(x',sin(x)',1,'061') //auto scale
```

The command *xbasc ()* is used to clear the existing graph before creating a new graph in the same window. It is similar to using the option *clear* in the *File* menu of the *SCILAB Graphic* window. Alternatively, you can use the command *xset('default')* to clear up a graphics window.

Plotting with symbols

To plot with symbols, use a negative integer in the style value. For example, the following statement will create a plots with symbols rather than a continuous line:

```
x = (0:1:20); y = 2.*sin(x) + rand();
xset('window',1);plot2d(x',y',-5)
```

The symbols available in a Windows-based version of SCILAB are:

```
-1  + (dot)         -2  X (cross)       -3  *               -4  diamond fill
-5  diamond         -6  triangle up     -7  triangle down   -8  trifle
-9  circle
```

You can change the size of the symbol or mark by using the command xset(*"mark",markid,marksize*), e.g.,

```
xset("mark",-4,10)
```

Repeat the plot in a new window to see the change in symbol size:

```
xset('window',0);plot2d(x',y',-5)
```

Plotting lines and symbols

The following commands plot a continuous line for the same function used above:

```
xc = (0:0.1:20);yc = 2.*sin(xc) + rand();
xset('window',2);plot2d(xc',yc',5)
```

You can plot the two graphs (line and symbols) together by keeping the window dimensions the same in two consecutive calls of the function *plot2d*:

```
xset('window',3)
plot2d(xc',yc',-5,'011','x',[0 -2 20 2],[5 20 10 10])
plot2d(xc',yc',5,'010','x',[0 -2 20 2])
```

Defining the grid

If you want to have more control not only on the grid characteristics, but other properties of the plot, use the command *plotframe*, whose general form is:

plotframe(rect, tics [,arg_opt1,arg_opt2,arg_opt3])

where, *rect* is the vector [xmin,ymin,xmax,ymax] representing the minimum and maximum values for x and y in the plot; *tics* is a vector [nx,mx,ny,my] where mx, nx are the number of x-axis intervals and subintervals, and my, ny intervals and subintervals for the y-axis. The parameters *arg_opt1*, *arg_opt2*, and *arg_opt3* are optional arguments that can be chosen from:

flags, given as a Boolean vector [*wantgrids,findbounds*] where *wantgrids* can take values of true(%t) or false(%f) depending on whether or not you want to have grids or not. The value *findbounds* can also take values of true(%t) or false(%f) depending on whether or not you want to use redefine the boundaries of the plot. If *findbounds* is %t, the bounds given in *rect* are slightly increase in order to have simpler graduations (in such a case, tics(2),tics(4) are ignored).

captions, given as a vector of 3 character strings [title, x-leg, y-leg]

subwin, a vector of size 4 specifying a sub-window definition. The sub-window is specified with the parameters [x,y,w,h], where (x,y) are the coordinates of the upper corner of the plot (with (0,0) being the upper left corner of the window), w is the plot's width, and h is the plot's height. The values of x,y,w,h are specified using proportion of the width or height of the current graphic window.

For example, to place a plot occupying the upper left quadrant of the SCILAB Graphic window, you would use the following *subwin* vector: [0.,0.,0.5,0.5]. This is interpreted as saying use a sub-window equal to half the width and the height of the SCILAB Graphic window, with its upper left corner starting at point (0,0) of the same window. Some examples are shown below.

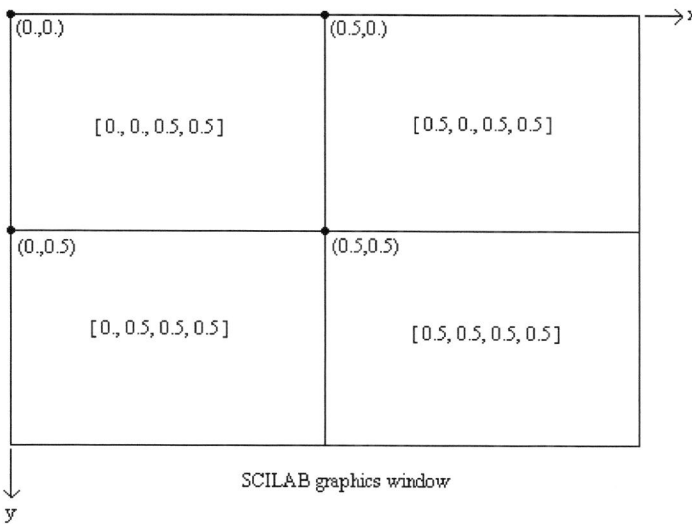

The *frameplot* command is to be used in conjunction with the *plot2d* command, rather than with the *plot* command. The following commands illustrate the use of *frameplot*:

```
x=[-0.3:0.8:27.3]'; y=rand(x);           // random number generator
rect=[min(x),min(y),max(x),max(y)];
tics=[4,10,2,5];                         //4 x-intervals and 2 y-intervals
plotframe(rect,tics,[%f,%f],['My plot','x','y'],[0,0,0.5,0.5]);
plot2d(x,y,2,'000')

plotframe(rect,tics,[%t,%f],['My plot with grids','x','y'],[0.5,0,0.5,0.5]);
plot2d(x,y,3,'000')

plotframe(rect,tics,[%t,%t],...
['My plot with grids and automatic bounds','x','y'],[0,0.5,0.5,0.5]);
plot2d(x,y,4,'000')

plotframe(rect,tics,[%f,%t],...
['My plot without grids but with automatic bounds','x','y'],...
[0.5,0.5,0.5,0.5]);
```

```
plot2d(x,y,5,'000');
```

The calls to the function *plot2d* in this example show as third argument a single value representing the style (i.e., the color) to be used for the single plot created in each call. Also, notice that, by using the string '000' in the call to *plot2d* we let *frameplot* take over in terms of defining the range and grids of the plots. This example also shows how to use the function *plotframe* to place four plots in the same window.

Calculating the grid

You can use the SCILAB command graduate to obtain a regular grid in your graphics. The call to the function graduate can take two forms:

```
[xi,xa,np]=graduate( xmi, xma, n1, n2)
[xi,xa,np]=graduate( xmi, xma)
```

where *xmi,xma* are real scalars; *n1, n2* are integers with default values 3 and 10, respectively. The function returns two real scalars *xi, xa*, and an integer value, *np*, representing a minimum interval [*xi,xa*] and a number of ticks, *np*, such that $xi \leq xmi \leq xma \leq xa$, $xa - xi / np = k(10^r)$, k in [1 3 5] for an integer r, and $n1 < np < n2$.

Try the following example:

```
y=(0:0.33:145.78)';
xbasc();plot2d1('enn',0,y)
[ymn,ymx,np]=graduate(mini(y),maxi(y))
rect=[1,ymn,prod(size(y)),ymx];
xbasc();plot2d1('enn',0,y,1,'011',' ',rect,[10,3,10,np])
```

The example shown above uses the function *plot2d1*, which is described below. Functions *mini*, *maxi*, and *prod* are also used. Use the help command with any of these functions to learn about their operation.

Other two-dimensional plot commands

The commands *plot* and *plot2d* produce continuous lines (or piecewise linear curves) for the curves being plotted. If you want to use other type of curves you want to consider using the commands *plot2d1*, *plot2d2*, *plot2d3*, and *plot2d4*. The type of curves produced by the different commands are as follows:

plot2d1: piecewise linear curves but with possible logarithmic scales
plot2d2: piecewise constant (stepped) curves
plot2d3: vertical bars
plot2d4: arrows style (used with ordinary differential equations in a phase space)

The general form for these commands is the following:

```
plot2di(str,x,y,[style,strf,leg,rect,nax])
```
(where i = 1, 2, 3, 4)

In this command, *str* is the string "*abc*", where if *a=e* the values of x are not used; if *a=o*, the x-values are the same for each curve; and *a=g* means general. If *b=l* a logarithmic scale is used on the x-axis. If $c=l$ a logarithmic scale is used on the y-axis. The other parameters in the *plot2di* command are the same as in the *plot2d* command shown earlier.

Examples of *plot2d1, plot2d2,* and *plot2d4* are shown below:

```
x = (1:0.1:10)'; z1 = 1.5+0.2*sin(x); z2 = 2+cos(x);
xset("font",2,3);         // Set font to times, size 3

plot2d1('oll',x,[z1 z2]); // Example of plot2d1 - log scale

xbasc()                   // Clear window
plot2d2('onn',x,[z1 z2]); // Example of plot2d2 - piecewise constant

xbasc()                   // Clear window
plot2d3('onn',x,[z1 z2]); // Example of plot2d3 - vertical bar plot
```

The commands below repeat the same plots as above, but selecting plot colors and adding captions to the curves. The first control string '111' indicates that logarithmic scales are to be used in the plot. The second control string '111' indicates that the graph will have captions, graph window limits ([1 10 1 10]), and a frame ([1 1 1 1]). The specifications following the second control string are the same that you would use in a call to *plot2d*.

```
xbasc()
plot2d1('oll',x,[z1 z2],[10 20], '111', 'z1@z2', [1 10 1 10], [1 1 1 1] );

xbasc()
plot2d2('onn',x,[z1 z2],[10 20], '111', 'z1@z2', [0 10 0 4], [10 10 5 8] );

xbasc()
plot2d3('onn',x,[z1 z2],[10 20], '111', 'z1@z2', [0 10 0 4], [10 10 5 8] );
```

Try also combining a piecewise constant plot with a vertical bar plot by using:

```
xbasc()
plot2d2('onn',x,[z1 z2],[10 20], '111', 'z1@z2', [0 10 0 4], [10 10 5 8] );
plot2d3('onn',x,[z1 z2],[10 20], '111', 'z1@z2', [0 10 0 4], [10 10 5 8] );
```

Histograms

Histograms are bar plots that show the frequency distribution of a data set. The data gets accumulated into classes, and the height of the histogram bars represents the count of data points in a particular class. SCILAB provides the function *histplot*, whose call is:

`histplot(npoint,data,[style,strf,leg,rect,nax])`

In this function call the parameter *npoint* is either an integer value, representing the number of classes to be included in the histogram, or a row vector of increasing values representing the class boundaries to be included. The parameter *data* is a real vector containing the data whose frequency distribution is to be obtained. The other optional parameters: *style,strf,leg,rect,* and *nax* follow the definition of function *plot2d*.

For example, try the following exercise:

```
x = rand(1:500);
classes = [0., 0.1, 0.2, 0.3, 0.4, 0.5, 1.0];
histplot(classes,x)
```

In this first exercise, there are 6 classes defined, the first 5 with the same width of 0.1, and a last class with a width of 0.5. The next exercise uses 10 classes of equal width (determined by SCILAB) by replacing the *classes* vector with the integer number 10:

```
xbasc(); histplot(10,x)
```

Because the data was generated using the uniform random number generator function *rand()*, the histogram shows a pretty uniform set of bars.

Creating sub windows with the command *xsetech*

The command *xsetech* is used to set the sub window of a graphic window for a specific graph. The general form of this command is:

xsetech(wrect [,frect,logflag])

where *wrect* = a vector of size 4 (sub window definition), *frect* = a vector of size 4 (just like the *rect* argument of *plot2d*); and, *logflag* = a string of size 2 "xy", where x and y can be "n" or "l". In this case, "n" stands for normal and "l" for log scale. x is for the x-axis, and y for the y-axis.

The following example will place four different versions of the same plot in a single window:

```
//Script to plot four different versions of a graph in the same window
x = (1:0.1:10)'; z1 = 2.5 + 0.2*sin(x); z2 = 3 + cos(x);
xset("font",2,3);
xbasc()
xsetech([0.,0.,0.5,0.5],[-1,1,-1,1]);        //Upper-left quadrant
plot2d([x,x],[z1,z2],[4 10]);
xtitle('Plot2d - piecewise linear');
xsetech([0.5,0.,0.5,0.5],[-1,1,-1,1]);       //Upper-right quadrant
plot2d1('oll',x,[z1,z2],[3 11]);
xtitle('Plot2d1 - with logarithmic scales');
xsetech([0.,0.5,0.5,0.5],[-1,1,-1,1]);       //Lower-left quadrant
plot2d2('onn',x,[z1,z2],[2,17]);
xtitle('Plot2d2 - piecewise constant');
xsetech([0.5,0.5,0.5,0.5],[-1,1,-1,1]);  //Lower-right quadrant
plot2d3('onn',x,[z1,z2],[12 22]);
xtitle('Plot2d3 - vertical bar plot');
```

Copy these commands into a text file to run it as a script.

A second example of using xetech() to split a graph is shown next:

```
xbasc();
t = (0:0.05:1)'; st=sin(2*%pi*t);
xsetech([0,0,1,0.5]);                //Upper half of window
plot2d2("onn",t,st);
xsetech([0.,0.5,1,0.5]);             //Lower half of window
plot2d3("onn",t,st);
```

Modifying plot properties

The following commands can be used to modify plot properties:

xgrid(style): adds a grid to a 2D graph; the calling parameter is the color number (see examples above).
xtitle(title,xlabel,ylabel,frame): adds title and axes labels, as well as a frame if required.
titlepage(string): places title page in the middle of the plot
xclea(x,y,w,h): clears the area in the plot defined by upper left corner = (x,y), width = w, height = h.
xstring(x,y,str,[angle,flag]): draws the string str starting at point (x,y).

File *plot3.txt* includes these commands to produce a plot. A listing of the file follows:

```
x=-2*%pi:%pi/100:2*%pi;              //Define x
y1=sin(x);y2=cos(x);y3=x;            //Calculate signals y1, y2, y3
X=[x;x;x]; Y = [y1;y2;y3];           //Create plot vectors
xbasc();                             //Clean graphs windows

//Plot the three signals using plot2d1
plot2d1("gnn",X',Y',[1 2 3]',"111","position@velocity@acceleration",...
[-3,-3,3,2],[2,20,5,5]);

xtitle(["Motion";"signals"],"time(s)","x(m), u(m/s), a(m/s^2)");  //Title
xgrid(15);                                                         //Grid
xclea(-2.7,1.5,1.5,1.5);                      //Clear a small window
xstring(-2.4,0.8,"Verify your results");      //Write to cleared window
titlepage("Non-Linear Motion");               //Place title in mid page
```

Use the help feature in SCILAB to find more information about these commands. To produce the plot use the command:

```
exec('plot3.txt')
```

Notes:
xtitle lets you place a title for the plot, but also label the axes – a feature that has been missing in our previous examples.
xstring lets you write notes in your plots at any location within the graph that you desire.
titlepage places a string in the middle of the plot window. This may not be desirable for many plots for it may muddle the plots.

Storing a plot as a pixmap – an example of animation

The contents of a plot can be temporarily stored as a pixmap by using the command

xset(*'pixmap',1*)

For example, try this exercise:

```
x = (0:0.1:10)'; y = sin(x); z = cos(x);
xset('pixmap',1)              //Activates pixmap option
plot(x,y)                     //Plot is not shown
xset('wshow')                 //Recalls pixmap to screen
```

```
plot(x,z)                    //New plot to pixmap, screen is cleared
xset('wshow')                //New plot is shown
```

The *plot* command is designed to clear out the current graph before plotting a new plot, therefore, there is no need to clear the pixmap when creating a new graph with plot. The following exercise illustrates the use of pixmaps with the command *plot2d*:

```
xbasc()                      //Clears the current graphics window
plot2d(x,y)                  //No plot is shown
xset('wshow')                //Recent plot is shown
plot2d(x,z)                  //No new plot is shown in graphics window
xset('wshow')                //Two plots shown in graphics window
```

<u>Clearing the pixmap</u>

The command *plot2d* does not clear the most recent screen (or pixmap) before creating a new plot. If you want to clear the pixmap for a new plot use the command:

```
xset('wwpc')
```

For example:

```
xbasc()                      //Clears the current graphics window
plot2d(x,y)                  //No plot is shown
xset('wshow')                //Recent plot is shown
xset('wwpc')                 //Clear out pixmap, but not graphics window
plot2d(x,z)                  //No plot is shown because pixmap is empty
xset('wshow')                //Two plots shown in graphics window
```

<u>Animation of a plot</u>

The following lines lets you produce an animation of the sine wave by using pixmaps:

```
xbasc()
x = (0:0.1:10)';
for j = 1:1000, y =sin(x+j./10); plot(x,y), xset('wshow'), end
```

This example takes advantage of the ability of the plot command to clear the graphics window after every pass. If we were to use the command *plot2d* to produce the animation, we need to include the command xset('wwpc') to clear the graphics window after every plot. Try the following exercise:

```
xbasc()
x = (0:0.1:10)';
for j = 1:1000, y =sin(x+j./10); plot2d(x,y), xset('wshow'), xset('wwpc'), end
```

The following example shows a second animation:

```
xbasc()
x = (0:0.1:10)';
for j = 1:1000, y =exp(-0.01.*j).*sin(x); plot(x,y), xset('wshow'), end
```

While this animation run you will see the shape of the graph changing slightly, however, if you observe the vertical scale carefully, you will notice that it covers smaller and smaller ranges of y as time increases. Because we are using the plot command to produce the graph, we have no control over the vertical scale and we cannot see very clearly the changes in the graph as the value of j increases. The following commands, using the *plot2d* function with grid control, lets you see the graph changes in more detail:

```
xbasc()
x = (0:0.1:10)';
for j = 1:1000, y =exp(-0.01.*j).*sin(x); ...
    plot2d(x,y,5,'010',' ',[0 -1 10 1]), ...
    xset('wshow'), xset('wwpc'), end
```

The command *plot2d* in this exercise was set such that no frame or grid is shown (the control string is '010). To include a frame in the plots use:

```
xbasc()
x = (0:0.1:10)';
for j = 1:1000, y =exp(-0.01.*j).*sin(x); ...
    plot2d(x,y,5,'011',' ',[0 -1 10 1],[5 10 5 10]), ...
    xset('wshow'), xset('wwpc'), end
```

The resulting animation will show a sinusoidal wave flattening out. The following command will produce a moving and flattening sinusoidal wave:

```
xbasc()
x = (0:0.1:10)';
for j = 1:50, y = exp(-0.01.*j).*sin(x+j./10); ...
    plot2d(x,y,5,'011',' ',[0 -1 10 1],[5 10 5 10]), ...
    xset('wshow'), xset('wwpc'), end
```

The colormap

The color map is a $m \times 3$ matrix, where m is the number of colors available. When SCILAB starts, a total of 32 colors are available. These are referred to by its color number. (A list of the basic 32 color numbers was presented in an earlier section.) A color number can be defined as the set of three values: *cmap(i,1)*, *cmap(i,2)*, and *cmap(i,3)*, corresponding, respectively, to *red*, *green,* and *blue* intensities expressed as numbers between 0 and 1. The colormap matrix would be, therefore, referred to as *map*. You can change the colormap by using the command

xset(*"colormap",cmap*).

An example of colormap modification

The following commands will let you create your own colormap with 100 colors. Before running these commands, click on the Restart menu to reset SCILAB. The first step after resetting is to create vectors R (red intensity), G (green intensity), and B (blue intensity), as follows (remember that lines preceded by / are comment lines):

```
// Define π as 100, red intensities from 1/m to 1
m = 100; R = [(1:m)/m];

// Green intensities go from 2/m to 1 and back to 2/m
n2=m/2; G1 = [(1:n2)/n2]; G2 = [(n2+1:m)]; G3 = (m-G2)/(m-n2);   G = [G1, G3];
```

```
// Blue intensities are zero for the first and last 25 values,
// and vary from 2/m to 1 for values 25 to 74.
B = [zeros(1:m/4),G1,zeros(1:m/4)];

// Create color map matrix with R, G, and B, and replace existing color map:
myColorMap1 = [R',G',B']; xset('colormap',myColorMap1);
```

Then, plot a series of lines corresponding to different colors in your colormap:

```
// Produce a graph illustrating the 100 different colors
xbasc();
x = (0:0.1:1)'; y = zeros(x);
for j = 1:100, y = y+2; plot2d(x,y,j,'010',' ',[0 0 1 200]), end
```

A script with many colormap examples

The following lines can be placed in a script, e.g., plot6.txt, and executed from the SCILAB command window. It illustrates other colormaps by plotting 100 or 120 lines of different colors. The comments in the script explain the way that the colormaps were created:

```
//---------------------------------------------------------------------------
// Case 2 (Different tones of red)
// Green and blue all set to zero

m=100; R=[(1:m)/m]; G = [zeros(1:m)]; B = [zeros(1:m)];
myColorMap2 = [R',G',B']; xset('colormap',myColorMap2);
xbasc();
x = (0:0.1:1)'; y = zeros(x);
for j = 1:100, y = y+2; plot2d(x,y,j,'010',' ',[0 0 1 200]), end
xtitle('Case 2')
pause



//Case 3 (different tones of light blue)
//Green and blue all set to one

m=100; R=[(1:m)/m]; G = [ones(1:m)]; B = [ones(1:m)];
myColorMap3 = [R',G',B']; xset('colormap',myColorMap3);
xbasc();
x = (0:0.1:1)'; y = zeros(x);
for j = 1:100, y = y+2; plot2d(x,y,j,'010',' ',[0 0 1 200]), end
xtitle('Case 3')
pause


//Case 4 (red to purple to blue)
//Green set to zero, blue set to one
m=100; R=[(1:m)/m]; G = [zeros(1:m)]; B = [ones(1:m)];
myColorMap4 = [R',G',B']; xset('colormap',myColorMap4);
xbasc();
x = (0:0.1:1)'; y = zeros(x);
for j = 1:100, y = y+2; plot2d(x,y,j,'010',' ',[0 0 1 200]), end
xtitle('Case 4')
pause
```

```
//Case 5 (different tones of green)
//Green set to one, blue set to zero
m=100; R=[(1:m)/m]; G = [ones(1:m)]; B = [zeros(1:m)];
myColorMap5 = [R',G',B']; xset('colormap',myColorMap5);
xbasc();
x = (0:0.1:1)'; y = zeros(x);
for j = 1:100, y = y+2; plot2d(x,y,j,'010',' ',[0 0 1 200]), end
xtitle('Case 5')
pause



//Case 6 (black, blue, green, red, black)
//Intensities in triangular shaped functions
m = 120; n1 = m/4;  n2 = m/2; n3 = 3*m/4;
//Red intensities peak at n1
R1 = [(1:n1)/n1]; R2 = [(n1+1:m)]; R3 = (m-R2)/(m-n1);  R = [R1, R3];
// Green intensities peak at n2
G1 = [(1:n2)/n2]; G2 = [(n2+1:m)]; G3 = (m-G2)/(m-n2);  G = [G1, G3];
//Blue intensities peak at n3
B1 = [(1:n3)/n3]; B2 = [(n3+1:m)]; B3 = (m-B2)/(m-n3);  B = [B1, B3];
myColorMap6 = [R',G',B']; xset('colormap',myColorMap6);
xbasc();
x = (0:0.1:1)'; y = zeros(x);
for j = 1:120, y = y+2; plot2d(x,y,j,'010',' ',[0 0 1 240]), end
xtitle('Case 6')
pause



//Case 7 (black, red, green, blue, black)
//Intensities in triangular shaped functions but peaks for red and blue
//are reversed
m = 120; n1 = m/4;  n2 = m/2; n3 = 3*m/4;
//Red intensities peak at n3
R1 = [(1:n3)/n3]; R2 = [(n3+1:m)]; R3 = (m-R2)/(m-n3);  R = [R1, R3];
// Green intensities peak at n2
G1 = [(1:n2)/n2]; G2 = [(n2+1:m)]; G3 = (m-G2)/(m-n2);  G = [G1, G3];
//Blue intensities peak at n1
B1 = [(1:n1)/n1]; B2 = [(n1+1:m)]; B3 = (m-B2)/(m-n1);  B = [B1, B3];
myColorMap7 = [R',G',B']; xset('colormap',myColorMap7);
xbasc();
x = (0:0.1:1)'; y = zeros(x);
for j = 1:120, y = y+2; plot2d(x,y,j,'010',' ',[0 0 1 240]), end
xtitle('Case 7')
pause
//-------------------------------------------------------------------------
```

When running the script, SCILAB will produce numbered prompts 1(->) at each pause. Type the command return at the prompt to continue the script execution. The graph below shows the intensity of the three basic colors red, green, and blue for case 7 in the script.

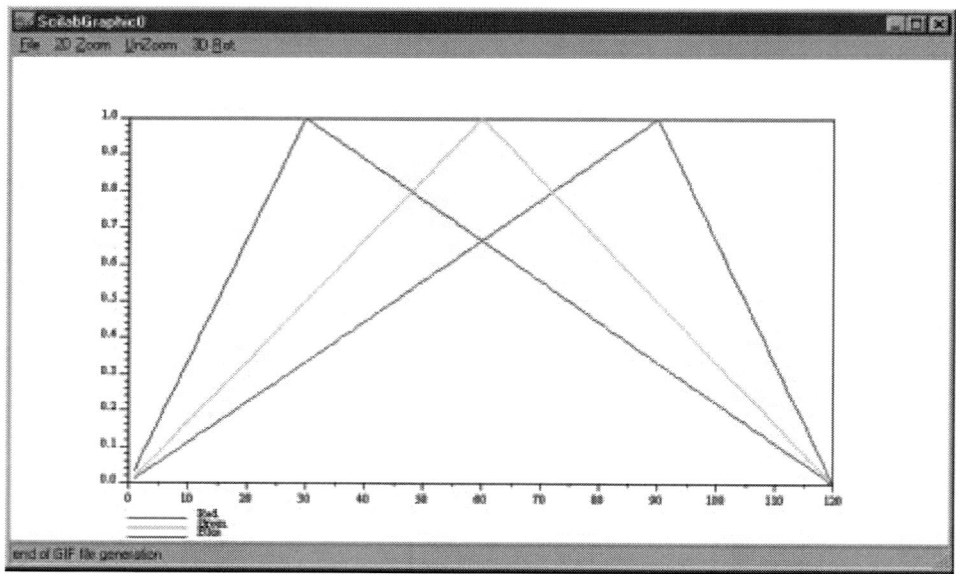

Obtaining a color map with the function *hotcolormap( )*

If you want to obtain a colormap with n colors, with a nice gradation of colors, use the function

```
hotcolormap(n)
```

where n is the number of colors requested. For example,

```
cMap = hotcolormap(40)
xset('colormap',cMap)
plot3d() // This is a demo of the use of function plot3d
```
(see below)

Obtaining a color map with the function *graycolormap( )*

The function *graycolormap()*, whose call is

```
cmap=graycolormap(n)
```

produces a colormap with *n* gradations of gray varying linearly from black to white. The exercise shown above for hotcolormap() is repeated below with the graycolormap() function:

```
cMap = graycolormap(40)
xset('colormap',cMap)
plot3d() // This is a demo of the use of function plot3d
```
(see below)

Density plots

A density plot is a two-dimensional representation of a three-dimensional function. The three-dimensional function $z = f(x,y)$ is projected onto the x-y plane with different gradations of gray (or color) showing the function values. In SCILAB, a density plot is also referred to as a grayplot. The grayplot command is described by the call:

grayplot(x,y,z,[strf,rect,nax])

where x and y are real row vectors of size n1 and n2, and z is a real matrix of size (n1,n2). The value $z(i,j)$ is the value of the function $z = f(x,y)$ at point $(x(i),y(j))$. The definition of the other optional parameters, *strf, rect*, and *nax* is the same as in the command *plot2d*.

Examples of grayplot applications

The *grayplot* command uses the current colormap to produce the gradation of the plot. Check the results of using the default colormap in SCILAB:

As an example, try the following commands:

```
xset('default'); xbasc();            // Set defaults, clear graphic
x=-10:10; y=-10:10;m1 =rand(21,21);  // Generate data for plot
grayplot(x,y,m1,"111",[-20,-20,20,20])  // Call grayplot function
```

The default colormap is a color scale. Try a second example:

```
t=-%pi:0.1:%pi; m2=sin(t)'*cos(t);   // Generate a second set of data
xbasc();grayplot(t,t,m2)             // Clear graph, call grayplot
```

Density plots in grayscale

The following exercise changes the colormap of the first example shown to different tones of gray:

```
R = [1:256]/256; cMap = [R', R', R']; xset('colormap',cMap);
grayplot(x,y,m1,"111",[-20,-20,20,20])
```

For the second example, we would get:

```
xbasc();grayplot(t,t,m2)
```

Density plots in a reddish scale

If you want to create a grayplot with different tones of red, use, for example:

```
R = [1:256]/256; G = 0.1*ones(R);
cMap = [R', G', G']; xset('colormap',cMap);
grayplot(x,y,m1,"111",[-20,-20,20,20])
```

For the second example under study:

```
xbasc();grayplot(t,t,m2)
```

Smooth density plots

The function *Sgrayplot* is an alternative to *grayplot* producing smoothed-out contours in the plane. The call to the function is the same as that of *grayplot*, thus, in the following script we repeat the exercises above using *Sgrayplot*. When running this script, type return to continue script execution after the pauses.

```
xset('default'); xbasc();
x=-10:10; y=-10:10;m1 =rand(21,21);
Sgrayplot(x,y,m1,"111",[-20,-20,20,20])
pause

t=-%pi:0.1:%pi; m2=sin(t)'*cos(t);
xbasc(); Sgrayplot(t,t,m2)
pause

R = [1:256]/256; cMap = [R', R', R']; xset('colormap',cMap);
xbasc(); Sgrayplot(x,y,m1,"111",[-20,-20,20,20])
pause

R = [1:256]/256; G = 0.1*ones(R);
cMap = [R', G', G']; xset('colormap',cMap);
xbasc(); Sgrayplot(x,y,m1,"111",[-20,-20,20,20])
pause

xbasc(); Sgrayplot(t,t,m2)
```

Color map of a matrix

The function *Maplot* (must use upper case), with call

`Matplot(a,[strf,rect,nax])`

is used to produce a color plot of the matrix a, of size (n1,n2). The color associated with element a(i,j) is placed in the square of side = 1 with center at location x=j, y=(n2-i+1). The optional parameters, *strf, rect*, and *nax* are the same as in function *plot2d*.

As an example, try the following commands:

```
x = (0:0.1:10)'; y = (0:0.1:10)';
m = x*y';
xbasc();
Matplot(a);
```

A second example uses the control string and provides graph frame and tick information:

`Matplot(a,'011',[-10,-10,110,110],[5 12 5 12])`

Plotting a function of the form y = f(x)

The command *fplot2d* can be used to plot a function in a manner similar to that produced by the plot command, except that in *fplot2d* the function is defined as an external function of the type $y = f(x)$. For example, the following commands, stored in the file *plot4.txt*, will plot the function $y = sin(x) + sin(2*x)$:

```
x = (0:0.025:10);
deff("[y]=f(x)","y = sin(x) + sin(2*x)");
fplot2d(x,f)
```

To generate the plot use the command:

```
exec('plot4.txt')
```

To add a grid and labels use, for example:

```
xgrid( )
xtitle("Wave signal","time(s)","signal(J)");
```

Plotting a function of two variables using grayscale

To produce a grayscale or density plot of a function $z = f(x,y)$ use the command *fgrayplot*. The general call to this function is:

```
fgrayplot(x,y,f,[strf,rect,nax])
```

where x, and y are real row vectors, and f is an external function of type y=f(x,y). This function can be defined as a function file or with the on-line function definition command deff. The optional arguments *strf, rect*, and *nax*, in fgrayplot, are the same as in the *plot2d* function.

As an example, try the following exercise:

```
R = [1:256]/256; cMap = [R',R',R']; xset('colormap',cMap); xbasc();
deff('[z] = f(x,y)','z = x^2+y^2');
x = -2:0.1:2; y = x;
fgrayplot(x,y,f,'111',[-2.2, -2.2, 2.2, 2.2]);
```

To embellish the graph, you could add a title such as:

```
xtitle(['Grayplot produced'; 'with fgrayplot command']);
```

Try the plot again with a green-type of scale:

```
G = [1:256]/256; R = 0.1*ones(G);
cMap = [R',G',R']; xset('colormap',cMap); xbasc();
fgrayplot(x,y,f,'111',[-2.2, -2.2, 2.2, 2.2]);
```

Smooth grayscale function plot

To produce a smoothed-out grayscale or colorscale contour plot use the function *Sfgrayplot*. The following script shows the exercises presented above for *fgrayplot* repeated using *Sfgrayplot*. Type return after each pause to continue script execution.

```
//Green colorscale
G = [1:256]/256; R = 0.1*ones(G);
cMap = [R',G',R']; xset('colormap',cMap); xbasc();
Sfgrayplot(x,y,f,'111',[-2.2, -2.2, 2.2, 2.2]);

pause

//Gray scale
R = [1:256]/256; cMap = [R',R',R']; xset('colormap',cMap); xbasc();
deff('[z] = f(x,y)','z = x^2+y^2');
x = -2:0.1:2; y = x;
Sfgrayplot(x,y,f,'111',[-2.2, -2.2, 2.2, 2.2]);
xtitle(['Grayplot produced'; 'with fgrayplot command']);
```

Plotting a vector field in the plane

SCILAB provides the function *fchamp* to plot a vector field in the plane defined by a function $v(x,y) = [v_1(x,y)\; v_2(x,y)]$. The general call to the function is

champ(*x,y,fx,fy,[arfact,rect,strf]*)

where *x* and *y* are vectors that define a grid in the x-y plane, *fx* and *fy* are matrices that contain the x- and y-components of the vector field at the gridpoints defined by x and y, e.g., fx(i,j) = x-component of vector field at (x(i),y(j)). The optional argument *arfact* is a real number representing a scale factor for the display of the arrow heads on the plot (default value is 1.0). The optional argument *rect* is a vector of four components [xmin,ymin,xmax,ymax] that provides the frame of the plot. Finally, the optional argument *strf* is a string of length 3 "xyz" similar to that used in command *plot2d*. However, the first character x of this string has no effect when used in the command champ.

As an example, try the following exercise:

```
xbasc(); x = (0:0.1:10); y = (0:0.1:10);
fx = sin(x)'*cos(y); fy = cos(x)'*sin(y);
champ(x,y,fx,fy);
```

A variant of the command *champ* is the command *champ1, which* uses color, besides arrow length, to indicate the intensity of the field. Command *champ1* uses the same arguments as *champ*. Try this example:

```
champ1(x,y,fx,fy);
```

Direction field vector plot for an ordinary differential equation

The function *fchamp*, whose call is given by

fchamp(f,t,x,y,[arfact,rect,strf])

can be used to plot the vector direction field corresponding to a given differential equation.

The argument f in the function call is an external (function or character string) or a list that describes an ordinary differential equation. The argument f can be a function name f, corresponding to a function of the form *y=f(t,x,[u])*, where f returns a column vector of size 2, y, which gives the value of the direction field f at point x and at time t. The parameter f can also be an object of type list, i.e., *list(f,u1)* where f is a function of type *y=f(t,x,u)* and u1 gives the value of the parameter u. The parameter *t* is the selected time for the plot. The parameters x and y are two row vectors of size n1 and n2 defining the grid on which the direction field is computed. The optional arguments *arfact, rect,* and *strf,* follow the same definition as in function *champ*.

For example, consider a system of differential equations defined by

$$\frac{d\mathbf{x}}{dt} = \begin{bmatrix} dx_1/dt \\ dx_2/dt \end{bmatrix} = \begin{bmatrix} x_1 + x_2 \\ x_1 + x_2(1-x_1) \end{bmatrix}$$

where x = [$x_1(t)$, $x_2(t)$], dx_1/dt = x_1+x_2 [=xx1], dx_2/dt = $x_1+x_2(1-x_1)$ [=xx2]. To plot a field vector plot in the domain -1 < xs < 1, -1 < ys < 1, at t = 0, we use:

-->deff('[dxdt]=der(t,x)',['xx1=x(1)+x(2)';'xx2=x(1)+x(2)*(1-x(1))';'dxdt= [xx1;xx2]'])

-->xs = -1:0.1:1; ys = -1:0.1:1;

-->fchamp(der,0,xs,ys)

THREE DIMENSIONAL GRAPHICS

Plotting data in 3D

SCILAB provides the function plot3d for plotting surfaces representing functions of the form z = f(x,y). The call to the function plot3d can take any of the following three forms:

plot3d(x,y,z,[theta,alpha,leg,flag,ebox])

plot3d(xf,yf,zf,[theta,alpha,leg,flag,ebox])

plot3d(xf,yf,list(zf,colors),[theta,alpha,leg,flag,ebox])

<u>First form of the function call</u>

In the first form of the call, namely,

plot3d(x,y,z,[theta,alpha,leg,flag,ebox])

the arguments x and y are row vectors of sizes n1 and n2, representing the x-axis and y-axis coordinates or the rectangular grid in x-y where the surface will be projected. These coordinates must be monotone, i.e., they must be in either increasing or decreasing order. The argument z is a matrix of size (n1,n2), so that z(i,j) represents the value of the surface at point (x(i),y(j)).

Simple example of plot3d and rotation of the three-dimensional graph

A simple example is:

x = (0:0.1:10)';y=x;z=x*y';

plot3d(x,y,z)

This example produces a three-dimensional plot with a point of view at 45° from the positive x- and z-axes, i.e., in the main diagonal of the positive octant in which space is divided by the Cartesian coordinate system. You can move the point of view by clicking on the menu item "*3D Rot*", then pointing and dragging the figure with your mouse. This will show the new location of the graphs borders. When you find one location that you like, press the mouse button and SCILAB will redraw the surface in its new orientation. Two positions for this example are shown below. First, the default position:

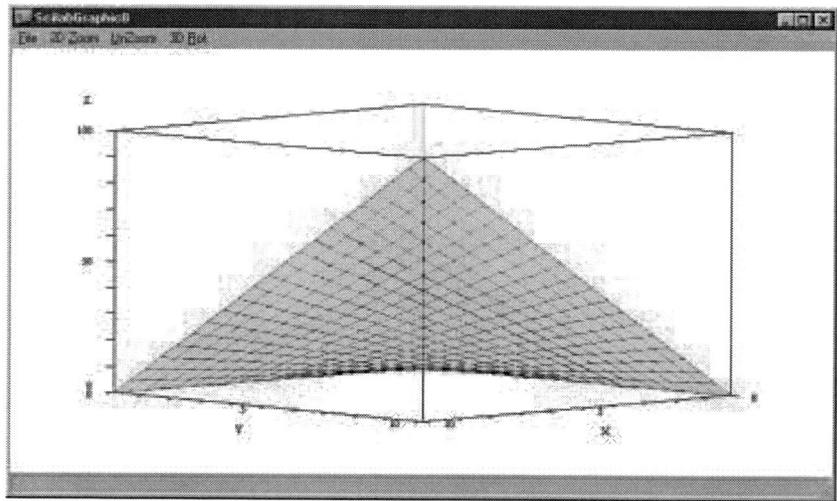

Next, after rotation:

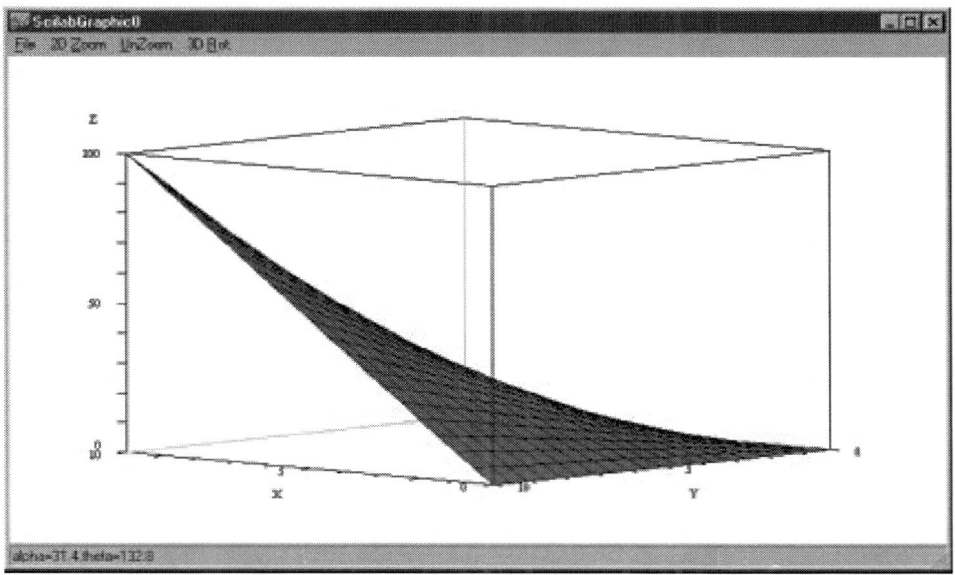

Additional arguments in the function call

The optional arguments, *theta, alpha, leg, flag*, and *ebox*, apply to the first form of the function call, as well as to the other two forms of the call listed above. These optional arguments are described as follows:

theta, and *alpha* are angles in degrees representing the spherical coordinates of the observation point. The angle theta is measured counterclockwise from the positive x-axis in the x-y plane, while the angle alpha is measured from the positive z-axis.

leg represents strings that define the captions for each axis with the character @ as field separator. The simplest implementation of this string is "X@Y@Z" or "x@y@z".

flag is a real vector of size three, i.e., flag=[mode,type,box], where

> *mode* is a string that controls the treatment of hidden parts of the surface as follows:
> If mode>0, the hidden parts of the surface are removed and the surface is painted solidly with the color whose number is represented by the value of mode.
> If mode=0, the hidden parts of the surface are drawn.
> If mode<0, then, only the shadow of the surface is painted with color or pattern id = mode.

> *type* is an integer representing the scaling of the surface according to:

>> If type=0 the plot is made using the current 3D scaling, which has been set by a previous call to *param3d, plot3d, contour* or *plot3d1*, or by SCILAB's default graphic parameters.

If type=1 the boundaries are specified by the value of the optional argument *ebox* (see below).
If type takes other values, the boundaries are computed using the given data.

box is an integer that controls the frame around the plot as follows:

If box=0 or 1, no frame is drawn.
If box=2, only the axes behind the surface are drawn.
If box=3, a box surrounding the surface is drawn and captions are added.
If box=4, a box surrounding the surface is drawn, captions and axes are added.

ebox is used when *type* in *flag* is equal to 1. It specifies the boundaries of the plot as the vector [xmin,xmax,ymin,ymax,zmin,zmax].

Examples using the additional parameters

This first example changes the angle for the point of view and adds captions to the axes:

plot3d(x,y,z,125,-45,'s(m)@r(m)@q(m)')

The next example does the same as the first but adds the flag option with *box*:

plot3d(x,y,z,75,-30,'s(m)@r(m)@q(m)',[1 4], [-1,11,-1,11,-1,105])

resulting in the following plot:

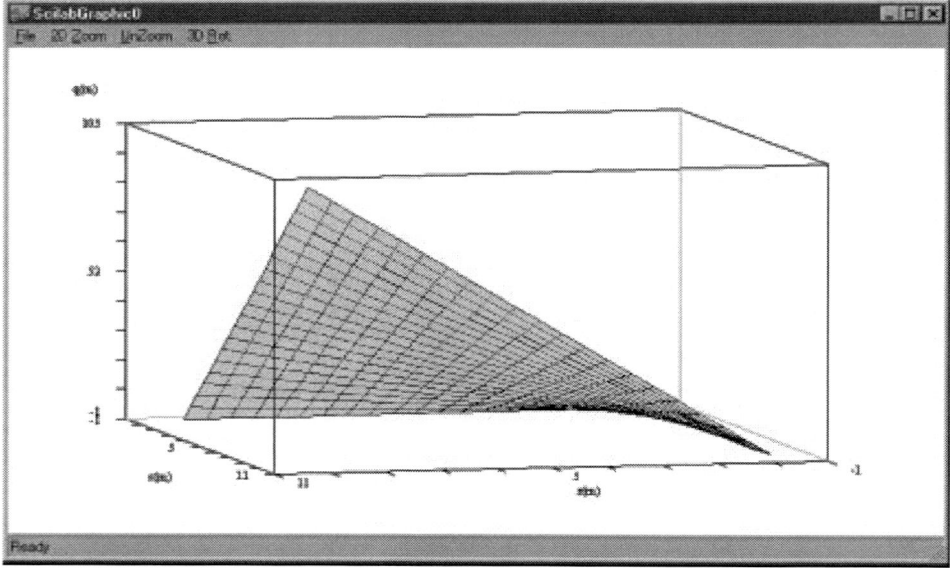

Call to plot3d using facets

The following call to the function plot3d, namely,

```
plot3d(xf,yf,zf,[theta,alpha,leg,flag,ebox])
```

requires as arguments the matrices xf,yf,zf of size (nf,n) that define the n facets used to draw the required surface. Each facet i is defined by a polygon with nf points. The x-, y-, and z-coordinates of the points of the i-th facet are given respectively by xf(:,i), yf(:,i) and zf(:,i).

A third call to the function plot3d is

```
plot3d(xf,yf,list(zf,colors),[theta,alpha,leg,flag,ebox])
```

which is used to assign a specific color to each facet by using the argument *list(zf,colors)* instead of zf. In this version of the call *colors* is a vector of size n, with *colors(i)* being the color of facet i. If *colors(i)* is negative, color id = colors(i) is used and the boundary of the facet is drawn.

Using the last two versions of the *plot3d* function call, you can draw multiple plots by replacing xf, yf and zf by multiple matrices assembled by rows as [xf1 xf2 ...], [yf1 yf2 ...] and [zf1 zf2 ...].

Obtaining facet information

Facet information can be obtained from measurements, as would be the case of plotting the surface of a solid object, or by using the function *genfac3d* to compute four sided facets from the surface z=f(x,y). This function uses the call

```
[xx,yy,zz]=genfac3d(x,y,z,[mask])
```

where xx,yy, and zz are matrices of size (4,n-1*m-1), and their elements xx(:,i) ,yy(:,i) and zz(:,i) are the x-, y-, and z-coordinates of the 4 points of the i-th four sided facet from the surface. The vectors x, and y are vectors of size m and n, respectively, representing a grid in the x-y plane, while the matrix z, of size (m,n), contains elements z(i,j) representing the function z = f(x(i),y(j)). The optional argument *mask* is a Boolean matrix with the same size as z, and is used to select the entries of z to be represented by facets.

For example, for the surface z = f(x,y) described by:

```
x = (0:0.1:10)';y=x;z=x*y';
```

the following call to genfac3d will provide the matrices representing the facets:

```
[xf,yf,zf]=genfac3d(x,y,z)
```

Type xf in the SCILAB command window to see the contents of matrix xf, for example.

Obtaining facet information given a parametric surface

If the surface is described by the parametric representation, x = x(u,v), y = y(u,v), and z = z(u,v), where u and v are real parameters, the command *eval3dp* can be used to provide facet information. The call for this command is:

```
[xx,yy,zz]=eval3dp(fun,u,v)
```

where xx, yy, and zz are described as in the call to *genfac3d*, *fun* is the name of the SCILAB function that describes the surface, and u and are vectors of size n, and m, respectively, representing a grid of the parameters u and v that will generate the surface.

For example, try this exercise to obtain facet information and plot the resulting surface:

```
x = (0:%pi/20:2*%pi)';y=x;
deff('[x,y,z] = spar(u,v)', ...
["x=u.*sin(u).*cos(v)";"y=u.*cos(u).*cos(v)";"z=u.*sin(u)"])
[xf, yf, zf] = eval3dp(spar,x,y)
plot3d(xf,yf,zf);
```

Three-dimensional surface plot with color or gray scales

An alternative to the use of *plot3d* is the function *plot3d1*, which produces a three-dimensional gray or color level plot of a surface z = f(x,y). The call to this function takes two forms, namely,

```
plot3d1(x,y,z,[theta,alpha,leg,flag,ebox])
plot3d1(xf,yf,zf,[theta,alpha,leg,flag,ebox])
```

The arguments used are exactly the same as those used in *plot3d*, with the caveat that only the sign of the flag(1), i.e., the mode, parameter is used. If this value is negative, a grid is not drawn.

An example follows:

```
x = (0:0.1:10)';y=x;z=x*y';
plot3d(x,y,z)
```

While this result does not show a color scale, by rotating the graph by about 180 degrees about the z-axis will show the color scale in the front face of the surface. You can accomplish that by dragging the curve around with the mouse, or by using the command:

```
plot3d1(x,y,z,225,45)
```

The following example will produce a parametric curve with color scale. The function plo3d1 is called with facet information as arguments.

```
x = (0:%pi/20:2*%pi)';y=x;
deff('[x,y,z] = spar(u,v)', ...
["x=u.*sin(u).*cos(v)";"y=u.*cos(u).*cos(v)";"z=u.*sin(u)"])
[xf, yf, zf] = eval3dp(spar,x,y)
plot3d1(xf,yf,zf);
```

Plotting functions in 3D

The command *fplot3d* produces the plot of a surface defined by a function f. The call to the command is:

fplot3d(x,y,f,[theta,alpha,leg,flag,ebox])

where x is a row vector of size n, y is a row vector of size m, and f is an external function of the type z=f(x,y). The vectors x and y define grid where the function is to be plotted. The remaining, optional, arguments are described above under function *plot3d*.

Try the following example:

```
x = (-10:0.5:10); y = (0:0.5,10);
deff('[z] = fs(x,y)','z = x^2+y^2');
fplot3d(x,y,fs);
```

Grayscale or colorscale three-dimensional plot for functions

The function *fplot3d1* produces a colorscale or grayscale plot of the surface defined by the SCILAB function z = f(x,y). The call and arguments are very similar to that of function fplot3d:

fplot3d1(x,y,f,[theta,alpha,leg,flag,ebox])

As an example, we repeat the exercise above using *fplot3d1*:

```
x = (-10:0.5:10); y = (0:0.5,10);
deff('[z] = fs(x,y)','z = x^2+y^2');
fplot3d(x,y,fs);
```

Parametric curves in space

Earlier we saw how to plot a parametric curve in space by combining the functions *eval3dp* and `plot3d`. SCILAB provides a function dedicated to the plotting of parametric curves:

param3d(x,y,z,[theta,alpha,leg,flag,ebox])

The arguments x,y, and z must be vectors of the same size representing the coordinates of points of the parametric curve. The remaining optional arguments (theta, alpha, leg, flag, and ebox) were described in the call to function *plot3d*.

Try the following examples:

```
x = (0:%pi/20:2*%pi)';y=x;    //parametric curve x,y,z, = f(u,v)
deff('[x,y,z] = spar(u,v)', ...
["x=u.*sin(u).*cos(v)";"y=u.*cos(u).*cos(v)";"z=u.*sin(u)"])
[xs, ys, zs] = spar(u,v);
param3d(xs,ys,zs);
```

```
t = (0:%pi/100:2*%pi)';      //parametric curve x,y,z, = f(t)
deff('[x,y,z] = helix(t)', ...
["x = 2.*sin(5.*t)";"y = 2.*cos(5.*t)";"z = 2.5.*t"]);
[xs, ys, zs] = helix(t);
param3d(xs,ys,zs);
```

Plotting multiple parametric curves in space

A companion function, *param3d1*, can be used to produce multiple plots. This function can be called in any of two ways:

param3d1(x,y,z,[theta,alpha,leg,flag,ebox])
param3d1(x,y,list(z,colors),[theta,alpha,leg,flag,ebox])

In these calls, x,y,z are matrices of the matrices of the same size (nl,nc). Each column i of the matrices corresponds to the coordinates of the i- th curve. You can assign a specific color for each curve by using the argument *list(z,colors)* instead of z, where *colors* is a vector of size nc. If *color(i)* is negative the curve is plotted using the mark with *id = abs(style(i))+1*. If *style(i)* is strictly positive, a plain line with *color id = style(i)* or a *dashed line with dash id = style(i)* is used. The remaining optional arguments *theta, alpha, leg, flag*, and *ebox*, are described in function *plot3d*.

An example follows:

```
x = (0:%pi/20:2*%pi)';y=x;
deff('[x,y,z] = spar(u,v)', ...
["x=u.*sin(u).*cos(v)";"y=u.*cos(u).*cos(v)";"z=u.*sin(u)"])
[xs, ys, zs] = spar(u,v);
param3d1(xs,ys,zs);
```

Contour plots in the plane and in space

Although contour plots are two-dimensional plots, they actually represent values of a three-dimensional function (or curve) projected onto the x-y plane. SCILAB provides the function contour, whose call is

contour(x,y,z,nz,[theta,alpha,leg,flag,ebox,zlev])

to produce contour plots. In the function call, x,y are two real row vectors of sizes n1 and n2, and z is real matrix of size (n1,n2) representing the values of the function, z = f(x,y). The number of level curves, nz, is the fourth required argument. If nz is an integer, its value gives the number of equally-spaced level curves selected by SCILAB in the range of values of z. The argument nz can also be a vector, so that the element nz(i) gives the value of the i-th level curve.

The remaining optional arguments in the function call, *theta, alpha, leg*, and *flag*, and *ebox*, are the same as in the function *plot3d*. In the call to function contour, however, only *flag(1)=mode* has a special meaning: If *mode=0*, the level curves are drawn on the surface defined by (x,y,z). If *mode=1*, the level curves are drawn on a 3D plot and on the plane defined by the equation *z=zlev*. Finally, if *mode=2*, the level curves are drawn on a 2D plot.

You can change the format of the floating point number printed on the levels by using xset("fpf",string) where string gives the format in C format syntax (for example string="%3f"). Use string="" to switch back to default format.

Contour plots in the plane (only)

The function contour2d is typically used to draw levels curves on a two-dimensional plot. The call to the function is

`contour2d`(x,y,z,nz,[style,strf,leg,rect,nax])

The description of this function call is similar to that of the function *contour*. The optional arguments, *style, strf, leg, rect*, and *nax*, are explained in the description of function *plot2d*.

Contour plots given a function z = f(x,y)

To produce contours if a curve is defined by the function z = f(x,y), use the function

`fcontour`(x,y,f,nz,[theta,alpha,leg,flag,ebox,zlev])

where x and y are two real row vectors of size n1 and n2, and f is an external function which defines the surface z=f(x,y). This function first calculates the matrix of values z = f(x,y) and then calls function contour to plot contours in space or in the plane.

Contour plots in a plane given a function z = f(x,y)

To produce contour plots in the plane given a function z = f(x,y), use the function

`fcontour2d`(x,y,f,nz,[style,strf,leg,rect,nax])

The argument description is the same as for function *contour2d*.

Contour examples

The following script contains examples of all the contour functions presented above:

```
//Contour plots
x = (-10:0.5:10); y = x;                //Generate x,y vectors
deff('[z] = fc(x,y)','z = x+y^2');      //Define function z = fc(x,y)
[nx mx] = size(x); [ny my] = size(y);   //Get sizes of vectors x and y

//Generate z matrix
for i = 1:mx, for j = 1:my, z(i,j) = fc(x(i),y(j)); end, end;

styles = [2:2:20];                      //Define styles for some plots

xbasc();                                //Case 1
contour(x,y,z,10);
xtitle('contour - 2D')
pause

xbasc();                                //Case 2
```

```
contour(x,y,z,10,45,45,'x1@x2@x3',[1 1 4],[-12.,12.,-12.,12.,-10.,100.], 40)
xtitle('contour - 3D')
pause

xbasc();                          //Case 3
contour2d(x,y,z,10)
xtitle('contour2d - simple')
pause

xbasc();                          //Case 4
contour2d(x,y,z,10,styles,'111','x1@x2@xx3',[-10 -10 10 10],[5 10 5 10])
xtitle('contour2d - complex')
pause

xbasc();                          //Case 5
fcontour(x,y,fc,10)
xtitle('fcontour - 2D')
pause

xbasc();                          //Case 6
fcontour(x,y,fc,10,45,45,'x1@x2@x3',[1 1 4],[-12., 12., -12., 12., -10., 100.],
40)
xtitle('fcontour - 3D')
pause

xbasc();                          //Case 7
fcontour2d(x,y,fc,10)
xtitle('fcontour2d - simple')
pause

xbasc();                          //Case 8
fcontour2d(x,y,fc,10,styles,'111','x1@x2@xx3',[-10 -10 10 10],[5 10 5 10])
xtitle('fcontour2d - complex')
```

Three dimensional histograms

A three-dimensional histogram will be a matricial representation of frequency counts where the classes are defined in a grid. There are two different calls available for this function, namely,

hist3d(f,[theta,alpha,leg,flag,ebox])
hist3d(list(f,x,y),[theta,alpha,leg,flag,ebox])

The argument f is a matrix of size (m,n) that defines the frequency count for the histogram, i.e., f(i,j)=F(x(i),y(j)), where x and y are taken as 0:m and 0:n. If you use the second call to the function, you need to provide as first argument a list: list(f,x,y), where f is a matrix of size (m,n) defining the frequency count as above, and x and y vectors of size (1,n+1) and (1,m+1), respectively. The remaining optional arguments are the same as in function plot3d.

Unlike the two-dimensional histogram function, histplot, in hist3d you need to provide the frequency count before the histogram is plotted.

An example is shown next in the form of a script:

```
xset('default');
x = (-10:5:10); y = x;
[nx mx] = size(x); [ny my] = size(y);
f = rand(mx,my)*100;

xbasc();
hist3d(f)
pause

xbasc();
hist3d(f,45,60,'x@y@freq')
pause
```

Animation of three-dimensional graphs

As with a two-dimensional plot, the animation of a three-dimensional surface requires us to set the pixmap option with the command xset('pixmap',1). As the plots are generated, with plot3d(xx,yy,zz,...), they are posted in the graphics window with xset('wshow') and removed with xset('wwpc'). The combined effect of posting and removing plots is to produce the animation of the surface. The values of the surface elevations, z = f(x,y), are produced in the line zz = feval(xx+k./10,yy+k./10) where the index k acts as a time value. Type the following script and run it from the SCILAB command window to see the animation of the curve, which, in this case, resembles a wave moving in a water surface.

```
deff('[z] = fs(x,y)',"z = sin(x).*cos(y)");  // Define function f(x,y)

xx = (-%pi:%pi/10:%pi); yy = xx;              // Generate xx,yy vectors
[nx mx] = size(xx); [ny my] = size(yy);       // Vectors size
xset('pixmap',1);                              // Activate pixmap

// The following loop produces the animation
for k = 1:50,
     zz = feval(xx+k./10,yy+k./10,fs);
     //plot3d(xx,yy,zz);
     plot3d(xx,yy,zz,45,45,'x@y@z',[3 1 4], [-%pi,%pi,-%pi,%pi,-1,1])
     xset('wshow');
     xset('wwpc');
end
```

Combination of two-dimensional and three-dimensional plots

The following examples show how to combine two-dimensional and three-dimensional plots in the same three-dimensional frame. The first example shows the use of the function geom3d() to project a curve onto a surface in space. You can type the following commands line by line, or create a scrip that is run from the SCILAB command window:

```
//Projecting 3D onto 2D
xbasc();
r =(%pi):-0.01:0; x = r.*cos(10.*r); y = r.*sin(10*r);
deff('[z] = surf(x,y)','z=sin(x).*cos(y)');
t=%pi*(-10:10)/10;
fplot3d(t,t,surf,35,45,'x@y@z',[-3,2,3]);   //Plots the surface
```

```
z = sin(x).*cos(y);                         //Generates curve
[x1 y1] = geom3d(x,y,z);                    //Projects curve onto surface
xpoly(x1,y1,"lines");                       //Creates polyline
[x1,y1] = geom3d([0,0],[0,0],[5,0]);        //Projects points on the surface
xsegs(x1,y1);                               //Draws segments
xstring(x1(1),y1(1),'the point (0,0,0)');   //Draws message in plot
```

The second example shows how to plot a surface and its contours in the same three-dimensional frame:

```
t = %pi*(-10:10)/10;
deff('[z] = surf(x,y)','z=sin(x).*cos(y)');    //Define function
rect = [-%pi,%pi,-%pi,%pi,-5,1];               //3-D frame dimensions
z = feval(t,t,surf);                           //Surface elevations
xbasc()                                        //Clear window
contour(t,t,z,10,35,45,'x@y@z',[1,1,0],rect,-5); //Plot contours on z = -5
plot3d(t,t,z,35,45,'x@y@z',[2,1,3],rect);      //Plot surface
title = ['Plot3d and contour'];                //Add title
```

These examples made use of functions *xpoly* and *xsegs*, which have not been presented in this chapter. To learn more about them use:

```
help xpoly
help xsegs
```

OVERVIEW OF SCILAB GRAPHICS FUNCTIONS

This is an overview of SCILAB graphic functions as presented in the SCILAB Help facility. We have presented the operation of many of these functions in relation to two-dimensional and three-dimensional graphics of functions. We also covered many of the graphic manipulation functions such as xbasc() and xset(). Use the *help* command with any of the functions listed below to obtain on-line information on the function.

Two-dimensional Plotting
    plot   : simple plot of a curve
    plot2d   : plot a curve
    plot2d1   : plot a curve, allows logarithmic axes
    plot2d2   : plot a curve as step function
    plot2d3   : plot a curve with vertical bars
    plot2d4   : plot a curve with arrows
    fplot2d   : plot a curve defined by a function
    champ   : 2D vector field
    champ1   : 2D vector field with colored arrows
    fchamp   : direction field of a 2D first order ODE
    contour2d   : level curves of a surface on a 2D plot
    fcontour2d : level curves of a surface defined by a function on a 2D plot
    grayplot   : 2D plot of a surface using colors
    fgrayplot   : 2D plot of a surface defined by a function using colors
    Sgrayplot   : smooth 2D plot of a surface using colors
    Sfgrayplot : smooth 2D plot of a surface defined by a function using colors
    xgrid   : add a grid on a 2D plot
    errbar   : add vertical error bars on a 2D plot

histplot	: plot a histogram
Matplot	: 2D plot of a matrix using colors

Three-dimensional plotting
plot3d	: plot a surface
plot3d1	: plot a surface with gray or color level
fplot3d	: plot a surface defined by a function
fplot3d1	: plot a surface defined by a function with gray or colcr level
param3d	: plot one curve
param3d1	: plots curves
contour	: level curves on a 3D surface
fcontour	: level curves on a 3D surface defined by a function
hist3d	: 3D representation of a histogram
genfac3d	: compute facets of a 3D surface
eval3dp	: compute facets of a 3D surface
geom3d	: projection from 3D on 2D after a 3D plot

Line and polygon plotting
xpoly	: draw a polyline or a polygon
xpolys	: draw a set of polylines or polygons
xrpoly	: draw a regular polygon
xsegs	: draw unconnected segments
xfpoly	: fill a polygon
xfpolys	: fill a set of polygons

Rectangle plotting
xrect	: draw a rectangle
xfrect	: fill a rectangle
xrects	: draw or fill a set of rectangles

Arc plotting
xarc	: draw a part of an ellipse
xarcs	: draw parts of a set of ellipses
xfarc	: fill a part of an ellipse
xfarcs	: fill parts of a set of ellipses

Arrow plotting
xarrows	: draw a set of arrows

Strings
xstring	: draw strings
xstringl	: compute a box, which surrounds strings
xstringb	: draw strings into a box
xtitle	: add titles on a graphics window
titlepage	: add a title inthe middle of a graphics window
xinfo	: draw an info string in the message subwindow

Frames and axes
xaxis	: draw an axis
graduate	: pretty axis graduations
plotframe	: plot a frame with scaling and grids

Coordinate transformations
- isoview : set scales for isometric plot (do not change the size of the window)
- square : set scales for isometric plot (change the size of the window)
- scaling : affine transformation of a set of points
- rotate : rotation of a set of points
- xsetech : set the sub window of a graphics window for plotting
- xgetech : get the current graphics scale
- xchange : transform real to pixel coordinates

Colors
- colormap : using colormaps
- getcolor : dialog to select colors in the current colormap
- addcolor : add new colors to the current colormap
- graycolormap : linear gray colormap
- hotcolormap : red to yellow colormap

Graphics context
- xset : set values of the graphics context
- xget : get current values of the graphics context
- xlfont : load a font in the graphics context or query loaded font
- getsymbol : dialog to select a symbol and its size

Save and load graphics
- xsave : save graphics into a file
- xload : load a saved graphics
- xbasimp : send graphics to a Postscript printer or in a file
- xs2fig : send graphics to a file in Xfig syntax

Graphics primitives
- xbasc : clear a graphics window and erase the associated recorded graphics
- xclear : clear a graphics window
- driver : select a graphics driver
- xinit : initialization of a graphics driver
- xend : close a graphics session
- xbasr : redraw a graphics window
- replot : redraw the current graphics window with new boundaries
- xpause : suspend SCILAB
- xselect : raise the current graphics window
- xclea : erase a rectangle
- xclip : set a clipping zone
- xdel : delete a graphics window
- winsid : return the list of graphics windows
- xname : change the name of the current graphics window

Mouse position
- xclick : wait for a mouse click
- locate : mouse selection of a set of points
- xgetmouse : get thecurrent position ofthe mouse

Interactive editor
- edit_curv : interactive graphics curve editor
- gr_menu : simple interactive graphic editor
- sd2sci : gr_menu structure to SCILAB instruction conversion

Graphics functions for automatic control applications
- bode : Bode plot
- gainplot : magnitude plot
- nyquist : Nyquist plot
- m_circle : M-circle plot
- chart : Nichols chart
- black : Black's diagram
- evans : Evans root locus
- sgrid : s-plane grid lines
- plzr : pole-zero plot
- zgrid : zgrid plot

Exercises

[1]. Plot the following functions in the ranges indicated below:
(a) $f(x) = (x+1)/(x+2)$, $x = 0..10$ (b) $g(t) = t + t/(1+\sin(t))$, $t = -2\pi..2\pi$

[2]. Plot the following functions using polar coordinates. First, generate the values $(\theta, f(\theta))$ and convert to Cartesian coordinates to produce the plot [e.g., see exercise [11] in Chapter 2].
(a) $r(\theta) = \sin(\theta)/(1+\cos(\theta))$, $\theta = 0..\pi/2$ (b) $r(\theta) = \sin(\theta)(1-\sin(\theta))$, $\theta = -\pi/2..\pi/2$

[3]. Plot the functions indicated by the following parametric equations using Cartesian coordinates:
(a) $x(t) = \sin(t+t^2/2)$, $y(t) = \exp(-t/10)\cos(2t)$, $t = 0..10$
(b) $x(s) = (1+s^2)^{1/3}$, $y(s) = 1-s^3$, $s = 0..10$

[4]. Plot the functions indicated by the following parametric equations that use polar coordinates (see exercise [2], above):
(a) $r(t) = \sin(t+t^2/2)$, $\theta(t) = \exp(-t/10)\cos(2t)$, $t = 0..10$
(b) $r(s) = (1+s^2)^{1/3}$, $\theta(s) = 1-s^3$, $s = 0..10$

[5]. Plot the following functions using the type of plot indicated:
(a) $f(x) = \exp(5t)$, $t = 1..20$, semi-logarithmic plot with f(x) using a logarithmic scale
(b) $f(x) = \exp(5t)$, $t = 1..1000$, double-logarithmic plot

[6]. Plot the three-dimensional function $f(x,y)$ as required. Note: to generate values of $z = f(x,y)$, define the function $f(x,y)$ using SCILAB function deff, e.g., for case (a), use

```
-->deff('[z]=f(x,y)','z=x^2+y^2')
```

Write vectors containing the ranges of values of x and y, e.g.,

```
-->x=[-10:0.5:10]; y = [-10:0.5:10];
```

Then, produce a matrix of values of $z=f(x,y)$ using either function $feval$ or function $eval3d$, i.e.,

```
--> z = feval(x,y,f);
```

(a) $f(x,y) = x^2+y^2$, $x = -10..10$, $y = -10..10$
(b) (b) $f(x,y) = x \sin y + y \sin x$, $x = -\pi..\pi$, $y = -\pi..\pi$

[7]. Plot the space curves described by the following parametric equations in Cartesian coordinates:

(a) $x(t) = \sin(t)$, $y(t) = 1+t^2$, $z(t) = t$, $t = 0..10$ (b) $x(t) = t$, $y(t) = 1/(1+t^2)$, $z(t) = t^3$, $t = 0..10$

[8]. Plot the three-dimensional surfaces described by the following parametric equations in Cartesian coordinates:

(a) $x(u,v) = u^2+v^2$, $y(u,v) = 2uv$, $z(u,v) = u+v$, $u = -10..10$, $v = -10..10$
(b) $x(u,v) = (u-v)/(u+v)$, $y(u,v) = uv$, $z(u,v) = \sin(u) \cos(v)$, $v = -10..10$

[9]. Produce a contour plot of the following functions:

(a) $f(x,y) = x^2+y^2-2x^2y+25$, $x = -2..2$, $y = -2..2$
(b) $f(x,y) = x \sin y + y \sin x$, $x = -2..2$, $y = -2..2$

[10]. Produce density plots of the functions of problem [9].

4 Vectors

A vector in two- or three-dimensions represents a *directed segment*, i.e., a mathematical object characterized by a magnitude and a direction in the plane or in space. Vectors in the plane or in space can be used to represent physical quantities such as the position, displacement, velocity, and acceleration of a particle, angular velocity and acceleration or a rotating body, forces and moments.

Operations with vectors

Vectors in two- or three-dimensions are represented by arrows. The length of the arrow represents the *magnitude* of the vector, and the arrowhead indicates the *direction* of the vector. The figure below shows a vector A, and its negative –A. As you can see *the negative of a vector* is a vector of the same magnitude, but with opposite sense.

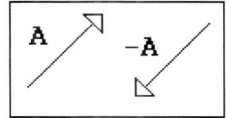

Vectors can be added and subtracted. To illustrate vector addition and subtraction refer to the figure below. Consider two vectors in the plane or in space, A and B, as shown in the figure below, item (a). There are two ways that you can construct *the vector sum*, A+B:

(1) By attaching the origin of the vector B to the tip of vector A, as shown in the figure, item (b). In this case, the vector sum is the vector extending from the origin of vector A to the tip of vector B.

(2) By showing the vectors A and B with a common origin, and completing the parallelogram resulting from drawing lines parallel to vectors A and B at the tips of vectors B and A, respectively, as shown in the figure below, item (c).

The vector sum, also known as the *resultant*, is the diagonal of the parallelogram that starts at the common origin of vectors A and B.

Subtraction is accomplished by using the definition:

$$A - B = A + (-B).$$

In other words, subtracting vector B from vector A is equivalent to adding vectors A and (–B),. This operation is illustrated in the figure below, item (d).

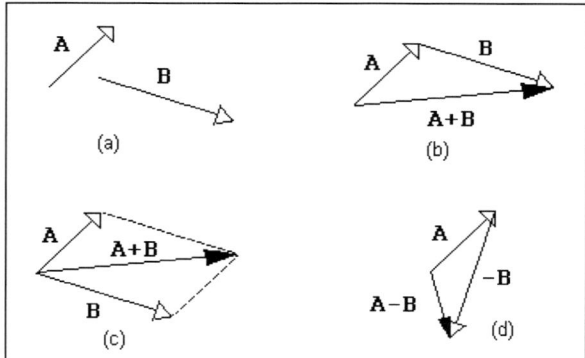

A vector A can be *multiplied by a scalar* c, resulting in a vector cA, parallel and oriented in the same direction as A, and whose magnitude is c times that of A. The figure below illustrates the case in which c = 2. If the scalar c is negative, then the orientation of the vector cA will be opposite that of A.

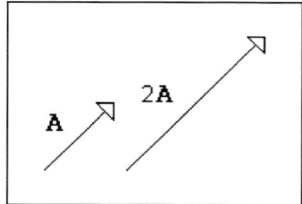

The *magnitude* of a vector A is represented by |A|. A *unit vector* in the direction of A is a vector of magnitude 1 parallel to A. The unit vector corresponding to a vector A is shown in the figure below, item (a). The unit vector along the direction of A is defined by

$$\mathbf{e}_A = \frac{\mathbf{A}}{|\mathbf{A}|}.$$

By definition, |e_A| = 1.0.

The *projection of vector B onto vector A*, $P_{B/A}$, is shown in the figure below, item (b). If θ represents the angle between the two vectors, we see from the figure that $P_{B/A}$ = |B|·cos θ = | e_A |·| B |·cos θ, or

$$P_{B/A} = \frac{|\mathbf{A}| \cdot |\mathbf{B}| \cdot \cos\theta}{|\mathbf{A}|}.$$

We will define the *dot product, or internal product*, of two vectors A and B as the scalar quantity

$$A \cdot B = |A| \cdot |B| \cdot \cos\theta,$$

where θ is the angle between the vectors when they have a common origin. Notice that A•B = B•A.

From the definition of the dot product it follows that the *angle between two vectors* can be found from

$$\theta = \arccos\left(\frac{\mathbf{A} \cdot \mathbf{B}}{|\mathbf{A}| \cdot |\mathbf{B}|}\right).$$

From the same definition it follows that if the angle between the vectors A and B is $\theta = 90° = \pi/2$ ^{rad}, i.e., if A is <u>perpendicular (or normal)</u> to B (A⊥B), cos θ = 0, and A•B = 0. The reverse statement is also true, i.e., if A•B = 0, then A⊥B.

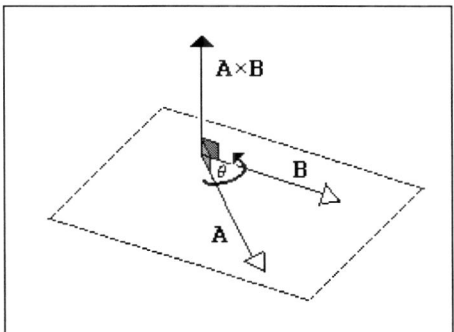

The *cross product, or vector product*, of two vectors in space is defined as the vector C = A×B, such that |C| = |A| · |B| · sin θ, where θ is the angle between the vectors, and A•C = 0 and B•C = 0 (i.e., C is perpendicular to both A and B). The cross product is llustrated in the figure below. Since there could be two orientations for a vector C perpendicular to both A and B, we need to refine the definition of C = A×B by indicating its orientation. The so-called <u>right-hand rule</u> indicates that if we were to curl the fingers of the right hand in the direction shown by the curved arrow in the figure (i.e., from A to B), the right hand thumb will point towards the orientation of C. Obviously, the order of the factors in a cross product affects the sign of the result, for the right-hand rule indicates that B×A = - C.

Three vectors A, B, and C, in space, having a common origin, determine a solid figure called a parallelepiped, as shown in the figure below. It can be proven that the *volume of the parallelepiped* is obtained through the expression $A \cdot (B \times C)$. This expression is known as the *vector triple product*.

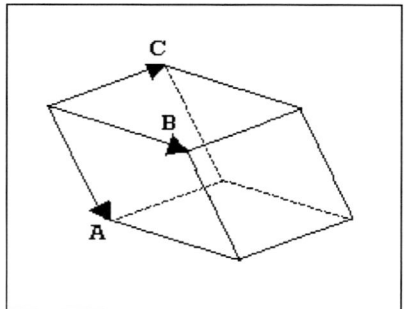

Vectors in Cartesian coordinates

The mathematical representation of a vector typically requires it to be referred to a specific coordinate system. Using a Cartesian coordinate system, we introduce the *unit vectors* i, j, and k, corresponding to the x-, y-, and z-directions, respectively. The unit vectors i, j, and k, are shown in the figure below. These unit vectors are such that

$$i \cdot j = i \cdot k = j \cdot k = 0,$$

and

$$i \times j = k, \quad j \times k = i, \quad k \times i = j, \quad i \times k = -j, \quad k \times j = -i, \quad j \times i = -k.$$

In terms of these unit vectors, any vector A can be written as

$$A = A_x \cdot i + A_y \cdot j + A_z \cdot k,$$

where the values A_x, A_y, and A_z, are called the *Cartesian components* of the vector A.

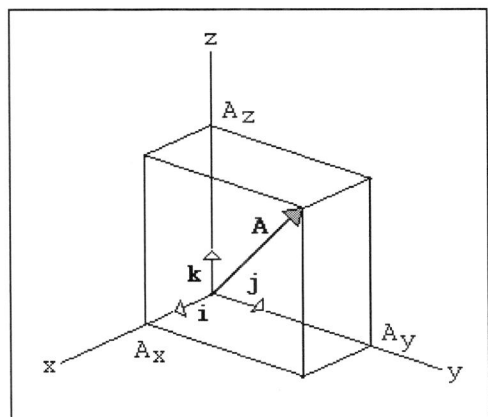

Using Cartesian components, therefore, we can also write $B = B_x \cdot i + B_y \cdot j + B_z \cdot k$, and define the following _vector operations:_

- negative of vector $-A = -(A_x \cdot i + A_y \cdot j + A_z \cdot k) = -A_x \cdot i - A_y \cdot j - A_z \cdot k$.

- addition: $A+B = (A_x + B_x) \cdot i + (A_y + B_y) \cdot j + (A_z + B_z) \cdot k$.

- subtraction: $A-B = (A_x - B_x) \cdot i + (A_y - B_y) \cdot j + (A_z - B_z) \cdot k$.

- multiplication by a scalar, c: $cA = c \cdot (A_x \cdot i + A_y \cdot j + A_z \cdot k) = c \cdot A_x \cdot i + c \cdot A_y \cdot j + c \cdot A_z \cdot k$.

- dot product: $A \bullet B = (A_x \cdot i + A_y \cdot j + A_z \cdot k) \bullet (B_x \cdot i + B_y \cdot j + B_z \cdot k) = A_x \cdot B_x + A_y \cdot B_y + A_z \cdot B_z$.

- magnitude: $|A|^2 = A \bullet A = A_x^2 + A_y^2 + A_z^2;\ |A| = \sqrt{(A \bullet A)} = (A_x^2 + A_y^2 + A_z^2)^{1/2}$.

- unit vector: $e_A = A/|A| = (A_x \cdot i + A_y \cdot j + A_z \cdot k)/(A_x^2 + A_y^2 + A_z^2)^{1/2}$.

- cross product: $A \times B = (A_x \cdot i + A_y \cdot j + A_z \cdot k) \times (B_x \cdot i + B_y \cdot j + B_z \cdot k) =$
    $(B_z \cdot A_y - B_y \cdot A_z) \cdot i + (A_z \cdot B_x - B_z \cdot A_x) \cdot j + (B_y \cdot A_x - A_y \cdot B_x) \cdot k$.

Vector operations in SCILAB

Consider the vectors $A = 3i+5j-k$ and $B = 2i+2j+3k$. You can enter these three-dimensional vectors as row vectors in SCILAB, i.e.,

```
-->A = [3, 5, -1], B = [2, 2, 3]
 A   =
```

```
!    3.    5.  - 1. !
 B  =
!    2.    2.    3. !
```

Addition and subtraction of vectors is straightforward:

```
-->A+B
 ans  =

!    5.    7.    2. !
-->A-B
 ans  =

!    1.    3.  - 4. !
```

The negative of these vectors are calculated as:

```
-->  -A
 A  =

!   -3.   -5.    1. !
-->  -B
 B  =

!   -2.   -2.   -3. !
```

The product of the vectors by a constant is also straightforward:

```
-->2*A,  -5*B
 ans  =

!    6.   10.  - 2. !
 ans  =

! - 10. - 10. - 15. !
```

The following is a linear combination of the two vectors:

```
-->5*A-3*B
 ans  =

!    9.   19.  - 14. !
```

The magnitude of a vector is obtained by using the function norm. For example, the magnitudes of vectors A and B are calculated as:

```
-->norm(A)
 ans  =

    5.9160798

-->norm(B)
```

ans =

   4.1231056

Unit vectors are calculated by dividing a vector by its magnitude. For example, unit vectors parallel to A and B (i.e., e_A and e_B) are given by:

```
-->eA = A/norm(A)
 eA  =

!    .5070926     .8451543  -  .1690309 !

-->eB = B/norm(B)
 eB  =

!    .4850713     .4850713     .7276069 !
```

You can check that these are indeed unit vectors by using norm:

```
-->norm(eA)
 ans  =

    1.

-->norm(eB)
 ans  =

    1.
```

The matrix multiplication of a row vector times the transpose of a second row vector (i.e., a column vector) which will produce a dot product, i.e.,

```
-->A*B'
 ans  =

    13.

-->B*A'
 ans  =

    13.
```

Following the rules of matrix multiplication (see Chapter…), the product of a column vector times a row vector produces a matrix, e.g.,

```
-->A'*B
 ans  =

!   6.      6.      9. !
!  10.     10.     15. !
! - 2.   - 2.   - 3. !

-->B'*A
 ans  =

!   6.    10.   - 2. !
!   6.    10.   - 2. !
```

```
!   9.    15.   - 3. !
```

When the multiplication symbol between two row (or column) vectors is preceded by a dot, the result is a vector whose components are the product of the corresponding components of the factors. This is referred to as a term-by-term multiplication. For example, try:

```
-->A.*B
 ans  =

!   6.    10.   - 3. !
-->B.*A
 ans  =

!   6.    10.   - 3. !
```

Term-by-term multiplication requires that the factors have the same dimensions. Thus, the term-by-term multiplication of a row vector and a column vector is not defined. The following term-by-term multiplications, for example, will produce error messages:

```
-->A.*B'
      !--error   9999
inconsistent element-wise operation

-->A'.*B
      !--error   9999
inconsistent element-wise operation
```

The dot product of two row or column vectors can be obtained by combining a term-by-term multiplication with the function sum. The function sum, when applied to a vector, produces the sum of the vector components, for example:

```
-->sum(A)
 ans  =

    7.
```

In the following examples, the function sum is used to calculate the dot product of two vectors:

```
-->sum(A.*B)
 ans  =

    13.
```

The cosine of the angle between two vectors is obtained from the dot product of the vectors divided by the product of their magnitudes. For example, the cosine of the angle between vectors A and B is given by

```
-->costheta = A*B'/(norm(A)*norm(B))
 costheta   =

    .5329480
```

The corresponding angle is obtained by using the function acos.

```
-->acos(costheta)
 ans  =

    1.0087155
```

Of course, the result is in radians, the natural angular units. To convert to degrees use:

```
-->theta = 180/%pi*acos(costheta)
 theta  =

    57.795141
```

The projection of vector B over vector A is calculated by dividing the dot product of the two vectors by the magnitude of A, i.e.,

```
-->PB_A = A*B'/norm(A)
 PB_A  =

    2.1974011
```

The calculation of cross products requires the use of determinants, as described in the following section.

Calculating 2×2 and 3×3 determinants

The calculation of a cross product can be simplified if the cross product is written as a determinant of a matrix of 3 rows and 3 columns (also referred to as a 3×3 matrix). A *determinant* is a number associated with a square matrix, i.e., a matrix with the same number of rows and columns. While there is a general rule to obtain the determinant of any square matrix, we concentrate our attention on 2×2 and 3×3 determinants. Next, we present a simple way to calculate the determinant for 2×2 and 3×3 matrices.

The elements of a matrix are identified with two sub-indices, the first representing the row and the second the column. Therefore, a 2×2 and a 3×3 matrix will be represented as:

$$\begin{bmatrix} a_{11} & a_{12} \\ a_{21} & a_{22} \end{bmatrix}, \quad \begin{bmatrix} a_{11} & a_{12} & a_{13} \\ a_{21} & a_{22} & a_{23} \\ a_{31} & a_{32} & a_{33} \end{bmatrix}.$$

The determinants corresponding to these matrices are represented by the same arrangement of elements enclosed between vertical lines, i.e.,

$$\begin{vmatrix} a_{11} & a_{12} \\ a_{21} & a_{22} \end{vmatrix}, \quad \begin{vmatrix} a_{11} & a_{12} & a_{13} \\ a_{21} & a_{22} & a_{23} \\ a_{31} & a_{32} & a_{33} \end{vmatrix}.$$

A 2×2 determinant is calculated by multiplying the elements in its diagonal and adding those products accompanied by the positive or negative sign as indicated in the diagram shown below.

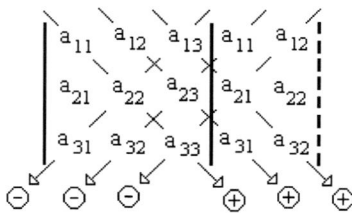

The 2×2 determinant is, therefore,

$$\begin{vmatrix} a_{11} & a_{12} \\ a_{21} & a_{22} \end{vmatrix} = a_{11} \cdot a_{22} - a_{12} \cdot a_{21}.$$

A 3×3 determinant is calculated by *augmenting* the determinant, an operation that consists on copying the first two columns of the determinant, and placing them to the right of column 3, as shown in the diagram below. The diagram also shows the elements to be multiplied with the corresponding sign to attach to their product, in a similar fashion as done earlier for a 2×2 determinant. After multiplication the results are added together to obtain the determinant.

Therefore, a 3×3 determinant produces the following result:

$$\begin{vmatrix} a_{11} & a_{12} & a_{13} \\ a_{21} & a_{22} & a_{23} \\ a_{31} & a_{32} & a_{33} \end{vmatrix} = a_{11} \cdot a_{22} \cdot a_{33} + a_{12} \cdot a_{23} \cdot a_{31} + a_{13} \cdot a_{21} \cdot a_{32}$$

$$- (a_{13} \cdot a_{22} \cdot a_{31} + a_{11} \cdot a_{23} \cdot a_{31} + a_{12} \cdot a_{21} \cdot a_{33}).$$

Determinants can be calculated with SCILAB by using the function *det*. The following commands shown examples of 2x2 and 3x3 determinant calculations in SCILAB.

```
-->A2x2 = [3, -1; 2, 5]
 A2x2  =

!   3.   - 1. !
!   2.    5.  !

-->det(A2x2)
 ans  =

    17.

-->A3x3 = [2,3, -1
-->        5,5, -2
-->        4, -3, 1]
 A3x3  =

!   2.    3.   - 1. !
!   5.    5.   - 2. !
!   4.  - 3.    1.  !

-->det(A3x3)
 ans  =

  - 6.

-->det([2,-2; 4, 5])
 ans  =

    18.
```

Cross product as a determinant

The cross product A×B in Cartesian coordinates can be expressed as a determinant if the first row of the determinant consists of the unit vectors i, j, and k. The components of vector A and B constitute the second and third rows of the determinant, i.e.,

$$\mathbf{A} \times \mathbf{B} = \begin{vmatrix} \mathbf{i} & \mathbf{j} & \mathbf{k} \\ A_x & A_y & A_z \\ B_x & B_y & B_z \end{vmatrix}.$$

Evaluation of this determinant, as indicated above, will produce the result

$$\mathbf{A} \times \mathbf{B} = (B_z \cdot A_y - B_y \cdot A_z) \cdot \mathbf{i} + (A_z \cdot B_x - B_z \cdot A_x) \cdot \mathbf{j} + (B_y \cdot A_x - A_y \cdot B_x) \cdot \mathbf{k}.$$

SCILAB does not provide a cross-product function of its own. The following function, *CrossProd*, calculates the cross product of two three-dimensional vectors:

```
function [p] = CrossProd(u,v)
//Calculates the cross-product of two vectors u and v.
//Vectors u and v can be columns or row vectors, but
//they must have only three elements each.

[nu,mu] = size(u);
[nv,mv] = size(v);

if nu*mu <> 3 | nv*mv   3 then
      error('Vectors must be three-dimensional only')
      abort;
end

A1 = [ u(2), u(3); v(2), v(3)];
A2 = [ u(3), u(1); v(3), v(1)];
A3 = [ u(1), u(2); v(1), v(2)];

px = det(A1); py = det(A2); pz = det(A3);

p = [px, py, pz]

//end function
```

An application of the function *CrossProd* follows:

```
-->getf('CrossProd')

-->u = [2, 3, -1], v = [-3, 1, 4]
 u  =

!   2.    3.   - 1. !
 v  =

! - 3.    1.    4. !

-->CrossProd(u,v)
 ans =

!   13.  - 5.   11. !
```

These operations are interpreted as $u = 2i+3j-k$, $v = -3i+j+4k$, and $u \times v = 13i+j+4k$.

Earlier in this chapter we indicated that the volume of the parallelepiped defined by vectors A, B, and C, is given by the magnitude of the vector triple product $A \cdot (B \times C)$. As an example in SCILAB, try the following calculation:

```
-->A = [2, 2, -1], B = [5, 3, 1], C = [1, 2, 3]
 A  =

!   2.    2.   - 1. !
 B  =

!   5.    3.    1. !
```

```
 C    =

!   1.    2.    3. !
-->abs(A*CrossProd(B,C)')
 ans  =

    21.
```

Polynomials as vector components

Although SCILAB is not a symbolic environment, some pseudo-symbolic calculations are possible using <u>polynomials</u>. Polynomials are a special type of SCILAB objects useful in linear system analysis. They are presented in more detail elsewhere in this book. In this section we present simple applications of polynomials as vector components.

Simple "symbolic" variables can be defined using the following call to the SCILAB function poly. For example, the following statement creates the symbolic variable c

```
-->c=poly(0,'c')
 c  =

    c
```

With the symbolic variable c defined above, you can produce the following vector operations:

```
-->c*A,  c*B,  c*(A+B),  c*(A-B)
 ans  =

!   3c     5c    - c  !
 ans  =

!   2c     2c     3c  !
 ans  =

!   5c     7c     2c  !
 ans  =

!   c      3c   - 4c  !
```

It should be kept in mind that these are not symbolic results in the most general sense of the word (i.e., as those obtained in a symbolic mathematical environment such as Maple or Mathematica). The results obtained above, in terms of the polynomial c, are three-dimensional vectors whose components are polynomials. Other examples of vectors with polynomial components would be:

```
-->u = [ 1+c, (c+1)^2, c^3+2*c^2 ]
 u  =
```

```
!                  2          2    3 !
!   1 + c    1 + 2c + c     2c + c  !

-->u+c*A+3*c*B
 ans =

!                   2           2    3 !
!   1 + 10c   1 + 13c + c    8c + 2c + c !
```

Operations such as term-by-term multiplication, or linear combinations, are permitted with vectors whose components are polynomials. For example,

```
-->A.*u
 ans =

!                  2           2    3 !
!   3 + 3c   5 + 10c + 5c    - 2c - c  !

-->u.*B
 ans =

!                  2          2    3 !
!   2 + 2c   2 + 4c + 2c    6c + 3c  !

-->A-B.*u
 ans =

!                   2             2    3 !
!   1 - 2c   3 - 4c - 2c   - 1 - 6c - 3c !

-->u +3*A.*u
 ans =

!                     2           2    3 !
!   10 + 10c   16 + 32c + 16c   - 4c - 2c !
```

Some operations, such as *norm*, are not defined when a vector has polynomial components:

```
-->norm(u)
         !--error    4
undefined variable : %p_norm


-->norm(c*A)
         !--error    4
undefined variable : %p_norm
```

Also, in keeping with SCILAB's numerical nature, operations that attempt to combine two polynomial variables (i.e., symbolic operations) are not allowed. For example, the following command defines a new polynomial "symbolic" variable *r*:

```
-->r=poly(0,'r')
 r =

    r
```

The following linear combination of the polynomial variables c and r fails to produce a result:

```
-->c*A+r*B
        !--error      4
undefined variable : %p_a_p
```

Assignment statements can replace the values of polynomial variables. In the next example, the value of *c*, which so far has been used as a polynomial variable, gets redefined as a constant:

```
-->c=2
 c  =

    2.
```

With the new value of *c* the following operation produces a constant vector:

```
-->c*A
 ans  =

!  6.    10.   - 2. !
```

As an application of polynomials as components of vectors, suppose that you want to determine the value of c such that vector $A = 2i+cj-k$ is normal to vector $B = -5i+3j-2k$. We will use the fact that if vectors A and B are perpendicular then their dot product is zero, i.e. $A \bullet B = 0$.
Using SCILAB:

```
-->c = poly(0,'c')
 c  =

    c

-->A = [2, c, -1], B = [-5, 3, -2]
 A  =

!   2      c    - 1 !
 B  =

! - 5.    3.   - 2. !

-->A*B'
 ans  =

   - 8 + 3c
```

This translates into the equation $-8 + 3c = 0$. From which we can find $c = 8/3$.

_____

Applications of vector algebra using SCILAB

In this section we present examples of operations with 2- and 3-dimensional vectors using SCILAB functions. The examples are taken from applications in different physical sciences.

Example 1 - Position vector

The position vector of a particle is a vector that starts at the origin of a system of coordinates and ends at the particle's position. If the current position of the particle is P(x,y,z), then the *position vector* is

$$r = x \cdot i + y \cdot j + z \cdot k,$$

as illustrated in the figure below.

If a particle is located at point P(3, -2, 5), the position vector for this particle is $r = 3i - 2j + 5k$. In SCILAB this position vector is written as [3 –2 5].

```
-->r = [3,-2,5]
 r  =

!   3.  - 2.    5. !
```

To determine the *magnitude* of the position vector the function *norm*.

```
-->abs_r = norm(r)
 abs_r  =

    6.164414
```

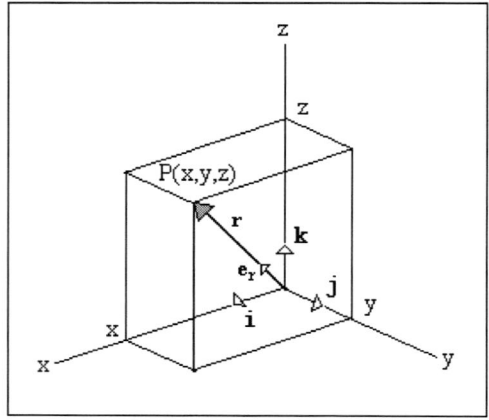

In paper, you can write $|r| = 6.164414$. To determine the unit vector, use:

```
-->e_r = r/abs_r
 e_r  =  !    .4866643    -    .3244428       .8111071  !
```

In paper, we can write: $e_r = r/|r| = [0.4866\ -0.3244\ 0.81111]$.

Example 2 - Center of mass of a system of discrete particles

Consider a system of discrete particles of mass m_i, located at position $P_i(x_i, y_i, z_i)$, with $i = 1, 2, 3, ..., n$. We can write position vectors for each particle as $r_i = x_i \cdot i + y_i \cdot j + z_i \cdot k$. The center of mass of the system of particles will be located at a position r_{cm} defined by

$$r_{cm} = \frac{\sum_{i=1}^{n} m_i \cdot r_i}{\sum_{i=1}^{n} m_i}.$$

A system of four particles is illustrated in the figure below.

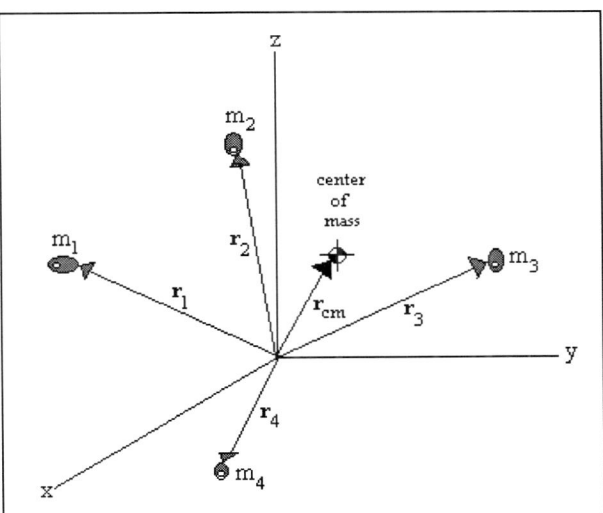

The following table shows the coordinates and masses of 5 particles. Determine their center of mass.

i	x_i	y_i	z_i	m_i
1	2	3	5	12
2	-1	6	4	15
3	3	-1	2	25
4	5	4	-7	10
5	5	3	2	30

First, we enter vectors containing the coordinates x_i, y_i, and z_i, as well as the masses m_i:

```
-->x = [2,-1,3,5,5]
 x  =

!   2.  - 1.    3.    5.    5. !

-->y = [3,6,-1,4,3]
 y  =

!   3.    6.  - 1.    4.    3. !

-->z = [5,4,2,-7,2]
 z  =

!   5.    4.    2.  - 7.    2. !

-->m = [12,15,25,10,30]
 m  =

!   12.   15.   25.   10.   30. !
```

Then, we proceed to calculate the coordinates of the center of mass, (x_{cm}, y_{cm}, z_{cm}) using the formulas:

$$x_{cm} = \frac{\sum_{i=1}^{n} x_i \cdot m_i}{\sum_{i=1}^{n} m_i}, \quad y_{cm} = \frac{\sum_{i=1}^{n} y_i \cdot m_i}{\sum_{i=1}^{n} m_i}, \quad x_{cm} = \frac{\sum_{i=1}^{n} z_i \cdot m_i}{\sum_{i=1}^{n} m_i}.$$

Using SCILAB, these formulas are calculated using the function sum:

```
-->x_cm = sum(x.*m)/sum(m)
 x_cm  =

    3.0869565

-->y_cm = sum(y.*m)/sum(m)
 y_cm  =

    2.5108696

-->z_cm = sum(z.*m)/sum(m)
 z_cm  =

    1.7391304
```

Example 3 - Resultant of forces

The figure below shows a vertical pole buried in the ground and supported by four cables EA, EB, EC, and ED. The magnitude of the tensions in each of those cables, as shown in the figure, are T_1 = 150 N, T_2 = 300 N, T_3 = 200 N, and T_4 = 150 N.

To find the vector resultant of all those forces you need to add the four tensions written out as vectors. The tension in cable i will be given by $T_i = T_i \cdot e_i$, where e_i is a unit vector in the direction of the cable where the tension acts. (The tension vectors act so that the cables pull away from point E, where the cables are attached to the pole.)

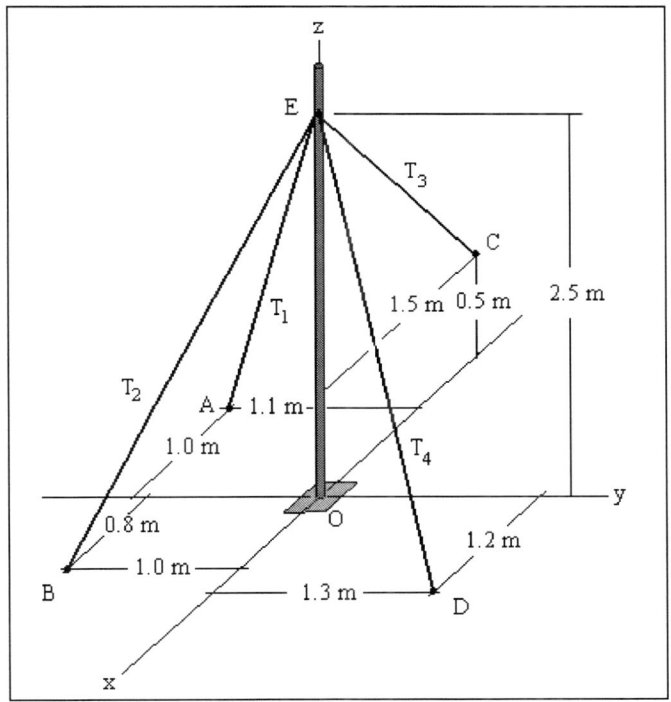

Writing out tension T_1

Tension T_1 acts along cable EA. To determine a unit vector along cable EA, you need to write the vector $r_{EA} = r_A - r_E$, where r_A is the position vector of point A (the tip of the vector r_{EA}), and r_A is the position vector of point A (the origin of the vector r_{EA}). The coordinates of these points, obtained from the figure, are A(-1.0 m, -1.1 m, 0) and E(0, 0, 2.5 m). Therefore, we can write r_E = (2.5k) m, and r_A = (-i −1.1j) m.

Using SCILAB we would calculate the vector r_{EA} as follows. First, enter r_E and r_A:

```
--> rE = [ 0 0 2.5]; rA = [-1 -1.1 0];
```

To obtain, $r_{EA} = r_A − r_E$, we will use

```
--> rEA = rA - rE;
rEA  =  !  -1.   -1.1   0. !
```

i.e., r_{EA} = -i −1.1j -2.5k.

To find the unit vector along which T first we find the magnitude,

```
--> rEA_abs = norm(rEA)
```

i.e., ($|r_{EA}|$ = 2.9086079).

Finally, the unit vector, is calculated as

```
--> eEA = rEA/rEA_abs
eEA  =  !  -0.344  - 0.378   -0.860 !
```

i.e., $e_{EA} = r_{EA}/|r_{EA}|$ = [-0.344 - 0.378 -0.860] = -0.344i 0.378j -0.860k. (To verify that this is indeed a unit vector, use the command -> `norm(eEA)`. You should get as a result 1.000).

The tension vector is calculated by multiplying the magnitude of the tension T = 150, times the unit vector e_{EA}, i.e.,

```
--> T1 = 150*eEA
T1  =  !  -51.57  -56.73  -128.93   !
```

The result is the vector [-51.57 -56.73 -128.93], or T = (-51.57i -56.73j -128.93k) N.

Writing the vector that joins two points in space

The vector that joints points A and B, where A(x_A, y_A, z_A) is the origin and point B(x_B, y_B, z_B) the tip of the vector, is written as

$$r_{AB} = r_B - r_A = (x_B - x_A)\cdot i + (y_B - y_A)\cdot j + (z_B - z_A)\cdot k,$$

where $r_A = x_A\cdot i + y_A\cdot j + z_A\cdot k$ is the position vector of point A, and $r_B = x_B\cdot i + y_B\cdot j + z_B\cdot k$ is the position vector of point B. This operation is illustrated in the figure below.

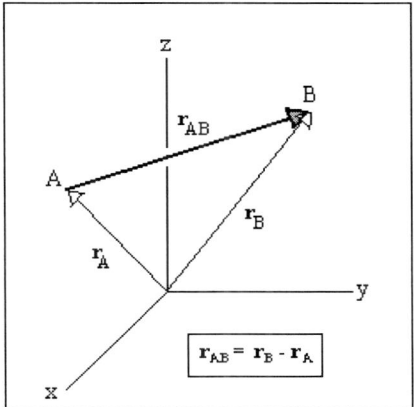

Relative position vector

The previous operation can also be interpreted as obtaining the relative position vector of point B(x_B, y_B, z_B) with respect to point A(x_A, y_A, z_A), and written as

$$r_{B/A} = r_B - r_A = (x_B - x_A)\cdot i + (y_B - y_A)\cdot j + (z_B - z_A)\cdot k.$$

Writing out tensions T_2, T_3, and T_4

Having developed a procedure to determine the unit vector along any of the cables, we can proceed to write out the vectors representing the tensions T_2, T_3, and T_4. First, we determine the coordinates of relevant points from the figure describing the problem. These points are: A(-1.0 m, -1.1m, 0) B(0.8 m, -1.0 m, 0.0), C(-1.5 m, 0.0, 0.5 m), D(1.2 m, 1.3m, 0.0), and E(0, 0, 2.5 m). The tensions, as vectors, will be written as $T_2 = T_2\cdot e_{EB}$, $T_3 = T_3\cdot e_{EC}$, and $T_4 = T_4\cdot e_{ED}$. (Recall that T_2 = 300 N, T_3 = 200 N, and T_4 = 150 N). Thus, we need to write out the vectors r_{EB}, r_{EC}, and r_{ED}, find their magnitudes, $|r_{EB}|$, $|r_{EC}|$, and $|r_{ED}|$, and calculate the unit vectors $e_{EB} = r_{EB}/|r_{EB}|$, $e_{EC} = r_{EC}/|r_{EC}|$, and $e_{ED} = r_{ED}/|r_{ED}|$, in order to obtain T_2, T_3, and T_4.

The following SCILAB commands perform the required calculations. First, we enter the position vectors for points A, B, C, D, and E:

```
-->rA =[-1, -1.1, 0], rB = [0.8, -1, 0], rC = [-1.5, 0,0.5]
 rA  =

!  - 1.   - 1.1     0. !
 rB  =

!    .8   - 1.      0. !
 rC  =
```

```
!  - 1.5    0.     .5 !
-->rD = [1.2, 1.3, 0], rE = [0, 0, 2.5]
 rD  =

!   1.2    1.3    0. !

 rE  =

!   0.    0.    2.5 !
```

Next, we calculate the relative position vectors r_{EB}, r_{EC}, and r_{ED}:

```
-->rEB = rB - rE, rEC = rC - rE, rED = rD - rE
 rEB  =

!    .8    - 1.    - 2.5 !
 rEC  =

!  - 1.5    0.    - 2. !
 rED  =

!   1.2    1.3    - 2.5 !
```

The magnitudes of the vectors, $|r_{EB}|$, $|r_{EC}|$, and $|r_{ED}|$, are calculated next:

```
-->abs_rEB = norm(rEB), abs_rEC = norm(rEC), abs_rED= norm(rED)
 abs_rEB  =

    2.8089144
 abs_rEC  =

    2.5
 abs_rED  =

    3.0626786
```

The unit vectors along the cables, $e_{EB} = r_{EB}/|r_{EB}|$, $e_{EC} = r_{EC}/|r_{EC}|$, and $e_{ED} = r_{ED}/|r_{ED}|$, are calculated as:

```
-->eEB = rEB/abs_rEB, eEC = rEC/abs_rEC, eED = rED/abs_rED
 eEB  =

!    .2848075    - .3560094    - .8900236 !
 eEC  =

!  - .6    0.    - .8 !
 eED  =

!    .3918139    .4244650    - .8162789 !
```

Next, we enter the magnitudes of the tensions, T_2 = 300 N, T_3 = 200 N, and T_4 = 150 N. These are identified in SCILAB as `T1m`, `T2m`, and `T3m`, respectively:

```
-->T2m = 300, T3m = 200, T4m = 150
 T2m  =

    300.
```

```
T3m  =

    200.
T4m  =

    150.
```

The tension vectors, themselves, are calculated by using $T_2 = T_2 \cdot e_{EB}$, $T_3 = T_3 \cdot e_{EC}$, and $T_4 = T_4 \cdot e_{ED}$. In SCILAB we use:

```
-->T2 = T2m*eEB, T3 = T3m*eEC, T4 = T4m*eED
 T2  =

!   85.442263  - 106.80283  - 267.00707 !
 T3  =

! - 120.         0.        - 160.  !
 T4  =

!   58.772083    63.669757  - 122.44184 !
```

The results are: T_2 = (85.44 $\vec{i}$ -106.80 $\vec{j}$ -267.0 $\vec{k}$) N, T_3 = (-120 $\vec{i}$ -160 $\vec{k}$) N, and for cable ED, T_4 = (58.77 $\vec{i}$ +63.67 $\vec{j}$ -122.4 $\vec{k}$) N.

The resultant of these four forces, namely $R = T_1 + T_2 + T_3 + T_4$, turns out to be

$$R = (-27.36 \vec{i} -99.86 \vec{j} -678.38 \vec{k}) \text{ N}.$$

Example 4 – Equation of a plane in space

The equation of a plane in space, in Cartesian coordinates, can be obtained given a point on the plane $A(x_A, y_A, z_A)$, and a vector normal to the plane $n = n_x i + n_y j + n_z k$. Let $P(x,y,z)$ be a generic point on the plane of interest. We can form a relative position vector $r_{P/A} = r_P - r_A = (x-x_A) \cdot i + (y-y_A) \cdot j + (z-z_A) \cdot k$, which is contained in the plane, as shown in the figure below.

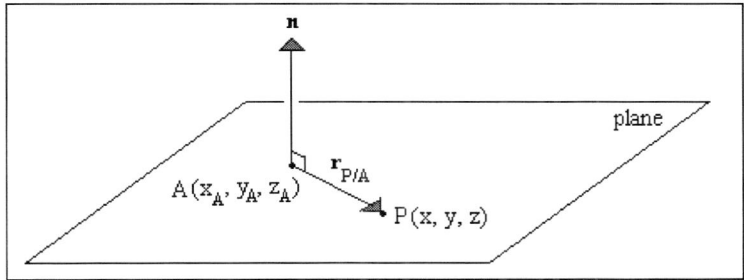

Because the vectors n and $r_{P/A}$ are perpendicular to each other, then, we can write $n \cdot r_{P/A} = 0$, or

$$(n_x i + n_y j + n_z k) \bullet ((x-x_A) i + (y-y_A) j + (z-z_A) k) = 0,$$

which results in the equation

$$n_x \cdot (x-x_A) + n_y \cdot (y-y_A) + n_z \cdot (z-z_A) = 0.$$

To implement a SCILAB function to produce the equation of a plane in space we use the fact that the equation can be re-written as $n_x \cdot x + n_y \cdot y + n_z \cdot z = n \bullet r_A$. The function *PlaneEquation*, shown below, calculates the right-hand side of the equation $n \bullet r_A$, and uses the function *string* to convert numerical results to strings. The final result of the function is a string representing the equation.

```
function [eq] = PlaneEquation(n,p)

//This function produces the equation of a plane
//in space given the normal vector n and the point p.

[nn,mn] = size(n);
[np,mp] = size(p);

if nn*mn <> 3 | np*mp <> 3 then
       error('Vector n or point p in PlaneEquation must have 3 elements')
       abort;
end

c = n*p';
eq = string(n(1))+'*x+'+string(n(2))+'*y+'+string(n(3))+'*z='+string(c)

//end function
```

The function requires as input the normal vector and the point A (referred to as p in the function), both entered as SCILAB vectors. For example, to find the equation of the plane with normal vector $n = 3i-5j+6k$ passing through point A(3, 6, -2) use:

```
-->getf('PlaneEquation')

-->n = [3, -5, 6], A = [3, 6, -2]

-->myEquation = PlaneEquation(n,A)
 myEquation  =

 3*x+-5*y+6*z=-33
```

To verify that the equation is satisfied by point A use:

```
-->x = 3, y = 6, z = -2
 x  =

     3.
 y  =

     6.
 z  =
```

```
    - 2.
-->3*x-5*y+6*z
 ans  =

    - 33.
```

Example 5 – Moment of a force

The figure below shows a force **F** acting on a point P in a rigid body. Suppose that the body is allowed to rotate about point O. Let **r** be the position vector of point P with respect to the point of rotation O, which we make coincide with the origin of our Cartesian coordinate system. The moment of the force **F** about point O is defined as **M** = **r**×**F**.

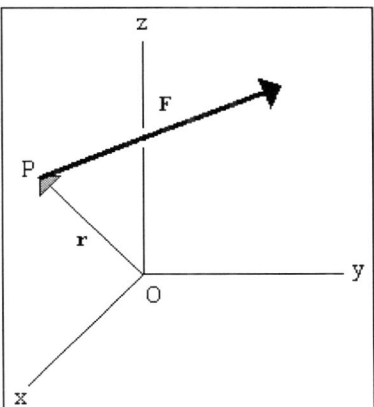

Referring to the figure of Example 3, if we want to calculate the moment of tension T_1 = (-51.57**i** -56.73**j** -128.93**k**) N, about point O, we will use as the position vector of the force's line of action through the pole, the vector r_{OE} = (2.5**k**) m. The moment $M_1 = r_{OE} \times T_1$, can be calculated as follows:

[0. 0. 2.5][ENTER]   Enter r_{OE}
[-57.51 –56.73 –128.93][ENTER]   Enter T_1
[↰][MTH][VECTR][CROSS]   Calculate $M_1 = r_{OE} \times T_1$

The result is [141.825 –143.775 0], M_1 = (141.825**i** –143.775**j**) m·N.

To find the magnitude of the moment, use [↰][ABS], thus, $|M_1|$ = M_1 = 201.954 m·N.

Note: Moments are vector quantities and obey all rules of vectors, i.e., they can be added, subtracted, multiplied by a scalar, undergo internal and external vector products. As an exercise, the reader may want to calculate the moments corresponding to the other tensions in Example 3, as well as the resultant moment from all four tensions.

Example 6 – Cartesian and polar representations of vectors in the x-y plane

A position vector in the x-y plane can be written simply as $r = x \cdot i + y \cdot j$. Let its magnitude be $r = |r|$. A unit vector along the direction of r is given by $e_r = r/r = (x/r) \cdot i + (y/r) \cdot j$. If we use polar coordinates, we recognize

$$x/r = \cos\theta, \text{ and } y/r = \sin\theta,$$

thus, we can write the unit vector as

$$e_r = r/r = \cos\theta \cdot i + \sin\theta \cdot j.$$

Thus, if we are given the magnitude, r, and the direction, θ, of a vector (i.e., its polar coordinates (r,θ)), we can easily put together the vector as

$$r = r \cdot e_r = r \cdot (\cos\theta \cdot i + \sin\theta \cdot j).$$

This result is illustrated in the figure below.

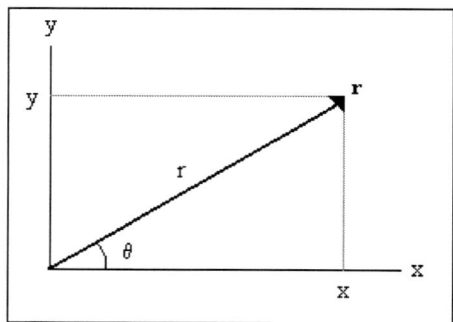

To enter a vector in SCILAB, given the magnitude r and the angle θ, you would use, for example:

```
-->r = 2.5*[cos(0.75), sin(0.75)]
 r =

!  1.8292222   1.7040969 !
```

In this case the angle represents radians. If you want to use an angle in degrees, you need to transform it to radians in the trigonometric functions, for example:

```
-->r = 5.2*[cos(32*%pi/180), sin(32*%pi/180)]
 r =

!  4.4098501   2.7555802 !
```

Example 7 – Planar motion of a rigid body

In the study of the planar motion of a rigid body the following equations are used to determine the velocity and acceleration of a point B (v_B, a_B) given the velocity and acceleration of a reference point A (v_A, a_A):

$$v_B = v_A + \omega_{AB} \times r_{B/A},$$

$$a_B = a_A + \alpha_{AB} \times r_{B/A} - \omega_{AB}^2 \cdot r_{B/A}.$$

The equations also use the angular velocity of the body connecting A and B, ω_{AB}, whose magnitude is ω_{AB}; the angular acceleration of the body connecting A and B, α_{AB}, and the relative position vector of point B with respect to point A, $r_{B/A}$. The following figure illustrates the calculation of relative velocity and acceleration in planar motion of a rigid body.

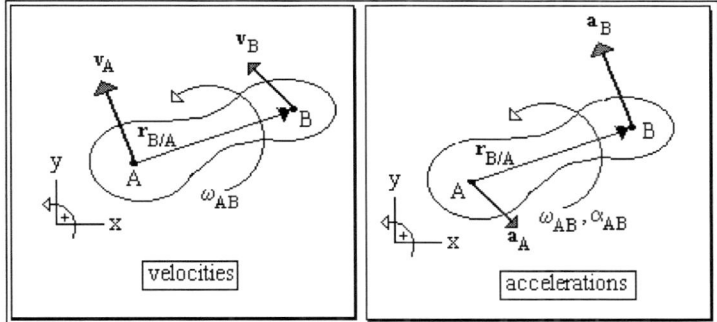

To present applications of this equation using the HP 49 G calculator, we use the data from the mechanism shown in the figure below.

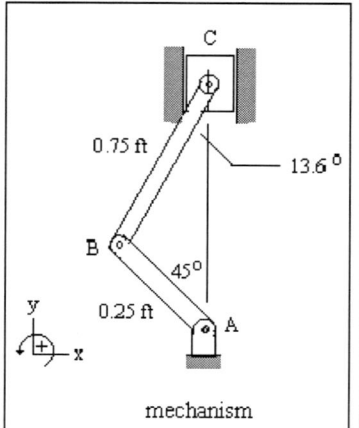
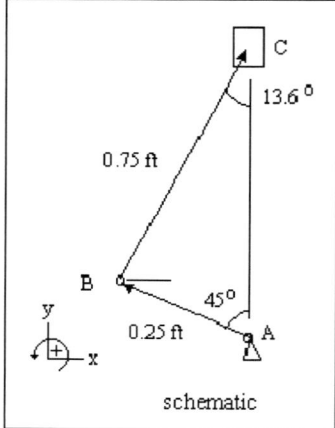

mechanism   schematic

In this mechanism there are two bars AB and AC pin-connected at B. Bar AB is pin supported at A, and bar BC is attached through a pin to piston C. Piston C is allowed to move in the vertical direction only. At the instant shown the angular velocity and acceleration of bar AB are 10 rad/s and 20 rad/s^2 clockwise. You are asked to determine the angular velocity and acceleration of bar BC and the linear velocity and acceleration of piston C.

Angular velocity and acceleration

Angular velocities and accelerations in the x-y plane are represented as vectors in the z-direction, i.e., normal to the x-y plane. These vectors are positive if the angular velocity or acceleration is counterclockwise. In general, thus we can write $\omega_{AB} = \pm\omega_{AB}\mathbf{k}$, and $\alpha_{AB} = \pm\alpha_{AB}\mathbf{k}$. For the data in this problem we can write, therefore,

$$\omega_{AB} = (-10\mathbf{k}) \text{ rad/s}, \quad \alpha_{AB} = (-20\mathbf{k})\text{rad/s}^2, \quad \omega_{BC} = (\omega_{BC}\mathbf{k}) \text{ rad/s}, \text{ and } \alpha_{BC} = (\alpha_{BC}\mathbf{k}).$$

Using SCILAB, we will write:

```
-->wAB = [0, 0, -10], alphaAB = [0, 0, -20]
 wAB  =

!  0.    0.   - 10. !
 alphaAB  =

!  0.    0.   - 20. !
```

The next statements define the polynomial variables *wBCm* (standing for ω_{BC}) and *alBCm* (standing for α_{BC}). The *m* in the polynomial variable names stands for 'magnitude':

```
-->wBCm = poly(0,'wBCm'), alBCm = poly(0,'alBC')
 wBCm  =
```

```
       wBCm
alBCm  =

    alBC
```

With the variables *wBCm* and *alBCm* we can define the vectors ω_{BC} and α_{BC} as:

```
-->wBC = [0, 0, wBCm], alBC = [0, 0, alBCm]
  wBC  =

 !  0   0   wBCm !
  alBC =

 !  0   0   alBC !
```

Relative position vector

The relative position vectors of interest in this problem are $r_{B/A}$ and $r_{C/B}$, which are obtained as follows:

- To obtain $r_{B/A}$, we use the fact that for the xy coordinate system shown, the angle corresponding to vector $r_{B/A}$ is $\theta_{B/A} = 90° + 45° = 135°$. Thus, we can write

```
-->rB_A = 0.25*[cos(135*%pi/180), sin(135*%pi/180), 0]
  rB_A =

 ! -  .1767767    .1767767    0. !
```

In paper, we would write, therefore, $r_{B/A} = (-0.177\hat{i} + 0.177\hat{j})$ ft.

- For $r_{C/B}$, the angle $\theta_{C/B} = 90° - 13.6° = 76.4°$. Thus, in SCILAB,

```
-->rC_B = 0.75*[ cos(76.4*%pi/180), sin(76.4*%pi/180), 0]
   rC_B =

 !   .1763566    .7289708    0. !
```

In paper, we write, $r_{C/B} = (0.175\hat{i} + 0.729\hat{j})$ ft.

Velocity

Since point A is fixed point, $v_A = 0$, and we can write $v_B = \omega_{AB} \times r_{B/A} = (-10\hat{k})$ rad/s $\times (-0.177\hat{i} + 0.177\hat{j})$ ft. Using SCILAB, we would write:

```
-->getf('CrossProd')

-->vA = 0
  vA  =

    0.
-->vB = vA + CrossProd(wAB,rB_A)
  vB  =
```

!   1.767767   1.767767   0. !

Thus,

$$\boxed{v_B = (1.77\mathbf{i}+1.77\mathbf{j}) \text{ ft/s.}}$$

Note: Radians are basically dimensionless units, thus rad·ft = ft, rad·m = m.

To find the velocity of point C, we use

$$v_C = v_B + \omega_{BC} \times r_{C/B} = (-1.77\mathbf{i}-1.77\mathbf{j}) \text{ ft/s} + (\omega_{BC}\mathbf{k}) \text{ rad/s} \times (0.175\mathbf{i} + 0.729\mathbf{j})\text{ft.}$$

With SCILAB, this operation is written as:

```
-->vC = vB + CrossProd(wBC,rC_B)
 vC    =
```

!   1.767767 - .7289708wBCm   1.767767 + .1763566wBCm   0 !

The result can be written in paper as:
$$v_C = ((1.77-0.729\omega_{BC})\cdot\mathbf{i} + (1.77+0.176\omega_{BC})\cdot\mathbf{j}) \text{ ft/s.}$$

The figure above shows that the piston C is forced to move in the vertical direction, thus, the velocity of point C can be written as

$$v_C = (v_C\mathbf{j}) \text{ ft/s.}$$

Equating the two results presented immediately above for v_C we get:

$$(1.77-0.729\omega_{BC})\cdot\mathbf{i} + (1.77+0.176\omega_{BC}) \cdot\mathbf{j} = 0\cdot\mathbf{i} + v_C\mathbf{j}.$$

Since the x- and y-components of the two vectors in each side of the equal sign must be the same, we can write the system of equations:

$$1.77-0.729\omega_{BC} = 0$$
$$1.77+ 0.176\omega_{BC} = v_C$$

Solution of equations – one at a time

Using SCILAB, we can solve for the two unknowns (ω_{BC} and v_C) as follows:

1. From the first equation, ω_{BC} = 1.77/0.729, i.e.,

    ```
    -->wBCm = 1.77/0.729
     wBCm   =  2.4279835
    ```

2. From the second equation, vC = 1.77+(0.176)(2.43), i.e.,

    ```
    -->vCm = 1.77+0.176*2.43
     vCm   =  2.19768
    ```

> Thus, the solution of the system of equations is:
>
> $$\omega_{BC} = 2.43 \text{ rad/s, and } v_C = 2.20 \text{ ft/s.}$$
>
> The positive sign in ω_{BC} means that the angular velocity is counterclockwise. The positive sign in v_C means that point C is moving upwards in the vertical direction.

Acceleration

Again, because A is a fixed point $a_A = 0$. Thus, the acceleration of point B is given by

$$a_B = \alpha_{AB} \times r_{B/A} - \omega_{AB}^2 \cdot r_{B/A} = (-20k)\text{rad/s}^2 \times (-0.177i + 0.177j)\text{ft} - (10 \text{ rad/s})^2 \times (-0.177i + 0.177j)\text{ft}$$

Using SCILAB we can obtain a_B as follows:

```
-->aA = 0
 aA  =

    0.
```

```
-->wABm = -10
 wABm  =

  - 10.
```

```
-->aB = aA + CrossProd(alphaAB,rB_A)-wABm^2*rB_A
 aB  =

!   21.213203  - 14.142136    0. !
```

The result is [21.240 -14.142 0.000], or

$$a_B = (21.24 i - 14.14 j)\text{ft/s}^2.$$

To calculate the acceleration of point C we use:

$$a_C = a_B + \alpha_{BC} \times r_{C/B} - \omega_{BC}^2 \cdot r_{C/B} =$$
$$(21.24 i - 14.14 j)\text{ft/s}^2 + (\alpha_{BC} k) \times (0.175 i + 0.729 j)\text{ft} - (-2.42 \text{ rad/s})^2 \cdot (0.175 i + 0.729 j)\text{ft}$$

In Scilab:

```
-->aC = aB + CrossProd(alphaBC,rC_B) - wBCm^2*rC_B
 aC  =

!   20.173563 - .7289708alBC   - 18.439494 + .1763566alBC    0 !
```

The result is:

$$a_C = ((20.17-0.729\alpha_{BC})\cdot i + (-18.44+0176\alpha_{BC})\cdot j) \text{ ft/s}^2.$$

Also, because the motion of point C is in the vertical direction, we can write

$$a_C = a_C \cdot j.$$

Equating the two expressions for the vector aC shown above, we get the following equations:

$$20.17 - 0.729\alpha_{BC} = 0,$$
$$-18.44 + 0176\alpha_{BC} = a_C.$$

Solution of a system of linear equations using matrices

The system of linear equations in two unknowns (α_{BC} and a_C) obtained above can be re-written in matricial form as follows:

1. The equations are first re-written as
$$a_c - 0.176\alpha_{BC} = -18.44$$
$$0.729\alpha_{BC} = 20.17$$

or, as a matrix equation:

$$\begin{bmatrix} 1 & -0.176 \\ 0 & 0.729 \end{bmatrix} \begin{bmatrix} a_C \\ \alpha_{BC} \end{bmatrix} = \begin{bmatrix} -18.44 \\ 20.17 \end{bmatrix}$$

2. This matrix equation can be solved by using the backward-slash operator (\), i.e., $x = A\backslash b$. This result follows from the original matrix equation $A \cdot x = b$, by "dividing" both sides of the equation by A. However, since A is a matrix, this "division" is not a regular arithmetic division. Typically, this operation would be represented as $x = A^{-1}b$, where A^{-1} is the inverse of matrix A. Modern matrix-based numerical environments, such as SCILAB, provide the user with the "backward-slash" operator instead of using the inverse matrix. The result, however, is exactly the same.

Using SCILAB, we would enter:

```
-->A = [1, -0.176; 0, 0.729], b = [-18.44;20.17]
 A   =

!    1.  -  .176 !
!    0.     .729 !

 b   =

! - 18.44 !
!   20.17 !

-->A\b
 ans  =

! - 13.570425 !
```

> ! 27.668038 !
>
> The results are interpreted as
>
> $$a_C = -13.57 \text{ ft/s}^2, \quad \alpha_{BC} = 27.67 \text{ rad/s}^2.$$
>
> The negative sign in a_C indicates that point C is decelerating. The positive sign in α_{BC} indicates that bar BC is accelerating angularly in the counterclockwise direction.

We have presented here two methods for solution of systems of linear equations. These methods, and others, are presented in more detail in a different chapter.

Exercises

For the following exercises use the Cartesian vectors:

$$u = 3i+2j-5k, \; v = -i-3k, \; w = 5i-10j-3k, \; r = -8i+10j-2.5k, \; s = -3i-2j-5k, \; t = 6i-2j+15k,$$

[1]. Determine the result of the following operations:
(a) $|u|$
(b) $|w|$
(c) $|v| \, |r|$
(d) $|s|/|w|$
(e) $a = u + v$
(f) $b = r-t$
(g) $c = 3r-2v$
(h) $d = -t + 2s$
(i) unit vectors: e_u, e_v, e_w
(j) angles between vectors u, v; r, s; and v, w.
(k) $u \bullet v$
(l) $w \bullet r$
(m) $s \times t$
(n) $u \times v$
(o) $r \times w$
(p) $u \bullet (v \times w)$
(q) $(s \times t) \bullet r$
(r) $w \times (r \times u)$
(s) $(u \times v) \times t$
(t) $(u \times v) \times (s \times t)$

[2]. Four different cables are attached to point E(0,0,0) on a structure. The four cables are anchored to points A(-1,-1,-1), B(2,3,-5), C(-2,2,4), and D(2,3,-1). The tensions in the four cables are: AE = 150 lb, BE = 250 lb, CE = 100 lb, DE = 50 lb. Determine the resultant force from the four cables.

[3]. Determine the torque of the following forces F given the arm r, i.e., $M = r \times F$:
(a) $F = (3i+2j-5k)$ N, $r = (-2i+5j-3k)$ m
(b) $F = (i-4j-3k)$ lb, $r = (i+8j-13k)$ ft
(a) $F = 100(i+j-k)$ lb, $r = (-2i+5j-3k)/2$ ft
(b) $F = 200(-4j-k)$ N, $r = 3(i+j-10k)$ m

[4]. Determine the equation of the plane through point A with normal vector n. Sketch the plane:
(a) A(-2,3,5), n = [2,-2,3]
(b) A(0, -1, 2), n = [5,5,-1]
(c) A(2,5,-1), n = [1, 1, 1]
(d) A(-1,5,-2), n = [3,3,-1]

[5]. Two vectors n and m are said to be orthogonal if $n \bullet m = 0$. Determine the missing components in the following vectors m and n so that they are orthogonal:
(a) n = [2, y, -2], m = [5,5,-1]
(b) n = [x,5,4], m = [-1,0,2]
(c) n = [4,2,y], m = [3,3,2]
(d) n = [5,5,2], m = [x,-2,3]

Note: define the unknown variable as a SCILAB polynomial variable, e.g., for (a):

```
-->y = poly(0,'y')
```

Then, define the vectors as follows:

```
--> n = [2,y,-2]; m = [5,5,1];
```

Calculate the dot product as a polynomial:

```
--> p = n*m'
```

and solve for y using function *roots*:

```
--> roots(p)
```

[6]. For the mechanism presented in Example 7, if the velocity of point C is v_c = 1.2 ft/s and its acceleration is a_c = -0.2 ft/s^2, determine the angular velocity and acceleration of bars AB and BC.

5 Matrices and Linear Algebra

A matrix is a rectangular arrangement of numbers in rows and columns enclosed in brackets. Examples of matrices follow:

■ A matrix with one row and three columns (a 1×3 matrix) is basically the same as a three-dimensional row vector, e.g.,

$$[5.\ 6.\ -2.]$$

■ A matrix with one column and five rows (a 5×1 matrix) is the same as a column vector of five elements, e.g.,

$$\begin{bmatrix} -5 \\ 3 \\ 2.5 \\ 0 \\ 4 \end{bmatrix}$$

■ The following is a matrix of two rows and four columns (a 2×4 matrix):

$$\begin{bmatrix} -5 & 2 & 3 & 0 \\ 11 & -7 & 0 & -1 \end{bmatrix}$$

■ A matrix can have variables and algebraic expressions as their elements, for example:

$$\begin{bmatrix} a_{11}^2 - \lambda & b \\ x & a_{22}^2 - 2\mu \end{bmatrix}$$

■ A matrix can have complex numbers as elements, for example:

$$\begin{bmatrix} -1+5i & 3 \\ 2i & \pi - 5i \\ 5 - i\sqrt{2} & e^{i\pi/2} \end{bmatrix}$$

Definitions

■ The _elements of a matrix_ are referred to by using two sub-indices: the first one representing the row, and the second one the column where the element is located. A matrix A with n rows and m columns can be represented by

$$\mathbf{A} = \begin{bmatrix} a_{11} & a_{12} & \cdots & a_{1,m-1} & a_{1,m} \\ a_{21} & a_{22} & \cdots & a_{2,m-1} & a_{2,m} \\ \vdots & \vdots & \ddots & \vdots & \vdots \\ a_{n-1,1} & a_{n-1,2} & \cdots & a_{n-1,m-1} & a_{n-1,m} \\ a_{n,1} & a_{n,2} & \cdots & a_{n,m-1} & a_{n,m} \end{bmatrix}$$

Thus, a generic element of matrix A belonging in row i and column j will be written as $a_{i,j}$ or a_{ij}. The matrix A, itself, can be written in a simplified form as

$$A_{n \times m} = [a_{ij}].$$

■ A matrix having the same number of rows and columns is called _square matrix_. The following is a 3×3 square matrix:

$$\begin{bmatrix} -2.5 & 4.2 & 2.0 \\ 0.3 & 1.9 & 2.8 \\ 2 & -0.1 & 0.5 \end{bmatrix}$$

■ The elements of a square matrix with equal sub-indices, i.e. a_{11}, a_{22}, ..., a_{nn}, belong to the matrix's _main diagonal_.

$$\begin{bmatrix} 12.5 & 0 & 0 \\ 0 & -9.2 & 0 \\ 0 & 0 & 0.75 \end{bmatrix}$$

■ A _diagonal matrix_ is a square matrix having non-zero elements only in the main diagonal. An example of a 3×3 diagonal matrix is:

$$\mathbf{I}_{3 \times 3} = \begin{bmatrix} 1 & 0 & 0 \\ 0 & 1 & 0 \\ 0 & 0 & 1 \end{bmatrix}$$

■ A diagonal matrix whose main diagonal elements are all equal to 1.0 is known as an _identity matrix,_ because multiplying I by any matrix results in the same matrix, i.e.,

$$I \cdot A = A \cdot I = A.$$

The identity matrix is typically given the symbol I. The following is a 3×3 identity matrix:

Matrices as tensors and the Kronecker's delta function

A sub-indexed variable, such as those used to identify a matrix, is also referred to as a *tensor*. The number of sub-indices determines the *order of the tensor*. Thus, a vector is a first-order tensor, and a matrix is a second order tensor. A scalar value is referred to as a zero-th order tensor.

The *Kronecker's delta function*, δ_{ij}, is a tensor function defined as $\delta_{ij} = 1.0$, if $i = j$, and $\delta_{ij} = 0$, if $i \neq j$.

Using the Kronecker's delta function, therefore, an $n \times n$ *identity matrix* can be written as

$$I_{n \times n} = [\delta_{ij}].$$

■ A *tridiagonal matrix* is a matrix having non-zero elements in the main diagonal and the upper and lower diagonals adjacent to the main diagonal. Tridiagonal matrices typically arise from numerical solution of partial differential equations, and, more often than not, the terms in the diagonals off the main diagonal are the same. An example of a 5×5 tridiagonal matrix follows:

$$\begin{bmatrix} -2.5 & 4 & 0 & 0 & 0 \\ 2 & -3.5 & 2 & 0 & 0 \\ 0 & -2 & 6.5 & -2 & 0 \\ 0 & 0 & 3 & -4 & 3 \\ 0 & 0 & 0 & 0 & 5 \end{bmatrix}$$

Matrix operations

■ The *transpose of a matrix* results from exchanging rows for columns and columns for rows. Therefore, given the matrix $A_{n \times m} = [a_{ij}]$, of n rows and m columns, its transpose matrix is $A^T_{n \times m} = [a^T_{ij}]$, of m rows and n columns, such that $a^T_{ij} = a_{ji}$, ($i = 1, 2, ..., n$; $j = 1, 2, ..., m$).

■ Consider the matrices $A_{n \times m} = [a_{ij}]$, and $B_{n \times m} = [b_{ij}]$, and $C_{n \times m} = [c_{ij}]$. The operations *of addition, subtraction, and multiplication by a scalar*, are defined as:

- Addition: $C_{n\times m} = A_{n\times m} + B_{n\times m}$, implies $c_{ij} = a_{ij} + b_{ij}$.
- Subtraction: $C_{n\times m} = A_{n\times m} + B_{n\times m}$, implies $c_{ij} = a_{ij} + b_{ij}$.
- Multiplication by a scalar, k: $C_{n\times m} = k \cdot A_{n\times m}$, implies $c_{ij} = k \cdot a_{ij}$.

- *Matrix multiplication* requires that the number of rows of the first matrix be equal to the number of columns of the second matrix. In other words, the only matrix multiplication allowed is such that,

$$A_{n\times m} \cdot B_{m\times p} = C_{n\times p},$$

with the elements of the matrix product given by

$$c_{ij} = \sum_{k=1}^{m} a_{ik} \cdot b_{kj}, \quad (i = 1, 2, \ldots, n; \ j = 1, 2, \ldots, p).$$

Schematically, the calculation of element c_{ij} of a matrix product $C_{n\times p} = A_{n\times m} \cdot B_{m\times p}$, is shown below:

Thus, element c_{ij} of the product results from the summation:

$$c_{ij} = a_{i1} \cdot b_{1j} + a_{i2} \cdot b_{2j} + \ldots + a_{ik} \cdot b_{kj} + \ldots + a_{i,m-1} \cdot b_{m-1,j} + a_{i,m} \cdot b_{m,j}.$$

which is the term-by-term multiplication of the elements of row i from A and column j from B which then are added together.

Note: *Matrix multiplication is, in general, non-commutative*, i.e., $A \cdot B \neq B \cdot A$. In fact, if one of these products exist, the other may not even be defined. The only case in which both $A \cdot B$ and $B \cdot A$ are defined is when both A and B are square matrices of the same order.

Einstein's summation convention for tensor algebra

When developing his general theory of relativity, Albert Einstein was faced with the daunting task of writing huge amounts of tensor summations. He figured out that he did not need to write the summation symbol, Σ, with its associated indices, if he used the convention that, *whenever two indices were repeated in an expression, the summation over all possible values of the repeating index was implicitly expressed.*

Thus, the equation for the generic term of a matrix multiplication, expressed above as a summation, can be simplified to read

$$c_{ij} = a_{ik} \cdot b_{kj}, \ (i = 1, 2, ..., n; \ j = 1, 2, ..., p).$$

Because the index k is repeated in the expression, the summation of all the products indicated by the expression is implicit over the repeating index, $k = 1, 2, ..., m$.

The dot or internal product of two vectors of the same dimension (see Chapter 9) $a = [a_1 \ a_2 \ ... \ a_n]$ and $b = [b_1 \ b_2 \ ... \ b_n]$, can be expressed, using Einstein's summation convention, as

$$a \bullet b = a_i \cdot b_i, \ \text{or} \ a \bullet b = a_k \cdot b_k, \ \text{or even} \ a \bullet b = a_r \cdot b_r,$$

The repeating index in this, or in the previous, expression is referred to as a *dummy index* and can be replaced by any letter, as long as we are aware of the range of values over which the summation is implicit.

The *inverse* of a square matrix $A_{n \times n}$, referred to as A^{-1}, is defined in terms of matrix multiplication and the $n \times n$ identity matrix, I, as

$$A \cdot A^{-1} = A^{-1} \cdot A = I.$$

Enter the following matrices and store them in the names suggested. Notice that the names of the variables correspond to an upper case letter of the alphabet followed by two numbers. The numbers represent the number of rows and columns that the matrix has. This way we can purposely select some particular matrices to illustrate matrix operations that are and that are not allowed. Thus, proceed to store the following variables:

$$\mathbf{A}11 = [[3]], \mathbf{B}11 = [[-2]], \mathbf{C}11 = [[5]]$$
$$\mathbf{A}12 = [[-5 \quad 6]], \mathbf{B}12 = [[3 \quad -2]], \mathbf{C}12 = [[-10 \quad 20]].$$
$$\mathbf{A}13 = [[1 \quad -2 \quad 6]], \mathbf{B}13 = [[0 \quad 3 \quad -4]], \mathbf{C}13 = [[5 \quad 3 \quad -10]].$$

$$\mathbf{A}21 = \begin{bmatrix} -7 \\ 3 \end{bmatrix}, \mathbf{B}21 = \begin{bmatrix} 3 \\ 5 \end{bmatrix}, \mathbf{C}21 = \begin{bmatrix} -2 \\ 2 \end{bmatrix}.$$

$$\mathbf{A}22 = \begin{bmatrix} -3 & 0 \\ 4 & -6 \end{bmatrix}, \mathbf{B}22 = \begin{bmatrix} 5 & -2 \\ 5 & 4 \end{bmatrix}, \mathbf{C}22 = \begin{bmatrix} -1 & 4 \\ 8 & 2 \end{bmatrix}.$$

$$\mathbf{A}23 = \begin{bmatrix} 8 & 0 & -1 \\ 5 & -2 & 3 \end{bmatrix}, \mathbf{B}23 = \begin{bmatrix} 1 & 0 & 1 \\ 0 & 1 & -1 \end{bmatrix}, \mathbf{C}23 = \begin{bmatrix} 2 & -3 & -5 \\ 6 & 4 & -2 \end{bmatrix}.$$

$$\mathbf{A}31 = \begin{bmatrix} -10 \\ 2 \\ 5 \end{bmatrix}, \mathbf{B}31 = \begin{bmatrix} 3 \\ -7 \\ -2 \end{bmatrix}, \mathbf{C}31 = \begin{bmatrix} 0 \\ 2 \\ 6 \end{bmatrix}.$$

$$\mathbf{A}32 = \begin{bmatrix} 1 & 0 \\ 1 & 2 \\ 5 & 2 \end{bmatrix}, \mathbf{B}32 = \begin{bmatrix} 9 & 2 \\ 3 & 0 \\ 6 & -5 \end{bmatrix}, \mathbf{C}32 = \begin{bmatrix} 5 & 8 \\ 6 & -7 \\ -3 & -2 \end{bmatrix}.$$

$$\mathbf{A}33 = \begin{bmatrix} 2 & -1 & 5 \\ 0 & 2 & 1 \\ -7 & 2 & -5 \end{bmatrix}, \mathbf{B}33 = \begin{bmatrix} 3 & 1 & 2 \\ 0 & 5 & 2 \\ -4 & 2 & 1 \end{bmatrix}, \mathbf{C}33 = \begin{bmatrix} 2 & 1 & 2 \\ 3 & -7 & 0 \\ 2 & 1 & 4 \end{bmatrix}.$$

To enter these matrices in SCILAB use:

```
-->A11 = [3]; B11 = [-2]; C11 = [5];
-->A12 = [-5, 6]; B12 = [3, -2]; C12 = [-10, 20];
-->A13 = [1, -2, 6]; B13 = [0, 3, -4]; C13 = [5, 3, -10];
-->A21 = [-7; 3]; B21 = [3; 5]; C21 = [-2; 2];
-->A22 = [-3, 0; 4, -6]; B22 = [5, -2; 5, 4]; C22 = [-1, 4; 8, 2];
-->A23 = [8, 0, -1; 5, -2, 3]; B23 = [1, 0, 1; 0, 1, -1];
-->C23 = [2, -3, -5; 6, 4, -2];
-->A31 = [-10; 2; 5]; B31 = [3; -7; -2]; C31 = [0; 2; 6];
-->A32 = [1, 0; 1, 2; 5, 2]; B32 = [9, 2; 3, 0; 6, -5];
```

```
-->C32 = [5, 8; 6, -7; 3, -2];
-->A33 = [2, -1, 5; 0, 2, 1;-7, 2, -5];
-->B33 = [3, 1, 2; 0, 5, 2; -4, 2, 1];
-->C33 = [2, 1, 2; 3, -7, 0; 2, 1, 4];
```

Note: the use of a semi-colon instead of a comma or blank space suppresses the output in SCILAB.

Addition and subtraction

Once these variables have been entered, try the following exercises

Addition and subtraction of 1x1 matrices (i.e., scalars)

```
-->A11 + B11
 ans  = 1.

-->A11 + C11
 ans  = 8.

-->A11 + B11 + C11
 ans  = 6.

-->A11 - B11
 ans  = 5.

-->A11 - C11
 ans  = - 2.

-->B11 - C11
 ans  = - 7.

-->A11 - (B11 - C11)
 ans  = 10.
```

Addition and subtraction of *2 matrices (i.e., two-dimensional row vectors)

```
-->A12 + B12
 ans  = ! - 2.    4. !

-->A12 + C12
 ans  = ! - 15.   26. !

-->A12 + B12 + C12
 ans  = ! - 12.   24. !

-->A12 - B12
 ans  = ! - 8.    8. !

-->A12 - C12
 ans  = !   5.  - 14. !

-->B12 - C12
 ans  = !  13.  - 22. !
```

```
-->A12 - (B12 - C12)
 ans  = ! - 18.    28. !
```

Addition and subtraction of 21 matrices (i.e., two dimensional column vectors)

```
-->A21 + B21 + C21
 ans  = ! - 6. !
        !  10. !
-->A21 - B21
 ans  = ! - 10. !
        ! -  2. !
-->A21 - C21
 ans  = ! - 5. !
        !   1. !
-->B21 - C21
 ans  = !  5. !
        !  3. !
-->A21 - (B21 - C21)
 ans  = ! - 12. !
        !    0. !
```

Addition and subtraction of 22 matrices

```
-->A22 + B22
 ans  = !  2.  - 2. !
        !  9.  - 2. !
-->A22 + C22
 ans  = ! - 4.    4. !
        !  12.  - 4. !
-->A22 + B22 + C22
 ans  = !  1.   2. !
        ! 17.   0. !
-->A22 - B22
 ans  = ! - 8.    2. !
        ! - 1.  - 10. !
-->A22 - C22
 ans  = ! - 2.  - 4. !
        ! - 4.  - 8. !
-->B22 - C22
 ans  = !  6.  - 6. !
        ! - 3.   2. !
-->A22 - (B22 - C22)
 ans  = ! - 9.    6. !
        !   7.  - 8. !
```

Addition and subtraction of *3 matrices

```
-->A13 + B13
 ans  =  !   1.    1.    2. !

-->A13 + C13
 ans  =  !   6.    1.  - 4. !

-->A13 + B13 + C13
 ans  =  !   6.    4.  - 8. !

-->A13 - B13
 ans  =  !   1.  - 5.   10. !

-->A13 - C13
 ans  =  ! - 4.  - 5.   16. !

-->B13 - C13
 ans  =  ! - 5.    0.    6. !

-->A13 - (B13 - C13)
 ans  =  !   6.  - 2.    0. !
```

Addition and subtraction of 23 matrices

```
-->A23 + B23
 ans  =  !   9.    0.    0. !
         !   5.  - 1.    2. !

-->A23 + C23
 ans  =  !  10.  - 3.  - 6. !
         !  11.    2.    1. !

-->A23 + B23 + C23
 ans  =  !  11.  - 3.  - 5. !
         !  11.    3.    0. !

-->A23 - B23
 ans  =  !   7.    0.  - 2. !
         !   5.  - 3.    4. !

-->A23 - C23
 ans  =  !   6.    3.    4. !
         ! - 1.  - 6.    5. !

-->B23 - C23
 ans  =  ! - 1.    3.    6. !
         ! - 6.  - 3.    1. !

-->A23 - (B23 - C23)
 ans  =  !   9.  - 3.  - 7. !
         !  11.    1.    2. !
```

Addition and subtraction of 31 matrices

```
-->A31 + B31
 ans  =  ! - 7. !
         ! - 5. !
         !   3. !
```

```
-->A31 + C31
 ans  = ! - 10. !
        !   4.  !
        !  11.  !
-->A31 + B31 + C31
 ans  = ! - 7. !
        ! - 3. !
        !   9. !
-->A31 - B31
 ans  = ! - 13. !
        !   9.  !
        !   7.  !
-->A31 - C31
 ans  = ! - 10. !
        !   0.  !
        ! - 1.  !
-->B31 - C31
 ans  = !   3. !
        ! - 9. !
        ! - 8. !
-->A31 - (B31 - C31)
 ans  = ! - 13. !
        !  11.  !
        !  13.  !
```

Addition and subtraction of 32 matrices

```
-->A32 + B32
 ans  = !  10.    2. !
        !   4.    2. !
        !  11.  - 3. !
-->A32 + C32
 ans  = !   6.    8. !
        !   7.  - 5. !
        !   8.    0. !
-->A32 + B32 + C32
 ans  = !  15.   10. !
        !  10.  - 5. !
        !  14.  - 5. !
-->A32 - B32
 ans  = ! - 8.  - 2. !
        ! - 2.    2. !
        ! - 1.    7. !
-->A32 - C32
 ans  = ! - 4.  - 8. !
        !   2.    4. !
-->B32 - C32
 ans  = !   4.  - 6. !
```

```
                  ! - 3.      7. !
                  !   3.    - 3. !
-->A32 - (B32 - C32)
 ans  = ! - 3.      6. !
        !   4.    - 5. !
        !   2.      5. !
```

Addition and subtraction of 3×3 matrices

```
-->A33 + B33
 ans  = !   5.      0.     7. !
        !   0.      7.     3. !
        ! - 11.     4.   - 4. !
-->A33 + C33
 ans  = !   4.      0.     7. !
        !   3.    - 5.     1. !
        ! - 5.      3.   - 1. !
-->A33 + B33 + C33
 ans  = !   7.      1.     9. !
        !   3.      0.     3. !
        ! - 9.      5.     0. !
-->A33 - B33
 ans  = ! - 1.    - 2.     3. !
        !   0.    - 3.   - 1. !
        ! - 3.      0.   - 6. !
-->A33 - C33
 ans  = !   0.    - 2.     3. !
        ! - 3.      9.     1. !
        ! - 9.      1.   - 9. !
-->B33 - C33
 ans  = !   1.      0.     0. !
        ! - 3.     12.     2. !
        ! - 6.      1.   - 3. !
-->A33 - (B33 - C33)
 ans  = !   1.    - 1.     5. !
        !   3.   - 10.   - 1. !
        ! - 1.      1.   - 2. !
```

Notes:

The subtraction A – B can be interpreted as A + (-B).

Addition is *commutative*, i.e., A + B = B + A, and *associative*, i.e., A+B+C = A+(B+C) = (A+B)+C.

Addition and subtraction can only be performed between matrices of the same dimensions. Verify this by trying [A23][A21][+]. You will get an error message: `-> + Error: Invalid Dimension`

Multiplication by a scalar

```
-->2*A11
 ans  =      6.

-->-3*A12
 ans  = !   15.   - 18. !

-->-1*A21
 ans  = !   7. !
        ! - 3. !

-->5*A22
 ans  = ! - 15.    0. !
        !   20.  - 30. !

-->-2*A13
 ans  = ! - 2.    4.   - 12. !

-->10*A31
 ans  = ! - 100. !
        !   20.  !
        !   50.  !

-->-5*A23
 ans  = ! - 40.    0.     5. !
        ! - 25.   10.   - 15. !

-->2*A32
 ans  = !   2.    0. !
        !   2.    4. !
        !  10.    4. !

-->1.5*A33
 ans  = !   3.   - 1.5    7.5 !
        !   0.     3.     1.5 !
        ! - 10.5    3.   - 7.5 !
```

Matrix multiplication

```
-->A11*B11
 ans  =    - 6.

-->B11*A11
 ans  =    - 6.

-->A12*B21
 ans  =      15.

-->B21*A12
 ans  = ! - 15.    18. !
        ! - 25.    30. !

-->A12*B22
 ans  = !   5.    34. !
```

```
-->A21*B12
 ans  = ! - 21.    14. !
        !   9.  -  6. !

-->B12*A21
 ans  =   - 27.

-->A22*B21
 ans  = ! - 9.  !
        ! - 18. !

-->A22*B22
 ans  = ! - 15.    6. !
        ! - 10. - 32. !

-->B22*A22
 ans  = ! - 23.   12. !
        !   1.  - 24. !

-->A13*B31
 ans  =    5.

-->B31*A13
 ans  = !   3.  -  6.    18. !
        ! - 7.    14.  - 42. !
        ! - 2.     4.  - 12. !

-->A13*B32
 ans  = !  39.  - 28. !

-->A11*B11
 ans  =   - 6.

-->A23*B31
 ans  = !  26. !
        !  23. !

-->A23*B32
 ans  = !  66.    21. !
        !  57.  - 5.  !

-->A32*B23
 ans  = !  1.    0.    1. !
        !  1.    2.  - 1. !
        !  5.    2.    3. !

-->A23*B33
 ans  = !  28.    6.   15. !
        !   3.    1.    9. !

-->A33*B31
 ans  = !   3. !
        ! - 16. !
        ! - 25. !

-->A23*B31
 ans  = !  26. !
        !  23. !
```

```
-->A23*B31
 ans  = !   26. !
        !   23. !

-->B33*A33
 ans  = ! - 8.      3.      6. !
        ! - 14.    14.    - 5. !
        ! - 15.    10.   - 23. !
```

Note: Some of the examples above illustrate the fact that $A_{m\times n} \cdot B_{n\times m} \neq B_{n\times m} \cdot A_{m\times n}$. That is, multiplication, in general, is not commutative.

```
-->A12* (B21*C12)
 ans  = ! - 150.    300. !

-->(A12* B21)*C12
 ans  = ! - 150.    300. !

-->A22* (B21*C12)
 ans  = !   90.   - 180. !
        !  180.   - 360. !

-->(A22* B21)*C12
 ans  = !   90.   - 180. !
        !  180.   - 360. !

-->A32* (B23*C32)
 ans  = !    8.      6. !
        !   14.   -  4. !
        !   46.     20. !

-->(A32* B23)*C32
 ans  = !    8.      6. !
        !   14.   -  4. !
        !   46.     20. !
```

Note: The examples above illustrate the fact that multiplication is associative:
$$A_{m\times n} \cdot B_{n\times m} \cdot C_{m\times p} = A_{m\times n} \cdot (B_{n\times m} \cdot C_{m\times p}) = (A_{m\times n} \cdot B_{n\times m}) \cdot C_{m\times p}.$$

Inverse matrices

Inverse matrices exists only for square matrices. In SCILAB, inverse matrices are calculated by using the function *inv*. The standard notation for the inverse matrix of A is A^{-1}. Try the following exercises:

```
-->inv(A11)
 ans  =      .3333333

-->inv(B11)
 ans  =   -  .5

-->inv(C11)
 ans  =      .2
```

```
-->inv(A22)
 ans   = ! -  .3333333     0.         !
         ! -  .2222222  -  .1666667 !

-->inv(B22)
 ans   = !    .1333333     .0666667 !
         ! -  .1666667     .1666667 !

-->inv(C22)
 ans   = ! -  .0588235     .1176471 !
         !    .2352941     .0294118 !

-->inv(A33)
 ans   = ! -  .2264151     .0943396  -  .2075472 !
         ! -  .1320755     .4716981  -  .0377358 !
         !    .2641509     .0566038     .0754717 !

-->inv(B33)
 ans   = !    .0285714     .0857143  -  .2285714 !
         ! -  .2285714     .3142857  -  .1714286 !
         !    .5714286  -  .2857143     .4285714 !

-->inv(C33)
 ans   = !    .8235294     .0588235  -  .4117647 !
         !    .3529412  -  .1176471  -  .1764706 !
         ! -  .5           0.           .5       !
```

Note: Some matrices has no inverse, for example, matrices with one row or column whose elements are all zeroes, or a matrix with a row or column being proportional to another row or column, respectively. These are called *singular* matrices.

Try the following examples:

```
-->A = [ 1 2 3; 0 0 0; -2 5 2], inv(A)
 A   = !   1.      2.      3. !
       !   0.      0.      0. !
       ! - 2.      5.      2. !
A = [ 1 2 3; 0 0 0; -2 5 2], inv(A)
                                  !--error    19
singular matrix

-->B = [ 1 2 3; 2 4 6; 5 2 -1], inv(B)
 A   = !   1.      2.      3. !
       !   2.      4.      6. !
       ! - 2.      5.      2. !
B = [ 1 2 3; 2 4 6; 5 2 -1], inv(B)
                                  !--error    19
singular matrix
```

Verifying properties of inverse matrices

```
-->inv(A22)*A22
 ans   =

!   1.      0. !
!   0.      1. !
```

```
-->A22*inv(A22)
 ans  =

!   1.    0. !
!   0.    1. !

-->inv(B22)*B22
 ans  =

!   1.    0. !
!   0.    1. !

-->B22*inv(B22)
 ans  =

!   1.    0. !
!   0.    1. !

-->inv(C22)*C22
 ans  =

!   1.    0. !
!   0.    1. !

-->C22*inv(C22)
 ans  =

!   1.    0. !
!   0.    1. !

-->inv(A33)*A33
 ans  =

!   1.    0.    0. !
!   0.    1.    0. !
!   0.    0.    1. !

-->A33*inv(A33)
 ans  =

!   1.           0.    0. !
!   0.           1.    0. !
! - 2.220E-16   0.    1. !

-->inv(B33)*B33
 ans  =

!   1.    0.    0. !
!   0.    1.    0. !
!   0.    0.    1. !

-->B33*inv(B33)
 ans  =

!   1.    0.    0. !
!   0.    1.    0. !
!   0.    0.    1. !
```

```
-->inv(C33)*C33
 ans  =

!    1.    0.    0. !
!    0.    1.    0. !
!    0.    0.    1. !

-->C33*inv(C33)
 ans  =

!    1.    0.    0. !
!    0.    1.    0. !
!    0.    0.    1. !
```

The last set of exercises verify the properties of inverse matrices, i.e., $A^{-1} A = A A^{-1} = I$, where I is the identity matrix.

Creating identity matrices in SCILAB

To obtain a nxn identity matrix in SCILAB use the function *eye*, e.g.,

```
-->I22 = eye(2,2)
 I22  =

!    1.    0. !
!    0.    1. !

-->I33 = eye(3,3)
 I33  =

!    1.    0.    0. !
!    0.    1.    0. !
!    0.    0.    1. !
```

If a square matrix A is already defined, you can obtain an identity matrix of the same dimensions by using *eye(A)*, for example:

```
-->A = [2, 3, 4, 2; -1, 2, 3, 1; 5, 4, 2, -2; 1, 1, 0, 1]
 A  =

!    2.    3.    4.    2. !
!  - 1.    2.    3.    1. !
!    5.    4.    2.  - 2. !
!    1.    1.    0.    1. !

-->eye(A)
 ans  =

!    1.    0.    0.    0. !
!    0.    1.    0.    0. !
!    0.    0.    1.    0. !
!    0.    0.    0.    1. !
```

The *eye* function call $A = eye(n,m)$ produces a matrix whose terms $a_{ii} = 1$, all other terms being zero. For example,

```
-->A = eye(3,2)
 A  =

!   1.    0. !
!   0.    1. !
!   0.    0. !


-->A = eye(2,3)
 A  =

!   1.    0.    0. !
!   0.    1.    0. !
```

Note: the name of the function *eye* comes from the name of the letter I typically used to refer to the identity matrix.

The Vandermonde matrix

A Vandermonde matrix of dimension n is based on a given vector of size n. The Vandermonde matrix corresponding to the vector $[x_1\ x_2\ ...\ x_n]$, is given by:

$$\begin{bmatrix} 1 & x_1 & x_1^2 & x_1^3 & ... & x_1^{n-1} \\ 1 & x_2 & x_2^2 & x_2^3 & ... & x_2^{n-1} \\ 1 & x_3 & x_3^2 & x_3^3 & ... & x_3^{n-1} \\ . & . & . & . & & . \\ . & . & . & . & & . \\ 1 & x_n & x_n^2 & x_n^3 & ... & x_n^{n-1} \end{bmatrix}$$

To produce a Vandermonde matrix given an input vector x, we can use the following function *vandermonde*:

```
function [v] = vandermonde(x)

//Produces the Vandermonde matrix based on vector x.
//If vector x has the components [x(1) x(2) ... x(n)],
//the corresponding Vandermonde matrix is written as:
//       [  1    x(1)   x(1)^2   x(1)^3 ... x(1)^(n-1) ]
//       [  1    x(2)   x(2)^2   x(2)^3 ... x(2)^(n-1) ]
//       [  .     .       .        .    ...    .       ]
//       [  .     .       .        .    ...    .       ]
//       [  1    x(n)   x(n)^2   x(n)^3 ... x(n)^(n-1) ]
//

[nx,mx] = size(x);
```

```
if nx<>1 & mx<>1 then
        error('Function vandermonde - input must be a vector');
        abort;
end;

if nx == 1 then
        u = x';
        n = mx;
else
        u = x;
        n = nx;
end;

// u = column vector = [x(1) x(2) ... x(n)]'
// n = number of elements in u
// v = first column of Vandermonde matrix (all ones)

v = ones(n,1);

for k = 1:(n-1)
        v = [v,u^k];
end;

//end function
```

For example, the Vandermonde matrix corresponding to the vector x = [2, -3, 5, -2], is calculated as follows:

```
-->x = [2, -3, 5, -2]
 x  =

!   2.   - 3.    5.   - 2. !

-->Vx = vandermonde(x)
 Vx   =

!   1.    2.    4.     8.  !
!   1.  - 3.    9.   - 27. !
!   1.    5.   25.    125. !
!   1.  - 2.    4.   - 8.  !
```

So, you wonder, what is the utility of the Vandermonde matrix? One practical application, which we will be utilizing in a future chapter, is the fact that the Vandermonde matrix corresponding to a vector $[x_1\ x_2\ ...\ x_n]$, which is in turn associated to a vector $[y_1\ y_2\ ...\ y_n]$, can be used to determine a polynomial fitting of the form

$$y = b_0 + b_1 \cdot x + b_2 \cdot x^2 + ... + b_{n-1} \cdot x^{n-1},$$

to the data sets (x,y).

The Hilbert matrix

The $n \times n$ Hilbert matrix is defined as $H_n = [h_{jk}]$, so that

$$h_{jk} = \frac{1}{j+k-1}.$$

The Hilbert matrix has application in numerical cue fitting by the method of linear squares.

In SCILAB, a Hilbert matrix can be generated by first using the function *testmatrix* with the option '*hilb*' and the size *n*. For example, for *n*=5, we have:

```
-->H_inv = testmatrix('hilb',5)
 H_inv  =

!    25.    - 300.      1050.     - 1400.       630.   !
!  - 300.    4800.    - 18900.     26880.    - 12600.  !
!   1050.  - 18900.    79380.   - 117600.     56700.   !
! - 1400.   26880.  - 117600.    179200.    - 88200.   !
!    630.  - 12600.    56700.    - 88200.     44100.   !
```

This function call produces the inverse of the Hilbert matrix. Use the function *inv* to obtain the actual Hilbert matrix, i.e.,

```
-->H = inv(H_inv)
 H  =

!   1.          .5         .3333333    .25         .2         !
!    .5         .3333333   .25         .2          .1666667   !
!    .3333333   .25        .2          .1666667    .1428571   !
!    .25        .2         .1666667    .1428571    .125       !
!    .2         .1666667   .1428571    .125        .1111111   !
```

Magic squares

The function *testmatrix* can also produce matrices corresponding to magic squares, i.e., matrices such that the sums of its rows and columns, as well as its diagonals, produce the same result. For example, a 3x3 magic square is obtained from:

```
-->A = testmatrix('magic',3)
 A  =

!   8.    1.    6.  !
!   3.    5.    7.  !
!   4.    9.    2.  !
```

The sum of elements in each column of the magic square is calculated as follows:

```
-->sum(A(:,1))
 ans  =

    15.

-->sum(A(:,2))
 ans  =

    15.
```

```
-->sum(A(:,3))
 ans  =

    15.
```

The sums corresponding to the rows of the magic square are:

```
-->sum(A(1,:))
 ans  =

    15.
-->sum(A(2,:))
 ans  =

    15.
-->sum(A(3,:))
 ans  =

    15.
```

The sums of the elements in the main diagonal is calculated using the function *trace*:

```
-->trace(A)
 ans  =

    15.
```

Finally, the sum of the elements in the second main diagonal of the matrix is:

```
-->A(3,1)+A(2,2)+A(1,3)
 ans  =

    15.
```

Thus, we have verified that matrix **A** is indeed a magic square.

Symmetric and anti-symmetric matrices

A square matrix, $A_{n \times n} = [a_{ij}]$, is said to be *symmetric* if $a_{ij} = a_{ji}$, for $i \neq j$, i.e., $A^T = A$. Also, a square matrix, $A_{n \times n} = [a_{ij}]$, is said to be *anti-symmetric* if $a_{ij} = -a_{ji}$, for $i \neq j$, i.e., $A^T = -A$.

The matrix **A** below is symmetric, while the matrix **C** below is anti-symmetric:

$$A = \begin{bmatrix} -2 & 3 & -5 \\ 3 & 6 & 4 \\ -5 & 4 & 2 \end{bmatrix}, \quad C = \begin{bmatrix} 12 & 1.3 & 15 \\ -1.3 & -2 & -2.4 \\ -15 & 2.4 & 5 \end{bmatrix}$$

Any square matrix, $B_{n\times n} = [b_{ij}]$ can be written as the sum of a symmetric $B'_{n\times n} = [b'_{ij}]$ and an anti-symmetric $B''_{n\times n} = [b''_{ij}]$ matrices. Because

$$b_{ij} = \tfrac{1}{2}\cdot(b_{ij} + b_{ji}) + \tfrac{1}{2}\cdot(b_{ij} - b_{ji}),$$

we can write

$$b'_{ij} = \tfrac{1}{2}\cdot(b_{ij} + b_{ji}), \text{ and } b''_{ij} = \tfrac{1}{2}\cdot(b_{ij} - b_{ji}).$$

Therefore,

$$B'_{n\times n} = \tfrac{1}{2}\cdot(B_{n\times n} + B^T_{n\times n}), \text{ and } B''_{n\times n} = \tfrac{1}{2}\cdot(B_{n\times n} - B^T_{n\times n}),$$

where $B^T_{n\times n} = [b^T_{ij}] = [b_{ji}]$ is the transpose of matrix B.

For example, take the matrix

$$B = \begin{bmatrix} 2 & -1 & 3 \\ 5 & 4 & -2 \\ 6 & 3 & -10 \end{bmatrix}$$

defined earlier, and use the following SCILAB commands to find its symmetric and anti-symmetric components:

```
-->B = [2, -1, 3; 5, 4, -2; 6, 3, -10];
```

The symmetric component:

```
-->B_sym = (B+B')/2
 B_sym   =

!    2.       2.       4.5 !
!    2.       4.        .5 !
!    4.5      .5     - 10. !
```

The anti-symmetric component is:

```
-->B_anti = (B-B')/2
 B_anti  =

!    0.     - 3.     - 1.5 !
!    3.       0.     - 2.5 !
!    1.5      2.5      0.  !
```

To verify that they add back to matrix B use:

```
-->B_sym + B_anti
 ans =

!    2.    - 1.       3.  !
!    5.      4.     - 2.  !
!    6.      3.    - 10.  !
```

This decomposition of a square matrix into its symmetric and anti-symmetric parts is commonly used in continuous mechanics to determine such effects as normal and shear strains or strain rates and rotational components.

Manipulating elements of vectors and matrices

Vectors and matrices are the basic data structures used in SCILAB. A vector or matrix is defined by simply assigning an array of values to a variable name. Many example defining vectors or matrices have been presented previously.

Determining the size of vectors and matrices

The function *size* is used to determine the number of rows and columns of a vector or matrix. Some examples of the use of the function *size* are presented next:

```
-->rv = [1, 3, 5, 7, 9, 11]          //A row vector
 rv  =

!    1.    3.    5.    7.    9.    11. !

-->cv = [2; 4; 6; 8; 10; 12]         //A column vector
 cv  =

!    2.  !
!    4.  !
!    6.  !
!    8.  !
!   10.  !
!   12.  !

-->size(rv)
 ans  =

!    1.    6. !                      // 1 row x 6 columns (1x6)

-->size(cv)
 ans  =

!    6.    1. !                      // 6 rows x 1 column (6x1)


-->M = [2,3;-2,1;5,4;1,3]            // A matrix
 M  =

!    2.    3. !
!  - 2.    1. !
!    5.    4. !
```

```
!   1.    3. !
-->size(M)
 ans  =

!   4.    2. !                                    //4 rows x 2 columns (4x2)
```

Extracting elements of vectors and matrices

Elements of vectors and matrices can be extracted and manipulated numerically by referring to them with the vector or matrix name with an appropriate set of indices (or sub-indices). For example,

```
-->u = [1:1:6], v = [10:-2:0]
 u  =

!   1.    2.    3.    4.    5.    6. !
 v  =

!   10.   8.    6.    4.    2.    0. !
-->u(1) + v(2), v(5)/u(2)
 ans  = 9.
 ans  = 1.
```

Generating vectors and matrices containing random numbers

The function *rand* can be used to generate a matrix whose elements are random numbers uniformly distributed in the interval (0,1). For example, to generate a matrix of random numbers with 3 rows and 5 columns, use:

```
-->m = rand(3,5)
 m  =

!   .2113249   .3303271   .8497452   .0683740   .7263507 !
!   .7560439   .6653811   .6857310   .5608486   .1985144 !
!   .0002211   .6283918   .8782165   .6623569   .5442573 !
```

If you want to generate a matrix of random integer numbers between 0 and 10, combine function *rand* with function *int* as follows:

```
-->A = int(10*rand(4,2))
 A =

!  2.  6. !
!  2.  3. !
!  2.  9. !
!  8.  2. !
```

Numerical operations involving elements of matrix A and of vector b are shown next:

```
-->A(2,1) + v(2), A(3,2)
 ans  =

    10.
 ans  =

    9.
```

Extracting rows and columns with the colon operator

The colon operator (:) can be used to extract rows or columns of a matrix. For example, the next two SCILAB expressions, with the colon operator as the first sub-index, extract the first and second rows from matrix A:

```
-->A(:,1), A(:,2)
 ans  =

!    2. !
!    2. !
!    2. !
!    8. !
 ans  =

!    6. !
!    3. !
!    9. !
!    2. !
```

The next two statements, with the colon operator as the second sub-index, extract the first and second rows from matrix A:

```
-->A(1,:), A(2,:)
 ans  =

!    2.    6. !
 ans  =

!    2.    3. !
```

Programming constructs with matrix elements

Programming constructs can be used to manipulate elements of a vector or matrix by using appropriate values of the sub-indices. As an example, the following commands create a 4x3 matrix A such that its elements are defined by $a_{ij} = i+j$:

```
-->for i = 1:4, for j = 1:3, A(i,j) = i+j; end, end
```

```
-->A
 A  =

!    2.    3.    4. !
!    3.    4.    5. !
!    4.    5.    6. !
!    5.    6.    7. !
```

Composing matrices by adding vectors

The next examples show how to create matrices by adding vectors to it as new columns or rows. We start by defining the 1x3 row vectors u1, u2, and u3:

```
-->u1 = [2,3,-5]; u2 = [7, -2, 1]; u3 = [2, 2, -1];
```

A 1x9 row vector composed of the elements of u1, u2, and u3 is put together by using:

```
-->[u1, u2, u3]
 ans  =

!    2.    3.   - 5.    7.   - 2.    1.    2.    2.   - 1. !
```

If the vector names are separated by semi-colons, the vectors are added as rows:

```
-->[u1; u2; u3]
 ans  =
!    2.    3.   - 5. !
!    7.   - 2.    1. !
!    2.    2.   - 1. !
```

The transpose vectors u1', u2', and u3' are column vectors. Therefore, the matrix that results from listing the vector names u1', u2', u3' is a 3x3 matrix whose columns are the vectors:

```
-->[u1' u2' u3']
 ans  =
!    2.    7.    2. !
!    3.   - 2.    2. !
!  - 5.    1.   - 1. !
```

If semi-colons are placed between the column vectors the result is a 9x1 column vector:

```
-->[u1';u2';u3']
 ans  =

!    2. !
!    3. !
!  - 5. !
!    7. !
!  - 2. !
!    1. !
!    2. !
!    2. !
!  - 1. !
```

Composing a matrix by adding vectors one at a time

The following exercises show how to build matrices by adding vectors one at a time. This procedure may be useful in programming when one needs to build a matrix out of a number of vectors. First, we define an empty matrix, by using B = [], and then the row vectors are added one at a time:

```
-->B = []; B = [B u1]
 B  =

!    2.    3.  - 5. !
-->B = [B;u2]
 B  =

!    2.    3.  - 5. !
!    7.  - 2.    1. !
-->B = [B; u3]
 B  =

!    2.    3.  - 5. !
!    7.  - 2.    1. !
!    2.    2.  - 1. !
```

In the next example, the row vectors are added one at a time to form a single row vector:

```
-->C = []; C = [C u1]
 C  =

!    2.    3.  - 5. !
-->C = [C u2]
 C  =

!    2.    3.  - 5.    7.  - 2.    1. !
-->C = [C u3]
 C  =

!    2.    3.  - 5.    7.  - 2.    1.    2.    2.  - 1. !
```

In the following example, column vectors are added one at a time:

```
-->D = []; D = [D u1']
 D  =
!    2. !
!    3. !
!  - 5. !
-->D = [D u2']
 D  =
!    2.    7. !
!    3.  - 2. !
!  - 5.    1. !
```

```
-->D = [D u3']
 D  =

!   2.     7.     2. !
!   3.  -  2.     2. !
! - 5.     1.  -  1. !
```

Finally, to construct a single column vector out of three column vectors, the composing column vectors are added one at a time:

```
-->E = []; E = [E; u1']
 E  =

!   2. !
!   3. !
! - 5. !

-->E = [E; u2']
 E  =

!   2. !
!   3. !
! - 5. !
!   7. !
! - 2. !
!   1. !

-->E = [E; u3']
 E  =

!   2. !
!   3. !
! - 5. !
!   7. !
! - 2. !
!   1. !
!   2. !
!   2. !
! - 1. !
```

Replacing elements of vectors or matrices

Individual elements in a vector or matrix can be replaced through assignment statements, for example:

```
-->B
 B  =
```

```
!    2.     3.   - 5. !
!    7.   - 2.     1. !
!    2.     2.   - 1. !
```

```
-->B(2,1) = 0
 B  =

!    2.     3.   - 5. !
!    0.   - 2.     1. !
!    2.     2.   - 1. !
```

```
-->B(3,2) = -10
 B  =

!    2.     3.   - 5. !
!    0.   - 2.     1. !
!    2.  - 10.   - 1. !
```

Notice that after each assignment statement the entire matrix is printed.

If need be to replace entire rows or columns in a matrix by a vector of the proper length, you can build the new matrix as illustrated in the examples below. In the first example, vector u1 replaces the second row of matrix B:

```
-->u1
 u1  =

!    2.     3.   - 5. !
```

```
-->[B(1,:);u1;B(3,:)]
 ans  =

!    2.     3.   - 5. !
!    2.     3.   - 5. !
!    2.  - 10.   - 1. !
```

In this second example we reconstruct the original matrix B and then replace its first row with vector u2:

```
-->B = [u1;u2;u3]
 B  =

!    2.     3.   - 5. !
!    7.   - 2.     1. !
!    2.     2.   - 1. !
```

```
--> [u2; B(2,:); B(3,:)]
```

```
ans  =

!   7.   - 2.     1. !
!   7.   - 2.     1. !
!   2.     2.   - 1. !
```

Sum and product of matrix elements

SCILAB provides the functions *sum* and *prod* to calculate the sum and products of all elements of a vector or matrix. In the following examples we use matrix B, defined above:

```
-->sum(B)
 ans  =

    9.

-->prod(B)
 ans  =

  -1680.
```

To calculate the sum or product of rows of a matrix use the qualifier 'r' in functions *sum* and *prod* (i.e., adding or multiplying by rows):

```
-->sum(B,'r')
 ans  =

!   11.     3.   - 5. !

-->prod(B,'r')
 ans  =

!   28.   - 12.    5. !
```

To obtain the sum or product of columns of a matrix use the qualifier 'c' in *sum* and *prod* (i.e., adding or multiplying by columns):

```
-->sum(B,'c')
 ans  =

!   0. !
!   6. !
!   3. !

-->prod(B,'c')
 ans  =

! - 30. !
! - 14. !
! -  4. !
```

Matrices and solution of linear equation systems

A system of n linear equations in m variables can be written as

$$
\begin{aligned}
a_{11} x_1 + a_{12} x_2 + a_{13} x_3 + \ldots + a_{1,m-1} x_{m-1} + a_{1,m} x_m &= b_1, \\
a_{21} x_1 + a_{22} x_2 + a_{23} x_3 + \ldots + a_{2,m-1} x_{m-1} + a_{2,m} x_m &= b_2, \\
a_{31} x_1 + a_{32} x_2 + a_{33} x_3 + \ldots + a_{3,m-1} x_{m-1} + a_{3,m} x_m &= b_3, \\
&\vdots \\
a_{n-1,1} x_1 + a_{n-1,2} x_2 + a_{n-1,3} x_3 + \ldots + a_{n-1,m-1} x_{m-1} + a_{n-1,m} x_m &= b_{n-1}, \\
a_{n1} x_1 + a_{n2} x_2 + a_{n3} x_3 + \ldots + a_{n,m-1} x_{m-1} + a_{n,m} x_m &= b_n.
\end{aligned}
$$

This system of linear equations can be written as a matrix equation,

$$A_{n \times m} \cdot x_{m \times 1} = b_{n \times 1},$$

if we define the following matrices:

$$
A = \begin{bmatrix} a_{11} & a_{12} & \cdots & a_{1m} \\ a_{21} & a_{22} & \cdots & a_{2m} \\ \vdots & \vdots & \ddots & \vdots \\ a_{n1} & a_{n2} & \cdots & a_{nm} \end{bmatrix}, \quad x = \begin{bmatrix} x_1 \\ x_2 \\ \vdots \\ x_m \end{bmatrix}, \quad b = \begin{bmatrix} b_1 \\ b_2 \\ \vdots \\ b_n \end{bmatrix}
$$

Using the matricial equation $A \cdot x = b$, we can solve for x by using the function *linsolve*. The function requires as arguments the matrices A and b. Some examples are shown below:

Solution to a system of linear equations using *linsolve*

The function *linsolve*, rather than solving the matricial equation described above, namely $A \cdot x = b$, solves the equation $A \cdot x + c = 0$, where $c = -b$. The general form of the function call is

$$[x0, nsA] = linsolve(A, c\,[, x0])$$

where A is a matrix with n rows and m columns, c is a $n \times 1$ vector, $x0$ is a vector (a particular solution of the system), and nsA is an $m \times k$ matrix known as the null space of matrix A.

Depending on the number of unknowns and equations (i.e., n and m), *linsolve* produces different results. Some examples are shown following:

Case 1. A system with the same number of equations and unknowns - unique solution exists:

If the number of unknowns is the same as the number of equations, the solution may be unique, in which case the null space returned by *linsolve* is empty. Consider the following case involving three equations with three unknowns:

$$2x_1 + 3x_2 - 5x_3 - 13 = 0,$$
$$x_1 - 3x_2 + 8x_3 + 13 = 0,$$
$$2x_1 - 2x_2 + 4x_3 + 6 = 0.$$

can be written as the matrix equation $A \cdot x + c = 0$, if

$$\mathbf{A} = \begin{bmatrix} 2 & 3 & -5 \\ 1 & -3 & 8 \\ 2 & -2 & 4 \end{bmatrix}, \quad \mathbf{x} = \begin{bmatrix} x_1 \\ x_2 \\ x_3 \end{bmatrix}, \quad and \quad \mathbf{c} = \begin{bmatrix} -13 \\ 13 \\ 6 \end{bmatrix}.$$

If a unique solution exists it represents the point of intersection of the three planes in the coordinate system (x_1, x_2, x_3). Using function *linsolve* to obtain a solution we write:

```
-->A = [2, 3, -5; 1, -3, 8; 2, -2, 4], c = [-13; 13; 6]
 A    =

    !   2.      3.    - 5.  !
    !   1.    - 3.      8.  !
    !   2.    - 2.      4.  !
 c    =

    ! - 13. !
    !   13. !
    !    6. !
-->[x0,nsA] = linsolve(A,c)
 nsA  =

       []
 x0   =

    !   1. !
    !   2. !
    ! - 1. !
```

The null space returned for A is empty, indicating a unique solution. To verify that the solution satisfies the system of equations we can use:

```
--> A*x0+c
 ans  =

    1.0E-14 *

    !   .1776357 !
    !   0.       !
    !   0.       !
```

Although the resulting vector $A*x0+c$, is not exactly zero, it is small enough (in the order of

10^{-14}) to indicate that the solution satisfies the linear system.

Case 2. A system with the same number of equations and unknowns - no unique solution exists:

A system of linear equations with the same number of equations and unknowns not always has a unique solution, as illustrated by the following system:

$$2x_1 + 3x_2 - 5x_3 - 13 = 0,$$
$$2x_1 + 3x_2 - 5x_3 + 13 = 0,$$
$$2x_1 - 2x_2 + 4x_3 + 6 = 0.$$

The system of linear equations can be written as the matrix equation $Ax + c = 0$, if

$$A = \begin{bmatrix} 2 & 3 & -5 \\ 2 & 3 & -5 \\ 2 & -2 & 4 \end{bmatrix}, \quad x = \begin{bmatrix} x_1 \\ x_2 \\ x_3 \end{bmatrix}, \quad and \quad c = \begin{bmatrix} -13 \\ 13 \\ 6 \end{bmatrix}.$$

Attempting a solution with *linsolve* in SCILAB produces the following:

```
-->A = [2, 3, -5; 2, 3, -5; 2, -2, 4], c = [-13, 13, 6]
 A   =

!   2.    3.   - 5. !
!   2.    3.   - 5. !
!   2.  - 2.    4. !
 c   =

! - 13.   13.    6. !

-->[x0,nsA] = linsolve(A,c)
WARNING:Conflicting linear constraints!
 nsA  =
     [ ]
 x0  =
     [ ]
```

The function *linsolve* fails to produce a solution because the first two equations represent parallel planes in Cartesian coordinates. This failure is reported as a warning indicating *conflicting linear constraints.*

Case 3 - A system with more unknowns than equations

The system of linear equations

$$2x_1 + 3x_2 - 5x_3 + 10 = 0,$$
$$x_1 - 3x_2 + 8x_3 - 85 = 0,$$

can be written as the matrix equation $A \cdot x + c = 0$, if

$$A = \begin{bmatrix} 2 & 3 & -5 \\ 1 & -3 & 8 \end{bmatrix}, \quad x = \begin{bmatrix} x_1 \\ x_2 \\ x_3 \end{bmatrix}, \quad \text{and} \quad c = \begin{bmatrix} 10 \\ -85 \end{bmatrix}.$$

This system has more unknowns than equations, therefore, it is not uniquely determined. Such a system is referred to as an *over-determined system*.

We can visualize the linear system by realizing that each of the linear equations represents a plane in the three-dimensional Cartesian coordinate system (x_1, x_2, x_3). The solution to the system of equations shown above will be the intersection of two planes in space. We know, however, that the intersection of two (non-parallel) planes is a straight line, and not a single point. Therefore, there is more than one point that satisfies the system. In that sense, the system is not uniquely determined.

Applying the function *linsolve* to this system results in:

```
-->A = [2, 3, -5; 1, -3, 8], c = [10; -85]
 A  =

 !   2.    3.   - 5. !
 !   1.  - 3.    8.  !
 c  =

 !   10. !
 ! - 85. !
-->[x0,nsA] = linsolve(A,c)
 nsA =

 ! -  .3665083 !
 !    .8551861 !
 !    .3665083 !
 x0  =

 !   15.373134 !
 !    2.4626866 !
 !    9.6268657 !
```

In this case, *linsolve* returns values for both $x0$, the particular solution, and for nsA, the null space of A. There is no unique solution to the equation system, instead, a multiplicity of solutions exist given by $x = x0 + nsA \cdot t$, where t can take any real value. For example, for t = 10, we calculate a solution that we call $x1$:

```
-->x1 = x + nsA*10
 x1  =

 !   11.708051 !
 !   11.014548 !
 !   13.291949 !
```

To check whether this solution satisfies the system of equation we calculate:

```
-->A*x1+c
 ans  =

   1.0E-12 *

 ! -   .0426326 !
 ! -   .1989520 !
```

The result, containing values in the order of 10^{-12}, is practically zero.

Case 4 – A system with more equations than unknowns

The system of linear equations

$$x_1 + 3x_2 - 15 = 0,$$
$$2x_1 - 5x_2 - 5 = 0,$$
$$-x_1 + x_2 - 22 = 0,$$

can be written as the matrix equation $\mathbf{A} \cdot \mathbf{x} + \mathbf{c} = 0$, if

$$\mathbf{A} = \begin{bmatrix} 1 & 3 \\ 2 & -5 \\ -1 & 1 \end{bmatrix}, \quad \mathbf{x} = \begin{bmatrix} x_1 \\ x_2 \end{bmatrix}, \quad and \quad \mathbf{c} = \begin{bmatrix} -15 \\ -5 \\ -22 \end{bmatrix}.$$

This system has more equations than unknowns, and is referred to as an *under-determined system*. The system does not have a single solution. Each of the linear equations in the system presented above represents a straight line in a two-dimensional Cartesian coordinate system (x_1, x_2). Unless two of the three equations in the system represent the same equation, the three lines will have three different intersection points. For that reason, the solution is not unique.

An attempt to solve this system of linear equations with function *linsolve* produces no result:

```
-->A = [1, 3; 2, -5; -1, 1], c = [-15; -5; -22]
 A  =

 !   1.     3. !
 !   2.   - 5. !
 ! - 1.     1. !
 c  =

 ! - 15. !
 ! - 5.  !
 ! - 22. !

-->[x0,nsA] = linsolve(A,c)
 WARNING:Conflicting linear constraints!
 nsA  = []
 x0   = []
```

Solution to an under-determined system of linear equations using the least-square method

The *method of least squares* can be used to force a "solution" to a system of linear equations by minimizing the sum of the squares of the distances from the presumptive solution point to each of the "lines" represented by the linear equations. For the case of a system of linear equations involving two unknowns only, the equations represent actual geometrical lines in the plane. Thus, the "solution" point can be visualized as that point such that the sum of the squares of the distances from the point perpendicular to each line is a minimum.

SCILAB provides the function *leastsqr* to obtain the parameters that minimize the sum of squares of the residuals of a function given a set of reference data. The residuals of a least-square problem are the differences between the reference data and the data reproduced by the function under consideration.

For the case of a system of linear equations the *function to be minimized* by the least-square method is

$$f(x) = A \cdot x + c,$$

where A and c describe the system $A \cdot x + c = 0$. The "parameters" of the function sought in this case are the elements of the least-square "solution" x. As it will be explained in more detail in a subsequent chapter, the method of least squares requires taking the derivatives of the function to be solved for with respect to the parameters sought. For this case, the derivative of interest is

$$g(x) = f'(x) = A.$$

This derivative is referred to as the *gradient of the function*.

A general call to function *leastsqr* in SCILAB is:

$$[SSE, xsol] = leastsq([imp,] \ fun \ [,Dfun], x0)$$

where *SSE* is the minimum value of the sum of the squared residuals. *SSE* stands for the "Sum of Squared Errors". Error is equivalent to residual in this context. *xsol* is the point that minimizes the sum of squared residuals. *imp* is an optional value that determines the type of output provided by the function. *fun* is the name of the function under consideration. *Dfun* is the gradient of the function under consideration, and *x0* is an initial guess to the least-square solution.

We will apply function *leastsq* to the under-determined system of linear equations presented earlier, namely,

$$\mathbf{A} = \begin{bmatrix} 1 & 3 \\ 2 & -5 \\ -1 & 1 \end{bmatrix}, \quad \mathbf{x} = \begin{bmatrix} x_1 \\ x_2 \end{bmatrix}, \quad and \quad \mathbf{c} = \begin{bmatrix} -15 \\ -5 \\ -22 \end{bmatrix}.$$

Using SCILAB, we first enter the matrix A and vector c, as well as an initial guess for the solution, vector x0, as follows:

```
--> A = [1,3;2,-5;-1,1],c=[-15;-5;-22]
```

```
 A    =

!   1.     3. !
!   2.   - 5. !
! - 1.     1. !
 c    =

! - 15. !
! -  5. !
! - 22. !
-->x0 = [1;1]
 x0   =

!   1. !
!   1. !
```

In order to use *leastsq* we need to define the functions $f(x) = A \cdot x + c$, and $g(x) = A$, as follows:

```
-->deff('y = f(x,A,c)','y = A*x+c')
-->deff('yp = g(x,A,c)','yp = A')
```

Now, we invoke function *leastsq* with the appropriate arguments to obtain our least-square solution as:

```
-->[SSE,xsol] = leastsq(f,g,x0)
 xsol =

!   3.0205479 !
!   1.890411  !
 SSE  =

    645.5411
```

The least-square solution to the system of linear equations is, therefore, the vector xsol = [3.02, 1.89], and the sum of squared errors is SSE = 645.5411. You can check that, by definition, SSE = $|Axsol+c|^2$, by using:

```
--> norm(A*xsol+c)^2
 ans  =

    645.5411
```

A user-defined function for least-square solution for systems of linear equations

As indicated in the example just solved, in order to obtain the least-square solution to a system of linear equations you need to define the function to be minimized and its derivative. You can incorporate such definitions and the call to function *leastsq* into a user-defined function, let's call it *LSlinsolve* (for *Least-Square linsolve*), which will perform the least-square solution for a system of linear equations. A listing of function *LSlinsolve* follows:

```
function [SSE,xsol] = LSlinsolve(A,c,x0)
```

```
//Uses the least-square method to obtain the point
//that minimizes the sum of squared residuals for
//the system of linear equations A*x+c = 0.
//
//    A   is a nxm matrix,
//    x0  is a mx1 vector, and
//    c   is a nx1 vector.

[nA,mA] = size(A);
[nx,mx] = size(x0);
[nc,mc] = size(c);

if nA  nc | mA <> nx then
      error('LSlinsolve - incompatible dimensions');
      abort;
end;

deff('y00 = ff(xx,A,c)', 'y00 = A*xx+c');
deff('yp0 = gg(xx,A,c)', 'yp0 = A');

[SSE,xsol] = leastsq(ff,gg,x0);

//end of function
```

Using the same matrix A and vectors c and x0 from the previous example, we can use function *LSlinsolve* to obtain the least-square solution to the linear system $A \cdot x + c$ as follows:

```
-->getf('LSlinsolve')

-->[SSE,xsol] = LSlinsolve(A,c,x0)
 xsol  =

!   3.0205479 !
!   1.890411  !
 SSE  =

    645.5411
```

Solution of a system of linear equations using the *left-division* operator

If you have a linear system of equations $A \cdot x = b$, such that its coefficient matrix, A, is square, you can solve the system directly by using the backward slash operator, i.e., $x = A\backslash b$. The backward slash operator represents a division of vectors and matrices in a similar fashion as the forward slash is used to represent a division of algebraic terms.

As an example, consider the linear system given by

$$A = \begin{bmatrix} 2 & -5 & 1 \\ 2 & 2 & -3 \\ 0 & 5 & -2 \end{bmatrix}, x = \begin{bmatrix} x_1 \\ x_2 \\ x_3 \end{bmatrix}, \text{ and } b = \begin{bmatrix} 18 \\ 23 \\ -51 \end{bmatrix}.$$

The solution using the backward slash operator with SCILAB is obtained as follows:

```
-->A = [2, -5, 1; 2, 2, -3; 0, 5, -2], b = [18; 23; -51]
 A   =

!    2.   - 5.     1. !
!    2.     2.   - 3. !
!    0.     5.   - 2. !
 b   =

!    18. !
!    23. !
!  - 51. !

-->x = A\b
 x   =

!  - 48.333333 !
!  - 35.666667 !
!  - 63.666667 !
```

To check the solution use:

```
-->A*x
 ans   =

!    18. !
!    23. !
!  - 51. !
```

Please notice that A\b is different from b\A:

```
-->b\A
 ans   =

!    .0237406  -  .0865663     .0147655 !
```

Solution using the inverse matrix

The traditional way of writing the solution to the system $A \cdot x = b$ is $x = A^{-1} \cdot b$. This results from multiplying the first equation by the inverse matrix A^{-1}, i.e., $A^{-1} \cdot A \cdot x = A^{-1} \cdot b$. By definition, $A^{-1} \cdot A = I$, therefore, $I \cdot x = A^{-1} \cdot b$. Also, $I \cdot x = x$, thus, the final result is,

$$x = A^{-1} \cdot b.$$

For the example used earlier we could first calculate the inverse of matrix A as:

```
-->Ainv = inv(A)
 Ainv   =

!    .9166667  -  .4166667    1.0833333 !
!    .3333333  -  .3333333     .6666667 !
!    .8333333  -  .8333333    1.1666667 !
```

The solution is, therefore:

```
-->x = Ainv*b
 x  =

!  - 48.333333 !
!  - 35.666667 !
!  - 63.666667 !
```

The solution can be calculated without first calculating the inverse by using:

```
-->x = inv(A)*b
 x  =

!  - 48.333333 !
!  - 35.666667 !
!  - 63.666667 !
```

Characterizing a matrix

In the previous section we mentioned that, under certain conditions, a system of linear equations with n unknowns may not have a unique solution. In order to determine when such situations occur, we can use certain measures or norms that characterize a matrix. Some of those measures are the rank, norm, and determinant of the matrix. These and other ways of characterizing a matrix are presented in this section.

Matrix decomposition - a brief introduction

To understand some of the numbers used in characterizing a matrix we will first introduce the ideas of matrix decomposition. Basically, matrix *decomposition* involves the determination of two or more matrices that, when multiplied in a certain order (and, perhaps, with some matrix inversion or transposition thrown in), produce the original matrix. For example, the so-called *LU decomposition*, of a square matrix A is accomplished by writing A = L·U, where L is a lower-triangular matrix, and U is an upper-triangular matrix. (A *lower-triangular matrix* is such that elements above and to the right of the main diagonal are zero, while a *upper-triangular matrix* is such that elements below and to the left of the main diagonal are zero.) An example of LU decomposition is shown below:

$$\mathbf{A} = \begin{bmatrix} 2 & 4 & -2 \\ 4 & 9 & -3 \\ -2 & -3 & 7 \end{bmatrix} = \begin{bmatrix} 1 & 0 & 0 \\ 2 & 1 & 0 \\ -1 & 1 & 1 \end{bmatrix} \cdot \begin{bmatrix} 2 & 4 & -2 \\ 0 & 1 & 1 \\ 0 & 0 & 4 \end{bmatrix} = \mathbf{L} \cdot \mathbf{U}$$

Such a decomposition can be obtained with SCILAB by using the function *lu*. A general call to function *lu* is

$$[L,U] = lu(A)$$

where A is as square matrix, and L, U are as defined above. The function can also be called by using

$$[L,U,P] = lu(A)$$

where P is a permutation matrix. When the permutation matrix P is included in the analysis, the relationship between the various matrices is given by $P \cdot A = L \cdot U$.

To illustrate the use of the function *lu* we use the matrix A defined above:

```
-->A = [2,4,-2;4,9,-3;-2,-3,7]
 A  =

!   2.    4.   - 2. !
!   4.    9.   - 3. !
! - 2.  - 3.    7.  !

-->[L,U] = lu(A)
 U =

!   4.    9.   - 3.        !
!   0.    1.5    5.5       !
!   0.    0.     1.3333333 !

 L =

!    .5  - .3333333   1. !
!   1.     0.         0. !
! -  .5    1.         0. !
```

While matrix L is a proper upper-triangular matrix, L is not a proper lower-triangular matrix. This results from the numerical algorithm used for the decomposition, which introduces a permutation in the rows or columns of the matrix. The following call of the function provides the required permutation matrix, as well as returning the L and U matrices of the decomposition:

```
-->[L1,U1,P1] = lu(A)
 P1 =

!   0.    1.    0. !
!   0.    0.    1. !
!   1.    0.    0. !
 U1 =

!   4.    9.   - 3.        !
!   0.    1.5    5.5       !
!   0.    0.     1.3333333 !
 L1 =

!   1.       0.         0. !
! -  .5     1.          0. !
!    .5   - .3333333    1. !
```

Solution to a system of linear equations using function *lu*

We indicated above that a call to the *lu* function of the form [L,U,P] = lu(A), where A is the nxn matrix of coefficients of a system of linear equations, returns the matrices L, U, and P, such that P·A = L·U. If the original system is A·x = b, then we can write, P·A·x = P·b, or L·U·x = c, where c = P·b. This system can be solved in two steps, the first one consisting in solving L·y = c, and the second one consisting in solving U·x = y.

Consider the system of linear equations:

$$A = \begin{pmatrix} 2 & 4 & 6 \\ 3 & -2 & 1 \\ 4 & 2 & -1 \end{pmatrix}, \quad x = \begin{bmatrix} x_1 \\ x_2 \\ x_3 \end{bmatrix}, \quad b = \begin{bmatrix} 14 \\ -3 \\ -4 \end{bmatrix}.$$

To solve the system of equations under consideration using function *lu* and the procedure outlined above, use:

```
-->A= [2,4,6;3,-2,1;4,2,-1], b = [14;-3;-4]
 A   =

!   2.      4.      6. !
!   3.    - 2.      1. !
!   4.      2.    - 1. !
 b   =
!   14. !
!  - 3. !
!  - 4. !

-->[L,U,P] = lu(A)
 P   =
!   0.      0.      1. !
!   0.      1.      0. !
!   1.      0.      0. !
 U   =

!   4.      2.    - 1.   !
!   0.    - 3.5    1.75  !
!   0.      0.      8.   !
 L   =

!   1.          0.             0. !
!    .75        1.             0. !
!    .5       - .8571429       1. !

-->c = P*b
 c   =

!  - 4. !
!  - 3. !
!   14. !
```

The first system to be solved is:

$$L \cdot y = c, \quad i.e., \quad \begin{bmatrix} 1 & 0 & 0 \\ 0.75 & 1 & 0 \\ 0.5 & -0.8571429 & 1 \end{bmatrix} \cdot \begin{bmatrix} y_1 \\ y_2 \\ y_3 \end{bmatrix} = \begin{bmatrix} -4 \\ -3 \\ 14 \end{bmatrix}$$

This system is equivalent to the three equations:

$$\begin{aligned} y_1 &= -4 \\ 0.75 y_1 + y_2 &= -3 \\ 0.5 y_1 - 0.8571429 y_2 + y_3 &= 14 \end{aligned}$$

This system of equations can be solved one equation at a time starting from the first one, $y_1 = -4$. The second equation produces $y_2 = -3 - 0.75(-4) = 0$. The third equation is used to solve for $y_3 = 14 - 0.5(-4) + 0.8571429(0) = 16$. Thus, the solution vector y, is written as:

$$y = \begin{bmatrix} -4 \\ 0 \\ 16 \end{bmatrix}.$$

Next, we proceed to solve the equation:

$$U \cdot x = y, \quad or \quad \begin{bmatrix} 4 & 2 & -1 \\ 0 & -3.5 & 1.75 \\ 0 & 0 & 8 \end{bmatrix} \cdot \begin{bmatrix} x_1 \\ x_2 \\ x_3 \end{bmatrix} = \begin{bmatrix} -4 \\ 0 \\ 16 \end{bmatrix}.$$

This produces the system of linear equations:

$$\begin{aligned} 4x_1 + 2x_2 - x_3 &= -4 \\ -3.5x_2 + 1.75x_3 &= -3 \\ 8x_3 &= 16 \end{aligned}$$

These equations can be solved one at a time, starting with the third equation, $x_3 = 16/8 = 2$. The second equation produces $x_2 = (-1.75)(2)/(-3.5) = 1$. Finally, the first equation produces $x_1 = (-4-2(1)+2)/4 = -1$. Thus, the solution is

$$x = \begin{bmatrix} -1 \\ 1 \\ 2 \end{bmatrix}.$$

In summary, the LU decomposition of a square matrix A helps in the solution of the linear system A·x = b, by generating two systems of equations that can be easily solved one at a time. With SCILAB, however, we need not be concerned with solving linear systems through LU decomposition. Instead we can use functions *linsolve* or the backward slash operator as illustrated earlier.

Singular value decomposition and rank of a matrix

The Singular Value Decomposition (SVD) of a rectangular matrix $A_{m \times n}$ is accomplished by obtaining the matrices U, S, and V, such that

$$A_{m \times n} = U_{m \times m} \cdot S_{m \times n} \cdot V^T_{n \times n},$$

Where U and V are orthogonal matrices, and S is a diagonal matrix. The diagonal elements of S are called the _singular values_ of A and are usually ordered so that $s_i \geq s_{i+1}$, for $i = 1, 2, ..., n-1$. The columns $[u_i]$ of U and $[v_i]$ of V are the corresponding _singular vectors_.

Orthogonal matrices are such that $U \cdot U^T = I$.

The _rank_ of a matrix can be determined from its SVD by counting the number of non-singular values.

SCILAB provides function _svd_ to obtain the singular value decomposition of a matrix A. A call of the form

$$[U,S,V] = svd(A)$$

will return matrices U, S, and V, as described above. A simpler call,

$$[s] = svd(A)$$

returns a vectors containing the singular values. If the rank of the matrix is also required, the appropriate function call is

$$[U,S,V,r] = svd(A,tol)$$

where _tol_ is a tolerance value. The rank is defined as the number of singular values larger than _tol_.

As an example, we will attempt the singular value decomposition of the following rectangular matrix,

$$A = \begin{bmatrix} 2 & -1 \\ -3 & 2 \\ 5 & 4 \end{bmatrix},$$

Using SCILAB:

```
-->A = [2,-1;-3,2;5,4]
 A   =

!   2.   - 1. !
! - 3.     2. !
!   5.     4. !
```

A vector of singular values is obtained with:

```
--> s = svd(A)
 s  =

!   6.6487173 !
!   3.8463696 !
```

The full singular value decomposition results from:

```
-->[U,S,V] = svd(A)
 V  =

! -  .8882616     .4593379 !
! -  .4593379  -  .8882616 !
 S  =

!   6.6487173    0.          !
!   0.           3.8463696 !
!   0.           0.          !
 U  =

! -  .1981112     .4697774  -  .8602681 !
!    .2626234  -  .8201336  -  .5083402 !
! -  .9443415  -  .3266344     .0391031 !
```

If the rank is included in the SVD we have:

```
-->tol= 1e-10
 tol  =

     1.000E-10

-->[U,S,V,rank] = svd(A,tol)
Warning :redefining function: rank

 rank  = 2.
 V  =

! -  .8882616     .4593379 !
! -  .4593379  -  .8882616 !
 S  =

!   6.6487173    0.          !
!   0.           3.8463696 !
!   0.           0.          !
 U  =

! -  .1981112     .4697774  -  .8602681 !
!    .2626234  -  .8201336  -  .5083402 !
! -  .9443415  -  .3266344     .0391031 !
```

To verify that U is an orthogonal matrix we use:

```
-->U*U'
 ans  =
!   1.    0.    0. !
!   0.    1.    0. !
!   0.    0.    1. !
```

To verify that V is also an orthogonal matrix use:

```
-->V*V'
 ans  =

!   1.    0. !
!   0.    1. !
```

The function *rank* in SCILAB

In the previous example, when the rank is included in the call to the function *svd*, you get a message indicating that the function *rank* is being redefined (Warning :redefining function: rank.) This occurs because SCILAB already provides a function *rank* and a new version of the function gets loaded through *svd*. If we attempt to use the function *rank* with a matrix or vector after using *svd* with the option *rank* included, we get an error message, i.e.,

```
--> rank(A)
       !--error    21
invalid index
```

To clear the name of the function *rank* use:

```
--> clear('rank')
Warning :redefining function: rank
```

To calculate the rank of matrix A we use:

```
--> rank(A)
  ans  =

2.
```

The rank of a square matrix

Consider the square matrix,

$$A = \begin{bmatrix} 3 & -2 & 1 \\ 1 & 1 & -2 \\ 3 & 5 & -1 \end{bmatrix}.$$

The rank of this matrix calculated with SCILAB is:

```
-->A = [3,-2,1;1,1,-2;3,5,-1]
 A  =

!   3.   - 2.    1. !
!   1.    1.   - 2. !
!   3.    5.   - 1. !
```

```
--> rank(A)
  ans  =

3.
```

The rank of the matrix is 3, i.e., the same as the number of rows or columns of matrix A. When the rank of a square matrix is the same as the number of rows or columns of the matrix, the corresponding system of linear equations $A \cdot x = b$ or $A \cdot x + c = 0$, has a unique solution. If the rank of the matrix is smaller than the number of rows or columns of the square matrix, the matrix is singular (i.e., it does not have an inverse), and the corresponding system does not have a unique solution.

Consider, for example, the system given by

$$\mathbf{A} = \begin{bmatrix} 1 & 2 & -5 \\ 2 & 4 & -10 \\ 2 & 2 & 5 \end{bmatrix}, \quad \mathbf{x} = \begin{bmatrix} x_1 \\ x_2 \\ x_3 \end{bmatrix}, \quad and \quad \mathbf{b} = \begin{bmatrix} 10 \\ 5 \\ 20 \end{bmatrix}.$$

We obtain the rank of the matrix A with function *rank* in SCILAB:

```
-->A = [1,2,-5;2,4,-10;2,2,5], b = [10;5;20]
 A  =

!   1.    2.   - 5.  !
!   2.    4.   - 10. !
!   2.    2.    5.   !
 b  =

!   10. !
!    5. !
!   20. !

--> rank(A)
  ans  =

2.
```

The rank of matrix A is 2. Therefore, the matrix is singular. We can check that by using:

```
-->A\b
    !--error    19
singular matrix
```

Norms of a matrix or vector

The norm of a matrix is a number that characterizes the matrix and helps identify some matrix properties in relation to linear algebra applications. There are many different types of matrix norms, some of which are defined next:

- The L_1 *norm* or *column norm* for a matrix $A_{m \times n} = [a_{ij}]$ is defined as the largest column sum of the matrix. The column sum is understood as the sum of the absolute values of the elements in a given column. Thus,

$$\|A\|_1 = \max_j \left(\sum_{i=1}^{n} |a_{ij}|, j = 1, 2, \ldots, m \right).$$

- The *infinity norm* or *row norm* of a matrix $A_{m \times n} = [a_{ij}]$ is defined as the maximum row sum of the matrix. Once more, this sum involves the absolute values of the elements. Thus,

$$\|A\|_\infty = \max_i \left(\sum_{j=1}^{m} |a_{ij}|, i = 1, 2, \ldots, n \right).$$

- The *Frobenius norm* of a matrix $A_{m \times n} = [a_{ij}]$ is defined as

$$\|\mathbf{A}\|_F = \sqrt{\sum_{i=1}^{n} \sum_{j=1}^{m} |a_{ij}|^2}.$$

- The *Euclidean norm* of a matrix $A_{m \times n} = [a_{ij}]$ is defined as the largest singular value of the matrix.

Norms for vectors are defined in a similar manner:

- The L_p-norm of a vector $v_{n \times 1} = [v_i]$, or $v_{1 \times n} = [v_i]$, is defined as

$$\|v\|_P = \left(\sum_{i=1}^{n} v_i^p \right)^{1/p}.$$

- The *Euclidean norm* is the same as the l_2-norm:

$$|v| = \|v\|_2 = \sqrt{\left(\sum_{i=1}^{n} v_i^2 \right)}.$$

- The infinite norm of $v_{n \times 1} = [v_i]$, or $v_{1 \times n} = [v_i]$, is the maximum absolute value of the elements of the vector, i.e.,

$$\|v\|_\infty = \max_i |v_i|.$$

All these norms can be calculated using SCILAB's function *norm*.

The function norm

We have used the function *norm* previously to determine the Euclidean magnitude of vectors. The function *norm* can also be used to produce a number of matrix norms. The general form of the function call is:

$$[y]=norm(x\ [,flag])$$

where *x* is a real or complex vector or matrix, and *flag* is a string or number that determines the type of norm sought. The default value for *norm* is 2, indicating the Euclidean norm of the matrix or vector.

If A is a matrix, according to the values of the *flag* argument, the function *norm* produces any of the following norms:

- norm(A), or norm(A,2):   Euclidean norm of the matrix
- norm(A,1):   The L_1-norm or column norm of the matrix.
- norm(A,'inf'),norm(A,%inf):   The infinity norm of the matrix.
- norm(A,'fro'):   Frobenius norm the matrix.

If v is a vector, the function *norm* produces any of the following norms:

- norm(v,p):   The L_p-norm of the vector.
- norm(v) or norm(v,2):   The L_2 or Euclidean norm (magnitude) of the vector.
- norm(v,'inf'):   The infinite norm of the vector.

In this description of the function *norm* we use the concept of the *singular values* of a matrix.

Some applications of the function *norm* for matrices and vectors are presented next:

```
-->A = [2,3;-2,1;0,5]
 A  =

!   2.    3. !
! - 2.    1. !
!   0.    5. !

-->norm(A)       //Default - Euclidean norm
 ans  =

    5.964908

-->norm(A,1)   //L1 norm
 ans  =

    9.

-->norm(A,'inf')    //Infinite norm
 ans  =

    5.

-->norm(A,'fro')  //Frobenius norm
 ans  =

    6.5574385
```

```
-->v = [3, 3, -5, 2]
 v  =

!  3.    3.   - 5.    2. !

-->norm(v,3)     //L3 norm
 ans  =

    5.7184791

-->norm(v,4)   //L4 norm
 ans  =

    5.3232748

-->norm(v)   //Default: Euclidean norm
 ans  =

    6.8556546

-->norm(v,'inf')    //Infinite norm
 ans  =

    5.
```

Determinants, singular matrices, and conditions numbers

In the chapter on vectors we introduce the concept of determinants for square matrices of dimensions 2×2 and 3×3. Calculation of determinants for matrices of higher order is described later in this section. It will be enough at this point to indicate that it is possible to calculate the determinant of any square matrix. If the determinant of matrix A, written *det A*, is zero, then the matrix A is said to be *singular*. Otherwise, it is *non-singular*. Singular matrices do not have an inverse.

The *condition number* of a square non-singular matrix is defined as the product of the matrix norm times the norm of its inverse, i.e.,

$$\text{cond}(A) = ||A|| \cdot ||A^{-1}||.$$

It is also defined as the ratio of the largest to the smallest singular values of the matrix.

The condition number of a non-singular matrix is a measure of how close the matrix is to being singular. The larger the value of the condition number, the closer it is to singularity.

The condition number of a matrix is calculated in SCILAB using the function *cond*. The following example illustrates the calculation of the condition number for a non-singular and a singular matrix:

Non-singular matrix:

```
-->A = [2,3,-1;5,5,2;1,1,-1]
 A  =
```

```
!   2.    3.  - 1. !
!   5.    5.    2. !
!   1.    1.  - 1. !

-->cond(A)
 ans  =

    20.765455
```

Singular matrix:

```
-->B = [2,3,-1;1,1,1;4,6,-2]
 B  =

!   2.    3.  - 1. !
!   1.    1.    1. !
!   4.    6.  - 2. !

-->cond(B)
 ans  =

    1.391E+16
```

A matrix very near singularity:

```
-->C = [2,2,-1;2.01,2.01,-0.99;1,5,-2]
 C  =

!   2.      2.     - 1.   !
!   2.01    2.01   -  .99 !
!   1.      5.     - 2.   !

-->cond(C)
 ans  =

    679.64701
```

The condition number for the singular matrix is practically infinity, while that for matrix C, which is near singularity, is a relatively large number compared to that of the non-singular matrix A. The ranks of these matrices are *rank(A) = rank(C) = 3*, and *rank(B) = 2*.

Both rank and condition numbers of a square matrix can be used to determine whether the matrix is singular or near singularity. This information will be useful in the analysis of the solution of a linear system.

The determinant of a matrix

For square matrices of order larger than 3, the determinant can be calculated by using smaller order determinants called *cofactors*. The general idea is to "expand" a determinant of an $n \times n$ matrix (also referred to as an $n \times n$ determinant) into a sum of the cofactors, which are $(n-1) \times (n-1)$ determinants, multiplied by the elements of a single row or column, with alternating positive and negative signs. This "expansion" is then carried to the next (lower) level, with cofactors of order $(n-2) \times (n-2)$, and so on, until we are left only with a long sum of 2×2

determinants. The 2×2 determinants are then calculated through the method presented in earlier.

The method of calculating a determinant by cofactor expansion is very inefficient in the sense that it involves a number of operations that grows very fast as the size of the determinant increases. A more efficient method, and the one preferred in numerical applications, is to use a result from Gaussian elimination. The method of Gaussian elimination is used to solve systems of linear equations. Details of this method are presented in a later part of this chapter.

To refer to the determinant of a matrix **A**, we write *det*(A). As mentioned in chapter 9, the determinant of a matrix can also be written as the elements of the matrix enclosed between vertical bars, for example, given

$$\mathbf{A} = \begin{bmatrix} 2 & -1 \\ 5 & 7 \end{bmatrix}, \quad \text{then} \quad \det(\mathbf{A}) = \begin{vmatrix} 2 & -1 \\ 5 & 7 \end{vmatrix} = 2 \cdot 7 - (-1) \cdot 5 = 19.$$

Determinants can be calculated in SCILAB by using the function *det*. For example, for the matrices used earlier to illustrate the use of *cond* we find:

```
-->det(A)
 ans   =

    7.
-->det(B)
 ans   =

    0.
-->det(C)
 ans   =

  -  .12
```

Notice that the determinant for a singular matrix, such as B in this example, is zero. The determinant of matrix C, which in nearly-singular, is very close to zero.

The determinant of a matrix, therefore, can also be used as a way to characterize a matrix.

Properties of determinants

The calculation of determinants by hand typically requires simplifying the determinant to reduce the number of operations in its calculation. Manipulation of the determinant includes operations such as multiplying or dividing a row or column by a constant, exchanging rows or columns, or replacing a row or column by a linear combination of other rows or columns. Whenever one of these operations take place, it is necessary to modify the expression for the determinant to ensure that its value does not change. Some of the rules of determinant manipulation are the following:

(1) Multiplying or dividing a row or column in a determinant by a constant is equivalent to multiplying or dividing the determinant by that constant. For example, consider the determinant used in the previous example

$$\det(\mathbf{A}) = \begin{vmatrix} 2 & -1 \\ 5 & 7 \end{vmatrix} = 19.$$

If we multiply any row by 2, the determinant gets multiplied by 2. For example (check these with your calculator):

$$\begin{vmatrix} 4 & -2 \\ 5 & 7 \end{vmatrix} = 2 \cdot 19 = 38, \quad \begin{vmatrix} 2 & -1 \\ 10 & 14 \end{vmatrix} = 38, \quad \begin{vmatrix} 4 & -1 \\ 10 & 7 \end{vmatrix} = 38, \quad \begin{vmatrix} 2 & -2 \\ 5 & 14 \end{vmatrix} = 38, \quad \begin{vmatrix} 4 & -2 \\ 10 & 14 \end{vmatrix} = 2 \cdot 2 \cdot 19 = 76.$$

(2) Switching any two rows or columns produces a change of sign in the determinant. For example, for the same case presented earlier we have:

$$\begin{vmatrix} 5 & 7 \\ 2 & -1 \end{vmatrix} = -19, \quad \begin{vmatrix} -1 & 2 \\ 7 & 5 \end{vmatrix} = -19.$$

(3) A row (or column) in a determinant can be replaced by a linear combination of rows (or columns) without changing the value of the determinant. For example, referring to $\det(\mathbf{A})$ above, we will replace the second row by the linear combination resulting from multiplying the first row by 2 and adding the second row multiplied by −1, i.e., 2·[5 7] +(-1) [2 −1] = [8 15], i.e.,

$$\begin{vmatrix} 5 & 7 \\ 8 & 15 \end{vmatrix} = 5 \cdot 15 - 7 \cdot 8 = 19.$$

Of course, with the HP 49 G calculator you no longer need to calculate determinants by hand. Still, to understand their calculation and some of the matrix elimination methods to be presented later, you need to keep in mind these rules.

Example: In the following example, we use determinant operations to simplify its calculation. First, we divide the first row by 5, the second by 3, and the third by 2.

$$\begin{vmatrix} 5 & 10 & -20 \\ 3 & -12 & 9 \\ 8 & 6 & -2 \end{vmatrix} = 5 \cdot 3 \cdot 2 \cdot \begin{vmatrix} 1 & 2 & -4 \\ 1 & -4 & 3 \\ 4 & 3 & -1 \end{vmatrix}$$

Next, we replace row 2 with (row 1 − row 2), and row 3 with (4·row1-row3):

$$5\cdot 3\cdot 2\cdot \begin{vmatrix} 1 & 2 & -4 \\ 1 & -4 & 3 \\ 4 & 3 & -1 \end{vmatrix} = 5\cdot 3\cdot 2\cdot \begin{vmatrix} 1 & 2 & -4 \\ 0 & -6 & -7 \\ 0 & 5 & -15 \end{vmatrix}$$

The next step in the simplification is to divide the second row by -6 and the third row by 5, to get

$$5\cdot 3\cdot 2\cdot \begin{vmatrix} 1 & 2 & -4 \\ 0 & 6 & -7 \\ 0 & 5 & -15 \end{vmatrix} = 5\cdot 3\cdot 2\cdot (-6)\cdot 5\cdot \begin{vmatrix} 1 & 2 & -4 \\ 0 & 1 & -7/6 \\ 0 & 1 & -3 \end{vmatrix}$$

Finally, we replace the third row with (row 2 − row 3), i.e.,

$$5\cdot 3\cdot 2\cdot (-6)\cdot 5\cdot \begin{vmatrix} 1 & 2 & -4 \\ 0 & 1 & -7/6 \\ 0 & 1 & -3 \end{vmatrix} = 5\cdot 3\cdot 2\cdot (-6)\cdot 5\cdot \begin{vmatrix} 1 & 2 & -4 \\ 0 & 1 & -7/6 \\ 0 & 0 & 11/6 \end{vmatrix}$$

Now we use the method for calculating 3×3 determinants presented in chapter 9, i.e.,

$$5\cdot 3\cdot 2\cdot (-6)\cdot 5\cdot \begin{vmatrix} 1 & 2 & -4 \\ 0 & 1 & -7/6 \\ 0 & 0 & 11/6 \end{vmatrix} = 5\cdot 3\cdot 2\cdot (-6)\cdot 5\cdot \begin{vmatrix} 1 & 2 & -4 & 1 & 2 \\ 0 & 1 & -7/6 & 0 & 1 \\ 0 & 0 & 11/6 & 0 & 0 \end{vmatrix} =$$

$$= 5\cdot 3\cdot 2\cdot (-6)\cdot 5\cdot (1\cdot 1\cdot 11/6 + 0 + 0 - (0 + 0 + 0)) = -1650.$$

You can check, using SCILAB's function *det*, that indeed, *det*(A) = -1650.

Cramer's rule for solving systems of linear equations

Cramer's rule for solving systems of n linear equations with n unknowns, consists in forming the matrix equation, $A \cdot x = b$, as presented earlier in the chapter and calculating the determinant $\Delta = \det(A)$. After that, for each unknown x_i, the matrix A_i is formed consisting of the matrix A with column i replaced by the components of vector b. The determinant corresponding to A_i is called $\Delta_i = \det(A_i)$. The unknown x_i is then calculated as $x_i = \Delta_i / \Delta$.

For example, we will use Cramer's rule to determine the solution to the following system of linear equations:

$$X + 2Y + 3Z + 4R = 4,$$
$$-X + 5Y + 2Z + 7R = 11,$$
$$4X + 2Y - Z + 6R = 2,$$
$$2X + Y - 4Z + 7R = 9.$$

To write the system as a matrix equation we use:

$$\mathbf{A} = \begin{bmatrix} 1 & 2 & 3 & 4 \\ -1 & 5 & 2 & 7 \\ 4 & 2 & -1 & 6 \\ 2 & 1 & -4 & 7 \end{bmatrix}, \quad \mathbf{x} = \begin{bmatrix} X \\ Y \\ Z \\ R \end{bmatrix}, \quad \text{and} \quad \mathbf{b} = \begin{bmatrix} 4 \\ 11 \\ 2 \\ 9 \end{bmatrix}.$$

Application of the Cramer's rule using SCILAB can be implemented as follows:

```
-->A = [1,2,3,4;-1,5,2,7;4,2,-1,6;2,1,-4,7]
 A   =

!   1.    2.    3.    4. !
! - 1.    5.    2.    7. !
!   4.    2.  - 1.    6. !
!   2.    1.  - 4.    7. !

-->b=[4;11;2;9]
 b   =

!   4.  !
!  11.  !
!   2.  !
!   9.  !

-->D = det(A)
 D   =

  - 258.

-->DX = det([b,A(:,2),A(:,3),A(:,4)])
```

```
    DX   =
         516.
-->DY = det([A(:,1),b,A(:,3),A(:,4)])
 DY   =
         258.
-->DZ = det([A(:,1),A(:,2),b,A(:,4)])
 DZ   =
         3.908E-14
-->DR = det([A(:,1),A(:,2),A(:,3),b])
 DR   =
       - 516.

-->X = DX/D, Y = DY/D, Z = DZ/D, R = DR/D
 X   = - 2.
 Y   = - 1.
 Z   = - 1.515E-16
 R   =   2.
```

The direct solution using matrices is:

```
-->A\b
 ans  =

 ! - 2. !
 ! - 1. !
 !   0. !
 !   2. !
```

Notice that Cramer's rule gives a value for Z of 1.515×10^{-16}, indicating that a negligible numerical error was introduced.

The function TRACE

The function TRACE calculates the trace of square matrix, defined as the sum of the elements in its main diagonal, or

$$tr(\mathbf{A}_{n \times n}) = \sum_{i=1}^{n} a_{ii}.$$

Using Einstein's repeated index convention we can write simply $tr(\mathbf{A}_{n \times n}) = a_{ii}$.

SCILAB provides the function *trace* to calculate the trace of a matrix. For example, for the matrix A used in the previous example:

```
--> trace(A)
 ans =

      12.
```

Gaussian and Gauss-Jordan elimination

Gaussian elimination is a procedure by which the square matrix of coefficients belonging to a system of n linear equations in n unknowns is reduced to an upper-triangular matrix (*echelon form*) through a series of row operations. This procedure is known as *forward elimination*. The reduction of the coefficient matrix to an upper-triangular form allows for the solution of all n unknowns, utilizing only one equation at a time, in a procedure known as *backward substitution*.

Gaussian elimination using a system of equations

To illustrate the Gaussian elimination procedure we will use the following system of 3 equations in 3 unknowns:

$$2X + 4Y + 6Z = 14,$$
$$3X - 2Y + Z = -3,$$
$$4X + 2Y - Z = -4.$$

Forward elimination

First, we replace the second equation by (equation 2 – (3/2)* equation 1), and the third by (equation 1 – (4/2)*equation 1), to get

$$2X + 4Y + 6Z = 14,$$
$$-8Y - 8Z = -24,$$
$$-6Y - 13Z = -32.$$

Next, replace the third equation with (equation 3 - (6/8)*equation2), to get

$$2X + 4Y + 6Z = 14,$$
$$-8Y - 8Z = -24,$$
$$-7Z = -14.$$

Backward substitution

The system of equations is now in an upper-triangular form, allowing us to solve for Z first, as

$$Z = -14/-7 = 2.$$

We then replace this value into equation 2 to solve for Y, as

$$Y = (-24 + 8Z)/(-8) = (-24 + 82)/(-8) = 1.$$

Finally, we replace the values of Y and Z into equation 1 to solve for X as

$$X = (14-4Y-6Z)/2 = (14-4(1)-6(2))/2 = -1.$$

The solution is, therefore, $\boxed{X = -1, Y = 1, Z = 2}$.

Gaussian elimination using matrices

The system of equations used in the example above, i.e.,

$$2X + 4Y + 6Z = 14,$$
$$3X - 2Y + Z = -3,$$
$$4X + 2Y - Z = -4.$$

Can be written as a matrix equation $A \cdot x = b$, if we use:

$$A = \begin{pmatrix} 2 & 4 & 6 \\ 3 & -2 & 1 \\ 4 & 2 & -1 \end{pmatrix}, \quad x = \begin{bmatrix} X \\ Y \\ Z \end{bmatrix}, \quad b = \begin{bmatrix} 14 \\ -3 \\ -4 \end{bmatrix}.$$

To obtain a solution to the system matrix equation using Gaussian elimination, we first create what is known as the _augmented matrix_ corresponding to A, i.e.,

$$A_{aug} = \begin{pmatrix} 2 & 4 & 6 & | & 14 \\ 3 & -2 & 1 & | & -3 \\ 4 & 2 & -1 & | & -4 \end{pmatrix}.$$

The matrix A_{aug} is nothing more than the original matrix A with a new row, corresponding to the elements of the vector b, added (i.e., augmented) to the right of the rightmost column of A.

Once the augmented matrix is put together, we can proceed to perform row operations on it that will reduce the original A matrix into an upper-triangular matrix similar to what we did with the system of equations shown earlier. If you perform the forward elimination by hand, you would write the following:

$$A_{aug} = \begin{pmatrix} 2 & 4 & 6 & | & 14 \\ 3 & -2 & 1 & | & -3 \\ 4 & 2 & -1 & | & -4 \end{pmatrix} \cong \begin{pmatrix} 2 & 4 & 6 & | & 14 \\ 0 & -8 & -8 & | & -24 \\ 0 & -6 & -13 & | & -32 \end{pmatrix} \cong \begin{pmatrix} 2 & 4 & 6 & | & 14 \\ 0 & -8 & -8 & | & -24 \\ 0 & 0 & -7 & | & -14 \end{pmatrix}$$

The symbol $\cong$ ("is congruent to") indicates that what follows is equivalent to the previous matrix with some row (or column) operations involved.

After the augmented matrix is reduced as shown above, we can proceed to perform the backward substitution by converting the augmented matrix into a system of equations and solving for x_3, x_2, and x_1 in that order, as performed earlier.

Gaussian elimination algorithm

In this section we present the algorithm for performing Gaussian elimination on an augmented matrix. The augmented matrix results from the system of linear equations represented by the matricial equation $A \cdot x = b$. The matrix A and vectors x and b are given by

$$A = \begin{bmatrix} a_{11} & a_{12} & \cdots & a_{1m} \\ a_{21} & a_{22} & \cdots & a_{2m} \\ \vdots & \vdots & \ddots & \vdots \\ a_{n1} & a_{n2} & \cdots & a_{nm} \end{bmatrix}, \quad x = \begin{bmatrix} x_1 \\ x_2 \\ \vdots \\ x_m \end{bmatrix}, \quad b = \begin{bmatrix} b_1 \\ b_2 \\ \vdots \\ b_n \end{bmatrix}$$

The augmented matrix is:

$$A_{aug} = \begin{bmatrix} a_{11} & a_{12} & \cdots & a_{1m} & b_1 \\ a_{21} & a_{22} & \cdots & a_{2m} & b_2 \\ \vdots & \vdots & \ddots & \vdots & \vdots \\ a_{n1} & a_{n2} & \cdots & a_{nm} & b_n \end{bmatrix}.$$

Thus, the augmented matrix can be referred to as $(A_{aug})_{n \times (n+1)} = [a_{ij}]$, with $a_{i,n+1} = b_i$, for $i = 1, 2, \ldots, n$.

Augmenting a matrix in SCILAB

In SCILAB augmenting a matrix A by a column vector b is straightforward. For example, for the linear system introduced earlier, namely,

$$\mathbf{A} = \begin{pmatrix} 2 & 4 & 6 \\ 3 & -2 & 1 \\ 4 & 2 & -1 \end{pmatrix}, \quad \mathbf{b} = \begin{bmatrix} 14 \\ -3 \\ -4 \end{bmatrix},$$

an augmented matrix, A_{aug}, is obtained as follows:

```
-->A = [2,4,6;3,-2,1;4,2,-1], b = [1;-3;-4]
 A  =

!   2.    4.    6. !
!   3.  - 2.    1. !
!   4.    2.  - 1. !
 b  =

!   1. !
! - 3. !
! - 4. !

-->A_aug = [A b]
 A_aug =

!   2.    4.    6.    1. !
!   3.  - 2.    1.  - 3. !
!   4.    2.  - 1.  - 4. !
```

Algorithm for first step in forward elimination

After the augmented matrix has been created the first elimination pass will fill with zeros those values in the first column below a_{11}, i.e.,

$$\begin{bmatrix} a_{11} & a_{12} & \cdots & a_{1m} & a_{1,n+1} \\ 0 & a^*_{22} & \cdots & a^*_{2m} & a^*_{2,n+1} \\ \vdots & \vdots & \ddots & \vdots & \vdots \\ 0 & a^*_{n2} & \cdots & a^*_{nm} & a^*_{n,n+1} \end{bmatrix}.$$

The procedure is indicated by the expressions:

$a^*_{21} = a^*_{31} = \ldots = a^*_{n1} = 0$; j = 1 (first column)

$a^*_{2,j} = a_{2j} - a_{1j} \cdot a_{21}/a_{11}$; j = 2,3, . . . , n+1
$a^*_{3,j} = a_{3,j} - a_{1j} \cdot a_{31}/a_{11}$; j = 2,3, . . . , n+1
 .   .   .
 .   .   .
 .   .   .
$a^*_{n,j} = a_{n,j} - a_{1j} \cdot a_{n1}/a_{11}$; j = 2,3, . . . , n+1

or, more concisely, as

$a^*_{ij} = a_{ij} - a_{1j} \cdot a_{i1}/a_{11}$; for i = 2,3, ...n; and, j = 2,3,. . .,n+1
$a^*_{ij} = 0$; for i = 2,3, ..., n; and, j = 1

SCILAB example for first step in forward elimination

To illustrate this first step using SCILAB, we first copy the augmented matrix we created into an array *a* by using:

```
-->a = A_aug
 a  =

!   2.    4.    6.    1. !
!   3.  - 2.    1.  - 3. !
!   4.    2.  - 1.  - 4. !
```

Next, we define n as 3 and implement the first step in the forward elimination through the use of *for..end* constructs:

```
--> n = 3;
-->for i=2:n, for j=2:n+1, a(i,j)=a(i,j)-a(1,j)*a(i,1)/a(1,1); end; a(i,1) = 0;
end;
```

To see the modified augmented matrix we use:

```
-->a
 a  =

!   2.    4.     6.    14. !
!   0.  - 8.   - 8.  - 24. !
!   0.  - 6.  - 13.  - 32. !
```

Algorithm for second step in forward elimination

After the second elimination pass, the generic augmented matrix is:

$$\begin{bmatrix} a_{11} & a_{12} & a_{13} & \cdots & a_{1n} & a_{1,n+1} \\ 0 & a^*_{22} & a^*_{23} & \cdots & a^*_{2n} & a^*_{2,n+1} \\ 0 & 0 & a^{**}_{33} & \cdots & a^{**}_{3n} & a^{**}_{3,n+1} \\ \vdots & \vdots & \vdots & \ddots & \vdots & \vdots \\ 0 & 0 & a^{**}_{n3} & \cdots & a^{**}_{nn} & a^{**}_{n,n+1} \end{bmatrix}$$

with rows i = 3, 4, ...n, recalculated as:

$$a^{**}_{ij} = a^*_{ij} - a^*_{2j} \cdot a^*_{i2}/a^*_{22}; \text{ for } i = 3,4,...n; \text{ and, } j = 3,4,...,n+1$$
$$a^{**}_{ij} = 0; \text{ for } i = 3,4,...,n; \text{ and, } j = 2$$

SCILAB example for second step in forward elimination

For the SCILAB example under consideration, this second step will be the final step in the forward elimination. This step is implemented as follows:

```
--> for i=3:n, for j=3:n+1, a(i,j)=a(i,j)-a(2,j)*a(i,2)/a(2,2); end; a(i,2) = 0; end;
```

The result is:

```
a  =

!   2.     4.     6.     14.  !
!   0.   - 8.   - 8.   - 24.  !
!   0.     0.   - 7.   - 14.  !
```

Algorithm for third and subsequent steps in the forward elimination

For a general $n \times (n+1)$ augmented matrix, we can predict that in the next (third) elimination pass the new coefficients in the augmented matrix can be written as:

$$a^{***}_{ij} = a^{**}_{ij} - a^{**}_{3j} \cdot a^{**}_{i3}/a^{**}_{33}; \text{ for } i = 4,5,\ldots n; \text{ and, } j = 4,5,\ldots,n+1$$
$$a^{***}_{ij} = 0; \text{ for } i = 4,5,\ldots,n; \text{ and, } j = 3$$

Notice that the number of asterisks in the new coefficients calculated for each elimination pass corresponds to the number of the elimination pass, i.e., we calculated a^*_{ij} in the first pass, a^{**}_{ij} in the second pass, and so on. We may venture to summarize all the equations we have written for the new coefficients as:

$$a^{(k)}_{ij} = a^{(k-1)}_{ij} - a^{(k-1)}_{kj} \cdot a^{(k-1)}_{ik}/a^{(k-1)}_{kk}; \text{ for } i = k+1,k+2,\ldots n; \text{ and, } j = k+1,k+2,\ldots,n+1,$$
$$a^{(k)}_{ij} = 0; \text{ for } i = k+1,k+2,\ldots,n; \text{ and, } j = 1,2,\ldots,k$$

where $k = 1,2,\ldots,n-1$.

Notice that k represents the order of the elimination pass, i represents the row index, and j represents the column index.

After the *forward elimination* passes have been completed, the modified augmented matrix should look like this:

$$\begin{bmatrix} a_{11} & a_{12} & a_{13} & \cdots & a_{1,n-1} & a_{1n} & a_{1,n-1} \\ 0 & a^{(1)}_{22} & a^{(1)}_{23} & \cdots & a^{(1)}_{2,n-1} & a^{(1)}_{2n} & a^{(1)}_{2,n+1} \\ 0 & 0 & a^{(2)}_{33} & \cdots & a^{(2)}_{3,n-1} & a^{(2)}_{3n} & a^{(2)}_{3,n+1} \\ \vdots & \vdots & \vdots & \ddots & \vdots & \vdots & \vdots \\ 0 & 0 & 0 & \cdots & a^{(n-2)}_{n-1,n-1} & a^{(n-2)}_{n-1,n} & a^{(n-2)}_{n-1,n+1} \\ 0 & 0 & 0 & \cdots & 0 & a^{(n-1)}_{n,n} & a^{(n-1)}_{n,n+1} \end{bmatrix}.$$

If we use the array a_{ij} to store the modified coefficients, we can simply write:

$$a_{ij} = a_{ij} - a_{kj} \cdot a_{ik}/a_{kk};\ i = k+1, k+2, \ldots, n;\ j = k+1, k+2, \ldots, n+1.$$
$$a_{ij} = 0,\ \text{for}\ i = k+1, k+2, \ldots, n;\ \text{and},\ j = k$$

for $k = 1, 2, \ldots, n-1$.

> Note: By using the array a_{ij} to store the newly calculated coefficients you loose the information stored in the original array a_{ij}. Therefore, when implementing the algorithm in SCILAB, if you need to keep the original array available for any reason, you may want to copy it into a different array as we did in the SCILAB example presented earlier.

SCILAB example implementing the full forward elimination algorithm

For the 3x4 augmented matrix presented earlier, the following SCILAB commands implement the algorithm for forward elimination:

```
-->a = A_aug
 a  =

!   2.    4.    6.    1. !
!   3.  - 2.    1.  - 3. !
!   4.    2.  - 1.  - 4. !

-->n=3;

-->for k=1:n-1, for i=k+1:n, for j=k+1:n+1, a(i,j)=a(i,j)-a(k,j)*a(i,k)/a(k,k);
end; for j = 1:k, a(i,j) = 0; end; end; end;


-->a
 a  =

!   2.    4.    6.    14. !
!   0.  - 8.  - 8.  - 24. !
!   0.    0.  - 7.  - 14. !
```

Algorithm for backward substitution

The next step in the algorithm is to calculate the solution $x_1, x_2, \ldots, x_n$, by *back substitution*, starting with

$$x_n = a_{n,n+1}/a_{nn}.$$

and continuing with

$$x_{n-1} = (a_{n-1,n+1} - a_{n-1,n} x_n)/a_{n-1,n-1}$$

$$x_{n-2} = (a_{n-2,n+1} - a_{n-2,n-1} x_{n-1} - a_{n-2,n} x_n)/a_{n-2,n-2}$$

.
.

$$x_1 = \frac{a_{1,n+1} - \sum_{k=2}^{n} a_{1k} x_k}{a_{11}}.$$

In summary, the solution is obtained by first calculating:

$$x_n = a_{n,n+1}/a_{nn}.$$

and, then, calculating

$$x_i = \frac{a_{i,n+1} - \sum_{k=i+1}^{n} a_{ik} x_k}{a_{ii}},$$

for i = n-1, n-2, ..., 2, 1 (i.e., counting backwards from (n-1) to 1).

SCILAB example for calculating the unknown x's

Using the current value of the matrix that resulted from the forward elimination, we can calculate the unknowns in the linear system as follows. First, the last unknown is:

`-->x(n) = a(n,n+1)/a(n,n);`

Then, we calculate the remaining unknowns using:

```
-->for i = n-1:-1:1, sumk=0; for k=i+1:n, sumk=sumk+a(i,k)*x(k); end;
x(i)=(a(i,n+1)-sumk)/a(i,i); end;
```

The solution is:

```
-->x
 x =

!  - 1. !
!    1. !
!    2. !
```

SCILAB function for Gaussian elimination

The following SCILAB function implements the solution of the system of linear equations, A·x=b. The function's arguments are a nxn matrix A and a nx1 vector b. The function returns the solution x.

```
function [x] = gausselim(A,b)

//This function obtains the solution to the system of
//linear equations A*x = b, given the matrix of coefficients A
//and the right-hand side vector, b

[nA,mA] = size(A)
[nb,mb] = size(b)

if nA<>mA then
                        error('gausselim - Matrix A must be square');
                        abort;
elseif mA<>nb then
        error('gausselim - incompatible dimensions between A and b');
        abort;
end;

a = [A b];  //Matrix augmentation

//Forward elimination

n = nA;
for k=1:n-1
    for i=k+1:n
                        for j=k+1:n+1
                          a(i,j)=a(i,j)-a(k,j)*a(i,k)/a(k,k);
                        end;
     end;
end;

//Backward substitution

x(n) = a(n,n+1)/a(n,n);

for i = n-1:-1:1
                        sumk=0
                        for k=i+1:n
```

```
                    sumk=sumk+a(i,k)*x(k);
                  end;
                  x(i)=(a(i,n+1)-sumk)/a(i,i);
end;

//End function
```

Note: In this function we did not include the statements that produce the zero values in the lower triangular part of the augmented matrix. These terms are not involved in the solution at all, and were used earlier only to illustrate the effects of the Gaussian elimination.

Application of the function *gausselim* to the problem under consideration produces:

```
->A = [2,4,6;3,-2,1;4,2,-1]; b = [14;-3;-4];

-->getf('gausselim')    //Loading the function

-->gausselim(A,b)    //Function call without assignment
 ans =

!  - 1. !
!    1. !
!    2. !

-->x = gausselim(A,b)   //Function call with assignment
  x =

!  - 1. !
!    1. !
!    2. !
```

This simple implementation of Gaussian elimination is commonly referred to as "naïve Gaussian elimination," because it does not account for the possibility of having zero terms in the diagonal. Such terms will produce a division by zero in the Gaussian elimination algorithm effectively terminating the process in SCILAB. A technique known as "partial pivoting" can be implemented to account for the case of zero diagonal terms. Details on pivoting are presented next.

Pivoting

If you look carefully at the row operations in the examples shown above, you will notice that many of those operations divide a row by its corresponding element in the main diagonal. This element is called a pivot element, or simply, *pivot*. In many situations it is possible that the pivot element become zero, in which case a division by zero occurs. Also, to improve the numerical solution of a system of equations using Gaussian or Gauss-Jordan elimination, it is recommended that the pivot be the element with the largest absolute value in a given column. This operation is called *partial pivoting*. To follow this recommendation is it often necessary to exchange rows in the augmented matrix while performing a Gaussian or Gauss-Jordan elimination.

While performing pivoting in a matrix elimination procedure, you can improve the numerical solution even more by seleting as the pivot the element with the largest absolute value in the column and row of interest. This operation may require exchanging not only rows, but also columns, in some pivoting operations. When row and column exchanges are allowed in pivoting, the procedure is known as _full pivoting_.

When exchanging rows and columns in partial or full pivoting, it is necessary to keep track of the exchanges because the order of the unknowns in the solution is altered by those exchanges. One way to keep track of column exchanges in partial or full pivoting mode, is to create a _permutation matrix_ $P = I_{n \times n}$, at the beginning of the procedure. Any row or column exchange required in the augmented matrix A_{aug} is also registered as a row or column exchange, respectively, in the permutation matrix. When the solution is achieved, then, we multiply the permutation matrix by the unknown vector to obtain the order of the unknowns in the solution. In other words, the final solution is given by $P \cdot x = b'$, where b' is the last column of the augmented matrix after the solution has been found.

A function such as _lu_ in SCILAB automatically take care of using partial or full pivoting in the solution of linear systems. No special provision is necessary in the call to this function to activate pivoting. The function _lu_ take care of reincorporating the permutation matrix into the final result.

Consider, as an example, the linear system shown below:

$$2Y + 3Z = 7,$$
$$2X + 3Z = 13,$$
$$8X + 16Y - Z = -3.$$

The augmented matrix is:

$$\mathbf{A}_{aug} = \begin{bmatrix} 0 & 2 & 3 & 7 \\ 2 & 0 & 3 & 13 \\ 8 & 16 & -1 & -3 \end{bmatrix}.$$

The zero in element (1,1) will not allow the simple Gaussian elimination to proceed since a division by zero will be required. Trying a solution with function _gausselim_, described earlier, produces an error:

```
-->A = [0,2,3;2,0,3;8,16,-1], b = [7;13;-3]
 A    =

!   0.    2.    3.  !
!   2.    0.    3.  !
!   8.   16.   -1.  !
 b   =

!   7.  !
!  13.  !
! - 3.  !
```

```
-->getf('gausselim')

-->x = gausselim(A,b)
 !--error    27
division by zero...
at line      26 of function gausselim              called by :
x = gausselim(A,b)
```

As expected, *gausselim* produces a division-by-zero error. However *lu*, which already incorporates pivoting, will produce the following solution through LU decomposition:

```
-->[L,U,P] = lu(A)
 P  =

!   0.    0.    1.  !
!   0.    1.    0.  !
!   1.    0.    0.  !
 U  =

!   8.    16.   - 1.       !
!   0.  - 4.     3.25   !
!   0.    0.     4.625  !
 L  =

!   1.     0.    0.  !
!    .25   1.    0.  !
!   0.   - .5    1.  !
```

The right-hand side vector is modified by using the permutation matrix:

```
-->c = P*b
 c  =

! - 3.  !
!  13.  !
!   7.  !
```

The solution to the system of linear equations through LU decomposition proceeds in two parts:

```
-->y = L\c
 y  =

! - 3.      !
!  13.75   !
!  13.875  !

-->x = U\y
 x  =

!   2.  !
! - 1.  !
!   3.  !
```

Gaussian elimination with partial pivoting

In this section we modify the function *gausselim* to incorporate partial pivoting. The resulting function is called *gausselimPP*. The algorithm for partial pivoting requires us to compare the current pivot at the *k-th* pass of the forward elimination part, namely a_{kk}, with all the elements of the same column, a_{ik}, for i>k. When the largest absolute value of the column is found, the corresponding row and row k are exchanged before proceeding with the forward elimination algorithm. The backward substitution part of the algorithm proceeds as in the original *gausselim* function.

Here is the listing of function *gausselimPP*.

```
function [x] = gausselimPP(A,b)

//This function obtains the solution to the system of
//linear equations A*x = b, given the matrix of coefficients A
//and the right-hand side vector, b.  Gaussian elimination with
//partial pivoting.

[nA,mA] = size(A)
[nb,mb] = size(b)

if nA<>mA then
      error('gausselim - Matrix A must be square');
      abort;
elseif mA<>nb then
       error('gausselim - incompatible dimensions between A and b');
      abort;
end;

a = [A b];     // Augmented matrix
n = nA   ;     // Matrix size

//Forward elimination with partial pivoting

for k=1:n-1
    kpivot = k; amax = abs(a(k,k));        //Pivoting
    for i=k+1:n
       if abs(a(i,k))>amax then
            kpivot = i; amax = a(k,i);
       end;
    end;
    temp = a(kpivot,:); a(kpivot,:) = a(k,:); a(k,:) = temp;

    for i=k+1:n                            //Forward elimination
       for j=k+1:n+1
            a(i,j)=a(i,j)-a(k,j)*a(i,k)/a(k,k);
       end;
    end;
end;

//Backward substitution

x(n) = a(n,n+1)/a(n,n);

for i = n-1:-1:1
      sumk=0
```

```
            for k=i+1:n
                sumk=sumk+a(i,k)*x(k);
            end;
            x(i)=(a(i,n+1)-sumk)/a(i,i);
    end;
```

//End function

Application of the function *gausselimPP* for the case under consideration is shown next:

```
-->A = [0,2,3;2,0,3;8,16,-1]; b = [7;13;-3];

-->getf('gausselimPP')

-->gausselimPP(A,b)
 ans =

!   2. !
! - 1. !
!   3. !
```

Solving multiple set of equations with the same coefficient matrix

Suppose that you want to solve the following three sets of equations:

$$\begin{array}{lll} x_1 + 2x_2 + 3x_3 = 14, & 2x_1 + 4x_2 + 6x_3 = 9, & 2x_1 + 4x_2 + 6x_3 = -2, \\ 3x_1 - 2x_2 + x_3 = 2, & 3x_1 - 2x_2 + x_3 = -5, & 3x_1 - 2x_2 + x_3 = 2, \\ 4x_1 + 2x_2 - x_3 = 5, & 4x_1 + 2x_2 - x_3 = 19, & 4x_1 + 2x_2 - x_3 = 12. \end{array}$$

We can write the three systems of equations as a single matrix equation $A \cdot X = B$, where

$$\mathbf{A} = \begin{bmatrix} 1 & 2 & 3 \\ 3 & -2 & 1 \\ 4 & 2 & -1 \end{bmatrix}, \quad \mathbf{X} = \begin{bmatrix} x_{11} & x_{12} & x_{13} \\ x_{21} & x_{22} & x_{23} \\ x_{31} & x_{32} & x_{33} \end{bmatrix}, \quad \mathbf{B} = \begin{bmatrix} 14 & 9 & -2 \\ 2 & -5 & 2 \\ 5 & 19 & 12 \end{bmatrix}.$$

In the unknown matrix X, the first sub-index identifies the original sub-index, while the second one identifies to which system of linear equations a particular variable belongs.

The solution to the system $A \cdot X = B$, can be found in SCILAB using the backward slash operator, i.e., $X = A \backslash B$, or the inverse matrix, $X = A^{-1}B$. For the matrices defined above we can write:

```
-->A = [1,2,3;3,-2,1;4,2,-1], B=[14,9,-2;2,-5,2;5,19,12]
 A  =
!   1.   2.    3. !
!   3. - 2.    1. !
!   4.   2.  - 1. !
 B  =
!  14.   9.  - 2. !
!   2. - 5.    2. !
!   5.  19.   12. !
```

Solution using the backward slash operator:

```
-->X1 = A\B
 X1  =

!   1.     2.     2. !
!   2.     5.     1. !
!   3.  -  1.  -  2. !
```

Solution using the inverse matrix of A:

```
-->X2 = inv(A)*B
 X2  =

!   1.     2.     2. !
!   2.     5.     1. !
!   3.  -  1.  -  2. !
```

In both cases, the result is:

$$x := \begin{bmatrix} 1 & 2 & 2 \\ 2 & 5 & 1 \\ 3 & -1 & -2 \end{bmatrix}.$$

Gaussian elimination for multiple sets of linear equations

In this section, function *gausselimPP* is modified to account for a multiple set of linear equations. The augmented matrix for this case is A_{aug} = [A B], where A is a nxn matrix, and B is a nxm matrix. The solution is now a nxn matrix X.

```
function [x] = gausselimm(A,B)

//This function obtains the solution to the system of
//linear equations A*X = B, given the nxn matrix of coefficients A
//and the nxm right-hand side matrix, B.  Matrix X is nxm.

[nA,mA] = size(A)
[nB,mB] = size(B)

if nA<>mA then
       error('gausselim - Matrix A must be square');
       abort;
elseif mA<>nB then
         error('gausselim - incompatible dimensions between A and b');
       abort;
end;

a = [A B];     // Augmented matrix
n = nA    ;    // Number of rows and columns in A, rows in B
m = mB    ;    // Number of columns in B
```

```
//Forward elimination with partial pivoting

for k=1:n-1
    kpivot = k; amax = abs(a(k,k));         //Pivoting
    for i=k+1:n
        if abs(a(i,k))>amax then
            kpivot = i; amax = a(k,i);
        end;
    end;
    temp = a(kpivot,:); a(kpivot,:) = a(k,:); a(k,:) = temp;

    for i=k+1:n                             //Forward elimination
        for j=k+1:n+m
            a(i,j)=a(i,j)-a(k,j)*a(i,k)/a(k,k);
        end;
    end;
end;

//Backward substitution

for j = 1:m
    x(n,j) = a(n,n+j)/a(n,n);
    for i = n-1:-1:1
        sumk=0
        for k=i+1:n
            sumk=sumk+a(i,k)*x(k,j);
        end;
        x(i,j)=(a(i,n+j)-sumk)/a(i,i);
    end;
end;

//End function
```

Next, function *gausselimm* is applied to the matrices A and B defined earlier:

```
-->A = [1,2,3;3,-2,1;4,2,-1]; B=[14,9,-2;2,-5,2;5,19,12];

-->getf('gausselimm')

-->gausselimm(A,B)
 ans =

!  1.    2.    2. !
!  2.    5.    1. !
!  3.  - 1.  - 2. !
```

Calculating an inverse matrix using Gaussian elimination

If the right-hand side matrix B of a set of multiple systems of linear equations is the nxn identity matrix, i.e., B = I_{nxn}, the solution X from the matrix system A·X = B, is the inverse of matrix A, i.e., X = A^{-1}.

For example, to find the inverse of the matrix A presented earlier through the use of function *gausselimm*, you can use the following SCILAB command:

```
-->Ainv = gausselimm(A,eye(3,3))
 Ainv  =

!   0.          .1428571     .1428571 !
!   .125     -  .2321429     .1428571 !
!   .25         .1071429  -  .1428571 !
```

You can check that this result is the same as that obtained from SCILAB's function *inv*:

```
-->inv(A)
 ans  =

!   0.          .1428571     .1428571 !
!   .125     -  .2321429     .1428571 !
!   .25         .1071429  -  .1428571 !
```

Calculating the determinant with Gaussian elimination

You can prove that the determinant of a matrix can be obtained by multiplying the elements in the main diagonal after the forward elimination part of a Gaussian elimination procedure is completed. In other words, after completing the forward elimination of a "naïve" Gaussian elimination, the determinant of a nxn matrix A = $[a_{ij}]$ is calculated as

$$\det(\mathbf{A}) = \prod_{k=1}^{n} a_{kk}.$$

If partial pivoting is included, however, the sign of the determinant changes according to the number of row switches included in the pivoting process. In such case, if N represents the number of row exchanges, the determinant is given by

$$\det(\mathbf{A}) = (-1)^{N} \cdot \prod_{k=1}^{n} a_{kk}.$$

The calculation of the determinant is included in the Gaussian elimination function called *gausselimd*. The call to this function includes return variables for the solution X to the system A·X = B as well as for the determinant of A. A listing of the function is shown below:

```
function [x,detA] = gausselimd(A,B)

//This function obtains the solution to the system of
//linear equations A*X = B, given the nxn matrix of coefficients A
//and the nxm right-hand side matrix, B.  Matrix X is nxm.
```

```
[nA,mA] = size(A);
[nB,mB] = size(B);

if nA<>mA then
        error('gausselim - Matrix A must be square');
        abort;
elseif mA<>nB then
         error('gausselim - incompatible dimensions between A and b');
        abort;
end;

a = [A B];      // Augmented matrix
n = nA    ;     // Number of rows and columns in A, rows in B
m = mB    ;     // Number of columns in B

//Forward elimination with partial pivoting

nswitch = 0;
for k=1:n-1
    kpivot = k; amax = abs(a(k,k));          //Pivoting
    for i=k+1:n
       if abs(a(i,k))>amax then
            kpivot = i; amax = a(k,i);
            nswitch = nswitch+1
       end;
    end;
    temp = a(kpivot,:); a(kpivot,:) = a(k,:); a(k,:) = temp;

    for i=k+1:n                              //Forward elimination
       for j=k+1:n+m
            a(i,j)=a(i,j)-a(k,j)*a(i,k)/a(k,k);
       end;
    end;
end;

//Calculating the determinant

detA = 1;
for k = 1:n
     detA = detA*a(k,k);
end;
detB = (-1)^nswitch*detA;

//Checking for singular matrix
epsilon = 1.0e-10;
if abs(detB)<epsilon then
      error('gausselimd - singular matrix');
      abort;
end;

//Backward substitution

for j = 1:m
      x(n,j) = a(n,n+j)/a(n,n);
      for i = n-1:-1:1
           sumk=0
           for k=i+1:n
                sumk=sumk+a(i,k)*x(k,j);
           end;
           x(i,j)=(a(i,n+j)-sumk)/a(i,i);
```

```
        end;
end;

//End function
```

An application of function *gausselimd* for a non-singular matrix A is shown next:

```
-->A = [3,5,-1;2,2,3;1,1,2]
 A  =

!   3.    5.   - 1. !
!   2.    2.    3. !
!   1.    1.    2. !

-->b = [-4;17;11]
 b  =

! - 4. !
!  17. !
!  11. !


-->getf('gausselimd')

-->[x,detA] = gausselimd(A,b)
 detA  =

  - 2.
 x  =

!   2. !
! - 1. !
!   5. !
```

For a singular matrix A, function *gausselimd* provides an error message:

```
-->A = [2,3,1;4,6,2;1,1,2]
 A  =

!   2.    3.    1. !
!   4.    6.    2. !
!   1.    1.    2. !


-->[x,detA] = gausselimd(A,b)
 !--error    9999
gausselimd - singular matrix
at line      53 of function gausselimd                called by :
[x,detA] = gausselimd(A,b)
```

Gauss-Jordan elimination

Gauss-Jordan elimination consists in continuing the row operations in the augmented matrix that results from the forward elimination from a Gaussian elimination process, until an identity matrix is obtained in place of the original A matrix. For example, for the following augmented matrix, the forward elimination procedure results in:

$$\mathbf{A}_{aug} = \begin{pmatrix} 2 & 4 & 6 & | & 14 \\ 3 & -2 & 1 & | & -3 \\ 4 & 2 & -1 & | & -4 \end{pmatrix} \cong \begin{pmatrix} 2 & 4 & 6 & | & 14 \\ 0 & -8 & -8 & | & -24 \\ 0 & -6 & -13 & | & -32 \end{pmatrix} \cong \begin{pmatrix} 2 & 4 & 6 & | & 14 \\ 0 & -8 & -8 & | & -24 \\ 0 & 0 & -7 & | & -14 \end{pmatrix}$$

We can continue performing row operations until the augmented matrix gets reduced to:

$$\begin{pmatrix} 1 & 2 & 3 & | & 7 \\ 0 & 1 & 1 & | & 3 \\ 0 & 0 & 1 & | & 2 \end{pmatrix} \cong \begin{pmatrix} 1 & 2 & 3 & | & 7 \\ 0 & 1 & 1 & | & 1 \\ 0 & 0 & 1 & | & 2 \end{pmatrix} \cong \begin{pmatrix} 1 & 2 & 0 & | & 1 \\ 0 & 1 & 0 & | & 1 \\ 0 & 0 & 1 & | & 2 \end{pmatrix} \cong \begin{pmatrix} 1 & 0 & 0 & | & -1 \\ 0 & 1 & 0 & | & 1 \\ 0 & 0 & 1 & | & 2 \end{pmatrix}.$$

The first matrix is the same as that one obtained before at the end of the forward elimination process, with the exception that all rows have been divided by the corresponding diagonal term, i.e., row 1 was divided by 2, row 2 was divided by -8, and row 3 was divided by –7. The final matrix is equivalent to the equations: X = -1, Y = 1, Z= 2, which is the solution to the original system of equations.

SCILAB provides the function *rref* (row-reduced echelon form) that can be used to obtain a solution to a system of linear equations using Gauss-Jordan elimination. The function requires as argument an augmented matrix, for example:

```
-->A = [2,4,6;3,-2,1;4,2,-1]; b = [14;-3;-4];

-->A_aug = [A b]
 A_aug   =

!   2.    4.    6.    14. !
!   3.  - 2.    1.  - 3.  !
!   4.    2.  - 1.  - 4.  !

-->rref(A_aug)
 ans =

!   1.    0.    0.  - 1. !
!   0.    1.    0.    1. !
!   0.    0.    1.    2. !
```

The last result indicates that the solution to the system is $x_1 = -1$, $x_2 = 1$, and $x_3 = 2$.

Calculating the inverse through Gauss-Jordan elimination

The calculation of an inverse matrix is equivalent to calculating the solution to the augmented system [A | I]. For example, for the matrix A

$$\mathbf{A} = \begin{bmatrix} 1 & 2 & 3 \\ 3 & -2 & 1 \\ 4 & 2 & -1 \end{bmatrix},$$

we would write this augmented matrix as

$$\mathbf{A}_{aug} = \begin{bmatrix} 1 & 2 & 3 & | & 1 & 0 & 0 \\ 3 & -2 & 1 & | & 0 & 1 & 0 \\ 4 & 2 & -1 & | & 0 & 0 & 1 \end{bmatrix}.$$

The SCILAB commands needed to obtain the inverse using Gauss-Jordan elimination are:

```
-->A = [1,2,3;3,-2,1;4,2,-1]    //Original matrix
 A  =
!    1.    2.    3. !
!    3.  - 2.    1. !
!    4.    2.  - 1. !

-->A_aug = [A eye(3,3)]     //Augmented matrix
 A_aug  =
!    1.    2.    3.    1.    0.    0. !
!    3.  - 2.    1.    0.    1.    0. !
!    4.    2.  - 1.    0.    0.    1. !
```

The next command produces the Gauss-Jordan elimination:

```
-->A_aug_inv = rref(A_aug)
 A_aug_inv  =
!    1.    0.    0.    0.       .1428571      .1428571 !
!    0.    1.    0.    .125   - .2321429      .1428571 !
!    0.    0.    1.    .25      .1071429  -   .1428571 !
```

The inverse is obtained by extracting rows 4, 5, and 6, of the previous result:

```
-->A_inv_1 = [A_aug_inv(:,4), A_aug_inv(:,5), A_aug_inv(:,6)]
 A_inv_1  =

!   0.         .1428571      .1428571 !
!    .125   -  .2321429      .1428571 !
!    .25       .1071429  -   .1428571 !
```

To check that the matrix A_inv_1 is indeed the inverse of A use:

```
-->A*A_inv_1
 ans  =
```

```
!   1.     0.     0. !
!   0.     1.     0. !
!   0.     0.     1. !
```

This exercise is presented to illustrate the calculation of inverse matrices through Gauss-Jordan elimination. In practice, you should use the function *inv* in SCILAB to obtain inverse matrices. For the case under consideration, for example, the inverse is obtained from:

```
-->A_inv_2 = inv(A)
 A_inv_2  =

!   0.          .1428571     .1428571 !
!   .125    -   .2321429     .1428571 !
!   .25         .1071429  -  .1428571 !
```

The result is exactly the same as found above using Gauss-Jordan elimination.

Eigenvalues and eigenvectors

Given a square matrix **A**, we can write the *eigenvalue equation*

$$\mathbf{A} \cdot \mathbf{x} = \lambda \cdot \mathbf{x},$$

where the values of λ that satisfy the equation are known as the *eigenvalues of matrix A*. For each value of λ, we can find, from the same equation, values of **x** that satisfy the eigenvalue equation. These values of **x** are known as the *eigenvectors of matrix A*.

The eigenvalues equation can be written also as

$$(\mathbf{A} - \lambda \cdot \mathbf{I}) \mathbf{x} = 0.$$

This equation will have a non-trivial solution only if the *characteristic matrix*, $(\mathbf{A} - \lambda \cdot \mathbf{I})$, is singular, i.e., if

$$\det(\mathbf{A} - \lambda \cdot \mathbf{I}) = 0.$$

The last equation generates an algebraic equation involving a polynomial of order *n* for a square matrix $\mathbf{A}_{n \times n}$. The resulting equation is known as the *characteristic polynomial* of matrix **A**. Solving the characteristic polynomial produces the *eigenvalues* of the matrix.

Using SCILAB we can obtain the characteristic matrix, characteristic polynomial, and eigenvalues of a matrix as shown below for a symmetric matrix

$$\mathbf{A} = \begin{bmatrix} 3 & -2 & 5 \\ -2 & 3 & 6 \\ 5 & 6 & 4 \end{bmatrix}.$$

First, we define the matrix A:

```
-->A = [3,-2,5;-2,3,6;5,6,4]
 A  =

!   3.    - 2.     5. !
! - 2.      3.     6. !
!   5.      6.     4. !
```

Next, the characteristic matrix $B = (A - \lambda \cdot I)$ corresponding to a square matrix A is calculated as follows. Notice that we define the symbolic variable 'lam' (for lambda) before forming the characteristic matrix:

```
-->lam = poly(0,'lam')
 lam =

    lam

-->charMat = A-lam*eye(3,3)

 charMat =

!   3 - lam      - 2             5          !
!                                            !
! - 2            3 - lam         6          !
!                                            !
!   5              6           4 - lam      !
```

The characteristic equation can be determined using function *poly* with matrix A and the variable name 'lam' as arguments, i.e.,

```
-->charPoly = poly(A,'lam')
 charPoly =

                    2      3
    283 - 32lam -10lam + lam
```

The function *spec* produces the eigenvalues for matrix A:

```
-->lam = spec(A)
 lam =

! - 5.4409348 !
!   4.9650189 !
!   10.475916 !
```

Calculating the first eigenvector

We can form the characteristic matrix for a particular eigenvalue, say λ = *lam(1)*, by using:

```
-->B1 = A - lam(1)*eye(3,3)
```

B1 =

```
!  8.4409348  - 2.       5.       !
! - 2.         8.4409348  6.       !
!  5.          6.         9.4409348 !
```

This, of course, is a singular matrix, which you can check by calculating the determinant of B1:

```
--> det(B1)
ans   =

5.973E-14
```

which, although not exactly zero, is close enough to zero to ensure singularity.

Because the characteristic matrix is singular, there is no unique solution to the problem $(A - \lambda_1 I)x = 0$. The equivalent system of linear equations is:

$$8.4409348 x_1 - 2 x_2 + 5 x_3 = 0$$
$$-2 x_1 + 8.4409348 x_2 + 6 x_3 = 0$$
$$5 x_1 + 6 x_2 + 9.4409348 x_3 = 0$$

The three equations are linearly dependent. This means that we can select an arbitrary value of one of the solutions, say, $x_3 = 1$, and solve two of the equations for the other two solutions, x_1 and x_2. We could try, for example, to solve the first two equations (with $x_3 = 1$), re-written as:

$$8.4409348 x_1 - 2 x_2 = -5$$
$$-2 x_1 + 8.4409348 x_2 = -6$$

Using SCILAB we can get the solution to this system as follows:

```
-->C1 = B1(1:2,1:2), b1 = -B1(3,1:2)
 C1   =

!   8.4409348   - 2.       !
! - 2.          8.4409348 !

-->b1 = -B1(1:2,3)
 b1   =

! - 5. !
! - 6. !
```

The solution for $\xi_1 = [x_1, x_2]^T$ is:

```
-->xi1 = C1\b1
 xi1 =

! - .8060249 !
! - .9018017 !
```

The eigenvector x_1 is, therefore:

```
-->x1 = [xi1;1]
 x1  =

! -   .8060249 !
! -   .9018017 !
!     1.       !
```

If we want to find the corresponding unit eigenvector e_{x1}, we can use:

```
-->e_x1 = x1/norm(x1)
 e_x1 =

! -  .5135977 !
! -  .5746266 !
!    .6371983 !
```

Calculating eigenvectors with a user-defined function

Following the procedure outlined above for calculating the first eigenvector, we can write a SCILAB user-defined function to calculate all the eigenvectors of a matrix. The following is a listing of this function:

```
function [x,lam] = eigenvectors(A)

//Calculates unit eigenvectors of matrix A
//returning a matrix x whose columns are
//the eigenvectors.  The function also
//returns the eigenvalues of the matrix.

[n,m] = size(A);

if m<>n then
      error('eigenvectors - matrix A is not square');
      abort;
end;

lam = spec(A)';            //Eigenvalues of matrix A

x = [];

for k = 1:n
      B = A - lam(k)*eye(n,n);    //Characteristic matrix
       C = B(1:n-1,1:n-1);        //Coeff. matrix for reduced system
      b = -B(1:n-1,n);            //RHS vector for reduced system
      y = C\b;                    //Solution for reduced system
      y = [y;1];                  //Complete eigenvector
      y = y/norm(y);              //Make unit eigenvector
      x = [x y];                  //Add eigenvector to matrix
end;

//End of function
```

Applying function *eigenvectors* to the matrix A used earlier produces the following eigenvalues and eigenvectors:

```
-->getf('eigenvectors')

-->[x,lam] = eigenvectors(A)
 lam  =

! - 5.4409348    4.9650189    10.475916 !
 x  =

! -  .5135977      .7711676      .3761887 !
! -  .5746266   -  .6347298      .5166454 !
!    .6371983      .0491799      .7691291 !
```

We can separate the eigenvectors x_1, x_2, x_3 from matrix x by using:

```
-->x1 = x(1:3,1), x2 = x(1:3,2), x3 = x(1:3,3)
 x1  =

! -  .5135977 !
! -  .5746266 !
!    .6371983 !
 x2  =

!    .7711676 !
! -  .6347298 !
!    .0491799 !
 x3  =

!    .3761887 !
!    .5166454 !
!    .7691291 !
```

The eigenvectors corresponding to a symmetric matrix are orthogonal to each other, i.e., $x_i \cdot x_j = 0$, for $i \neq j$. Checking these results for the eigenvectors found above:

```
-->x1'*x2, x1'*x3, x2'*x3
 ans  =

  - 3.678E-16
 ans  =

  - 5.551E-17
 ans  =

    9.576E-16
```

For a non-symmetric matrix, the eigenvalues may include complex numbers:

Example 1 - non-symmetric matrix, real eigenvalues

```
-->A = [3, 2, -1; 1, 1, 2; 5, 5, -2]    A  =

!   3.    2.  - 1. !
!   1.    1.    2. !
!   5.    5.  - 2. !

-->[x,lam] = eigenvectors(A)
```

```
lam  =

!    .9234927      4.1829571    - 3.1064499 !
x  =

! -  .5974148      .3437456       .2916085 !
!    .7551776      .5746662    -  .4752998 !
!    .2698191      .7426962       .8300931 !
```

Example 2 - non-symmetric matrix, complex eigenvalues

```
-->A = [2, 2, -3; 3, 3, -2; 1, 1, 1]
A  =

!   2.    2.   - 3. !
!   3.    3.   - 2. !
!   1.    1.     1. !

-->[x,lam] = eigenvectors(A)
warning
matrix is close to singular or badly scaled.
results may be inaccurate. rcond =    7.6862E-17

lam  =

!   4.646E-16    3. - i      3. + i   !
x  =

! -  .7071068    .25 -  .25i    .25 +  .25i !
!    .7071068    .75 -  .25i    .75 +  .25i !
!    2.826E-16   .5             .5          !
```

Generating the characteristic equation for a matrix

This section represents an additional exercise on SCILAB function programming, since we already know that SCILAB can generate the characteristic equation for a square matrix through function *poly*. The method coded in the function uses the equations:

$$p_{n+1} = -1.0, \; B_{n+1} = A$$

$$B_j = A \cdot (B_{j+1} - p_{j+1} I), \; \text{for } j = n, n-1, \ldots, 3, 2, 1$$

$$P_j = (-1)^j p_j, \; j = 1, 2, \ldots, n+1$$

The matrix I shown in the formula is the nxn identity matrix. The coefficients of the polynomial will be contained in the 1x(n+1) vector

$$p = [p_1 \; p_2 \; \ldots \; p_{n+1}].$$

The characteristic equation is given by

$$p_1 + p_2 \lambda + p_3 \lambda^2 + \ldots + p_n \lambda^{n-1} + p_{n+1} \lambda^n = 0.$$

Here is a listing of the function:

```
function [p]=chreq(A)
//This function generates the coefficients of the characteristic
//equation for a square matrix A
[m n]=size(A);
if(m n)then
      error('matrix is not square.')
      abort
end;
I = eye(n,n);                    //Identity matrix
p = zeros(1,n);                  //Matrix (1xn) filled with zeroes
p(1,n+1) = -1.0;
B = A;
p(1,n)=trace(B);
for j = n-1:-1:1,
      B = A*(B-p(1,j+1)*I),
      p(1,j) = trace(B)/(n-j+1),
end;
p = (-1)^n*p;
p = poly(p,"lmbd","coeff");
p
//end function chreq
```

In this function we used the function *poly* to generate the final result in the function. In the call to *poly* shown above, we use the vector of coefficients p as the first argument, "lmbd" is the independent variable λ, and "coeff" is required to indicate that the vector p represent the coefficients of the polynomial. The following commands show you how to load the function and run it for a particular matrix:

```
-->getf('chreq')

-->A = [1 3 1;2 5 -1;2 7 -1]
 A  =

!   1.     3.     1. !
!   2.     5.   - 1. !
!   2.     7.   - 1. !

-->CheqA = chreq(A)
 CheqA =

                      2          3
  - 6 - 21mbd - 5lmbd + lmbd
```

Generalized eigenvalue problem

The *generalized eigenvalue problem* involves square matrices A and B of the same size, and consists in finding the values of the scalar λ and the vectors x that satisfy the matricial equation:

$$A \cdot x = \lambda \cdot B \cdot x.$$

The following function, *geingenvectors* (generalized *eigenvectors*), calculates the eigenvalues and eigenvectors from the generalized eigenvalue problem $A \cdot x = \lambda \cdot B \cdot x$, or $(A-\lambda B)x = 0$.

```
function [x,lam] = geigenvectors(A,B)

//Calculates unit eigenvectors of matrix A
//returning a matrix x whose columns are
//the eigenvectors.  The function also
//returns the eigenvalues of the matrix.

[nA,mA] = size(A);
[nB,mB] = size(B);

if (mA<>nA | mB<>nB) then
        error('geigenvectors - matrix A or B not square');
        abort;
end;

if nA<>nB then
        error('geigenvectors - matrix A and B have different dimensions');
        abort;
end;

lam = poly(0,'lam');               //Define variable "lam"
chPoly = det(A-B*lam);             //Characteristic polynomial
lam = roots(chPoly)';              //Eigenvalues of matrix A

x = []; n = nA;

for k = 1:n
        BB = A - lam(k)*B;         //Characteristic matrix
         CC = BB(1:n-1,1:n-1);     //Coeff. matrix for reduced system
        bb = -BB(1:n-1,n);         //RHS vector for reduced system
        y = CC\bb;                 //Solution for reduced system
        y = [y;1];                 //Complete eigenvector
        y = y/norm(y);             //Make unit eigenvector
        x = [x y];                 //Add eigenvector to matrix
end;

//End of function
```

An application of this function is presented next:

```
-->A = [4,1,6;8,5,8;1,5,5]
 A  =

!   4.    1.    6. !
!   8.    5.    8. !
!   1.    5.    5. !

-->B = [3,9,7;3,3,2;9,3,4]
 B  =

!   3.    9.    7. !
!   3.    3.    2. !
!   9.    3.    4. !
```

```
-->getf('geigenvectors')

-->[x,lam] = geigenvectors(A,B)
 lam  =

!  - .2055713 - 1.1759636i   - .2055713 + 1.1759636i   - 1.5333019 !
 x  =

!  - .2828249 -  .0422024i   - .2828249 +  .0422024i   -  .0202307 !
!  - .5392352 +  .2691247i   - .5392352 -  .2691247i   -  .7437197 !
!    .7450009                  .7450009                   .6681854 !
```

Sparse matrices

Sparse matrices are those that have a large percentage of zero elements. When a matrix is defined as sparse in SCILAB, only those non-zero elements are stored. The regular definition of a matrix, also referred to as a *full* matrix, implies that SCILAB stores all elements of the matrix, zero or otherwise.

Creating sparse matrices

SCILAB provides the function *sparse* to define sparse matrices. The simplest call to the function is

$$A\_sparse = sparse(A)$$

Where A is a sparse or full matrix. Obviously, if A is already a sparse matrix, no action is taken by the call to function *sparse*. If A is a full matrix, the function *sparse* squeezes out those zero elements from A. For example,

```
-->A = [2, 0, -1; 0, 1, 0; 0, 0 , 2]
 A  =

!   2.     0.    - 1. !
!   0.     1.      0. !
!   0.     0.      2. !

-->As = sparse(A)
 As  =

(     3,     3) sparse matrix

(     1,    1)         2.
(     1,    3)       - 1.
(     2,    2)         1.
(     3,    3)         2.
```

Notice that SCILAB reports the size of the matrix (3,3), and those non-zero elements only. These are the only elements stored in memory. Thus, sparse matrices are useful in minimizing memory storage particularly when large-size matrices, with relatively small density of non-zero elements, are involved.

Alternatively, a call to *sparse* of the form

$$A\_sparse = sparse(index, values)$$

Where *index* is a nx2 matrix and *values* is a nx1 vector such that *values(i,1)* represents the element in row *index(i,1)* and column *index(i,2)* of the sparse matrix. For example,

```
-->row = [2, 2, 3, 3, 6, 6, 10]   //row position for non-zero elements
 row  =

!   2.    2.    3.    3.    6.    6.    10. !
```

```
-->col = [1, 2, 2, 3, 1, 4, 2]    //column position for non-zero elements
  col =

!   1.    2.    2.    3.    1.    4.    2. !

-->val = [-0.5, 0.3, 0.2, 1.5, 4.2, -1.1, 2.0] //values of non-zero elements
  val =

! -  .5    .3    .2    1.5    4.2  - 1.1    2. !

-->index = [row' col']    //indices of non-zero elements (i,j)
  index =

!   2.    1. !
!   2.    2. !
!   3.    2. !
!   3.    3. !
!   6.    1. !
!   6.    4. !
!  10.    2. !

-->As = sparse(index,val)    //creating the sparse matrix
  As =

(   10,    4) sparse matrix

(    2,    1)        -  .5
(    2,    2)           .3
(    3,    2)           .2
(    3,    3)          1.5
(    6,    1)          4.2
(    6,    4)        - 1.1
(   10,    2)          2.
```

The function *full* converts a sparse matrix into a full matrix. For example,

```
-->A = full(As)
  A =

!   0.     0.    0.     0.  !
! - .5     .3    0.     0.  !
!   0.     .2   1.5     0.  !
!   0.     0.    0.     0.  !
!   0.     0.    0.     0.  !
!  4.2     0.    0.   - 1.1 !
!   0.     0.    0.     0.  !
!   0.     0.    0.     0.  !
!   0.     0.    0.     0.  !
!   0.     2.    0.     0.  !
```

The following call to *sparse* includes defining the row and column dimensions of the sparse matrix besides providing indices and values of the non-zero values:

$$A\_sparse = sparse(index, values, dim)$$

Here, *dim* is a 1x2 vector with the row and column dimensions of the sparse matrix. As an example, we can try:

```
-->As = sparse(index,val,[10,12])
 As  =

(    10,     12) sparse matrix

(     2,      1)        -   .5
(     2,      2)            .3
(     3,      2)            .2
(     3,      3)           1.5
(     6,      1)           4.2
(     6,      4)        - 1.1
(    10,      2)           2.
```

Getting information about a sparse matrix

The function *spget*, through a call of the form

$$[index, val, dim] = spget(As)$$

returns the location of the values contained in *val* described by the row and column indices (listed in the first and second columns of *index*), as well as the row and column dimensions of the matrix contained in vector *dim*. For example, for the matrix *As* defined above, function *spget* produces:

```
-->[index, values, dim] = spget(As)
 dim   =

!   10.    12. !
 values   =

! -   .5 !
!     .3 !
!     .2 !
!    1.5 !
!    4.2 !
! - 1.1 !
!    2.  !
 index    =

!    2.      1. !
!    2.      2. !
!    3.      2. !
!    3.      3. !
!    6.      1. !
!    6.      4. !
!   10.      2. !
```

Sparse matrix with unit entries

To create a matrix including values of 1.0 with the same structure of an existing sparse matrix use the function *spones*, for example:

```
-->A1 = spones(As)
 A1   =

(    10,    12) sparse matrix

(     2,     1)        1.
(     2,     2)        1.
(     3,     2)        1.
(     3,     3)        1.
(     6,     1)        1.
(     6,     4)        1.
(    10,     2)        1.
```

Sparse identity matrices

To create a sparse identity matrix use the function *speye*. For example, giving the dimensions of the desired identity matrix we can use:

```
-->speye(6,6)
 ans   =

(     6,     6) sparse matrix

(     1,     1)        1.
(     2,     2)        1.
(     3,     3)        1.
(     4,     4)        1.
(     5,     5)        1.
(     6,     6)        1.
```

To produce a sparse identity matrix with the same dimensions of an existing matrix *As* use:

```
-->speye(As)
 ans   =

(    10,    12) sparse matrix

(     1,     1)        1.
(     2,     2)        1.
(     3,     3)        1.
(     4,     4)        1.
(     5,     5)        1.
(     6,     6)        1.
(     7,     7)        1.
(     8,     8)        1.
(     9,     9)        1.
(    10,    10)        1.
```

Sparse matrix with random entries

The function *sprand* generates a sparse matrix with random non-zero entries. The function requires the dimensions of the matrix as the two first arguments, and a density of non-zero elements as the third argument. The density of non-zero values is giver as a number between zero and one, for example:

```
-->As = sprand(6,5,0.2)
 As   =

(     6,     5) sparse matrix

(     1,     3)        .0500420
(     2,     1)        .9931210
(     2,     4)        .7485507
(     3,     2)        .6488563
(     3,     5)        .4104059
(     4,     2)        .9923191
```

To see the full matrix use:

```
-->full(As)
 ans   =

!    0.          0.         .0500420    0.          0.          !
!    .9931210    0.          0.         .7485507    0.          !
!    0.          .6488563    0.          0.         .4104059    !
!    0.          .9923191    0.          0.          0.         !
!    0.          0.          0.          0.          0.         !
!    0.          0.          0.          0.          0.         !
```

Sparse matrices with zero entries

The function *spzeros* is used to define a sparse matrix given the dimensions of the matrix. Since all the elements of the matrix are zero, what the function does is to reserve memory space for the matrix ensuring its sparse character. A couple of examples of application of *spzeros* are shown next:

```
->spzeros(As)
 ans =
(     6,     5) zero sparse matrix

-->spzeros(6,4)
 ans =
(     6,     4) zero sparse matrix
```

The function *spzeros* can be used, for example, in programming SCILAB functions that require sparse matrices to reserve a matrix name for future use.

Visualizing sparse matrices

The following function, *spplot* (sparse matrix *plot*), can be used to visualize the distribution of non-zero elements for relatively large sparse matrices. A listing of the function follows:

```
function spplot(As)

//Plot a schematic of non-zero elements
//for a sparse matrix As

wnumber = input('Enter graphics window number:');
A = sparse(As);
[index,vals,dim] = spget(A);
xx=index(:,1);yy=index(:,2);
xset('window',wnumber);
xset('mark',-2,2);
plot2d(xx,yy,-2);

//end function
```

The function requires as input the name of the sparse matrix and it requests the number of the graphics window where the plot is to be displayed. The following is an example that uses this function to visualize a sparse matrix of dimensions 40x40 with a density of non-zero numbers of 0.2:

```
-->As = sprand(40,40,0.2);
-->getf('spplot')
-->spplot(As)

 Enter graphics window number:

--> 2
```

The result, shown in SCILAB graphics window number 2 is reproduced next:

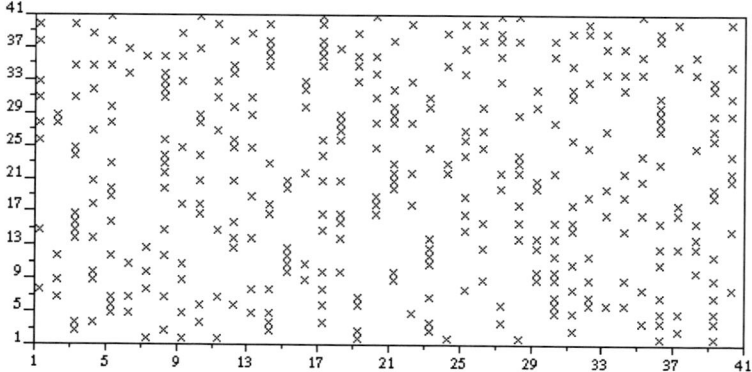

Factorization of sparse matrices

SCILAB provides functions *lufact*, *luget*, and *ludel*, to produce the LU factorization of a sparse matrix A. Function *lufact* returns the rank of the matrix as well as a pointer or handle to the LU factors, which are then retrieved with function *luget*. Function *ludel* is required after performing a LU factorization to clear up the pointer or handle generated with *lufact*.

The call to function *lufact* has the general form:

$$[hand, rk] = lufact(As)$$

where *hand* is the handle or pointer, *rk* is the rank of sparse matrix *As*. Be aware that *hand* is a pointer to locate the LU factors in memory. SCILAB produces no display for *hand*.

The call to function *luget* has the general form:

$$[P,L,U,Q] = luget(hand)$$

where P and Q are permutation matrices and L and U are the LU factors of the sparse matrix that generated *hand* through a call to function *lufact*. Matrices P, Q, L, and U are related to matrix As by P*Q*L*U = As.

After a LU factorization is completed, it is necessary to call function *ludel* to clear the pointer generated in the call to function *lufact*, i.e., use

$$ludel(hand)$$

The following example shows the LU factorization of a 6x6 randomly-generated sparse matrix with a density of non-zero numbers of 0.5:

```
-->As = sprand(5,5,0.5);
```

To see the full matrix just generated try:

```
-->full(As)
 ans  =

!    .7019967    .7354560    0.          0.          .5098139 !
!    .5018194    0.          .6522234    .2921187    .3776263 !
!    0.          .4732295    .9388094    .6533222    0.       !
!    .7860680    0.          0.          .9933566    0.       !
!    0.          .9456872    .2401141    .4494063    0.       !
```

The first step in the LU factorization is:

```
-->[hand,rk] = lufact(As)
 rk  =

    5.
 hand  =
```

The rank of the matrix is 5. Notice that SCILAB shows nothing for the handle or pointer hand. The second step in the LU factorization is to get the matrices P, L, U, and Q, such that P*L*U*Q = As, i.e.,

```
-->[P,L,U,Q] = luget(hand);
```

These matrices are shown in full as follows:

```
-->full(P)
 ans  =

!   0.    0.    1.    0.    0. !
!   0.    0.    0.    1.    0. !
!   0.    1.    0.    0.    0. !
!   1.    0.    0.    0.    0. !
!   0.    0.    0.    0.    1. !

-->full(L)
 ans  =

!  .9933566    0.          0.          0.          0.         !
!  .6533222    .9388094    0.          0.          0.         !
!   0.          0.         .7019967    0.          0.         !
!  .2921187    .6522234    .6298297  - .9886182    0.         !
!  .4494063    .2401141  - .2233988   1.0586985    .0768072   !

-->full(U)
 ans  =

!   1.    0.      .7913251    0.          0.         !
!   0.    1.   -  .5506871    .5040741    0.         !
!   0.    0.     1.          1.047663    .726234     !
!   0.    0.     0.          1.          .0806958    !
!   0.    0.     0.          0.          1.          !

-->full(Q)
 ans  =

!   0.    0.    0.    1.    0. !
!   0.    0.    1.    0.    0. !
!   1.    0.    0.    0.    0. !
!   0.    1.    0.    0.    0. !
!   0.    0.    0.    0.    1. !
```

To check if the product P*L*U*Q is indeed equal to the original sparse matrix As, use:

```
-->full(P*L*U*Q-As)
 ans  =

!   0.    1.110E-16    0.    0.    0. !
!   0.    0.           0.    0.    0. !
!   0.    0.           0.    0.    0. !
!   0.    0.           0.    0.    0. !
!   0.    1.110E-16    0.    0.    0. !
```

The resulting matrix has a couple of small non-zero elements. These can be cleared by using the function *clean* as follows:

```
-->clean(full(P*L*U*Q-As))
 ans  =

!  0.    0.    0.    0.    0. !
!  0.    0.    0.    0.    0. !
!  0.    0.    0.    0.    0. !
!  0.    0.    0.    0.    0. !
!  0.    0.    0.    0.    0. !
```

At this point we can use function *ludel* to clear up the handle or pointer used in the factorization:

```
--> ludel(hand)
```

Solution to system of linear equations involving sparse matrices

The solution to a system of linear equations of the form $A \cdot x = b$, where A is a sparse matrix and b is a full column vector, can be accomplished by using functions *lufact* and *lusolve*. Function *lufact* provides the handle or pointer *hand*, from [hand,rk] = lufact(A), which then used by *lusolve* through the function call

$$x = lusolve(hand,b)$$

The following example illustrates the uses of *lufact* and *lusolve* to solve a system of linear equations whose matrix of coefficients is sparse:

```
-->A=sprand(6,6,0.6);         //Generate a random, sparse matrix of coefficients

-->b=rand(6,1);               //Generate a random, full right-hand side vector
```

First, we get the rank and handle for the LU factorization of matrix A:

```
-->[hand,rk] = lufact(A)
 rk  =

    5.
 hand  =
```

Next, we use function *lusolve* with the handle *hand* and right-hand side vector *b* to obtain the solution to the system of linear equations:

```
-->x = lusolve(hand,b)
 x  =

! -  .8137973 !
! -  .5726203 !
!    .8288245 !
!    .9152823 !
!    .4984395 !
!    0.       !
```

Function *lusolve* also allows for the direct solution of the system of linear equations without having to use *lufact* first. For the case under consideration the SCILAB command is:

```
-->x = lusolve(A,b)
            !--error    19
singular matrix
```

However, matrix A for this case is singular (each we found that its rank was 5, i.e., smaller than the number of rows or columns, thus indicating a singular matrix), and no solution is obtained. The use of *lufact* combined with *lusolve*, as shown earlier, forces a solution by making one of the values equal to zero and solving for the remaining five values.

After completing the solution we need to clear the handle for the LU factorization by using:

```
-->ludel(hand)
```

A second example of solving a system of linear equations is shown next:

```
-->A = sprand(5,5,0.5);
-->b = full(sprand(5,1,0.6));
```

Notice that to generate b, which must be a full vector, we first generated a sparse random vector with a non-zero value density of 0.6. Next, we used the function *full* to convert that sparse vector into a full one.

A call to function *lufact* will provide the rank of matrix A:

```
-->[hand,rk] = lufact(A)
 rk  =

    5.
 hand  =
```

Because the matrix has full rank (i.e., its rank is the same as the number of rows or columns), it is possible to find the solution by using:

```
-->x = lusolve(A,b)
 x  =

!  -  .2813594  !
!     .5590971  !
!    1.0143263  !
!  -  .1810458  !
!  - 1.1233045  !
```

Do not forget to clear the handle generated with *lufact* by using: `-->ludel(hand)`

Solution to system of linear equations using the inverse of a sparse matrix

If sparse matrix A in the system of linear equations $A \cdot x = b$ is non-singular (i.e., a full-rank matrix), it is possible to find the inverse of A, A^{-1}, through function *inv*. The solution x can then be found with $x = A^{-1} \cdot b$. For example, using matrix A from the previous example we can write:

```
-->Ainv = inv(A)              //Calculate inverse of a sparse matrix
```

```
 Ainv  =

(    5,     5) sparse matrix

(    1,    1)    -  .7235355
(    1,    2)    -  .7404212
(    1,    3)       .3915968
(    1,    4)      2.0631067
(    1,    5)       .1957261
(    2,    1)      1.4075482
(    2,    2)      1.2851264
(    2,    3)    -  .6179589
(    2,    4)       .0607043
(    2,    5)    -  .5012662
(    3,    1)      2.9506345
(    4,    1)    - 2.1683689
(    4,    3)      1.8737551
(    5,    1)    - 2.4138658
(    5,    2)    -  .0298745
(    5,    3)    -  .9542841
(    5,    4)    - 2.1488971
(    5,    5)      2.5469151

-->x = Ainv*b
 x  =

! -  .2813594 !
!    .5590971 !
!   1.0143263 !
! -  .1810458 !
! - 1.1233045 !
```

Alternatively, you can also use left-division to obtain the solution:

```
-->x=A\b
 x  =

! -  .2813594 !
!    .5590971 !
!   1.0143263 !
! -  .1810458 !
! - 1.1233045 !
```

Solution to a system of linear equations with a tri-diagonal matrix of coefficients

A tri-diagonal matrix is a square matrix such that the only non-zero elements are those in the main diagonal and those in the two diagonals immediately off the main one. A tri-diagonal matrix system will look as follows:

$$\begin{bmatrix} a_{11} & a_{12} & 0 & \cdots & 0 & 0 & 0 \\ a_{21} & a_{22} & a_{23} & \cdots & 0 & 0 & 0 \\ 0 & a_{32} & a_{33} & \cdots & 0 & 0 & 0 \\ \vdots & \vdots & \vdots & \ddots & \vdots & \vdots & \vdots \\ 0 & 0 & 0 & \cdots & a_{n-2,n-2} & a_{n-2,n-1} & 0 \\ 0 & 0 & 0 & \cdots & a_{n-1,n-2} & a_{n-1,n-1} & a_{n-1,n} \\ 0 & 0 & 0 & \cdots & 0 & a_{n-1,n} & a_{nn} \end{bmatrix} \begin{bmatrix} x_1 \\ x_2 \\ x_3 \\ \vdots \\ x_{n-2} \\ x_{n-1} \\ x_n \end{bmatrix} = \begin{bmatrix} b_1 \\ b_2 \\ b_3 \\ \vdots \\ b_{n-2} \\ b_{n-1} \\ b_n \end{bmatrix}$$

This system can also be written as $A \cdot x = b$, where the nxn matrix A, and the nx1 vectors x and b are easily identified from the previous expression.

Since each column in the matrix of coefficients only uses three elements, we can enter the data as the elements of a nx3 matrix,

$$\mathbf{A} = \begin{bmatrix} a_{11} & a_{12} & 0 \\ a_{21} & a_{22} & a_{23} \\ a_{31} & a_{32} & a_{33} \\ \vdots & \vdots & \vdots \\ a_{n-1,1} & a_{n-1,2} & a_{n-1,3} \\ 0 & a_{n,n-1} & a_{nn} \end{bmatrix}$$

Thomas algorithm for the solution of the tri-diagonal system of linear equations is an adaptation of the Gaussian elimination procedure. It consists of a forward elimination accomplished through the recurrence formulas:

$a_{i2} = a_{i2} - a_{i1}\, a_{i-1,3}/a_{i-1,2}$, $b_i = b_i - a_{i1} b_{i-1}/a_{i-1,2}$, for i = 2, 3, ..., n

The backward substitution step is performed through the following equations:

$$x_n = b_n/a_{n2},$$

and

$x_i = (b_i - a_{i3} x_{i+1}/a_{i2})$, for i = n-1, n-2, ..., 3, 2, 1 (counting backwards).

The following function implements the Thomas algorithm for the solution of a system of linear equations whose matrix of coefficients is a tri-diagonal matrix:

```
function [x] = Tridiag(A,b)
//Uses Thomas algorithm for tridiagonal matrices
//The matrix A is entered as a matrix of three columns and n rows
//containing the main diagonal and its two closest diagonals
[n m] = size(A);   // determine matrix size
//Check if number of columns = 3.
if m <> 3 then
        error('Matrix needs to have three columns only.')
        abort;
end
```

```
        [nv mv] = size(b);   // determine vector size
        if ((mv  1) | (nv  n)) then
              error('Vector needs to be a column vector or it does not have same
        number of rows as matrix')
        end
        //Recalculate matrix A and vector b
        AA = A; bb = b;
        for i = 2:n
              AA(i,2) = AA(i,2)-AA(i,1)*AA(i-1,3)/AA(i-1,2);
              bb(i)   = bb(i) - AA(i,1)*bb(i-1)/AA(i-1,2);
        end;
        //Back calculation of solution
        x(n) = bb(n)/AA(n,2);
        for i = n-1:-1:1
              x(i) = (bb(i)-AA(i,3)*x(i+1))/AA(i,2)
        end;
        //show solution
        x
        //end function
```

As an exercise, enter the following SCILAB commands:

```
-->A = [0,4,-1;-1,4,-1;-1,4,-1;-1,4,0]; b=[150;20;150;100];

-->getf('Tridiag')

-->x = Tridiag(A,b)
 x =

!    44.976077 !
!    29.904306 !
!    54.641148 !
!    38.660287 !
```

Solution to tri-diagonal systems of linear equations using sparse matrices

Because a tri-diagonal matrix is basically a sparse matrix, we can use function *lufact* and *lusolve* to obtain the solution to a tri-diagonal system of linear equations. The following function takes the nx3 matrix that represents a tri-diagonal matrix and produces the index and values of the corresponding sparse matrix:

```
function [index,val] = tritosparse(A)

//Converts the nx3 matrix A that represents
//a tri-diagonal matrix, into the corresponding
//nxn sparse matrix

krow = 0; kcol = 0; kval = 0;

krow = krow+1; row(krow) = 1;
kcol = kcol+1; col(kcol) = 1;
kval = kval+1; val(kval) = A(1,2);
krow = krow+1; row(krow) = 1;
```

```
      kcol = kcol+1; col(kcol) = 2;
      kval = kval+1; val(kval) = A(1,3)

      for i = 2:n-1
            krow = krow+1; row(krow) = i;
            kcol = kcol+1; col(kcol) = i-1;
            kval = kval+1; val(kval) = A(i,1)
            krow = krow+1; row(krow) = i;
            kcol = kcol+1; col(kcol) = i;
            kval = kval+1; val(kval) = A(i,2)
            krow = krow+1; row(krow) = i;
            kcol = kcol+1; col(kcol) = i+1;
            kval = kval+1; val(kval) = A(i,3)
      end;

      krow = krow+1; row(krow) = n;
      kcol = kcol+1; col(kcol) = n-1;
      kval = kval+1; val(kval) = A(n,1)
      krow = krow+1; row(krow) = n;
      kcol = kcol+1; col(kcol) = n;
      kval = kval+1; val(kval) = A(n,2)

      index = [row col];

      //end function
```

An application, using the compact tri-dimensional matrix A presented earlier is shown below:

First, we load the function:

```
-->getf('tritosparse')
```

A call to the function with argument A produces the values and index for a sparse matrix:

```
-->[index,val] = tritosparse(A)
 val  =
!   4. !
! - 1. !
! - 1. !
!   4. !
! - 1. !
! - 1. !
!   4. !
! - 1. !
! - 1. !
!   4. !

 index  =
!   1.    1. !
!   1.    2. !
!   2.    1. !
!   2.    2. !
!   2.    3. !
!   3.    2. !
!   3.    3. !
!   3.    4. !
!   4.    3. !
!   4.    4. !
```

Next, we put together the sparse matrix using the matrix *index* and the vector *val*:

```
-->As = sparse(index,val)
 As  =

(    4,    4) sparse matrix

(    1,    1)          4.
(    1,    2)        - 1.
(    2,    1)        - 1.
(    2,    2)          4.
(    2,    3)        - 1.
(    3,    2)        - 1.
(    3,    3)          4.
(    3,    4)        - 1.
(    4,    3)        - 1.
(    4,    4)          4.
```

To see the full form of the sparse matrix we use:

```
-->full(As)
 ans  =

!   4.   - 1.    0.    0. !
! - 1.     4.  - 1.    0. !
!   0.   - 1.    4.  - 1. !
!   0.     0.  - 1.    4. !
```

For the right-hand side vector previously defined we can use function *lusolve* to obtain the solution of the tri-diagonal system of linear equations:

```
-->x = lusolve(As,b)
 x  =

!   44.976077 !
!   29.904306 !
!   54.641148 !
!   38.660287 !
```

Iterative solutions to systems of linear equations

With a powerful numerical environment like SCILAB, which provides a number of pre-programmed functions to obtain the solution to systems of linear equations, there is really no need to use iterative methods. They are presented here only as programming exercises.

Iterative methods result from re-arranging the system of linear equations

$$a_{11} \cdot x_1 + a_{12} \cdot x_2 + a_{13} \cdot x_3 + \ldots + a_{1,n-1} \cdot x_{n-1} + a_{1,n} \cdot x_n = b_1,$$
$$a_{21} \cdot x_1 + a_{22} \cdot x_2 + a_{23} \cdot x_3 + \ldots + a_{2,n-1} \cdot x_{n-1} + a_{2,n} \cdot x_n = b_2,$$
$$\vdots$$
$$a_{n1} \cdot x_1 + a_{n2} \cdot x_2 + a_{n3} \cdot x_3 + \ldots + a_{n,n-1} \cdot x_{n-1} + a_{n,n} \cdot x_n = b_n.$$

as

$$x_1 = (b_1 - a_{12}x_2 - a_{13}x_3 - \ldots - a_{1n}x_n)/a_{11}$$
$$x_2 = (b_2 - a_{22}x_2 - a_{23}x_3 - \ldots - a_{2n}x_n)/a_{22}$$
$$\vdots$$
$$x_n = (b_n - a_{n2}x_2 - a_{n3}x_3 - \ldots - a_{nn}x_n)/a_{nn}$$

The solution is obtained by first assuming a first guess for the solution $x_{(0)} = [x_{10}, x_{20}, \ldots, x_{n0}]$, which is then replaced in the right-hand side of the recursive equations shown above to produce a new solution $x_{(1)}$. With this new value in the right-hand side, a new approximation, $x_{(2)}$ is obtained, and so on until the solution converges to a fixed value.

If you replace each value of x in the recursive equations as it gets calculated the approach is called the Gauss-Seidel method. An alternative, presented below as a SCILAB function, is the Jacobi iterative method.

Jacobi iterative method

In the Jacobi iterative method the new values of x_i's are replaced only once in each iteration. This method calculates the residual, R, from the equation $A \cdot x = b$, as $R = A \cdot x - b$, and adjusts the value of R recalculating x until the average of the residuals is smaller than a set value of tolerance, ε.

To program the Jacobi iterative method we create three files, as follows:

```
function [x]= Jacobi(A,b)
//Uses Jacobi iterative process to calculate x
getf('xbar.txt'); // this function calculates average absolute value
getf('Nextx.txt');// this function calculates a new value of x
[n m] = size(A);   // determine size of matrix A
// check if matrix is square
if n <> m then
        error('Matrix must be square');
        abort;
end;
//initialize variables
x = zeros(n,1);                      //x = [0 0 ... 0]
Itmax = 100.; eps = 0.001;           //max iterations and tolerance
Iter = 1; R = b-A*x; Rave = xbar(R); //first value of residuals
disp(Iter, 'iteration'); disp(Rave,' Average residual:')
while ((Rave > eps) & (Iter < Itmax))    //Loop while no convergence
        x = Nextx(x,R,A)
        R = b-A*x;
        Rave = xbar(R);
        Iter = Iter + 1
        disp(Iter, 'iteration'); disp(Rave,' Average residual:')
end;
x
//end function Jacobi
```

```
function [xb] = xbar(x)
//Calculates average of absolute values of vector x
[n m] = size(x);
suma = 0.0;
for i = 1:n
      suma = suma + abs(x(i,1));
end;
xb = suma/n
//end function xbar


function [x]=Nextx(x,R,A)
//calculates residual average for the system A*x = b
[n m] = size(A);
for i = 1:n
      x(i,1) = x(i,1) + R(i,1)/A(i,i)
end;
x
//end function Nextx
```

As an exercise, within SCILAB enter the following:
-->A = [4 -1 0 0; -1 4 -1 0; 0 -1 4 -1; 0 0 -1 4]; b = [150; 200; 150; 100]:
-->getf('Jacobi.txt')
-->Jacobi(A,b)

A few things to notice in these functions:

1.   Function *Jacobi* loads the functions *xbar.txt* and *Nextx.txt*.
2.   The function *size*, when used with a matrix or vector, requires two components. For that reason, whenever we use it in any of the functions *Jacobi*, *xbar* or *Nextx*, we always use `[n m] = size(…)`. Therefore, n = number of rows, m = number of columns.
3.   To initialize the vector x we use the statement `x = zeros(n,1)`. The general form of the function zeros is *zeros(m,n)*. See also, *help ones*.
4.   The vector x having one column is treated as a matrix. See also the use of vector x in functions *xbar.txt* and *Nextx.txt*.
5.   The function *disp* (display) prints the values in the list of variables, from the last to the first. Thus, the command `disp(iter, 'iteration: ')` prints a line with *'iteration:'* and the next line with the value of *iter*.
6.   A while loop is used in function *Jacobi.txt*, which uses a compound logical expression, namely, `((Rave > eps) & (Iter < Itmax))`. So, as long as the average residual is larger than the tolerance (eps) and the number of iterations is less than the maximum number of iterations allowed (Itmax), the loop statements are repeated.
7.   In function *xbar*, the word *suma* is used to hold a sum. The word *sum* is reserved by SCILAB (try `help sum`) and cannot be redefined as a variable. By the way, *suma* is Spanish for sum.

Matrix applications

In this section we explore some applications of matrices in the physical sciences.

Electric circuits

Consider the simple electrical circuit shown in the figure below.

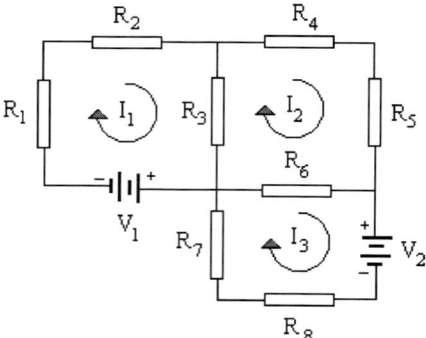

Given the values of the electric resistance, $R_1 = R_3 = R_5 = R_7 = 1.5$ kΩ, $R_2 = R_4 = R_6 = R_8 = 800 \Omega$, and the known steady voltages $V_1 = 12$ V, $V_2 = 24$ V. We are asked to determine the electrical currents I_1, I_2, and I_3, associated with the circulation loops shown in the figure.

The circulation loops shown pre-determine for us a preferred direction in each loop to write Kirchoff law of voltage in a closed loop. Basically, we start at a node in the circuit and move around a given loop subtracting voltages $R \cdot I$ if the current is in the same direction as the loop direction, or adding voltages if the current and the loop directions are opposite. When encountering a voltage source, the voltage from the source is added or subtracted according to the orientation of the voltage source with respect to the loop circulation direction. We stop back at the same node were we started to complete the voltage equation for a given loop.

For the case shown in the figure we can write:

I_1: $-R_1 \cdot I_1 - R_2 \cdot I_1 - R_3 \cdot (I_1 - I_2) - V_1 = 0$
I_2: $-R_4 \cdot I_2 - R_5 \cdot I_2 - R_6 \cdot (I_2 - I_3) - R_3 \cdot (I_2 - I_1) = 0$
I_3: $-V_2 - R_8 \cdot I_3 - R_7 \cdot I_3 - R_6 \cdot I_3 = 0$

Replacing the values of the resistances and voltage sources:

I_1: $-1500 I_1 - 800 I_1 - 1500 (I_1 - I_2) - 12 = 0$
I_2: $-800 I_2 - 1500 I_2 - 800 (I_2 - I_3) - 1500 (I_2 - I_1) = 0$
I_3: $-24 - 800 I_3 - 1500 I_3 - 800 (I_3 - I_2) = 0$

Algebraic manipulation of the equations reduce them to the following system of linear equations:

$$-3800 I_1 + 1500 I_2 = 12$$
$$1500 I_1 - 4600 I_2 + 800 I_3 = 0$$
$$ 800 I_2 - 3100 I_3 = 24$$

This system can be written as a matricial system:

$$\mathbf{A} = \begin{bmatrix} -3800 & 1500 & 0 \\ 1500 & -4600 & 800 \\ 0 & 800 & -3100 \end{bmatrix}, \quad \mathbf{x} = \begin{bmatrix} I_1 \\ I_2 \\ I_3 \end{bmatrix}, \quad \mathbf{b} = \begin{bmatrix} 12 \\ 0 \\ 24 \end{bmatrix}.$$

A solution can be obtained by using left division, an inverse matrix, or function *linsolve*. The three methods are illustrated below:

```
-->A=[-3800,1500,0;1500,-4600,800;0,800,-3100]
 A  =

 ! - 3800.     1500.      0.    !
 !   1500.   - 4600.    800.    !
 !     0.      800.   - 3100.   !

-->b = [12;0;24]
 b  =

 !   12. !
 !    0. !
 !   24. !
```

Using left division:

```
-->x = A\b
 x  =

 ! -  .0042929 !
 ! -  .0028753 !
 ! -  .0084840 !
```

Using the inverse of matrix A:

```
-->x = inv(A)*b
 x  =

 ! -  .0042929 !
 ! -  .0028753 !
 ! -  .0084840 !
```

Using *linsolve*:

```
-->c = -b
 c  =
```

```
!  - 12. !
!    0. !
!  - 24. !

-->x = linsolve(A,c)
 x  =

!  -  .0042929 !
!  -  .0028753 !
!  -  .0084840 !
```

Regardless of the method used to obtain the solution, the final results are:

$I_1 = -0.0042929$ A $= -4.2929$ mA, $I_2 = -0.0028753$ A $= -2.8753$ mA, $I_3 = -0.0084840$ A $= 8.484$ mA.

Structural mechanics

Consider the truss structure shown in the figure below. Horizontal and vertical bars are of length 1.0 m, and diagonal bars 1.4142 m. All acute angles in the truss are $45°$

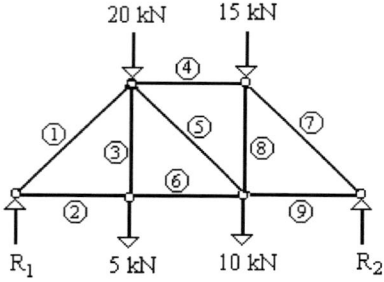

By isolating each node, as shown in the figure below, we can write the following equations for node equilibrium (i.e., $\Sigma Fx = 0, \Sigma Fy = 0$):

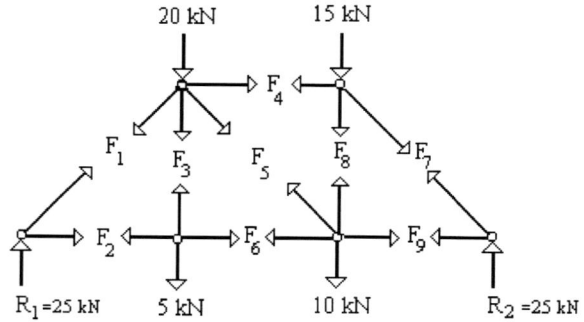

$$F_2 + F_1 \cos 45° = 0,$$
$$25 + F_1 \sin 45° = 0,$$
$$-F_2 + F_6 = 0,$$
$$-5 + F_3 = 0,$$
$$F_4 - F_1 \cos 45° + F_5 \cos 45° = 0,$$
$$-20 - F_3 - F_1 \cos 45° - F_5 \cos 45° = 0,$$
$$-F_4 + F_7 \cos 45° = 0,$$
$$-15 - F_8 - F_7 \cos 45° = 0,$$
$$-F_6 + F_9 - F_5 \cos 45° = 0,$$
$$-10 + F_8 + F_5 \cos 45° = 0,$$
$$-F_9 - F_7 \cos 45° = 0,$$
$$25 + F_7 \cos 45° = 0.$$

With $\sin 45° = \cos 45° = 0.866$, then we have:

$0.866 F_1$	$+ F_2$							$= 0$
$0.866 F_1$								$= -25$
	$-F_2$			$+ F_6$				$= 0$
		F_3						$= 5$
$-0.866 F_1$			$+F_4$	$+0.866 F_5$				$= 0$
$-0.866 F_1$		$-F_3$		$-0.866 F_5$				$= 20$
			$-F_4$		$+ 0.866 F_7$			$= 0$
					$-0.866 F_7$	$- F_8$		$= 15$
				$-0.866 F_5$	$- F_6$		$+ F_9$	$= 0$
				$0.866 F_5$		$+F_8$		$= 10$
					$-0.866 F_7$		$- F_9$	$= 0$
					$0.866 F_7$			$= -25$

We have a total of 12 equations with 9 unknowns. The system is over-determined, so we choose, arbitrarily, the first 9 equations:

$0.866 F_1$	$+ F_2$							$= 0$
$0.866 F_1$								$= -25$
	$-F_2$			$+ F_6$				$= 0$
		F_3						$= 5$
$-0.866 F_1$			$+F_4$	$+0.866 F_5$				$= 0$
$-0.866 F_1$		$-F_3$		$-0.866 F_5$				$= 20$
			$-F_4$		$+ 0.866 F_7$			$= 0$
					$-0.866 F_7$	$- F_8$		$= 15$
				$-0.866 F_5$	$- F_6$		$+ F9$	$= 0$

Writing the system as a matrix equation:

$$\begin{bmatrix} 0.866 & 1 & 0 & 0 & 0 & 0 & 0 & 0 & 0 \\ 0.866 & 0 & 0 & 0 & 0 & 0 & 0 & 0 & 0 \\ 0 & -1 & 0 & 0 & 0 & 1 & 0 & 0 & 0 \\ 0 & 0 & 1 & 0 & 0 & 0 & 0 & 0 & 0 \\ -0.866 & 0 & 0 & 1 & 0.866 & 0 & 0 & 0 & 0 \\ -0.866 & 0 & -1 & 0 & -0.866 & 0 & 0 & 0 & 0 \\ 0 & 0 & 0 & -1 & 0 & 0 & 0.866 & 0 & 0 \\ 0 & 0 & 0 & 0 & 0 & 0 & -0.866 & -1 & 0 \\ 0 & 0 & 0 & 0 & -0.866 & -1 & 0 & 0 & 1 \end{bmatrix} \cdot \begin{bmatrix} F_1 \\ F_2 \\ F_3 \\ F_4 \\ F_5 \\ F_6 \\ F_7 \\ F_8 \\ F_9 \end{bmatrix} = \begin{bmatrix} 0 \\ -25 \\ 0 \\ 5 \\ 0 \\ 20 \\ 0 \\ 15 \\ 0 \end{bmatrix}$$

The coefficient matrix for this problem is a *sparse matrix*. To solve this problem using SCILAB we need to load vectors containing the indices and the values of the non-zero elements of the matrix A, i.e.,

```
-->index =
[1,1;1,2;2,1;3,2;3,6;4,3;5,1;5,4;5,5;6,1;6,3;6,5;7,4;7,7;8,7;8,8;9,5;9,6;9,9];
```

```
-->values = [0.866,1,0.866,-1,1,1,-0.866,1,0.866,-0.866,-1,-0.866,-1,0.866,-0.866,-1,-0.866,-1,1];
```

```
-->dim = [9,9];
```

To check that the dimensions of the matrix *index* and vector *values* are compatible use the function *size*

```
-->size(index), size(values)
 ans =

!   19.    2. !
 ans =

!   1.    19. !
```

Next, we create the matrix of coefficients A as a sparse matrix:

```
-->A = sparse(index,values,dim);
```

The full matrix can be seen by using:

```
-->full(A)
 ans =

!   .866    1.    0.    0.    0.    0.    0.    0.    0. !
```

```
!   .866      0.      0.      0.      0.      0.      0.      0.     0. !
!    0.     - 1.      0.      0.      0.      1.      0.      0.     0. !
!    0.       0.      1.      0.      0.      0.      0.      0.     0. !
! -  .866     0.      0.      1.      .866    0.      0.      0.     0. !
! -  .866     0.    - 1.      0.    - .866    0.      0.      0.     0. !
!    0.       0.      0.    - 1.      0.      0.      .866    0.     0. !
!    0.       0.      0.      0.      0.      0.    - .866  - 1.     0. !
!    0.       0.      0.      0.    - .866  - 1.      0.      0.     1. !
```

Next, we define the right-hand side vector:

```
-->b = full(sparse(indexb,valuesb,dimb));

-->b
 b  =

!    0.  !
!  - 25. !
!    0.  !
!    5.  !
!    0.  !
!   20.  !
!    0.  !
!   15.  !
!    0.  !
```

The solution to the system is:

```
-->x = lusolve(A,b)
 x  =

! - 28.86836 !
!   25.      !
!    5.      !
! - 25.      !
!    0.      !
!   25.      !
! - 28.86836 !
!   10.      !
!   25.      !
```

i.e.,

$$F_1 = -28.87 \text{ kN}, F_2 = 25 \text{ kN}, F_3 = 5 \text{ kN},$$
$$F_4 = -25 \text{ kN}, F_5 = 0 \text{ kN}, F_6 = 25 \text{ kN},$$
$$F_7 = -28.87 \text{ kN}, F_8 = 10 \text{ kN}, F_9 = 25 \text{ kN}.$$

Dimensionless numbers in fluid mechanics

Dimensional analysis is a technique used in fluid mechanics, and other sciences, to reduce the number of variables involved in an experiment by creating *dimensionless numbers* that combine the original set of variables. In order to obtain these dimensionless numbers, we make use of the principle of *dimensional homogeneity*, which basically states that an equation derived from conservation laws and material properties should have the same dimensions on both sides of the equation. For example, the equation for the distance traveled by a projectile dropped from rest at a certain elevation above the ground is given by $d = \frac{1}{2}gt^2$ where $g = 9.806$ m/s^2, is the acceleration of gravity, and t is the time in seconds. The distance d is given in meters. Instead of dealing with units, we refer to three (sometimes more) fundamental dimensions: length (L), time (T), and mass (M). We use brackets to refer to the dimensions of a quantity, thus, $[d] = L$, $g = [LT^{-2}]$, and $t = [T]$. Replacing dimensions in the formula for d we have:

$$[d] = [1/2][g][t]^2 = 1 \cdot LT^{-2} \cdot T^2 = L,$$

as expected. Thus, we say that the equation $d = \frac{1}{2}gt^2$ is dimensionally homogeneous.

Suppose that we have an experiment that involves the following variables (showed with their dimensions attached):

D = a diameter (L)
V = a flow velocity (LT^{-1})
ν = kinematic viscosity of the fluid (L^{2}T^{-1})
ρ = density of the fluid (ML^{-3})
E = bulk density of the fluid (ML^{-1}T^{-2})
σ = surface tension of the fluid (MT^{-2})
Δp = a characteristic pressure drop in the flow (ML^{-1}T^{-2})
g = acceleration of gravity (LT^{-2})

There are m = 8 variables which need n = 3 dimensions to be expressed (i.e., L, T, and M). Buckingham's Π theorem indicates that you can form r = m − n = 8 − 3 = 5 dimensionless parameters. The technique consists in selecting one geometric variable, in this case we have no choice but to select D, the only variable that represents geometry alone; a kinematic variable, V (you can also choose ν), i.e., a variable involving length and time; and, finally, a dynamic variable, say ρ, i.e., a variable involving length, time, and mass. These three variables, D, V and ρ, become repeating variables, i.e., variables that will participate in each of the dimensionless parameters to be formed. Each dimensionless parameter, Π number, is formed by multiplying the repeating variables raised to a certain unknown power and multiplying one of the remaining variables. For example, we can form for this case the following Π parameters:

$$\Pi_1 = \rho^x \cdot D^y \cdot V^z \cdot \nu,$$
$$\Pi_2 = \rho^x \cdot D^y \cdot V^z \cdot E,$$
$$\Pi_3 = \rho^x \cdot D^y \cdot V^z \cdot \sigma,$$
$$\Pi_4 = \rho^x \cdot D^y \cdot V^z \cdot \Delta p,$$
$$\Pi_5 = \rho^x \cdot D^y \cdot V^z \cdot g.$$

Since the Π numbers are dimensionless, we can write $[\Pi_i] = L^0 \cdot T^0 \cdot M^0$, for i = 1, 2, 3, 4, 5. Replacing the dimensions of the variables involved in each dimensionless parameters we can write, for example, for Π_1:

$$L^0 \cdot T^0 \cdot M^0 = (ML^{-3})^x \cdot (L)^y \cdot (LT^{-1})^z \cdot (L^2 T^{-1}) = (L)^{-3x+y+z+2} (T)^{-z-1} \cdot (M)^x,$$

From which we get the following equations:

$$-3x+y+z+2 = 0$$
$$-z - 1 = 0$$
$$x = 0$$

Or,

$$\begin{bmatrix} -3 & 1 & 1 \\ 0 & 0 & -1 \\ 1 & 0 & 0 \end{bmatrix} \cdot \begin{bmatrix} x \\ y \\ z \end{bmatrix} = \begin{bmatrix} -2 \\ 1 \\ 0 \end{bmatrix}$$

If we replace the dimensions of the non-repeating variables in the remaining π parameters, we can expand the matrix equation shown above to read:

$$\begin{bmatrix} -3 & 1 & 1 \\ 0 & 0 & -1 \\ 1 & 0 & 0 \end{bmatrix} \cdot \begin{bmatrix} x \\ y \\ z \end{bmatrix} = \begin{bmatrix} -2 & 1 & 0 & 1 & -1 \\ 1 & 2 & 2 & 2 & 2 \\ 0 & -1 & -1 & -1 & 0 \end{bmatrix}$$

So, the independent vector b has become a matrix B, and we can write the matrix equation A·X = B. The columns of B are the negatives of the exponents of the dimensions, L, T, and M, in that order, of each of the non-repeating variables as shown in the π parameters that we set up.

To solve for the variables x,y,z for each parameter using SCILAB, we propose using function *gausselimd*:

```
-->A = [-3,1,1;0,0,-1;1,0,0]
 A   =

! - 3.    1.    1. !
!   0.    0.  - 1. !
!   1.    0.    0. !

-->B = [-2,1,0,1,-1;1,2,2,2,2;0,-1,-1,-1,0]
 B   =

! - 2.    1.    0.    1.  - 1. !
!   1.    2.    2.    2.    2. !
!   0.  - 1.  - 1.  - 1.    0. !

-->getf('gausselimd')

-->[x,detA]=gausselimd(A,B)
 detA  =

    1.
 x   =
```

```
!   0.   - 1.   - 1.   - 1.    0. !
! - 1.     0.   - 1.     0.    1. !
! - 1.   - 2.   - 2.   - 2.  - 2. !
```

The result is the matrix

$$X = \begin{pmatrix} 0 & -1 & -1 & -1 & 0 \\ -1 & 0 & -1 & 0 & 1 \\ -1 & -2 & -2 & -2 & -2 \end{pmatrix},$$

each column representing the values of x,y,z, for the repeating variables in each of the dimensionless parameters, thus we have:

$$\Pi_1 = \rho^0 \cdot D^{-1} \cdot V^1 \cdot v = v/DV,$$
$$\Pi_2 = \rho^{-1} \cdot D^0 \cdot V^2 \cdot E = E/\rho V^2,$$
$$\Pi_3 = \rho^{-1} \cdot D^{-1} \cdot V^2 \cdot \sigma = \sigma/\rho DV^2$$
$$\Pi_4 = \rho^{-1} \cdot D^0 \cdot V^2 \cdot \Delta p = \Delta p/\rho V^2,$$
$$\Pi_5 = \rho^0 \cdot D^1 \cdot V^2 \cdot g = gD/V^2.$$

Note: if you don't want to use function *gausselimd* you can use, for example, left-division:
```
-->A\B
 ans    =

!   0.   - 1.   - 1.   - 1.    0. !
! - 1.     0.   - 1.     0.    1. !
! - 1.   - 2.   - 2.   - 2.  - 2. !
```

Or, a Gauss-Jordan elimination with function *rref:*
```
-->A_aug = [A B]
 A_aug   =

! - 3.    1.     1.   - 2.    1.     0.    1.  - 1. !
!   0.    0.   - 1.     1.    2.     2.    2.    2. !
!   1.    0.     0.     0.  - 1.   - 1.  - 1.    0. !

-->rref(A_aug)
 ans    =

!   1.    0.     0.     0.  - 1.   - 1.  - 1.    0. !
!   0.    1.     0.   - 1.    0.   - 1.    0.    1. !
!   0.    0.     1.   - 1.  - 2.   - 2.  - 2.  - 2. !
```

Stress at a point in a solid in equilibrium

Consider a solid body in equilibrium under the action of a system of forces and moments, as illustrated in the figure below. If we were to make an imaginary cut through the solid body, so that we can separate it into two parts at section S.

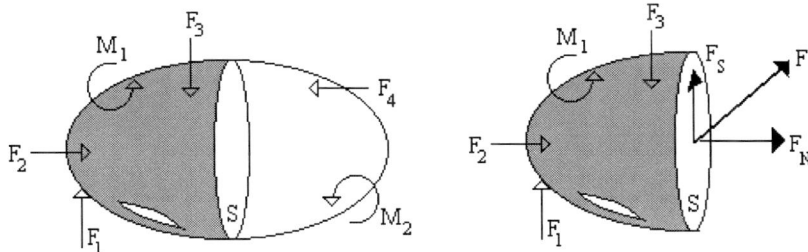

The effect of the part that we remove to the right of the cut surface S is replaced by the force F, which in turn can be decomposed into a normal component F_N, and a shear or tangential component F_S.

Suppose now that we isolate a small particle off this solid body, and we do it by cutting the body with four planes so that we can draw the particle as shown in the left-hand side of the figure below.

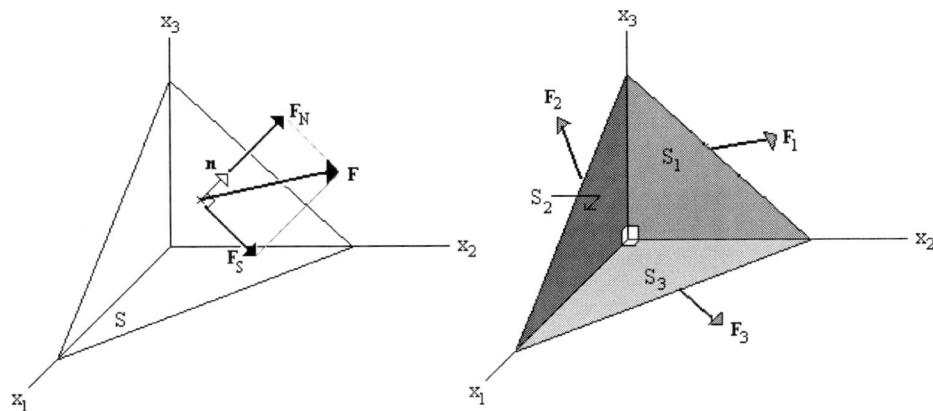

Three of the planes are chose to be perpendicular to each other so that they help us identify a Cartesian coordinate system (x_1, x_2, x_3) as shown above. The surface S, limiting the particle from above, has a normal unit vector $n = [\cos\alpha_1, \cos\alpha_2, \cos\alpha_3]$, where $\cos\alpha_1$, $\cos\alpha_2$, and $\cos\alpha_3$ are the direction cosines of n. The other three surfaces limiting the particle are S_1, S_2, and S_3, where the sub-index indicates the axis that is normal to the surface. The effect of the solid body on this particle is represented by the forces, F_1, F_2, and F_3, acting, respectively, upon surfaces S, S_1, S_2, and S_3. Let the areas corresponding to each surface S, S_1, S_2, and S_3 be given by A, A_1, A_2, and A_3. It is possible to show, from the geometry of the figure, that

$$A_1 = A \cdot \cos \alpha_1, \; A_2 = A \cdot \cos \alpha_2, \text{ and } A_3 = A \cdot \cos \alpha_3.$$

The force F on surface S can be decomposed into a normal component,

$$F_N = F_N \cdot n = F_N \cdot [\cos \alpha_1, \cos \alpha_2, \cos \alpha_3] = F_N \cdot (\cos \alpha_1 \cdot e_1 + \cos \alpha_2 \cdot e_2 + \cos \alpha_3 \cdot e_3) = F_N \cdot \cos \alpha_j \cdot e_j, \; (*)$$

(*) using Einstein's repeated index convention.

and a shear component,

$$F_S = F - F_N,$$

as shown in the figure above. The vectors are the unit vectors corresponding to the three coordinate directions.

The forces on surfaces S_1, S_2, and S_3 can be written in terms of the stress components σ_{ij}, shown in the figure below, as

$$F_i = [-\sigma_{i1}, -\sigma_{i2}, -\sigma_{i3}] \cdot A_i = (-\sigma_{i1} \cdot e_1 - \sigma_{i2} \cdot e_2 - \sigma_{i3} \cdot e_3) \cdot A_i = (-\sigma_{i1} \cdot e_1 - \sigma_{i2} \cdot e_2 - \sigma_{i3} \cdot e_3) \cdot A \cdot \cos \alpha_i \; (i = 1,2,3).$$

Using Einstein's repeated index convention we can write

$$F_i = [-\sigma_{i1}, -\sigma_{i2}, -\sigma_{i3}] \cdot A_i = -\sigma_{ij} \cdot e_j \cdot A_i = -\sigma_{ij} \cdot e_j \cdot A \cdot \cos \alpha_i \; (i = 1,2,3).$$

The sub-indices identifying each stress components are chosen so that the first sub-index represents the sub-index of the axis normal to the surface of interest, and the second represents the direction along which the stress acts.

Stresses with the same sub-index σ_{ii} ($i = 1,2,3$) act normal to the appropriate surface and are known as *normal stresses*. The other two components on each of the surfaces S_1, S_2, and S_3, are known as *shear stresses*, i.e., σ_{ij}, $i \neq j$. The direction of action as shown in the figure below is the conventional way to represent the stresses, namely, the stresses are positive when acting in the negative coordinate directions, so that the resulting forces have a negative sign, as shown in the equation above.

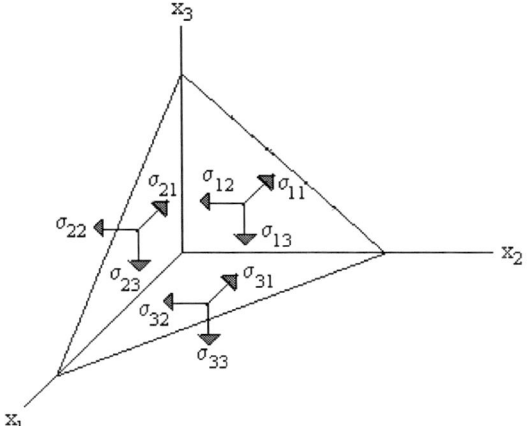

The stress components illustrated in the figure above can be written as a matrix known as the *stress tensor*,

$$T = \begin{bmatrix} \sigma_{11} & \sigma_{12} & \sigma_{13} \\ \sigma_{21} & \sigma_{22} & \sigma_{23} \\ \sigma_{31} & \sigma_{32} & \sigma_{33} \end{bmatrix}.$$

The set up of the Cartesian coordinate system and the stresses in the particle under consideration can be used to define the stress condition at a point in the limit when the dimensions of the particle tend to zero. Under such conditions you can prove that the stress tensor is symmetric, i.e., $\sigma_{ij} = \sigma_{ji}$. Therefore, to define completely the state of stress at a point we need only to know the three normal stresses and three of the shear stresses.

For the equilibrium of force on the particle we can write

$$F + \Sigma F_i = F + \Sigma(-\sigma_{ij} \cdot e_j \cdot A \cos \alpha_i) = 0, \text{ or } F = \sigma_{ij} \cdot e_j \cdot A \cos \alpha_i$$

[using Einstein's convention, with both i and j repeated]

If we let

$$F = \sigma \cdot A,$$

where s is the stress vector on surface S, and replace this value in the previous equation we get

$$\sigma = \sigma_{ij} \cdot \cos \alpha_i \cdot e_j = \cos \alpha_i \cdot e_j \cdot \sigma_{ij} = n \cdot T$$

To find the magnitude of the normal component of the stress vector, i.e., the projection of the stress σ along the unit normal vector n, we use

$$\sigma_n = \sigma \bullet n / |n| = \sigma \bullet n = (\sigma_{ij} \cdot \cos\alpha_i \cdot e_j) \bullet (\cos\alpha_k \cdot e_k) = \sigma_{ij} \cdot \cos\alpha_i \cdot \cos\alpha_k \cdot (e_j \bullet e_k).$$

We can prove that for the unit vectors in the Cartesian coordinate system,

$$e_j \bullet e_k = \delta_{jk},$$

where δ_{jk} is Dirac's delta function. Thus, the normal component of the stress on surface S is

$$\sigma_n = \sigma_{ij} \cdot \cos\alpha_i \cdot \cos\alpha_k \cdot \delta_{jk}$$

Since the product indicated in this expression is zero if $j \neq k$, then the only terms surviving are those for which $j = k$, i.e.,

$$\sigma_n = \sigma_{ij} \cdot \cos\alpha_i \cdot \cos\alpha_j = \cos\alpha_j \cdot \sigma_{ij} \cdot \cos\alpha_i.$$

You can prove that this latter result can be written in vector and matrix notation as the quadratic form

$$\sigma_n = n \cdot T \cdot n^T,$$

where

$$n = \cos\alpha_j \cdot e_j.$$

Thus, the normal stress magnitude can be written as a quadratic form for any normal unit vector $n = n_j \cdot e_j$, written as a row vectors, with $n_j = \cos\alpha_j$, $j = 1, 2, 3$. Also, the normal stress as a vector will be written as

$$\sigma_n = \sigma_n \cdot n = (n \cdot T \cdot n^T) \cdot n$$

The normal force is given by

$$F_N = \sigma_n \cdot A = (\sigma_n \cdot A) \cdot n.$$

The shear force can be written in terms of shear stress on surface $F_S = F - F_N = \sigma_S A$, so that

$$\sigma_S = \sigma - \sigma_n.$$

Example:

Let the stress at a point be given by

$$T = \begin{bmatrix} 25 & -10 & 20 \\ -10 & 30 & 15 \\ 20 & 15 & 40 \end{bmatrix} \cdot Pa$$

Determine the total stress $\vec{\sigma}$, the normal stress σ_n, and shear stress σ_s if the surface S has a normal unit vector n = [0.5 0.25 0.8292]. What are the total force F, the normal force F_n, and the shear force F_s, if the surface S has an area of 0.00001 m^2

Solution:

To calculate the total stress we use

$$\vec{\sigma} = n \cdot T \cdot \vec{e} = \begin{bmatrix} 25 & -10 & 20 \\ -10 & 30 & 15 \\ 20 & 15 & 40 \end{bmatrix} \cdot \begin{bmatrix} 0.5 \\ 0.25 \\ 0.8292 \end{bmatrix}$$

This result can be obtained by using SCILAB as follows:

```
-->T = [25,-10,20;-10,30,15;20,15,40], n = [0.5,0.25,0.829]
 T  =

!   25.   - 10.    20. !
! - 10.     30.    15. !
!   20.     15.    40. !
 n  =

!    .5      .25    .829 !

-->sigma = T*n'
 sigma  =

!   26.58  !
!   14.935 !
!   46.91  !
```

To calculate the normal stress, use:

$$\vec{\sigma} = n \cdot T \cdot \vec{e} = \begin{bmatrix} 25 & -10 & 20 \\ -10 & 30 & 15 \\ 20 & 15 & 40 \end{bmatrix} \cdot \begin{bmatrix} 0.5 \\ 0.25 \\ 0.8292 \end{bmatrix}$$

Using SCILAB:

```
-->sigma_n = n*T*n'
 sigma_n  =

    55.91214
```

The result is $\boxed{\sigma_n = 55.93\ Pa}$

The shear stress is given by

$$\sigma_S = \sigma - \sigma_n,$$

or, using SCILAB:

```
-->sigma_s = sigma - sigma_n*n'
 sigma_s   =

!  - 1.37607   !
!     .956965  !
!     .5588359 !
```

The forces can be calculated by multiplying the stresses times the area of the surface S, i.e., $F = \sigma \cdot A$, $F_n = \sigma_n \cdot A$, and $F_t = \sigma_t \cdot A$. Using Maple, the forces are calculated as:

```
-->A = 0.00001
 A   =

       .00001

-->Fn = sigma_n*n'*A
 Fn   =

!     .0002796 !
!     .0001398 !
!     .0004635 !

-->Ft = sigma_s*A
 Ft   =

!  -  .0000138 !
!     .0000096 !
!     .0000056 !

-->F = sigma*A
 F   =

!     .0002658 !
!     .0001494 !
!     .0004691 !
```

In paper, these forces are written as

$$F_n = (2.79\mathbf{i} + 1.39\mathbf{j} + 4.63\mathbf{k}) \times 10^{-4} \text{ N},$$
$$F_s = (-1.38\mathbf{i} + 0.96\mathbf{j} + 0.54\mathbf{k}) \times 10^{-5} \text{ N},$$
$$F = (2.66\mathbf{i} + 1.49\mathbf{j} + 4.69\mathbf{k}) \times 10^{-4} \text{ N}.$$

Principal stresses at a point

Given the stress tensor T representing the state of stress at a point P in a Cartesian coordinate system (x_1, x_2, x_3), suppose that you want to find the normal vector, or vectors, for which the stress is only in the normal direction. In other words, we are trying to find $\mathbf{n}$ and σ_n such that

$$T \cdot n = \sigma_n \cdot n.$$

This equation is the eigenvalue equation for the matrix T with eigenvalues σ_n and eigenvectors n.

Recall that this equation can be written also as

$$(T - \sigma_n \cdot I) \cdot n = 0,$$

which has non-trivial solution if

$$det(T - \sigma_n \cdot I) = 0.$$

For the previous example, we can write

$$\det(\mathbf{T} - \sigma_n \cdot \mathbf{I}) = \begin{vmatrix} 25 - \sigma_n & -10 & 20 \\ -10 & 30 - \sigma_n & 15 \\ 20 & 15 & 40 - \sigma_n \end{vmatrix} = 0.$$

To obtain the eigenvalues and eigenvectors of T we use function *eigenvectors* in SCILAB:

```
-->getf('eigenvectors')
-->[x,sigm] = eigenvectors(T)
 sigm  =

!   1.1203785    37.800525    56.079096 !
 x =

! - .6673642  - .6009826    .4398237 !
! - .5119885    .7991229    .3150721 !
!   .5408260    .0149168    .8410022 !
```

In paper we would write:

$$n_1 = [-0.667\ -0.512\ 0.541], (\sigma_n)_1 = 1.12,$$
$$n_2 = [-0.601\ 0.800\ 0.015], (\sigma_n)_2 = 37.80,$$
$$n_3 = [0.440\ 0.315\ 0.841], (\sigma_n)_3 = 56.08.$$

The three normal stresses found are known as the *principal stresses* at the point. The eigenvalues represent the normal vectors to the surfaces where those principal stresses act. These directions are known as the *principal axes*.

Multiple linear fitting

Consider a data set of the form

x_1	x_2	x_3	...	x_n	y
x_{11}	x_{21}	x_{31}	...	x_{n1}	y_1
x_{12}	x_{22}	x_{32}	...	x_{n2}	y_2
x_{13}	x_{32}	x_{33}	...	x_{n3}	y_3
.	.	.		.	.
.	.	.		.	.
$x_{1,m-1}$	$x_{2,m-1}$	$x_{3,m-1}$	...	$x_{n,m-1}$	y_{m-1}
$x_{1,m}$	$x_{2,m}$	$x_{3,m}$	...	$x_{n,m}$	y_m

Suppose that we search for a data fitting of the form

$$y = b_0 + b_1 \cdot x_1 + b_2 \cdot x_2 + b_3 \cdot x_3 + ... + b_n \cdot x_n.$$

You can obtain the least-square approximation to the values of the coefficients

$$b = [b_0 \; b_1 \; b_2 \; b_3 ... b_n],$$

by putting together the matrix X

$$\begin{bmatrix} 1 & x_{11} & x_{21} & x_{31} & ... & x_{n1} \\ 1 & x_{12} & x_{22} & x_{32} & ... & x_{n2} \\ 1 & x_{13} & x_{32} & x_{33} & ... & x_{n3} \\ . & . & . & . & & . \\ . & . & . & . & & . \\ 1 & x_{1,m} & x_{2,m} & x_{3,m} & ... & x_{n,m} \end{bmatrix}$$

Then, the vector of coefficients is obtained from

$$b = (X^T \cdot X)^{-1} \cdot X^T \cdot y,$$

where y is the vector

$$y = [y_1 \; y_2 \; ... \; y_m]^T.$$

For _example_, use the following data to obtain the multiple linear fitting

$$y = b_0 + b_1 \cdot x_1 + b_2 \cdot x_2 + b_3 \cdot x_3,$$

x_1	x_2	x_3	y
1.20	3.10	2.00	5.70
2.50	3.10	2.50	8.20
3.50	4.50	2.50	5.00
4.00	4.50	3.00	8.20
6.00	5.00	3.50	9.50

With SCILAB you can proceed as follows:

First, enter the vectors x_1, x_2, x_3, and y, as row vectors:

```
-->x1 = [1.2,2.5,3.5,4.0,6.0]
 x1  =

!   1.2    2.5    3.5    4.    6. !

-->x2 = [3.1,3.1,4.5,4.5,5.0]
 x2  =

!   3.1    3.1    4.5    4.5    5. !

-->x3 = [2.0,2.5,2.5,3.0,3.5]
 x3  =

!   2.    2.5    2.5    3.    3.5 !

-->y = [5.7,8.2,5.0,8.2,9.5]
 y  =

!   5.7    8.2    5.    8.2    9.5 !
```

Next, we form matrix X and replace y by its transpose:

```
-->X = [ones(5,1) x1' x2' x3']
 X  =

!   1.    1.2    3.1    2.  !
!   1.    2.5    3.1    2.5 !
!   1.    3.5    4.5    2.5 !
!   1.    4.     4.5    3.  !
!   1.    6.     5.     3.5 !
```

The vector of coefficients for the multiple linear equation is calculated as:

```
-->b =inv(X'*X)*X'*y
 b  =

! - 2.1649851 !
! -  .7144632 !
! - 1.7850398 !
!   7.0941849 !
```

Thus, the multiple-linear regression equation is:

$$\hat{y} = -2.1649851 - 0.7144682 x_2 + 1.7850398 x_2 + 7.0941849 x_3.$$

This function can be used to evaluate y for values of x given as $[x_2,x_3]$. For example, for $[x_1,x_2,x_3] = [3,4,2]$, construct a vector xx = [1,3,4,2], and multiply xx times b, to obtain y(xx):

```
-->xx = [1,3,4,2]
 xx =

!  1.    3.    4.    2. !

-->xx*b
 ans =

    2.739836
```

The fitted values of y corresponding to the values of x_1, x_2, and x_3 from the table are obtained from y = X·b:

```
-->X*b
 ans =

!    5.6324056 !
!    8.2506958 !
!    5.0371769 !
!    8.2270378 !
!    9.4526839 !
```

Compare these fitted values with the original data as shown in the table below:

x_1	x_2	x_3	y	y-fitted
1.20	3.10	2.00	5.70	5.63
2.50	3.10	2.50	8.20	8.25
3.50	4.50	2.50	5.00	5.04
4.00	4.50	3.00	8.20	8.23
6.00	5.00	3.50	9.50	9.45

Polynomial fitting

Consider the x-y data set

x	y
x_1	y_1
x_2	y_2
x_3	y_3
.	.
.	.
x_{n-1}	y_{n-1}
x_n	y_n

Suppose that we want to fit a polynomial or order p to this data set. In other words, we seek a fitting of the form

$$y = b_0 + b_1 \cdot x + b_2 \cdot x^2 + b_3 \cdot x^3 + \ldots + b_p \cdot x^p.$$

You can obtain the least-square approximation to the values of the coefficients

$$b = [b_0 \quad b_1 \quad b_2 \quad b_3 \ldots b_p],$$

by putting together the matrix X

$$\begin{bmatrix} 1 & x_1 & x_1^2 & x_1^3 & \ldots & x_1^{p-2} & x_1^{p-1} \\ 1 & x_2 & x_2^2 & x_2^3 & \ldots & x_2^{p-2} & x_2^{p-1} \\ 1 & x_3 & x_3^2 & x_3^3 & \ldots & x_3^{p-2} & x_3^{p-1} \\ \cdot & \cdot & \cdot & \cdot & & \cdot & \cdot \\ \cdot & \cdot & \cdot & \cdot & & \cdot & \cdot \\ 1 & x_n & x_n^2 & x_n^3 & \ldots & x_n^{p-2} & x_n^{p-1} \end{bmatrix}$$

Then, the vector of coefficients is obtained from $b = (X^T \cdot X)^{-1} \cdot X^T \cdot y$, where y is the vector $y = [y_1 \; y_2 \ldots y_n]^T$.

Earlier on, in this chapter, we defined the Vandermonde matrix corresponding to a vector $x = [x_1 \; x_2 \ldots x_n]$ as

$$\begin{bmatrix} 1 & x_1 & x_1^2 & x_1^3 & \ldots & x_1^{n-1} \\ 1 & x_2 & x_2^2 & x_2^3 & \ldots & x_2^{n-1} \\ 1 & x_3 & x_3^2 & x_3^3 & \ldots & x_3^{n-1} \\ \cdot & \cdot & \cdot & \cdot & & \cdot \\ \cdot & \cdot & \cdot & \cdot & & \cdot \\ 1 & x_n & x_n^2 & x_n^3 & \ldots & x_n^{n-1} \end{bmatrix}$$

Notice that this matrix is similar to the matrix X of interest to the polynomial fitting, but having only n, rather than $(p+1)$ columns.

We can take advantage of the VANDERMONDE function to create the matrix X if we observe the following rules:

If $p = n-1$, $X = V_n$.
If $p < n-1$, then we need to remove columns $p+2, \ldots, n-1, n$ from matrix V_n to form matrix X.
If $p > n-1$, then we need to add columns $n+1, \ldots, p-1, p+1$, to matrix V_n to form matrix X.

After X is ready, and having the vector y available, the calculation of the coefficient vector b is the same as in multiple linear fitting (the previous matrix application).

Because we can fit a polynomial of any degree tour data, we need to be able to evaluate the fitting by checking on a couple of parameters, namely, the sum of squared errors (SSE) and the correlation coefficient, r. These parameters are defined as follows:

Given the vectors x and y of data to be fit to the polynomial equation, we form the matrix X and use it to calculate a vector of polynomial coefficients b. We can calculate a *vector of fitted data*, y', by using

$$y' = X \cdot b.$$

An *error vector* is calculated by

$$e = y - y'.$$

The *sum of square errors* is equal to the square of the magnitude of the error vector, i.e.,

$$SSE = |e|^2 = e \cdot e = \Sigma\, e_i^2 = \Sigma\, (y_i - y'_i)^2.$$

To calculate the correlation coefficient we need to calculate first what is known as the *sum of squared totals*, SST, defined as

$$SST = \Sigma\, (y_i - \bar{y})^2,$$

where $\bar{y}$ is the *mean value* of the original y values, i.e.,

$$\bar{y} = (\Sigma y_i)/n.$$

In terms of SSE and SST, the *correlation coefficient* is defined by

$$r = \sqrt{1 - \frac{SSE}{SST}}.$$

This value is constrained to the range $-1 < r < 1$. The closer r is to +1 or –1, the better the data fitting.

The following function, *polyfit*, takes as input the vectors x and y and the polynomial order p and returns the *coefficients* of the polynomial fitting (vector b), the sum of square errors (SSE), and the correlation coefficient (r):

```
function [SSE,r,b] = polyfit(xx,yy,p)

//Calculates the polynomial fitting
//y^ = b(1) + b(2)*x + b(3)*x^2 + ... + b(p)*x^p
//given data sets xx, yy, and the polynomial
//degree p.
//Vectors xx and yy are row vectors.

[n m] = size(xx');

getf('vandermonde');

V = vandermonde(xx);    //Get Vandermonde matrix for xx

//Get matrix X for solution
if p == n-1 then
    X = V;
```

```
elseif p<n-1 then
   X = V(1:n,1:p+1);
else
  X = V;
  for k = n+1:p+1
      X = [X xx'^k]
  end
end;

//Calculating coefficients b, SSE, and r
b=inv(X'*X)*X'*yy';
yfit = X*b;
err = yy'-yfit;
SSE = err'*err;
ybar = sum(yy)/n;
ybarv = ybar*ones(n,1);
SST = sum((yy'-ybarv)^2);
r = sqrt(1-SSE/SST);

//end function
```

As an *example*, use the following data to obtain a polynomial fitting with p = 2, 3, 4, 5, 6.

x	y
2.30	179.72
3.20	562.30
4.50	1969.11
1.65	65.87
9.32	31220.89
1.18	32.81
6.24	6731.48
3.45	737.41
9.89	39248.46
1.22	33.45

First, we enter:

```
--> x =[2.30,3.20,4.50,1.65,9.32,1.18,6.24,3.45,9.89,1.22];
-->
y=[179.72,562.30,1969.11,65.87,31220.89,32.81,6731.48,737.41,39248.46,33.45];
```

To fit the data to polynomials of order p = 2, 3, 4, 5, 6, 7, and 8 we use the following calls to function *polyfit*.

```
-->getf('polyfit')

-->[SSE,r,b] = polyfit(x,y,2)
 b  =

!   4527.7303 !
! - 3958.5178 !
!   742.23219 !
 r  =

     .9971908
 SSE   =
```

```
     10731140.

-->[SSE,r,b] = polyfit(x,y,3)
 b  =

!  - 998.0541  !
!    1303.2053 !
!  - 505.27432 !
!    79.229744 !
 r  =

      .9999768
 SSE  =

    88619.368

-->[SSE,r,b] = polyfit(x,y,4)
 b  =

!    20.917344 !
!  - 2.6108313 !
!  - 1.5247295 !
!    6.0491773 !
!    3.5068553 !
 r  =

    1.
 SSE  =

       7.4827578

-->[SSE,r,b] = polyfit(x,y,5)
 b  =

!    19.083718 !
!     .1745033 !
!  - 2.9383508 !
!    6.3611564 !
!    3.475986  !
!     .0011220 !
 r  =

    1.
 SSE  =

       7.4140764

-->[SSE,r,b] = polyfit(x,y,6)
 b  =

!  - 16.807588 !
!    67.398517 !
!  - 48.814654 !
!    21.163051 !
!    1.0603971 !
!     .1930681 !
!  -  .0058903 !
 r  =
```

```
         1.
   SSE   =

      3.8884213

-->[SSE,r,b] = polyfit(x,y,7)
 warning
 matrix is close to singular or badly scaled.
 results may be inaccurate. rcond =    1.1558E-19

   b   =

 !    117.79067 !
 !  - 237.32895 !
 !    218.31856 !
 !  - 96.918027 !
 !    29.689084 !
 !  - 3.6422545 !
 !      .25902    !
 !  -  .0073389 !
   r   =

         1.
   SSE   =

      1.2829472

-->[SSE,r,b] = polyfit(x,y,8)
 warning
 matrix is close to singular or badly scaled.
 results may be inaccurate. rcond =    1.7245E-23

   b   =

 !    68.081558 !
 !  - 100.44092 !
 !    65.29768  !
 !  - 6.3024667 !
 !  - 1.3844292 !
 !    2.6919754 !
 !  -  .4920537 !
 !     .0401628 !
 !  -  .0012344 !
   r   =

        .9999909
   SSE   =

      34695.662
```

Selecting the best fitting

The following table summarizes the values of r and SSE found for the different polynomial orders:

p	r	SSE
2	0.9971908	10731140
3	0.9999768	88619.37
4	1	7.482758
5	1	7.414076
6	1	3.888421
7	1	1.282947
8	0.9999909	34695.66

While the correlation coefficient is very close to 1.0 for all values of p, the values of SSE vary widely. The smallest value of SSE corresponds to p = 7. However, a warning is reported for values of p = 7 and 8, indicating that the results may be inaccurate. Thus, we eliminate from the analysis values for p = 7 and 8.

Discarding those values, the best fitting in terms of the minimum value of SSE is p = 6, however, there is very little difference in the values of SSE for values of p = 4, 5, or 6 (at least when compared to those values for p = 2, 3, or 8). Thus, any of the polynomial degrees p = 4, 5, or 6, will produce a good fitting of the original data.

To visualize the original data and the fitted data, we can use the following function *plotpoly*, which calls on function *polyfit*. Function *plotpoly* requires the user to provide the (row) vectors x and y, as well as the polynomial degree *p*. During execution, *plotpoly* requests from the user the number of the graphics window where the plot will be produced. The function returns the plot of the original data points and the polynomial fitting. A listing of the function follows:

```
function plotpoly(xx,yy,p)

//Plots original data and polynomial fitting
//for degree p

[m n] = size(xx);
xmin = min(xx); xmax = max(xx);
xs = [xmin:(xmax-xmin)/100:xmax];
[mm nn] = size(xs);

getf('polyfit');
[SSE,r,b] = polyfit(xx,yy,p);


XX = ones(1,nn);
for j = 1:p
    XX = [XX;xs^j];
end;

yfit = b'*XX;
ymin = min(yfit); ymax = max(yfit);

nwindow = input('Enter the graphic window number:');
xset('window',nwindow);
xset('mark',-9,3);

//plot2d(xs,yfit);
//plot2d(xx,yy,-9);
```

```
plot2d(xx',yy',-9,'010','x',[xmin ymin xmax ymax])
plot2d(xs',yfit',1,'011','x',[xmin ymin xmax ymax])

//end function
```

Calling the function for p = 5, for example, produces the following:

```
-->getf('plotpoly')

-->plotpoly(x,y,5)

 Enter the graphic window number:
-->   2
```

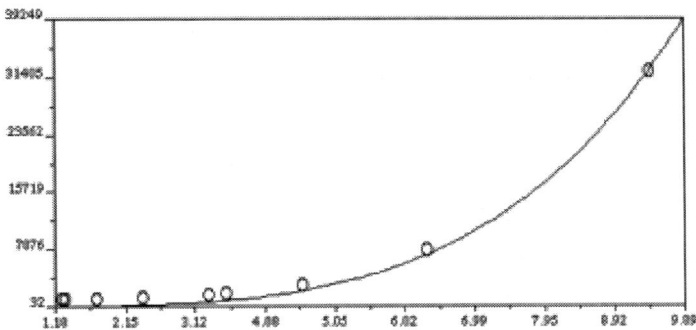

Exercises

[1]. Using *SCILAB* *rand* function to generate a matrix A_{2x2} (`-->A = rand(2,2)`) and a matrix B_{2x2} (`-->B = rand(2,2)`). Then, calculate the following:

(a) A^T (b) A^{-1} (c) B^T (d) B^{-1} (e) $A+B$ (f) $A-B$
(g) $2A$ (h) $-5B$ (i) $2A-5B$ (j) $A^T - B^T$ (k) $3A^{-1}+5B^T$ (l) $A \cdot B$
(m) $B \cdot A$ (n) $A^{-1} \cdot A$ (o) $A^{-1} \cdot A^T$ (p) $B^{-1} \cdot A$ (q) $A^{-1} \cdot B^T$ (r) $A \cdot B \cdot B^T$
(s) $B^T \cdot B$ (t) $B^T \cdot B + A^{-1} \cdot A^T$ (u) $A^{-1} \cdot A^T \cdot B^T$ (v) norm(A,2)   (w) det(A)   (x) trace(A)
(y) rank(B)   (z) cond(A)

[2]. Using *SCILAB rand* function generate a matrix A_{3x3} and a matrix B_{3x3}. Then, calculate the following:

(a) A^T (b) A^{-1} (c) B^T (d) B^{-1} (e) $A+B$ (f) $A-B$
(g) $2A$ (h) $-5B$ (i) $2A-5B$ (j) $A^T - B^T$ (k) $3A^{-1}+5B^T$ (l) $A \cdot B$
(m) $B \cdot A$ (n) $A^{-1} \cdot A$ (o) $A^{-1} \cdot A^T$ (p) $B^{-1} \cdot A$ (q) $A^{-1} \cdot B^T$ (r) $A \cdot B \cdot B^T$
(s) $B^T \cdot B$ (t) $B^T \cdot B + A^{-1} \cdot A^T$ (u) $A^{-1} \cdot A^T \cdot B^T$ (v) norm(A,2)   (w) det(A)   (x) trace(A)
(y) rank(B)   (z) cond(A)

[3]. Using *SCILAB rand* function generate a matrix $A_{3\times 2}$ and a matrix $B_{3\times 2}$. Then, if possible, calculate the following:

(a) A^T (b) A^{-1} (c) B^T (d) B^{-1} (e) $A+B$ (f) $A-B$
(g) $2A$ (h) $-5B$ (i) $2A-5B$ (j) $A^T - B^T$ (k) $3A^{-1}+5B^T$ (l) $A \cdot B$
(m) $B \cdot A$ (n) $A^{-1} \cdot A$ (o) $A^{-1} \cdot A^T$ (p) $B^{-1} \cdot A$ (q) $A^{-1} \cdot B^T$ (r) $A \cdot B \cdot B^T$
(s) $B^T \cdot B$ (t) $B^T \cdot B + A^{-1} \cdot A^T$ (u) $A^{-1} \cdot A^T \cdot B^T$ (v) norm(A,2) (w) norm(A_F) (x) rank(A)

[4]. Using *SCILAB rand* function generate a matrix $A_{3\times 2}$ and a matrix $B_{2\times 3}$. Then, if possible, calculate the following:

(a) A^T (b) A^{-1} (c) B^T (d) B^{-1} (e) $A+B$ (f) $A-B$
(g) $2A$ (h) $-5B$ (i) $2A-5B$ (j) $A^T - B^T$ (k) $3A^{-1}+5B^T$ (l) $A \cdot B$
(m) $B \cdot A$ (n) $A^{-1} \cdot A$ (o) $A^{-1} \cdot A^T$ (p) $B^{-1} \cdot A$ (q) $A^{-1} \cdot B^T$ (r) $A \cdot B \cdot B^T$
(s) $B^T \cdot B$ (t) $B^T \cdot B + A^{-1} \cdot A^T$ (u) $A^{-1} \cdot A^T \cdot B^T$ (v) norm(A,2) (w) norm(A_F) (x) rank(A)

[5]. Using *SCILAB rand* function generate matrices $A_{2\times 2}$ and $B_{3\times 3}$. Then, obtain symmetric matrices A' and B', and anti-symmetric matrices A" and B" such that A = A'+A", and B = B'+B". Verify the results.

[6]. Generate the Vandermonde matrix, V, corresponding to the following vectors:
(a) [2,3,-1] (b) [5,5,-2,4] (c) [1,1,2,3,9] (d) [1,2,3,4,5,6]

[7]. For the matrices generated in [6] determine:
(a) determinant (b) rank (c) condition number (e) inverse

[8]. Generate the Hilbert matrix, H, of dimensions (a) 2×2, (b) 3×3, (c) 4×4, and (d) 5×5.

[9]. For the matrices generated in [6] determine:
(a) determinant (b) rank (c) condition number (e) inverse

[10]. Consider the system of linear equations given by:

$$\begin{bmatrix} X + 2Y - Z \\ 2X + 2Y - Z - 3W \\ 2X + 5Y + Z + W \\ X + 2Z + 2W \end{bmatrix} = \begin{bmatrix} 3 \\ -1 \\ 9 \\ 1 \end{bmatrix}$$

(a) Solve the system of linear equations using Cramer's rule
(b) solve the system of linear equations using matrices and the function *linsolve*
(c) solve the system of linear equations using x = $^{-1}A b$
(d) solve the system of linear equations using Gaussian elimination and back substitution
(e) solve the system of linear equations using Gauss-Jordan elimination
(f) solve the system of linear equations using left division, i.e., x = A\b

[11]. Consider the system of linear equations:

$$2x+4y=2$$
$$x+y=2$$
$$2x+3y=2$$

(a) Sketch the lines represented by the equations in the x-y plane with -5<x<5, -5<y<5. Is there a unique solution for the system?
(b) Obtain a "solution" to the system by using SCILAB function *leastsq*. Sketch the solution point together with the lines.
(c) Determine the error involved in this "solution".

[12]. Consider the system of linear equations:

$$5x - 2y + 3z = 10$$
$$x - 3y + 4z = 20$$

(a) Obtain a solution to the system using the function *linsolve*
(b) Obtain a solution to the system using the function *leastsq*
(c) What is the rank of the matrix of coefficients for this linear system

[13]. Consider the following systems of linear equations:

X +2Y+3Z = 28,   2X +4Y+6Z = 18,   2X +4Y+6Z = -4,
3X -2Y+ Z = 4,   3X -2Y+ Z = -10,   3X -2Y+ Z = 4,
4X +2Y -Z = 10,   4X +2Y -Z = 38,   4X +2Y -Z = 24.

(a) Solve the multiple linear system by using matrices and the function *linsolve*
(b) Solve the multiple linear system by using an augmented matrix and Gauss-Jordan elimination
(c) Solve the multiple linear system by using the inverse matrix of coefficients
(d) Obtain the inverse of the matrix of coefficients by using the appropriate augmented matrix and Gauss-Jordan elimination. Verify this solution by using the function *inv*

[14]. Given the matrix

$$A := \begin{bmatrix} -1 & 0 & 5 & 4 \\ 0 & 3 & -2 & 2 \\ 5 & -2 & 4 & 1 \\ 4 & 2 & 1 & 3 \end{bmatrix}$$

corresponding to the eigenvalue problem $Ax = \lambda x$,

(a) Obtain the characteristic matrix for the eigenvalue problem
(b) Obtain the characteristic polynomial corresponding to matrix A
(c) Plot the characteristic polynomial in the range $-6 \le \lambda < 10$
(d) Solve the characteristic polynomial to obtain the eigenvalues, λ, of matrix A

(e) Obtain the eigenvalue, λ, of matrix A using the function *spec*
(f) Obtain the eigenvectors, x, of matrix A using the user-defined function *eigenvectors*

[15]. Given the matrices

$$A = \begin{bmatrix} -1 & 3 & 5 \\ 3 & 4 & 2 \\ 5 & 2 & 3 \end{bmatrix} \quad B = \begin{bmatrix} 2 & -3 & 2 \\ -3 & 4 & 2 \\ 2 & 2 & 10 \end{bmatrix}$$

corresponding to the generalized eigenvalue problem $Ax = \lambda Bx$,

(a) Obtain the characteristic matrix for the eigenvalue problem
(b) Obtain the characteristic polynomial corresponding to matrix A
(g) Plot the characteristic polynomial in the range -6 < λ < 10
(h) Solve the characteristic polynomial to obtain the eigenvalues, of matrix A
(i) Obtain the generalized eigenvalues λ, of matrix A using the function *geigenvectors*
(j) Obtain the eigenvectors, x, of matrix A using the function *geigenvectors*

[16]. Determine the matrices L, U, and P corresponding to the LU decomposition of
   (a) matrix A in problem [14]
   (b) matrix A in problem [15]
   (c) matrix B in problem [15].

[17]. Determine the matrices Q and R corresponding to the QR decomposition of
   (a) matrix A in problem [14]
   (b) matrix A in problem [15]
   (c) matrix B in problem [15].

[18]. Determine the matrices U and V of left and right vectors and the vector of singular values s corresponding to
   (a) matrix A in problem [14]
   (b) matrix A in problem [15]
   (c) matrix B in problem [15].

[19]. Expand the quadratic form $f(x) = x^T A x$ for $x = [X, Y, Z]^T$, where matrix A represents
   (a) matrix A in problem [14]
   (b) matrix A in problem [15]
   (c) matrix B in problem [15].

[20]. For the electric circuit shown below

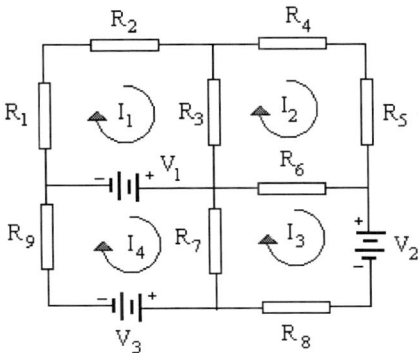

Determine the electrical currents I_1, I_2, I_3, and I_4, associated with the circulation loops shown in the figure, if

(a) $R_1 = R_3 = R_5 = R_7 = R_9 = 1.5$ kΩ, $R_2 = R_4 = R_6 = R_8 = 800\Omega$, $V_1 = 12$ V, $V_2 = 24$ V, $V_3 = 6$ V
(b) $R_1 = R_3 = R_5 = R_7 = R_9 = R_2 = R_4 = R_6 = R_8 = 1.2$ kΩ, $V_1 = 12$ V, $V_2 = V_3 = 6$ V
(c) $R_1 = R_3 = R_5 = R_7 = R_9 = 2.2$ kΩ, $R_2 = R_4 = R_6 = R_8 = 1.2$ kΩ, $V_1 = V_2 = V_3 = 18$ V
(d) $R_1 = R_3 = R_5 = R_7 = R_9 = 0.5$ kΩ, $R_2 = R_4 = R_6 = R_8 = 0.8$ kΩ, $V_1 = 6$ V, $V_2 = 12$ V, $V_3 = 6$ V

[21]. The truss shown in the figure below is such that all horizontal and vertical bars are of length 1.0 m, diagonal bars of length 1.4142 m, and all acute angles in the truss are 45°

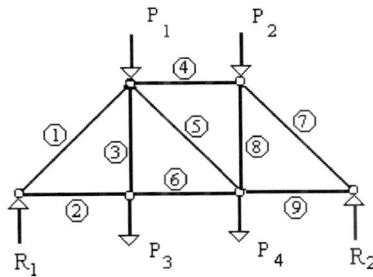

Determine the axial forces in the truss elements if

(a) P_1 = 100 kN, P_2 = 200 kN, P_3 = 200 kN, P_4 = 100 kN.
(b) P_1 = P_2 = P_3 = P_4 = 200 kN.
(c) P_1 = 50 kN, P_2 = 150 kN, P_3 = 50 kN, P_4 = 150 kN.
(d) P_1 = 50 kN, P_2 = 150 kN, P_3 = 200 kN, P_4 = 250 kN.

To determine the reactions use the equations of moments taken about the points of application of R_1 and R_2, respectively:

$$-3P_2 + 1 \cdot (P_1 + P_3) + 2 \cdot (P_2 + P_4) = 0$$
$$3P_1 - 1 \cdot (P_2 + P_4) - 2 \cdot (P_1 + P_3) = 0$$

[22]. Obtain dimensionless numbers to describe a fluid mechanics experiment that involves the following variables:

H = a characteristic water depth (L)
Q = a flow rate (L^3T^{-1})
μ = dynamic viscosity of a fluid $(ML^{-1}T^{-1})$
γ = specific weight of a fluid $(ML^{-2}T^{-2})$
P_0 = a characteristic pressure in the flow $(ML^{-1}T^{-2})$
g = acceleration of gravity (LT^{-2})

Let, H, Q and γ, be the repeating variables in the dimensionless numbers.

[23]. The state of stress at a point within a solid in equilibrium is given by the stress tensor

$$T := \begin{bmatrix} 12 & -22 & 40 \\ -22 & -10 & 5 \\ 40 & 5 & 15 \end{bmatrix}$$

where the components of T represent stresses in kPa. For a plane passing through the point of interest with a normal vector given by $n = [5, -5, 2]$, determine:

(a) the total stress on the plane
(b) the normal stress on the plane
(c) the shear stress on the plane
(d) the total, normal, and shear forces on the plane if the area of the plane is $0.0005\ m^2$

[24]. For the stress tensor given in problem [23] determine:

(a) the principal stresses
(b) the vectors corresponding to the principal axes

[25]. The table below shows sediment load data (y, in kg/min) obtained in a laboratory flume under controlled conditions. The sediment load, y, is known to be a function of the water discharge, x_1 (lt/sec), of the mean sediment diameter, x_2 (cm), and of the flume slope, x_3 (10^{-3} m/m). Using matrices determine a multiple linear fitting of the form

$$y = b_0 + b_1x_1 + b_2x_2 + b_3x_3$$

for the data provided in the table.

x_1	x_2	x_3	y
1.20	0.50	3.5	27.35
1.40	0.75	4.5	29.86
1.60	1.00	5.5	35.15
1.80	1.50	3.5	33.45
2.00	2.00	4.5	38.98
2.20	2.50	5.5	43.35
2.40	0.50	3.5	30.72
2.60	0.75	4.5	34.13
2.80	1.00	5.5	38.45
3.00	1.50	3.5	37.12
3.20	2.00	4.5	42.83
3.40	2.50	5.5	47.12

[26]. The table below shows the water discharge, y(cubic feet per second), measured at a gage station in a large river as a function of time, x(days), during a 40-day period in the early spring season. A plot of y vs. x is known as a hydrograph.

x	y
1.5	101.42
5.0	176.73
8.5	311.22
12.0	389.61
15.5	546.24
19.0	638.14
22.5	716.99
26.0	743.60
29.5	737.96
33.0	623.16
36.5	492.53
40.0	15.84

(a) Determine a polynomial fitting for this hydrograph with p = 2, 3, 4, 5, and 6, where the polynomial fitting is of the form

$$y = b_0 + b_1 x + b_2 x^2 + \ldots + b_p x^p$$

(b) Select the best polynomial fitting for the hydrograph based on the values of the correlation coefficient and of the sum of squared errors, SSE.
(c) Plot the original hydrograph data and the fitted polynomial in the same set of axes.
(d) The area under the curve for 0 < x < 40 days, represents the total volume of water passing through the mouth of the river in that period. Using the fitted polynomial and the function *int* (*int*egral) estimate the volume of water passing through the gage station in the 40-day period of interest.

6 Solution to non-linear equations

Non-linear equations covered in this chapter include quadratic, cubic, and polynomial equations. These are known as algebraic equations. We also consider equations involving non-algebraic terms such as exponential, logarithmic, trigonometric, and hyperbolic functions. These would be referred to as transcendental equations, since those types of functions are known as transcendental functions (i.e., they *transcend* the realm of algebraic equations). Even the simplest of algebraic equations, namely, quadratic equations, may produce a complex solution. Therefore, we start this chapter with a quick introduction to complex numbers. The chapter continuous with numerical solutions to quadratic, cubic, polynomial, and transcendental equations. Methods presented include bisection, Newton-Raphson, and secant. The chapter concludes with the analysis of systems of non-linear equations.

Introduction to complex numbers

A *complex number* z is a number written as

$$z = x + iy,$$

where x and y are real numbers, and i is the *imaginary unit* defined by $i^2 = -1$.

The complex number $x+iy$ has a *real part*,
$$x = Re(z),$$
and an *imaginary part*,
$$y = Im(z).$$

We can think of a complex number as a point $P(x,y)$ in the x-y plane, with the x-axis referred to as the *real axis*, and the y-axis referred to as the *imaginary axis*. Thus, a complex number represented in the form $x+iy$ is said to be in its *Cartesian representation*.

A complex number can also be represented in polar coordinates (*polar representation*) as

$$z = re^{i\theta} = r \cdot \cos\theta + I \, r \cdot \sin\theta$$

where

$$r = |z| = (x^2+y^2)^{1/2}$$

is the *magnitude* of the complex number z, and

$$\theta = Arg(z) = \arctan(y/x)$$

is the *argument* of the complex number z.

The relationship between the Cartesian and polar representation of complex numbers is given by the Euler formula:

$$re^{i\theta} = \cos\theta + I\sin\theta$$

The *complex conjugate* of a complex number $z = x + iy = re^{i\theta}$, is

$$\bar{z} = x - iy = re^{-i\theta}.$$

The complex conjugate of z can be thought of as the reflection of z about the real (x-) axis. Similarly, the *negative* of z,

$$-z = -x - iy = -re^{i\theta},$$

can be thought of as the reflection of z about the origin.

Examples of basic complex number operations in SCILAB

The unit imaginary number, $i = \sqrt{(-1)}$, is represented in SCILAB by the symbol %i. A sequence of the first 10 powers of I can obtained by using:

```
-->ipow = []; for j=1:10, ipow=[ipow %i^j]; end; ipow
 ipow  =

!   i    - 1.   - i    1.    i    - 1.   - i    1.    i    - 1. !
```

A complex number, say $z = 3+5i$, is written as:

```
-->z =3+5*%i
 z  =

    3. + 5.i
```

The functions *real* and *imag* can be used to obtain the real and imaginary parts, respectively, of a complex number, for example:

```
-->real(z), imag(z)
 ans  =

    3.
 ans  =

    5.
```

The magnitude and argument of the complex number are obtained as:

```
-->abs(z), atan(imag(z)/real(z))
 ans  =

    5.8309519
 ans  =

    1.0303768
```

If we write the polar representation of a complex number as r exp(%I*theta), SCILAB returns the Cartesian representation. For example,

```
-->5*exp(0.25*%i)
 ans  =

    4.8445621 + 1.2370198i
```

SCILAB provides the function *polar* to obtain the magnitude and argument of a complex number. The following example illustrates its application:

```
-->[r,theta] = polar(z)
 theta  =

    1.0303768
 r  =

    5.8309519
```

The complex conjugate of a complex number is obtained by using the function *conj*:

```
-->conj(z)
 ans  =

    3. - 5.i
```

The negative is simply obtained by adding a minus sign to the number, i.e.,

```
-->-z
 ans  =

  - 3. - 5.i
```

Matrices in SCILAB can have complex numbers as elements. The following commands, for example, produce a 3x4 matrix of complex numbers. First, we generate random matrices with integer numbers to be the real and imaginary parts of the complex numbers:

```
-->xMs = int(10*rand(3,3)), yMs = int(10*rand(3,3))
 xMs  =

!   2.    5.    2. !
!   4.    5.    6. !
!   2.    1.    7. !
 yMs  =

!   0.    3.    4. !
!   6.    8.    2. !
!   2.    5.    8. !
```

Next, the complex-number matrix is put together by using:

```
-->zMs = xMs + yMs*%i
 zMs  =

!   2.         5. + 3.i    2. + 4.i !
!   4. + 6.i   5. + 8.i    6. + 2.i !
!   2. + 2.i   1. + 5.i    7. + 8.i !
```

To obtain the magnitude of the elements of the matrix just defined we simply apply the function *abs* to the matrix name, i.e.,

```
-->abs(zMs)
 ans  =

!   2.          5.8309519    4.472136  !
!   7.2111026   9.4339811    6.3245553 !
!   2.8284271   5.0990195    10.630146 !
```

To find the arguments of the elements we can use the function *atanm* applied to the term-by-term division of the imaginary part by the real part of the elements. The function *atanm* is a generalization of the function *atan* used when the argument is a matrix. Here is the calculation of the arguments:

```
-->atanm(yMs./xMs)
 ans  =

! -  .8101607     .5954016     .9174249 !
!    .7153096  -  .0687575     .2626142 !
!    .6906707    2.5474625  -  .2654686 !
```

Complex number calculations

Complex numbers can be added, subtracted, multiplied, and divided. The rules for these operations are shown below:

Let $\quad z = x + i \cdot y = r \cdot e^{i\theta}$, $z_1 = x_1 + i \cdot y_1 = r_1 \cdot e^{i\theta_1}$, and $z_2 = x_2 + i \cdot y_2 = r_2 \cdot e^{i\theta_2}$,

be complex numbers. In these definitions the numbers x, y, x_1, x_2, y_1, and y_2 are real numbers.

Addition: $\quad z_1 + z_2 = (x_1 + x_2) + i \cdot (y_1 + y_2)$

Subtraction: $\quad z_1 - z_2 = (x_1 - x_2) + i \cdot (y_1 - y_2)$

Multiplication: $\quad z_1 \cdot z_2 = (x_1 \cdot x_2 - y_1 \cdot y_2) + i \cdot (x_1 \cdot y_2 + x_2 \cdot y_1) = r_1 \cdot r_2 \cdot e^{i(\theta_1 + \theta_2)}$.

Multiplication of a number by its conjugate results in the square of the number's magnitude, i.e.:

$$z \cdot \bar{z} = (x + i \cdot y)(x - i \cdot y) = x^2 + y^2 = r^2 = |z|^2$$

Division:

$$\frac{z_1}{z_2} = \left(\frac{z_1}{z_2}\right) \cdot \left(\frac{\bar{z_2}}{\bar{z_2}}\right) = \frac{z_1 \cdot \bar{z_2}}{|z_2|^2} = \frac{x_1 \cdot x_2 + y_1 \cdot y_2}{x_2^2 + y_2^2} + i \cdot \frac{y_1 \cdot x_2 - x_1 \cdot y_2}{x_2^2 + y_2^2} = \frac{r_1}{r_2} \cdot e^{i(\theta_1 - \theta_2)}.$$

Powers: $$z^n = (r \cdot e^{i \cdot \theta})^n = r^n \cdot e^{i \cdot n\theta}$$

Roots: because the argument θ of a complex number z has a periodicity of 2π, we can write
$$z = r \cdot e^{i \cdot (\theta + 2k\pi)}, \quad \text{for } k = 0, 1, 2, \ldots$$

There are n n-th roots of z calculated as

$$\sqrt[n]{z} = z^{1/n} = r^{1/n} \cdot e^{i \cdot \frac{(\theta + 2k\pi)}{n}}, \quad k = 0, 1, 2, \cdots (n-1).$$

More details on the calculation of roots of complex numbers are presented later in the chapter.

Examples of operations with complex numbers

The following are operations with complex numbers using SCILAB:

```
-->z1 = -5+2*%i, z2 = 3+4*%i
 z1  =

  - 5. + 2.i
 z2  =

    3. + 4.i
```

Addition, subtraction, multiplication, and division:

```
-->z1+z2
 ans  =

  - 2. + 6.i

-->z1-z2
 ans  =

  - 8. - 2.i

-->z1*z2
 ans  =

  - 23. - 14.i

-->z1/z2
 ans  =

  - .28 + 1.04i
```

The following sequence provides the first 5 integer powers of z1:

```
-->z1pow = []; for j=1:5, z1pow=[z1pow z1^j]; end; z1pow
 z1pow  =

         column 1 to 4

!  - 5. + 2.i    21. - 20.i   - 65. + 142.i    41. - 840.i !

         column 5

!   1475. + 4282.i !
```

The following SCILAB command attempts to find one cubic root of z1:

```
-->z1^(1/3)
 ans  =    1.0613781 + 1.394917i
```

There are, in fact, three cubic roots for any real or complex number. These are calculated, using the formulas indicated earlier, as follows. First, we calculate the magnitude and argument of complex number z1:

```
-->r1=abs(z1), theta1 = atan(imag(z1)/real(z1))
 r1      =    5.3851648
 theta1  = - .3805064
```

Next, we create an empty vector called *cubic_roots_of_z1*:

```
-->cubic_roots_of_z1 = [];
```

The vector is then filled with the three roots of z1 as follows:

```
-->for k = 0:2
-->    cubic_roots_of_z1 = [cubic_roots_of_z1 r1^(1/3)*exp(%i*((theta1+2*k*%pi)/3))];
-->end;
```

To see the final result, enter the name of the vector:

```
-->cubic_roots_of_z1
 cubic_roots_of_z1  =

         column 1 to 2

!   1.7387226 - .2217219i   - .6773445 + 1.6166389i !

         column 3

! - 1.0613781 - 1.394917i !
```

More details on the calculation of roots of real and complex numbers are presented in a subsequent section of this chapter.

Solution to quadratic and cubic equations

Quadratic equations, of the form $ax^2+bx+c = 0$, and cubic equations, of the form $ax^3+bx^2+cx+d = 0$, are the simplest non-linear, polynomial equations. SCILAB provides function *roots* to solve polynomial equations of any order. Therefore, function *roots* can be used to solve quadratic and cubic equations. The methods presented next for solving quadratic and cubic equations, therefore, are not strictly necessary, however, they are presented here as SCILAB programming exercises.

Quadratic equations

Quadratic equations are those algebraic equations with one unknown that can be reduced to the form

$$ax^2+bx+c = 0,$$

where a, b, and c are real numbers.

The solution to a quadratic equation can be accomplished by re-writing the equation as

$$x^2+(b/a)x = -(c/a)$$

and completing the square of a binomial in the left hand side. To complete the square of a binomial, add the term $b^2/(4a^2)$ to both sides of the equation:

$$x^2+(b/a)x+b^2/(4a^2) = -(c/a)+b^2/(4a^2)$$

The equation can now be re-written as

$$(x+b/(2a))^2 = (b^2-4ac)/(4a^2).$$

Taking the square root of both sides of the equation results in

$$x+b/(2a) = \pm (b^2-4ac)^{1/2}/(2a).$$

Solving for x results in

$$x = [-b \pm (b^2-4ac)^{1/2}]/(2a).$$

The quantity under the square root in this result is known as the *discriminant* of the equation, i.e.,

$$D = b^2-4ac.$$

According to the sign of the discriminant, the equation can have one or two real solutions, or two complex conjugate solutions:

If D>0, the quadratic equation has two distinct real solutions:

$$x_{1,2} = (-b \pm D^{1/2})/(2a).$$

If D=0, the quadratic equation has one real (double) solution,

$$x_1 = x_2 = -b/(2a).$$

If D<0, the quadratic equation has two conjugate complex solutions,

$$x_{1,2} = (-b \pm i \cdot (-D)^{1/2})/(2a),$$

where $i = (-1)^{1/2}$ is the unit imaginary number.

The basic algorithm (written in pseudo-code) for solving a quadratic equation, would look something like this:

```
Enter equation coefficients a, b, c

Calculate discriminant, D = b²-4ac

If D > 0,
      Indicate that two distinct real solutions exist
      Calculate roots as x₁ = (-b+D^(1/2))/(2a), and x₂ = (-b-D^(1/2))/(2a)
      Display roots x₁ and x₂

Else If D = 0,
      Indicate that only one real solution exist
      Calculate root as x = -b/(2a)
      Display single root x

Else (default case D<0)
      Indicate that two conjugate complex solutions exist
      Calculate the real part of the complex roots as xᵣ = -b/(2a)
      Calculate the imaginary part of the roots as xᵢ = (-D)^(1/2)
      Display the roots as 'x₁ =xᵣ +i*xᵢ' and 'x₂ =xᵣ -i*xᵢ'
```

The reader is invited to write a SCILAB function to solve the quadratic equation given the values a, b, and c.

Note: *Pseudo-code* is a way to present an algorithm using English-like statements that are later coded into a particular computer language. The statements are general enough to be understood by any programmer and easily translated into a computer language.

Cubic equations

The *canonical* (simplest) *form* of the cubic equation is

$$x^3 + ax^2 + bx + c = 0,$$

where *a, b, c* are real numbers.

Substituting the auxiliary variable

$$y = x + a/3$$

leads to the reduced form

$$y^3 + py + q = 0,$$

with

$$p = (3b - a^2)/3,$$

and

$$q = c + 2a^3/27 - a \cdot b/3.$$

A *discriminant* for the reduced cubic equation is given by

$$D = (p/2)^2 + (q/3)^3.$$

An Italian mathematician, Gierolimo Cardano, proposed the following solutions to the cubic equation:

$$x_1 = -(a/3) + u + v$$

$$x_{2,3} = -(a/3) - (u+v)/2 \pm i \cdot \sqrt{3} \cdot (u-v)/2$$

where

$$u = \sqrt[3]{-\frac{q}{2} + \sqrt{D}}, \quad v = \sqrt[3]{-\frac{q}{2} - \sqrt{D}}.$$

Depending on the sign of the discriminant, D, the solutions to the cubic equation can be classified as follows:

If D > 0, one real and two complex conjugate solutions (calculated using the formulas shown above).
If D = 0, three real solutions including a double solution (x_2 and x_3).
If D < 0, three distinct real solutions (this case is known as the irreducible case).

In the irreducible case, the formulas shown above for the three roots of the cubic equation will introduce complex expressions because the calculation of u and v involves the square root of D<0. To avoid introducing such complex expressions, we can use the so-called trigonometric form of the solution:

$$x_1 = -\frac{a}{3} + 2\sqrt{\frac{|p|}{3}} \cos(\frac{\phi}{3}),$$

$$x_2 = -\frac{a}{3} + 2\sqrt{\frac{|p|}{3}}\cos\left(\frac{\phi-\pi}{3}\right),$$

and

$$x_3 = -\frac{a}{3} + 2\sqrt{\frac{|p|}{3}}\cos\left(\frac{\phi+\pi}{3}\right),$$

where

$$\cos(\phi) = -\frac{q}{2\sqrt{\left(\frac{|p|}{3}\right)^3}}.$$

The algorithm for solving the cubic equation can be written in pseudo-code as follows:

```
Enter coefficients for the cubic equation:  a,b,c
Calculate p and q
Calculate the discriminant D

If D > 0
        Indicate that there one real and two complex conjugate solutions
        Calculate u and v (use subroutine for cubic equation - see below)
        Calculate the real root, x₁ = -(a/3)+u+v
        Calculate the real part of roots x₂,₃, xᵣ = -(a/3)+(u+v)/2
        Calculate the imaginary part of roots x₂,₃, xᵢ = √3˙(u-v)/2
        Display roots x₁, 'x₂ = xᵣ + xᵢ*i' and 'x₃ = xᵣ - xᵢ*i'

Else D = 0
        Indicate that there are three real solutions with one double root
        Calculate x₁ = -(a/3)+u+v, x₂,₃ = -(a/3) - (u+v)/2
        Display roots x₁, x₂ = x₃

Else (Default case, D<0)
        Indicate that there are three distinct real solutions
        Calculate cos(ϕ) and ϕ
        Calculate the three roots using the trigonometric form, i.e.,

        ϕ₁ = ϕ/3,       x₁ = -a/3 + 2(|p|/3)^(1/2) cos ϕ₁
        ϕ₂ = (ϕ-π)/3,   x₁ = -a/3 + 2(|p|/3)^(1/2) cos ϕ₂
        ϕ₃ = (ϕ+π)/3,   x1 = -a/3 + 2(|p|/3)^(1/2) cos ϕ₃

        Display roots x1, x2, and x3
```

The calculation of u and v for the case D>0 requires us to calculate cubic roots, namely,

$$\sqrt[3]{-\frac{q}{2}+\sqrt{D}},\ \sqrt[3]{-\frac{q}{2}-\sqrt{D}}.$$

I suggest you use the following user-defined SCILAB function to obtain those cubic roots:

```
function RealCubicRoot(x)
//This function calculates the cubic root of a real number
    One_Third = 1.0/3.0
    if x < 0 then
        RealCubicRoot = -(Abs(x)^One_Third)
    elseif x == 0 then
        RealCubicRoot = 0
    else
        Real CubicRoot = Abs(x)^One_Third
    end
//End of the function
```

The function *RealCubicRoot* calculates the real cubic root corresponding to a real number. The functions is designed so that if the real number is positive so is its cubic root, and if the number is negative so is its cubic root. With this function we ensure that we always get a real cubic root and that the calculation is not encumbered with complex number operations.

The many roots of a real or complex number

Consider a complex number

$$z = r \cdot e^{i\theta} = r \cdot \cos\theta + i \cdot r \cdot \sin\theta.$$

Because the functions *sin* and *cos* are periodic functions of period 2π in θ, the complex number z can be written as

$$z = r \cdot e^{i(\theta+2k\pi)},\ k = 0, \pm 1, \pm 2, \pm 3, \ldots$$

In other words, there are infinite ways to represent the complex number z. The most general representation being

$$z = r \cdot e^{i(\theta+2k\pi)}.$$

To obtain the *n*-th root of this complex number we can write

$$z^{1/n} = r^{1/n} \cdot e^{i[(\theta/n)+2k\pi/n]}.$$

You can check that we need only use the values $k = 0, 1, 2, \ldots (n-1)$, to produce all *n* independent roots of the number z.

Example 1: Consider the number $z = 16 e^{i\pi} = 16 \cdot \cos\pi + i \cdot 16 \cdot \sin\pi = -16$, which is actually a real number. Calculate the roots corresponding to $z^{1/4}$:

From

$$z = 16 \cdot e^{i\pi} = 16 \cdot e^{i(\pi+2k\pi)} = 16 \cdot e^{i(1+2k)\pi},$$

it follows that

$$r = z^{1/4} = 16^{1/4} \cdot e^{i(1+2k)(\pi/4)} = 2 \cdot e^{i(1+2k)(\pi/4)}, \; k = 0, 1, 2, 3$$

Thus,

- For k = 0, $r_1 = 2 \cdot e^{i(1+2 \cdot 0)(\pi/4)} = 2 \cdot e^{i\pi/4} = 2\cdot\cos(\pi/4) + i\cdot 2\cdot\sin(\pi/4) = \sqrt{2}\cdot(1 + i)$
- For k = 1, $r_2 = 2 \cdot e^{i(1+2 \cdot 1)(\pi/4)} = 2 \cdot e^{i3\pi/4} = 2\cdot\cos(3\pi/4) + i\cdot 2\cdot\sin(3\pi/4) = \sqrt{2}\cdot(-1 + i)$
- For k = 2, $r_3 = 2 \cdot e^{i(1+2 \cdot 2)(\pi/4)} = 2 \cdot e^{i5\pi/4} = 2\cdot\cos(5\pi/4) + i\cdot 2\cdot\sin(5\pi/4) = -\sqrt{2}\cdot(1 + i)$
- For k = 3, $r_3 = 2 \cdot e^{i(1+2 \cdot 3)(\pi/4)} = 2 \cdot e^{i7\pi/4} = 2\cdot\cos(7\pi/4) + i\cdot 2\cdot\sin(7\pi/4) = \sqrt{2}\cdot(-1 + i)$

Using values such as k = -1 or k = 4 in the general expression for the 4-th root of z = -16 will produce values already accounted for in the four results found above. This example, therefore, verifies that there are exactly n independent n-th roots of a complex number, with n = 4 for this case.

Notice that the results of this example actually correspond to the 4-th roots of a real number, z = -16. Since real numbers are special cases of complex numbers, the approach outlined above for finding the n-th root of a complex number is also applicable to a real number. The only requirement is that the number be written in the Polar form, $z = r \cdot e^{i\theta}$.

Using SCILAB, the previous calculations are performed as follows:

```
-->z = -16; r=abs(z); theta = -%pi;

-->roots_of_z = [];

-->for k = 0:3
-->   roots_of_z = [roots_of_z r^(1/4)*exp(%i*((theta+2*k*%pi)/n))];
-->end;

-->roots_of_z
 roots_of_z  =

         column 1 to 2

!   1.4142136 - 1.4142136i    1.4142136 + 1.4142136i !

         column 3 to 4

! - 1.4142136 + 1.4142136i   - 1.4142136 - 1.4142136i !
```

Principal values of a cubic root

The principal value for the n-th root of a complex (or real) number,

$$z = r \cdot e^{i\theta},$$

is the value corresponding to $k = 0$ in the general expression:

$$z^{1/n} = r^{1/n} \cdot e^{i[(\theta/n)+2k\pi/n]},$$

i.e.,

$$z^{1/n} = r^{1/n} \cdot e^{i\theta/n}.$$

For the case of cubic root ($n = 3$), if the number z is a positive real number $\theta = 0$, and the result is straightforward, $z^{1/3} = r^{1/3}$. If the number z is a negative real number $\theta = \pi$, and the principal value is $z^{1/3} = r^{1/3} \cdot e^{i\pi/3} = r^{1/3} \cdot (\cos \pi/3 + i \cdot \sin \pi/3)$. Thus, the principal value of the root of a complex number is not necessarily always a real number.

The following SCILAB exercise shows the three cubic roots of a positive and a negative number.

<u>Example 1</u> - Cubic roots of a positive number:

To calculate the cubic roots of $z = 81$, with $r = 81$ and $\theta = 0$, we use:

```
-->z = 81, r = abs(z), theta = 0
 z  =

    81.
 r  =

    81.
 theta  =

    0.
-->for k = 0:2
-->    r^(1/3)*exp(%i*(theta+2*k*%pi)/3)
-->end
 ans  =

    4.3267487
 ans  =

  - 2.1633744 + 3.7470743i
 ans  =

  - 2.1633744 - 3.7470743i
```

Example 2 - Cubic roots of a negative number:

To calculate the cubic roots of $z = 8$, with $r = 9$ and $\theta = \pi$, we use:

```
-->z = -8, r = abs(z), theta = %pi
 z  =

  - 8.
 r  =

    8.
 theta  =

    3.1415927

-->for k = 0:2
-->    r^(1/3)*exp(%i*(theta+2*k*%pi)/3)
-->end
 ans  =

    1. + 1.7320508i
 ans  =

  - 2. + 2.449E-16i       // Note: this is equivalent to -2.0
 ans  =

    1. - 1.7320508i
```

Polynomials and solutions to polynomial equations

Polynomials are one of the categories of SCILAB data types. Polynomials are defined using the function *poly*. In Chapter 5 we indicated, for example, that for a square matrix A, the characteristic equation can be obtained by using *poly(A,'lam')*, where *lam* is the independent variable defining the resulting polynomial. We also indicated that we can define a simple symbolic variable, say, s, by using *s = poly(0,'s')*.

In this section we are interested in defining a polynomial of order n, namely

$$P = a_0 + a_1 x + a_2 x^2 + a_3 x^3 + \ldots + a_n x^n,$$

we use a row vector containing the coefficients as $[a_0\ a_1\ a_2\ \ldots\ a_n]$, and call function *poly* using this vector, the independent variable that defines the polynomial, say '*x*', and the qualifier "coeff". For example, to define a fourth-order polynomial with coefficients [1 -5 0 3 2], use:

```
-->p4 = poly([1 -5 0 3 2],'x','coeff')
 p4  =

                    3     4
    1 - 5x + 3x + 2x
```

A polynomial of order 10 in y is generated next. The coefficients of the polynomial are stored in vector *c*:

```
-->c = [23 0 -122 34 -20 0 4 525 -2 11 3]
 c   =

        column  1 to 10

 !   23.     0.   - 122.    34.   - 20.     0.    4.    525.   - 2.    11. !

        column 11

 !   3. !
```

The resulting polynomial is:

```
-->p10 = poly(c,'y','coeff')
 p10 =
                    2         3         4        6         7        8        9       10
      23 -  122y  + 34y   -  20y   + 4y  +  525y  -  2y  + 11y  + 3y
```

To find the roots of a polynomial use the function *roots*. For example, the roots of the fourth-order polynomial *p4* are:

```
-->roots(p4)
 ans =

 !    .2059620              !
 !  - 1.3030302  +  .9995932i !
 !  - 1.3030302  -  .9995932i !
 !    .9000985              !
```

The following example provides the roots of the polynomial *p10*:

```
-->roots(p10)
 ans =

 !    .2308180  +  .7299993i !
 !    .2308180  -  .7299993i !
 !  - .3995841              !
 !  - .5911741  +  .5126340i !
 !  - .5911741  -  .5126340i !
 !    .4935580              !
 !    .6187957              !
 !  - 7.1652026             !
 !    1.7532393 + 4.6211667i !
 !    1.7532393 - 4.6211667i !
```

The next example combines functions *roots* and *poly* to calculate the roots of a polynomial given its coefficients in the vector [2 -3 5 4 2 100]:

```
-->roots(poly([2 -3 5 4 2 100],'s','coeff'))
 ans  =
```

```
!     .3143499  +   .2557167i  !
!     .3143499  -   .2557167i  !
! -   .0539859  +   .4715218i  !
! -   .0539859  -   .4715218i  !
! -   .5407282                 !
```

The *fundamental theorem of algebra* indicates that a polynomial of integer order n has a total of n roots, among real and complex roots. It also indicates that if a complex number z is a root of a polynomial, then its complex conjugate $\bar{z}$ is also a root of the polynomial. These facts are illustrated in the examples worked above.

More information on polynomials is provided in Chapter 7.

Solution of a single non-linear equation

In an earlier section of this chapter we presented algorithms for the solution of quadratic and cubic equations. These two types of equations are examples of polynomial equations of the form:

$$a_n \cdot x^n + a_{n-1} \cdot x^{n-1} + a_{n-2} \cdot x^{n-2} + \ldots + a_2 \cdot x^2 + a_1 x + a_0 = 0,$$

with $n = 2$ corresponding to the quadratic equation, and $n = 3$ to the cubic equation. A linear equation would be one for which $n = 1$, and its solution is straightforward. Equations that can be cast in the form of a polynomial are referred to as *algebraic equations*. Equations involving more complicated terms, such as trigonometric, hyperbolic, exponential, or logarithmic functions are referred to as *transcendental equations*.

No general algorithms for solution exist for algebraic (or polynomial) equations of order ≥ 4, or for transcendental equations. The methods presented in this section are numerical methods that can be applied to the solution of such equations, to which we will refer, in general, as *non-linear equations*.

In general, we will we searching for one, or more, solutions to the equation,

$$f(x) = 0.$$

We will present the methods of *interval halving* (or *bisection* method, the *Newton-Raphson* algorithm, the *secant* method, and the *fixed iteration* method. In the interval-halving method as well as in the secant method we need to provide two initial values of x to get the algorithm started. In the fixed iteration and Newton-Raphson methods only one initial value is required.

Because the solution is not exact, the algorithms for any of the methods presented herein will not provide the exact solution to the equation $f(x) = 0$, instead, we will stop the algorithm when the equation is satisfied within an allowed tolerance or error, ε. In mathematical terms this is expressed as

$$|f(x_R)| < \varepsilon.$$

The value of x for which the non-linear equation $f(x)=0$ is satisfied, i.e., $x = x_R$, will be the solution, or root, to the equation within an error of ε units.

Interval-halving or bisection method

This method starts by identifying two values of x, a and b, with $a<b$, for which the corresponding function values, namely $f(a)$ and $f(b)$, have opposite signs, i.e., $f(a) \cdot f(b) < 0$. Figure 1, below, presents two of such cases.

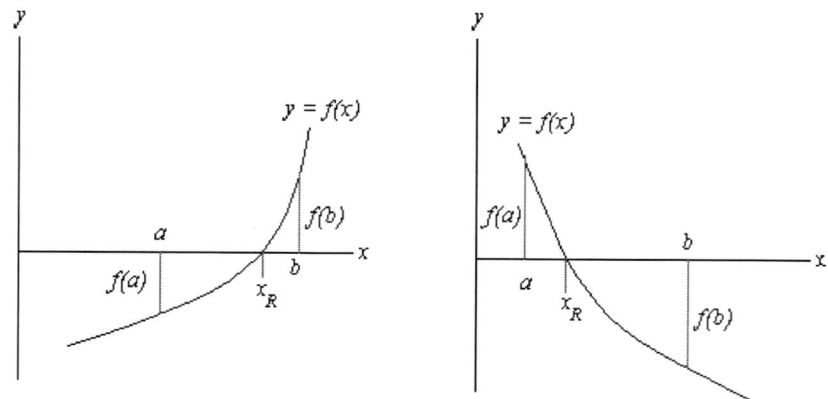

Obviously, since the function $y = f(x)$ changes sign as x goes from $x = a$ to $x = b$, somewhere within the interval (a,b), x must take a value x_R for which $f(x) = 0$. The mid-point of the interval, namely,

$$c = 1/2(a+b),$$

will be closer to x_R than either a or b can be.

Two situations are possible, as illustrated in the figure below: (1) $a < x_R < c < b$; or, (2) $a < c < x_R < b$. In the first case, $f(a) \cdot f(c) < 0$, while $f(b) \cdot f(c) > 0$, and x_R is contained in the interval (a,c). In the second case, $f(a) \cdot f(c) > 0$, while $f(b) \cdot f(c) < 0$, and x_R is contained in the interval (c,b). We can think of c replacing b in the first case in a general interval (a,b), while c replaces a in the interval (a,b) in the second case. In other words, in the first case b takes the value of c, $b \leftarrow c$, and in the second case, $a \leftarrow c$. We can think of the method, therefore, as finding the center-point of an ever-decreasing interval. The mid-point value replaces the interval extreme for which the product of its function and that of the mid-point is a positive number.

The process is then repeated until a value of is found so that (3) is satisfied, i.e., until

$$|f(c)| < \varepsilon.$$

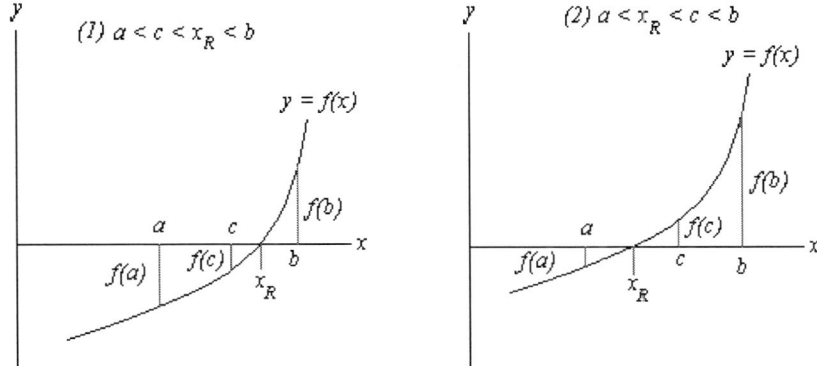

Pseudo-code for the interval-halving or bisection method

The following is one possible pseudo-code for the interval-halving method:

1. Function $f(x)$ must be loaded through *deff* or *getf*.
2. Enter initial values of *a* and *b*.
3. Check that $a < b$, if not, send message indicating error in input data and requesting user to re-enter values of *a* and *b*.
4. When input data is correct, check that $f(a) \cdot f(b) < 0$. If that is not the case, inform the user that his/her initial values of *a* and *b* do not satisfy the problem conditions for solution.
5. If problem conditions are satisfied, proceed to calculate c according to $c = 1/2(a+b)$.
6. Check if convergence condition $|f(c)| < \varepsilon$, is satisfied. If it is so, print the solution and stop.
7. If convergence solution is not satisfied, replace values of *a* or *b* according to the following procedure: If $f(b) \cdot f(c) > 0$, $b \leftarrow c$, else $a \leftarrow c$.
8. Repeat procedure from step 5 on. Stop if the number of iterations is too large. Send a message to user indicating that the process is not converging after a large number of iterations.

SCILAB function for interval-halving or bisection

The following function, *half.txt*, can be used to obtain a solution using interval halving. The function looks like this:

```
function [x]=half(a,b,f)
//interval halving routine
N = 100; eps = 1.e-5; // define max. no. iterations and error
if (f(a)*f(b) > 0) then
      error('no root possible f(a)*f(b) > 0')
      abort;
end;
if(abs(f(a)) < eps) then
      error('solution at a')
      abort;
end;
```

```
if(abs(f(b)) < eps) then
      error('solution at b')
      abort;
end;
while (N > 0)
      c = (a+b)/2;
      if(abs(f(c)) < eps) then
            x = c;
            x
            return;
      end;
      if(f(a)*f(c) < 0)then
            b = c;
      else
            a = c;
      end;
      N = N - 1;
end;
error('No convergence')
abort;
//end function
```

Example of interval-halving (bisection) method application

Let's apply it to an example, first define the function p(x) as follows:

```
-->deff('[y]=p(x)',['y=x^3-2*x^2-2*x-1'])
```

We will produce a plot of the function to check possible solutions visually, for example:

```
-->xx = 0:0.1:5; yy = p(xx);            //(x,y) data
-->size(xx)                              //size of x to produce the x-axis
 ans  =!   1.     51. !

-->zeroLine = zeros(1,51);               //data for the x-axis (all zeros)
-->plot2d([xx' xx'],[yy' zeroLine'])     //plot function and x-axis
```

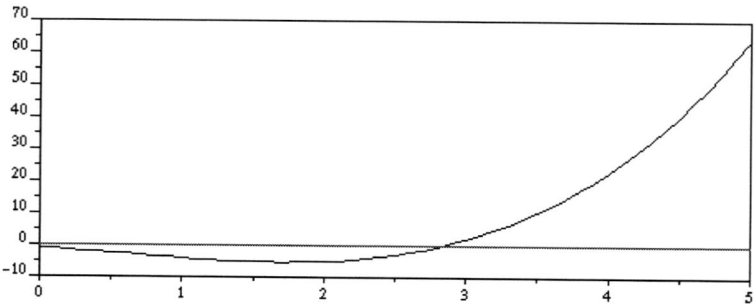

The figure shows a root between 2 and 3. The next step in the solution is to load function *half*, and call it with the proper arguments:

```
-->getf('half');

-->x = half(2,3,p)
 x  =

    2.8311768
```
To check the solution evaluate the function at the value of x:

```
-->p(x)
 ans =

  - .0000048
```

The function does not evaluates to zero. However, the error involved is in the order of 5×10^{-6}, small enough to accept the solution provided.

The Newton-Raphson method

Consider the Taylor-series expansion of the function $f(x)$ about a value $x = x_o$:

$$f(x) = f(x_o) + f'(x_o)(x-x_o) + (f''(x_o)/2!)(x-x_o)^2 + \ldots$$

Using only the first two terms of the expansion, a first approximation to the root of the equation

$$f(x) = 0$$

can be obtained from

$$f(x) = 0 \approx f(x_o) + f'(x_o)(x_1 - x_o)$$

Such approximation is given by,

$$x_1 = x_o - f(x_o)/f'(x_o).$$

The Newton-Raphson method consists in obtaining improved values of the approximate root through the recurrent application of equation (8). For example, the second and third approximations to that root will be given by

$$x_2 = x_1 - f(x_1)/f'(x_1),$$

and

$$x_3 = x_2 - f(x_2)/f'(x_2),$$

respectively.

This iterative procedure can be generalized by writing the following equation, where i represents the iteration number:

$$x_{i+1} = x_i - f(x_i)/f'(x_i).$$

After each iteration the program should check to see if the convergence condition, namely,

$$|f(x_{i+1})| < \varepsilon,$$

is satisfied.

The figure below illustrates the way in which the solution is found by using the Newton-Raphson method. Notice that the equation $f(x) = 0 \approx f(x_o) + f'(x_o)(x_1 - x_o)$ represents a straight line tangent to the curve $y = f(x)$ at $x = x_o$. This line intersects the x-axis (i.e., $y = f(x) = 0$) at the point x_1 as given by $x_1 = x_o - f(x_o)/f'(x_o)$. At that point we can construct another straight line tangent to $y = f(x)$ whose intersection with the x-axis is the new approximation to the root of $f(x) = 0$, namely, $x = x_2$. Proceeding with the iteration we can see that the intersection of consecutive tangent lines with the x-axis approaches the actual root relatively fast.

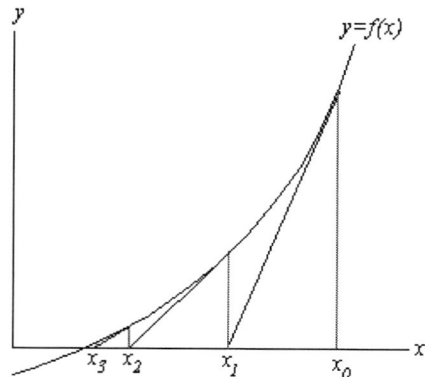

The Newton-Raphson method converges relatively fast for most functions regardless of the initial value chosen. The main disadvantage is that you need to know not only the function f(x), but also its derivative, f'(x), in order to achieve a solution. The secant method, discussed in the following section, utilizes an approximation to the derivative, thus obviating such requirement.

The programming algorithm of any of these methods must include the option of stopping the program if the number of iterations grows too large. How large is large? That will depend of the particular problem solved. However, any interval-halving, fixed iteration, Newton-Raphson, or secant method solution that takes more than 1000 iterations to converge is either ill-posed or contains a logical error. Debugging of the program will be called for at this point by changing the initial values provided to the program, or by checking the program's logic.

A SCILAB function for the Newton-Raphson method

The function *newton*, listed below, implements the Newton-Raphson algorithm. It uses as arguments an initial value and expressions for f(x) and f'(x).

```
function [x]=newton(x0,f,fp)
//newton-raphson algorithm
N = 100; eps = 1.e-5; // define max. no. iterations and error
```

```
maxval = 10000.0;      // define value for divergence
xx = x0;
while (N>0)
      xn = xx-f(xx)/fp(xx);
      if(abs(f(xn))<eps)then
            x=xn
            disp(100-N);
            return(x);
      end;
      if (abs(f(xx))>maxval)then
            disp(100-N);
            error('Solution diverges');
            abort;
      end;
      N = N - 1;
      xx = xn;
end;
error('No convergence');
abort;
//end function
```

We will use the Newton-Raphson method to solve for the equation $f(x) = x^3 - 2x^2 + 1 = 0$. The following SCILAB commands define the function $f(x)$ and its derivative, $fp(x)$, and load the function newton.txt:

```
-->deff('[y]=f(x)','y=x^3-2*x^2+1');

-->deff('[y]=fp(x)','y=3*x^2-2');

-->getf('newton')
```

To have an idea of the location of the roots of this polynomial we'll plot the function using the following SCILAB commands:

```
-->x= (-0.8:0.01:2.0)'; y = f(x);

-->plot(x,y,'x','f(x)','my plot');

-->xgrid()
```

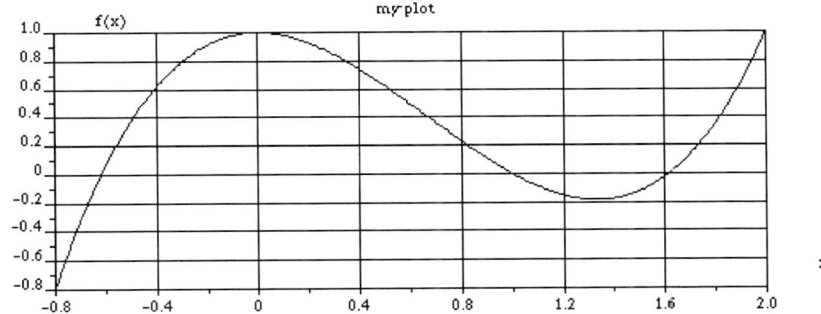

We see that the function graph crosses the x-axis somewhere between -.8 and -.4, between .8 and 1.2, and between 1.6 and 2.0. The following commands use the function *newton* with different initial values. The nature of the function is such that most initial values converge to either of the two real roots, a few diverge, but it is very difficult to make the algorithm converge to the negative root. The number listed before the variable name *ans* in each solution is the number of iterations required to obtain a solution.

```
-->newton(-1,f,fp)

    0.
 ans  =

    1.
-->newton(-10,f,fp)

    52.
 ans  =

    1.6180279
-->newton(-5,f,fp)

    44.
 ans  =

    1.6180278
-->newton(-0.1,f,fp)

    49.
 ans  =

    1.6180279
-->newton(-2,f,fp)

    45.
 ans  =

    1.6180405
-->newton(0,f,fp)

    1.
 ans  =

    1.
-->newton(0.5,f,fp)

    0.
 ans  =

    1.
-->newton(-0.8,f,fp)

    47.
```

```
 ans  =

    1.6180408

-->newton(-0.2,f,fp)

    43.
 ans  =

    1.6180405

-->newton(-0.1,f,fp)

    49.
 ans  =

    1.6180279

-->newton(-100,f,fp)

    0.
 !--error    9999
Solution diverges
at line       15 of function newton              called by :
newton(-100,f,fp)


-->newton(-10,f,fp)

    52.
 ans  =

    1.6180279

-->newton(100,f,fp)

    0.
 !--error    9999
Solution diverges
at line       15 of function newton              called by :
newton(100,f,fp)


-->newton(10,f,fp)

    48.
 ans  =

    1.6180405
```

The Secant Method

In the secant method, we replace the derivative $f'(x_i)$ in the Newton-Raphson method with

$$f'(x_i) \approx (f(x_i) - f(x_{i-1}))/(x_i - x_{i-1}).$$

With this replacement, the Newton-Raphson algorithm becomes

$$x_{i+1} = x_i - \frac{f(x_i)}{f(x_i) - f(x_{i-1})} \cdot (x_i - x_{i-1}).$$

To get the method started we need two values of x, say x_0 and x_1, to get the first approximation to the solution, namely,

$$x_2 = x_1 - \frac{f(x_1)}{f(x_1) - f(x_o)} \cdot (x_1 - x_0).$$

As with the Newton-Raphson method, the iteration is stopped when

$$|f(x_{i+1})| < \varepsilon.$$

Figure 4, below, illustrates the way that the secant method approximates the solution of the equation $f(x) = 0$.

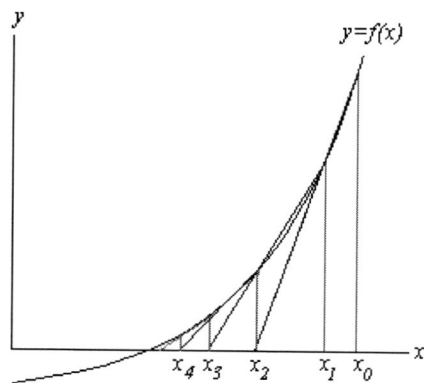

A SCILAB function for the secant method

The function *secant*, listed below, uses the secant method to solve for non-linear equations. It requires two initial values and an expression for the function, f(x).

```
function [x]=secant(x0,x00,f)
//newton-raphson algorithm
N = 100; eps = 1.e-5; // define max. no. iterations and error
maxval = 10000.0;    // define value for divergence
xx1 = x0; xx2 = x00;
while (N>0)
      gp = (f(xx2)-f(xx1))/(xx2-xx1);
```

```
        xn = xx1-f(xx1)/gp;
        if(abs(f(xn))<eps)then
              x=xn
              disp(100-N);
              return(x);
        end;
        if (abs(f(xn))>maxval)then
              disp(100-N);
              error('Solution diverges');
              abort;
        end;
        N = N - 1;
        xx1 = xx2;
        xx2 = xn;
end;
disp(100-N);
error('No convergence');
abort;
//end function
```

Application of secant method

The following SCILAB commands define the function f(x), load the function *secant.txt*:

```
-->deff('[y]=f(x)','y=x^3-2*x^2+1')

-->getf('secant.txt')
```

The following commands call the function *secant.txt* and converge to a solution:

```
-->secant(-10.,-9.8,f)

    11.
 ans  =

 -   .6180354

-->secant(1.0,1.2,f)

    0.
 ans  =

    1.

-->secant(5.0,5.2,f)

    10.
 ans  =

    1.6180341
```

Fixed-point iteration

Fixed point iteration consists in re-writing the equation $f(x)=0$ in the form

$$x = g(x).$$

This equation will now represent a recursive relation by writing it as

$$x_{n+1} = g(x_n).$$

To get the process started we use an initial value, $x = x_0$. Then, we calculate $x_1 = g(x_0)$, $x_2 = g(x_1)$, etc. Convergence is achieved whenever $|f(x)| < \varepsilon$, or whenever $|x_{n+1} - x_n| < \varepsilon$.

A SCILAB function for fixed iteration

The following function will perform the iterations, it will stop if there is divergence or if convergence is achieved. The function is stored in file *fixedp*:

```
function [x]=fixedp(x0,f)
//fixed-point iteration
N = 100; eps = 1.e-5; // define max. no. iterations and error
maxval = 10000.0;    // define value for divergence
xx = x0;
while (N>0)
      xn = f(xx);
      if(abs(xn-xx)<eps)then
            x=xn
            disp(100-N);
            return(x);
      end;
      if (abs(f(xx))>maxval)then
            disp(100-N);
            error('Solution diverges');
            abort;
      end;
      N = N - 1;
      xx = xn;
end;
error('No convergence');
abort;
//end function
```

Applications of fixed-point iteration

We use fixed-point iteration to solve the equation

$$f(x) = 3x - exp(x) + 2 = 0,$$

with the following recurrence equations:

(a) $x = g1(x) = exp(x) - (2x+2)$; (b) $x = g2(x) = (exp(x)-2)/3$; and, (c) $x = g3(x) = ln(3x+2)$.

The following SCILAB commands define the three functions required:

```
-->deff('[y]=g1(x)','y=exp(x)-(2*x+2)');

-->deff('[y]=g2(x)','y=(exp(x)-2)/3');

-->deff('[y]=g3(x)','y=log(3*x+2)');
```

Next, we get the function fixedp:

```
-->getf('fixedp')
```

The following calls using function *g1* diverge:

```
-->fixedp(1.0,g1)
 !--error    9999
No convergence
at line       21 of function fixedp              called by :
fixedp(1.0,g1)


-->fixedp(-1.0,g1)
 !--error    9999
No convergence
at line       21 of function fixedp              called by :
fixedp(-1.0,g1)


-->fixedp(0.0,g1)
 !--error    9999
No convergence
at line       21 of function fixedp              called by :
fixedp(0.0,g1)
```

The next examples converge to one root:

```
-->fixedp(1.0,g2)

     9.
 ans  =

   - .4552324

-->fixedp(-1.0,g2)

     7.
 ans  =

   - .4552349

-->fixedp(0.0,g2)

     7.
 ans  =

   - .4552309
```

These three examples converge to a second root.

```
-->fixedp(1.0,g3)

    12.
 ans  =

    2.1253885

-->fixedp(-1.0,g3)

    13.
 ans  =

    2.1253935 +   .0000049i

-->fixedp(0.0,g3)

    13.
 ans  =

    2.1253872
```

The number shown before the variable *ans* in these results indicates the number of iterations.

The fixed-point iteration method does not always converge. There is no convergence pattern for this method. Whether the method converges or not depends on the form of the function *g(x)* as well as on the initial value chosen.

Solving systems of non-linear equations

Consider the solution to a system of n non-linear equations in m unknowns given by

$$f_1(x_1, x_2, \ldots, x_n) = 0$$
$$f_2(x_1, x_2, \ldots, x_n) = 0$$
$$\vdots$$
$$f_n(x_1, x_2, \ldots, x_n) = 0$$

The system can be written in a single expression using vectors, i.e.,

$$f(x) = 0,$$

where the vector **x** contains the independent variables, and the vector **f** contains the functions $f_i(x)$:

$$\mathbf{x} = \begin{bmatrix} x_1 \\ x_2 \\ \vdots \\ x_n \end{bmatrix}, \quad \mathbf{f}(\mathbf{x}) = \begin{bmatrix} f_1(x_1, x_2, \ldots, x_n) \\ f_2(x_1, x_2, \ldots, x_n) \\ \vdots \\ f_n(x_1, x_2, \ldots, x_n) \end{bmatrix} = \begin{bmatrix} f_1(\mathbf{x}) \\ f_2(\mathbf{x}) \\ \vdots \\ f_n(\mathbf{x}) \end{bmatrix}.$$

Newton-Raphson method to solve systems of non-linear equations

A Newton-Raphson method for solving the system of linear equations requires the evaluation of a determinant, known as the _Jacobian_ of the system, which is defined as:

$$\mathbf{J} = \frac{\partial(f_1, f_2, \ldots, f_n)}{\partial(x_1, x_2, \ldots, x_n)} = \begin{bmatrix} \partial f_1/\partial x_1 & \partial f_1/\partial x_2 & \cdots & \partial f_1/\partial x_n \\ \partial f_2/\partial x_1 & \partial f_1/\partial x_2 & \cdots & \partial f_1/\partial x_n \\ \vdots & \vdots & \ddots & \vdots \\ \partial f_n/\partial x_1 & \partial f_n/\partial x_2 & \cdots & \partial f_n/\partial x_n \end{bmatrix} = [\frac{\partial f_i}{\partial x_j}]_{n \times n}.$$

If $\mathbf{x} = \mathbf{x}_0$ (a vector) represents the first guess for the solution, successive approximations to the solution are obtained from

$$\mathbf{x}_{n+1} = \mathbf{x}_n - \mathbf{J}^{-1} \cdot \mathbf{f}(\mathbf{x}_n) = \mathbf{x}_n - \Delta \mathbf{x}_n,$$

with $\Delta \mathbf{x}_n = \mathbf{x}_{n+1} - \mathbf{x}_n$.

Convergence criteria for the solution of a system of non-linear equation could be, for example, that the maximum of the absolute values of the functions $f_i(\mathbf{x}_n)$ is smaller than a certain tolerance ε, i.e.,

$$\max_i |f_i(\mathbf{x}_n)| < \varepsilon.$$

Another possibility for convergence is that the magnitude of the vector $\mathbf{f}(\mathbf{x}_n)$ be smaller than the tolerance, i.e.,

$$|\mathbf{f}(\mathbf{x}_n)| < \varepsilon.$$

We can also use as convergence criteria the difference between consecutive values of the solution, i.e.,

$$\max_i |(x_i)_{n+1} - (x_i)_n| < \varepsilon.,$$

or,

$$|\Delta \mathbf{x}_n| = |\mathbf{x}_{n+1} - \mathbf{x}_n| < \varepsilon.$$

The main complication with using Newton-Raphson to solve a system of non-linear equations is having to define all the functions $\partial f_i/\partial x_j$, for $i,j = 1,2, \ldots, n$, included in the Jacobian. As the number of equations and unknowns, n, increases, so does the number of elements in the Jacobian, n^2.

SCILAB function for Newton-Raphson method for a system of non-linear equations

The following SCILAB function, *newtonm*, calculates the solution to a system of n non-linear equations, $f(x) = 0$, given the vector of functions f and the Jacobian J, as well as an initial guess for the solution x_0.

```
function [x] = newtonm(x0,f,J)

//Newton-Raphson method applied to a
//system of linear equations f(x) = 0,
//given the jacobian function J, with
//J = del(f1,f2,...,fn)/del(x1,x2,...,xn)
//x = [x1;x2;...;xn], f = [f1;f2;...;fn]
//x0 is an initial guess of the solution

N = 100;            //define max. number of iterations
epsilon = 1e-10;    //define tolerance
maxval = 10000.0;   //define value for divergence
xx = x0;            //load initial guess

while (N>0)
      JJ = J(xx);
      if(abs(det(JJ))<epsilon) then
            error('newtonm - Jacobian is singular - try new x0');
            abort;
      end;
      xn = xx - inv(JJ)*f(xx);
      if(abs(f(xn))<epsilon)then
            x=xn;
            disp(1000-N);
            return(x);
      end;
      if (abs(f(xx))>maxval)then
            disp(100-N);
            error('Solution diverges');
            abort;
      end;
      N = N - 1;
      xx = xn;
end;
error('No convergence');
abort;
//end function
```

The functions f and the Jacobian J need to be defined as separate functions. To illustrate the definition of the functions consider the system of non-linear equations:

$$f_1(x_1,x_2) = x_1^2 + x_2^2 - 50 = 0,$$
$$f_2(x_1,x_2) = x_1 \cdot x_2 - 25 = 0,$$

whose Jacobian is

$$\mathbf{J} = \begin{bmatrix} \dfrac{\partial f_1}{\partial x_1} & \dfrac{\partial f_1}{\partial x_2} \\ \dfrac{\partial f_2}{\partial x_1} & \dfrac{\partial f_2}{\partial x_2} \end{bmatrix} = \begin{bmatrix} 2x_1 & 2x_2 \\ x_2 & x_1 \end{bmatrix}.$$

We can define the function f as the following user-defined SCILAB function $f2$:

```
function [f] = f2(x)

//f2(x) = 0, with x = [x(1);x(2)]
//represents a system of 2 non-linear equations

f(1) = x(1)^2 + x(2)^2 - 50;
f(2) = x(1)*x(2) -25;

//end function
```

The corresponding Jacobian is calculated using the user-defined SCILAB function $jacob2x2$:

```
function [J] = jacob2x2(x)

//Evaluates the Jacobian of a 2x2
//system of non-linear equations

J(1,1) = 2*x(1); J(1,2) = 2*x(2);
J(2,1) = x(2);   J(2,2) = x(1);

//end function
```

Illustrating the Newton-Raphson algorithm for a system of two non-linear equations

Before using function *newtonm*, we will perform some step-by-step calculations to illustrate the algorithm. We start by loading functions $f2$ and *jacob2x2*:

```
-->getf('f2')
```

```
-->getf('jacob2x2')
```

Next, we define an initial guess for the solution as:

```
-->x0 = [2;1]
 x0  =

!   2. !
!   1. !
```

Let's calculate the function $f(x)$ at $x = x_0$ to see how far we are from a solution:

```
-->f2(x0)
 ans =
```

```
!  - 45. !
!  - 23. !
```

Obviously, the function $f(x_0)$ is far away from being zero. Thus, we proceed to calculate a better approximation by calculating the Jacobian $J(x_0)$:

```
-->J0 = jacob2x2(x0)
 J0 =

!   4.    2. !
!   1.    2. !
```

The new approximation to the solution, x_1, is calculated as:

```
-->x1 = x0 - inv(J0)*f2(x0)
 x1 =

!   9.3333333 !
!   8.8333333 !
```

Evaluating the functions at x_1 produces:

```
-->f2(x1)
 ans =
!   115.13889 !
!   57.444444 !
```

Still far away from convergence. Let's calculate a new approximation, x_2:

```
-->x2 = x1 - inv(jacob2x2(x1))*f2(x1)
 x2 =
!   6.0428135 !
!   5.7928135 !
```

Evaluating the functions at x_2 indicates that the values of the functions are decreasing:

```
-->f2(x2)
 ans =
!   20.072282 !
!   10.004891 !
```

A new approximation and the corresponding function evaluations are:

```
-->x3 = x2 - inv(jacob2x2(x2))*f2(x2)
 x3 =
!   5.1336734 !
!   5.0086734 !

-->f2(x3)
 ans =
!   1.4414113 !
!    .7128932 !
```

The functions are getting even smaller suggesting convergence towards a solution.

Solution using function newtonm

Next, we use function newtonm to solve the problem postulated earlier. We start by loading function newtonm:

```
-->getf('newtonm')
```

A call to the function using the values of x0, f2, and jacob2x2, already loaded is:

```
-->[x] = newtonm(x0,f2,jacob2x2)

           16.
    x  =

    !   5.0000038 !
    !   4.9999962 !
```

The result shows the number of iterations required for convergence (16) and the solution found as x_1 = 5.0000038 and x_2= 4.9999962. Evaluating the functions for those solutions results in:

```
-->f2(x)
 ans  =

    1.0E-10 *

 !     .2910383 !
 ! -   .1455192 !
```

The values of the functions are close enough to zero (error in the order of 10^{-10}).

> Note: The functions f2 and jacob2x2 can be loaded as line functions by using deff:
>
> ```
> -->deff('[f]=f2(x)',['f_1=x(1)^2+x(2)^2-50';'f_2=x(1)*x(2)-25';'f=[f_1;f_2]'])
> --
> >deff('[J]=jacob2x2(x)',['J11=2*x(1)';'J12=2*x(2)';'J21=x(2)';'J22=x(1)';'J=[J11,J12;J21,J22]'])
> ```

"Secant" method to solve systems of non-linear equations

We use the term "secant" to refer to a method for solving systems of non-linear equations through the Newton-Raphson algorithm, namely $x_{n+1} = x_n - J^{-1} \cdot f(x_n)$, but approximating the Jacobian through finite differences. This approach is a generalization of the secant method for a single non-linear equation. For that reason, we refer to the method applied to a system of non-linear equations as a "secant" method, although the geometric origin of the term not longer applies.

The "secant" method for a system of non-linear equations free us from having to define the n^2 functions necessary to define the Jacobian for a system of n equations. Instead, we approximate the partial derivatives in the Jacobian with

$$\frac{\partial f_i}{\partial x_j} \approx \frac{f_i(x_1, x_2, \cdots, x_j + \Delta x, \cdots, x_n) - f_i(x_1, x_2, \cdots, x_j, \cdots, x_n)}{\Delta x},$$

where Δx is a small increment in the independent variables. Notice that $\partial f_i/\partial x_j$ represents element J_{ij} in the jacobian $J = \partial(f_1, f_2, \ldots, f_n)/\partial(x_1, x_2, \ldots, x_n)$.

To calculate the Jacobian we proceed by columns, i.e., column j of the Jacobian will be calculated as shown in the function *jacobFD* (*jacob*ian calculated through *F*inite *D*ifferences) listed below:

```
function [J] = jacobFD(f,x,delx)

//Calculates the Jacobian of the
//system of non-linear equations:
//f(x) = 0, through finite differences.
//The Jacobian is built by columns

[m n] = size(x);

for j = 1:n
    xx = x;
    xx(j) = x(j) + delx;
    J(:,j) = (f(xx)-f(x))/delx;
end;
//end function
```

Notice that for each column (i.e., each value of j) we define a variable *xx* which is first made equal to x, and then the *j*-th element is incremented by *delx*, before calculating the j-th column of the Jacobian, namely, J(:,j). This is the SCILAB implementation of the finite difference approximation for the Jacobian elements $J_{ij} = \partial f_i/\partial x_j$ as defined earlier.

Illustrating the "secant" algorithm for a system of two non-linear equations

To illustrate the application of the "secant" algorithm we use again the system of two non-linear equations defined earlier through the function *f2*. We start by loading functions *f2* and *jacobFD*:

```
-->getf('f2')
```

```
-->getf('jacobFD')
```

We choose an initial guess for the solution as $x_0 = [2;3]$, and an increment in the independent variables of $\Delta x = 0.1$:

```
-->x0 = [2;3]
 x0  =
```

```
!    2. !
!    3. !

 -->dx = 0.1
 dx  =
     .1
```

Variable J0 will store the Jacobian corresponding to x_0 calculated through finite differences with the value of Δx defined above:

```
-->J0 = jacobFD(f2,x0,dx)
 J0  =
!   4.1      6.1 !
!   3.       2.  !
```

A new estimate for the solution, namely x_1, is calculated using the Newton-Raphson algorithm:

```
-->x1 = x0 - inv(J0)*f2(x0)
 x1  =
!   6.1485149 !
!   6.2772277 !
```

The finite-difference Jacobian corresponding to x_1 gets stored in J1:

```
-->J1 = jacobFD(f2,x1,dx)
 J1  =
!   12.39703     12.654455 !
!   6.2772277    6.1485149 !
```

And a new approximation for the solution x_2 is calculated as:

```
-->x2 = x1 - inv(J1)*f2(x1)
 x2  =
!   6.1417644 !
!   3.9045469 !
```

The next two approximations to the solution (x_3 and x_4) are calculated without first storing the corresponding finite-difference Jacobians:

```
-->x3 = x2 - inv(jacobFD(f2,x2,dx))*f2(x2)
 x3  =
!   5.5599859 !
!   4.4403496 !
-->x4 = x3 - inv(jacobFD(f2,x3,dx))*f2(x3)
 x4  =
!   5.2799174 !
!   4.7200843 !
```

To check the value of the functions at $x = x_4$ we use:

```
-->f2(x4)
 ans =

!     .1567233 !
! -   .0783449 !
```

The functions are close to zero, but not yet an acceptable error (i.e., something in the order of 10^{-6}). Therefore, we try one more approximation to the solution, i.e x_5:

```
-->x5 = x4 - inv(jacobFD(f2,x4,dx))*f2(x4)
 x5  =

!   5.1399583 !
!   4.8600417 !
```

The functions are even closer to zero than before, suggesting a convergence to a solution.

```
-->f2(x5)
 ans  =

!   .0391768 !
! - .0195883 !
```

SCILAB function for "secant" method to solve systems of non-linear equations

To make the process of achieving a solution automatic, we propose the following SCILAB user-defined function, *secantm*:

```
function [x] = secantm(x0,x1,f)

///Secant-type method applied to a
//system of linear equations f(x) = 0,
//given the jacobian function J, with
//JJ approximated by (f(x(n)-f(x(n-1)))/(x(n)-x(n-1))
//x = [x1;x2;...;xn], f = [f1;f2;...;fn]
//x0,x1 are the initial guesses of the solution

N = 100;              //define max. number of iterations
epsilon = 1e-10;      //define tolerance
maxval = 10000.0;     //define value for divergence

if abs(x0-x1)<epsilon then
        error('x1=x0 - use different values');
        abort;
end;

xn    = x0;           //load initial guesses
xnm1  = x1;

[n m] = size(x1);

while (N>0)
        fxn   = f(xn);
        fxnm1 = f(xnm1);
        for i = 1:n
             for j = 1:n
                  JJ(i,j) = (fxn(i)-fxnm1(i))/(xn(j)-xnm1(j))
             end;
        end;

        if abs(det(JJ))<epsilon then
```

```
                error('newtonm - Jacobian is singular - try new x0,x1');
                abort;
        end;

        xnp1 = xn - inv(JJ)*f(xn);

        if abs(f(xnp1))<epsilon then
                x=xnp1;
                disp(1000-N);
                return(x);
        end;

        if abs(f(xnp1))>maxval then
                disp(100-N);
                error('Solution diverges');
                abort;
        end;

        N = N - 1;
        xnm1 = xn;
        xn   = xnp1;
end;
error('No convergence');
abort;
//end function
```

Solution using function *secantm*

To solve the system represented by function *f2*, we start by loading function *secantm*:

-->getf('secantm')

The following call to function *secantm* produces a solution after 18 iterations:

-->x = secantm(x0,dx,f2)

     18.
 x =

 !   4.9999964 !
 !   5.0000036 !

Solving non-linear equations with the *fsolve* function

SCILAB provides function *fsolve* for the solution of non-linear equations. In calling the function you can either include a derivative (for a Newton-Raphson method) or only the function f(x) (for a secant-type method). The *fsolve* function can be called by using:

$$[x [,v [,info]]] = fsolve(x0, fct [,fjac] [,tol])$$

where *x0* is a real vector representing an initial guess for the solution; *fct* is an external (i.e function or list or string) representing the equation *fct(x) = 0*; *fjac* is an external (i.e function or list or string) representing a Jacobian or derivative; and *tol* is a real scalar representing the tolerance for convergence. The default value of *tol*, if not provided in the function call, is *tol*=1.0x10^{10}.

Termination of a *fsolve* function call occurs when the algorithm estimates that the relative error between x and the solution is at most *tol*.

In the left-hand side of the function call, *x* is a real vector representing the final value of the solution; *v* is a real vector representing the value of the function at *x*; and *info* is an integer representing a termination indicator. *Info* can take any of the following values corresponding to different termination conditions:

> 0 : improper input parameters.
> 1 : relative error between x and the solution is at most *tol*.
> 2 : number of calls to *fcn* reached
> 3 : *tol* is too small. No further improvement in the approximate solution x is possible.
> 4 : iteration is not making good progress.

As indicated above, this function can be used to solve for a system of linear equations, including a Jacobian matrix (*jac*). For a single non-linear equation *fjac* is the derivative.

Solving single non-linear equations with *fsolve*

The following examples show how to use the *fsolve* function for solving equations of the form *f(x) = 0*. First, we define *f(x)* and its derivative, *fp(x)*:

```
-->deff('[y]=f(x)','y=x^3-2*x^2+1')

-->deff('[y]=fp(x)','y=x*x^2-4*x')
```

Then, we perform different calls to the function *fsolve*:

```
-->fsolve(2.0,f)       //No left-hand side, no Jacobian
 ans  =

    1.618034

-->fsolve(2.0,f,fp)    //No left-hand side, Jacobian provided
 ans  =

    1.618034

-->fsolve(2.0,f,fp,0.001)   //No left-hand side, Jacobian and tol provided
 ans  =

    1.9999745

-->x = fsolve(1.0,f,fp)    //solution name, x, in left-hand side
 x  =
    1.
```

```
-->[x,f_x] = fsolve(-10,f,fp)    //solution and function value in LHS
 f_x  =

    2.220E-16
 x =

  - .6180340
-->[x,f_x,msg] = fsolve(-2.0,f)   //solution, function, message in LHS
 msg  =

    1.
 f_x  =

  - 2.220E-16
 x =

  - .6180340
```

Solving a system of non-linear equations with *fsolve*

We use function *fsolve* to solve the system of two non-linear equations defined by function *f2*. To begin with, we load the function *f2*, and the corresponding Jacobian *jacob2x2*:

```
-->getf('f2')
```

```
-->getf('jacob2x2')
```

Next, we define an initial value for the solution, *x0*, and call function *fsolve* using *f2*, *jacob2x2*:

```
-->x0 = [3;-2]
 x0  =
 !   3. !
 ! - 2. !
-->fsolve(x0,f2,jacob2x2)
 ans  =
 !   5. !
 !   5. !
```

A second call to the function includes a left-hand side specifying the solution, *x*, the value of the function at the solution, *f_x*, and information about the solution *info*:

```
-->[x,f_x,info] = fsolve(x0,f2,jacob2x2)
 info  =
    1.

 f_x  =
 !   0. !
 !   0. !
```

```
      x  =

!   5.  !
!   5.  !
```

You can also call function *fsolve* without including the Jacobian:

```
-->[x,f_x,info] = fsolve(x0,f2)
  info =

     1.
  f_x  =

!     0.         !
! -  3.553E-15 !
  x  =

!   5.0000001 !
!   4.9999999 !
```

A second example involves the solution of the system of 3 non-linear equations without using the Jacobian:

$$f_1(x_1, x_2, x_3) = x_1^2 - x_2^2 + x_3^2 - 4$$
$$f_2(x_1, x_2, x_3) = x_1 x_2 - x_3 + 1$$
$$f_3(x_1, x_2, x_3) = (x_1 x_2 x_3)^{1/2} - 1.4142$$

First, we define the system of equations as function $f3$:

```
-->deff('[y]=f3(x)',['f_1=x(1)^2-x(2)^2+x(3)^2-4','f_2=x(1)*x(2)-x(3)+1',...
-->'f_3=sqrt(x(1)*x(2)*x(3))-1.4142','y=[f_1;f_2;f_3]'])
```

We use the following values as first guesses for the solution:

```
-->x0 = [3,3,3]
  x0 =

!   3.    3.    3. !
```

A call to *fsolve* produces:

```
-->[xs,fxs,m] = fsolve(x0',f3)
  m  =
     1.
  fxs  =
     1.0E-15 *

! -  .4440892 !
!    0.       !
! -  .2220446 !
  xs =
!   1.0000064 !
!    .9999808 !
!   1.9999872 !
```

Applications of non-linear equations

In this section we present solutions of non-linear equations that arise from applications to the physical sciences.

Projectile motion

The motion of a projectile in a Cartesian coordinate system as shown in the figure below is described by the equations:

$$a_x = 0, \; a_y = -g,$$

$$v_x = v_0 \cos(\theta_0), \; v_y = v_0 \sin(\theta_0) - gt,$$

$$x = x_0 + v_0 \cos(\theta_0) \cdot t, \; y = y_0 + v_0 \sin(\theta_0) \cdot t - g \cdot t^2/2,$$

where a stands for acceleration, v for velocity, and (x,y) are the positions of the projectile at time t. It is implied that the projectile was launched from point (x_0, y_0) at time $t = 0$ with an initial velocity of magnitude $v = v_0$ at an angle above the positive x-axis of $\theta = \theta_0$. The variable g represents the acceleration of gravity ($g = 9.806$ m/s^2 = 32.2 ft/s^2).

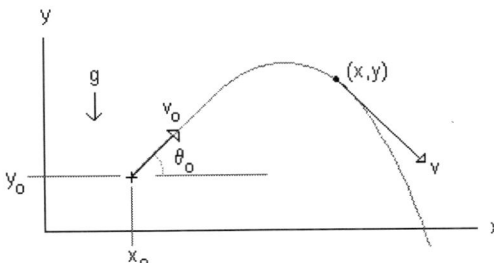

The velocity vector, illustrated in the figure, can be written as $v = v_x i + v_y j$. The equation of the trajectory can be obtained by replacing $t = (x-x_0)/(v_0 \cos(\theta_0))$, into the equation for y, resulting in

$$y = y_0 + \tan(\theta_0) \cdot (x - x_0) - \frac{g}{2 \cdot v_0^2 \cdot \cos^2(\theta_0)} \cdot (x - x_0)^2.$$

Example 1. A projectile is launched from point $(x_0, y_0) = (0,0)$ with a velocity $v = 25$ m/s at an unknown angle θ_0. If the projectile passes through point $(x,y) = (2,3)$, determine the angle.

Replacing the values of the data given in the problem statement together with the appropriate value of g in the equation of the trajectory, we can form a single non-linear equation on θ_0 defined by

$$f(\theta_0) = y_0 + \tan(\theta_0) \cdot (x - x_0) - \frac{g}{2 \cdot v_0^2 \cdot \cos^2(\theta_o)} \cdot (x - x_0)^2 - y = 0.$$

The solution using SCILAB can be found as follows:

First, we enter the known data:

```
-->x0 = 0, y0 = 0, v0 = 25, x = 2, y = 3, g = 9.806
 x0  =

    0.
 y0  =

    0.
 v0  =

    25.
 x   =

    2.
 y   =

    3.
 g   =

    9.806
```

Next, we define the function $f(\theta_o)$.

```
-->deff('[f]=traj(theta0)',...
-->'f = y0+tan(theta0).*(x-x0)-g.*(x-x0)^2.\(2.*v0^2.*cos(theta0)^2)-y')
```

Notice that in the definition we used the left division (\) in the third term of the function. We do this in order to be able to plot the function given an array of values of θ_0 as will be shown next. The variable *th* is an array of values of θ_0, starting at 0.1 and ending at $6.28 \approx 2\pi$. The variable *fth* stores the values of the function *traj(theta0)*, representing $f(\theta_0)$, and corresponding to *th*.

```
-->th = [0.1:0.1:6.28]'; fth = traj(th);
```

We use those variables, *th* and *fth*, to plot the function $f(\theta_0)$ with the purpose of identifying possible solutions.

```
-->plot(th,fth,'theta0','f_trajectory','projectile motion')

-->xgrid()
```

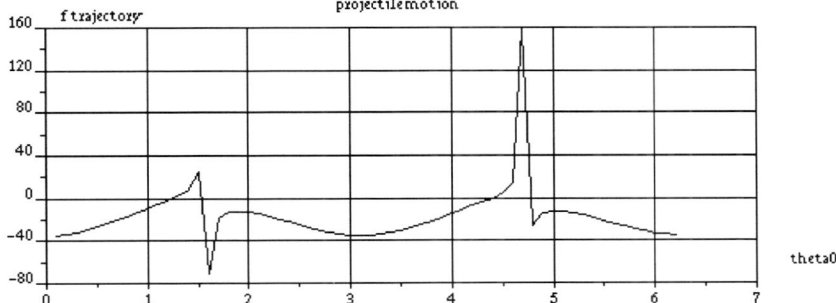

The figure is shown above. From the figure we notice that there are two possible solutions, one near 1.0 and one near 4.0. To obtain the solutions we use SCILAB'S function *fsolve*. The two solutions are shown next. The solutions are given in radians, the natural unit of angular measurement. We also show the equivalent values in degrees, through the formula,

$$\theta^o = 180 \cdot \theta / \pi.$$

```
-->th0 = fsolve(1,traj)
 th0  =

    1.2538009

-->180*th0/%pi
 ans  =

    71.8375

-->th0 = fsolve(4,traj)
 th0  =

    4.3953936

-->180*th0/%pi
 ans  =
    251.8375
```

Next, we produce a plot of the projectile trajectory corresponding to θ_0 = 1.2538009 rad. We start by clearing the variables and defining the equation of the trajectory:

```
-->clear

-->deff('[y]=f(x)',...
-->'y=y0+tan(theta0)*(x-x0)-g*(x-x0)^2/(2*v0^2*cos(theta0)^2)')
```

Next, we load the constant values:

```
-->x0 = 0; y0 = 0; v0 = 25; x = 2; y = 3; g = 9.806; theta0 = 1.2538009;
```

The plot is produced by the following statements:

```
-->xx = [0:0.1:40]';
```

```
-->yy = f(xx);

-->plot(xx,yy,'x','y','projectile trajectory')
```

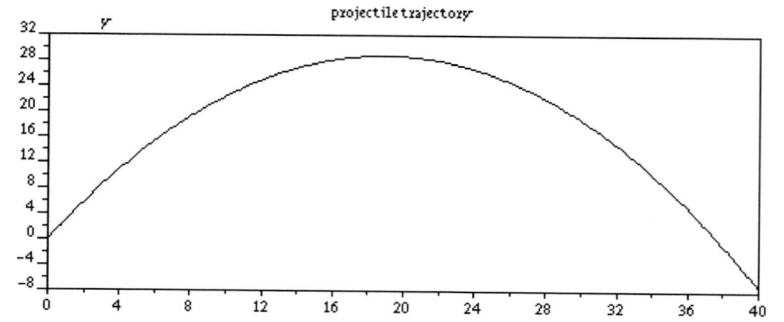

Solving the equation *tan(x) = x*

The equation *tan(x) = x* shows up in problems of differential equations when determining so-called eigenvalues and eigenfunctions. In this example we solve the equation for values of x > 0. To see possible solutions we plot the functions $f_1(x) = x$ and $f_2(x) = tan(x)$ in the same set of axes by using:

```
-->deff('[y]=f1(x)','y=x')

-->deff('[y]=f2(x)','y=tan(x)')

-->xx = [0:0.1:20]'; yy1 = f1(xx); yy2 = f2(xx);

-->plot2d([xx xx],[yy1 yy2],[1,2],'111','x@tan(x)',[0 0 10 10])
```

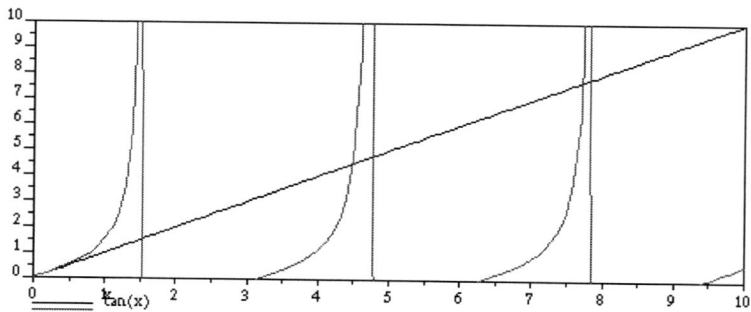

We can see at least three roots one is zero, the other two are near 4 and 7.5. To solve the corresponding equation we define the function $f_x(x) = \tan(x)-x$, and solve it using SCILAB's function *fsolve*:

```
-->deff('[y]=fx(x)','y=tan(x)-x')

-->x1 = fsolve(0.5,fx)
 x1  =

    9.218E-09

-->x2 = fsolve(4.1,fx)
 x2  =

    4.4934095

-->x3 = fsolve(7.5,fx)
 x3  =

    7.7252518
```

To verify that the solutions satisfy the equation $f_x(x) = 0$, try:

```
-->fx(x1), fx(x2), fx(x3)
 ans  =

    0.
 ans  =

    8.882E-16
 ans  =

  - 2.309E-14
```

Analysis of a simple three-bar mechanism

Consider the mechanism shown in the figure below. Bar SR has a fixed hinge at S, while bar PQ has a fixed hinge at P. Bar SR is animated by a rotational motion about point S that drives the mechanism forcing bar PQ to rotate about point P. The analysis in this case consists in determining the angle γ (output angle) given the angle α (input angle).

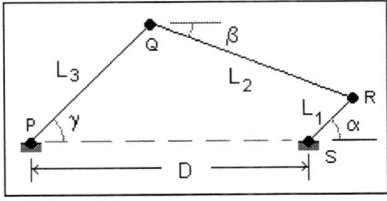

You can verify from the figure that:

$$L_3 \sin \gamma = L_1 \sin \alpha + L_2 \sin \beta$$
$$L_3 \cos \gamma + L_2 \cos \beta - L_1 \cos \alpha = D$$

This is a system of two non-linear equations in two unknowns β and γ, for a given value of α. The system can be written as follows:

$$f_1(\beta, \gamma) = -L_2 \sin \beta + L_3 \sin \gamma - L_1 \sin \alpha = 0$$
$$f_2(\beta, \gamma) = L_2 \cos \beta + L_3 \cos \gamma - L_1 \cos \alpha - D = 0$$

These system of non-linear equations can be entered into SCILAB as the following file function:

```
function [f] = fmech(angle)

//evaluates f1(beta,gama) & f2(beta,gamma)
//for the case of a three-bar mechanism
//angle(1) = beta, angle(2) = gamma

f = zeros(2,1);
f(1) = -L2*sin(angle(1))+L3*sin(angle(2))-L1*sin(alpha);
f(2) =  L2*cos(angle(1))+L3*cos(angle(2))-L1*cos(alpha)-D;

//end function
```

Next, we will use SCILAB function *fsolve* to obtain a table of values of γ given a set of values of α. We will use the values D = 4, L_1 = 6, L_2 = 3, L_3 = 7, and α = 0, $\pi/20$, $2\pi/20$, ..., $19\pi/20$. First, we load the function fmech:

```
-->getf('fmech')
```

Next, we define the constant values:

```
-->L1=6;L2=3;L3=7;D=4;

-->alphav = [0:%pi/20:19*%pi/20];
```

The size of *alphav* (the *v* stands for vector) will be used later in calculating the angles β and γ.

```
-->[m n] = size(alphav)
 n =
    20.
 m =
    1.
```

The angles β and γ will be obtained as rows in the matrix angles, which is first defined as an empty array:

```
-->angles = [];
```

The next *for* loop will solve for values of angles β and γ for each value of *alphav*, which is temporarily stored in variable *alpha*:

```
-->for j = 1:m
-->    alpha = alphav(j);
-->    angles = [angles, fsolve([alpha;alpha],fmech)];
-->end;
```

The following assignment statements load the values of the angles β and γ in separate vectors:

```
-->beta = angles(1,:);
```

```
-->gama = angles(2,:);
```

Next, we produce a plot of β-vs-α (both in radians):

```
-->plot(alphav,beta,'alpha','beta','three-bar mechanism analysis')
```

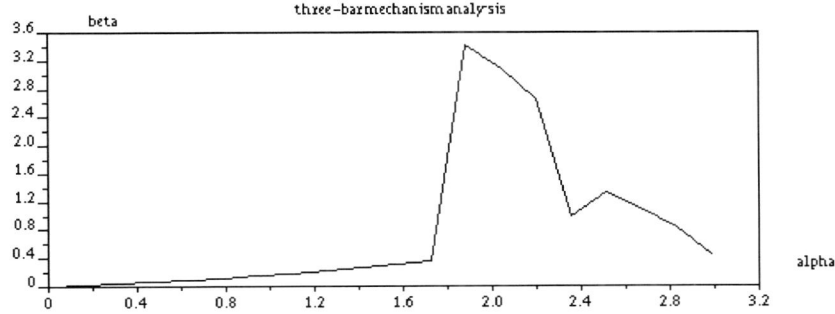

The following is a plot of γ-vs-α (both in radians):

```
-->plot(alphav,gama,'alpha','gamma','three-bar mechanism analysis')
```

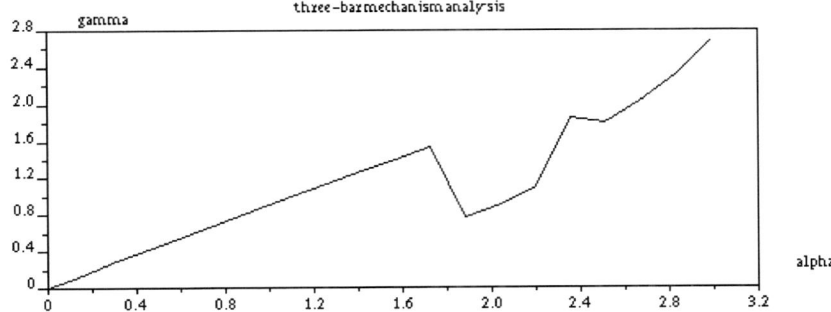

Solving the Darcy-Weisbach and Coolebrook-White equations for pipeline flow

The figure below shows the components of the energy equation for turbulent flow in a pipe. The datum is a horizontal reference level from which the elevation of the pipe centerline is measured. The energy line (E.L.) is a graphical representation of the total head along the pipe. The hydraulic grade line (H.G.L.) represents the piezometric head along the pipe.

Let the pipe length between cross-sections 1 and 2 be L. The slope of the energy line is defined as $S = h_f/L$, where h_f is the energy losses due to friction on the length L.

The energy equation for the figure above can be written by simply adding the lengths of the different energy heads shown, i.e.,

$$z_1 + \frac{p_1}{\gamma} + \frac{V_1^2}{2g} = z_2 + \frac{p_2}{\gamma} + \frac{V_2^2}{2g} + h_f$$

For a constant-diameter pipeline $V_1 = V_2$, and using the *piezometric head*, $h = z + p/\gamma$, the energy loss is equal to the difference in piezometric heads, i.e.,

$$h_f = h_1 - h_2 = (z_1 + p_1/\gamma) - (z_2 + p_2/\gamma).$$

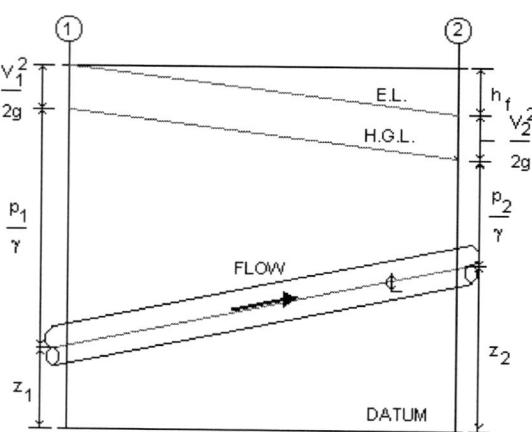

The <u>Darcy-Weisbach equation</u> provides a way to calculate the friction head loss, h_f, based of fluid properties and flow characteristics:

$$h_f = f \cdot \frac{L}{D} \cdot \frac{V^2}{2g},$$

in which, L and D are the length and diameter of the pipe, V is the mean flow velocity, g is the acceleration of gravity, and f is known as the Darcy-Weisbach friction factor. The friction factor, $f = f(e/D, Re)$, is a function of the parameters e/D or *relative roughness*, and the *Reynolds number*, Re. The parameter *e*, known as the absolute roughness of the pipeline is a measure of the roughness heights of the pipeline's inner wall, and the Reynolds number defined as

$$Re = \frac{\rho V D}{\mu} = \frac{VD}{\nu},$$

where ν is the fluid's kinematic viscosity.

An expression describing the variation of $f = f(e/D, Re)$ for turbulent flow is the Coolebrook-White equation given by:

$$\frac{1}{\sqrt{f}} = -2 \cdot \log\left(\frac{e}{3.7D} + \frac{2.51}{Re\sqrt{f}}\right)$$

Here, *log* represents the logarithm of base 10. In SCILAB, the function *log* represents the natural logarithm, i.e., the logarithm of base $e = 2.718281828$, which is typically written in paper as *ln*. Using natural logarithms, we re-write the Coolebrook-White equation to read:

$$\frac{1}{\sqrt{f}} = -0.8686 \cdot \ln\left(\frac{e}{3.7 \cdot D} + \frac{2.51}{Re\sqrt{f}}\right).$$

This function is implicit on *f*, therefore, suitable for solution through the methods of non-linear equations presented in this chapter.

Example 1. Determining the friction factor.

As an example, try using the following values e = 0.00001m, D = 0.25 m, Re=10^6 to determine the corresponding friction factor. Here is the solution using SCILAB: First, we define the function for the Coolebrook-White equation:

```
-->deff('[P]=CW(f)','...
-->P=1/sqrt(f)+0.8686*log(e/(3.7*D)+2.51/(Re*sqrt(f)))')
```

Next, we enter the constant values:

```
-->e = 0.00001; D = 0.25; Re = 1e6;
```

The corresponding friction factor is calculated as:

```
-->f = fsolve(0.02,CW)
 f  =

    .0124687
```

Example 2 Plotting the Moody diagram.

The function described by the Coolebrook-White equation is typically plotted in log-log scale with the Reynolds number, Re, in the x-axis and the friction factor, f, as curves corresponding to different values of the relative roughness, e/D. The following SCILAB script is used to plot a simplified version of the Moody diagram for selected values of the relative roughness. The script is called *PlotMoody* and it is stored in SCILAB's working directory:

```
//Script to plot Moody diagram

//First we define the function for the Coolebrook-
//White equation:

deff('[P]=CW(f)','...
P=1/sqrt(f)+0.8686*log(e/(3.7*D)+2.51/(Re*sqrt(f)))')

D = 0.025; //Diameter of 2.5 cm, approx. 1.0 inch

//The next two vectors contain values of the relative
//roughness and the Reynolds number
e_v = [0.01 0.001 0.0001 0.00001 0.000001 0.0000001];
Re_v = [1e4 1e5 1e6 1e7 1e8];

[ne me] = size(e_v);     //size of vectors
[nR mR] = size(Re_v);    //e_v and Re_v

fMoody = zeros(mR,me);   //Create matrix for f values

//Calculating friction factors for combinations of values
//of e_v(i) and Re_v(j):
for j = 1:me
    for i = 1:mR
        Re = Re_v(i); e = D*e_v(j);
        if e < 1e-5 then
            f0 = 0.01;
        else
            f0 = 0.02;
        end;
        fMoody(i,j) = fsolve(f0,CW);
    end;
end;

//Plotting the Moody diagram
plot2d1('oll',Re_v,[fMoody(:,1),fMoody(:,2),...
fMoody(:,3),fMoody(:,4), fMoody(:,5), fMoody(:,6)],...
[1:6],'121','0.01@0.001@0.0001@0.00001@0.000001@0.0000001');

xtitle('Moody diagram','Reynolds number','friction factor');

//end script
```

To execute the script use:

```
-->exec('PlotMoody')
```

SCILAB produces a listing of the script before producing the following graph:

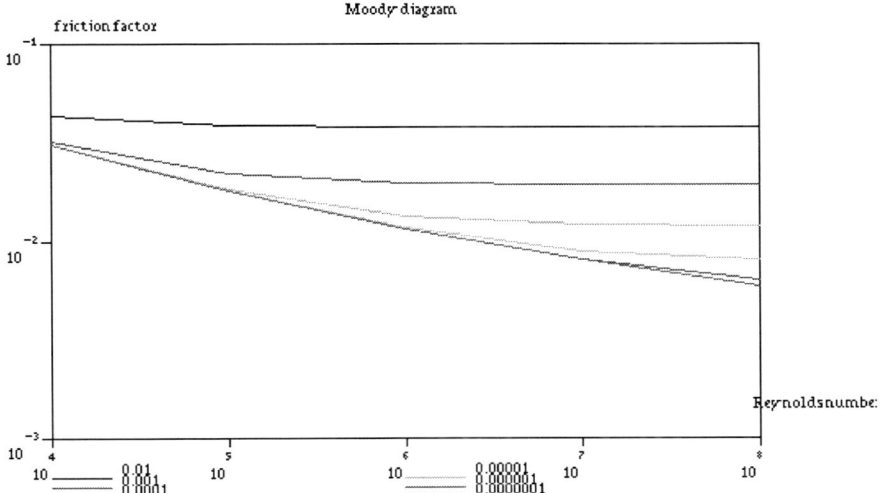

Example 3 Determining pipe diameter given the flow velocity or discharge

Eliminating the friction factor from the Darcy-Weisbach and Coolebrook-White equation we get the following equation relating velocity (V) to pipe length (L), diameter (D), and absolute roughness (e), energy loss (h_f), and kinematic viscosity (ν):

$$V = -1.2283 \cdot \sqrt{\frac{g \cdot h_f \cdot D}{L}} \cdot \ln\left(\frac{e}{3.7 \cdot D} + \frac{1.77 \cdot \nu}{D^{3/2} \cdot \sqrt{\frac{g \cdot h_f}{L}}}\right)$$

Suppose that we are given the values g = 9.806 m²/s, h_f = 1.0 m, e = 0.0001 m, L = 2000 m, ν = 1x10⁵ m²/s, V = 1.1 m/s, and asked to determine the value of D. We can define the following SCILAB function:

```
-->deff('[P]=VCW(D)',...
-->'P=V+1.2283*sqrt(g*D*hf/L)*log(e/(3.7*D)+1.77*Nu/(D^1.5*sqrt(g*hf/L)))')
```

The problem data is entered next:

```
-->V=1.1;g=9.806;hf=1;L=2000;e=0.0001;Nu=1e-5;
```

The solution is found by using the following call to SCILAB function *fsolve* with an initial guess D = 0.5:

```
-->D = fsolve(0.5,VCW)
```

```
   D  =  1.9543027
```

Using continuity, i.e., $Q = AV = \pi D^2 V/4$, an equation can be written in terms of Q as,

$$Q = -0.9648 \cdot D^{5/2} \cdot \sqrt{\frac{g \cdot h_f}{L}} \cdot \ln\left(\frac{e}{3.7 \cdot D} + \frac{1.78 \cdot v}{D^{3/2} \cdot \sqrt{\frac{g \cdot h_f}{L}}}\right)$$

For design problems, this equation is often more useful than the previous one given in terms of the velocity because more often than not the discharge rather than the velocity is given. To solve for the diameter given the discharge, we present the following SCILAB example. Given g = 9.806 m/s^2, h_f = 1.0 m, e = 0.0001 m, L = 2000 m, v = 1x10^5 m^2/s, Q = 2.2 m^3/s, find the corresponding pipe diameter. We start by defining the function:

```
-->deff('[P]=QCW(D)',...
--
>'P=Q+0.9648*D^2.5*sqrt(g*hf/L)*log(e/(3.7*D)+1.78*Nu/(D^1.5*sqrt(g*hf/L)))');
```

Next, we enter the problem data:

```
-->Q=2.2;g=9.806;hf=1;L=2000;e=0.0001;Nu=1e-5;
```

Finally, we solve for D:

```
-->D = fsolve(0.5,QCW)
  D  =  1.6782603
```

Solving pipe flow with the Swamee-Jain equation

To avoid the implicit nature of f in the Coolebrook-White equation we can use the following explicit approximation for f, referred to as the Swamee-Jain equation:

$$f = \frac{1.3254}{\left[\ln\left(\frac{e}{3.75D} + \frac{5.74}{Re^{0.9}}\right)\right]^2}.$$

With the definition of the Reynolds number $Re = VD/v$, the resulting expression for the friction factor is

$$f = \frac{1.3254}{\left[\ln\left(\frac{e}{3.75D} + \frac{5.74 v^{0.9}}{V^{0.9} D^{0.9}}\right)\right]^2}.$$

In design problems it is more convenient to work with the discharge Q. Replacing the velocity $V = 4Q/(\pi D^2)$ into the Swamee-Jain equation we get

$$f = \frac{1.3254}{\left[\ln\left(\dfrac{e}{3.75 \cdot D} + 4.618 \cdot \left(\dfrac{D \cdot v}{Q}\right)^{0.9}\right)\right]^2}$$

If we write the Darcy-Weisbach equation in terms of the discharge, i.e.,

$$h_f = f \cdot (L/D) \cdot V^2/(2g) = 8fLQ^2/(\pi^2 g D^5),$$

and then introduce the latest version of the Swamee-Jain equation, we will get the following equation for the friction losses in a pipe:

$$h_f = \frac{1.074 \cdot L \cdot Q^2}{g \cdot D^5 \left[\ln\left(\dfrac{e}{3.75 \cdot D} + 4.618 \cdot \left(\dfrac{D \cdot v}{Q}\right)^{0.9}\right)\right]^2}$$

A SCILAB function to solve the Darcy-Weisbach equation with the Swamee-Jain equation

The following function, *DWSJ* (*D*arcy-*W*eisbach equation with *S*wamee-*J*ain friction factor) can be used to solve for any of the variables in the previous equation given appropriate values of the remaining variables. The function also requires that the user provide an initial value of the variable that he or she is solving for. Function *DWSJ* uses SCILAB function *fsolve* to solve for the particular unknown of interest. A listing of the function follows:

```
function [result] = DWSJ(index,gindex,L,D,e,nu,hf,Q)

//This function solves for one of the variables
//in the Darcy-Weisbach equation with the friction
//factor approximated through the Swamee-Jain
//equation.   The string variable 'index' determines
//which variable to solve for.  Possible values of
//index are:
//       'L'    - to solve for the length of the pipe
//       'D'    - to solve for the diameter
//       'e'    - to solve for the absolute wall roughness
//       'nu'   - to solve for the kinematic viscosity
//       'hf'   - to solve for the friction losses
//       'Q'    - to solve for the discharge
//The variable 'gindex' can take the values 'SI' or
//'ES' corresponding to the system of units to be used:
//       'SI'   - for the Systeme International
//       'ES'   - for the English (or Imperial) System
//Make sure that the values of the variables are given
//in consistent units, i.e.,
// L(m or ft), D(m or ft), e(m or ft),
```

```
// nu(m^2/s or ft^2/s), hf(m or ft), Q(m^3/s or ft^3/s)
// The order of the variables does not change in the call
// to the function.  The user needs to provide an initial
// guess for the variable he/she is solving for in the
// appropriate position in the function call.

if gindex == 'SI' then
      g = 9.806;
elseif gindex == 'ES' then
      g = 32.2;
else
      error('DWSJ - wrong index for unit system');
      abort;
end;

if index == 'L' then
      deff('[P] = DWSJEq(LL)',...
      'P=1.074*LL*Q^2/(g*D^5*(log(e/(3.75*D)+4.618*(D*nu/Q)^0.9))^2)-hf');
      result = fsolve(L,DWSJEq);
elseif index == 'D' then
      deff('[P] = DWSJEq(DD)',...
      'P=1.074*L*Q^2/(g*DD^5*(log(e/(3.75*DD)+4.618*(DD*nu/Q)^0.9))^2)-hf');
      result = fsolve(D,DWSJEq);
elseif index == 'e' then
      deff('[P] = DWSJEq(ee)',...
      'P=1.074*L*Q^2/(g*D^5*(log(ee/(3.75*D)+4.618*(D*nu/Q)^0.9))^2)-hf');
      result = fsolve(e,DWSJEq);
elseif index == 'nu' then
      deff('[P] = DWSJEq(nnu)',...
      'P=1.074*L*Q^2/(g*D^5*(log(e/(3.75*D)+4.618*(D*nnu/Q)^0.9))^2)-hf');
      result = fsolve(nu,DWSJEq);
elseif index == 'hf' then
      deff('[P] = DWSJEq(hhf)',...
      'P=1.074*L*Q^2/(g*D^5*(log(e/(3.75*D)+4.618*(D*nu/Q)^0.9))^2)-hhf');
      result = fsolve(L,DWSJEq);
elseif index == 'Q' then
      deff('[P] = DWSJEq(QQ)',...
      'P=1.074*L*QQ^2/(g*D^5*(log(e/(3.75*D)+4.618*(D*nu/QQ)^0.9))^2)-hf');
      result = fsolve(L,DWSJEq);
else
      error('DWSJ - index is L, D, e, nu, hf, or Q enclosed in quotes');
      abort;
end;
```

The function may provide an error message if the initial value for the unknown variable is too far away from the solution, particularly for those unknowns whose values are typically very small, such as the viscosity (of the order of 10^{-6} to 10^{-5}) or the absolute roughness (anywhere from 0.000001 to 0.1). Whenever you receive an error message in a solution, try using different initial values of the unknown to improve the convergence of the function.

Applications of function*DWSJ* to pipe flow

Examples of applications of the function*DWSJ* follow. Recall that the general call to the function is

[result] = DWSJ(index,gindex,L,D,e,nu,hf,Q)

With *index* determining the unknown to solve for *('L','D','e','nu','hf','Q')*, and *gindex* determining the system of units *('SI', 'ES')*.

```
-->getf('DWSJ')                              //Load the function

-->DWSJ('L','SI',100,0.5,0.0001,1e-5,2,0.5)  //Solve for pipe length
 ans  =

    165.70807

-->DWSJ('D','SI',100,0.5,0.0001,1e-5,2,0.5)  //Solve for pipe diameter
 ans  =

    .4511914

-->DWSJ('e','SI',100,0.5,0.0001,1e-5,2,0.5)  //Solve for pipe roughness
 ans  =

    .0022291

-->DWSJ('nu','SI',100,0.5,0.0001,1e-5,2,0.5) //Solve for kinematic viscosity
 ans  =

    .0001117

-->DWSJ('hf','SI',100,0.5,0.0001,1e-5,2,0.5) //Solve for friction loss
 ans  =

    1.2069418

-->DWSJ('Q','SI',100,0.5,0.0001,1e-5,2,0.5)  //Solve for discharge
 ans  =

    .6567565
```

Solving for discharge and head for a pipe-pump system

Consider the flow through a horizontal pipe between two reservoirs as shown in the figure below. A pump is necessary to overcome the difference in water surface levels between the two reservoirs, $\Delta h = z_2 - z_1$. The pump inserts an energy head H into the system. If we neglect minor losses (entrance into the pipe, exit out of the pipe, valves, etc.), the energy equation for this system is given by

$$z_1 + 0 + 0 + H = z_2 + 0 + 0 + h_f.$$

Using the equation presented earlier for h_f that combines the Darcy-Weisbach and Swamee-Jain equations, we can write the so-called *system equation*:

$$H = \Delta h + \frac{1.074 \cdot L \cdot Q^2}{g \cdot D^5 \left[\ln\left(\frac{e}{3.75 \cdot D} + 4.618 \cdot \left(\frac{D \cdot v}{Q} \right)^{0.9} \right) \right]^2}.$$

The discharge through the pump Q and the energy head H that the pump provides to the system are related by the *pump rating curve*, typically described by a quadratic equation, i.e.,

$$H = a + bQ + cQ^2.$$

For a given system, the pipe characteristics, i.e., length(L), diameter (D), and roughness (e), as well as the kinematic viscosity of the liquid (v) are known. For a given value of Δh, the two equations listed above are solved for the unknowns H and Q. The solution can be accomplished through graphical means by plotting the two equations in the same set of axis and determining their point of intersection. This approach is shown next, using SCILAB.

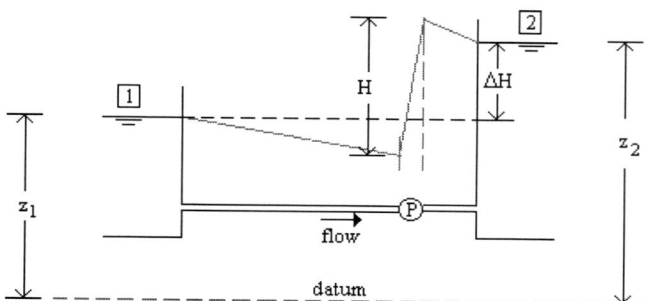

Graphical solution to the pump-pipeline system

To obtain the graphical solution we define the following functions that represent, respectively, the system equation and the pump rating curve:

```
-->deff('[HH]=H1(Q)',...
-->'HH = Dh+1.074*L*Q^2/(g*D^5*log(e/(3.75*D)+4.618*(D*nu/Q)^0.9)^2)')

-->deff('[HH]=H2(Q)','HH = a+b*Q+c*Q^2')
```

Next, we enter the constant values:

```
-->Qp = [0.1:0.1:2.0]; Hp1 = feval(Qp,H1); Hp2 = feval(Qp,H2);
```

The next step is to define a vector of values of Q, which we call Qp, and evaluate the two functions for those values of Q using function *feval* (function *eval*uation). Thus, vectors Hp1 and Hp2 store, respectively, the values of H corresponding to the system equation and the pump rating curve.

```
-->Dh = 20; L = 150; g = 9.806; e = 0.00001;

-->D = 0.25; nu = 1e-6; Q = 0.20;

-->a = 500; b = 0; c = -100;
```

The plot is obtained by using:

```
->plot2d([Qp',Qp'],[Hp1',Hp2'],[1,2])

-->xtitle('Pump-pipeline system','Q(m^3/s)','H(m)')
```

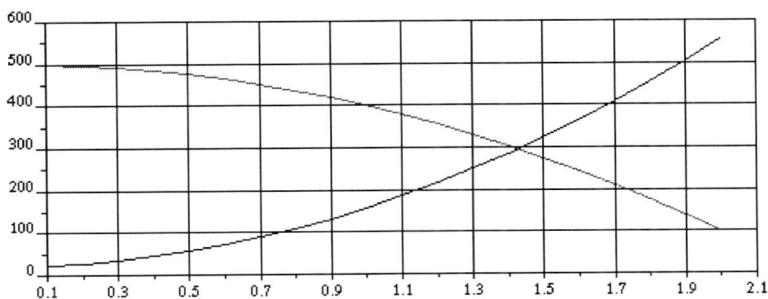

We can estimate the solution from the graphics as Q = 1.42 m^3/s and H = 290 m.

A function to solve a pipe-pump system

The following SCILAB function *PipePump*, is used to code the functions

$$f_1(Q,H) = H - \Delta h - \frac{1.074 \cdot L \cdot Q^2}{g \cdot D^5 \left[\ln\left(\frac{e}{3.75 \cdot D} + 4.618 \cdot \left(\frac{D \cdot v}{Q} \right)^{0.9} \right) \right]^2},$$

$$f_2(Q,H) = H - a - b \cdot Q - c \cdot Q^2.$$

This is the listing of the function:

```
function [P] = PipePump(X)

//This function codes the system equation
//and the pump rating curve for a pipe-pump
//system representing pumping between two
//reservoirs.  X(1) = Q and X(2) = H.
```

```
P = zeros(2,1);

P(1)=X(2)-Dh-1.074*L*X(1)^2/(g*D^5*(log(e/(3.75*D)+4.618*(D*nu/X(1))^0.9))^2);

P(2)=X(2)-a-b*X(1)-c*X(1)^2;

//end function
```

To load the function we use:

```
-->getf('PipePump')
```

The following call to function *fsolve* produces the solution:

```
-->fsolve([1.4;300],PipePump)
 ans  =

!    1.4275835 !
!    296.20053 !
```

To verify the solution use:

```
-->PipePump(ans)
 ans  =

   1.0E-11 *

!     .5798029 !
! -   .4490630 !
```

Notice that the results found through the use of *fsolve* and *PipePump*, i.e., Q = 1.4275835 m^3/s and H = 296.20053 m, are very close to the estimates we obtained from the graphical solution.

Exercises

In problems [1] through [6], use the following definitions:

$$z_1 = -3 + 2i, \; z_2 = 5 - i, \; z_3 = -4+3i, \; z_4 = -2-4i$$

[1]. Determine the following magnitudes and arguments:

(a) $|z_1|$ (b) $Arg(z_1)$ (c) $|z_2|$ (d) $Arg(z_2)$
(e) $|z_3|$ (f) $Arg(z_3)$ (g) $|z_4|$ (h) $Arg(z_4)$

[2]. Write the following complex numbers in polar form:

(a) 3-5i   (b) 4-4i   (c) 3-5i   (d) -2-6i
(e) -5+6i   (f) π+3i   (g) (5-i)/2 (h) 7+5i

[3]. Plot the complex numbers of problem [2] in the x-y plane using the function *complexplot*.

[4]. Determine the result of the following complex number operations:

(a) z_1+3z_2 (b) $z_1-z_2+4z_3$ (c) $(z_1-2)\cdot(z_4-z_3)$ (d) $z_4/z_2 + z_3/z_1$
(e) $z_1\cdot z_2\cdot z_3$ (f) $(z_1-2z_2)\cdot(z_3/\pi)$ (g) $z_1\cdot z_2 -1/z_3$ (h) $(z_2+z_3)/(z_1+3z_2)$

[5]. Determine the result of the following complex number operations:

(a) $\overline{z_1}+z_1$ (b) $\overline{z_2}\cdot z_2$ (c) $\overline{z_3/\,z_3}$ (d) $(\overline{z_1}+\overline{z_2})/(z_3-5\,\overline{z_4})$
(e) $\overline{z_1-z_1}$ (f) $2(\overline{z_1-z_1})$ (g) $1/\overline{z_2}+1/z_2$ (h) $|z_1|(\overline{z_2}+z_3)$

[6]. Determine the result of the following complex number operations:

(a) z_3^3 (b) $z_2(z_1-2z_3)^2$ (c) z_2/z_3^4 (d) z_3^2/z_1^3
(e) $z_1+1/z_2+1/z_3^2$ (f) $(1+1/z_2)^3$ (g) $z_1^3+(z_2-z_3)^2$ (h) $(z_2+1)^5/z_3$

[7]. Solve for z in the following equations:

(a) $z^2+3-2i = 0$ (b) $(z+1)^2 = 3^{1/2}$ (c) $z^3-i = 0$ (d) $z^4+(i-2)^3 = 0$
(e) $z^2+2z=4$ (f) $\overline{z}=-1$ (g) $1/(z+1)^3 = i$ (h) $z(z-1)=2$

[8]. Write a SCILAB function to calculate the roots of the quadratic equation $ax^2+bx+c = 0$. Use the function to solve the quadratic equations whose coefficients are:

(a) $a = 2, b = -5, c = 3$ (b) $a = 12, b = 22, c = -3$
(c) $a = 10, b = 25, c = 33$ (d) $a = -5, b = -5, c = 2$

[9]. Write a SCILAB function to calculate the roots of the cubic equation $ax^3+bx^2+cx+d=0$. (a)

(a) $a = 2, b = -5, c = 3, d = 23$ (b) $a = 12, b = 22, c = -3, d = 1$
(c) $a = 10, b = 25, c = 33, d = -10$ (d) $a = -5, b = -5, c = 2, d = 10$

[10]. Use function *roots* to solve problems [8] and [9].

[11]. Use function *roots* to solve the following polynomial equations:

(a) $s^5 + 6s^3 - 27 = 0$ (b) $y^4 - 23y^3 + 5y^2 - 3y + 2 = 0$
(c) $r^6 + r^2 + r - 2345 = 0$ (d) $(s+1)^7 - s^2 + 2 = 0$

In problems [12] through [16], you are required to solve the equation $f(x) = 0$. Plot the corresponding function $y = f(x)$ to obtain guesses of the solution(s), then solve for as many solutions as possible using:

(a) the bisection method
(c) the secant method
(b) the Newton-Raphson method
(d) SCILAB function $fsolve$

[12] $f(x) = x^3 + 18x^2 - 22x + \sin(2x^2+x) - 255$

[13] $f(x) = x^4 + \exp(x-2) + x^3 - 200$

[14] $f(x) = \exp(-0.1x)\cos(2x-\pi/2)$

[15] $f(x) = x^5 + 5x^2 - 23x - 19$

[16] $f(x) = \ln((x^2+x+2)/(\sin x + 1) - 5$, for $x > 0$

In problems [17] through [21], solve the system of equations shown using (a) SCILAB function $fsolve$, and (b) the "Secant" method for multiple equations

[17] $x^2 + y^2 - 2xy = 1$, $(x-2)(y-3) + e^x + y = 10.39$

[18] $x^2 + y^2 + z^2 = 17$, $xy + yz + zx = -4$, $(x+1)(y+1)(z-3) + xyz = -8$

[19] $\tan(x-1/2) + 5\cos y + z = 0.75$, $xyz + \sin(y) = 4.05$, $\exp(-xyz) + \cos(z) = 0.58$

[20] $ab + bc^2 + abc = 26$, $\sin(a+b) + \exp(c) - \ln(a) = -2.05$, $a + b + c = 0$

[21] $x \ln(y+z) = -3.83$, $xy^2 + yz^2 + zx^2 = -27.20$, $(x+y)^{1/2} + x = 0.60$

[22]. Manning's equation is used to calculate the discharge on an open channel of slope S (typically a relatively small value, i.e., $0.00000001 < S_0 < 0.001$), whose surface roughness is characterized by a parameter known as the Manning's coefficient n (typical values between 0.001 and 0.3. The larger the value of n, the rougher the surface. For example, concrete surfaces have $n = 0.012$). The equation is written as

$$Q = \frac{C_u}{n} \cdot \frac{A^{5/3}}{P^{2/3}} \cdot \sqrt{S_0},$$

where C_u is a coefficient that depends on the system of units used, with $C_u = 1.0$ for the Systeme Internationale (S.I.) and $C_u = 1.486$ for the English (or Imperial) System of units (E.S.), A is the cross-sectional area, P is the wetted perimeter of the cross-section (i.e., the length of the cross-sectional boundary in contact with the water), and Q is the discharge.
For a symmetric trapezoidal cross section, as shown below, the area and wetted perimeter are given by

$$A = (b+zy)y, \quad P = b + 2y\sqrt{1+z^2},$$

where b is the bottom width of the cross-section, y is the cross-sectional depth, and z is the (dimensionless) side slope.

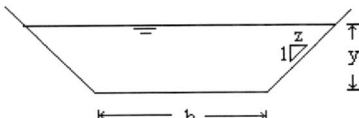

Write a function, along the lines of function wSJ, that allows the user to select which element to solve for out of the Manning's equation for a trapezoidal cross-section. Use the function thus developed to solve for the missing terms in each line of the following table:

Case	System of Units	b	y	z	n	So	Q
(a)	S.I.	b=?	0.6	1.5	0.012	0.0001	0.2
(b)	S.I.	1.5	y=?	0.5	0.023	0.00001	0.15
(c)	S.I.	0.5	0.25	z=?	0.01	0.001	0.35
(d)	S.I.	1.4	0.4	1	n=?	0.0001	0.6
(e)	S.I.	1.2	0.6	0.5	0.018	S=?	0.8
(f)	S.I.	0.6	0.3	0.75	0.015	0.0001	Q=?
(g)	E.S.	b=?	0.6	1.5	0.012	0.0001	3.5
(h)	E.S.	3	y=?	0.5	0.023	0.00001	7.2
(i)	E.S.	2	1.2	z=?	0.01	0.001	4.5
(j)	E.S.	3.5	0.75	1	n=?	0.0001	10
(k)	E.S.	4.25	2.1	0.5	0.018	S=?	25
(l)	E.S.	5	2.5	0.75	0.015	0.0001	Q=?

[23]. Critical flow conditions in open channel flow are given by the equation

$$\frac{Q^2 T}{gA^3} = 1,$$

where Q is the flow discharge, T is the top width of the cross-section (for a trapezoidal channel, $T = b+2zy$), g is the acceleration of gravity ($g = 9.806$ m/s^2 in the S.I. and $g = 32.2$ ft/s^2 in the E.S.), and A is the cross-sectional area. Use SCILAB function solve to obtain the critical depth, y_c, (i.e., the water depth at critical conditions) for the data shown in the following table:

Case	System of units	b	z	Q
(a)	S.I.	0.6	1.5	0.2
(b)	S.I.	1.5	0.5	0.15
(c)	S.I.	0.5	1	0.35
(d)	E.S.	1.4	1	0.6
(e)	E.S.	1.2	0.5	0.8
(f)	E.S.	0.6	0.75	1

[24]. The conditions of open channel flow at the entrance from a reservoir are determined by the simultaneous solution of the energy equation and Manning's equation. The energy equation, for an available head of H_0 at the reservoir, is written as

$$H_0 = y + \frac{Q^2}{2g[A(y)]^2},$$

while the Manning's equation is written as

$$Q = \frac{C_u}{n} \cdot \frac{[A(y)]^{5/3}}{[P(y)]^{2/3}} \cdot \sqrt{S_0},$$

where C_u is a coefficient that depends on the system of units used, with $C_u = 1.0$ for the Systeme Internationale (S.I.) and $C_u = 1.486$ for the English (or Imperial) System of units (E.S.), n is the Manning's coefficient (typically, between 0.001 and 0.3), $A(y)$ is the cross-sectional area, $P(y)$ is the wetted perimeter of the cross-section (i.e the length of the cross-sectional boundary in contact with the water), and Q is the discharge.

Typically the values of n, g, C_u, S_0, and the geometry of the cross-section are known. The simultaneous solution of these two equations produces as a result the values of the water depth, y, and the flow discharge Q.

For a trapezoidal cross-section of bottom width b and side slope z, the area and wetted perimeter are given by

$$A(y) = (b + zy)y, \quad P(y) = b + 2y\sqrt{1 + z^2}.$$

Use SCILAB function *fsolve* to obtain the simultaneous solution of the energy and Manning's equation at the entrance from a reservoir into an open channel using the following data values:

Case	System of units	Ho	b	z	n	So
(a)	S.I.	4.5	1.2	1.5	0.012	0.0001
(b)	S.I.	3.5	0.8	0.5	0.023	0.00001
(c)	S.I.	2.5	0.4	1	0.01	0.001
(d)	E.S.	6	5	1	0.012	0.0001
(e)	E.S.	3	3	0.5	0.018	0.00001
(f)	E.S.	10	7.5	0.75	0.015	0.0001

7 Numerical integration using SCILAB

Integrals can be interpreted as the area under the curve of the function f(x) in a given interval a < x < b. Such an integral is written as

$$\int_a^b f(x)dx$$

where the term *dx*, referred to as the differential of x, indicates the variable of integration. In the next section, we present methods to estimate the value of an integral by using summations.

Integrals calculated through summation of rectangles

The integral of a function *f(x)* in an interval *(a,b)*, is defined as the limit of the sum

$$S_n = \sum_{i=1}^{n} f(\xi_i)\Delta x_i,$$

as $\Delta x_i \to 0$, or $n \to \infty$. The values Δx_i represent the length of *n* sub-intervals in *(a,b)*, so that the values ξ_i are contained within the *i*-th sub-interval, i.e., $x_i \leq \xi_i \leq x_{i+1}$. The sub-intervals are limited by the values $x_1, x_2, \ldots, x_n, x_{n+1}$, therefore, $\Delta x_i = x_{i+1} - x_i$.

The figure below illustrates the meaning of the terms in the summation. The terms $f(\xi_i)\Delta x_i$ represent increments of area ΔA_i, under the curve *y = f(x)* in the interval *(a,b)*.

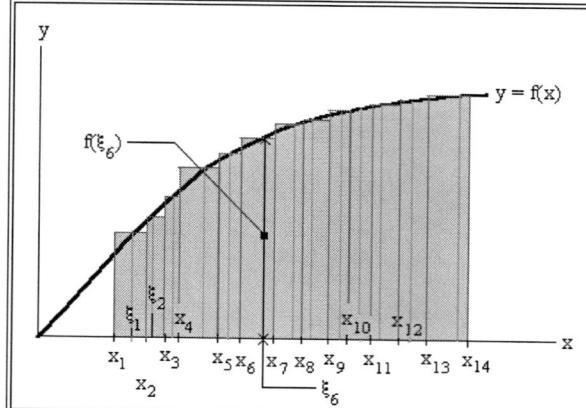
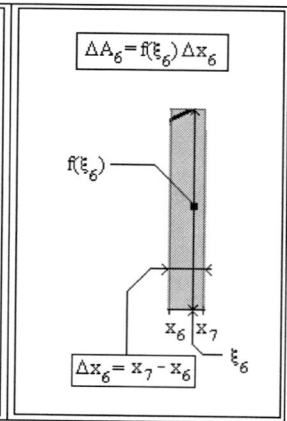

While there are no restrictions in the way we may divide the interval (a,b) to generate n sub-intervals, or where to select ξ_i within a sub-interval, dividing it into n equally-spaced sub-intervals, and selecting the values of ξ_i in a regular fashion, facilitates the calculation of the summation.

To divide the interval (a,b) into n sub-intervals we take,

$$\Delta x = (b-a)/n,$$

therefore,

$$x_1 = a,\ x_2 = x_1 + \Delta x,\ x_3 = x_1 + 2\cdot\Delta x,\ \ldots,\ x_i = x_1 + (i-1)\cdot\Delta x,\ \ldots,\ x_n = x_1 + (n-1)\cdot\Delta x = b.$$

The value of can be selected to be the leftmost value in the sub-interval (x_i, x_{i+1}), i.e., $\xi_i = x_i$, the center of the sub-interval, i.e. $\xi_i = (x_i + x_{i+1})/2$, or the right-most value of the sub-interval, i.e., $= x_{i+1}$. Suppose that we call SL_n the summation when $\xi_i = x_i$, then we can write:

$$SL_n = \left(\frac{b-a}{n}\right)\cdot\sum_{i=1}^{n} f(x_i).$$

If we call SM_n the summation when $\xi_i = (x_i + x_{i+1})/2$, then we have

$$SM_n = \left(\frac{b-a}{n}\right)\cdot\sum_{i=1}^{n} f\left(\frac{x_i + x_{i+1}}{2}\right).$$

Finally, for the summation when $\xi_i = x_{i+1}$, we have

$$SU_n = \left(\frac{b-a}{n}\right)\cdot\sum_{i=1}^{n} f(x_{i+1}).$$

The following function, *Sumint* (*Sum*mation as *int*egrals), can be used to calculate the summations SL_n, SM_n, and SU_n, as defined above, given the values of the integration limits a and b, the number of sub-intervals for the summation n, and the function to be integrated f. The general call to the function is

$$[I] = Sumint(sum\_type, a, b, n, f)$$

where *sum_type* can take the values *'L'* for SL_n, *'M'* for SM_n, and *'U'* for SU_n. The function returns the value of the summation requested as well as a graph showing the function $f(x)$ in the interval $a<x<b$ and the rectangles whose area represent the summation. The graph for SL_n is shown in SCILAB graphics window 1, that for SM_n is shown in SCILAB graphics window 2, and that for SU_n is shown in SCILAB graphics window 3.

A listing of function *Sumint* follows:

```
function [I] = Sumint(stype,a,b,n,f)

//Calculates the summation corresponding
//to the integral:
//I = integral from a to b of f(x) dx
//
//The variable 'stype' can be one of the
//following:
//
//   'L' - lower sum
//   'M' - middle sum
//   'U' - upper sum
//
//n is the number of sub-intervals in [a,b]

//Checking that the proper value of 'stype' is used:
if (stype<>'L') & (stype<>'M') & (stype<>'U') then
      error('Sumint - stype must be L, M, or U between brackets');
      abort;
end;

//Calculating parameters for sum and plot
Dx = (b-a)/(n-1);        //Increment in x
x = [a:Dx:b];            //List of values of x
y = feval(x,f);          //List of values of the function, y = f(x)
[n m] = size(x);         //Size of vectors x and y
xmin = min(x);           //Minimum value of x
xmax = max(x);           //Minimum value of y
ym = f(xmax);            //Value of y = f(xmax)
yy = [y(2:m), ym];       //Vector of values of y shifted one Dx to the right
ymin = min(y);           //Minimum value of y
ymax = max(y);           //Maximum value of y

//Change ymin to zero if ymin is larger than zero:
if ymin>0 then
      ymin = 0
end;

//Draw plot of function and rectangles, and calculate summation
if stype == 'L' then
      xset('window',1);xbasc(1);
        plot2d1('onn',x',y',[1],'011','y',[xmin ymin xmax ymax]);   //[1]
      plot2d2('onn',x',y',[1],'000');                                //[2]
      plot2d3('onn',x',y',[1],'000');                                //[3]
      xtitle('Left sum','x','y');                                    //[4]
      I = sum(y(1:m-1))*Dx;                                          //[5]
elseif stype == 'M' then
      xset('window',2);xbasc(2);
      yyy = (y+yy)/2;
      plot2d1('onn',x',y',[1],'011','y',[xmin ymin xmax ymax]);
        plot2d2('onn',x',yyy',[1],'000');
      plot2d3('onn',x',yyy',[1],'000');
      xtitle('Middle sum','x','y');
      I = sum(yyy(1:m-1))*Dx;
else
      xset('window',3);xbasc(3);
      plot2d1('onn',x',y',[1],'011','y',[xmin ymin xmax ymax]);
        plot2d2('onn',x',yy',[1],'000');
      plot2d3('onn',x',yy',[1],'000');
      xtitle('Right sum','x','y');
```

```
        I = sum(yy(1:m-1))*Dx;
end;

//     Notes:
//        [1] Plot the curve y=f(x).
//        [2] Plot step function for y = f(x).
//        [3] Plot vertical lines for y = f(x).
//        [4] Plot title and labels.
//        [5] Calculate summation.

//Draw the x-axis if ymin is negative:
if ymin<0 then
    xpoly([xmin,xmax],[0,0],'lines'); //draw x-axis if any
end;

//end function
```

Applications of function *Sumint* for calculating integrals

We use function *Sumint* to approximate the integral of functions $f(x) = 1-x^2$ and $g(x) = sin(x) + sin(2x)$. First, we define the functions:

```
-->deff('[y]=f(x)','y=1-x^2')
-->deff('[y]=g(x)','y=sin(x)+sin(2*x)')
```

Next, function *Sumint* is loaded into SCILAB: `-->getf('Sumint')`

The following calls to function *Sumint* calculate the integral of f(x) with a = 0 and b = 1.5 using n = 20. The figures illustrating the summation calculations are shown after the function calls.

```
-->Sumint('L',0,1.5,40,f)
 ans  = .4178994
```

```
-->Sumint('M',0,1.5,20,f)
 ans  = .3734418
```

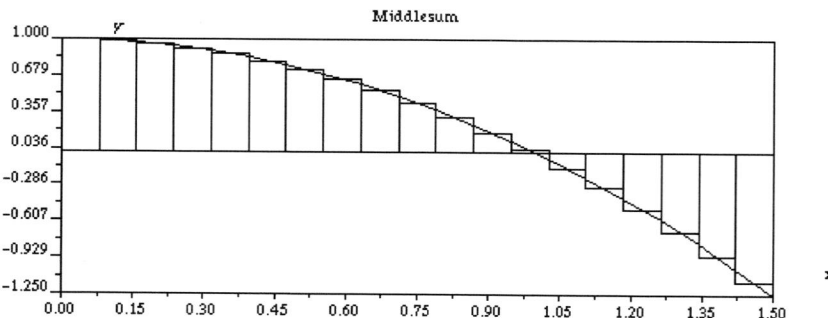

```
-->Sumint('U',0,1.5,20,f)
 ans  = .2846260
```

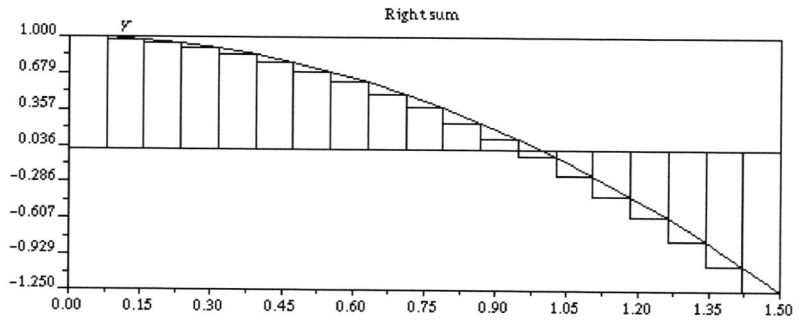

The actual value of the integral for $f(x)$ between $a = 0$ and $b = 1.5$ is

$$\int_0^{1.5} f(x)dx = \int_0^{1.5} (1-x^2)dx = (x - \frac{1}{3}x^3)\Big|_0^1 = 1.5 - \frac{1.5^3}{3}$$

i.e.,

```
-->1.5-1.5^3/3
 ans =

    .375
```

The values calculated through the summations differ from the actual value of the integral with relative errors of 11.44% for SL_n, 0.41% for SM_n, and 24.09% for SU_n, as shown next:

```
-->error_SLn = (0.4178994-0.375)/0.375*100
 error_SLn  =

     11.43984
```

```
-->error_SMn = (0.3734418-0.375)/0.375*100
 error_SMn  =

   -  .41552

-->error_SUn = (0.2846260-0.375)/0.375*100
 error_SUn  =

   - 24.099733
```

The summation SM_n, with an error of less than 1%, provides the best approximation to the integral out of the three summations calculated above. Improved values of the summation approximations can be obtained by increasing the number of sub-intervals in the summation. The following calls to function *Sumint* use values of n = 100 (graphics are omitted):

```
-->Sumint('L',0,1.5,100,f)
 ans  =

      .3919881

-->Sumint('M',0,1.5,100,f)
 ans  =

      .3749426

-->Sumint('U',0,1.5,100,f)
 ans  =

      .3578972
```

The corresponding errors are:

```
-->error_SL100 = (0.3919881-0.375)/0.375*100
 error_SL100  =

     4.53016

-->error_SM100 = (0.374926-0.375)/0.375*100
 error_SM100  =

   -  .0197333

-->error_SMU100 = (0.357872-0.375)/0.375*100
 error_SMU100  =

   - 4.5674667
```

Thus, SL_n and SU_n show errors of the order of 4.5% for $n = 100$. The middle-sum, SM_n, on the other hand, shows an error of about 2/10%. Thus, the middle sum seems to provide the smallest relative error. Also, as the value of n grows larger, the better the approximation to the integral. The following sequence of SCILAB statements use function *Sumint* to approximate the integral with values of n = 10, 100, 1000, 10000, 100000.

```
-->nn = [10,100,1000,10000,100000];

-->SumintSeq = [];
```

```
-->for j = 1:5
-->    n = nn(j);
-->    SumintSeq = [SumintSeq Sumint('M',0,1.5,n,f)];
-->end;
```

SCILAB may take longer than usual to finish this operation since the last integral requires calculation 100000 values of y before summing. After the summation calculations end, the sequence of values of the integral is:

```
-->SumintSeq
 SumintSeq  =

!   .3680556    .3749426    .3749994    .3751875    .375 !
```

These results verify the observation that the approximation to the integral improves as the value of n increases.

The following calls to function Sumint calculate the integral of $g(x) = sin(x) + sin(2x)$, with $a = 0$ and $b = \pi$ using $n = 40$. The figures illustrating the summation calculations are shown after the function calls.

```
-->Sumint('L',0,%pi,40,g)
 ans  = 1.9989184
```

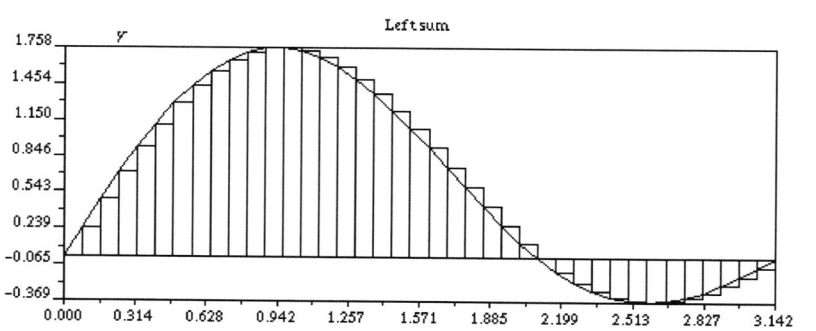

```
-->Sumint('M',0,%pi,40,g)
 ans  = 1.9989184
```

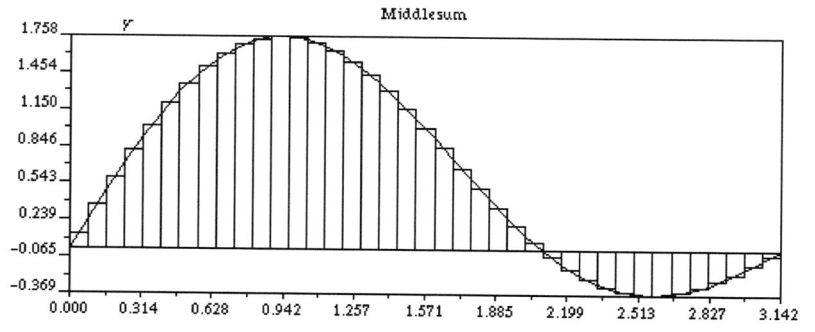

```
-->Sumint('U',0,%pi,40,g)
 ans  = 1.9989184
```

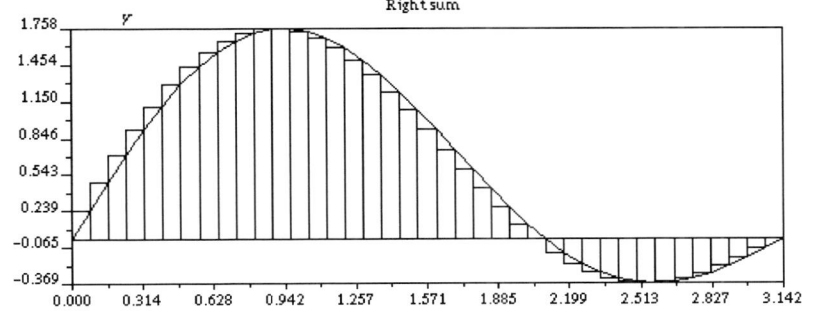

The actual value of the integral for $g(x)$ between $a = 0$ and $b = \pi$ is

$$\int_0^\pi g(x)dx = \int_0^\pi (\sin x + \sin 2x)dx = (-\cos x - \frac{1}{2}\cos 2x)\Big|_0^\pi$$

i.e.,

```
--> -cos(%pi)-(1/2)*cos(2*%pi)-(-cos(0)-(1/2)*cos(2*0))
ans  =

 2.
```

For the function y = g(x) = sin(x) + sin(2x) the three summation approximations to the integral with n = 40, produce results that are very close to the actual value of 2.0.

The examples presented in this section, thus, illustrate the fact that there is always an error involved in estimating an integral through summations. In the next section we present the trapezoidal rule for integration, which reduces the error in the numerical calculation of the integral with respect to the summation of rectangles used in this section.

Trapezoid Rule for Numerical Integration

Numerical methods are often used to calculate integrals, particularly when the integrand does not have a closed-formed anti-derivative. One such integral, which is used very often in probability and statistics, as well as in the study of dispersion of contaminants in fluid flow, is the integral of the Gaussian curve:

$$\int_a^b \exp(-\frac{z^2}{2})dz$$

We will develop herein a general method to estimate the integral,

$$I = \int_a^b f(x)\, dx.$$

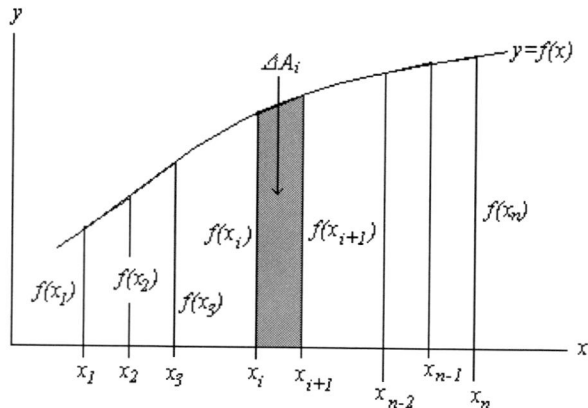

As illustrated in the figure above we can divide the interval (a, b), where $a = x_1$, and $b = x_n$, into (n-1) sub-intervals: (x_1, x_2), (x_2, x_3),...,(x_{n-1}, x_n), or (x_i, x_{i+1}) for $i = 1, 2, ..., n-1$. Recalling that the integral represents the area under the curve $y = f(x)$ between values of $x = a$ and $x = b$, we can estimate the area under the curve corresponding to sub-intervals as

$$\Delta A_i = 1/2(x_{i+1} - x_i)(f(x_i)+f(x_{i+1})) = 1/2 \cdot \Delta x_i \cdot (f(x_i)+f(x_{i+1}))$$

where,

$$\Delta x_i = x_{i+1} - x_i.$$

We can simplify the calculation by taking the interval width to be a constant value, say. In such case, the integral is approximated by

$$I = \sum_{i=1}^{n} \Delta A_i = \frac{1}{2} \cdot [f(x_1) + 2\cdot \sum_{i=1}^{n} f(x_i) + f(x_n)] \cdot \Delta x$$

Because the area calculated in this equation is the area of the trapezoid limited by the sub-interval (x_i, x_{i+1}), and the curve $y = f(x)$, this method is known as the *trapezoid rule*.

For the case of a constant sub-interval width the following relationships apply:

$$\Delta x = (x_n - x_1)/(n-1),$$

and

$$x_i = x_1 + (i-1)\Delta x,$$

for $i = 1, 2, ..., n$.

Trapezoid rule calculation using SCILAB function *inttrap*

SCILAB provides function *inttrap* to calculate the numerical integral of a function using the trapezoid rule. The general call to the function is:

$$[v] = inttrap([x,] y),$$

where x is the vector of increasing x coordinate data, its default value being = [1, 2, ..., m], where m is the size of vector y, y is the vector of y coordinate data, and v is the value of the integral.

The function calculates

$$v = \int_a^b f(x)dx,$$

where f is a function described by the data set of data $y_i = f(x_i)$, with $a = x_1$, and $b = x_n$.

To check the operation of function *inttrap* we will use the functions f(x) and g(x) used in the previous section when approximating integrals through the summation of rectangles. First, we calculate the integral of $f(x) = 1 - x^2$ in the interval [0, 1.5] using x increments of Δx = 0.5, 0.25, 0.10, 0.05, and 0.01, corresponding to n = 3, 6, 15, 30, 150 sub-intervals.

```
-->x=[0:0.5:1.5];inttrap(x,f(x))
 ans  =

     .3125

-->x=[0:0.25:1.5];inttrap(x,f(x))
 ans  =

     .359375

-->x=[0:0.1:1.5];inttrap(x,f(x))
 ans  =

     .3725

-->x=[0:0.05:1.5];inttrap(x,f(x))
 ans  =

     .374375

-->x=[0:0.01:1.5];inttrap(x,f(x))
 ans  =

     .374975
```

The next set of examples shows the integral of function $g(x) = sin(x) + sin(2x)$ in the interval [0, π], with values of $\Delta x = \pi/2, \pi/3, \pi/5, \pi/10, \pi/20$, and $\pi/100$, corresponding to n = 2, 3, 5, 10, 20, and 100.

```
-->x = [0:%pi/2:%pi];inttrap(x,g(x))
 ans  =

    1.5707963

-->x = [0:%pi/3:%pi];inttrap(x,g(x))
 ans  =

    1.8137994

-->x = [0:%pi/5:%pi];inttrap(x,g(x))
 ans  =

    1.9337656

-->x = [0:%pi/10:%pi];inttrap(x,g(x))
 ans  =

    1.9835235

-->x = [0:%pi/20:%pi];inttrap(x,g(x))
 ans  =

    1.995886

-->x = [0:%pi/50:%pi];inttrap(x,g(x))
 ans  =

    2.0013068

-->x = [0:%pi/100:%pi];inttrap(x,g(x))
 ans  =

    2.0003284
```

As observed in the case of the summation of rectangles presented in the previous section, the approximation of the integral improves as the number of sub-intervals used in the calculation increases.

Additional examples for function *inttrap*

The following examples illustrate different forms for calling function *inttrap*. The exercises are provided for the user to try on his or her own.

In this first example, a call to a SCILAB function, namely *sin(x)*, is included as the second argument to function *inttrap*:

```
x=(0:0.1:1.5);
inttrap(x,sin(x))
```

In the next example, a user-defined SCILAB function is included as the second argument to function *inttrap*:

```
x = (0:0.1:1.0);
deff('[y]=f(x)','y = x^3 - 2*x + sin(x)');
```

```
inttrap(x,f(x))
```

In the next three examples, both x and y are defined as vectors before calling function *inttrap*:

```
x = (0.4:0.2:2.0);
y=[5.16, 3.6922, 3.14, 3.0, 3.1067, 3.3886, 3.81,4.3511, 5.0];
inttrap(x,y)

x = (1.0:0.1:2.0);
y=x^(-1) ;
inttrap(x,y)

x=[0., 0.05, 0.1, 0.2, 0.5, 0.6, 0.9, 1.0];
y=[1.2, 1.3, 1.25, 1.45, 2.3, 4.5, 5.0, 1.2];
inttrap(x,y)
```

Plotting the trapezoidal approximation

To illustrate the trapezoidal approximation to an integral we propose the following user-defined function *plottrap* (*plot trap*ezoidal approximation):

```
function plottrap(x,f)

//This function plots the trapezoidal approximation
//to a function y = f(x) as well as plotting the
//original function on the range of values of x.

[n m] = size(x);                //Size of vector x
y = f(x);                       //Data for trapezoidal fitting
xx = [x(1):(x(m)-x(1))/100:x(m)];  //Generate 100 points xx on x
yy = f(xx);                     //Generate y = f(xs) for xx

xmin = min(xx);                 //Minimum value of xx
xmax = max(xx);                 //Maximum value of xx
ymin = min(yy);                 //Minimum value of yy
ymax = max(yy);                 //Maximum value of yy

//Change ymin to zero if ymin is larger than zero:
if ymin>0 then
      ymin = 0
end;

//Draw plot of function and trapezoids
xset('window',1);xbasc(1);
plot2d1('onn',xx',yy',[1],'011','y',[xmin ymin xmax ymax]); //[1]
xpoly(x',y','lines');                                       //[2]
plot2d3('onn',x',y',[1],'000');                             //[3]
xtitle('Trapezoid rule','x','y');                           //[4]

//   Notes:
//   [1] Plot the curve y=f(x).
//   [2] Plot trapezoid top for y = f(x).
//   [3] Plot vertical lines for y = f(x).
//   [4] Plot title and labels.

//Draw the x-axis if ymin is negative:
```

```
if ymin<0 then
   xpoly([xmin,xmax],[0,0],'lines'); //draw x-axis if any
end;

//end function
```

The call to the function requires that the user provide an ordered vector of values x and the function f to be plotted. The general call to the function is *plottrap(x,f)*. An example of its application is shown below:

```
-->xx = [0:%pi/10:%pi];

-->deff('[y]=g(x)','y=sin(x)+sin(2*x)')

-->plottrap(xx,g)
```

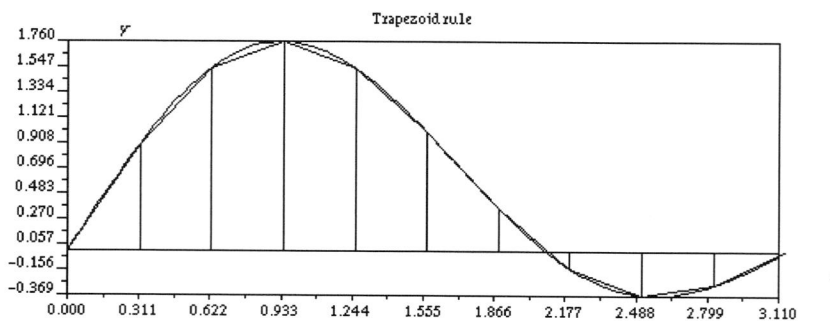

Simpson's 1/3 Rule

The summation of rectangles for estimating integrals can be though of as approximating the function to a constant value (the height of the rectangle) in each sub-interval $[x_i, x_{i+1}]$. The trapezoid rule can be thought of as fitting a straight line between the points $(x_i, f(x_i))$ and $(x_{i+1}, f(x_{i+1}))$ in each sub-interval. Simpson's 1/3 rule results from fitting a quadratic equation, say,

$$y = px^2 + qx + r,$$

using the three consecutive points $(x_i, f(x_i))$, $(x_{i+1}, f(x_{i+1}))$, and $(x_{i+2}, f(x_{i+2}))$ that link the two consecutive sub-intervals $[x_i, x_{i+1}]$ and $[x_{i+1}, x_{i+2}]$, as illustrated in the figure below (with $y_i = f(x_i)$):

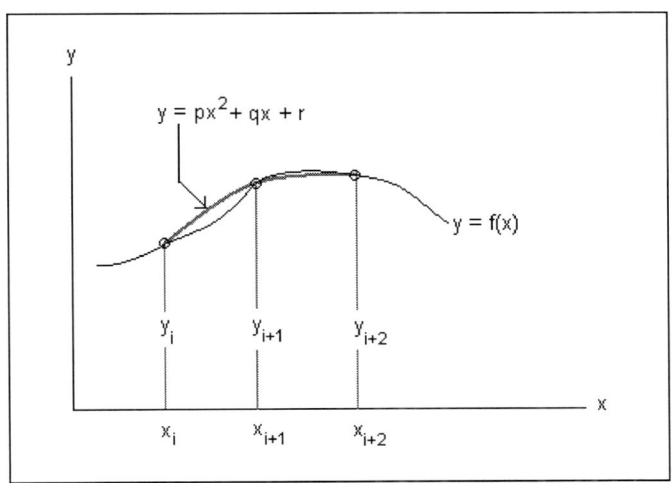

You can verify that, for sub-intervals of the same length $\Delta x = x_{i+1} - x_i = x_{i+2} - x_i$, the expression for the integral in the two sub-intervals limited by $[x_i, x_{i+2}]$ is given by

$$\int_{x_i}^{x_{i+2}} f(x)dx \approx \frac{\Delta x}{3}(y_i + 4y_{i+1} + y_{i+2}).$$

A similar expression can be found for the integral in the next pair of sub-intervals $[x_{i+2}, x_{i+3}]$ and $[x_{i+3}, x_{i+4}]$, i.e.,

$$\int_{x_{i+2}}^{x_{i+4}} f(x)dx \approx \frac{\Delta x}{3}(y_{i+2} + 4y_{i+3} + y_{i+4}).$$

Combining the last two expressions we get an approximation to the integral in the interval $[x_i, x_{i+4}]$, i.e.,

$$\int_{x_i}^{x_{i+4}} f(x)dx \approx \frac{\Delta x}{3}(y_i + 4y_{i+1} + 2y_{i+2} + 4y_{i+3} + y_{i+4}).$$

Following this pattern of summation, we can write the integral in the next 4 sub-intervals as

$$\int_{x_{i+4}}^{x_{i+8}} f(x)dx \approx \frac{\Delta x}{3}(y_{i+4} + 4y_{i+5} + 2y_{i+6} + 4y_{i+7} + y_{i+8}).$$

Adding the last two expressions we can write the integral for the 8 sub-intervals enclosed in $[x_i, x_{i+8}]$ as:

$$\int_{x_i}^{x_{i+8}} f(x)dx \approx \frac{\Delta x}{3}(y_i + 4y_{i+1} + 2y_{i+2} + 4y_{i+3} + 2y_{i+4} + 4y_{i+5} + 2y_{i+6} + 4y_{i+7} + y_{i+8}),$$

or,

$$\int_{x_i}^{x_{i+8}} f(x)dx \approx \frac{\Delta x}{3}[y_i + 4(y_{i+1} + y_{i+3} + y_{i+5} + y_{i+7}) + 2(y_{i+2} + 2y_{i+4} + 2y_{i+6}) + y_{i+8}].$$

We can see the general pattern of the integral in the latter expression. One obvious result is that the number of sub-intervals for the calculation of the integral must be even. This is so that we can fit quadratic equations through pairs of consecutive sub-intervals. Thus, if we divide the interval [a,b] into 2n sub-intervals, referring to the values of x limiting those sub-intervals as $x_0(=a)$, x_1, x_2, ..., $x_{2n}(=b)$, (make i=0 in the previous expression) we can write the general expression for Simpson's 1/3 rule as

$$\int_a^b f(x)dx \approx \frac{\Delta x}{3} \cdot [y_0 + 4(y_1 + y_3 + y_5 + \cdots + y_{2n-1}) + 2(y_2 + 2y_4 + 2y_6 + \cdots + y_{2n-2}) + y_{2n}].$$

From the last expression it is obvious why this approach is referred to as the 1/3 rule. The following function, *simpson13*, calculates an integral using Simpson's 1/3 rule given the vectors x and y containing an odd number of elements. Vector x must contain the limits of the even number of sub-intervals into which the integration interval [a,b] is divided:

```
function [I] = simpson13(x,f)
//This function calculates the numerical integration of f(x)dx
//between limits x(1) and x(n) using Simpson's 1/3 rule
//Check that x and y have the same size (which must be an odd number)
//Also, the values of x must be equally spaced with spacing Dx
[nrx,ncx]=size(x)
[nrf,ncf]=size(f)
if((nrx<>1)|(nrf<>1))then
        error('x or f, or both, not column vector(s)');
        abort;
end;
if((ncx<>ncf))then
        error('x and f are not of the same length');
        abort;
end;
//check that the size of the vector x and f is odd
if(modulo(ncx,2)==0)then
        disp(ncx,"list size =")
        error('list size must be an odd number');
        abort
end;
n = ncx;
xdiff = mtlb_diff(x);
h = xdiff(1,1);
I = f(1,1) + f(1,n);
for j = 2:n-1
        if(modulo(j,2)==0) then
                I = I + 4*f(1,j);
        else
                I = I + 2*f(1,j);
        end;
```

```
end;
I = (h/3.0)*I
//end of function simpson13
```

The following commands show applications of the function *simpson13* for calculating integrals. The function *inttrap* is also used to compare the results of the two integration procedures. The main restriction in using the *simpson13* function is that the number of elements in the x,f vectors must be an odd number. Also, the spacing in the values of x must be constant.

```
-->getf('simpson13')              //Load function

-->x = (0:0.1:1.6);               //Generate vector of x values

-->simpson13(x,sin(x))            //Simpson 1/3 rule - Example 1
 ans  =

    1.0292001

-->inttrap(x,sin(x))              //Compare with inttrap
 ans  =

    1.0283417

-->x = (0.4:0.2:2.0);             //New vector of values of x

-->y = [5.16, 3.69, 3.14, 3.0, 3.11, 3.39, 3.81, 4.35, 5.0];

-->simpson13(x,))                 //Simpson 1/3 rule - Example 2

 ans  =

    5.8666667

-->inttrap(x,y)                   //Compare with inttrap
 ans  =

    5.914

-->x = (1.0:0.1:2.0);             //New vector of values of x

-->y=x^(-1);                      //Vector y = 1/x

-->simpson13(x,y)                 //Simpson 1/3 rule - example 3
 ans  =

    .6931502

-->inttrap(x,y)                   //Compare with inttrap
 ans  =

    .6937714

-->deff('[y]=f(x)','y=x^3-2*exp(x)')   //User-defined function

-->x = (1.0:0.1:2.0);             //New vector of values of x

-->yp = f(x);                     //Vector of values of y

-->simpson13(x,yp)                //Simpson 1/3 rule - example 4
```

```
 ans  =

  - 5.5915537

-->inttrap(x,yp)          //Compare with inttrap
 ans  =

  - 5.5918319
```

Simpson's 3/8 Rule

In the previous section we demonstrated that Simpson's 1/3 rule results from fitting quadratic equations to the three points $x_i, f(x_i)$) defining two consecutive sub-intervals in the integration interval (a,b). Simpson's 3/8 rule follows from fitting cubic equations to the four points that define three consecutive sub-intervals in the integration interval. Skipping the details of the derivation, we present the general form of the integral approximated by Simpson's 3/8 rule as:

$$\int_a^b f(x)dx \approx$$

$$\frac{3}{8}\Delta x \cdot [y_0 + 3(y_1 + y_4 + \cdots + y_{3n-2}) + 3(y_2 + y_5 + \cdots + y_{3n-1}) + 2(y_3 + y_6 + \cdots + y_{3n-3}) + y_{3n}].$$

The method requires that the integration interval be divided into a number of sub-intervals that is a multiple of three. As in the case of Simpson's 1/3 rule, we define $y_i = f(x_i)$, and take $x_0 = a$ and $x_{3n} = b$.

The following function, *simpson38*, calculates an integral using Simpson's 3/8 rule given a vector of equally-spaced values of $x = [a=x_0, x_1,..., x_{3n} = b]$, the corresponding vector of values of $y = [y_0\ y_1\ ...\ y_{3n}] = [\ f(x_0)\ f(x_1)\ ...\ f(x_{3n})]$. The function checks that the number of sub-intervals is indeed a multiple of 3, producing an error otherwise.

```
function [I] = simpson38(x,f)

//This function calculates the numerical integration of f(x)dx
//between limits x(1) and x(n) using Simpson's 3/8 rule
//Check that x and y have the same size (which must be of the form 3*i+1,
//where i is an integer number)
//Also, the values of x must be equally spaced with spacing h

[nrx,ncx]=size(x);
[nrf,ncf]=size(f);

if((nrx<>1)|(nrf<>1))then
       error('x or f, or both, not column vector(s)');
       abort;
end;
if((ncx<>ncf))then
       error('x and f are not of the same length');
       abort;
end;

//check that the size of the lists xL and f is odd
```

```
if(modulo(ncx-1,3)<>0)then
      disp(ncx,"list size =")
      error('list size must be of the form 3*i+1, where i=integer');
      abort
end;
n = ncx;
xdiff =  mtlb_diff(x);
h = xdiff(1,1);
I = f(1,1) + f(1,n);
for j = 2:n-1
      if(modulo(j-1,3)==0) then
            I = I + 2*f(1,j);
      else
            I = I + 3*f(1,j);
      end;
end;
I = (3/8)*h*I;
//end of function simpson38
```

The following commands show applications of the function *simpson38* for calculating integrals. The function *inttrap* is also used to compare the results of the two integration procedures. The main restriction in using the *simpson38* function is that the number of elements in the x,f vectors must be a number of the form *3*i+1*, where *i* is an integer. Also, the spacing in the values of x must be constant.

```
-->getf('simpson38')          //Load function

-->x=(0:0.1:1.8);             //Vector of values of x

-->simpson38(x,sin(x))        //Simpson's 3/8 rule - example 1
 ans  =

    1.2272036

-->inttrap(x,sin(x))          //Compare with inttrap
 ans  =

    1.2261793

-->x = (0.4:0.2:2.2);         //New vector of values of x

-->y = [5.16, 3.70, 3.4, 3.0, 3.11, 3.39, 3.81, 4.35, 5.0, 5.2];

-->simpson38(x,y)             //Simpson's 3/8 rule - example 2
 ans  =

    6.96225

-->inttrap(x,y)               //Compare with inttrap
 ans  =

    6.988

-->x = (1.0:0.1:1.9);         //New vector of values of x

-->y = x^(-1);                //Vector of values of y = 1/x

-->simpson38(x,y)             //Simpson's 3/8 rule - example 3
```

```
    ans  =

         .6418605

-->inttrap(x,y)              //Compare with inttrap
    ans  =

         .6424556

-->deff('[y]=f(x)','y=x^3-2*exp(x)')   //User defined function for integration

-->x = (1.0:0.1:1.9);        //New vector of values of x

-->yp = f(x);                //Vector of values of y = f(x)

-->simpson38(x,yp)           //Simpson's 3/8 rule - example 4
    ans  =

       - 4.9272101

-->inttrap(x,yp)             //Compare with inttrap
    ans  =

       - 4.9272868
```

Newton-Cotes Formulas

The trapezoidal rule and Simpson's 1/3 and 3/8 rules are the first three of a collection of formulas based on equally spaced values of the independent variable and commonly known as Newton-Cotes Formulas. The Newton-Cotes formulas are based on fitting polynomials of orders n = 1, 2, 3, etc. to 2, 3, 4, etc. consecutive points determining the sub-intervals into which the integration interval [a,b] is divided.. The general expression for the formulas is

$$\int_a^b f(x)dx \approx n \cdot \kappa \cdot \Delta x \cdot (\beta_0 y_0 + \beta_1 y_1 + ...),$$

where n represents the number of intervals and the degree of the polynomial fitted, and β's are coefficients given in the following table:

n	β_0	β_1	β_2	β_3	β_4	β_5	β_6	β_7	κ
1	1	1							1/2
2	1	4	1						1/6
3	1	3	3	1					1/8
4	7	32	12	32	7				1/90
5	19	75	50	50	75	19			1/288
6	41	216	27	272	27	216	41		1/840
7	751	3577	1323	2989	2989	1323	3577	751	1/17280

The following function, *NewtonCotes*, allows the estimation of an integral using the Newton-Cotes formulas up to seventh degree. It is implemented only for functions defined as *y = f(x)* (i.e., the function f must be defined using *deff* or by a file-defined function loaded with *getf*). The function *NewtonCotes* requires the limits of integration *(a,b)*, the function name *f(x)*, and the degree of the polynomial to be used *n* (*1 ≤ n ≤ 7*).

```
function [I] = NewtonCotes(a,b,f,n)

//This function calculates the numerical integration of f(x)dx
//between limits a and b using Newton-Cotes integration of degree n.

if((n<1)|(n>7))then
      disp(n,"n =");
      error('n must be an integer between 1 and 7.');
      abort;
end;

kappa = [1/2, 1/6, 1/8, 1/90, 1/288, 1/840, 1/17280];
beta = [[1 1 0 0 0 0 0 0];
        [1 4 1 0 0 0 0 0];
        [1 3 3 1 0 0 0 0];
        [7 32 12 32 7 0 0 0];
        [19 75 50 50 75 19 0 0];
        [41 216 27 272 27 216 41 0];
        [751 3577 1323 2989 2989 1323 3577 751]];
h = (b-a)/n;
x = zeros(n+1,1);
y = x;
I = 0.0
for j = 1:n+1
      x(j,1) = a + (j-1)*h;
      y(j,1) = f(x(j,1));
      I = I + beta(n,j)*y(j,1);
end;
I = n*kappa(n)*h*I
//end function NewtonCotes
```

The following examples show applications of the Newton-Cotes integration formulas. In each example we define a function using SCILAB's function *deff* and produce a vector containing the integrals using polynomials of orders *n = 1* to *n = 7*:

```
-->getf('NewtonCotes')

-->deff('[y]=f(x)','y=1/x');

-->I = []; for k=1:7, I=[I NewtonCotes(1,2,f,k)]; end; I
 I  =

        column 1 to 6

!   .75       .6944444     .69375     .6931746     .6931630     .6931481  !

        column 7

!   .6931477  !
```

```
-->deff('[y]=f(x)','y=x');

-->I = []; for k=1:7, I=[I NewtonCotes(1,2,f,k)]; end; I
 I  =

!   1.5     1.5     1.5     1.5     1.5     1.5     1.5  !

-->deff('[y]=f(x)','y=x^2');

-->I = []; for k=1:7, I=[I NewtonCotes(1,2,f,k)]; end; I
 I  =

        column 1 to 6

!   2.5     2.3333333    2.3333333    2.3333333    2.3333333    2.3333333 !

        column 7

!   2.3333333 !

-->deff('[y]=f(x)','y=exp(x)');

-->I = []; for k=1:7, I=[I NewtonCotes(1,2,f,k)]; end; I
 I  =

        column 1 to 6

!   5.053669    4.672349    4.6714765    4.6707766    4.6707756    4.6707743 !

        column 7

!   4.6707743 !

-->deff('[y]=f(x)','y=log(x)')

-->I = []; for k=1:7, I=[I NewtonCotes(1,2,f,k)]; end; I
 I  =

        column 1 to 6

!   .3465736    .3858346    .3860838    .3862879    .3862906    .3862942 !

        column 7

!   .3862943 !
```

Romberg Integration

The Romberg algorithm consists in improving the approximation of an integral by first calculating the integral using a constant increment Δx and then re-calculating it with an increment $\Delta x/2$. The two values of the integral thus calculated are then combined through the formula:

$$I(Romberg) = I_{\Delta x/2} + \frac{1}{3}\left[I_{\Delta x/2} + I_{\Delta x}\right],$$

where $I_{\Delta x/2}$ is the integral calculated with a sub-interval size of $\Delta x/2$ and $I_{\Delta x}$ is the integral calculated with a sub-interval size of Δx.

To calculate the values $I_{\Delta x/2}$ and $I_{\Delta x}$ we can simply use the trapezoidal rule (i.e., SCILAB's *inttrap* function), such as illustrated in function *Romberg*, listed below:

```
function [I]=Romberg(a,b,f,h)

//This function calculates the numerical integral of f(x) between
//x = a and x = b, with intervals h.  Intermediate results are obtained
//by using SCILAB's own inttrap function

x=(a:h:b);
y=f(x);
I1 = inttrap(x,y);
x=(a:h/2:b);
y=f(x);
I2 = inttrap(x,y);
I = I2 + (1.0/3.0)*(I2-I1);
//end function Romberg
```

The call to function *Romberg* is similar to that of *NewtonCotes* except that the increment h is used in place of a polynomial order. Some examples of Romberg integration are shown below:

```
-->getf('Romberg.txt')

-->Dx = [0.1,0.05,0.01,0.005,0.001];

-->deff('[y]=f(x)','y=x^(-1)')

-->I=[];for j=1:5, h=Dx(j); I = [I Romberg(1,2,f,h)]; end; I
 I  =

!   .6931474    .6931472    .6931472    .6931472    .6931472 !

-->deff('[y]=f(x)','y=exp(-0.02*x).*sin(x)')

-->I=[];for j=1:5, h=Dx(j); I = [I Romberg(1,2,f,h)]; end; I
 I  =

!   .9280852    .9280852    .9280852    .9280852    .9280852 !

-->deff('[y]=f(x)','y=x^3-3*x+2')

-->I=[];for j=1:5, h=Dx(j); I = [I Romberg(1,2,f,h)]; end; I
 I  =

!   1.25    1.25    1.25    1.25    1.25 !

-->deff('[y]=f(x)','y=exp(-x^2/2)/sqrt(2*%pi)')

-->I=[];for j=1:5, h=Dx(j); I = [I Romberg(0,1,f,h)]; end; I
```

```
  I  =

!    .3413448      .3413447      .3413447      .3413447      .3413447  !

-->deff('[y]=f(x)','y=sin(x)')

-->I=[];for j=1:5, h=Dx(j); I = [I Romberg(0.1,1,f,h)]; end; I
  I  =

!    .4547019      .4547019      .4547019      .4547019      .4547019 !
```

Other integrating functions provided by SCILAB

This section presents functions provided by SCILAB that produce integration by quadrature, by spline fitting, and by definite integration.

Integration by quadrature

By integration by quadrature we must understand the integral of an external function, as opposite to the integral of a function provided as a vector of values, such as those obtained with *inttrap*. Integration by quadrature is accomplished with the function *integrate*. The general call to the function *integrate* is

$$[x]=integrate(f,v,a,b\ [,ea\ [,er]])$$

where f = external SCILAB function, v = integration variable entered as a string, a,b = real numbers (bounds of integration), and ea, er = real numbers (absolute and relative errors). The presence of errors

Some examples of applications of the integrate function are shown below. The first example is the integral $\int_0^\pi sin(x)\ dx$:

```
--> integrate('sin(x)','x',0,%pi)
 ans  =

    2.
```

The following call to *integrate* uses a function defined by an *if...else...end* programming construct:

```
-->integrate('if x<0 then x, else x^2-1, end','x',-2,2)
 ans  =

    4.6666667
```

The following is the integral $\int_0^\pi dx/sin(x)$:

```
-->integrate('1/sin(x)','x',%pi/10,%pi/2)
 ans  =1.84273
```

In the next example the function f(x) is defined using *deff*. Notice that the call to function *integrate* includes the name of the function '*f(x)*' as a string.

```
-->deff('[y]=f(x)','y=sin(x)+sin(2*x)')

-->integrate('f(x)','x',0,%pi)
 ans  =   2.
```

The following example is the integral $\int_0^\pi dx/x$:

```
-->integrate('1/x','x',1,5)
 ans  =

    1.6094379
```

Integration by spline interpolation

Integration by spline interpolation is accomplished by using the function *intsplin*, whose general call is given by

$$I = intsplin([x,] y),$$

where x = vector of increasing x coordinate data, y = vector of y coordinate data, and I = value of the integral. This function computes the integral of $f(x)$ between $x = x_0$ and $x = x_1$, where the values of $f(x)$ are represented by the vector y. The vector $x = \{x_0, ..., x_n\}$, and $y_i = f(x_i)$. The function between discrete values is interpolated using splines. [Note: Splines are piece-wise curves used to fit data between consecutive data points. Splines are covered in a different chapter of this book.]

Examples of interpolation using splines follow:

```
-->x = 0:0.1:%pi; y = sin(x) + sin(2*x);

-->intsplin(x,y)
 ans  =  2.0008637

-->x = (-4:0.1:0); y = exp(-x^2/2)/sqrt(2*%pi);

-->intsplin(x,y)
 ans  =   .4999685
```

Calculation of definite integrals

SCILAB offers a function, called *intg*, that calculates the definite integral of a function. The general call to function *intg* is

$$[I,err]=intg(a,b,f [,ea [,er])$$

where a, b = limits of integration, f = represents a function, list or string, ea = absolute error required on the result (default value, ea = 0), er = relative error required on the result (default value, er = 1.d-8), I = integral value, and err = estimated absolute error on the result.

If f is function its definition must be as follows: y = f(t). If is a list the list must be as follows: *list(f,x1,x2,...)*, where f is a function with calling sequence $f(t,x1,x2,...)$. Finally, if f is a string it refers to the name of a Fortran subroutine.

An application of function *intg* follows:

```
-->deff('[y]=f(x)','y=cos(x)+0.5*cos(2*x)+1.5*cos(3*x)')

-->[I,err] = intg(0,1,f)
 err  =
    1.668E-14
 I  =
    1.1393553
```

Integrals of functions of a complex variable

SCILAB provides a couple of functions *intl* and *intc* for calculation of integrals of functions of a complex variable $z = x + iy$, where x and y are real variables and $\sqrt{-1}$ is the unit imaginary number. While the application of the functions is simple and straightforward, we need to provide some definitions related to complex variables and their functions for the benefit of those who have not covered functions of a complex variable.

Functions of a complex variable

We defined a complex variable z as $z = x + iy$, where x and y are real variables, and $i = (-1)^{1/2}$. We can also define another complex variable

$$w = F(z) = \Phi + i\Psi,$$

where, in general,

$$\Phi = \Phi(x,y), \text{ and } \Psi = \Psi(x,y),$$

are two real functions of (x, y). These real functions can also be given in terms of the polar coordinates (r, θ) if we use the polar representation for z, i.e.,

$$z = r \cdot e^{i\theta} = r(\cos\theta + i \cdot \sin\theta).$$

In such case,

$$\Phi = \Phi(r, \theta), \text{ and } \Psi = \Psi(r, \theta).$$

Recall that the coordinate transformations between Cartesian and polar coordinates are:

$$r = (x^2 + y^2)^{1/2}, \qquad \tan\theta = y/x,$$

$$x = r \cos\theta, \qquad y = r \sin\theta$$

The complex variable w is also known as a *complex function*. Another name for a complex function is "*mapping*." Thus, we say $F(z)$ is a mapping of z. In geometric terms, this means that any figure in the x-y plane gets "mapped" onto a different figure on the Φ-Ψ plane by the complex function $F(z)$.

As an example, take the function

$$w = F(z) = \ln(z) = \ln(r \cdot e^{i\theta}) = \ln(r) + i\theta.$$

We can identify the functions

$$\Phi = \Phi(r,\theta) = \ln(r), \text{ and } \Psi = \Psi(r,\theta) = \theta,$$

as the real and imaginary components, respectively, of the function $\ln(z)$. Using the transformations indicated above we can also write,

$$\Phi = \Phi(x,y) = \ln[(x^2+y^2)^{1/2}] = (1/2)\ln(x^2+y^2), \text{ and } \Psi = \Psi(x,y) = \tan^{-1}(y/x).$$

Derivative of a complex function

The derivative of the complex variable $f(z)$, to be referred to as $f'(z) = df/dz$, is, by definition,

$$f'(z) = \frac{df}{dz} = \lim_{\Delta z \to 0} \frac{f(z+\Delta z) - f(z)}{\Delta z}.$$

The definition of a complex derivative requires us to evaluate the function $f(z)$ at a point $P(x,y)$ corresponding to $z = x + iy$, and at point $Q(x+\Delta x, y+\Delta y)$, as illustrated in the figure below.

The figure also illustrates the fact that to get from point z to point $z+\Delta z$ in the complex x-y plane you can follow a multitude of paths. In general, the value of the derivative will depend on the path we follow to define Δz. Because we want the derivative df/dz to be uniquely defined, we need to find some criteria such that, regardless of the path selected to define z, the value of df/dz remains the same.

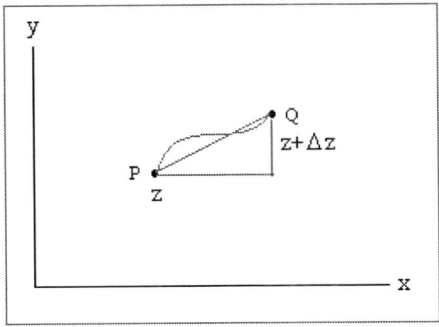

In general, we will write $\Delta z = \Delta x + i\Delta y$. Let's calculate the derivative df/dz utilizing paths for Δz along the x-axis alone, i.e., $\Delta z = \Delta x$, and along the y-axis alone, i.e. $\Delta z = i\Delta y$. Thus, for $\Delta z = \Delta x$, we can write

$$\frac{df}{dz} = \lim_{\Delta x \to 0} \frac{[\Phi(x+\Delta x, y) + i\Psi(x+\Delta x, y)] - [\Phi(x, y) + i\Psi(x, y)]}{\Delta x}$$

$$\frac{df}{dz} = \lim_{\Delta x \to 0} \left(\frac{[\Phi(x+\Delta x, y) - \Phi(x, y)]}{\Delta x} + i\frac{[\Psi(x+\Delta x, y) - \Psi(x, y)]}{\Delta x} \right)$$

You can prove, by expressing the derivative in terms of $\Delta z = i\Delta y$, that

$$\frac{df}{dz} = \frac{\partial \Psi}{\partial y} - i\frac{\partial \Phi}{\partial y}.$$

In order for the last two expressions for df/dz to be the same, we require that

$$\frac{\partial \Phi}{\partial x} = \frac{\partial \Psi}{\partial y}, \qquad \frac{\partial \Phi}{\partial y} = -\frac{\partial \Psi}{\partial x}.$$

These two equations are known as the *Cauchy-Riemann differentiability conditions* for complex functions (or, simply, the Cauchy-Riemann conditions). Thus, if the functions $\Phi(x,y) = Re[f(z)]$ and $\Psi(x,y) = Re[f(z)]$, satisfy the Cauchy-Riemann conditions, the derivative $f'(z) = df/dz$ is uniquely defined. In such case, the function $f(z)$ is said to be an *analytical complex function*, and the functions $\Phi(x,y)$ and $\Psi(x,y)$ are said to be *harmonic functions*.

More importantly, if a complex function $f(z)$ is analytical, the rules used for univariate derivatives can be applied to $f(z)$. For example, we indicated earlier that the function

$$w = f(z) = \ln(z) = \ln(r \cdot e^{i\theta}) = \ln(r) + i\theta.$$

can be written in terms of (x,y) as

$$\Phi = \Phi(x,y) = \ln[(x^2+y^2)^{1/2}] = (1/2)\ln(x^2+y^2), \text{ and } \Psi = \Psi(x,y) = \tan^{-1}(y/x).$$

You can check that the functions $\Phi(x,y)$ and $\Psi(x,y)$ satisfy the Cauchy-Riemann conditions. The function $f(z) = \ln(z)$ is, therefore, analytical, and its derivative can be calculated by using:

$$\frac{df}{dz} = \frac{d}{dz}(\ln z) = \frac{1}{z}.$$

Note: Most of the functions that we commonly use with real variables, e.g. exp, ln, sin, cos, tan, asin, acos, atan, hyperbolic functions, polynomials, 1/x, square root, etc., are analytical functions when used with the complex variable $z = x + iy$. Thus, the rules of derivatives for these functions are the same as in real variables, e.g. $d(sin(z))/dz = cos(z)$, $d(z^2+z)/dz = 2z+1$, etc.

Integrals of complex functions

If $f(z) = \phi(x,y) + i\psi(x,y)$ is a complex analytic function in a given region of the plane, we define the integral of $f(z)$ along a path C from point $z_1 = x_1 + iy_1$ to point $z_2 = x_2 + iy_2$, as:

$$\int_C f(z)dz = \int_{z_1}^{z_2} f(z)dz = \int_{(x_1,y_1)}^{(x_2,y_2)} [\phi(x,y) + i\psi(x,y)] \cdot (dx + idy)$$

$$= \int_{(x_1,y_1)}^{(x_2,y_2)} (\phi dx - \psi dy) + i \int_{(x_1,y_1)}^{(x_2,y_2)} (\psi dx + \phi dy)$$

where $dz = dx + i\,dy$.

If the integral evaluates to the same value regardless of the nature of path C, we say that the integral is independent of the path. It depends only on the limits of integration z_1 and z_2. We can prove that if the function $f(z)$ is analytic, then the resulting integrals

$$\int_{(x_1,y_1)}^{(x_2,y_2)} (\phi dx - \psi dy) + i \int_{(x_1,y_1)}^{(x_2,y_2)} (\psi dx + \phi dy)$$

are independent of the path. The conditions for independence of the path for these two integrals are

$$\frac{\partial}{\partial y}\phi = -\left(\frac{\partial}{\partial x}\psi\right) \text{ and } \frac{\partial}{\partial x}\psi = \frac{\partial}{\partial y}\phi,$$

respectively, which are the Cauchy-Riemann conditions necessary for analycity.

Thus, integrals of any analytic function $f(z)$ can be evaluated as a simple univariate integral treating the function z as a real variable and evaluating the complex integration limits, $z_1 = x_1 + iy_1$, and $z_2 = x_2 + iy_2$, once the anti-derivative of $f(z)$ has been found.

SCILAB functions for integrals of complex functions

SCILAB provides functions *intc* and *intl* for the numerical calculation of integrals of a complex function. Function *intc* integrates the complex function $f(z)$ between complex numbers z and

z_2 along the straight line connecting the two numbers. Since line integrals of analytic functions are independent of the path, function *intc* can be used to evaluate integrals of any analytic function. The general call of the function is *[y]=intc(z_1,z_2,f)*, where *f* is an external SCILAB function representing the complex function *f(z)*.

The following examples show how to calculate the integral of the complex function *f(z)* between complex numbers z_1 and z_2 along the straight line joining the two points.

```
-->deff('[w]=f(z)','w=1/z');

-->intc(2+3*%i,-5+4*%i,f)
 ans  =

    .5743114 + 1.484058i

-->deff('[w]=f(z)','w=log(z)')

-->intc(2,3,f)
 ans  =

    .9095425

-->intc(2-%i,%i,f)
 ans  =

  - .7165866 -  .2679858i

-->deff('[w]=f(z)','w=z+2/z^2')

-->intc(2-4*%i,3-%i,f)
 ans  = 9.6 + 5.2i
```

Function *intl* calculates the line integral of the function of a complex variable $w = f(z)$ on the curve *C* represented by the arc of a circle centered at point $z = z_0$ with radius *r* extending between the angles θ_1 and θ_2. The figure below illustrates the geometry of the problem.

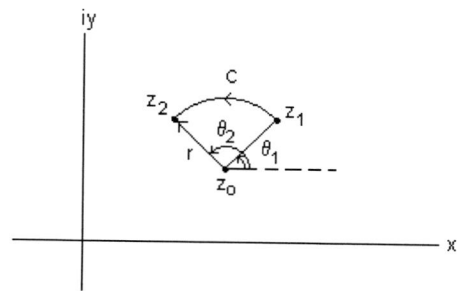

The general call to the function is *[y] = intl(θ_1, θ_2, z_0, r, f)*, where *f* is the name of a SCILAB external function. The other terms in the function call have been defined above.

The following examples show some cases of line integrals of function of a complex variable on circular arc paths.

```
-->deff('[w]=f(z)','w=z^2')
-->intl(%pi/6,%pi/2,2-3*%i,0.5,f)
 ans  =

    22.82069 - 35.377982i

-->intl(0.1,3.14,0,1.2,f)
 ans  =

  - 1.1262672 -  .1674675i

-->deff('[w]=f(z)','w=1/z+z')

-->intl(%pi/6,%pi/6+2*%pi,2+%i,1,f)
 ans  =

  - 25.132741 + 25.132741i
```

The current definition of function f(z) has a discontinuity a z = 0, so if we select the center of the circle as z_0 = 0, the integral does not converge:

```
-->intl(0,2*%pi,0,0.5,f)
 !--error    24
convergence problem...
at line       19 of function intl              called by :
intl(0,2*%pi,0,0.5,f)
```

Other examples of function *intl* follow:

```
-->intl(0.1,2*%pi+0.1,2+2*%i,0.5,f)
 ans  = - 50.265482 + 6.2831853i

-->intl(0.1,2*%pi+0.1,0.1+0.1*%i,0.5,f)
 ans  =

  -  .1256637 + 6.2831853i
```

The following example of an integral path centered at z_0 = 0.2i with radius r = 0.5 fails to converge:

```
-->intl(0.1,2*%pi+0.1,0.2*%i,0.5,f)
 !--error    24
convergence problem...
at line       19 of function intl              called by :
intl(0.1,2*%pi+0.1,0.2*%i,0.5,f)
```

However, moving the center of the circle to z_0 = 0.1(1+i) produces a convergent integral:

```
-->intl(0.1,2*%pi+0.1,0.1+0.1*%i,0.5,f)
 ans  =

  -.1256637 + 6.2831853i
```

Applications of integrals of one variable

In this section we present applications of integrals for the solution of problems from the physical sciences.

Areas under curves

A simple physical interpretation of the integral $I = \int_a^b f(x)\,dx$, is the area under the curve $y = f(x)$ and above the x-axes, between the values $x = a$ and $x = b$.

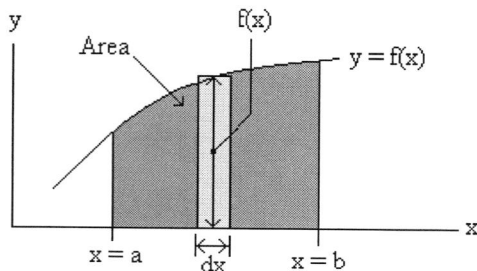

A representative differential of area (or area element) is the rectangle of base dx and height $y = f(x)$ shown in the figure. We will write the area of the differential element as $dA = f(x)\,dx$. The total area is,

$$A = \int_R dA = \int_a^b f(x)\,dx$$

For example, to find the area between x = 2 and x = 4, under the curve $y = ln(x+1)$, use:

```
-->integrate('log(x+1)','x',2,4)
 ans  =   2.7513527
```

The region under consideration can be depicted as shown below:

```
-->x=[0:0.1:6];y=log(x+1);

-->xvv = [2:0.1:4];yvv=log(xvv+1);

-->xva=[2 2 xvv 4 4];yva=[0 log(3) yvv log(5) 0];

-->plot(x,y,'x','y','Integral example')

-->xfpoly(xva,yva,2)
```

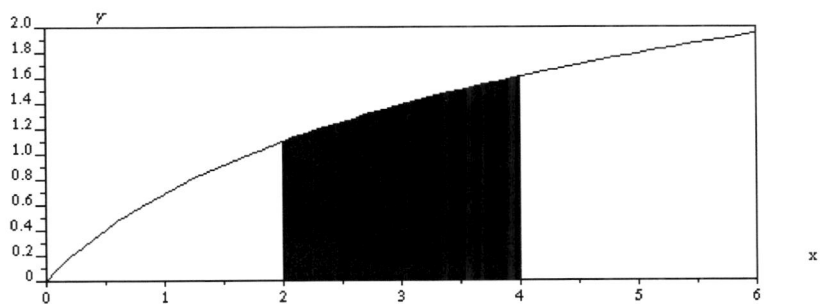

Area between curves

The area between the curves $y = f_1(x)$ and $y = f_2(x)$, and $x = a$ and $x = b$, assuming that in (a,b), $f_2(x) \leq f_1(x)$, is given by $\int_a^b f_1(x) - f_2(x)\, dx$.

For example, let $y = f_1(x) = x$ and $y = f_2(x) = x^2$, for $a=0.25$ and $b=0.75$. The following statements define the functions in SCILAB and produce the graph of the area to be calculated:

```
-->deff('[y]=f1(x)','y=x');deff('[y]=f2(x)','y=x^2');a=0.25;b=0.75;

-->x=[a:0.01:b];y1=f1(x);y2=f2(x);

-->xv1=[a,a];yv1=[f1(a),f2(a)];xv2=[b,b];yv2=[f1(b),f2(b)];

-->plot2d([x' x'],[y1' y2'],[1,2],'011',' ',[0 0 1 1])

-->xsegs(xv1,yv1,3);xsegs(xv2,yv2,4);

-->xtitle('Area between y1=x and y2 = x^2, 0.25<x<0.75','x','y')
```

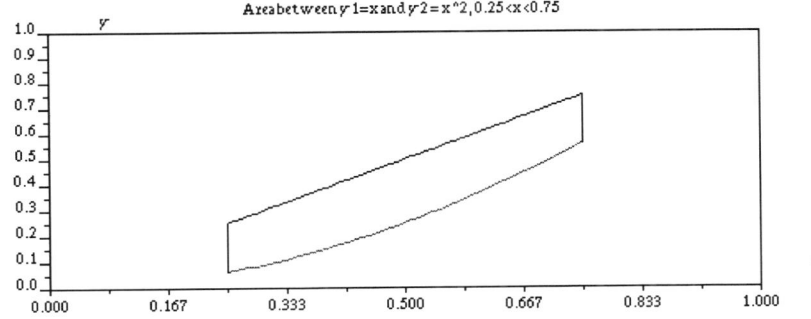

The differential of area used for this exercise is shown below.

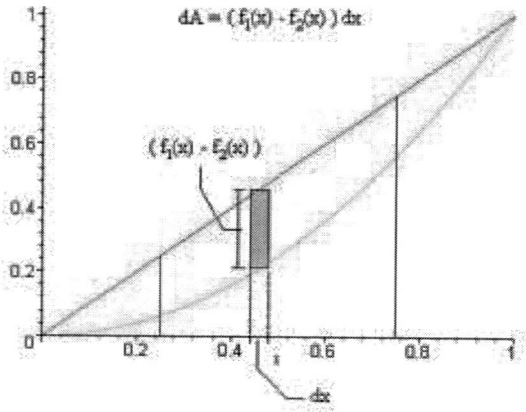

To calculate the area we use SCILAB function *inttrap*:

```
--> x = [0.25:0.01:0.75];y1=f1(x);y2=f2(x);y=y1-y2;inttrap(x,y);
ans  =   0.11475
```

Center of mass of an area

Consider the rectangular element of area in the figure below, $dA = f(x) \, dx$. If the base of the rectangle is centered at x, then the center of mass of the rectangle is the point

$$C[x, \frac{f(x)}{2}],$$

i.e.,

$$x_c = x, \text{ and } y_c = \frac{f(x)}{2}.$$

First moments of the areas with respect to the x-and y-axes are:

$$M_x = \int y_c \, dA = \int_a^b \frac{f(x) f(x)}{2} dx = \frac{1}{2} \int_a^b f(x)^2 \, dx, \text{ and } M_y = \int x_c \, dA = \int_a^b x f(x) \, dx$$

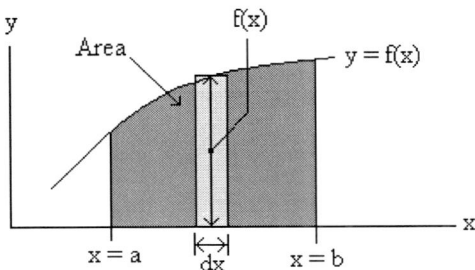

For example, for the region $0 < y < \ln(1+x)$, $2<x<4$:

```
-->deff('[y]=f(x)','y=log(x+1)');a=2;b=4;
-->Mx = integrate('f(x)^2','x',a,b)/2
 Mx   = 1.9139498
-->My = integrate('x*f(x)','x',a,b)
 My   = 8.4228659
```

The center of mass has coordinates,

$$X_c = \frac{M_y}{A}, \text{ and } Y_c = \frac{M_x}{A}.$$

Where,

$$A = \int_a^b f(x)\, dx$$

```
-->A = integrate('f(x)','x',a,b)
 A   = 2.7513527

-->xc = My/A, yc = Mx/A
 xc  = 3.0613545
 yc  = .6956396
```

The following plot shows the center of mass (centroid) of the area

```
-->x=[2:0.1:4];y=log(x+1);xv1=[2 2];yv1=[0 log(3)];xv2=[4 4];yv2=[0 log(5)];
-->plot2d(x,y,1,'011',' ',[0 0 6 2]);xsegs(xv1,yv1,1);xsegs(xv2,yv2,1);
-->xset('mark',-1,1);plot2d([xc],[yc],-1,'010',' ',[0 0 6 2])
```

```
-->xstring(xc,yc,'C')

-->xtitle('Centroid of an area','x','y')
```

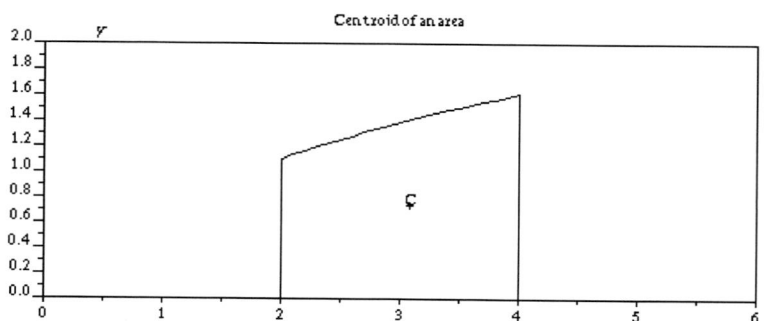

Volume of a solid of revolution

The figure below shows a body of revolution generated by the rotation of the curve f(x), a<x<b, about the x-axis. The shadowed rectangle represents the area differential of width dx, and height f(x), centered at x. The rotation of that differential of area about the x-axis generates a differential of volume in the shape of a disk (a cylinder) of height dx and base area equal to $\pi f(x)^2$. The volume of the elementary disk is $dV = \pi f(x)^2 dx$. Therefore, the volume of the body of revolution is $V = \int 1\, dV = \int_a^b \pi f(x)^2\, dx$

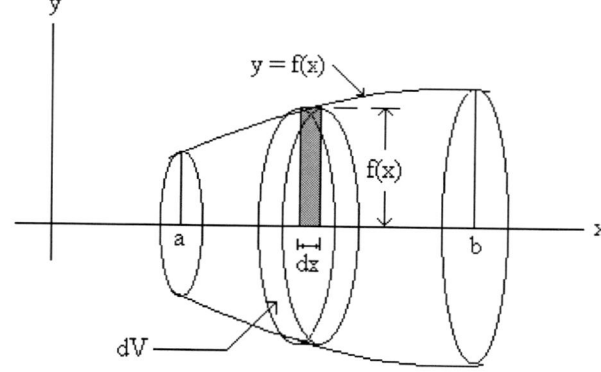

or example, for the region used earlier to find the centroid of the area, the volume of a body of revolution generated by the rotation of the curve $y = \ln(1+x)$, 2<x<4, about the x axis is given by:

```
-->V = integrate('%pi*f(x)^2','x',a,b)
```

V = 12.025702

Moment of inertia of an area

Consider the rectangular region defined by 0<x<B, 0<y<H, as shown below:

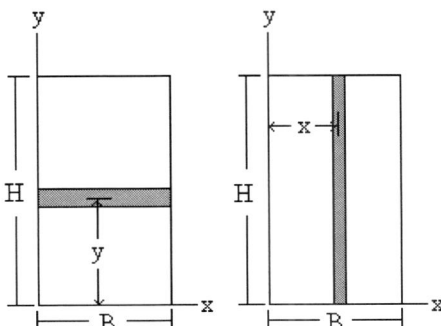

The horizontal element of area shown in the left-hand side figure, is a rectangle of width dy and height L, and centered at y. The element's area is $dA = B\,dy$. The distance from the area element to the x-axis is y, therefore, the moment of inertia of the area element with respect to the x-axis is $dI_x = y^2\,dA = y^2 B\,dy$. The moment of inertia of the area with respect to the x-axis is

$$I_x = \int 1\,dI_x = \int y^2\,dA = \int_0^H y^2 B\,dy,$$

i.e.,

$$I_x = \frac{1}{3}BH^3$$

For the vertical element shown in the right-hand side figure above, we can write $dA = H\,dx$. Its moment of inertia with respect to the y-axis is $dI_y = x^2\,dA = x^2 H\,dx$, and the total moment of inertia with respect to the y-axis is

$$I_y = \int 1\,dI_y = \int x^2\,dA = \int_0^L x^2 H\,dx,$$

i.e.,

$$I_y = \frac{1}{3} H B^3$$

These two results can be used to obtain moments of inertia of areas limited by curves in the x-y plane. For example, for the element of area shown in the figure below we can write,

$$B = dx,$$

$$H = f(x),$$

$$dI_x = \frac{1}{3} \, dx \, f(x)^3 \,,$$

and

$$I_x = \frac{1}{3} \int_a^b f(x)^3 \, dx.$$

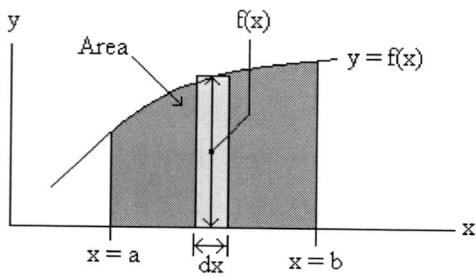

For example, to find the moment of inertia of the semi-circle shown below with respect to the x-axis, we use:

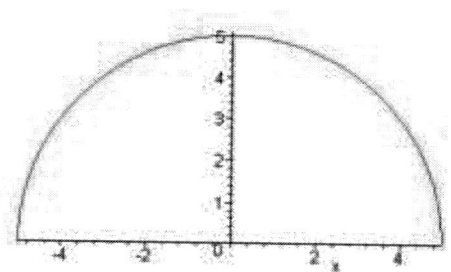

```
-->deff('[w]=f(x)','w=sqrt(25-x^2)')
-->Ix = integrate('f(x)^3','x',-5,5)/3
 Ix  = 245.43693
```

In general, for a semi-circle of radius R:

$$\frac{1}{3}\int_{-R}^{R} f(x)^3 \, dx$$

$$Inertia_x := \frac{1}{8} R^4 \pi$$

Suppose that we want to find the moment of inertia of the same semicircle, but with respect to the x-axis, we will use the element of area shown in the figure below:

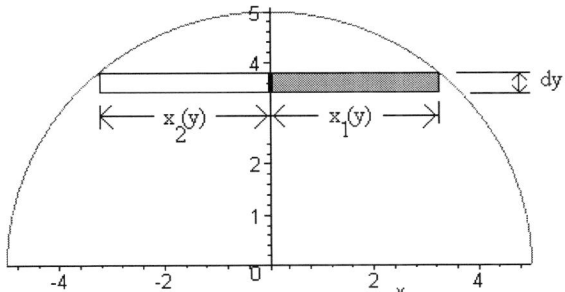

The element of area actually consists of two rectangles, of base dy, height $x_1(y)$ and $x_2(y)$, centered at y. The values of the functions $x_1(y)$ and $x_2(y)$ are obtained by solving for x in the equation, $x^2 + y^2 = 25$, thus, $x_1 = \sqrt{25-y^2}$, $x_2 = -\sqrt{25-y^2}$.

The moment of inertia of the right-hand side element, is $dI_{y,1} = \frac{1}{3} \, dy \, |x_1(y)|^3$, while that of the left-hand side element is, $dI_{y,2} = \frac{1}{3} \, dy \, |x_2(y)|^3$. The absolute value is used to indicate that the moment of inertia of the element is based on that of a rectangle, where only the rectangle's dimensions, and not their signs are important. Since $|x_1(y)| = \sqrt{25-y^2} = |x_2(y)|$, then the moment of inertia of the two elements is $dI_y = dI_{y,1} + dI_{y,2} = \frac{2}{3}(25-y^2)^{\left(\frac{3}{2}\right)} dy$, and the moment of inertia of the entire semicircle, with respect to the y axis, is

$$I_y = \frac{2}{3}\int_0^5 (25-y^2)^{\left(\frac{3}{2}\right)} dy, \text{ i.e.,}$$

```
-->Iy=(2/3)*integrate('(25-y^2)^(3/2)','y',0,5)
Iy  = 245.43693
```

This result turns out to be the same as the moment of inertia of the semicircle with respect to the x-axis. Since the moment of inertia is a measure of the resistance of a body (or an area) to angular acceleration about the axis of interest, in the same sense that a mass is a measure of the resistance of a body to linear acceleration, the fact that $I_x = I_y$ indicates that is equally difficult to provide the same angular acceleration to a thin body shaped like a semicircle whether you try to make it rotate about the x- or the y-axis.

Parallel axes theorem

The figure below shows an area in the x-y plane indicating its centroid and a couple of axes, x_c, y_c, parallel to the x- and y-axes, respectively, and passing through the area's centroid. The distance between the x- and x_c-axes is d_y, and that between the y- and y_c-axes is d_x.

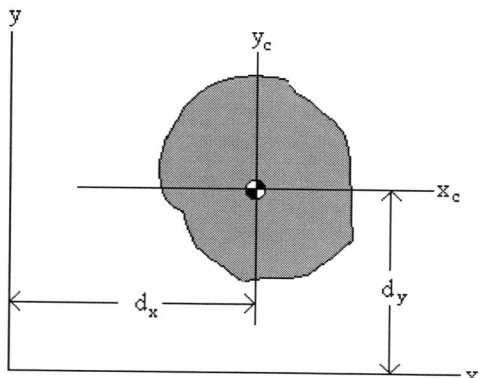

The parallel axes theorem states that if I_x represents the moment of inertia of the area with respect to the x-axis, and I_{xc} represents the moment of inertia of the area with respect to the x_c-axis, the following relationship holds: $I_x = I_{xc} + A d_y^2$
Similarly, for the moment of inertia with respect to the y-axis, I_y, in terms of the moment of inertia with respect to the y_c-axis, we can write, $I_y = I_{yc} + A d_x^2$

Centroidal moments of inertia for a rectangle

Earlier we found the moments of inertia of a rectangle whose sides lay on the coordinate axes, width (along the x-axis) = L, height (along the y-axis) = H, with respect to those axes as,

$I_x = \frac{1}{3} B H^3$, and $I_y = \frac{1}{3} H B^3$. With, $A = H L$, and $d_x = \frac{B}{2}$, and $d_y = \frac{H}{2}$, we can find the centroidal moments of inertia of a rectangle as shown below:

The parallel axes theorem indicates that: $I_x = I_{xc} + A d_y^2$, $I_y = I_{yc} + A d_x^2$.

For the rectangle:

$$\text{Inertia}_x := \frac{1}{3} B H^3$$

$$\text{Inertia}_y := \frac{1}{3} H B^3$$

$$A := B H$$

$$d_x := \frac{1}{2} B$$

$$d_y := \frac{1}{2} H$$

Solving for the centroidal moments of inertia:

$$\{\text{Inertia}_{xc} = \frac{1}{12} B H^3\}$$

$$\{\text{Inertia}_{yc} = \frac{1}{12} H B^3\}$$

Moment of inertia of the semicircle using centroidal axes

Noticing that moment of inertia of the rectangle of height can attack the problem of finding the moment of inertia of the semicircle used earlier with respect to the y-ax $|x_1(y)| + |x_2(y)|$, and width dy, about the y-axis is the centroidal moment of inertia, i.e.,

$$dI_y = dI_{yc} = \frac{1}{12} dy \ (|x_1(y)| + |x_2(y)|)^3 = \frac{1}{12} (2\sqrt{25 - y^2})^3 = \frac{2}{3} (25 - y^2)^{\left(\frac{3}{2}\right)} dy,$$

which is the same value for dI_y found earlier.

Area enclosed by a curve in polar coordinates

Consider the area enclosed by the curve $r = r(\theta)$ between the rays $\theta = a$, and $\theta = b$. An element of area in polar coordinates is shown in the figure below. The area of the element shown is approximated by that of a triangle of height $r(\theta)$ and base equal to $(r d) \cdot \theta$, i.e.,

$$dA = \frac{1}{2} (r(\theta) \ d \cdot \theta) r(\theta) = \frac{1}{2} r(\theta)^2 d\theta.$$

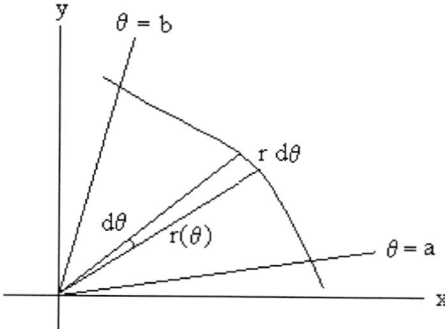

For example, find the area enclosed by the curve $r(\theta) = 5\cos(\theta)$, between the values of $\theta = \frac{\pi}{10}$ and $\frac{\pi}{2}$, we use the integral

```
-->th1 = %pi/10; th2 = %pi/2; A = integrate('0.5*(5*cos(th))^2','th',th1,th2)
 A  = 6.0171527
```

Fluid dynamics: calculating discharge in pipe for laminar flow

The figure below shows the profile of laminar flow velocity as a function of the radial distance r in a pipe.

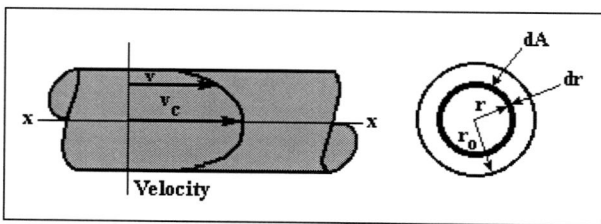

The velocity distribution is given by the expression,

$$v(r) = v_s[1-(r/r_o)^2],$$

where v_c is the centerline velocity and r is the radius of the pipe.

We can use this expression to obtain the discharge (volumetric flow) in the pipe by using the definition

$$Q = \int_A v \cdot dA.$$

Because the velocity distribution in a pipe depends on the radial distance only, we can use an element of area consisting of a ring of thickness dr and length $2\pi r$, thus, the area is

$$dA = 2\pi\, r dr.$$

With this element of area, the discharge is calculated, in general, as

$$\int_0^R v(r)\, 2\pi r\, dr$$

For the specific case of a laminar flow velocity distribution, you will need to set up the integral:

$$\int_0^R vc\left(1 - \left(\frac{r}{R}\right)^2\right) 2\pi r\, dr$$

The result is $\frac{vc\, r0^2\, \pi}{2}$. The mean velocity is defined as $V = Q/A$, with $A = \pi r0^2$, then $V = v_c/2$ for laminar flow.

Line integrals

A line integral is an integral calculated along a curve C in space or in the plane with the integrand defined at each point of C. Suppose that the curve C has the representation

$$r(s) = x(s)\,\mathbf{i} + y(s)\,\mathbf{j} + z(s)\,\mathbf{k}, \quad a \leq s, s \leq b,$$

so that $r(s)$ is continuous and has a non-zero, continuous first derivative dr/ds for $a \leq s, s \leq b$. Then C is said to be a *smooth curve*, i.e., C has a unique tangent at each of its points whose direction varies continuously as we travel along the curve. Let $f(x, y, z)$ be a function defined (at least) at each point of C, and let f be a continuous function of s (i.e. $f[x(s),y(s),z(s)] = g(s)$). Then, the *line integral* of f along C from A to B (where $s = a$, and $s = b$, respectively) is calculated as

$$\int_C f(x,y,z)ds = \int_a^b f[x(s),y(s),z(s)]ds$$

The curve C is called the *path of integration*.

For a line integral over a closed path C, the symbol $\oint_C$ is sometimes used in the literature.

In the exercises presented in next sub-section is it assumed that all the integration paths are **piecewise smooth**, i.e., it consists of finitely many smooth curves.

Some properties of line integrals are shown below.

$$\int_C kf\,ds = k\int_C f\,ds; \quad \int_C (f+g)\,ds = \int_C f\,ds + \int_C g\,ds; \quad \int_C f\,ds = \int_{C_1} f\,ds + \int_{C_2} f\,ds;$$

where C is composed of C_1 and C_2.

Evaluation of line integrals

The formula for evaluating a line integral over a curve C when the curve is described by the vector **r**(s), was given earlier as:

$$\int_C f(x,y,z)\,ds = \int_a^b f[x(s),y(s),z(s)]\,ds$$

If the curve is given by a parameter, so that the curve C is defined by **r** = **r**(t), with $t_0 \le t, t \le t_1$, then it can be shown that

$$\int_C f(x,y,z)\,ds = \int_{t_0}^{t_1} f[x(t),y(t),z(t)]\left(\frac{ds}{dt}\right)dt$$

Example 1
Integrate the function $f(x,y) = 3(x^2 + y^2)$, along the path y = x from (0,0) to (1,1). First, we sketch the path of integration:

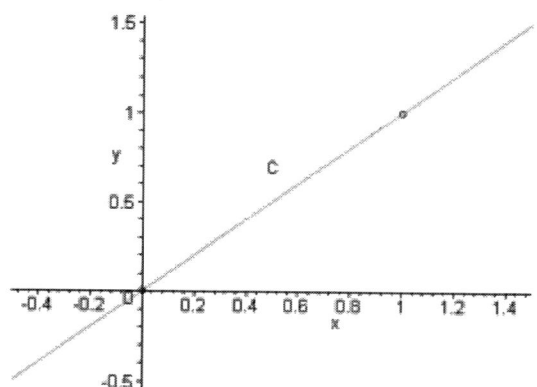

For the path of integration $y = x$, we can arbitrarily set $x(s) = s$, and $y(s) = s$, and use

$$\int_C f(x,y)\,ds = \int_a^b f[x(s),y(s)]\,ds$$

with a = 0, b = 1, i.e., $f[x(s),y(s)] = g(s) = 3(s^2+s^2) = 6s^2$, and the integral reduces to

$$\int_C f(x,y)ds = \int_0^1 6s^2 ds.$$

Using SCILAB:

```
--> integrate('6*s^2','s',0,1)
ans = 2
```

Example 2
Calculate the line integral of $f(x,y) = k(x^2+y^2)$, $k = 1$, counterclokwise along the circle $x^2 + y^2 = r^2$, with r=5, from (0,r) to (r,0): One possible representation of the circle $x^2+y^2=r^2$ is the parametric equations, $x = r\cos(s)$, and $y = r\sin(s)$, with $s = \frac{\pi}{2}$ at (0,r) and $s=0$ at (r,0). Thus, $f[x(s),y(s)] = k(r^2 \cdot \sin^2 s + r^2 \cdot \cos^2 s) = kr^2$. The line integral is simply,

$$\int_C f(x,y)ds = \int_{\pi/2}^{0} kr^2 ds = -\frac{1}{2}\pi kr^2.$$

Example 3
Using the curve of *Example 2* that the with the integrand being $f(x,y) = x^2 \sin(y)$, we replace $x = r\cos(s)$, and $y = r\sin(s)$, in the function *f(x,y)* to obtain $f[x(s),y(s)] = r^2 \cos^2 s \sin(r \sin(s))$, with *s* from $a = \pi/2$ to $b = 0$. The integral, using SCILAB, can be calculated as follows:

```
--> integrate('r^2*cos(s)^2*sin(r*sin(s))','s',%pi/2,0)
ans = -6.3445402
```

Example 4
Evaluate the line integral of $f(x,y) = xy^3$, along the line represented by $r(t) = t\,i + 2t\,j$, for $-1 \le t, t \le 1$.

The formula to use is

$$\int_C f(x,y,z)ds = \int_{t_0}^{t_1} f[x(t),y(t),z(t)]\left(\frac{ds}{dt}\right)dt$$

Notice that $\dfrac{ds}{dt} = \left|\dfrac{dr}{dt}\right| = |v| = v_s$, the speed of a particle moving with position vector r(t) if t represents time. The velocity vector is

$$v = dr/dt = i + 2j,$$

and the speed is

$$v_s = ds/dt = |dr/dt| = \sqrt{5}.$$

We also need to define *f[x(t),y(t)]*, with x(t) = t, and y(t) = 2t, i.e., $f[x(t),y(t)] = (t)(2t)^3 = 8t^4$, thus, the integral reduces to

$$\int_C f(x,y)ds = \int_{-1}^{=1} 8t^4 \cdot \sqrt{5}dt.$$

Using SCILAB:

```
-->integrate('8*t^4*sqrt(5)','t',-1,1);
```

ans = 7.1554175

==

In many applications the integrands of the line integrals are of the form $g(x,y,z)\dfrac{dx}{ds}$, $g(x,y,z)\dfrac{dy}{ds}$, or $g(x,y,z)\dfrac{dz}{ds}$, where s = variable expressing a length on the integration path, and x=x(s), y=y(s), z=z(s). Then, the line integrals are

$$\int_C g(x,y,z)\frac{dx}{ds}ds = \int_C g(x,y,z)ds,$$

and similarly for the other two cases.

For sums of these types of integrals along the same path C we use the following notation:

$$\int_C f\,dx + \int_C g\,dx + \int_C h\,dx = \int_C (f\,dx + g\,dy + h\,dz)$$

==

Example 5

Evaluate the line integral whose integrand is $[y^2\,dx + (x-z)\,dy + xyz\,dz]$ where C is the arc of the parabola $y = x^2$ in the plane z = 2 from A[0,0,2] to B[1,1,2].
Here is a plot of the path of integration:

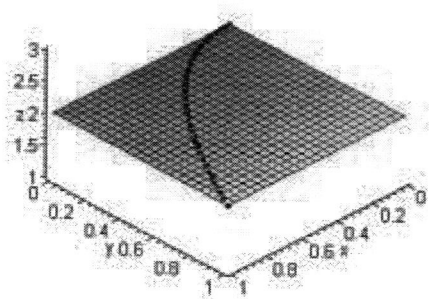

We can calculate the integral by writing all the terms in terms of x, i.e., replacing $y = x^2$, $dy = 2x\,dx$, z = 2, $dz = 0$. Therefore,

$$[x^2 y\, dx + (x-z)\, dy + x y z\, dz\,] = [x^2 x^2\, dx + (x-2)\, 2x\, dx + x y z\, 0] = (x^4 + 2x(x-2))\, dx.$$

The integral is now,

$$\int_0^1 (x^4 + 2x(x-2))\, dx.$$

To calculate the integral using SCILAB:

```
-->integrate('x^4+2*x*(x-2)','x',0,1)
 ans  = -1.1333333
```

Line integrals independent of path

Definitions:

(1) An expression of the form $f\, dx + g\, dy + h\, dz$ is known as a first-order differential form.

(2) If $f = \dfrac{\partial}{\partial x} u,\ g = \dfrac{\partial}{\partial y} u,\ h = \dfrac{\partial}{\partial z} u$, then the differential form shown above is said to be an **exact differential** of a function $u(x, y, z)$, i.e., $du = f\, dx + g\, dy + h\, dz$, or

$$du = \left(\frac{\partial}{\partial x} u\right) dx + \left(\frac{\partial}{\partial y} u\right) dy + \left(\frac{\partial}{\partial z} u\right) dz.$$

In general, a line integral of a differential form, i.e., $\int f\, dx + g\, dy + h\, dz$, over a path C will be dependent not only on the endpoints of the integration (say from point P to point Q), but also on the path followed to perform that integration, i.e., on the curve C. However, if the integrand is an exact differential then the line integral is independent of the path and we can write:

$$\int_C (f\, dx + g\, dy + h\, dz) = \int_P^Q du = u\Big|_Q^P = u(P) - u(Q)$$

For example, the expression

$$e^x \cos(y)\, dx - e^x \sin(y)\, dy + 2\, dz$$

is an exact differential form, which you can prove by checking the conditions

$$\frac{\partial}{\partial y} h = \frac{\partial}{\partial z} g, \qquad \frac{\partial}{\partial z} f = \frac{\partial}{\partial x} h, \qquad \frac{\partial}{\partial x} g = \frac{\partial}{\partial y} f.$$

Therefore, $e^x \cos(y)\, dx - e^x \sin(y)\, dy + 2\, dz = du$, is an exact differential. To find the function $u(x, y, z)$ we write: $\dfrac{\partial}{\partial x} u = f = e^x \cos(y)$, and integrate with respect to x, i.e.,

$$u := e^x \cos(y) + C(y, z)$$

Next, take the derivative of this function with respect to y and make it equal to g(x,y), i.e.,

$$-e^x \sin(y) + \left(\frac{\partial}{\partial y} C(y, z)\right) = -e^x \sin(y)$$

which indicates that,

$$\frac{\partial}{\partial y} C(y, z) = 0$$

Integrating with respect to y, we get:

$$C(y, z) = E(z) + K$$

Thus,

$$u := e^x \cos(y) + E(z) + K$$

Now, take the derivative of this last expression with respect to z and make it equal to h, i.e.,

$$\frac{\partial}{\partial z} E(z) = 2$$

Which indicates that

$$E(z) = 2z$$

Therefore, the function $u(x, y, z)$ is:

$$u := e^x \cos(y) + 2z + K$$

If we want to evaluate the line integral of $e^x \cos(y)\, dx - e^x \sin(y)\, dy + 2\, dz = du$ between points P(0,0,0) and Q(2, π, 2), we only need to evaluate u(x,y,z) at Q and P and take the difference, i.e.,

```
--> exp(2)*cos(%pi)+ 2*2 - exp(0)*cos(0) + 2*0
ans  =    -4.3890561
```

Work of a force as a line integral

A force field can be represented by a vector function $F(x,y,z) = f(x,y,z)i + g(x,y,z)j + h(x,y,z)k$. If the force acts on a particle of mass m along a path defined by a curve C starting at point P and ending at point Q, the work exerted by the force field on the particle is, by definition,

$$W = \int_C \mathbf{F} \bullet d\mathbf{r} = \int_P^Q [f(x,y,z)dx + g(x,y,z)dy + h(x,y,z)dz],$$

where

$$d\mathbf{r} = dx\, \mathbf{i} + dy\, \mathbf{j} + dz\, \mathbf{k}.$$

If the quantity $\mathbf{F} \bullet d\mathbf{r}$ is an exact differential, there exists a function $U(x,y,z)$ such that

$$dU = \mathbf{F} \bullet d\mathbf{r} = f(x,y,z)dx + g(x,y,z)dy + h(x,y,z)dz,$$

thus, the integral for calculating the work exerted by force $\mathbf{F}(x,y,z)$ between points P and Q is independent of the path. The function $U(x,y,z)$ represents the *potential energy function* associated with the force $\mathbf{F}(x,y,z)$, and the force field itself is said to be *conservative*. The force field can be obtained out of the potential energy function by using the gradient operator, i.e.,

$$\mathbf{F}(x,y,z) = \frac{\partial U}{\partial x}\mathbf{i} + \frac{\partial U}{\partial x}\mathbf{j} + \frac{\partial U}{\partial x}\mathbf{k}.$$

For example, for a potential energy function $U(x,y,z) = x^2+y^2+z^2$, the force field is given by $\mathbf{F}(x,y,z) = 2(x\mathbf{i}+y\mathbf{j}+z\mathbf{k})$. To calculate the work performed by the force $\mathbf{F}(x,y,z)$ along a path given by $x(s) = 2\sin s$, $y(s) = 2\cos s$, and $z = 2s$, from point $P(0,2,0)$, for $s=0$, to point $Q(\sqrt{3},1,2\pi/3)$, for $s=\pi/3$, we calculate the integrand

$$\mathbf{F} \bullet d\mathbf{r} = 2xdx + 2ydy + 2zdz = 2(2\sin s)(2\cos s\, ds) + 2(2\cos s)(-2\sin s\, ds) + 2(2s)(2\, ds),$$

$$\mathbf{F} \bullet d\mathbf{r} = (8\sin s \cos s - 8\sin s \cos s + 8s)ds = 8s\, ds.$$

The work performed by the force is

$$W = \int_{s=0}^{s=\pi/3} \mathbf{F} \bullet d\mathbf{r} = \int_0^{\pi/3} 8s\, ds = 4s^2 \Big|_0^{\pi/3} = \frac{4\pi^2}{9}.$$

Alternatively, since the force field is conservative,

$$W = U(Q) - U(P) = 3+1+4\pi^2/9 - 4 = 4\pi^2/9.$$

Double integral in a rectangular domain

As the integral of a single variable, say $\int_a^b f(x)dx$, can be interpreted as the area under the curve $y = f(x)$ between $x = a$ and $x = b$, the double integral

$$I = \int_a^b \int_c^d f(x,y)dy\, dx,$$

can be interpreted as the volume of the solid that extends between the xy plane and the surface defined by $z = f(x,y)$ above the rectangular region $R = \{a < x < b,\ c < y < d\}$, as illustrated in the figure below.

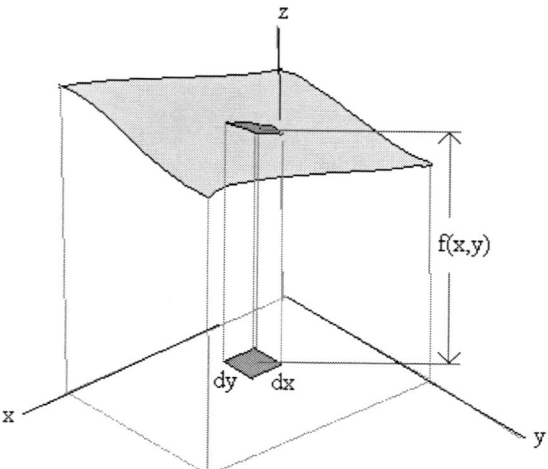

To approximate the volume representing the double integral we first divide the region R into a grid of x and y values as shown in the figure below. There will be n sub-intervals in x and m in y. Consider the volume element limited by $x_i < x < x_{i+1}$ and $y_j < y < y_{j+1}$. The base of the volume element is the shaded rectangle shown in the figure.

The height of the element, h_{ij}, is taken to be the average of the four values of the function $z = f(x_i, y_j)$ evaluated in the four corners of the element of area, i.e.,

$$h_{ij} = \frac{1}{4}\left(y_{ij} + y_{i,j+1} + y_{i+1,j} + y_{i+1,j+1}\right),$$

for $i = 0, 1, 2, \ldots, n-1$, and $j = 0, 1, 2, \ldots, m-1$. Thus, the element of volume corresponding to the shaded rectangle in the x-y plane is

$$\Delta V_{ij} = h_{ij} \cdot \Delta x_i \cdot \Delta y_j = \frac{1}{4}\left(y_{ij} + y_{i,j+1} + y_{i+1,j} + y_{i+1,j+1}\right) \cdot \Delta x_i \cdot \Delta y_j,$$

where $\Delta x_i = x_{i+1} - x_i$, and $\Delta y_j = y_{j+1} - y_j$. In practice, the values of Δx_i and Δy_j are typically taken as constant values although not necessarily the same. Thus, the double integral is approximated by

$$V \approx \sum_{i=1}^{n}\sum_{j=1}^{m} V_{ij} = \frac{1}{4}\Delta x \cdot \Delta y \cdot \sum_{i=1}^{n}\sum_{i=1}^{m}\left(y_{ij} + y_{i,j+1} + y_{i+1,j} + y_{i+1,j+1}\right).$$

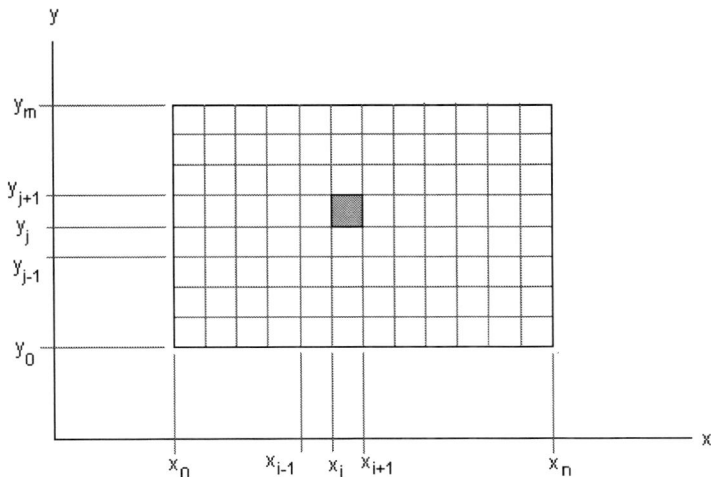

User-defined function for calculating double integrals

The function *DoubleIntegral*, shown below, calculates a double integral over a rectangular domain using the approximation outlined above. The function call requires the x integration limits and the number of x sub-intervals, *a, b, n*, the y integration limits and number of y sub-intervals, *c, d, m*, and the function name, *f*. The function *f* is a SCILAB external function (e.g., a function defined with command *deff*.)

```
function [I]=DoubleIntegral(a,b,n,c,d,m,f)

//This function calculates the double integral of f(x,y)
//in the rectangular domain a < x < b, c < y < d through a
//generalization of the trapezoidal rule.

Dx = (b - a)/n;
Dy = (d - c)/m;
x = zeros(1,n+1);
y = zeros(1,m+1);
F = zeros(n+1,m+1);

for i = 1:n+1
      x(1,i) = a + (i-1)*Dx;
end;

for j = 1:m+1
      y(1,j) = c + (j-1)*Dy;
end;

for i = 1:n+1
      for j = 1:m+1
            F(i,j) = f(x(1,i),y(1,j));
      end;
```

```
end;
I = F(1,1) + F(1,m+1) + F(n+1,1) + F(n+1,m+1);
for i = 2:n
    I = I + 2*(F(i,1) + F(i,m+1));
end;
for j = 2:m
    I = I + 2*(F(1,j) + F(n+1,j));
end;
for i = 2:n
    for j = 2:m
        I = I + 4*F(i,j);
    end;
end;
I = I*Dx*Dy/4;
//end of DoubleIntegral function
```

Applications of function *DoubleIntegral*

The following commands show applications of the function *DoubleIntegral*. First, we load the function

```
-->getf('DoubleIntegral.txt')
```

Next, we will calculate the double integral of the function $z = f(x,y) = x+y$, in the interval $0<x<2$, $0<y<2$. Before doing that, however, we produce a plot of the function:

```
-->deff('[z]=f(x,y)','z=x+y')                              //define z = f(x,y)
-->xx = [0:0.2:2]; yy = [0:0.2:2]; zz = feval(xx,yy,f);    //calculate z = f(x,y)
-->plot3d(xx,yy,zz)                                        //produce plot
```

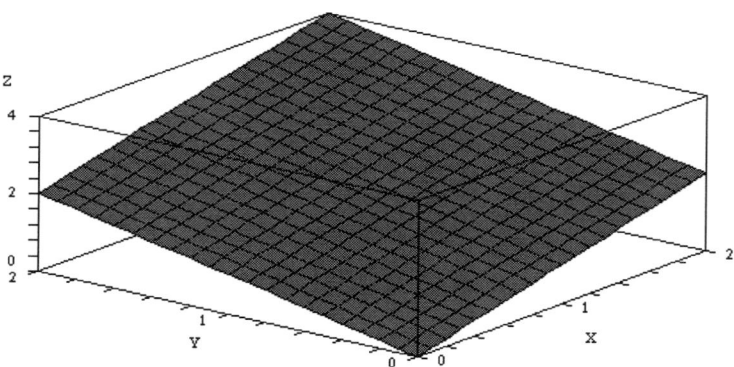

To calculate the double integral using 10 sub-intervals in both x and y use:

```
-->DoubleIntegral(0,2,10,0,2,10,f)
 ans   =
```

8.

Note: Notice that the plot shows a box extending between 0<x<2, 0<y<2, 0<z<4, whose volume is 2×2×4 = 16. Since the plane representing the function z = x+y divides the box into two halves, the volume representing the double integral will be half of the volume of the box, namely, 8.

The following calls to function *DoubleIntegral* for $0 < x < 1$ and $0 < y < 1$, use 5, 10, and 20 sub-intervals with $z = f(x,y) = x+y$:

```
-->DoubleIntegral(0,1,5,0,1,5,f)
 ans  = 1.

-->DoubleIntegral(0,1,10,0,1,10,f)
 ans  = 1.

-->DoubleIntegral(0,1,20,0,1,20,f)
 ans  = 1.
```

In the next exercise we use the function $z=f(x,y)=\sin(x+y)$. First, we define the function and produce a plot for $0<x<2\pi$ and $0<y<2\pi$:

```
-->deff('[z]=f(x,y)','z=sin(x+y)')

-->xx = [0:%pi/10:2*%pi]; yy = xx; zz = feval(xx,yy,f);

-->plot3d(xx,yy,zz)
```

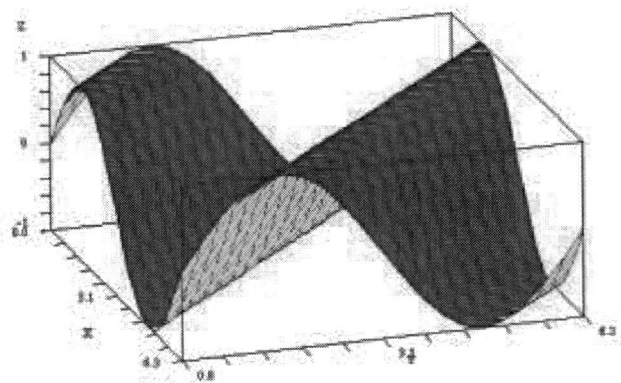

Due to the symmetry of the function above and below the xy plane, we suspect that the double integral will add to zero. A call to function *DoubleIntegral* in the interval under consideration confirms our suspicion:

```
-->DoubleIntegral(0,2*%pi,20,0,2*%pi,20,f)
 ans  = - 2.049E-15
```

Similar symmetry occurs for the function in the interval $0<x<2\pi$ and $0<y<2\pi$, the double integral on those intervals producing again a zero result:

```
-->DoubleIntegral(0,%pi,20,0,%pi,20,f)
ans  =  3.137E-16
```

The following plot shows the function $z = \sin(x+y)$ for the interval $0<x<1$ and $0<y<2$.

```
-->xx = [0:0.1:1]; yy = [0:0.1:2]; zz = feval(xx,yy,f);plot3d(xx,yy,zz)
```

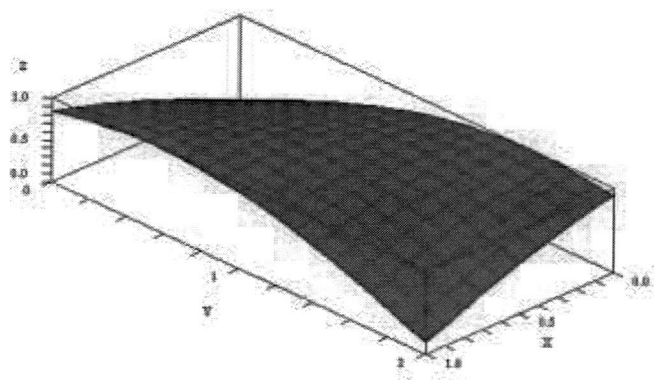

The figure does not show the same symmetry of the surface above and below the x-y plane as in the two previous intervals. The integral of the function on this region produces indeed a non-zero value:

```
-->DoubleIntegral(0,1,20,0,2,20,f)
ans  =  1.6079717
```

Double integrals transforming integration region into a rectangle

Suppose we are to calculate the double integral

$$I = \int_a^b \int_{g_1(x)}^{g_2(x)} f(x,y) dy dx$$

in the region $R = \{g_1(x) \le y \le g_2(x), a \le x \le b\}$, illustrated in part [a] of the figure below.

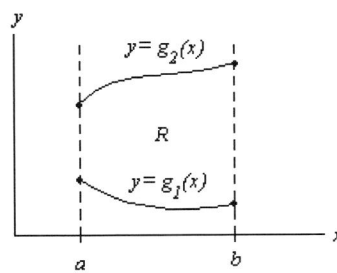
[a] Original region R in the x-y plane

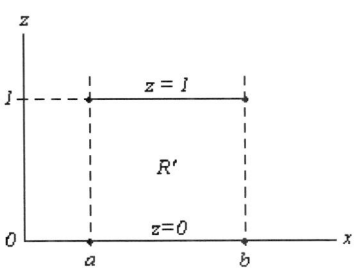
[b] Transformed region in the x-z plane

We can use function *DoubleIntegral* to calculate the double integral indicated above if we transform the original region of integration R in the x-y plane into a rectangular region of integration through the coordinate transformation

$$y = [g_2(x)-g_1(x)]z + g_1(z).$$

The resulting rectangular region $R' = \{0 \leq z \leq 1, a \leq x \leq b\}$ is illustrated in part [b] of the figure above. Function $f(x,y)$ gets transformed into function $\phi(x,z)$ through

$$\phi(x,y) = f(x, [g_2(x)-g_1(x)]z + g_1(z)) = \phi(x,z).$$

To put together the double integral in the x-z plane we need to replace the value dy with

$$dy = g_2(x)-g_1(x).$$

Thus, the double integral to be calculated is now

$$I = \int_a^b \int_{g_1(x)}^{g_2(x)} f(x,y) dy dx = \int_a^b \int_0^1 \phi(x,z) \cdot [g_2(x)-g_1(x)] \cdot dz dx = \int_a^b \int_0^1 \psi(x,z) \cdot dz dx,$$

where

$$\psi(x,y) = \phi(x,z) \cdot [g_2(x)-g_1(x)] = f(x, [g_2(x)-g_1(x)]z + g_1(z)) \cdot [g_2(x)-g_1(x)]$$

is the new integrand function.

As an example, to calculate the double integral

$$I = \int_0^3 \int_1^{\sqrt{x/3}} \exp(y^3) dy dx$$

we identify $g_1(x) = 1$, $g_2(x) = (x/3)^{1/2}$, and use the transformation $y = ((x/3)^{1/2}-1)z+1$, to obtain a new function $\phi(x,z) = \exp([((x/3)^{1/2}-1)z+1]^3)$. With $dy = ((x/3)^{1/2}-1)$, the double integral itself gets transformed to

$$I = \int_0^3 \int_0^1 \exp([(\sqrt{x/3}-1)z+1]^3) \cdot (\sqrt{x/3}-1) \cdot dz dx.$$

For the purpose of calculating the integral with function *DoubleIntegral* we need to define the function

$$\psi(x,z) = \exp([((x/3)^{1/2}-1)z+1]^3) \cdot ((x/3)^{1/2}-1).$$

The SCILAB commands to calculate the double integral are

```
-->deff('[p]=psi(x,z)',...
--> 'p=exp(((sqrt(x/3)-1)*z+1)^3)*(sqrt(x/3)-1)')

-->I=DoubleIntegral(0,3,100,0,1,100,psi)
 I  =  - 1.7189023
```

Simpson's 1/9 rule for double integrals

In this section we present an outline of the application of Simpson's rule to double integrals on a rectangular domain. The domain is divided as indicated in the figure below.

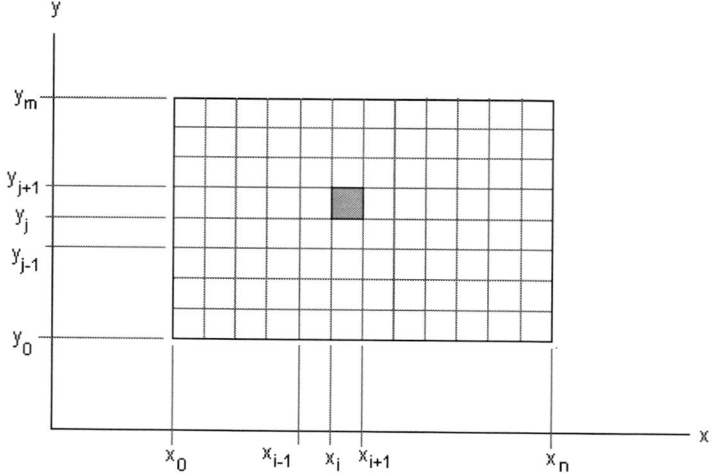

The function to be integrated is discretized to values $f_{ij} = f(x_i, y_j)$, $i=0,1,\ldots,n$, $j=0,1,\ldots,m$. The increments in x and y are Δx and Δy, respectively. Also, as with the single-variable Simpson's 1/3 rule, the values n and m must be even for the Simpson's 1/9 rule for double integrals.

Applying the Simpson's 1/3 rule to the nine points in the sub-region

$$R_{1,1} = \{x_0 \leq x \leq x_2,\ y_0 \leq y \leq y_2\}$$

results in the expression

$$\int_{x_0}^{x_2}\int_{y_0}^{y_2} f(x,y)dydx \approx \frac{1}{9}\Delta x \cdot \Delta y \cdot [f_{0,0} + f_{0,2} + f_{2,0} + f_{2,2} + 4\{f_{0,1} + f_{1,0} + f_{1,2} + f_{2,1}\} + 16 f_{1,1}].$$

In general, the integral on the nine points contained in each of the 9-point sub-regions

$$R_{ij} = \{x_{i-1} \leq x \leq x_{i+1},\ y_{i-1} \leq y \leq y_{i+2}\},$$

for $i = 1,2,..,n-1$, and $j = 1,2,...,m-1$, is calculated as

$$S_{ij} = \frac{1}{9}\Delta x \cdot \Delta y \cdot [f_{i-1,0=i-1} + f_{i-1,i+1} + f_{i+1,i-1} + f_{i+1,i+1} + 4\{f_{i-1,i} + f_{i,i-1} + f_{i,i+1} + f_{i+1,i}\} + 16 f_{i,i}].$$

To calculate the integral through the full region, i.e., in

$$R = \{x_0 \leq x \leq x_n,\ y_0 \leq y \leq y_m\},$$

one needs to calculate the $(n-1)(m-1)$ summations S_{ij} for $i = 1,2,..,n-1$, and $j = 1,2,...,m-1$, and add them all together. Thus, we can write

$$I = \int_{x_0}^{x_n}\int_{y_0}^{y_m} f(x,y)dydx \approx \sum_{i=1}^{n-1}\sum_{j=1}^{m-1} S_{ij},$$

where the sums S_{ij} were defined above.

The implementation of Simpson's 1/9 rule for double integrals is left as an exercise for the reader.

SCILAB function for calculating double integrals

SCILAB provides function *int2d* to calculate the integral of a function $z = f(x,y)$ over a region R defined by a number of triangles. The simplest call to the function is

[Int,er] = int2d(X,Y,f),

where *Int* is the value of the integral, *er* is the error involved in the calculation. X and Y are matrices of 3 rows and n columns representing the abscissas and ordinates, respectively, of the n triangles into which region R is divided.

As an example consider the integral of the function $f(x,y) = \cos(x+y)$ in the region $R = \{0 < x < 5,\ 0 < y < 5\}$. The figure below shows two possible ways of triangulating the region.

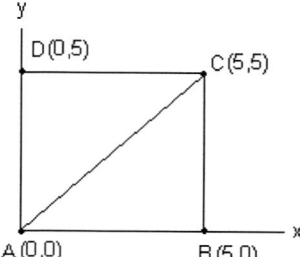 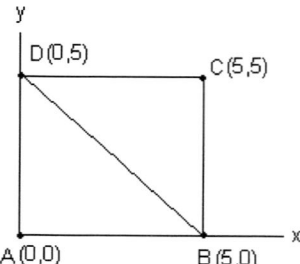

In the first case we will define the matrices X and Y as

$$X = \begin{bmatrix} 0 & 0 \\ 1 & 1 \\ 1 & 0 \end{bmatrix}, \quad Y = \begin{bmatrix} 0 & 0 \\ 0 & 1 \\ 1 & 1 \end{bmatrix},$$

while in the second case they will be defined as

$$X = \begin{bmatrix} 0 & 1 \\ 1 & 1 \\ 0 & 0 \end{bmatrix}, \quad Y = \begin{bmatrix} 0 & 0 \\ 0 & 1 \\ 1 & 1 \end{bmatrix}.$$

The following SCILAB commands show the calculation of the double integral for the two triangulations shown above:

```
-->deff('z=f(x,y)','z=cos(x+y)')
```

Triangles ABC-ACD:

```
-->X = [0,0;1,1;1,0]; Y = [0,0;0,1;1,1];

-->[Int,er] =int2d(X,Y,f)
 er  = 3.569E-11
 Int = .4967514
```

Triangles ABD-BCD:

```
-->X = [0,1;1,1;0,0]; Y = [0,0;0,1;1,1];

-->[Int,er] =int2d(X,Y,f)
 er  =  6.088E-14
 Int =  .4967514
```

If the region of integration is a single triangle, you need to provide only the coordinates of that triangle to obtain and integral with function int2d. Consider the case of the double integral of the function $z = f(x,y) = x^2+y^2$ in the triangular region shown below.

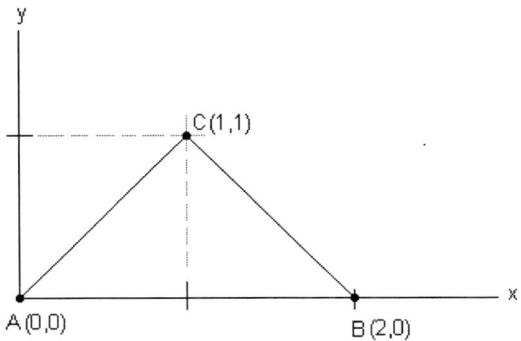

The SCILAB commands to calculate this integral are as follows:

```
-->deff('[z]=f(x,y)','z=x^2+y^2')

-->X = [0;2;1]; Y =[0;0;1];

-->[Int,er] =int2d(X,Y,f)
 er   =   2.961E-16
 Int  = 1.3333333
```

Consider now the double integral of the function $z = f(x,y) = x + y$, in the region defined by $R = \{ 0<y<1-x^2, 0<x<1\}$. The figure below shows the region R with a triangulation based on a partition of the range 0<x<1 into 10 sub-intervals, x = 0, 0.1, 0.2, ..., 1.0. The following SCILAB commands are used to generate the graph:

```
--> x = [0:0.1:1]; yT = 1-x.^2; yB = zeros(x);

--> xset('mark',-9,1)

--> plot2d([x',x',x'],[yT',yT',yB'],[1,-9,-9])

--> xtitle('triangulation of a region','x','y')

--> n = length(x)
 n  =    11.

--> for j = 1:n
-->    xpoly([x(j),x(j)],[yB(j),yT(j)],"lines")
--> end;


--> for j = 1:n-2
-->    xpoly([x(j),x(j+1)],[yB(j),yT(j+1)],"lines")
--> end;
```

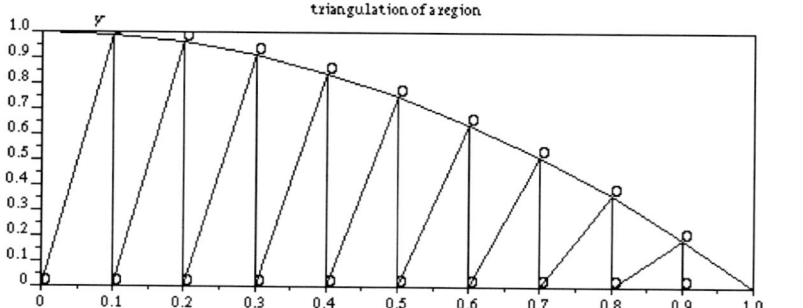

The following *for..end* loops generate the matrices X ad Y required for the application of function *int2d*:

```
--> X=[];Y=[];
--> for j = 1:n-2
-->     X = [X [x(j);x(j);x(j+1)]]; X = [X [x(j);x(j+1);x(j+1)]];
-->     Y = [Y [yB(j);yT(j);yT(j+1)]]; Y = [Y [yB(j);yT(j+1);yB(j+1)]];
-->end;

-->X = [X [x(n-1);x(n-1);x(n)]]; Y = [Y [yB(n-1);yT(n-1);yB(n)]];
```

The following statement defines the function to integrate:

```
-->deff('[z]=f(x,y)','z=x+y')
```

The integral is calculated as follows:

```
-->[Int,er] = int2d(X,Y,f)
 er =

    1.283E-16
 Int =

    .5147233
```

Application of double integrals

As their one-dimensional counterparts, double integrals can be used to calculate properties of areas and volumes. Some applications of double integrals are presented in this section.

Area properties with double integrals

For the calculation of area properties through the use of double integrals, refer to the following figure:

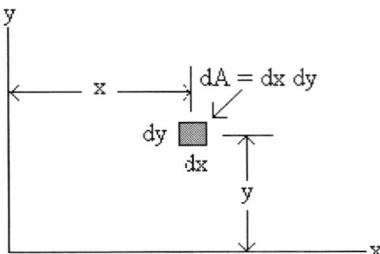

Area: since $dxdy$ represent an element of area in the plane, $dA = dxdy$, then,

$$A = \iint_R dA = \iint_R dy\,dx.$$

Centroid: Let (x_c, y_c) represents the centroid of the region R, then

$$x_c = \frac{1}{A}\iint_R x\,dA, \quad y_c = \frac{1}{A}\iint_R y\,dA.$$

Areal moments of inertia: Let I_x, I_y, and I_0, represent areal moments of inertia with respect to the x-, y- and z-axes, respectively, then

$$I_x = \iint_R y^2\,dA, \text{ and } I_y = \iint_R x^2\,dA, \text{ and } I_0 = I_x + I_y = \iint_R (x^2 + y^2)\,dA.$$

Radius of gyration: The radii of gyration of an area with respect to the x-, y-, and z-axes are given by

$$k_x = \sqrt{\frac{I_y}{A}}, \quad k_y = \sqrt{\frac{I_x}{A}}, \text{ and } k_0 = \sqrt{\frac{I_0}{A}},$$

respectively.

Mass: if $f(x,y)$ represents the *density (mass/unit area)* of a body in the shape of the region of integration, then a differential of mass associated with the differential of area $dA = dy\, dx$, is $dM = f(x,y)\, dA = dM = f(x,y)\, dy\, dx$, and the mass of the region is

$$M = \iint_R dM = \iint_R f(x,y)\, dA = \iint_R f(x,y)\, dy\, dx.$$

Center of mass: The center of mass of the region R has coordinates x_c, y_c, given by:

$$x_c = \frac{1}{M}\iint_R x f(x,y)\, dA, \quad y_c = \frac{1}{M}\iint_R y f(x,y)\, dA.$$

Moments of inertia of the mass: The moments of inertia I_x and I_y of the mass represented by region R about the x and y axes, respectively, are

$$I_x = \iint_R y^2 f(x,y)\, dA, \text{ and } I_y = \iint_R x^2 f(x,y)\, dA,$$

and the polar moment of inertia (i.e., moment of inertia with respect to the origin, or, more correctly, with respect to the z-axis) is

$$I_0 = I_x + I_y = \iint_R (x^2 + y^2) f(x,y)\, dA.$$

Radius of gyration of the mass: The radii of gyration of the mass represented by region R with respect to the x-, y-, and z-axes are given by

$$k_x = \sqrt{\frac{I_y}{M}}, \quad k_y = \sqrt{\frac{I_x}{M}}, \text{ and } k_0 = \sqrt{\frac{I_0}{M}},$$

respectively.

Volume: the volume between the x-y plane and the surface $= f(x,y)$ is provided by the double integral,

$$V = \iint_R f(x,y)\, dA = \iint_R f(x,y)\, dy\, dx.$$

Calculation of areal properties in Cartesian coordinates

For the quarter of circle defined by the region $R = \{x^2+y^2 = a^2, 0<x<a\}$, for $a = 2$, find the area, the centroid, and the areal moments of inertia with respect to the x-, y-, and Z-axes in a Cartesian coordinate system (x,y,Z). [Note: Z is used here instead of z to avoid confusing the Z coordinate of the Cartesian system with the z variable used in a transformation that converts the original region into a rectangular region as shown below].

The region of integration can be described as $R = \{ 0 < y < (a^2-x^2)^{1/2}, 0 < x < a\}$. To calculate the double integrals using the user-defined function *DoubleIntegral* we need to transform the region R in the x-y plane into a rectangular region $R' = \{0<z<1, 0<x<a\}$ in the z-x plane, by using the transformation

$$y = z \cdot (a^2-x^2)^{1/2},$$

$$dy = (a^2-x^2)^{1/2} \, dz.$$

The function to be integrated $f(x,y)$ in the x-y plane gets transformed into

$$\phi(x,z) = f(x, z \cdot (a^2-x^2)^{1/2}),$$

thus, we will calculate

$$\int_0^a \int_0^{\sqrt{a^2-x^2}} f(x,y) \, dy \, dx = \int_0^a \int_0^1 \phi(x, z\sqrt{a^2-x^2}) \cdot \sqrt{a^2-x^2} \, dz \, dx.$$

The area is calculated by taking $f(x,y) = 1.0$ as follows:

$$A = \int_0^a \int_0^{\sqrt{a^2-x^2}} dy \, dx = \int_0^a \int_0^1 \sqrt{a^2-x^2} \, dz \, dx.$$

Using SCILAB and the user-defined function *DoubleIntegral* we find the following approximation to the area:

```
-->deff('[w]=g(x,y)','w=sqrt(4-x^2)')

-->A = DoubleIntegral(0,2,1000,0,1,50,g)
 A  =  3.1415555
```

The coordinates of the centroid are calculated using $x_c = M_y/A$, and $y_c = M_x/A$, with

$$M_y = \iint_R x \, dA = \int_0^a \int_0^{\sqrt{a^2-x^2}} x \, dy \, dx = \int_0^a \int_0^1 x\sqrt{a^2-x^2} \, dz \, dx,$$

and

$$M_x = \iint_R y \, dA = \int_0^a \int_0^{\sqrt{a^2-x^2}} y \, dy \, dx = \int_0^a \int_0^1 (z\sqrt{a^2-x^2})(\sqrt{a^2-x^2}) \, dz \, dx =$$

$$\int_0^a \int_0^d z(a^2 - x^2) \, dz \, dx.$$

Using SCILAB we calculate the centroidal coordinates as

```
-->deff('[w]=my(x,z)','w=x*sqrt(4-x^2)')

-->deff('[w]=mx(x,z)','w=z*(4-x^2)')

-->My = DoubleIntegral(0,2,1000,0,1,50,my)
 My  = 2.6665916

-->Mx = DoubleIntegral(0,2,1000,0,1,50,mx)
 Mx  = 2.666666

-->xc=My/A, yc=Mx/A
 xc  = .8488125
 yc  = .8488362
```

The moments of inertia of the area are

$$I_y = \iint_R x^2 \, dA = \int_0^a \int_0^{\sqrt{a^2-x^2}} x^2 \, dy \, dx = \int_0^a \int_0^d x^2 \sqrt{a^2 - x^2} \, dz \, dx,$$

and

$$I_x = \iint_R y^2 \, dA = \int_0^a \int_0^{\sqrt{a^2-x^2}} y^2 \, dy \, dx = \int_0^a \int_0^d (z\sqrt{a^2 - x^2})^2 (\sqrt{a^2 - x^2}) \, dz \, dx =$$

$$\int_0^a \int_0^d z^2 (a^2 - x^2)^{3/2} \, dz \, dx.$$

Using SCILAB:

```
-->deff('[w]=ix(x,z)','w=x^2*sqrt(4-x^2)')

-->deff('[w]=iy(x,z)','w=z^2*(4-x^2)^(3/2)')

-->Ix=DoubleIntegral(0,2,1000,0,1,50,ix)
 Ix  = 3.1414439

-->Iy=DoubleIntegral(0,2,1000,0,1,50,iy)
 Iy  = 3.142221
```

The radii of gyration are $k_x = (I_x/A)^{1/2}$ and $k_y = (I_y/A)^{1/2}$, i.e.,

```
-->kx=sqrt(Ix/A), ky=sqrt(Iy/A)
 kx  = .9999823
 ky  = 1.0001059
```

Change of variables in double integrals

Let R is a region in the x-y plane. Suppose that we want to evaluate the double integral,

$$\iint_R f(x,y)dA_{x,y} = \iint_R f(x,y)dydx$$

by changing variables through the coordinate transformation $x = x(u,v)$, $y = y(u,v)$. The transformation of coordinates maps the region R in the x-y plane into a region R* in the u-v plane. The double integral in terms of the variables u and v incorporates a quantity known as the Jacobian of the transformation. We define the *Jacobian* of the coordinate transformation as the determinant

$$J = \frac{\partial(x,y)}{\partial(u,v)} = \begin{vmatrix} \frac{\partial x}{\partial u} & \frac{\partial x}{\partial v} \\ \frac{\partial y}{\partial u} & \frac{\partial y}{\partial v} \end{vmatrix}$$

With this definition, then we can write

$$\iint_R f(x,y)dA_{x,y} = \iint_R f(x,y)dydx = \iint_{R^*} f[x(u,v),y(u,v)]dA_{u,v} = \iint_{R^*} f[x(u,v),y(u,v)]|J|dudv$$

The latter equation suggests that the differential of area in the u-v plane is:

$$dA_{u,v} = |J|dudv$$

Jacobian functions can be obtained for any coordinate transformations in systems of three or more coordinates. Thus, a generalized definition of the Jacobian corresponding to the transformation $(x_1, x_2, ..., x_n) \rightarrow (\phi_1, \phi_2, ..., \phi_n)$, is

$$J = J\left(\frac{x_1, x_2, ..., x_n}{\phi_1, \phi_2, ..., \phi_n}\right) = \begin{vmatrix} \frac{\partial x_1}{\partial \phi_1} & \frac{\partial x_1}{\partial \phi_2} & \cdots & \frac{\partial x_1}{\partial \phi_n} \\ \frac{\partial x_2}{\partial \phi_1} & \frac{\partial x_2}{\partial \phi_2} & \cdots & \frac{\partial x_2}{\partial \phi_n} \\ \vdots & \vdots & \ddots & \vdots \\ \frac{\partial x_n}{\partial \phi_1} & \frac{\partial x_2}{\partial \phi_n} & \cdots & \frac{\partial x_n}{\partial \phi_n} \end{vmatrix}$$

Area calculation using double integrals with polar coordinates

Suppose we want to find the area of a circle of radius R using polar coordinates. The transformations are:

$$x := (r, \theta) \to r \cos(\theta)$$
$$y := (r, \theta) \to r \sin(\theta)$$

The Jacobian of the transformation (x,y) to (r,θ) is:

$$\begin{bmatrix} \cos(\theta) & -r\sin(\theta) \\ \sin(\theta) & r\cos(\theta) \end{bmatrix}$$

$$J := r$$

Therefore, the differential of area $dA_{r,\theta}$ in the r-θ plane is $dA_{r,\theta} = |J| dr d\theta = r \, dr \, d\theta$. The shaded element in the figure below is a typical area differential in polar coordinates. Although it is not shaped as a rectangle, because we are dealing with small quantities, we can approximate it to a rectangle of dimensions rdθ and dr, from which the value $dA_{r,\theta} = r \, dr \, d\theta$, follows.

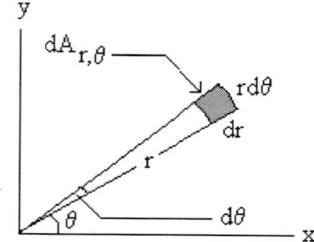

Since we are trying to obtain the area of a region in x-y (a circle of radius R), the function to integrate is $f(x, y) = 1.0$, which transforms to $f[x(r, \theta), y(r, \theta)] = 1.0$. The region in the x-y plane is the circle itself, $R = \{x^2 + y^2 \leq R^2\}$, which in polar coordinates is mapped as $R^* = \{0 \leq r, r \leq R, \text{ and } 0 \leq \theta, \theta \leq 2\pi\}$. Therefore, the integral $\iint 1.0 \, dy \, dx$ over R, becomes:

$$\int_0^{2\pi} \int_0^R J \, dr \, d\theta = R^2 \pi$$

Double integral applications in polar coordinates

Some double integral applications using polar coordinates are shown below:

Area: since $dxdy$ represent an element of area in the plane, $dA = dxdy$, then,

$$A = \iint_{R^*} dA_{r,\theta} = \iint_{R^*} r \, dr \, d\theta$$

Centroid: Let (r_c, θ_c) represents the centroid of the region R*, then

$$r_c = \frac{1}{A}\iint_R r\,dA_{r,\theta}, \quad \theta_c = \frac{1}{A}\iint_{R^*} \theta\,dA.$$

Polar areal moment of inertia: The moment of inertia I_0, represents the so-called polar of inertia, i.e., with respect to the z-axis, is

$$I_0 = \iint_{R^*} r^2\,dA_{r,\theta}.$$

Radius of gyration: The radii of gyration of an area with respect to the z-axis is given by

$$k_0 = \sqrt{\frac{I_0}{A}}.$$

Mass: if f(r, θ) represents the *density (mass/unit area)* of a body in the shape of the region of integration, then a differential of mass associated with the differential of area $dA_{r,\theta} = r\,dr\,d\theta$, is dM= f($r, \theta$) $dA_{r,\theta}$ = f(r, θ) $r\,dr\,d\theta$, , and the mass of the region is

$$M = \iint_{R^*} dM = \iint_{R^*} f(r, \theta)\,dA_{r,\theta} = \iint_{R^*} f(r, \theta)\,r\,dr\,d\theta.$$

Center of mass: The center of mass of the region R has coordinates r_c, θ_c, given by:

$$r_c = \frac{1}{M}\iint_{R^*} r f(r, \theta)\,dA_{r,\theta}, \quad \theta_c = \frac{1}{M}\iint_{R^*} \theta f(r, \theta)\,dA_{r,\theta}.$$

Moments of inertia of the mass: The polar moment of inertia (i.e., moment of inertia with respect to the origin) is

$$I_0 = \iint_{R^*} r^2 f(r, \theta)\,dA_{r,\theta}.$$

Radius of gyration of the mass: The radii of gyration of the mass represented by region R with respect to the z-axes is given by

$$k_0 = \sqrt{\frac{I_0}{M}}.$$

Volume: the volume between the x-y plane and the surface = f(r, θ) is provided by the double integral,

$$V = \iint_{R^*} f(r, \theta)\,dA = \iint_{R^*} f(r, \theta)\,r\,dr\,d\theta.$$

Calculation of areal properties in polar coordinates

Calculate the area, centroid, polar moment of inertia, and radius of gyration of the region defined by $R^* = \{0 < r < \sin(2\theta), 0 < \theta < \frac{\pi}{2}\}$.

A plot of the region follows:

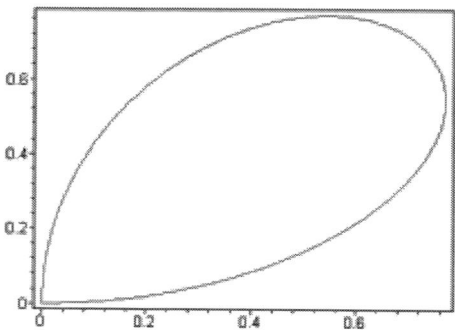

The area is calculated as

$$A = \int_0^{\pi/2} \int_0^{\sin(2\theta)} r\, dr\, d\theta.$$

The region of integration in the r-θ plane (not the x-y plane using polar coordinates, but a plane where the abscissas are represented by r and the ordinates by θ) will be an irregularly shaped region R which can be transformed into a rectangular region R' in a z-plane. The transformation to use is $r = z \sin(2\theta)$, $dr = \sin(2\theta)dz$. The area is calculated now as

$$A = \int_0^{\pi/2} \int_0^1 z\sin(2\theta)\sin(2\theta) dz d\theta = \int_0^{\pi/2} \int_0^1 z\sin^2(2\theta) dz d\theta.$$

Using SCILAB:

```
-->deff('[w]=g(z,th)','w=z*(sin(2*th))^2')

-->A = DoubleIntegral(0,1,100,0,%pi/2,100,g)
 A  =  .3926991
```

The coordinates of the centroid are $r_c = (1/A) \iint_A r^2 dr d\theta$, $\theta_c = (1/A) \iint_A \theta\, r\, dr d\theta$. Using the transformation $r = z \sin(2\theta)$, $dr = \sin(2\theta)dz$, the integrals are calculated as

$$r_c = \frac{1}{A}\int_0^{\pi/2}\int_0^1 z^2 \sin^3(2\theta) dz d\theta, \quad \theta_c = \frac{1}{A}\int_0^{\pi/2}\int_0^1 z\theta \sin^2(2\theta) dz d\theta.$$

Using SCILAB:

```
-->deff('[w]=mr(z,th)','w=z^2*(sin(2*th))^3')

-->deff('[w]=mt(z,th)','w=z*th*(sin(2*th))^2')
```

```
-->rc = DoubleIntegral(0,1,100,0,%pi/2,100,mr)/A
 rc  = .5659125

-->thc = DoubleIntegral(0,1,100,0,%pi/2,100,mt)/A
 thc = .7853982
```

The polar moment of inertia is calculated with $I_c = \iint_A r^3 dr d\theta$. With the coordinate transformation $r = z\sin(2\theta)$, $dr = \sin(2\theta)dz$, the integral to calculate is

$$I_0 = \frac{1}{A} \int_0^{\pi/2} \int_0^1 z^3 \sin^4(2\theta) dz d\theta.$$

Using SCILAB

```
-->deff('[w]=i0(z,th)','w=z^3*(sin(2*th))^4')

-->I0 = DoubleIntegral(0,1,100,0,%pi/2,100,i0)
 I0 = .1472769
```

The radius of gyration about the origin is calculated as $k_0 = (I_0/A)^{1/2}$, i.e.,

```
-->k0=sqrt(I0/A)
 k0 = .6124031
```

A final note on the numerical calculation of double integrals

All the examples of applications of numerical calculation of double integrals presented here have been calculated using the user-defined function *DoubleIntegral* with coordinate transformations that convert the original integration region into a rectangular region. It should be indicated that the approach followed in function *DoubleIntegral* is based on approximating the volume represented by the integral $\iint_A f(x,y) \, dxdy$ by the sum of parallelepiped elements whose base has an area $\Delta x \cdot \Delta y$, and whose height is $f(x_i, y_j)$. Function *DoubleIntegral* uses a fixed and uniform grid to approximate the integral. The error incurred in the approximation is of first order, i.e. $O(\Delta x \cdot \Delta y)$. Thus, you may have to use a very fine grid to obtain reasonable results with this function.

Improved results for double integrals can be obtained by coding Simpson's 1/9 rule as indicated in a previous section, or by using SCILAB function *int2d*. Function *int2d* uses an adaptive algorithm by which regions in which the function varies rapidly are divided into finer grids and the integral recalculated until a convergence is achieved. Adaptive methods can also be used to calculate integrals of one variable. Such algorithms are incorporated in many of SCILAB's predefined integral functions such as *intg* or *integrate*.

Exercises

For problems [1] through [10], use the user-defined function *sumint* to produce the approximation to the integral of $f(x)$ between the limits $a<x<b$ using n subintervals. Calculate the integrals using (a) the left sum, (b) the middle sum, and (c) the right sum.

[1] $f(x) = 1/(1+ \ln(x))$, $a = 1$, $b = 5$, $n = 30$

[2] $f(x) = 1 + x^2 + x^3 + 1/x$, $a = 1$, $b = 3.5$, $n = 90$

[3] $f(x) = \exp(-x/5)/(1+x^2)$, $a = -2$, $b = 2$, $n = 50$

[4] $f(x) = (x^2+1)^{1/2}$, $a = -1$, $b = 1$, $n = 20$

[5] $f(x) = (x^2+1)^{1/3} + 2.5(x^2+1) + 1.5$, $a = 0$, $b = 5$, $n = 60$

[6] $f(x) = \sinh(x)/(1+x^3)$, $a = 0$, $b = 3$, $n = 40$

[7] $f(x) = \exp(-x^2/2)/(2\pi)^{1/2}$, $a = -4$, $b = 4$, $n = 100$

[8] $f(x) = 2.5(1+x^2+x^3/3)\cos(3x^2+2)$, $a = 0$, $b = 2\pi$, $n = 25$

[9] $f(x) = 4.2x^{1/3} + 3.245x^{1/2} + 1.4142$, $a = 0.25$, $b = 1.25$, $n = 20$

[10] $f(x) = 0.33 \ln((x+1)/(x^2+5x+2))$, $a = 0$, $b = 20$, $n = 40$

[11] - [20] Repeat problems [1] through [10] using (a) the trapezoidal rule through SCILAB function *inttrap*; (b) Simpson's 1/3 rule through function *simpson13* if the number of subintervals is even, and/or Simpson's 3/8 rule through function *simpson38* if the number of subintervals is a multiple of 3.

[21] - [30] Repeat problems [1] through [10] using the Newton-Cotes formulas with (a) $n=3$, (b) $n=4$, (c) $n=5$, (d) $n=6$, (e) $n=7$.

[31] - [40] Repeat problems [1] through [10] using (a) SCILAB function *integrate*; (b) integration by splines using SCILAB function *intsplin*; (c) SCILAB function *intg*.

In problems [41] through [50], given a function of a complex variable $w = F(z)$, with $z = x + iy$, identify the real and imaginary components $\Phi(x,y)$ and $\Psi(x,y)$ such that $F(z) = \Phi(x,y) + i\Psi(x,y)$. Also, produce contour plots of the functions $\Phi(x,y)$ and $\Psi(x,y)$.

[41] $F(z) = 1/z$

[42] $F(z) = z + 1/z$

[43] $F(z) = \exp(z)$

[44] $F(z) = z^3$

[45] $F(z) = z^{1/2}$

[46]-[50]. For problems [46] through [50], integrate the function of a complex variable from problems [41] through [45] using SCILAB function $intl$ along the straight line joining the points z_1 and z_2, where (a) $z_1 = 3$, $z_2 = 2-i$; (b) $z_1 = -5+2i$, $z_2 = 2-2i$; (c) $z_1 = 3i$, $z_2 = 5+2i$; (d) $z_1 = (1+i)/2$, $z_2 = 3+\sqrt{2}i$; (e) $z_1 = i/2$, $z_2 = -i/2$.

[51]-[55]. For problems [51] through [55] use function $intl$ to calculate the integral of the function of a complex variable from problems [41] through [45] along the curve defined by $z_0 + r \cdot e^{i\theta}$, within the limits θ_1 and θ_2, using the following values: (a) $z_0 = 2+3i$, $r = 1$, $\theta_1 = 0$, $\theta_2 = \pi/4$; (b) $z_0 = 1+i$, $r = 0.2$, $\theta_1 = -\pi/2$, $\theta_2 = \pi/2$; (c) $z_0 = 0$, $r = 1$, $\theta_1 = \pi$, $\theta_2 = 2\pi$; (d) $z_0 = -1-2i$, $r = 0.75$, $\theta_1 = 0$, $\theta_2 = 3\pi/4$; (e) $z_0 = 3$, $r = 1$, $\theta_1 = -\pi/2$, $\theta_2 = \pi$.

For problems [56]-[60] use the user-defined function $DoubleIntegral$ to calculate the double integral of function $f(x,y)$ in the rectangular domain $a < x < b$, $c < y < d$.

[56]. $f(x,y) = x^2+y^2$, $a = -2$, $b = 2$, $c = -1$, $d = 1$.

[57]. $f(x,y) = x \sin y + y \sin x$, $a = -\pi/2$, $b = \pi/2$, $c = 0$, $d = \pi$.

[58]. $f(x,y) = 2xy(x^2+y^2+1)^{1/2}$, $a = 0$, $b = 2$, $c = 0$, $d = 2$.

[59]. $f(x,y) = x \ln(y/x) + y \ln(x/y)$, $a = 1$, $b = 2$, $c = 0.5$, $d = 0.75$.

[60]. $f(x,y) = 1-\exp(-(x^2+y^2)/25)$, $a = -2$, $b = 2$, $c = -2$, $d = 2$.

[61]-[65]. Repeat problems [56] through [60] using SCILAB function $int2d$ by dividing the rectangular region of integration into two triangles.

[66]-[70]. For problems [66] through [70] use function $int2d$ to calculate the double integral of the functions in problems [56] through [60] on the integration region defined by: (a) $R = \{-1 < x < 1, 0 < y < (1-x^2)\}$; (b) $R = \{0<x< 1, x^2 < y < x\}$; (c) $R = \{-1 < x < 1, 0 < y < 1 - x^2\}$; (d) $R = \{-3 < x < 3, |x| < y < 3\}$; (e) $R = \{-4 < x < 4, (25-x^2)^{1/2} < y < (16-x^2)^{1/2}\}$.

[71]. Determine the area under the curve $y = f(x)$ limited by the values $x = a$ and $x = b$:
(a) $f(x) = x^2$, $a=2$, $b=5$
(b) $f(x) = \ln(x)$, $a = 2$, $b = 3$
(c) $f(x) = 1/(1+x^2)$, $a = 0$, $b =1$
(d) $f(x) = (1-x^2)^{1/2}$, $a = -0.5$, $b = 0.5$

[2]. Determine the area between the curves $y = f_1(x)$ and $y = f_2(x)$ and the values $x =a$ and $y = b$. Plot the region to be integrated:
(a) $f_1(x) =x^{1/2}$, $f_2(x) = x^2$, $a = 0$, $b = 1$
(b) $f_1(x) = (1-x^2)^{1/2}$, $f_2(x) = -(1-x^2)^{1/2}$, $a = -1$, $b = 1$
(c) $f_1(x) = 10(1-x/5)$, $f_2(x) = 2$, $a =0$, $b =3$
(d) $f_1(x) = (1-x^2)^{1/2}$, $f_2(x) = x$, $a = 0$, $b = $ point of intersection

[73]. Determine the center of mass (centroid) of the figure limited by the x-axis and the curve $y = f(x)$ between the values $x = a$ and $x = b$ for the functions of problem [71].

[74]. Determine the volume of the solid of revolution generated by the rotation of the curve $y = f(x)$ between the values $x = a$ and $x = b$ about the x axis for the functions of problem [71].

[75]. Determine the moments of inertia and radii of gyration $k_x (= (I_x/A)^{1/2}$, $k_y = (I_y/A)^{1/2})$ with respect to the x-axis, y-axis, and the origin of the area limited by the x-axis and the curve $f(x)$ between the values $x = a$ and $x = b$, for the functions of problem [71].

[76]. For the figures in problem [75] determine the moments of inertia and radii of gyration with respect to the centroidal axes and the centroid. Use the parallel axes moment.

[77]. Determine the area defined by $r = f(\theta)$ and the radii $r = \theta_1$ and $r = \theta_2$. Plot the region using polar coordinates:
(a) $f(\theta) = 3\cos\theta$, $\theta_1 = 0$, $\theta_2 = \pi/2$
(b) $f(\theta) = 1-\sin\theta$, $\theta_1 = -\pi/2$, $\theta_2 = \pi/2$
(c) $f(\theta) = 1/(1+\cos\theta)$, $\theta_1 = 0$, $\theta_2 = \pi/2$
(d) $f(\theta) = \theta$, $\theta_1 = 0$, $\theta_2 = \pi$

[78]. Calculation of discharge in a pipe. Calculate the discharge in a pipe of radius $R = 2.5$ ft, if the velocity distribution in the pipe cross-section is given by:
(a) $v(r) = v_0(1-r/R)$
(b) $v(r) = v_0[1-(r/R)^3]$
(c) $v(r) = v_0[1-(r/R)^{1/2}]$
The value of $v_0 = 3.5$ fps.

[79]. Integrate the function $f(x,y,z)$ along curve C using the suggested variable substitutions:
(a) $f(x,y,z) = 1-x^2-y^2$, $x(s) = \sin(s)$, $y(s) = \cos(s)$, $z(s) = 0$, $s = 0..\pi$
(b) $f(x,y,z) = xyz$, $x(s) = 2\sin(s)$, $y(s) = 3\cos(s/2)$, $z(s) = s$, $s = 0..\pi$
(c) $f(x,y,z) = \sin x \cos y$, $x(s) = s$, $y(s) = s^2/2$, $z(s) = 0$, $s = 0..2$
(d) $f(x,y,z) = 1/(x^2+y^2+1)$, $x(s) = s^2$, $y(s) = \ln s$, $z(s) = 0$, $s = 1..10$

[80]. Calculate the line integral for the differential $f(x,y,z)dx + g(x,y,z)dy + h(x,y,z)dz$ along the curve C specified:
(a) $f(x,y,z)=x+y$, $g(x,y,z)=xy$, $h(x,y,z)=z^2$, C:$\{y=x+2, z=x-1, 0<x<5\}$
(b) $f(x,y,z)=x+yz$, $g(x,y,z)=y+xz$, $h(x,y,z)=z+xy$, C:$\{x^2+y^2=1, 0<x<1, y>0, z=2\}$
(c) $f(x,y,z)=\sin x$, $g(x,y,z)=\sin y$, $h(x,y,z)=\sin z$, C:$\{z=x+1, y=2, 0<x<2\}$
(d) $f(x,y,z)=x\exp(y)$, $g(x,y,z)=\exp(z)$, $h(x,y,z)=y^2$, C: $\{x=2, y=z^2+1, 0<z<1\}$

[81]. Check if the differential $f(x,y,z)dx + g(x,y,z)dy + h(x,y,z)dz$ is an exact differential, and calculate the line integral between the selected points A and B:
(a) $f(x,y,z)=2x$, $g(x,y,z)=2y$, $h(x,y,z)=2z$, A: (0,0,0), B(1,-1,2)
(b) $f(x,y,z)=z\cos(x)\exp(y)$, $g(x,y,z) = z^2\sin(x)\exp(y)$, $h(x,y,z) = 2z\sin(x)\exp(y)$, A:(1,1,1), B:(2,2,2)
(c) $f(x,y,z)= g(x,y,z) = h(x,y,z) = 2(x+y+z)$, A:(2,-2,1), B:(5,5,-2)
(d) $f(x,y,z)=y\cos(xy)$, $g(x,y,z) = x\cos(xy)$, $h(x,y,z) = 0$, A:(-1,1,0), B:(2,2,2)

[82]. Calculate the following double integrals using function DoubleIntegral:

(a) $\int_0^2 \int_{-x}^{\pi} (x+xy)dydx$ (b) $\int_{-2}^{2} \int_{-y}^{0} (x+xy)dxdy$ (c) $\int_0^2 \int_{-x}^{x} \sqrt{x}dxdy$ (d) $\int_0^2 \int_{-2}^{\xi^2-1} \xi\eta\, d\eta d\xi$

[83]. Using double integrals, calculate the area, coordinates of the centroid, areal moments of inertia with respect to the x- and y-axes and with respect to the origin of the area described by the region R. Plot the region of interest:
(a) R: $\{0<y<x^2+1, 0<x<1\}$
(b) R: $\{-1 < y < (1-x^2), 0 < x < 1\}$
(c) R: $\{0<y<1-x, 0<x<1\}$
(d) R: $\{0 < x < (1-y^2)^{1/2}, -1 < y < 1\}$

[84]. Calculate the mass, coordinates of the center of mass, mass moments of inertia with respect to the x- and y-axes and with respect to the origin of the area described for the regions R from problem [83] if the corresponding areal densities are given by f(x,y):
(a) $f(x,y) = x$ (b) $f(x,y) = (x+1)^{1/2}$ (c) $f(x,y) = \sin(x)$ (d) $f(x,y) = 1/(x^2+y^2)$

[85]. Determine the volume of the three-dimensional region described by the surface $f(x,y)$ and limited by the region R:
(a) $f(x,y) = x^2+y$, R:$\{x = -2..2, y = -2..x^{1/2}\}$
(b) $f(x,y) = \sin(x)\cos(y)$, R:$\{x = -2\pi..2\pi, y = -2\pi..\sin(x)\}$
(c) $f(x,y) = \exp(-0.05^*x)^*\cos(y+2)$, R:$\{x = 0..5, y = 0..25\}$
(d) $f(x,y) = |\ln(x^2+y^2+10)|$, R:$\{x = -2..2, y = -2..2\}$

[86]. Calculate the area, coordinates of the centroid, areal moments of inertia with respect to the x- and y-axes and with respect to the origin of the area described by the region R (polar coordinates):
(a) R:$\{0 < r < 3\theta, 0 < \theta < \pi\}$
(b) R:$\{0 < r < \sin\theta, 0 < \theta < \pi/2\}$
(c) R:$\{0 < r < (\cos\theta - 1), 0 < \theta < \pi\}$
(d) R:$\{0 < r < 1/(1+\cos\theta), -\pi/2 < \theta < \pi/2\}$

[87]. Calculate the mass, coordinates of the center of mass, mass moments of inertia with respect to the x- and y-axes and with respect to the origin of the area described by the regions R in problem [11], if the corresponding areal densities $f(r,\theta)$:
(a) $f(r,\theta) = 2.5$ (b) $f(r,\theta) = \sin(\theta)$ (c) $f(r,\theta) = 1 - \sin(\theta)$ (d) $f(r,\theta) = |\theta|$

[88]. Determine the volume of the three-dimensional region described by the surface $f(r,\theta)$, as shown below, and limited by the region R (polar coordinates) from problem [86]:
(a) $f(r,\theta) = 2.5 \exp(-\theta)$ (b) $f(r,\theta) = \sin^2(\theta)$ (c) $f(r,\theta) = 1+\theta$ (d) $f(r,\theta) = (1+\sin(\theta))^{1/2}$

[89]. The outline for the calculation of double integrals using Simpson's 1/9 rule was presented earlier. Write a SCILAB function that takes as input the limits of a rectangular region in the x-y plane, $R = \{x_0 < x < x_n, y_0 < y < y_m\}$, the (even) values n and m, and the function $f(x,y)$, and returns the approximation to the double integral

$$I = \int_{x_0}^{x_n} \int_{y_0}^{y_m} f(x,y) dy dx.$$

[90]. Use the function for calculating double integrals through Simpson's 1/9 rule developed in problem [89] to solve problem [82].

[91]. Use the function for calculating double integrals through Simpson's 1/9 rule developed in problem [89] to solve problem [83].

[92]. Use the function for calculating double integrals through Simpson's 1/9 rule developed in problem [89] to solve problem [84].

[93]. Use the function for calculating double integrals through Simpson's 1/9 rule developed in problem [89] to solve problem [85].

[94]. The table below shows the flow velocity v(fps), and suspended sediment concentration, C(mg/l), as functions of the distance from the channel bed y(ft), measured at a cross-section of a 800-ft-wide (b = 800 ft), 7.8-ft-deep (h = 7.8 ft) river cross-section that can be approximated by a rectangle.

y(ft)	v(ft/s)	C(mg/l)
0.7	4.30	411
0.9	4.50	380
1.2	4.64	305
1.4	4.77	299
1.7	4.83	277
2.2	5.12	238
2.7	5.30	217
2.9	5.40	211
3.2	5.42	196
3.4	5.42	188
3.7	5.50	184
4.2	5.60	165
4.8	5.60	148
5.8	5.70	130
6.8	5.95	80

The flow discharge, Q(cfs), is defined by the integral

$$Q = \int_A v(y)\,dA = \int_0^h v(y)\cdot b\,dy,$$

with the mean flow velocity calculated as $V = Q/A$, where $A = b\cdot h$ being the cross-sectional area.

The total flux of suspended sediment through the cross-section is defined as

$$Q_s = \int_A v(y)\cdot C(y)\cdot dA = \int_0^h v(y)\cdot C(y)\cdot b\,dy,$$

with the *flux-averaged concentration* given by $C_f = Q_s/Q$.

The terms used in the definitions above are illustrated in the figure below:

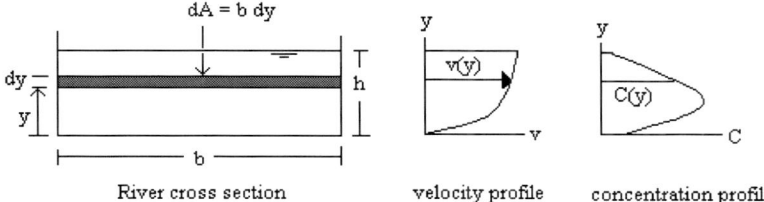

(a) Plot the velocity profile $v(y)$-vs-y and the concentration profile $C(y)$-vs-y.
(b) Determine the flow discharge, mean velocity, sediment flux, and flux averaged concentration for the data given using integration by splines.

8 Data fitting and interpolation

In this chapter we present SCILAB polynomials and their applications, as well as presenting a number of numerical methods for fitting data to polynomial and other non-linear functions.

Simple linear interpolation

Simple linear interpolation is typically applied to a table of values { (x_1,y_1), (x_2,y_2), ..., (x_n,y_n) } in order to obtain the value y corresponding to a value x located within the range of values of x. It is assumed that the values of x are shown in increasing order in the table. Suppose that the value of x is such that $x_i < x_k < x_{i+1}$ for a certain value of i. The situation is illustrated in the table below:

x	y
x_1	y_2
:	:
x_i	y_i
x_k	y_k
x_{i+1}	y_{i+2}
:	:
x_n	x_n

Assuming a linear variation for y as function of x in the range $_i,[xx_{i+1}]$ we can write the following relationship involving values (x_i,y_i), (x_k,y_k), and (x_{i+1},y_{i+1}):

$$\frac{y_k - y_i}{x_k - x_i} = \frac{y_{i+1} - y_i}{x_{i+1} - x_i},$$

from which,

$$y_k = y_i + \frac{y_{i+1} - y_i}{x_{i+1} - x_i} \cdot (x_k - x_i).$$

SCILAB provides function *interpln* to obtain linear interpolations out of a matrix of two rows representing pairs of data values (x_i,y_i). The general call to this function is

[y]=interpln(xy_table,x)

where *xy_table* is a two-row matrix with the first row representing values of x and the second row representing values of y from the table, and is a vector of values. The function returns a vector of values y corresponding to the linear interpolation of the table for the values in vector x.

An example of application for function *interpln* follows. First, we define the table of values for interpolation:

```
-->TableXY = [[1,2,3,4,5,6];[2,5,6,8,10,11]]
 TableXY  =

!   1.    2.    3.    4.    5.    6.  !
!   2.    5.    6.    8.   10.   11.  !
```

The following call to function *interpln* is used to obtain the value of y for x = 2.5:

```
-->interpln(TableXY,2.5)
 ans  =

    5.5
```

Next, we use function *interpln* to interpolate a vector of values:

```
-->xx = [1.5, 2.5, 3.5, 4.5, 5.5]
 xx  =

!   1.5    2.5    3.5    4.5    5.5 !

-->yy = interpln(TableXY,xx)
 yy  =

!   3.5    5.5    7.    9.    10.5 !
```

To produce a plot of the data from the table and the interpolated data we use the following SCILAB commands:

```
-->ymax1 = max(TableXY(2,:))             //Max & min values of y
 ymax1  =

    11.

-->ymax2 = max(yy)
 ymax2  =

    10.5

-->rect = [0,0,6,11];                    // define the plot rectangle

-->plot2d(TableXY(1,:),TableXY(2,:),9,'011','y',rect)   //Plot table

-->xset('mark',-9,1)
```

```
-->plot2d(xx,yy,-9,'010','y',rect)          //Plot interpolated data
-->xtitle('linear interpolation','x','y')    //Place title
```

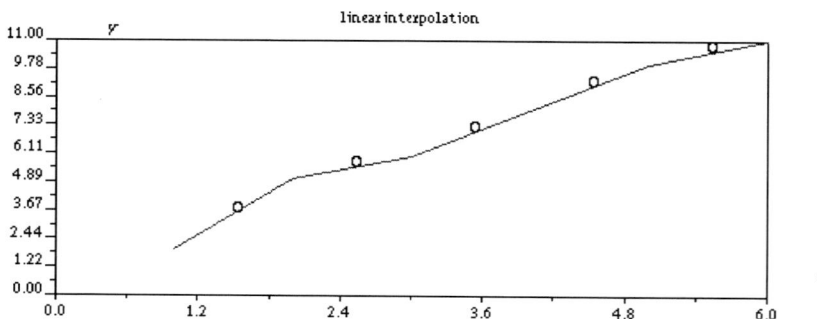

Polynomials in SCILAB

As indicated in previous chapters, SCILAB recognizes polynomials as a particular data type and provides the function *poly* with the purpose of defining such data types. The simplest polynomial that can be defined is a variable name, say *x*, *y*, *z*, etc. By defining a variable name as a polynomial type, simple algebraic manipulations, resulting in polynomial forms, can be accomplished.

Defining a polynomial variable

In the following example, the variable *s* is defined as a polynomial and used in some simple operations:

```
-->s=poly(0,'s')         //Defining variable s as a polynomial
 s  =

       s

-->s+2                   //Simple algebraic operation
 ans =

       2 + s

-->y = (s+2)^2           //Defining a new polynomial (y)
 y =
                2
       4 + 4s + s
```

Identifying the polynomial variable, degree, and coefficients

SCILAB function *varn* can be used to identify the variable in a polynomial, for example:

```
-->varn(y)
 ans  =
  s
```

SCILAB function *degree* is used to determine the degree of a polynomial, for example:

```
-->degree(y)
 ans  =

    2.
```

Function *coeff* can be used to obtain a vector with the coefficients of the polynomial listed in increasing order of powers of the polynomial variable. For example,

```
-->x=poly(0,'x')            //Define polynomial variable
 x  =
     x

-->p = 3.5*x^2+2*x-5        //Create a polynomial
 p  =
                 2
   - 5 + 2x + 3.5x

-->c = coeff(p)             //Determine the coefficients of the polynomial
 c  = !  - 5.    2.    3.5 !
```

Some operations with polynomials

The next command defines a polynomial in terms of polynomial variable s:

```
-->p = (s+1)^2
 p  =
             2
   1 + 2s + s
```

Polynomials in the same variable can be added:

```
-->p+y
 ans  =
              2
   5 + 6s + 2s
```

The next statement defines a polynomial out of a multiplication of monomial expressions:

```
-->q = (s+1)*(s+3)
 q  =
             2
   3 + 4s + s
```

Polynomial division

The following example uses polynomial division resulting in the simplification of the result:

```
-->p/(s+1)
 ans  =

          1 + s
          -----
            1
```

Function *pdiv* can be used to obtain the quotient and residual of a polynomial division, for example:

```
-->[res,quo] = pdiv(p,q)
 quo  =    1
 res  = - 2 - 2s
```

The quotient *quo* and the residual *res* are such that p/q = *quo* + *res*/*q*. For the case under consideration, in which $p = s^2+2s+1$ and $q = s^2+4s+3$, we can write:

$$\frac{s^2+2s+1}{s^2+4s+3} = 1 + \frac{-2s-2}{s^2+4s+3}.$$

Polynomial long division

A polynomial division, such as the one just performed, stops whenever the degree of the residual is smaller than that of the divisor. (For the example shown above, the degree of the residual is 1 while that of the divisor is 2.) Through the operation of long division we can continue generating terms for the division allowing for negative powers of the polynomial variable. SCILAB provides function *ldiv* to perform the polynomial long division. Since, in general, one can obtain an infinite number of negative powers of the polynomial variable while performing the long division, function *ldiv* requires that the user provides the number of coefficients to be generated. For example, consider the following polynomial long division in which 7 coefficients are generated:

```
-->ldiv(s^3+5,s+1,7)
 ans  =

!    1.  !
!  - 1.  !
!    1.  !
!    4.  !
!  - 4.  !
!    4.  !
!  - 4.  !
```

This result is to be interpreted in the following manner:

$$\frac{s^3+5}{s+1} = s^2 - s + 1 + \frac{4}{s} - \frac{4}{s^2} + \frac{4}{s^3} - \frac{4}{s^4} + \cdots$$

Thus, the degree of the polynomial variables, in the first term of the quotient is equal to the difference between the degree of the numerator and that of the denominator, i.e., 3-1 = 2. The degree of subsequent terms decreases by one. Note: An expression, such as the one shown above, would be referred to as a *Laurent series* if the variable s represents the complex variable $x+iy$, where i is the unit imaginary number.]

The following example uses the polynomials p and q defined earlier:

```
-->ldiv(p,q,5)
 ans  =

!    1.   !
!  - 2.   !
!    6.   !
!  - 18.  !
!    54.  !
```

Since both p and q have the same degree (2), the first term in the expression resulting from the long division of p by q is multiplied by $s^0 = 1$. Subsequent terms will have increasing negative powers of s:

$$\frac{s^2 + 2s + 1}{s^2 + 4s + 3} = 1 - \frac{2}{s} + \frac{6}{s^2} - \frac{18}{s^3} + \frac{54}{s^4} + \cdots.$$

Polynomial fractions

SCILAB allows the construction of polynomial fractions, i.e., one in which both the numerator and denominator are polynomials. For example, a SCILAB polynomial fraction is:

```
-->t = (s+1)*(s+2)/((s-2)*(s+3))
 t  =

                2
    2 + 3s + s
    ----------
                2
    - 6 + s + s
```

Functions *numer* and *denom* are used to extract the numerator and denominator of a polynomial fraction, e.g.,

```
-->numer(t)
 ans  =

                2
    2 + 3s + s

-->denom(t)
 ans  =

                2
    - 6 + s + s
```

The function *simp* is used to simplify the ratio of two polynomials. For the following call to function *simp* we seek two polynomials *p1* and *q1* so that $p1/q1 = p/q$, and *p1* and *q1* have no common factors:

```
-->[p1,q1] = simp(p,q)
 q1 =

       3 + s
 p1 =

       1 + s
```

Matrices with polynomial elements

Polynomials can also be used as elements of a matrix, for example:

```
-->A = [ s+1    s-2;  (s+1)^2  s^2/2]
 A =

 !   1 + s              - 2 + s   !
 !                                !
 !              2              2  !
 !   1 + 2s + s           .5s     !
```

Determinant of a polynomial matrix

The determinant of matrix A can be calculated using either of function *determ, det,* or *detr*:

```
-->determ(A)
 ans =

                    2      3
     2 + 3s +   .5s  -   .5s

-->det(A)
 ans =

                    2      3
     2 + 3s +   .5s  -   .5s

-->detr(A)
 ans =

                    2      3
     2 + 3s +   .5s  -   .5s
```

Inverse of a polynomial matrix

The function *inv* can be used to obtain the inverse of a polynomial matrix:

```
-->inv(A)
 ans  =
```

```
!                2                                           !
!              .5s                          2 - s            !
!      ---------------------         --------------------    !
!              2         3                  2         3     !
!      2 + 3s + .5s  -  .5s          2 + 3s + .5s  -  .5s   !
!                                                            !
!          2 + 2s                           - 2              !
!         ----------                      ---------          !
!                 2                                2          !
!       - 4 - 2s + s                       - 4 - 2s + s      !
```

To check that the properties of inverses hold for polynomial matrices too use:

```
-->inv(A)*A
 ans  =
```

```
!    1                              0   !
!    -                              -   !
!    1                              1   !
!                                       !
!   5.773E-15 + 6.217E-15s           1   !
!   ----------------------           -   !
!              2                         !
!        - 4 - 2s + s                1   !
```

The result is not exactly an identity matrix due to some small numerical error. The coefficients shown in the term belonging to the second row and first column, however, are negligible small. To eliminate such small coefficients we can use SCILAB function *clean*:

```
-->clean(ans)
 ans  =
```

```
!   1    0  !
!   -    -  !
!   1    1  !
!           !
!   0    1  !
!   -    -  !
!   1    1  !
```

The result verifies that the matrix is indeed an identity matrix.

The inverse of a polynomial matrix can be written as $A^{-1} = N_s/d$, where N_s is a square matrix and d is a polynomial. The matrix N_s and the polynomial d are returned as separate factors by function *coffg*, for example:

```
-->[Ns,d] = coffg(A)
 d  =
                  2        3
       2 + 3s +  .5s  -  .5s
```

```
Ns  =

!        2                      !
!     .5s            2 - s      !
!                               !
!                    2          !
!  - 1 - 2s - s      1 + s      !
```

Evaluating a polynomial or polynomial matrix

To evaluate a polynomial or polynomial matrix, say $p(x)$, at a particular value of x use the function *horner*, for example:

```
-->horner(p,2)
 ans  =

    9.

-->horner(A,3)
 ans  =

!   4.    1.  !
!  16.    4.5 !
```

Characteristic matrix and characteristic equations

Polynomial matrices can be used, for example, to write the characteristic matrix and the characteristic equation of a square matrix (see chapter 5). To illustrate this applications, we create a square random matrix B:

```
-->B = int(10*rand(3,3))
 B  =

!  2.   3.   8.  !
!  7.   6.   6.  !
!  0.   6.   8.  !
```

The characteristic matrix is calculated as $\mathbf{B} - s \cdot \mathbf{I}_{3 \times 3}$:

```
-->B-s*eye(3,3)
 ans  =

!  2 - s      3          8       !
!                                !
!  7          6 - s       6      !
!                                !
!  0          6           8 - s  !
```

The determinant of the characteristic matrix is the characteristic polynomial of the matrix

```
-->det(B-s*eye(3,3))
 ans  =
```

```
                    2     3
      192 - 19s + 16s  - s
```

Polynomial functions applied to polynomial matrices

Many of the functions whose application was illustrated above for single polynomials apply as well to matrices of polynomial elements as illustrated with the following examples:

```
-->M = [(2-s)/(s^2+s) s^2; 1/(s+1) (s+1)/(s+2)]
 M   =

!                  2          !
!    2 - s        s           !
!    -----        -           !
!         2                   !
!    s + s        1           !
!                             !
!      1        1 + s         !
!    -----      -----         !
!    1 + s      2 + s         !

-->denom(M)
 ans  =

!       2                     !
!    s + s        1           !
!                             !
!    1 + s      2 + s         !

-->numer(M)
 ans  =

!                  2          !
!    2 - s        s           !
!                             !
!      1        1 + s         !
```

This introduction to polynomials in SCILAB is by no means a comprehensive one. Polynomials and polynomial matrices are commonly used in signal processing and control system analysis. The reader is invited to check extensive applications of polynomials and polynomial matrices in the document *Signals.pdf*, available in the documentation section of SCILAB's web page:

http://www-rocq.inria.fr/scilab/doc.html

Derivatives of polynomials

While SCILAB is basically a numerical environment, it allows a few symbolic operations using polynomials. One of such functions is the function *derivat* which is used to calculate the derivative of polynomials or rational expressions. In the next applications we define a polynomial variable x and apply function *derivat* to it and to polynomial and rational expressions involving variable x.

First, define the polynomial variable x:

```
-->x=poly(0,'x')
 x  =

    x
```

Next, we obtain the derivatives of functions $y = x$, $y = x^2$, $y = 1/x$, and $y = 2x^3-2x$:

```
-->derivat(x)
 ans  =

    1

-->derivat(x^2)
 ans  =

    2x

-->derivat(1/x)
 ans  =

    - 1
    ---
     2
    x

-->derivat(2*x^3-2*x)
 ans  =

             2
    - 2 + 6x
```

An attempt to obtain the derivative of function $y = sin(x)$ fails since function *derivat* applies only to polynomials and rational expressions:

```
-->derivat(sin(x))
              !--error     4
undefined variable : %p_sin
```

A rational expression is simply a fraction or combination of fractions involving polynomials. The following is an application of function *derivat* to a rational expression:

```
-->derivat((2*x^2-5*x)/(x^3-x^2+2))
 ans  =

                  2     3      4
    - 10 + 8x - 5x + 10x  - 2x
    --------------------------
              2     3    4     5    6
      4 - 4x + 4x + x  - 2x + x
```

Generating a polynomial given its coefficients

We define the polynomial of order n as

$$P_n(x) = a_0 + a_1 x + a_2 x^2 + ... + a_{n-1} x^{n-1} + a_n x^n$$

Using SCILAB we can obtain a polynomial expression by using the function *poly*. The general form of the function is:

$$[p] = poly(a, "x", ["flag"])$$

where *a* is a vector, matrix or real number, *x* is a symbolic variable; and, *"flag"* is a string (either *"roots"*, *"coeff"* -- the default value is *"roots"*) that determines whether the values in *a* represent the roots of the polynomial or its coefficients. If *a* is a vector representing the coefficients of the polynomial, the vector should be defined or entered as $[a_1\ a_2\ ...\ a_{n-1}\ a_n]$. (Note: If *a* is a matrix, p is the characteristic polynomial for the eigenvalues of the matrix, i.e., $p = det(xI-a)$, x being the symbolic variable.)

For example, if you want to obtain the polynomial whose coefficients are given by a = [3. -5. 1.], use the following command:

```
-->p = poly([3. -5. 1.],"x","coeff")
 p =
              2
    3 - 5x + x
```

The command above will store the polynomial expression $3-5x+x^2$ into variable *p*. You can also define the vector of coefficients into a variable before calling *poly*. For example:

```
-->v = [4. -2. -1. 7.];

-->k = poly(v,"y","coeff")
 k =
              2     3
    4 - 2y - y + 7y
```

will produce the polynomial '$4-2y-y^2+7y^3$' and store it into variable *k*.

Generating a polynomial given its roots

To obtain a polynomial given its roots use the same function poly as above, but replace *"coeff"* for *"roots"* in the last argument of the function. For example, to generate the polynomial whose roots are [1. 1. -1.], try:

```
-->q = poly([1. 1. -1.],"z","roots")
 q =
            2    3
    1 - z - z + z
```

The result is the polynomial '$1-z-z^2+z^3$' stored into the variable *q*. Because "roots" is the default value of the "flag" argument in the definition of poly, we could have use

```
-->q = poly([1. 1. -1.],"z")
```

to produce the polynomial.
The vector containing the roots of the polynomial can be stored into a variable and the variable name used as the first argument in the call of function *poly*. For example, to obtain the polynomial whose roots are [2. 3. -1.], we could use:

```
-->w = [2. 3. -1.];

-->r = poly(w,"n")
 r =

              2    3
     6 + n - 4n + n
```

The variable *r* will now contain the polynomial '$6+n-4n^2+n^3$'.

Obtaining the roots of a polynomial

To obtain the roots of a polynomial expression use the function *roots*. Some examples are shown below, using the polynomials *k*, *p*, *q*, and *r* defined above :

```
-->roots(k)

-->roots(p)

-->roots(q)

-->roots(r)
```

Verify the following results using SCILAB: *roots(k)* =[0.5180404 + .6094027 0.5180404 - .6094027, - 0.8932236], and *roots(p)* = [0.6972244, 4.3027756]. The results *roots(q)* and *roots(r)* should be pretty obvious.

Indefinite integrals for polynomials

Indefinite integrals for polynomials can be obtained using the following function *intpoly*:

```
function [pInt] = intpoly(p)

//This function calculates the indefinite integral
//of polynomial p

c = coeff(p);
n = length(c)-1;
d = [1];
for j=1:n+1
      d = [d j];
end;
cc = [0 c];
cc = cc./d;
```

```
disp('Indefinite integral - Add integration constant');
printf(' \n');
pInt = poly(cc,varn(p),'coeff');

//end function intpoly
```

Some examples follow:

```
-->getf('intpoly')

-->p1 = poly([5 0 -2 3 1 0 2],'s','coeff')
 p1  =

              2      3    4        6
     5  -  2s  +  3s  +  s   +  2s

-->intpoly(p1)

 Indefinite integral - Add integration constant

 ans  =

                   3          4         5              7
     5s  -  .6666667s  +  .75s  +  .2s  +  .2857143s

-->p2 = poly([-2 3 -5],'t','roots')
 p2  =

                  2     3
    - 30  -  11t  +  4t  +  t

-->intpoly(p2)

 Indefinite integral - Add integration constant

 ans  =

                  2              3          4
    - 30t  -  5.5t  +  1.3333333t  +  .25t
```

Numerical Methods with Polynomials

In this section we present numerical methods used for evaluation of polynomials and of its first derivative, as well as methods for fitting polynomials to tables of data.

Polynomial deflation

Polynomial deflation refers to the procedure by which a polynomial of degree $n-1$, say $Q_{n-1}(x)$, is obtained from a polynomial of degree n, say $P_n(x)$, by dividing out the factor $(x-r)$. Polynomials $P_n(x)$ and $Q_{n-1}(x)$ and the value r are related by:

$$P_n(x) = (x-r) \cdot Q_{n-1}(x) + R,$$

Where R is a constant remainder, i.e. $P_n(r) = R$. If for a particular value of r, say $r = r_0$, $P_n(x) = (x-r) \cdot Q_{n-1}(x)$, (i.e., $R = 0$) then r_0 is a root of $P_n(x)$.

The derivative of $P_n(x)$, in terms of $Q_n(x)$ and r is:

$$P'_n(x) = (x-r) \cdot Q'_{n-1}(x) + Q_{n-1}(x).$$

Thus, $P'_n(r) = Q_{n-1}(r)$.

The SCILAB commands shown below can be used for polynomial deflation, which in turn allows us to calculate the first derivative of a polynomial at a given value. For example, using the polynomial

$$P_5(x) = -120 + 274x - 225x^2 + 85x^3 - 15x^4 + x^5,$$

we can evaluate $P_5(2.5)$ and $P'_5(2.5)$, as follows:

```
-->P5 = poly([-120 274 -225 85 -15 1],'x','coeff')   //Define P5(x)
 P5  =

                    2       3        4     5
   - 120 + 274x - 225x + 85x  - 15x + x

-->R = horner(P5,2.5)     //Evaluate P5(2.5)
 R  =

   - 1.40625

-->d5 = x - 2.5           //Prepare factor (x-2.5)
 d5  =

   - 2.5 + x

-->[R4,Q4] = pdiv(P5,d5)  //Deflate polynomial
 Q4  =

                           2         3     4
     47.4375 - 90.625x + 53.75x - 12.5x + x
 R4  =

   - 1.40625

-->P5prime = horner(Q4,2.5)   //Evaluate derivative P5'(x) at x = 2.5
 P5prime  =

      .5625

-->P5prime = derivat(P5)      //Evaluate derivative P5'(x) with derivat

 P5prime  =

                    2      3     4
     274 - 450x + 255x - 60x + 5x
```

```
-->horner(P5prime,2.5)    //Evaluate derivative
 ans  =

    .5625
```

For x=2, try the following SCILAB commands:

```
horner(P5,2)
d5=x-2
[R4,Q4]=pdiv(P5,d5)
horner(Q4,2)
```

Direct fitting of a polynomial

Suppose that we have a set of $n+1$ data values $\{(x_0,y_0), (x_1,y_1), (x_2,y_2), ..., (x_n,y_n)\}$ and we want to fit a polynomial of degree n,

$$y = P_n(x) = a_0 + a_1 x + a_2 x^2 + ... + a_n x^n,$$

to these data. A direct fitting of the polynomial will involve the solution of the system of $n+1$ equations resulting from replacing each pair of data values (x_i, y_i), $i = 0, 1, 2, ..., n$, into the polynomial, i.e.,

$$a_0 + a_1 x_0 + a_2 x_0^2 + ... + a_n x_0^n = y_0$$
$$a_0 + a_1 x_1 + a_2 x_1^2 + ... + a_n x_1^n = y_1$$
$$\vdots$$
$$a_0 + a_1 x_n + a_2 x_n^2 + ... + a_n x_n^n = y_n$$

The unknowns in this system are the coefficients of the polynomial, $a_1, ..., a_n$.

The following function, *dfp*, will produce a direct polynomial fitting given the sets of paired data values (x_i, y_i), $i = 0, 1, 2, ..., n$:

```
function [a]=dfp(x,f)

//Performs direct data fitting for a polynomial given
//data sets {(x0,f0), (x1,f1), ..., (xn,fn)}.

//check if x,f are of the same length
[m1,n1]=size(x);
[m2,n2]=size(f);
if((m1  m2) | (n1  n2)) then
     error('x and f are not of the same size');
     abort;
end;
m = n1;
n = m - 1; //define order of polynomial
B = ones(m,m); //fill matrix coefficients with 1.0
//Calculate rest of matrix
for i = 1:m
```

```
        for j = 2:m
            B(i,j) = x(i)^(j-1);
        end;
end;
a = linsolve(B,-f); //solve for the coefficients
a=a';               //show result as a row vector
//end function dfp
```

The call to the function is simply *dfp(x,f)*. Values of x and f need to be defined as column vectors. Try the following example:

```
-->getf('dfp')

-->x = [3.4 3.5 3.6]; y = [0.294118, 0.285714, 0.277778];

-->a = dfp(x',y')
 a  =

!   .858314  -  .2455      .0234 !
```

To generate the polynomial, use:

```
-->p = poly(a,'x','coeff')
 p  =
                              2
    .858314 -  .2455x  +  .0234x
```

The evaluation of the polynomial for the values of x given above verifies the polynomial fitting:

```
-->horner(p,x)
 ans =

!   .294118     .285714     .277778 !
```

Lagrange polynomials

Lagrange polynomials are used to fit a data set $\{(x_1,y_1), (x_2,y_2), ..., (x_n,y_n)\}$. A Lagrange polynomial is expanded from the formula:

$$p_{n-1}(x) = \sum_{j=1}^{n} \frac{\prod_{k=1,k\neq j}^{n}(x-x_k)}{\prod_{k=1,k\neq j}^{n}(x_j-x_k)} \cdot y_j.$$

For example, for n = 2, we will write:

$$p_1(x) = \frac{x-x_2}{x_1-x_2} \cdot y_1 + \frac{x-x_1}{x_2-x_1} \cdot y_2 = \frac{(y_1-y_2)\cdot x + (y_2 \cdot x_1 - y_1 \cdot x_2)}{x_1-x_2}.$$

The following function, *LagPol*, will evaluate the Lagrange polynomial of order n at $x = x0$, using the data in column vectors x and f.

```
function [y]=lagpol(x0,x,f,n)

//Evaluates the Lagrange polynomial corresponding
//to the data set {(x1,f1), (x2,f2), ..., (xn,fn)}
//at point x = x0.

//check if x,f are of the same length
[m1,n1]=size(x);
[m2,n2]=size(f);
if((m1  m2) | (n1  n2)) then
        error('x and f are not of the same size');
        abort;
end;
m = n1;
if(n>m-1)then
        disp(n,"polynomial degree =")
        disp(m,"vector size=")
        error('use smaller polynomial degree n');
        abort
end;
m = n + 1;
N = ones(1,m);
D = N;
C = N;
y = 0.0;
for j = 1:m
        for k = 1:m
                if(k  j) then
                        N(j) = N(j)*(x0-x(k));
                        D(j) = D(j)*(x(j)-x(k));
                end;
        end;
        C(j) = N(j)/D(j);
        y = y + C(j)*f(j);
end;

//end LagPol function
```

As an example, try the following SCILAB statements:

```
-->getf('lagpol')

-->x = [3.4 3.5 3.55 3.65]; y = [0.294118,0.285714,0.281690,0.273973];

-->lagpol(3.44,x,y,1)
 ans  =

     .2907564

-->lagpol(3.44,x,y,2)
 ans  =

     .2906994

-->lagpol(3.44,x,y,3)
```

```
      ans  =

          .2906977

-->lagpol(3.44,x,y,4)

  polynomial degree =

      4.

  vector size=

      4.
  !--error    9999
  use smaller polynomial degree n
  at line        18 of function lagpol                    called by :
  lagpol(3.44,x,y,4)
```

The following example demonstrate the use of Lagrange polynomials of orders n = 1, 2, 3, 4, 5, and 6 to the following data set.

x	0.0	1.2	3.5	4.2	6.2	8.1	11.2
y	15.0	29.0	13.3	-6.4	2.9	17.1	-8.0

The SCILAB commands that follow load the original data and produce Lagrange polynomials for orders n = 1 to 6. A plot showing the different polynomials and the original data is also produced.

```
-->getf('lagpol')
-->x = [0.0,1.2,3.5,4.2,6.2,8.1,11.2];           //Original x data
-->y = [15.0,29.0,13.3,-6.4,2.9,17.1,-8.0];      //Original y data
-->xx = [0.0:0.1:12.0];                          //x data for fitting

-->yy1 = []; yy2 = []; yy3 =[]; yy4 = []; yy5 = []; yy6 =[];

-->for j = 1:n                                   //Lagrange polynomial fittings
-->      yy1 = [yy1 lagpol(xx(j),x,y,1)];
-->      yy2 = [yy2 lagpol(xx(j),x,y,2)];
-->      yy3 = [yy3 lagpol(xx(j),x,y,3)];
-->      yy4 = [yy4 lagpol(xx(j),x,y,4)];
-->      yy5 = [yy5 lagpol(xx(j),x,y,5)];
-->      yy6 = [yy6 lagpol(xx(j),x,y,6)];
-->end;
```

The plot is produced with the following statements:

```
-->plot2d([xx',xx',xx',xx',xx',xx'],[yy1',yy2',yy3',yy4',yy5',yy6'],...
-->[1:1:6],'111','n=1@n=2@n=3@n=4@n=5@n=6',[0 -50 12 50])
-->plot2d(x,y,-9,'011','y',[0 -50 12 50])
-->xtitle('Lagrange polynomials', 'x', 'y')
```

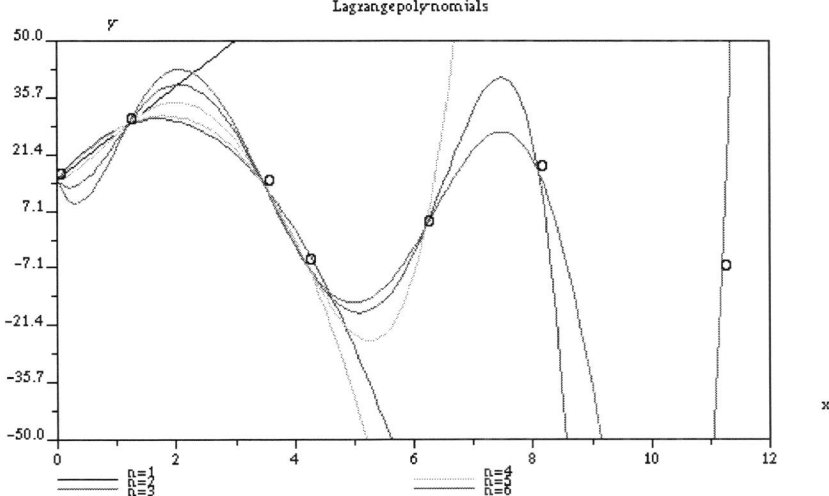

SCILAB function *mtlb_diff*

SCILAB provides function *mtlb_diff* which we will use to generate tables of differences in subsequent sections. This function can be used, for example, to calculate the differences between consecutive elements in a vector. The following application uses a vector with 7 elements:

```
-->u = [0, 1, 3, 6, 11, 15, 23]
 u   =

!   0.    1.    3.    6.    11.    15.    23. !
```

function *mtlb_diff* produces a vector of 6 elements representing the differences between consecutive elements of the original vector:

```
-->Du = mtlb_diff(u)
 Du  = !   1.    2.    3.    5.    4.    8. !
```

Consecutive applications of the function *mtlb_diff* produce vectors of differences with one less element than the previous vector:

```
-->D2u = mtlb_diff(Du)
 D2u  = !   1.    1.    2.  - 1.    4. !

-->D3u = mtlb_diff(D2u)
 D3u  = !   0.    1.  - 3.    5. !

-->D4u = mtlb_diff(D3u)
 D4u  = !   1.  - 4.    8. !

-->D5u = mtlb_diff(D4u)
```

```
       D5u   = ! - 5.     12. !

-->D6u = mtlb_diff(D5u)
  D6u  =    17.
```

The following example shows the application of function *mtlb_diff* to a column vector v of six elements, and consecutive applications to the resulting vector until a single value is obtained:

```
-->v = [1;3;5;9;12;23]
  v  =
!    1.  !
!    3.  !
!    5.  !
!    9.  !
!   12.  !
!   23.  !

-->Dv = mtlb_diff(v)
  Dv  =
!    2.  !
!    2.  !
!    4.  !
!    3.  !
!   11.  !

-->D2v = mtlb_diff(Dv)
  D2v  =
!    0.  !
!    2.  !
!  - 1.  !
!    8.  !

-->D3v = mtlb_diff(D2v)
  D3v  =
!    2.  !
!  - 3.  !
!    9.  !
-->D4v = mtlb_diff(D3v)
  D4v  =
!  - 5.  !
!   12.  !

-->D5v = mtlb_diff(D4v)
  D5v  =
       17.
```

The following example shows the application of function *mtlb_diff* to a 5 4 matrix. The result of *mtlb_diff*, when applied to matrices, is another matrix containing the differences between consecutive rows of the original matrix:

```
-->A = int(10*rand(5,4))
  A  =
!    2.    9.    5.    4. !
!    2.    2.    4.    2. !
!    8.    3.    3.    6. !
!    6.    3.    5.    4. !
!    3.    2.    5.    9. !
```

```
-->DA = mtlb_diff(A)
DA  =
!    0.   - 7.   - 1.   - 2. !
!    6.     1.   - 1.     4. !
!  - 2.     0.     2.   - 2. !
!  - 3.   - 1.     0.     5. !
```

Continuous application of function *mtlb_diff* to the resulting matrix continues until the matrix is reduced to a row vector:

```
-->D2A = mtlb_diff(DA)
D2A =
!    6.     8.    0.     6. !
!  - 8.   - 1.    3.   - 6. !
!  - 1.   - 1.  - 2.     7. !

-->D3A = mtlb_diff(D2A)
D3A =

!  - 14.   - 9.     3.   - 12. !
!     7.     0.   - 5.     13. !

-->D4A = mtlb_diff(D3A)
D4A =

!    21.    9.   - 8.    25. !
```

From this point on, further applications of *mtlb_diff* will produce row vectors of smaller sizes until a single value results:

```
-->D5A = mtlb_diff(D4A)
D5A =
!  - 12.   - 17.    33. !

-->D6A = mtlb_diff(D5A)
D6A =
!  - 5.    50. !

-->D7A = mtlb_diff(D6A)
D7A =

     55.
```

Difference Tables

A difference table corresponding to a data set $\{(x_0,y_0), (x_1,y_1), (x_2,y_2), ..., (x_n,y_n)\}$ is illustrated below:

x	y	Δy	Δ²y	Δ³y	Δ⁴y
x_0	y_0				
		$\Delta y_0 = y_1 - y_0$			
x_1	y_1		$\Delta^2 y_0 = \Delta y_1 - \Delta y_0$		
		$\Delta y_1 = y_2 - y_1$		$\Delta^3 y_0 = \Delta^2 y_1 - \Delta^2 y_0$	
x_2	y_2		$\Delta^2 y_1 = \Delta y_2 - \Delta y_1$		$\Delta^4 y_0 = \Delta^3 y_1 - \Delta^3 y_0$
		$\Delta y_2 = y_2 - y_1$		$\Delta^3 y_1 = \Delta^2 y_2 - \Delta^2 y_1$	
x_3	y_3		$\Delta^2 y_2 = \Delta y_2 - \Delta y_1$		
		$\Delta y_3 = y_3 - y_2$			
x_4	y_4				

This table corresponds to what is referred to as *forward differences*. The first two columns are simply the data values. The third column is the difference of values of y, the fourth column is the difference of values of the third column, and so forth. The table illustrated above starts with five points and is able to calculate differences up to the fourth order.

Consider, for example, the following table of forward differences corresponding to the function $y = \exp(x)$ in the range [2,3] with x increments of 0.1:

x	y	Δy	Δ²y	Δ³y	Δ⁴y	Δ⁵y	Δ⁶y	Δ⁷y
2.00	7.389056							
		0.777114						
2.10	8.16617		0.08173					
		0.858844		0.008596				
2.20	9.025013		0.090325		0.000904			
		0.949169		0.0095		9.51E-05		
2.30	9.974182		0.099825		0.000999		1E-05	
		1.048994		0.010499		0.000105		1.05E-06
2.40	11.02318		0.110324		0.001104		1.11E-05	
		1.159318		0.011603		0.000116		1.16E-06
2.50	12.18249		0.121926		0.00122		1.22E-05	
		1.281244		0.012823		0.000128		1.28E-06
2.60	13.46374		0.13475		0.001349		1.35E-05	
		1.415994		0.014172		0.000142		1.42E-06
2.70	14.87973		0.148921		0.00149		1.49E-05	
		1.564915		0.015662		0.000157		
2.80	16.44465		0.164584		0.001647			
		1.729499		0.017309				
2.90	18.17415		0.181893					
		1.911392						
3.00	20.08554							

The following SCILAB commands will generate the columns of the table of differences shown above:

```
-->x=[3.0:0.1:4.0]'; y = exp(x);
-->Dy = mtlb_diff(y)
 Dy   =
!    2.1124144 !
!    2.3345789 !
!    2.5801087 !
!    2.8514611 !
!    3.1513519 !
!    3.4827825 !
!    3.8490699 !
!    4.2538801 !
!    4.7012646 !
!    5.1957009 !

-->x=[2.0:0.1:3.0]'; y = exp(x);
-->Dy = mtlb_diff(y)
 Dy   =
!     .7771138 !
!     .8588436 !
!     .9491690 !
!    1.0489939 !
!    1.1593176 !
!    1.2812441 !
!    1.4159937 !
!    1.564915  !
!    1.7294986 !
!    1.9113916 !

-->D2y = mtlb_diff(Dy)
 D2y   =
!     .0817298 !
!     .0903254 !
!     .0998250 !
!     .1103237 !
!     .1219265 !
!     .1347496 !
!     .1489214 !
!     .1645836 !
!     .1818930 !

-->D3y = mtlb_diff(D2y)
 D3y   =
!     .0085956 !
!     .0094996 !
!     .0104987 !
!     .0116028 !
!     .0128231 !
!     .0141717 !
!     .0156622 !
!     .0173094 !

-->D4y = mtlb_diff(D3y)
 D4y   =
!     .0009040 !
!     .0009991 !
!     .0011042 !
!     .0012203 !
```

```
!    .0013486 !
!    .0014905 !
!    .0016472 !

-->D5y = mtlb_diff(D4y)
 D5y  =

!    .0000951 !
!    .0001051 !
!    .0001161 !
!    .0001283 !
!    .0001418 !
!    .0001568 !

-->D6y =mtlb_diff(D5y)
 D6y  =

!    .0000100 !
!    .0000111 !
!    .0000122 !
!    .0000135 !
!    .0000149 !

-->D7y = mtlb_diff(D6y)
 D7y  =

!    .0000011 !
!    .0000012 !
!    .0000013 !
!    .0000014 !
```

A function to produce a forward-difference table

The following function, called *Difference_Table(f,n)*, where *f* is a column vector and *n* is the highest order of the difference, is shown below:

```
function [Df]=Difference_Table(f,n)
//This function calculates a difference table starting with
//a column vector f
[m,nc]=size(f)
//check that it is indeed a column vector
if(nc<>1)then
        error('f is not a column vector.');
        abort
end;
//check the difference order
if(n > m)then
        disp(n,"n=");
        disp(m,"m=");
        error('n must be less than or equal to m');
        abort
end;
//
Df=zeros(m,n);
for i = 1:m
        Df(i,1) = f(i,1);
end;
delf = f;
for j = 2:n
```

```
        delf = mtlb_diff(delf)
        [m,nc]=size(delf);
        for i = 1:m
            Df(i,j) = delf(i,1);
        end;
end;
//end of function Difference_Table
```

The following SCILAB commands will generate a difference table for the values of y defined previously. The resulting matrix contains the same information than the table of differences shown earlier, except for the location of entries. However, the interpretation of the entries is straightforward. The first column in the matrix is the vector y, the second is the first difference, the third column is the second difference, and so on. Furthermore, the top row in the table of differences contains the values of y_0, Δy_0, $\Delta^2 y_0$, and so on:

```
-->Difference_Table(y,5)
 ans  =

!    7.3890561    .7771138    .0817298    .0085956    .0009040  !
!    8.1661699    .8588436    .0903254    .0094996    .0009991  !
!    9.0250135    .9491690    .0998250    .0104987    .0011042  !
!    9.9741825   1.0489939    .1103237    .0116028    .0012203  !
!   11.023176    1.1593176    .1219265    .0128231    .0013486  !
!   12.182494    1.2812441    .1347496    .0141717    .0014905  !
!   13.463738    1.4159937    .1489214    .0156622    .0016472  !
!   14.879732    1.564915     .1645836    .0173094   0.         !
!   16.444647    1.7294986    .1818930   0.          0.         !
!   18.174145    1.9113916   0.          0.          0.         !
!   20.085537   0.           0.          0.          0.         !
```

Newton Forward-Difference Polynomial

A Newton forward-difference polynomial uses a table of forward differences to approximate the function of interest, $y = f(x)$, to a polynomial on the variable

$$s = (x-x_0)/\Delta x,$$

where x is a particular value of the independent variable where the polynomial is evaluated, x_0 is the first value of x in the table of differences, and Δx is the increment in the independent variable. The expression for the Newton forward-difference polynomial is

$$f(x) \approx P_n(x) = y_0 + \binom{s}{1} \cdot \Delta y_0 + \binom{s}{2} \cdot \Delta^2 y_0 + \binom{s}{3} \cdot \Delta^3 y_0 + \cdots,$$

where the terms

$$\binom{n}{r} = \frac{n!}{r!(n-r)!},$$

are binomial coefficients.

The following function calculates the Newton forward-difference polynomial of order n, evaluated at x. The polynomial needs as input a column vector representing values of x (we call the vector xL), and a second column vector representing the values of f. The first value of xL represents x_o. The function is called *NFDP*. Notice that in the listing of this function we also include the listing of functions *factorial* and *binomial*, used to calculate, respectively, factorials and binomial coefficients:

```
function [P]=NFDP(x,n,xL,f)
//This function calculates a Newton Forward-Difference Polynomial of
//order n, evaluated at x, using column vectors xL, f as the reference
//table.  The first value of xL and of f, represent, respectively,
//xo and fo in the equation for the polynomial.
[m,nc]=size(f)
//check that it is indeed a column vector
if(nc<>1)then
        error('f is not a column vector.');
        abort
end;
//check the difference order
if(n >= m)then
        disp(n,"n=");
        disp(m,"m=");
        error('n must be less than or equal to m-1');
        abort
end;
//
xo = xL(1,1);
delx = mtlb_diff(xL);
h = delx(1,1);
s = (x-xo)/h;
P = f(1,1);
delf = f;
for i = 1:n
        delf = mtlb_diff(delf)
        P = P + Binomial(s,i)*delf(1,1)
end;
//end of function NFDP
function[C]=Binomial(s,i)
        C = 1.0;
        for k = 0:i-1
                C = C*(s-k);
        end;
        C = C/factorial(i)
//end of function Binomial
function[fact]=factorial(nn)
        fact = 1.0
        for k = nn:-1:1
                fact=fact*k
        end;
//end of function factorial
```

The following SCILAB commands will generate the third-order Newton forward-difference polynomial evaluated at x = 3.44, for the function $f(x) = 1/x$, with xL a column vector with values of x: 3.4, 3.5, 3.6, 3.7, 3.8, 3.9, 4.0:

```
-->getf('NFDP.txt')

-->x = [3.4:0.1:4.0]; y = 1./x; //Note: y is a column vector
```

```
-->y
 y  =

!    .0353761  !
!    .0364166  !
!    .0374571  !
!    .0384976  !
!    .0395380  !
!    .0405785  !

-->NFDP(3.44,3,x',y)
 ans  =

    .0357923
```

With the same values of x and f, the following command will show the Newton forward-difference polynomial of degrees 0, 1, 2 and 3:

```
-->for n=0:3, NFDP(3.44,n,x',y), end
 ans  = .0353761
 ans  = .0357923
 ans  = .0357923
 ans  = .0357923
```

Newton Backward-Difference Polynomial

A backward-difference table is illustrated below. The reference value is the last value, $y(x)$, thus the table starts with a negative sub-index which increases in value until reaching the value of zero at the bottom of the table. Backward differences are represented through the use of the *del* or *nabla* operator ∇, i.e., ∇y for the first difference, $\nabla^2 y$ for the second, and so on.

x	y	∇y	$\nabla^2 y$	$\nabla^3 y$	$\nabla^4 y$
x_{-4}	y_{-4}				
		$\nabla y_{-3} = y_{-3} - y_{-4}$			
x_{-3}	y_{-3}		$\nabla^2 y_{-2} = \Delta y_{-2} - \Delta y_{-3}$		
		$\nabla y_{-2} = y_{-2} - y_{-3}$		$\nabla^3 y_{-1} = \Delta^2 y_{-1} - \Delta^2 y_{-2}$	
x_{-2}	y_{-2}		$\nabla^2 y_{-1} = \Delta y_{-1} - \Delta y_{-2}$		$\nabla^4 y_0 = \Delta^3 y_0 - \Delta^3 y_{-1}$
		$\nabla y_{-1} = y_{-1} - y_{-2}$		$\nabla^3 y_0 = \Delta^2 y_0 - \Delta^2 y_{-1}$	
x_{-1}	y_{-1}		$\nabla^2 y_0 = \Delta y_0 - \Delta y_{-1}$		
		$\nabla y_0 = y_0 - y_{-1}$			
x_0	y_0				

A Sterling centered-difference polynomial uses a table of centered differences to approximate the function of interest, $y = f(x)$, to a polynomial on the variable

$$s = (x-x_0)/\Delta x,$$

where x is a particular value of the independent variable where the polynomial is evaluated, x_0 is the last value of x in the table of differences, and Δx is the increment in the independent variable. The expression for the Newton backward-difference polynomial is

$$f(x) \approx P_n(x) = y_0 + \binom{s}{1}\cdot\nabla y_0 + \binom{s+1}{2}\cdot\nabla^2 y_0 + \binom{s+2}{3}\cdot\nabla^3 y_0 + \cdots.$$

The following function calculates the Newton backward-difference polynomial of order n, evaluated at x. The polynomial needs as input a column vector representing values of x (we call the vector xL), and a second column vector representing the values of f. The last value of xL represents x_0. The function is called NBDP and is stored in file NBDP.txt:

```
function [P]=NBDP(x,n,xL,f)
//This function calculates a Newton Forward-Difference Polynomial of
//order n, evaluated at x, using column vectors xL, f as the reference
//table.  The first value of xL and of f, represent, respectively,
//xo and fo in the equation for the polynomial.
[m,nc]=size(f)
//check that it is indeed a column vector
if(nc<>1)then
        error('f is not a column vector.');
        abort
end;
//check the difference order
if(n >= m)then
        disp(n,"n=");
        disp(m,"m=");
        error('n must be less than or equal to m-1');
        abort
end;
//
xo = xL(m,1);
delx = mtlb_diff(xL);
h = delx(1,1);
s = (x-xo)/h;
P = f(m,1);
delf = f;
for i = 1:n
        delf = mtlb_diff(delf);
        [m,nc] = size(delf);
        P = P + Binomial(s+i-1,i)*delf(m,1)
end;
//end of function NBDP
function[C]=Binomial(s,i)
        C = 1.0;
        for k = 0:i-1
                C = C*(s-k);
        end;
        C = C/factorial(i)
//end of function Binomial
function[fact]=factorial(nn)
        fact = 1.0
        for k = nn:-1:1
```

```
        fact=fact*k
    end;
//end of function factorial
```

The following SCILAB commands will generate the third-order Newton backward-difference polynomial evaluated at x = 3.44, for the function f(x) = 1/x, with xL a column vector with values of x: 3.0, 3.1, 3.2, 3.3, 3.4, 3.5:

```
-->getf('NBDP.txt')

-->x = [3.0:0.1:3.5]'; y = x^(-1);   //both x & y are column vectors

-->NBDP(3.44,3,x,y)
 ans  =

    .2906979
```

With the same values of x and f, the following command will show the Newton forward-difference polynomial of degrees 0, 1, 2 and 3:

```
-->for n=0:3, NBDP(3.44,n,x,y), end
 ans  =  .2857143
 ans  =  .2907563
 ans  =  .2906952
 ans  =  .2906979
```

Stirling centered-difference polynomial

A centered-difference table is illustrated below. The reference value is the middle value (x_0, y_0), thus the table should contain an odd number of data points. Centered differences are represented through the use of the δ symbol, i.e., δy for the first difference, $\delta^2 y$ for the second, and so on.

x	y	δy	$\delta^2 y$	$\delta^3 y$	$\delta^4 y$
x_{-2}	y_{-2}				
		$\delta y_{-3/2} = y_{-1} - y_{-2}$			
x_{-1}	y_{-1}		$\delta^2 y_{-1} = \delta y_{-1/2} - \delta y_{-3/2}$		
		$\delta y_{-1/2} = y_0 - y_{-1}$		$\delta^3 y_{-1/2} = \delta^2 y_0 - \delta^2 y_{-1}$	
x_0	y_0		$\delta^2 y_0 = \delta y_{1/2} - \delta y_{-1/2}$		$\delta^4 y_0 = \delta^3 y_{1/2} - \delta^3 y_{-1/2}$
		$\delta y_{1/2} = y_1 - y_0$		$\delta^3 y_{1/2} = \delta^2 y_1 - \delta^2 y_0$	
x_1	y_1		$\delta^2 y_1 = \delta y_{3/2} - \delta y_{1/2}$		
		$\delta y_{3/2} = y_2 - y_1$			
x_2	y_2				

A Stirling centered-difference polynomial uses a table of centered differences with an odd number of data points to approximate the function of interest, y = f(x), to a polynomial on the variable

$$s = (x-x_0)/\Delta x,$$

where x is a particular value of the independent variable where the polynomial is evaluated, x_0 is the middle value of x in the table of differences, and Δx is the increment in the independent variable. The expression for the Sterling centered-difference polynomial is

$$f(x) \approx P_n(x) = y_0 + \binom{s}{1} \cdot \frac{1}{2}(\delta y_{1/2} + \delta y_{-1/2}) + \frac{1}{2}\left(\binom{s+1}{2} + \binom{s}{2}\right) \cdot \delta^2 y_0$$

$$+ \binom{s+1}{3} \cdot \frac{1}{2}(\delta^3 y_{1/2} + \delta^3 y_{-1/2}) + \frac{1}{2}\left(\binom{s+2}{4} + \binom{s+1}{4}\right)\delta^4 y_0 + \cdots.$$

The following function calculates the Stirling centered-difference polynomial of order n, evaluated at x. The polynomial needs as input a column vector representing values of x (we call the vector xL), and a second column vector representing the values of f. The length of the vectors xL and f must be an odd number. The middle value of the vectors xL and f will represent x_o and f_o. The function is called *stirling* and is stored in file *stirling.txt*:

```
function [P]=stirling(x,n,xL,f)
//This function calculates a Stirling-Difference Polynomial of
//order n, evaluated at x, using column vectors xL, f as the reference
//table.  The length of the vectors xL and f must be an odd number,
//with xo, fo being the middle value in the corresponding lists.
[m,nc]=size(f)
//check that it is indeed a column vector
if(nc<>1)then
        error('f is not a column vector.');
        abort
end;
//check that the size of the lists xL and f is odd
if(modulo(m,2)==0)then
        disp(m,"list size =")
        error('list size must be an odd number');
        abort
end;
//check the difference order
if(n > (m-1)/2)then
        disp(n,"n=");
        disp(m,"m=");
        error('n must be less than or equal to (m-1)/2');
        abort
end;
//
i0 = floor(m/2)+1
xo = xL(i0,1);
delx = mtlb_diff(xL);
h = delx(1,1);
s = (x-xo)/h;
P = f(i0,1);
delf = f;
for i = 1:n
        delf = mtlb_diff(delf)
```

```
        [m,nc]=size(delf)
        j = m/2
        k = j+1
        P = P + 0.5*Binomial(s+i-1,i)*(delf(j,1)+delf(k,1))
        delf = mtlb_diff(delf)
        [m,nc]=size(delf)
        j = floor(m/2)+1
        P = P + 0.5*(Binomial(s+i,2*i)+Binomial(s+i-1,2*i))*delf(j,1)
end;
//end of function stirling
function[C]=Binomial(s,i)
        C = 1.0;
        for k = 0:i-1
                C = C*(s-k);
        end;
        C = C/factorial(i)
//end of function Binomial
function[fact]=factorial(nn)
        fact = 1.0
        for k = nn:-1:1
                fact=fact*k
        end;
//end of function factorial
```

The following SCILAB commands will generate the third, fourth and, if possible, the fifth-order Stirling centered-difference polynomial evaluated at x = 3.44, for the function $f(x) = 1/x$, with xL a column vector with values of x: 3.0, 3.1, 3.2, 3.3, 3.4, 3.5, 3.6, 3.7, 3.8 (i.e., vector size = 9):

```
-->getf('stirling.txt')

-->x = [3.0:0.1:3.8]'; y = x^(-1);

-->stirling(3.44, 3, x, y)
 ans  =

    .2906824

-->stirling(3.44, 4, x, y)
 ans  =

    .2906823

-->stirling(3.44, 5, x, y)

 n=

    5.

 m=

    9.
 !--error    9999
n must be less than or equal to (m-1)/2
at line       22 of function stirling                called by :
stirling(3.44, 5, x, y)
```

With the same values of x and f, the following command will show the Stirling centered-difference polynomial of degrees 0 through 4:

```
-->for n = 0:4, stirling(3.44, n, x, y), end
 ans  = .2941176
 ans  = .2906952
 ans  = .2906825
 ans  = .2906824
 ans  = .2906823
```

Bessel centered-difference polynomial

A Bessel centered-difference polynomial uses a table of centered differences with an even number of data points to approximate the function of interest $y = f(x)$, to a polynomial on the variable

$$s = (x-x_0)/\Delta x,$$

where x is a particular value of the independent variable where the polynomial is evaluated, is a middle value of x in the table of differences, and Δx is the increment in the independent variable. Bessel centered differences are based on a point between and x_1. The expression for the Bessel centered-difference polynomial is

$$f(x) \approx P_n(x) = \frac{1}{2}(y_0 + y_1) + \frac{1}{2}\left(\binom{s}{1} + \binom{s-1}{1}\right) \cdot \delta y_{1/2} + \binom{s}{2} \cdot \frac{1}{2}(\delta^2 y_0 + \delta^2 y_1)$$
$$+ \frac{1}{2}\left(\binom{s+1}{3} + \binom{s}{3}\right) \cdot \delta^3 y_{1/2} + \binom{s+1}{4} \frac{1}{2}(\delta^4 y_0 + \delta^4 y_1) + \cdots.$$

The following function calculates the Bessel centered-difference polynomial of order n, evaluated at x. The polynomial needs as input a column vector representing values of x (we call the vector xL), and a second column vector representing the values of f. The length of the vectors xL and f must be an odd number. The middle value of the vectors xL and f will represent x_o and f_o. The function is called *stirling* and is stored in file *stirling.txt*:

```
function [P]=bessel(x,n,xL,f)
//This function calculates a Bessel Centered-Difference Polynomial of
//order n, evaluated at x, using column vectors xL, f as the reference
//table.  The length of the vectors xL and f must be an even number (m),
//with xo, fo being the value number m/2 in the corresponding lists.
[m,nc]=size(f)
//check that it is indeed a column vector
if(nc<>1)then
        error('f is not a column vector.');
        abort
end;
//check that the size of the lists xL and f is odd
if(modulo(m,2)<>0)then
```

```
        disp(m,"list size =")
        error('list size must be an even number');
        abort
end;
//check the difference order
if(n > (m-1)/2)then
        disp(n,"n=");
        disp(m,"m=");
        error('n must be less than or equal to (m-1)/2');
        abort
end;
//
i0 = floor(m/2)
xo = xL(i0,1);
delx = mtlb_diff(xL);
h = delx(1,1);
s = (x-xo)/h;
P = 0.5*(f(i0,1)+f(i0+1,1));
delf = f;
for i = 1:n
        delf = mtlb_diff(delf)
        [m,nc]=size(delf)
        j = (m+1)/2;
        P = P + 0.5*(Binomial(s+i-1,i)+Binomial(s+i-2,i))*delf(j,1)
        delf = mtlb_diff(delf)
        [m,nc]=size(delf)
        j = m/2;
        k = j+1
        P = P + 0.5*Binomial(s+i-1,2*i)*(delf(j,1)+delf(k,1))
end;
//end of function bessel
function[C]=Binomial(s,i)
        C = 1.0;
        for k = 0:i-1
                C = C*(s-k);
        end;
        C = C/factorial(i)
//end of function Binomial
function[fact]=factorial(nn)
        fact = 1.0
        for k = nn:-1:1
                fact=fact*k
        end;
//end of function factorial
```

The following SCILAB commands will generate the third, fourth, and, if possible, the fifth-order Bessel centered-difference polynomial evaluated at x = 3.44, for the function f(x) = 1/x, with xL a column vector with values of x: 3.0, 3.1, 3.2, 3.3, 3.4, 3.5, 3.6, 3.7, 3.8 (i.e., vector size = 9):

```
-->x = [3.0:0.1:3.9]'; y = x^(-1);

-->getf('bessel.txt')

-->bessel(3.44,3,x,y)
 ans  =   .2906944

-->bessel(3.44,4,x,y)
 ans  =     .2906944
```

With the same values of x and f, the following command will show the Bessel centered-difference polynomial of degrees 0 through 4:

```
-->for n = 0:4, bessel(3.44,n,x,y), end
 ans  = .2899160
 ans  = .2906977
 ans  = .2906944
 ans  = .2906944
 ans  = .2906944
```

Least Squares Polynomial Approximation

Given a set of N data points (x_1, Y_1), (x_2, Y_2), ..., (x_N, Y_N), we try to obtain a polynomial

$$y = b_o + b_1 x + b_2 x^2 + \ldots + b_{n-1} x^{n-1} + b_n x^n,$$

such that the sum of the squares of the estimation errors $e_i = Y_i - y_i$, i.e.,

$$S(b_o, b_1, \ldots, b_n) = \sum_{i=1}^{N} e_i^2 = \sum_{i=1}^{N} (Y_i - y_i)^2$$

is minimized.

The following method (e.g., Johnson, R.A., 1994, "Miller & Freund's Probability and Statistics for Engineers," Prentice Hall, Englewood Cliffs, New Jersey) uses matrices to obtain the vector of coefficients $b = [b_o \; b_1 \; b_2 \ldots b_{n-1} \; b_n]$, by creating the matrix X,

$$X = \begin{bmatrix} 1 & x_1 & x_1^2 & \cdots & x_1^n \\ 1 & x_2 & x_2^2 & \cdots & x_2^n \\ 1 & x_3 & x_3^2 & \cdots & x_3^n \\ \vdots & \vdots & \vdots & \vdots & \vdots \\ 1 & x_N & x_N^2 & \cdots & x_N^n \end{bmatrix},$$

and solving for b, from

$$b = (X^T X)^{-1} X^T y,$$

where y is the column vector, $y = [y_1 \; y_2 \ldots y_{n-1} \; y_N]^T$. For implementation in SCILAB, we use two column vectors, $x = [x_1 \; x_2 \ldots x_{N-1} \; x_N]^T$, and $y = [y_1 \; y_2 \ldots y_{N-1} \; y_N]^T$, as well as the polynomial degree, n, as input to a function PolyFit, listed below.

```
function [b]=PolyFit(x,y,n)
//Least-square method fitting a polynomial equation
//x and y are column vectors
//Check that x and y have the same size
[nrx,ncx]=size(x)
```

```
[nry,ncy]=size(y)
if((ncx<>1)|(ncy<>1))then
        error('x or y, or both, not column vector(s)');
        abort;
end;
if((nrx<>nry))then
        error('x and y have not the same length');
        abort;
end;
N = nrx;
X = ones(N,n+1);
for j = 2:n+1
        for i = 1:N
                X(i,j) = x(i,1)^(j-1)
        end;
end;
XT = X';
M = XT*X;
M = inv(M);
M = M*XT;
b = M*y;
//end PolyFit function
```

For example, to fit a second-order polynomial to the following data, use the SCILAB commands shown below:

x	y
0	12.0
1	10.5
2	10.0
3	8.0
4	7.0
5	8.0
6	7.5
7	8.5
8	9.0

```
-->getf('PolyFit.txt')

-->x = [0:1:8]
 x  =

!   0.    1.    2.    3.    4.    5.    6.    7.    8. !

-->Y = [12,10.5,10,8,7,8,7.5,8.5,9]
 Y  =

!   12.    10.5    10.    8.    7.    8.    7.5    8.5    9. !

-->b = PolyFit(x',Y',2)
 b  =

!    12.184848  !
!  - 1.8465368  !
!     .1829004  !
```
The vector b now can be used in the function *poly* to generate the polynomial $y = f(x)$, which can be evaluated at x = 6.5 by using the function *horner*, as shown below:

```
-->y = poly(b,'x','coeff')
 y  =

                              2
    12.184848 - 1.8465368x +  .1829004x

-->horner(y,6.5)
 ans  =

    7.9099026
```

Linear Data Fitting

The function PolyFit, when called with $n = 1$, can be used to fit a linear function to the data, namely,

$$y = b_o + b_1 x.$$

For example, fit a linear relationship to the following data using *PolyFit*:

x	y
20	0.18
60	0.37
100	0.35
140	0.78
180	0.56
220	0.75
260	1.18
300	1.36
340	1.17
380	1.65

The SCILAB commands to use are:

```
-->x = [20:40:380]';

-->Y = [0.18, 0.37, 0.35, 0.78, 0.56, 0.75, 1.18, 1.36, 1.17, 1.65]';

-->b  = PolyFit(x,Y,1)
 b  =

!   .0692424 !
!   .0038288 !

-->y = poly(b,'x','coeff')
 y  =

    .0692424 +  .0038288x
```

To evaluate y = f(x) at, say, x = 190, use:

```
-->horner(y,190)
 ans   =

     .7967121
```

We can also obtain the errors for the original data by using the following commands:

```
-->yh = horner(y,x)
 yh  =

!     .1458182  !
!     .2989697  !
!     .4521212  !
!     .6052727  !
!     .7584242  !
!     .9115758  !
!    1.0647273  !
!    1.2178788  !
!    1.3710303  !
!    1.5241818  !

-->e = Y-yh
  e  =

!     .0341818  !
!     .0710303  !
!  -  .1021212  !
!     .1747273  !
!  -  .1984242  !
!  -  .1615758  !
!     .1152727  !
!     .1421212  !
!  -  .2010303  !
!     .1258182  !
```

Other Linearized Data Fittings

The table below shows other functions that can easily be linearized and their coefficients obtained by using the *PolyFit* function with n = 1.

Type of Fitting	Actual Model	Linearized Model	Independent variable ξ	Dependent Variable η
Linear	$y = a + bx$	$y = a + bx$ [same]	x	y
Logarithmic	$y = a + b \ln(x)$	$y = a + b \ln(x)$ [same]	$\ln(x)$	y
Exponential	$y = a\, e^{bx}$	$\ln(y) = \ln(a) + bx$	x	$\ln(y)$
Power	$y = a\, x^b$	$\ln(y) = \ln(a) + b \ln(x)$	$\ln(x)$	$\ln(y)$
Simplified polynom.	$y = a + bx^m$	$y = a + bx^m$ [same]	x^m	y
Reciprocal linear	$y = 1/(a+bx)$	$1/y = a + bx$	x	$1/y$

The functions listed can be re-written as

$$\eta = a + b\xi,$$

by using the variable transformation shown above. Other combinations of variables can also be linearized, for example, $y = 1/(a+bx^m)$, and $y = a + b\,(lnx)^m$.

For example, fit an expression of the form $y = a + bx^2$, to the following data:

X	Y
0	100
110	90
180	80
250	60
300	40
340	20

Use the variables $\xi = x^2$ and $\eta = y$. The following SCILAB commands will perform the linear fitting:

```
-->x = [0;110;180;250;300;340]
 x  =

!    0.   !
!   110.  !
!   180.  !
!   250.  !
!   300.  !
!   340.  !

-->Y = [100;90;80;60;40;20]
 Y  =
!   100.  !
!    90.  !
!    80.  !
!    60.  !
!    40.  !
!    20.  !

-->x2 = x^2
 x2 =
!      0.    !
!   12100.   !
!   32400.   !
!   62500.   !
!   90000.   !
!  115600.   !
```

```
-->b = PolyFit(x2,Y,1)
 b  =

!   100.35736  !
! -   .0006786  !

-->y = poly(b,'x','coeff')
 y  =

    100.35736 -  .0006786x
```

Interpolation with splines

The term *splines* or *spline curves* refers to a technique by which a set of points $\{(x_1,y_1), (x_2,y_2), ..., (x_n,y_n)\}$ are fitted with a series of functions (typically, cubic polynomials) that satisfy continuity of the functions and some of their derivatives at the points being fitted. The term *spline* is borrowed from instruments used to fit a continuous smooth shape through a number of points in drafting. A *spline* or *French curve* consists of a flexible ruler that a draftsman can mold to fit points in paper.

Cubic splines

The method of cubic splines consists in fitting a number of cubic polynomials of the form

$$y = f_k(x) = b_0 + b_1 x + b_2 x^2 + b_3 x^3,$$

through the data set $\{(x_1,y_1), (x_2,y_2), ..., (x_n,y_n)\}$, requiring that not only the functions $f_k(x)$ but also their first and second derivatives,

$$s = f_k'(x) = b_1 + 2b_2 x + 3b_3 x^2,$$

and

$$\kappa = f_k''(x) = 2b_2 + 6b_3 x,$$

be continuous at the "interior" points $(x_2,y_2), (x_3,y_3), ..., (x_{n-1},y_{n-1})$. The first derivatives $f'(x)$ are referred to as the *slope* and the second derivatives as the *curvature* of the data fitting.

Suppose that we seek $n-1$ cubic polynomials to fit the n data points $\{(x_1,y_1), (x_2,y_2), ..., (x_n,y_n)\}$. Because each cubic polynomial requires 4 coefficients to be determined, we have a total of $4(n-1) = 4n-4$ unknowns. To satisfy continuity of the fitting function, we let polynomial number 1, $f_1(x)$, fit the data through points x_1, and x_2, polynomial number 2, $f_2(x)$, through points x_2, and x_3, and so on. Thus, there are two data values that satisfy each of the $n-1$ polynomials, i.e., $y_1 = f_1(x_1)$, $y_2 = f_1(x_1)$, $y_2 = f_2(x_2)$, $y_3 = f_2(x_3)$, ..., $y_{n-1} = f_{n-2}(x_{n-1})$, $y_{n-1} = f_{n-1}(x_{n-1})$, and $y_n = f_{n-1}(x_n)$. These results constitute a total of $2(n-1)$ equations.

Continuity of the slope at the interior points requires that $f'_1(x_2) = f'_2(x_2)$, $f'_2(x_2) = f'_3(x_2),...,$ $f'_{n-2}(x_{n-1}) = f'_{n-1}(x_{n-1})$, which adds an additional $n-2$ equations to the system. An additional set of $n-2$ equations result from continuity of curvature at the interior points, i.e. $f''_1(x_2) = f''_2(x_2)$, $f''_2(x_2) = f''_3(x_2),..., f''_{n-2}(x_{n-1}) = f''_{n-1}(x_{n-1})$. At this point, we count with $2(n-1) + 2(n-2) = 4n-6$

equations for the 4n-4 unknown coefficients. Therefore, we need to come up with two additional equations to uniquely solve for all the unknown coefficients.

There are several options for the additional two equations including:

- Set the slope of the fitting curve at the extreme points $x = x_1$ and $x = x_n$ to fixed values, i.e., $f'_1(x_1) = h_1$ and $f'_{n-1}(x_n) = h_n$.
- Use zero curvature at the extreme points, i.e. $f''_1(x_1) = f''_{n-1}(x_n) = 0$.
- Make the curvature at the extreme points equal to that of the closest points, i.e., $f''_1(x_1) = f''_1(x_2)$ and $f''_{n-1}(x_{n-1}) = f''_{n-1}(x_n)$.
- Use a linear extrapolation of the curvature at points x_2 and x_3 to get the curvature at point x_1, and a linear extrapolation of the curvature at points x_{n-2} and x_{n-1} to get the curvature at point x_n.
- Make the third derivative of the cubic polynomials, $f_k'''(x) = 6b_3$, continuous at points x_2 and x_{n-1}, i.e., $f_1'''(x_2) = f_2'''(x_2)$, and $f_{n-2}'''(x_{n-1}) = f_{n-1}'''(x_{n-1})$. This condition ensures continuity of the fitting function and all its derivatives not only at the interior points but also at the extreme points, making the fitting function, in fact, periodic.

SCILAB functions for cubic splines

SCILAB provides functions *splin* and *interp* to obtain the spline fitting of a set of data and to interpolate data after the spline fitting is completed. Function *splin* requires as input data vectors x and y, and returns a vector of derivatives of the fitting function. The general form of the function call is

$$d = splin(x, y [, "periodic"])$$

The optional argument "*periodic*" is used when a periodic spline function is sought.

Function *interp* is used after function *splin* has been invoked to produce values of the fitted function y, as well as values of the first, second, and third derivatives, if needed, for a vector of values xd. The general call to the function is:

$$[y0 [,y1 [,y2 [,y3]]]] = interp(xd, x, y, d)$$

Notice that all the terms in the left-hand side of the call are optional. These terms represent the data fitting ($y0$), first derivatives ($y1$), second derivatives ($y2$), and third derivatives ($y3$).

An example of application of functions *splin* and *interp* is shown next using the data in the following table:

x	0.0	1.2	3.5	4.2	6.2	8.1	11.2
y	15.0	29.0	13.3	-6.4	2.9	17.1	-8.0

First, we define the data vectors and use function *splin* to get the derivatives of the fitting functions:

```
-->x = [0.0,1.2,3.5,4.2,6.2,8.1,11.2]
 x  =

!   0.    1.2    3.5    4.2    6.2    8.1    11.2 !
```

```
-->y = [15.0,29.0,13.3,-6.4,2.9,17.1,-8.0]
 y  =

 !   15.     29.     13.3  - 6.4    2.9    17.1   - 8. !

-->//simple spline

-->d = splin(x,y)
 d =
         column 1 to 5

 !   13.47637    8.3035909   - 27.66225   - 21.025873    13.960103 !

         column 6 to 7

 !   1.2037304  - 16.821038 !
```

To produce the curve representing the fitting spline curve we generate x data in the range (0,11.2) and use function *interp* to generate the fitted data:

```
-->xx = [0:0.1:11.2];

-->[y0,y1,y2,y3] = interp(xx,x,y,d);
```

To produce the plot we need to know about the minimum and maximum values in the plotting rectangle:

```
-->min(y),max(y)
 ans  =  - 8.
 ans  =    29.

-->min(y0), max(y0)
 ans  = - 11.862191
 ans  =   32.468457
```

Based on the minimum and maximum values of the original data x,y and of the fitted data y0 we select the following plotting rectangle:

```
-->rect = [0 -12 12 40]
 rect  =

 !   0.   - 12.    12.    40. !
```

A plot of the fitted spline and the original data follows:

```
-->plot2d(xx,y0,9,'011','y',rect)

-->xset('mark',-9,1)

-->plot2d(x,y,-9,'010','y',rect)

-->xtitle('Cubic spline fitting','x','y')
```

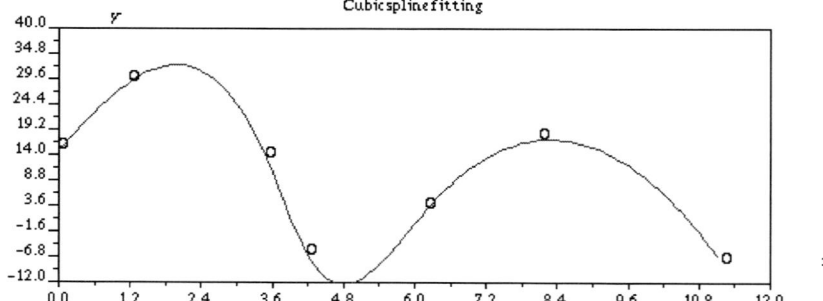

If we want to fit a periodic spline to the original data we need to have the first and last values in the y data set be the same:

```
-->y
y =

!    15.     29.     13.3   - 6.4    2.9     17.1   - 8. !

-->y(7) = y(1)
y =

!    15.     29.     13.3   - 6.4    2.9     17.1    15. !
```

The following SCILAB commands produce the spline fitting and the corresponding graph:

```
-->d = splin(x,y,'periodic')
d =
         column 1 to 5

!   8.6838537    9.9142635   - 27.872184   - 20.968424    14.116738 !

         column 6 to 7

!    .5382762    8.6838537 !

-->xx = [0:0.1:11.2];

-->[y0,y1,y2,y3] = interp(xx,x,y,d);

-->plot2d(xx,y0,9,'011','y',rect)

-->xset('mark',-9,1)

-->plot2d(x,y,-9,'010','y',rect)

-->xtitle('Periodic cubic spline fitting','x','y')
```

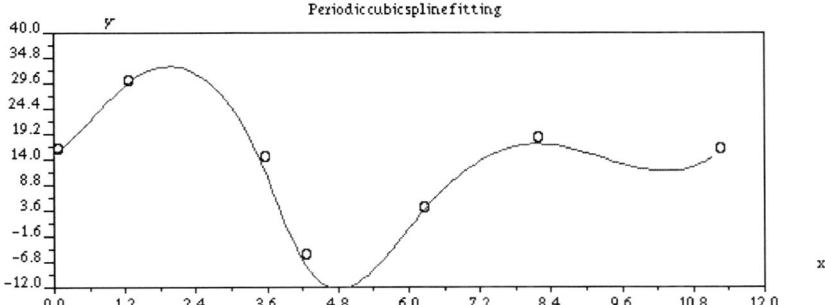
Periodic cubic spline fitting

The function *smooth*

Function smooth is used to generate a data set (x_1, ys_1), $(x_2 = x_1 + \Delta x, ys_2)$, $(x_2 = x_1 + 2\Delta x, ys_3)$, ..., (x_n, ys_n) from a cubic spline fitting $ys = f(x)$ based on the data set $\{(x_1, y_1), (x_2, y_2), ..., (x_n, y_n)\}$. The general call to the function is

[xy_Fitted_Data]=smooth(xy_Original_Table [,step])

xy_Original_Table is a two-row matrix with the first row containing the values of and the second row containing the values of *y* from the original data set, *step* is the value of Δx that generates a set of values of *x* for the fitted data. The *x* data generated consists of values $x_1 + \Delta x$, $x_2 + \Delta x$, ..., etc. If no value of *step* is provided, SCILAB uses a default value that generates 100 data points for *x*. The *y* data generated by function *smooth* follows a cubic spline fitting. The (x,y) data generated by function *smooth* is returned in the form of a two-row matrix with the first row corresponding to values of x and the second row corresponding to values of y.

The application of function *smooth* is equivalent to the application of functions *splin* and *interp* for the range of values of *x* in the original data table. The following example shows how to fit the following data through cubic splines by applying function *smooth*:

x	1.2	4.2	6.2	11.2	12.5	13.9	14.1	15.6	16.5	18.4
y	32.3	-4.2	13.6	-1.7	2.8	22.1	29.7	11.5	14.3	18.5

First, we enter the data for x and y:

```
-->x = [1.2,4.2,6.2,11.2,12.5,13.9,14.1,15.6,16.5,18.4];

-->y = [32.3,-4.2,13.6,-1.7,2.8,22.1,29.7,11.5,14.3,18.5];
```

Next, we put together the matrix *xy_Original_Table* as a two-row matrix:

```
-->xy_Original_Table = [x;y]
 xy_Original_Table  =
```

```
           column  1 to 8

!   1.2      4.2      6.2      11.2     12.5     13.9     14.1     15.6 !
!  32.3    - 4.2    13.6    - 1.7      2.8     22.1     29.7     11.5 !

           column   9 to 10

!  16.5    18.4 !
!  14.3    18.5 !
```

To generate the fitted data use:

`-->xy_Fitted_Data = smooth(xy_Original_Table,0.1);`

Next, we separate the rows of data into vectors xx and yy:

`-->xx=xy_Fitted_Data(1,:); yy = xy_Fitted_Data(2,:);`

To determine the plot rectangle to use, we get information on the minimum and maximum values of xx and yy:

```
-->min(xx),max(xx),min(yy),max(yy)
 ans  =      .2
 ans  =    18.4
 ans  =  - 7.8229563
 ans  =   34.685766

-->rect = [0 -10 20 40]
 rect  = !   0.   - 10.    20.     40. !
```

The following commands plot the original and the fitted data in the same set of axes:

```
-->xset('mark',-9,1)
-->plot2d(x,y,-9,'011',' ',rect)
-->plot2d(xx,yy,1,'010',' ',rect)
-->xtitle('Spline through use of function smooth','x','y')
```

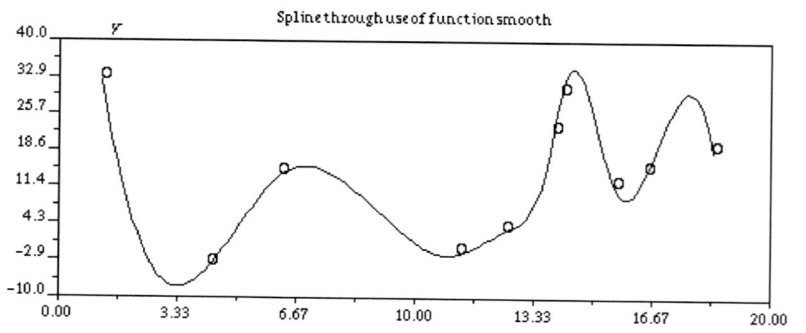

Obtaining the spline polynomials

The user-defined function *splinepol*, listed below, can be used to generate the $n-1$ cubic polynomials that constitute the spline fitting for a data set $\{(x_1,y_1), (x_2,y_2),...,(x_n,y_n)\}$. The function requires as input the vectors *x* and *y* containing the data set, as well as the vector of derivatives *d* obtained from function *splin*, i.e., $d = splin(x,y)$ or $d = splin(x,y,'periodic')$. Also, the user must provide a polynomial variable (*var*), say 'x', 's', etc., to generate the polynomials.

The general call to this function is

$$[ps] = splinepol(x,y,d,var)$$

A listing of the function is provided next:

```
function [ps] = splinepol(x,y,d,var)

//Produces the (n-1) cubic splines that fit the
//data set [(x1,y1),(x2,y2),...,(xn,yn)] of size n.
//Input to the function consists of vectors x, y, d
//and polynomial variable var, where
//    x = [x1,x2,...,xn], y = [y1,y2,...,yn].
//Vector d results from the application of function
//splin: d = splin(x,y) or d = splin(x,y,'periodic')

[y0,y1,y2,y3] = interp(x,x,y,d);

n = length(x);

yy0=y0(2:n);yy1=y1(2:n);yy2=y2(2:n);yy3=y3(2:n);
xx = x(2:n);

a = zeros(n-1,4);

a(:,4) = yy3./6;
a(:,3) = (yy2-6.*a(:,4).*xx')./2;
a(:,2) = yy1-2.*a(:,3).*xx'-3.*a(:,4).*xx'.^2;
a(:,1) = yy0'-a(:,2).*xx'-a(:,3).*xx'.^2-a(:,4).*xx'.^3;

ps = zeros(n-1,1);

for j = 1:n-1
    ps(j) = poly(a(j,:),var,'coeff');
end;

//end of function splinepol
```

To accompany function *splinepol* we also create the following function *intersplin*, to interpolate data out of the polynomials *ps* generated with *splinepol*. The general call to function *intersplin* is

$$[yy] = intersplin(xx,x,ps)$$

where *xx* is a vector containing the values of x for the interpolation, x is a vector of *n* elements representing the original x data used in generating the *n-1* cubic polynomials listed in vector *ps*. The function returns values of y in vector *yy* of length n.

A listing of function *intersplin* follows:

```
function [yy] = intersplin(xx,x,ps)

//interpolates spline polynomials in the range given
//by vector xx.  The spline polynomials are
//passed to the function as a column vector
//of polynomials (as generated by function
//splinepol).  Vector x represents the original
//x data from which the polynomials were generated.

n = length(x);
m = length(xx);

yy = [];

for i = 1:m
        if xx(i) <= x(1) | xx(i) >= x(n) then
            yy = [yy 0];
        else
            for j = 1:n-1
                if xx(i)>x(j) & xx(i)<=x(j+1) then
                    yy = [yy horner(ps(j),xx(i))];
                end;
            end;
        end;
end;
```

The purpose of including function *splinpol* is to provide a way to list the cubic polynomials for a given spline data fitting. The purpose of function *intersplin* is to be able to interpolate those polynomials to check the data fitting. The results out of function *intersplin* are not different of those generated with SCILAB function *interp*, as will be demonstrated in the following examples.

In the examples that follow, we take vectors *x* and *y*, of the same length, and generate the vector of derivatives *d* from function *splin*. Next, we interpolate data for y (vector *yy*) using function *interp* given a vector *xx*. We also use function *splinpol* to generate the cubic polynomials corresponding to the spline fitting, and interpolate values of y (vector *yy*) using function *intersplin*. Finally, we produce a joint plot of the original data (circles), the data from *interp* (continuous line), and the data from *intersplin* (crosses), to verify that the results provided by the polynomials generated with *splinpol* coincide with those generated through SCILAB functions *interp*. Two examples are presented, one for a non-periodic spline and one for a periodic spline.

First, we load functions splinepol and intersplin:

```
-->getf('splinepol')

-->getf('intersplin')
```

The (x,y) data used for a non-periodic spline fitting are generated with

```
-->x = [0.5:0.5:5]
 x  = !    .5    1.    1.5    2.    2.5    3.    3.5    4.    4.5    5. !

-->y = [0.2 1.4 2.3 1.0 0.4 -0.6 -1.0 -0.5 0.2 1.2]
```

```
y = !    .2    1.4    2.3    1.    .4  -  .6  - 1.  -  .5    .2    1.2 !
```

Next, we produce the spline fitting and generate information for the plot:

```
-->d = splin(x,y);              //vector of derivatives

-->xx = [0:0.1:5];              //values of x for interpolation

-->yy = interp(xx,x,y,d);       //values of y from interp

-->ps = splinepol(x,y,d,'x')    //cubic spline polynomials
 ps  =

!                                 2              3 !
!   2.2156991 - 9.5908966x + 13.462796x - 4.6875988x  !
!                                                     !
!                                 2              3 !
!   2.2156991 - 9.5908966x + 13.462796x - 4.6875988x  !
!                                                     !
!                                 2             3  !
! - 41.408176 + 77.656853x - 44.70237x + 8.2379938x   !
!                                                     !
!                                 2             3  !
!   65.010787 - 81.971591x + 35.111852x - 5.0643765x  !
!                                                     !
!                                 2             3  !
! - 64.424974 + 73.351323x - 27.017314x + 3.2195122x  !
!                                                     !
!                                 2            3  !
!   17.471007 - 8.5446582x +  .2813466x +  .1863277x  !
!                                                     !
!                                 2           3  !
!   92.551597 - 72.89945x + 18.66843x - 1.5648231x    !
!                                                     !
!                                 2            3  !
! - 37.866816 + 24.914359x - 5.7850223x + .4729646x   !
!                                                     !
!                                 2            3  !
! - 37.866816 + 24.914359x - 5.7850223x + .4729646x   !

-->yyy = intersplin(xx,x,ps);    //interpolating using polynomials

-->min([y yy yyy]), max([y yy yyy])  //determining values for plot
 ans  = - 1.0050396
 ans  =   2.3127536

-->rect = [0 -2 5 4];            //define plot rectangle
```

The next SCILAB commands produce the required plot:

```
-->plot2d(xx,yy,1,'011',' ',rect)

-->xset('mark',-9,1)

-->plot2d(x,y,-9,'011',' ',rect)

-->plot2d(xx,yyy,-1,'011',' ',rect)
```

```
-->xtitle('Spline fittin -- interp + interspline','x','y')
```

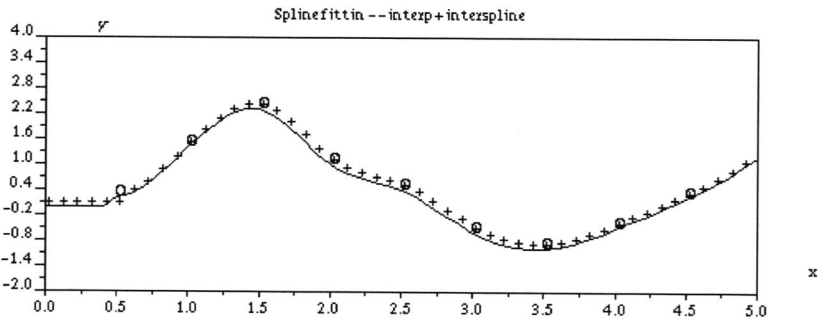

Next, we modify the data in y to produce a periodic spline fitting:

```
-->x
 x  = !   .5    1.   1.5    2.    2.5    3.    3.5    4.    4.5    5. !

-->y
 y  = !   .2   1.4   2.3    1.    .4  -  .6  - 1.  -  .5    .2    1.2 !

-->y(10) = y(1)
 y  = !   .2   1.4   2.3    1.    .4  -  .6  - 1.  -  .5    .2    .2 !
```

Next, we generate the vector of derivatives using *splin*, and interpolate data using *interp*, *splinepol*, and *intersplin*:

```
-->d = splin(x,y,'periodic');

-->xx = [0:0.1:5];

-->yy = interp(xx,x,y,d);

-->ps = splinepol(x,y,d,'x')
 ps  =

!                           2                3 !
!   1.2431373 - 5.8509804x + 9.0509804x - 3.0431373x  !
!                                                     !
!                            2                 3 !
!   3.3294118 - 12.109804x + 15.309804x - 5.1294118x  !
!                                                     !
!                           2            3           !
! - 42.2 + 78.94902x - 45.396078x + 8.3607843x        !
!                                                     !
!                             2            3 !
!   65.596078 - 82.745098x + 35.45098x - 5.1137255x   !
!                                                     !
!                             2             3 !
! - 65.776471 + 74.901961x - 27.607843x + 3.2941176x  !
!                                                     !
```

```
!                                   2               3 !
!    24.858824 - 15.733333x + 2.6039216x - .0627451x !
!                                                    !
!                                   2               3 !
!    49.743137 - 37.062745x + 8.6980392x - .6431373x !
!                                                    !
!                                   2               3 !
!    198.32353 - 148.49804x + 36.556863x - 2.9647059x !
!                                                    !
!                                   2               3 !
! -  554.97647 + 353.70196x - 75.043137x + 5.3019608x !
```

```
-->yyy = intersplin(xx,x,ps);
```

The following SCILAB commands produce the comparative plot:

```
-->plot2d(xx,yy,1,'011',' ',rect)
-->xset('mark',-9,1)
-->plot2d(x,y,-9,'011',' ',rect)
-->plot2d(xx,yyy,-1,'011',' ',rect)
-->xtitle('Spline fitting/periodic function -- interp + interspline','x','y')
```

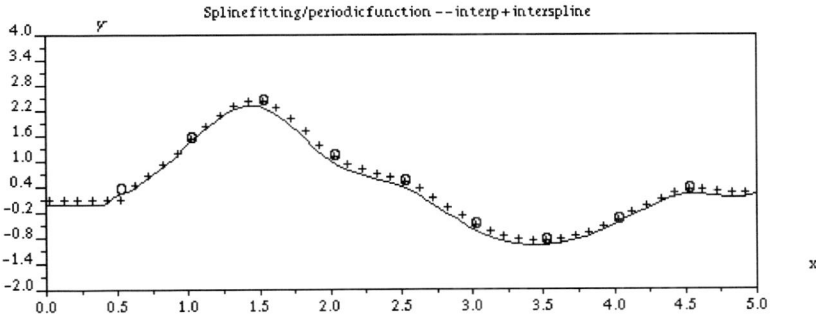

Multi-variate data fitting

In this section we consider interpolation and fitting of the data in a table of values, (x_i, z_{ij}), for $i=1,2,...,n$; $j=1,2,...,m$, through a function $z = f(x,y)$. A typical table will look as follows:

x\y	y_1	y_2	...	y_j	...	y_m
x_1	z_{11}	z_{12}	...	z_{1j}	...	z_{1m}
x_2	z_{21}	z_{22}	...	z_{2j}	...	z_{2m}
:	:	:		:	:	:
x_i	z_{i1}	z_{i2}	...	z_{ij}	...	z_{im}
:	:	:		:	:	:
x_n	z_{n1}	z_{n2}	...	z_{nj}	...	z_{nm}

Successive univariate polynomial interpolation

By successive univariate polynomial interpolation we mean to interpolate data by columns of the table first, and then by rows using a univariate polynomial in each direction. For example, we can select polynomials of order k to fit data for the columns of the table, i.e.,

$$ZC_j(x) = a_{0j} + a_{1j}x + a_{2j}x^2 + \ldots + a_{kj}x^k,$$

for $j = 1,2,\ldots,m$. Quadratic polynomials to fit data for the rows of the table would have the form

$$ZR_i(y) = a_{i0} + a_{i1}y + a_{i2}y^2 + \ldots + a_{ik}y^k,$$

for $i = 1,2,\ldots,n$.

If we are interested in interpolating the value of the function $z = f(x,y)$ for $x = x_r$ and $y = y_s$, we can start by first generating the polynomial fittings $ZC_j(x) = a_{0j} + a_{1j}x + a_{2j}x^2 + \ldots + a_{kj}x^k$, for $j = 1,2,\ldots,m$. From these fittings we can get the data set $\{zc_1, zc_2, \ldots, zc_m\}$, where $zc_j = ZC_j(x_r)$. Next, we attempt a fitting of the form $ZR(y) = a_{i0} + a_{i1}y + a_{i2}y^2 + \ldots + a_{ik}y^k$, using the data set $\{(y_1,zc_1), (y_2,zc_2),\ldots,(y_m,zc_m)\}$. The value we are searching for is $z = f(x_r,y_s) = ZR(y_s)$.

Consider, for example, the following table of values $z = f(x,y)$:

x \ y	12.00	13.00	14.00
2.00	71.09	76.94	81.70
3.00	77.07	82.13	87.34
4.00	85.22	91.63	96.67

Suppose that we want to interpolate the value of z for $x = 2.5$, $y = 13.2$, using quadratic polynomials in both directions. We start by loading the vectors x and y and the table of values z:

```
-->x = [2,3,4];y=[12,13,14];
-->z = [71.09,76.94,81.70;77.07,82.13,87.34;85.22,91.63,96.67];
```

A plot of the z data can be obtained by using:
```
-->plot3d(x,y,z)
```

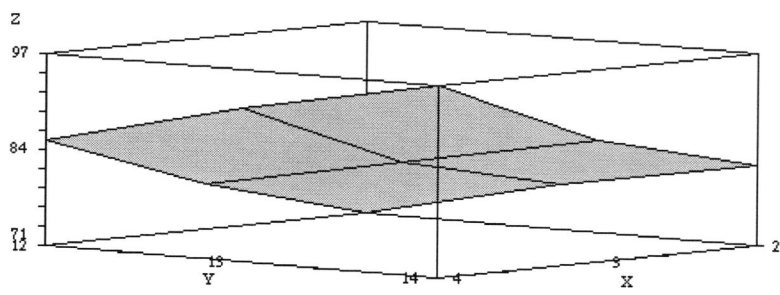

The first step in the successive univariate polynomial fitting requires using function *dfp* (*direct polynomial fitting*) to fit quadratic equations by columns. The polynomials corresponding to rows 1, 2, and 3 are called *p1(x)*, *p2(x)*, and *p3(x)*, respectively. The coefficients of each of these polynomials results from the use of function *dfp* for the data in vector *x* (passed on to the function as a column vector, i.e., *x'*) and the data in the corresponding columns of the table, i.e., *z(:,1)*, *z(:,2)*, and *z(:,3)*.

```
-->[a1] = dfp(x',z(:,1)), p1 = poly(a1,'xx','coeff')
 a1  =

!   65.64      .555      1.085 !
 p1  =

                              2
     65.64  +  .555xx + 1.085xx

-->[a2] = dfp(x',z(:,2)), p2 = poly(a2,'xx','coeff')
 a2  =

!   79.49   - 5.585      2.155 !
 p2  =

                              2
     79.49  - 5.585xx + 2.155xx

-->[a3] = dfp(x',z(:,3)), p3 = poly(a3,'xx','coeff')
 a3  =

!   81.49   - 3.585      1.845 !
 p3  =

                              2
     81.49  - 3.585xx + 1.845xx
```

After obtaining the polynomial fittings per column, we proceed to generate the data *zc* corresponding to x = 2.5, by using:

```
-->zc(1)=horner(p1,2.5);zc(2)=horner(p2,2.5);zc(3)=horner(p3,2.5); zc
 zc =

!   73.80875    78.99625    84.05875 !
```

These data are next fit to a quadratic polynomial on y:

```
-->b = dfp(y',zc'), zz = poly(b,'yy','coeff')
 b  =

!   1.80875    6.75    - .0625 !
 zz =

                              2
     1.80875 + 6.75yy - .0625yy
```

The evaluation of the resulting polynomial, zz(y), for y = 13.2, will produce the required interpolation:

```
-->zfit = horner(zz,13.2)
 zfit  =

    80.01875
```

The interpolation performed above can be repeated by first fitting data by rows, i.e., generating polynomials p1(y), p2(y), and p3(y) corresponding to the rows of the table. A data set zc is then generated by evaluating these polynomials for y = 13.2. Fitting data to the data sets x and zc produces a polynomial zz(x) which is then evaluated at x = 2.5 to obtain the desired result. The corresponding SCILAB commands are shown next:

```
-->x = [2,3,4];y=[12,13,14];

-->z = [71.09,76.94,81.70;77.07,82.13,87.34;85.22,91.63,96.67];

-->[b1] = dfp(y',z(1,:)'), p1 = poly(b1,'yy','coeff')
 b1  =

!  - 84.13      19.475   -   .545 !
 p1  =

                              2
   - 84.13 + 19.475yy -  .545yy

-->[b2] = dfp(y',z(2,:)'), p2 = poly(b2,'yy','coeff')
 b2  =

!    28.05      3.185        .075 !
 p2  =

                              2
     28.05 + 3.185yy +   .075yy

-->[b3] = dfp(y',z(3,:)'), p3 = poly(b3,'yy','coeff')

 b3  =

!  - 98.56      23.535   -   .685 !
 p3  =

                              2
   - 98.56 + 23.535yy -  .685yy

-->zc(1)=horner(p1,13.2);zc(2)=horner(p2,13.2);zc(3)=horner(p3,13.);zc
 zc  =

!    77.9792    83.16       91.63 !

-->a = dfp(x',zc'), zz = poly(a,'xx','coeff')
 a  =

!    77.4852  - 3.0422     1.6446 !
 zz  =

                              2
     77.4852 - 3.0422xx + 1.6446xx
```

```
-->z_fit = horner(zz,2.5)
  z_fit =

     80.15845
```

The interpolation results obtained through the two approaches shown above are z = 80.01875 and z = 80.15845. Although they are very close to each other, they are not exactly the same as expected. You may report as the final interpolation the average of these two results, namely, z = (80.01875 +80.15845)/2 = 80.0886.

Notes:
[1] Function *dfp* requires that the vectors of data used in the direct polynomial fitting be passed to the function as column vectors.
[2] The degree of the polynomial whose coefficients are returned by function *dfp* is n-1 where n is the length of the vectors *x* or *y* passed to the function. Therefore, the 3x3 table of data used in the examples above had the right size for quadratic polynomial fittings.
[3] Polynomial fittings for any polynomial order can be obtained if we use function *polyfit* instead of *dfp*.

Direct multivariate polynomial fitting

Direct multivariate polynomial fitting is a generalization of the direct (univariate) polynomial fitting presented earlier in the chapter. We will use a very general multivariate polynomial function of degree *n* given by:

$$z = f(x,y) = a_0 + a_1 x + a_2 y + a_3 x^2 + a_4 xy + a_5 y^2 + a_6 x^3 + a_7 x^2 y + a_8 xy^2 + a_9 y^3 + \ldots$$

The degree of the polynomial for direct fitting is determined by the number of data values available. For example, for the table used in the previous example:

x \ y	12.00	13.00	14.00
2.00	71.09	76.94	81.70
3.00	77.07	82.13	87.34
4.00	85.22	91.63	96.67

which contains nine entries, we can, in principle, fit a function with nine coefficients. One possibility is to use:

$$z = f(x,y) = a_0 + a_1 x + a_2 y + a_3 x^2 + a_4 xy + a_5 y^2 + a_6 x^3 + a_7 x^2 y + a_9 y^3$$

However, the matrix of data for the linear system that results from replacing values *x* and *y* in the equation, is an ill-conditioned matrix (i.e., a singular matrix or a matrix close to singularity). Thus, direct multivariate polynomial fitting fails for this case.

One alternative is to try to fit a simpler function, say,

$$z = f(x,y) = a_0 + a_1 x + a_2 y + a_3 xy,$$

using only four data points from the table. Suppose that we use the following data points:

1. $x = 2, y = 12, z = 71.09$, $a_0 + 2a_1 + 12a_2 + 24a_3 = 71.09$
2. $x = 3, y = 12, z = 85.22$, $a_0 + 3a_1 + 12a_2 + 36a_3 = 77.07$
3. $x = 2, y = 14, z = 81.70$, $a_0 + 2a_1 + 14a_2 + 28a_3 = 81.70$
4. $x = 4, y = 14, z = 96.67$, $a_0 + 4a_1 + 14a_2 + 56a_3 = 71.09$

The solution to the linear system that results is obtained using SCILAB as follows:

```
-->A = [1,2,12,24;1,3,12,36;1,2,14,28;1,4,14,56]     //Matrix of coefficients
 A  =

!    1.    2.    12.    24. !
!    1.    3.    12.    36. !
!    1.    2.    14.    28. !
!    1.    4.    14.    56. !

-->det(A)                         //Verifying that the matrix is not singular
 ans  = 8.

-->b = [71.09;77.07;81.70;71.09]
 b  =

!    71.09 !
!    77.07 !
!    81.7  !
!    71.09 !

-->a = A\b                        //Function coefficients
 a  =

!  - 139.95 !
!    73.69  !
!    16.59  !
!  - 5.6425 !

-->deff('[z]=f(x,y)','z=a(1)+a(2)*x+a(3)*y+a(4)*x*y')     //Defining function

-->[f(2,12),f(3,12),f(2,14),f(4,14)]'                     //Verifying solution
 ans  =

!    71.09 !
!    77.07 !
!    81.7  !
!    71.09 !
```

Least-square multivariate polynomial fitting

The method of least-squares presented earlier for univariate polynomials can be generalized for a multivariate polynomial fitting. For example, a simple multivariate linear fitting given by

$$z = a_0 + a_1 x + a_2 y,$$

produces a sum-of-squared-errors given by

$$SSE(a_0, a_1, a_2) = \sum_{i=1}^{n} (z_i - a_0 - a_1 x - a_2 y)^2.$$

To minimize function SSE, we set up the equations $\partial(SSE)/\partial a_0 = 0$, $\partial(SSE)/\partial a_1 = 0$, and $\partial(SSE)/\partial a_2 = 0$, which result in the set of equations:

$$a_0 n + a_1 \Sigma x_i + a_2 \Sigma y_i = \Sigma z_i$$
$$a_0 \Sigma x_i + a_1 \Sigma x_i^2 + a_2 \Sigma x_i y_i = \Sigma x_i z_i$$
$$a_0 \Sigma y_i + a_1 \Sigma x_i y_i + a_2 \Sigma y_i^2 = \Sigma y_i z_i$$

The solution to the resulting linear system provides the coefficients of the function a_0, a_1, and a_2.

For example, to fit the data in the bivariate table presented earlier, namely,

x \ y	12.00	13.00	14.00
2.00	71.09	76.94	81.70
3.00	77.07	82.13	87.34
4.00	85.22	91.63	96.67

to the proposed bivariate function $z = a_0 + a_1 x + a_2 y$, using SCILAB, we proceed as follows:

First, we define the x, y, and z data:
```
-->x = [2,3,4]; y = [12,13,14];

-->z = [71.09,76.94,81.70;77.07,82.13,87.34;85.22,91.63,96.67];
```

To calculate the summations in the set of linear equations presented above, we need to create matrices of values of x and y corresponding to the entries in the bivariate table. These matrices, called xx and yy, respectively, are determined as follows:

```
-->xx = [x',x',x']
xx  =

!   2.    2.    2. !
!   3.    3.    3. !
!   4.    4.    4. !

-->yy = [y;y;y]
yy  =

!   12.   13.   14. !
!   12.   13.   14. !
!   12.   13.   14. !
```

The next step is to produce the matrix of coefficients for the system:

```
-->A = zeros(3,3)
A  =
!   0.    0.    0. !
!   0.    0.    0. !
!   0.    0.    0. !
```

```
-->A(1,1) = n; A(1,2) = sum(xx); A(1,3) = sum(yy);

-->A(2,1) = sum(xx); A(2,2)=sum(xx^2); A(2,3) = sum(xx.*yy);

-->A(3,1) = sum(yy); A(3,2)=sum(xx.*yy); A(3,3) = sum(yy^2);

-->A
 A  =

!    9.      27.      117.   !
!   27.     243.      351.   !
!  117.     351.     4563.   !
```

The vector of right-hand side terms in the system of equations is:

```
-->b = [sum(z);sum(xx.*z);sum(yy.*z)]
 b  =
!   749.79  !
!  2293.16  !
!  9779.6   !
```

Before solving the linear system we check that the matrix is not singular:

```
-->det(A)
 ans  = 4435236.
```

The coefficients of the function are obtained by using left division:

```
-->a = A\b
 a  =
!  82.360912  !
!    .2703086 !
!    .0106279 !
```

The following is the definition of the function:

```
-->deff('[z]=f(x,y)','z=a(1)+a(2)*x+a(2)*y')
```

To evaluate the function in a grid we can use function *feval* as follows:

```
-->feval(x,y,f)
 ans  =

!  86.145233   86.415541   86.68585   !
!  86.415541   86.68585    86.956159  !
!  86.68585    86.956159   87.226467  !
```

Compared with the original values of *z* we find that the simple linear fitting does not reproduces those original values very well.

```
-->z
 z  =
```

```
!    71.09    76.94    81.7  !
!    77.07    82.13    87.34 !
!    85.22    91.63    96.67 !
```

Bivariate quadratic fitting

To improve the fitting we may want to try using a bivariate quadratic fitting given by the expression

$$z = a_0 + a_1 x + a_2 y + a_3 x^2 + a_4 xy + a_5 y^2,$$

whose sum of squared errors is given by

$$SSE(a_0, a_1, a_2) = \sum_{i=1}^{n} (z_i - a_0 - a_1 x - a_2 y - a_3 x^2 - a_4 xy - a_5 y^2)^2.$$

To minimize the function SSE, we set up the equations: $\partial(SSE)/\partial a_0 = 0$, $\partial(SSE)/\partial a_1 = 0$, $\partial(SSE)/\partial a_2 = 0$, $\partial(SSE)/\partial a_3 = 0$, $\partial(SSE)/\partial a_4 = 0$, and $\partial(SSE)/\partial a_5 =$, which result in the system:

$$\begin{aligned}
a_0 n + a_1 \Sigma x_i + a_2 \Sigma y_i + a_3 \Sigma x_i^2 + a_4 \Sigma y_i^2 + a_5 \Sigma x_i y_i &= \Sigma z_i \\
a_0 \Sigma x_i + a_1 \Sigma x_i^2 + a_2 \Sigma x_i y_i + a_3 \Sigma x_i^3 + a_4 \Sigma x_i y_i^2 + a_5 \Sigma x_i^2 y_i &= \Sigma x_i z_i \\
a_0 \Sigma y_i + a_1 \Sigma x_i y_i + a_2 \Sigma y_i^2 + a_3 \Sigma x_i^2 y_i + a_4 \Sigma y_i^3 + a_5 \Sigma x_i y_i^2 &= \Sigma y_i z_i \\
a_0 \Sigma x_i^2 + a_1 \Sigma x_i^3 + a_2 \Sigma x_i^2 y_i + a_3 \Sigma x_i^4 + a_4 \Sigma x_i^2 y_i^2 + a_5 \Sigma x_i^3 y_i &= \Sigma x_i^2 z_i \\
a_0 \Sigma y_i^2 + a_1 \Sigma x_i y_i^2 + a_2 \Sigma y_i^3 + a_3 \Sigma x_i^2 y_i^2 + a_4 \Sigma y_i^4 + a_5 \Sigma x_i y_i^3 &= \Sigma y_i^2 z_i \\
a_0 \Sigma x_i y_i + a_1 \Sigma x_i^2 y_i + a_2 \Sigma x_i y_i^2 + a_3 \Sigma x_i^3 y_i + a_4 \Sigma x_i y_i^3 + a_5 \Sigma x_i^2 y_i^2 &= \Sigma x_i y_i z_i
\end{aligned}$$

We will use the data from the table presented above to generate the coefficients for this matrix. Considering the number of evaluations involved we are going to prepare a function, *multiquad*, to produce the coefficients of the function:

```
function [a] = multiquad(xyzMatrix)

//produces the coefficients a = [a1 a2 a3 ... a6]
//from the function
//   f(x,y) = a1+a2*x+a3*y+a4*x^2+a5*x*y+a6*z^3
//xyzMatrix = [x(col1) y(col2) z(col3)]

xx = xyzMatrix(:,1);
yy = xyzMatrix(:,2);
zz = xyzMatrix(:,3);
n = length(xx);
A=zeros(6,6);
A(1,1)=n; A(1,2)=sum(xx);A(1,3)=sum(yy);A(1,4)=sum(xx^2);
A(1,5)=sum(yy^2);A(1,6)=sum(xx.*yy);
A(2,1)=A(1,2);A(2,2)=sum(xx^2);A(2,3)=sum(xx.*yy);
A(2,4)=sum(xx^3);A(2,5)=sum(xx.*(yy^2));A(2,6)=sum((xx^2).*yy);
A(3,1)=A(1,3);A(3,2)=A(2,3);A(3,3)=sum(yy^2);
A(3,4)=sum((xx^2).*yy);A(3,5)=sum(yy^3);A(3,6)=sum(xx.*(yy^2));
A(4,1)=A(1,4);A(4,2)=A(2,4);A(4,3)=A(3,4);
A(4,4)=sum(xx^4);A(4,5)=sum((xx^2).*(yy^2);
A(5,4)=A(4,5);A(5,5)=sum(yy^4);A(5,6)=sum(xx.*(yy^3));
A(6,1)=A(1,6);A(6,2)=A(2,6);A(6,3)=A(3,6);
A(6,4)=A(4,6);A(6,5)=A(5,6);A(6,6)=sum((xx^2).*(yy^2));
```

```
b=[sum(zz);sum(xx.*zz);sum(yy.*zz);sum((xx^2).*zz);sum((yy^2).*zz);sum(xx.*yy.*
zz)];
a=A\b;
disp('Coefficients in the function z = f(x,y)')
disp('z=a(1)+a(2)*x+a(3)*y+a(4)*x^2+a(5)*x*y+a(6)*y^2')

//end function multiquad
```

The function requires as input a matrix of three columns where the columns correspond to values of x, y, and z.

In the following example, we use function *multiquad* to produce a fitting of the form

$$z = a_0 + a_1 x + a_2 y + a_3 x^2 + a_4 xy + a_5 y^2,$$

for the data in the table below:

x \ y	700	800	900
9000	0.031980	0.037948	0.043675
10000	0.028345	0.033827	0.039053
11000	0.025360	0.030452	0.035270

First, we prepare the matrix of data:

```
-->x = [9000,10000,11000]; y = [700,800,900];

-->z = [.031980,.037948,.4675;.028345,.033827,.039053;.025360,.030452,.035270]
 z =

!    .03198      .037948     .4675     !
!    .028345     .033827     .039053   !
!    .02536      .030452     .03527    !

-->xx = [x';x';x']; yy = [y(1) y(1) y(1) y(2) y(2) y(2) y(3) y(3) y(3)]';

-->zz = [z(:,1);z(:,2);z(:,3)];

-->M = [xx yy zz]
 M  =

!    900.    700.    .03198    !
!    1000.   700.    .028345   !
!    1100.   700.    .02536    !
!    900.    800.    .037948   !
!    1000.   800.    .033827   !
!    1100.   800.    .030452   !
!    900.    900.    .4675     !
!    1000.   900.    .039053   !
!    1100.   900.    .03527    !
```

To obtain the coefficients of the data fitting, we use:

```
-->a = multiquad(M)

warning
```

```
matrix is close to singular or badly scaled.
results may be inaccurate. rcond =    1.1496E-21


Coefficients in the function z = f(x,y)

z=a(1)+a(2)*x+a(3)*y+a(4)*x^2+a(5)*x*y+a(6)*y^2
 a  =

 !    3.2238377  !
 ! -   .0006434  !
 !     .0001190  !
 !    7.101E-08  !
 !     .0000071  !
 ! -   .0000011  !
```

To check how well the fitting reproduces the data we use:

```
-->deff('[z]=f(x,y)','z=a(1)+a(2)*x+a(3)*y+a(4)*x^2+a(5)*x*y+a(6)*y^2')

-->feval(x,y,f)
 ans  =

 !   47.167934    53.366045    59.542874  !
 !   52.809383    59.712584    66.594503  !
 !   58.592852    66.201143    73.788152  !
```

Obviously, the proposed data fitting does not work very well with this data set. The reader should be advised that there is no guarantee that a given function will fit a particular data set. The purpose of using the least-square method is to minimize the sum of square errors, SSE, which is a measure of the overall error involved in the data fitting. However, this procedure does not ensure that the fitting will be acceptable. There are statistical inference techniques that can be used as guidelines for the goodness of fit of a particular function to a given data set. These techniques are covered in a separate chapter.

SCILAB function *datafit*

Function *datafit* is used for fitting data to a model by defining an error function $e = G(p,z)$ where p is a column vector of m rows representing the parameters of the model, and z is a column vector of n rows representing the variables involved in the model. Function *datafit* finds a solution to the set of k equations

$$e_i = G(p, z_i) = 0,$$

by minimizing the functional

$$G^T(p,z_1) \cdot W \cdot G(p,z_1) + G^T(p,z_2) \cdot W \cdot G(p,z_2) + \ldots + G^T(p,z_n) \cdot W \cdot G(p,z_n),$$

where z_i, $i = 1, 2, \ldots, n$, are specific values of the vector of variables z, and W is a $k \times k$ weight matrix (default value $W = I_{k \times k}$, the identity matrix).

The simplest call to function *datafit* is

$$[p,err] = datafit(G,Z,p0)$$

where G is the name of the error function $G(p,z)$, Z is a matrix whose rows consists of the different vectors of variables, i.e. $Z = [z_1; z_2; ...; z_n]$, and $p0$ is a column vector representing initial guesses of the parameters p sought.

Example 1 - quadratic polynomial

As an example, we will generate data using the function $y = a_1 + a_2 x + a_3 x^2 + 100r$, where $a_1 = 20$, $a_2 = 30$, $a_3 = 50$, and r is a random component to be generated in SCILAB through the expression $r = 100*(rand()-0.5)$. Because function $rand$ generates uniform random numbers in the range (0,1), the values of r will be random numbers uniformly distributed in the range (-50,50). Thus, the data generated for y is based on the quadratic function $a_1 + a_2 x + a_3 x^2$, but modified by a random number in the range (-50,50). We will generate data for x in the range (0,10) with increments of 0.1, and calculate the corresponding values of y. Then, the data will be placed in a matrix Z with values of x in the first row and values of y in the second row. This matrix Z will be used in the call to function $datafit$.

The function to fit will be defined as $G(a,z) = z(2) - a(1) - a(2)*z(1) - a(3)*z(1)^2$, and we will provide an initial value for the vector of parameters a as $a0 = [10;20;30]$ for the call to function $datafit$.

The following SCILAB commands will take care of generating the data and finding the parameters a that produce the best fitting. The process by which the best fitting for the model is obtained is an iterative procedure and may take some time to produce a result. Therefore, be patient if SCILAB does not produce a result right away. Depending on the complexity of the function to be fitted or on the number data points involved $datafit$ may take up to 10 minutes to return a result.

For this example we start by defining the values of x and y that we want to fit. These are stored in vectors X and Y, which then get put together into matrix Z:

```
-->X = [0:0.1:10]; Y=20+30.*X+50.*X^2+100*(rand()-0.5); Z = [X;Y];
```

Next, we define a function $G(a,z) = y - a_1 - a_2 x - a_3 x^2$, that will be used to obtain the parameters $a = [a_1\ a_2\ a_3]$ that define the expression $y = a_1 + a_2 x + a_3 x^2$, with $z = [x\ y]^T$.

```
-->deff('[e]=G(a,z)','e=z(2)-a(1)-a(2)*z(1)-a(3)*z(1)^2')
```

Initial values of the parameters a are given by:

```
-->a0 = [10;20;30];
```

Application of function $datafit$ produces, after a few minutes, the following results for the coefficients a_i:

```
-->[aa,er] = datafit(G,Z,a0)
 er =

    3.161E-10
```

```
aa   =

!    20.644345  !
!    30.000002  !
!    50.         !
```

To verify the fitting of the data we define function $f(x)$, and produce data YY = f(X) to plot the original and fitted data:

```
-->deff('[yy]=f(x)','yy=aa(1)+aa(2)*x+aa(3)*x^2')

-->YY = f(X);

-->min([Y YY]), max([Y YY])
 ans  =

    20.644345
 ans  =

    5320.6443

-->rect = [0 0 10 5500]
 rect =

!  0.    0.    10.    5500. !

-->xset('mark',-9,1)
-->plct2d(X,YY,1,'011',' ',rect)
-->plct2d(X,Y,-9,'011',' ',rect)
-->xtitle('datafit for y = a1+a2*x+a3*x^3','x','y')
```

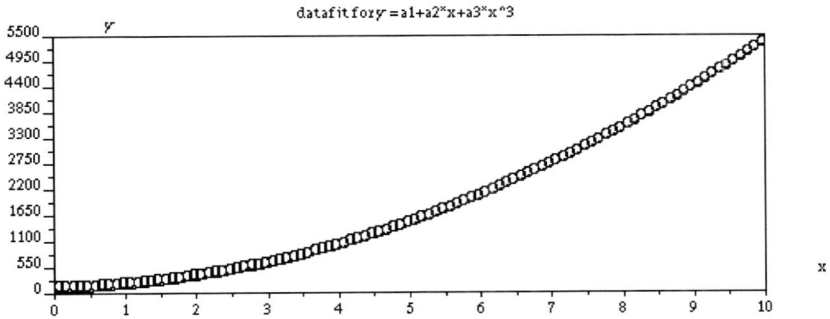

Example 2 - cubic polynomial

Suppose that we want to fit the data to a cubic polynomial, i.e., $y = a_1 + a_2 x + a_3 x^2 + a_4 x^3$, we can use the following SCILAB commands to obtain the coefficients:

```
-->deff('[e]=G(a,z)','e=z(2)-a(1)-a(2)*z(1)-a(3)*z(1)^2-a(4)*z(1)^3')
Warning :redefining function: G
```

```
-->a0 = [10;20;30;10];

-->[aa,er] = datafit(G,Z,a0)
 er =

    2.012E-07
 aa =

!   20.644456 !
!   29.999865 !
!   50.000034 !
! -  .0000023 !
```

The results indicates that the last coefficient $a_4 \approx 0$, thus, confirming that the quadratic fitting is sufficient to reproduce the data. Notice also that the error is relatively small $er = 2.012 \times 10^{-7}$, indicating a very good fitting of the data. Such a good fitting is to be expected since the data was originated from a quadratic function

Example 3 - exponential function

In this example we try to fit an exponential function of the form $m = f(x) = a_1 + a_2 \exp(a_3 x)$ to data generated out of a quadratic function. The data is obtained as follows:

```
-->X=[0:0.1:5];Y = 2.3+5.8.*X+3.2.*X^2;Z=[X;Y];
```

The next two function definitions are used to specify functions $G(a,z) = y - a_1 + a_2 \exp(a_3 x)$, with $a = [a_1; a_2; a_3]$, $z = [x;y]$, and a vector of derivatives corresponding to $= [\partial G/\partial a_1, \partial G/\partial a_2, \partial G/\partial a_3] = [-1, -\exp(a_3 x), -a_2 x \exp(a_3 x)]$:

```
-->deff('[e]=G(a,z)','e=z(2)-a(1)-a(2).*exp(a(3).*z(1))')

-->deff('[s]=DG(a,z)','s=[-1,-exp(a(3).*z(1)),-a(2).*z(1).*exp(a(3).*z(1))]')
```

Using this vector of derivatives, the call to function *datafit* is now:

```
-->[aa,er] = datafit(G,DG,Z,a0)
 er =

    2606.3157
 aa =

!   5.         !
!   4.7859729  !
!    .6494727  !
```

To verify the fitting we define the function $y = a_1 + a_2 \exp(a_3 x)$, and obtain data points corresponding to the values of x stored in X:

```
-->deff('[y]=f(x)','y=aa(1)+aa(2)*exp(aa(3)*x)')

-->YY = f(X);
```

A plot of the original data (symbols) along with the fitted data (continuous line) is obtained as follows:

```
-->plot2d(X,YY,1,'011',' ',rect)
-->plot2d(X,Y,-1,'011',' ',rect)
-->xtitle('Function data fit - y = a1+a2*exp(a3*x)','x','y')
```

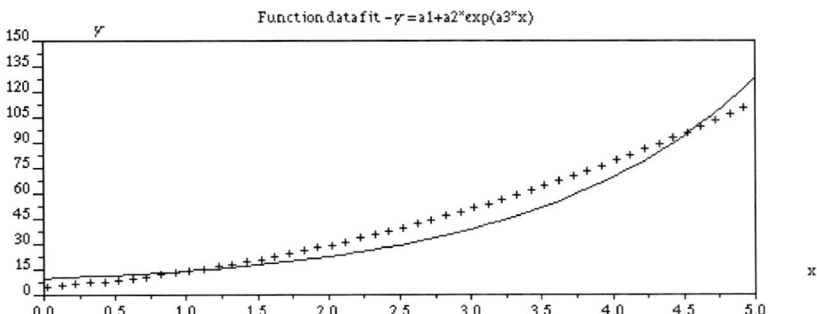

Example 4 - fitting data to a function r = f(x,y)

In this example we will attempt fitting a data set (x,y,r) to a function of the form

$$r = a_1 + a_2 x + a_3 y + a_4 x^2 + a_5 xy + a_6 y^2.$$

The function $G(a,z)$, defined below, represents $e = r - (a_1 + a_2 x + a_3 y + a_4 x^2 + a_5 xy + a_6 y^2)$.

```
-->deff('[e]=G(a,z)',...
--> 'e=a(1)+a(2)*z(1)+a(3)*z(2)+a(4)*z(1)^2+a(5)*z(1)*z(2)+a(6)*z(2)^2-z(3)')
```

The data is generated from the function $f_1(x,y) = exp(0.1x)+exp(0.2y)$, as shown next:

```
--> xx = [0:0.1:10]; yy = [0:0.1:10];
-->n = length(X), m = length(Y)
 n  = 121.
 m  = 121.
```

The following commands creates vectors of data X, Y and R, which are then put together into matrix Z:

```
-->X = []; Y = []; R = [];

-->for i = 1:n
-->    for j = 1:m
-->        X = [X xx(i)]; Y = [Y yy(j)];
-->        R = [R exp(0.1*xx(i))+exp(0.2*yy(j))];
-->    end;
-->end;
-->Z = [X;Y;R];
```

The initial value of the function parameters is given (arbitrarily) as:

```
-->a0=10*ones(6,1)
 a0  =
 !    10.  !
 !    10.  !
 !    10.  !
 !    10.  !
 !    10.  !
 !    10.  !
```

The following call to function *datafit*, which took about 5 minutes in produce a result, provides the best fitting for the parameters. Notice that the overall error is relatively small.

```
-->[a,err]=datafit(G,Z,a0)
 err  =

      1.0343445
 a  =

 !    2.1356627  !
 !     .0856497  !
 !     .0204965  !
 !     .0084165  !
 !  -  6.695E-08 !
 !     .0590437  !
```

Next, we will attempt the same calculation using derivatives of the function G(a,z) with respect to the parameters a

```
-->deff('[s]=DG(a,z)',...
-->'s=[1,z(1),z(2),z(1)^2,z(1)*z(2),z(2)^2]')
```

Using the derivatives the call to function *datafit* takes only about 1.5 minutes:

```
-->[a,err]=datafit(G,DG,Z,a0)
 err  =

      1.0343445

 a  =

 !    2.1356698  !
 !     .0856476  !
 !     .0204943  !
 !     .0084167  !
 !    0.         !
 !     .0590439  !
```

Notice the difference in value of a(5) in the two results. The next commands are used to reproduce the original data and the fitted data as three-dimensional plots:

```
-->deff('[z]=ff(x,y)','z=exp(0.1.*x)+exp(0.2.*y)')

-->deff('[r]=f(x,y)',...
```

```
-->'r=a(1)+a(2).*x+a(3).*y+a(4).*x.^2+a(5).*x.*y+a(6).*y.^2'

-->zz = feval(xx,yy,ff); zzz = feval(xx,yy,f);

-->plot3d(xx,yy,zz)

-->xtitle('original function')
```

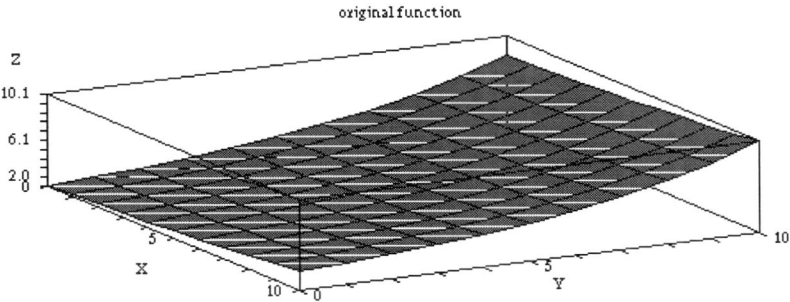

```
-->plot3d(xx,yy,zzz)

-->xtitle('fitted function')
```

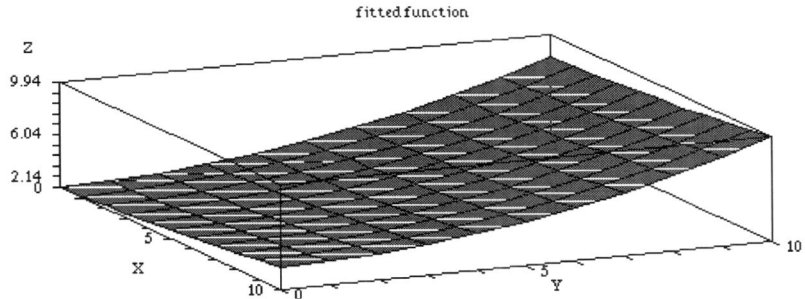

Function *datafit* provides other options for calculation which are not presented in this book. For more information use:

```
--> help datafit
```

Exercises

The following table shows values of the discharge Q (cfs) of a 1.75-ft long spillway as a function of stage (i.e., water surface elevation) above spillway crest h (ft) for a weir. The table also shows the storage available in the reservoir S (cu.ft), for the different stages.

h(ft)	Q(cfs)	S(cu.ft)
0.0	0.0	0
0.5	1.9	16641
1.0	5.4	33911
1.5	10.0	51246
2.0	15.3	69103
2.5	21.4	86901
3.0	28.2	104796
3.5	35.5	122772
4.0	43.4	140817
4.5	51.8	158924
5.0	60.7	177085
5.5	70.0	195296
6.0	79.7	213551

Use the data in this table to solve problems [1] through [14].

[1]. Use simple linear interpolation, through function *interpln*, to obtain the values of the discharge Q for stage values of h = 0.25, 0.75, 1.25, 1.75, 2.25, 2.75, 3.25, 3.75, 4.25, 4.75, 5.25, and 5.75 ft.

[2]. Use simple linear interpolation, through function *interpln*, to obtain the values of the storage S for stage values of h = 0.25, 0.75, 1.25, 1.75, 2.25, 2.75, 3.25, 3.75, 4.25, 4.75, 5.25, and 5.75 ft.

[3]. Solve problem [1] using Lagrange polynomials of order = 2,3, and 4.

[4]. Solve problem [2] using Lagrange polynomials of order = 2, 3, and 4.

[5]. Produce a forward difference table for the Q-h data.

[6]. Produce a forward difference table for the S-h data.

[7]. Solve problem [1] using a Newton forward-difference polynomial.

[8]. Solve problem [2] using a Newton forward-difference polynomial.

[9]. Solve problem [1] using a Newton backward-difference polynomial.

[10]. Solve problem [2] using a Newton backward-difference polynomial.

[11]. Solve problem [1] using a Sterling centered-difference polynomial.

[12]. Solve problem [2] using a Sterling centered-difference polynomial.

[13]. Solve problem [1] using a Bessel centered-difference polynomial.

[14]. Solve problem [2] using a Bessel centered-difference polynomial.

Use the following SCILAB polynomials in the solution of problems [15] through [21]:

$p = x^3 + 3x - 2$, $q = x+2$, $r = \frac{1}{2}x^3 - x^2 - x - 1$, $s = (2x+2)^3 - (5x+3)$

[15]. Calculate the following polynomial operations:
(a) p+q   (b) q+r   (c) r+s   (d) p+s   (e) p-q   (f) q-2r
(g) p+q+r   (h) p-2r+q (i) q+2p-r (j) pq   (k) pqr   (l) pq + rs
(m) $2pq-r^2$ (n) (p+q)(r+s) (o) q^3-x^3 (p) p/q   (q) r/q   (r) q+2/p

[16]. Determine the quotient and residual of the following polynomial divisions

(a) p/q   (b) r/q   (c) s/q   (d) (p+2s)/q   (e) $(s+q^2)/q$ (f) r/p

[17]. Obtain an expression for the polynomial long division defined by the following expressions. Use 5 terms in the expansion.

(a) 1/p   (b) 1/q   (c) 1/r   (d) 1/s   (e) p/q   (f) q/p
(g) p/s   (h) s/p   (i) r/q   (j) q/r   (k) s/p   (l) q/p^2

[18]. Use function *horner* to evaluate the polynomials calculated in problem [15] at values of x = 0, 2, 6, 10, and 20.

[19]. Determine the derivative of the polynomials obtained in problem [15] and evaluate those derivatives at values of x = 0, 2, 6, 10, and 20.

[20]. Obtain the roots of the polynomials obtained in problem [15].

[21]. Use user-defined function *intpoly* to obtain the indefinite integrals of the polynomials obtained in problem [15].

The following data shows the elevation of the bed surface in a flume, $y(ft)$, against the distance from one of the flume walls $x(ft)$. The data is to be used in problems [22] - [26].

x(ft)	0.5	1.0	1.5	2.0	2.5	3.0	3.5	4.0
y(ft)	0.23	0.45	0.48	0.40	0.31	0.40	0.59	0.37

[22]. Use the 8 data points to generate a direct-fit polynomial of order 7 that fits the data. Plot the original data and the fitted polynomial.

[23]. Fit Lagrange polynomials of orders 2, 3, 4, 5, and 6 to the bed profile data. Plot the original data and the fitted polynomials.

[24]. Produce a forward difference table out of the bed profile data.

[24]. Use (a) a Newton forward-difference polynomial; (b) a Newton backward-difference polynomial; (c) a Stirling centered-difference polynomial; and (d) a Bessel centered-difference polynomial to obtain the bed elevation at points x = 2.75 ft and x = 3.65 ft.

[25]. Fit polynomials of order 2, 3, 4, 5, and 6 for the bed profile data, using a least-square method.

[26]. Use cubic spline curves to fit the bed profile data. (a) Plot the original data and the fitted splines. (b) Produce the equations of the cubic spline curves that fit the data.

The following data shows the peak monthly concentration of a certain hydrocarbon component, C(ppm), measured in a monitoring well throughout the past year.

t(month)	0	1	2	3	4	5	6	7	8	9	10	11
C(ppm)	450	420	150	180	430	620	610	520	320	106	110	190

Use these data in problems [27] through [32].

[27]. Use the 12 data points to generate a direct-fit polynomial of order 11 that fits the data. Plot the original data and the fitted polynomial.

[28]. Fit Lagrange polynomials of orders 2, 3, 4, 5, and 6 to the concentration-vs-time data. Plot the original data and the fitted polynomials.

[29]. Produce a forward difference table out of the concentration-vs-time data.

[30]. Use (a) a Newton forward-difference polynomial; (b) a Newton backward-difference polynomial; (c) a Stirling centered-difference polynomial; and (d) a Bessel centered-difference polynomial to estimate the hydrocarbon concentration at times t = 2.5 months and t = 6.2 months.

[31]. Fit polynomials of order 2, 3, 4, 5, and 6 for the concentration-vs-time data, using a least-square method.

[32]. Use cubic spline curves to fit the concentration-vs-time data. (a) Plot the original data and the fitted splines. (b) Produce the equations of the cubic spline curves that fit the data.

[33]. Develop a SCILAB function to produce successive univariate polynomial approximation for a function z = f(x,y) based on nine data points as illustrated in the following table:

x\y	y_{k-1}	y_k	y_{k+1}
x_{m-1}	$z_{m-1,k-1}$	$z_{m-1,k}$	$z_{m-1,k+1}$
x_m	$z_{m,k-1}$	$z_{m,k}$	$z_{m,k+1}$
x_{m+1}	$z_{m+1,k-1}$	$z_{m+1,k}$	$z_{m+1,k+1}$

The table entries are values of $z_{m,k} = f(x_m, y_k)$. The function should use quadratic polynomials to obtain the value of $z_0 = f(x_0, y_0)$, for $x_{m-1} < x_0 < x_{m+1}$, $y_{k-1} < y_0 < y_{k+1}$, along rows and then columns, and vice versa. The function should return the values produced by the two approaches for interpolation, as well as the average.

The following table represents the entropy $s(kJ/(kg\ K))$, for superheated steam.

T(°C)\P(kPa)	20	40	s(kJ/(kg K)) 60	80	101.33
100	8.126	7.801	7.608	7.470	7.607
150	8.367	8.045	7.855	7.719	7.828
200	8.584	8.262	8.074	7.939	8.028
250	8.780	8.460	8.271	8.131	8.210
300	8.961	8.641	8.454	8.320	8.380
350	9.130	8.810	8.622	8.489	8.538
400	9.288	8.968	8.780	8.647	8.687

Use this table for problems [33] through [].

[33]. Using successive univariate polynomial interpolation with quadratic equations calculate the value of the superheated steam entropy for the following cases:

(a) T = 156°C, P = 42 kPa   (b) T = 310°C, P = 63 kPa
(c) T = 116°C, P = 22 kPa   (d) T = 156°C, P = 42 kPa
(e) T = 210°C, P = 92 kPa   (f) T = 343°C, P = 25 kPa
(g) T = 107°C, P = 58 kPa   (h) T = 280°C, P = 88 kPa
(i) T = 155°C, P = 42 kPa   (j) T = 306°C, P = 21 kPa

[34]. Solve problem [33] by fitting the given data to a function of the form

$$s(T,P) = b_0 + b_1 T + b_2 P.$$

[35]. Solve problem [33] by fitting the given data to a function of the form

$$s(T,P) = b_0 + b_1 T + b_2 P + b_3 SP$$

[36]. Solve problem [33] by fitting the given data to a function of the form

$$s(T,P) = b_0 + b_1 T + b_2 P + b_3 SP + b_4 S^2 + b_5 P^2.$$

[37]. Data from radiation counts of a radioactive material is shown in the table below.

t, months	0	2	4	5.5	6	9	10	14	18
N, counts/hour	1260	794	500	454	315	158	125	50	20

The equation for the radiation count as a function of time $N(t) = N_0 \exp(-\lambda t)$. Using the data in the table above determine the values of the parameters N_0 and λ, (a) using a simple linear fitting of the linearized equation $\ln(N) = -\lambda t + \ln(N_0)$; and (b) using SCILAB function datafit for the original equation, $N = N_0 \exp(-\lambda t)$. (c) Plot the original data against the data generated from the fittings in (a) and (b). (d) The half-life of the radioactive material is that value of time t for which the mass (or radiation count) falls by one half, i.e., $N = N_0/2$. Determine the half-life for this material.

[38]. The table below shows the flow velocity v(fps), and suspended sediment concentration, C(mg/l), as functions of the distance from the channel bed y(ft), measured at a cross-section of a 800-ft-wide (b = 800 ft), 7.8-ft-deep (h = 7.8 ft) river cross-section that can be approximated by a rectangle.

y(ft)	v(ft/s)	C(mg/l)
0.7	4.30	411
0.9	4.50	380
1.2	4.64	305
1.4	4.77	299
1.7	4.83	277
2.2	5.12	238
2.7	5.30	217
2.9	5.40	211
3.2	5.42	196
3.4	5.42	188
3.7	5.50	184
4.2	5.60	165
4.8	5.60	148
5.8	5.70	130
6.8	5.95	80

(a) Fit the velocity data, $v(y)$, to a logarithmic function, i.e., $v(y) = b_0 + b_1 \ln(y)$. Plot the original data and the fitted data in the same set of axes.
(b) Fit the concentration data, $C(y)$, to a function of the form $\ln(C) = b_0 + b_1 \ln((h-y)/y)$. Plot the original data and the fitted data in the same set of axes.

[39]. For the data in problem [38], the flow discharge Q(cfs), is defined by the integral

$$Q = \int_A v(y)dA = \int_0^h v(y) \cdot b dy,$$

with the mean flow velocity calculated as $V = Q/A$, where $A = b \cdot h$ being the cross-sectional area. The total flux of suspended sediment through the cross-section is defined as

$$Q_s = \int_A v(y) \cdot C(y) \cdot dA = \int_0^h v(y) \cdot C(y) \cdot b dy,$$

with the flux-averaged concentration given by $C_f = Q_s/Q$.

The terms used in the definitions above are illustrated in the figure below:

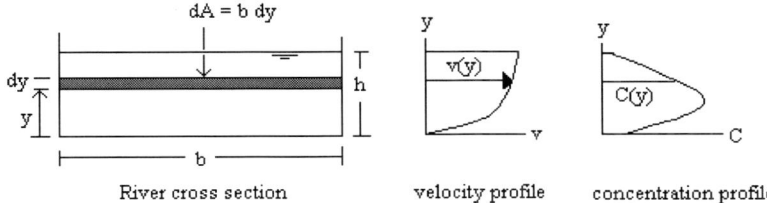

(c) Determine the flow discharge, mean velocity, sediment flux, and flux averaged concentration for the data given using for the integration the functions $v(y)$ and $C(y)$ obtained in problem [38]. Compare the results with those obtained in problem [94], Chapter 7.

9 Ordinary Differential Equations

The chapter starts with a review of concepts of differential equations and symbolic solution techniques that can be applied using SCILAB. Since SCILAB is not a symbolic environment, its applications to symbolic solutions of ordinary differential equations (ODEs) is limited. However, SCILAB can be used to calculate intermediate numerical steps in the solutions. The strength of SCILAB in solving ODEs is in its numerical applications. Thus, the chapter also includes a number of numerical solutions to ODEs through user-programmed and pre-programmed SCILAB functions.

Introduction to differential equations

Differential equations are equations involving derivatives of a function. Because many physical quantities are given in terms of rates of change of a certain quantity with respect to one or more independent quantities, derivatives appear frequently in the statement of physical laws. For example, the flux of heat, q [J/m^2], in a one-dimensional direction is given by

$$q = -k \cdot (dT/dx),$$

where T[K or °C] is the temperature, x [m] is positions, and k [J/(m K) or J/(m oC)]. This equation can be considered as a differential equation if and k are known, and we are trying to solve for the temperature as a function of x, i.e. $T = T(x)$. The equation of conservation of energy for heat transfer in one-dimension, where there are no sources or sink of heat, requires that the rate of change of the heat flux across an area perpendicular to the axis be zero, i.e., $dq/dx = 0$, or,

$$\frac{d}{dx}\left[-k \cdot \frac{dT}{dx}\right] = 0.$$

If k is a constant, i.e., not a function of x, then, the equation of conservation of energy reduces to

$$d^2T/dx^2 = 0.$$

The last two expressions are also differential equations. The solution for these equations will be a function $T = T(x)$ representing the temperature.

Definitions

The following definitions allow us to classify equations, thus providing general guidelines for obtaining solutions.

Ordinary and partial differential equations

When the dependent variable is a function of a single independent variable, as in the cases presented above, the differential equation is said to be a _ordinary differential equation (ODE)_. If the dependent variable is a function of more than one variable, a differential equation involving derivatives of this dependent variable is said to be _partial differential equation (PDE)_. An example of a partial differential equation would be the time-dependent would be the Laplace's equation for the stream function $\psi(x,y,z)$, of a three-dimensional, inviscid flow:

$$\partial^2\psi/\partial x^2 + \partial^2\psi/\partial y^2 + \partial^2\psi/\partial z^2 = 0.$$

Order and degree of an equation

The _order_ of a differential equation is the order of the highest-order derivative involved in the equation. Thus, the ODE

$$dy/dx + 3xy = 0$$

is a first-order equation, while Laplace's equation (shown above) is a second-order equation.

The _degree_ of a differential equation is the highest power to which the highest-order derivative is raised. Therefore, the equation

$$(d^3y/dt^3)^2 + (d^2y/dx^2)^5 - xy = e^x,$$

is a third order, second-degree ODE, while the equation

$$\partial y/\partial t = c \cdot (\partial y/\partial x),$$

is a first-order, first-degree PDE.

Linear and non-linear equations

An equation in which the dependent variable and all its pertinent derivatives are of the first degree is referred to as a _linear differential equation_. Otherwise, the equation is said to be _non-linear_. Examples of linear differential equations are:

and
$$d^2x/dt^2 + \beta \cdot (dx/dt) + \omega_0 \cdot x = A \sin \omega_f t,$$
$$\partial C/\partial t + u \cdot (\partial C/\partial x) = D \cdot (\partial^2 C/\partial x^2).$$

Constant or variable coefficients

The following equation:
$$d^3y/dt^3 + \pi \cdot (d^2y/dx^2)^2 - 5 \cdot y = e^x,$$

where all the coefficients accompanying the dependent variable and its derivative are constant, would be classified as a third order, linear ODE *with constant coefficients*. Instead, the equation

$$\partial^2 C/\partial t^2 - u(x,t) \cdot (\partial C/\partial x) = 0,$$

would be classified as a second-order, linear PDE *with variable coefficients*.

Homogeneous and non-homogeneous equations

Typically, differential equations are arranged so that all the terms involving the dependent variable are placed on the left-hand side of the equation leaving only constant terms or terms involving the independent variable(s) only in the right-hand side. When arranged in this fashion, a differential equation that has a zero right-hand side is referred to as *homogeneous equation*. Examples of homogeneous equations are:

$$d^2x/dt^2 + \beta \cdot (dx/dt) + \omega_0 \cdot x = 0,$$
and
$$(x-1) \cdot (dy/dx) + 2 \cdot x \cdot y = 0.$$

On the other hand, if the right-hand side of the equation, after placing the terms involving the dependent variable and its derivatives on the left-hand side, is non-zero, the equation is said to be *non-homogeneous*. Non-homogeneous versions of the last two equations are:

$$d^2x/dt^2 + \beta \cdot (dx/dt) + \omega_0 \cdot x = A_0 \cdot e^{-t/\tau},$$
and
$$(x-1) \cdot (dy/dx) + 2 \cdot x \cdot y = x^2 - 2x.$$

Solutions

A _solution_ to a differential equation is a function of the independent variable(s) that, when replaced in the equation, produces an expression that can be reduced through algebraic manipulation, to the form 0 = 0. For example, the function

$$y = \sin x,$$

is a solution to the equation

$$d^2y/dx^2 + y = 0,$$

because when we replace y into the equation we have

$$-\sin x + \sin x = 0,$$

or, 0 = 0, for all values of x. This follows from the fact that $dy/dx = \cos(x)$, and $d^2y/dx^2 = -\sin(x)$.

General and particular solutions

A _general solution_ is one involving integration constants so that any choice of those constants represents a solution to the differential equation. For example, the function

$$x = C \cdot e^{-t},$$

is a general solution to the equation

$$dx/dt + x = 0,$$

because, substituting $C e^{-t}$ for x in the equation produces

$$-C \cdot e^{-t} + C \cdot e^{-t} = 0.$$

A _particular solution_ is a solution corresponding to a specific value of the integration constants. For example, the function

$$y = x^2/2$$

is a particular solution to the equation,

$$dy/dx - x = 0.$$

A general solution for this equation would be

$$y = x^2/2 + C,$$

where C is an arbitrary integration constant.

Given the solution of the homogeneous equation, $y_h(x)$, the solution of the corresponding non-homogeneous equation, y(x), can be written as

$$y(x) = y_h(x) + y_p(x),$$

where $y_p(x)$ is a particular solution to the ODE.

Verifying solutions using SCILAB

Since SCILAB is not a symbolic environment it is not suitable for the verification of solutions other than polynomial solutions. As indicated in Chapter 8, SCILAB provides function *derivat* to calculate derivatives of polynomials. If we have a function that can be expressed as a polynomial, we can use function *derivat* to check if that function satisfies a particular differential equation as illustrated in the example below:

Check that the function $y(x) = x^3-2x+4$ is a solution to the differential equation $d^2y/dx^2 - 6x = 0$ using SCILAB:

```
-->x = poly(0,'x'); y = x^3-2*x+4;
```

```
-->derivat(derivat(y))-6*x
 ans  =

    0
```

Initial conditions and boundary conditions

To determine the specific value of the constant(s) of integration, we need to provide values of the solution, or of one or more of its derivatives, at specific points. These values are referred to as the _conditions_ of the solution. For example, we could specify that the solution to the equation

$$d^2y/dt^2+y = 0,$$

must satisfy the conditions

$$y(0) = -5,$$

and

$$dy/dt = -1 \text{ at } t = 5.$$

Initial conditions are provided at a single value of the independent variable so that after evaluating those conditions at that point all the integration constants are uniquely specified. In general, first order differential equations include one integration constant, requiring only one condition to be evaluated to uniquely determine the solution. Thus, this type of equations needs only one initial condition. The term "initial condition" is used because many first order equations involve a derivative with respect to time, and the condition given to specify the solution is typically the value of the function at time equal to zero, i.e., an initial value of the function. _Boundary conditions_, on the other hand, are provided at more then one value of the independent variable(s). The term "boundary conditions" is used because the function is evaluated at the "boundaries" of the solution domain in order to specify the solution.

An example of _initial conditions_ used in a solution will be to solve the equation

$$d^2u/dt^2 + 2 \cdot (du/dt) = 0,$$

given

$$u(0) = 1, \; du/dt|_{t=0} = -1.$$

An example of boundary conditions used in a solution will be to solve the equation

$$d^2y/dx^2 + y = A \sin x,$$

using

$$y(0) = A/2, \text{ and } y(1) = -A/2.$$

In general, the solution of an n-th order ODE requires n conditions.

Symbolic solutions to ordinary differential equations

By symbolic solutions we understand those solutions that can be expressed as a closed-form function of the independent variable. Because solution of first-order differential equations imply integrating the derivative involved in the equation, many of the techniques used for solving first-order ODEs follow from integration techniques. Details of some techniques used for solving ordinary differential equations follow.

Solution techniques for first-order, linear ODEs with constant coefficients

A first order equation is an equation of the form

$$a \cdot (dy/dx)^n + b \cdot y^m = f(x),$$

where a, b, n and m are, in general, real numbers. Some specific techniques <u>for linear equations</u>, i.e., when n = m = 1, follow. This catalog of solutions for linear ODEs is intended as a review of the techniques. Numerical solutions using SCILAB will be presented in a later chapter.

▪ *Equations of the form: dy/dx = f(x) -- Direct integration*

An equation of the form dy/dx = f(x) can be re-written as

$$dy = f(x)dx,$$

and a general solution found by direct integration,

$$\int dy = \int f(x)dx,$$

or

$$y = \int f(x)dx + C.$$

If an initial condition $y(x_o) = y_o$, is given, then the integration can be calculated as

$$\int_{y_o}^{y} dy = \int_{x_o}^{x} f(x)dx,$$

or,

$$y - y_0 = \int_{x_0}^{x} f(x)dx.$$

If the function f(x) is a polynomial, we can use the SCILAB user-defined function *intpoly* to produce the indefinite integral. Consider the example in which dy/dx = f(x) = $3x^3$ +x + 2. The solution, with the help of SCILAB, is calculated as:

```
-->f = poly([2,1,0,3],'x','coeff')
 f =
                3
    2 + x + 3x

-->getf('intpoly')

-->fInt = intpoly(f)

   Indefinite integral - Add integration constant

   fInt =
                2        4
    2x +  .5x +   .75x
```

Thus, the general solution is :

$$y(x) = 2x+0.5*x^2+0.75*x^4 + C$$

■ *Equations of the form: dy/dx = g(y) -- Inversion and direct integration*

Equations of the form *dy/dx = g(y)*, can be re-written as

$$dy/g(y) = dx.$$

Thus, an indefinite integral will be given by

$$\int dy/g(y) = \int dx,$$

or

$$\int dy/g(y) = x + C.$$

From the latter expression, the dependent variable y may be solved for.   A similar approach is followed when using a definite integral, i.e., one with initial condition y(x = y_0. The integration in this case reads:

$$\int_{y_0}^{y} \frac{dy}{g(y)} = \int_{x_0}^{x} dx = x - x_0.$$

■ Equations of the form: dy/dx = f(x)g(y) -- Separation of variables

Equations of the form $dy/dx = f(x)g(y)$, can be separated into

$$dy/g(y) = dx/g(x),$$

and then integrated using indefinite integrals for general solutions, or definite integrals with initial conditions for particular solutions.

■ Equations of the form: dy/dx = g(y/x)

Using the change of variable
$$u = y/x,$$
we have
$$y = u \cdot x,$$
$$dy = u \cdot dx + x \cdot du,$$
then
$$(u \cdot dx + x \cdot du)/dx = g(u),$$
$$u \cdot dx + x \cdot du = g(u) \cdot dx,$$
$$[g(u)-u] \cdot dx = x \cdot du,$$

from which the variables x and u can be separated as

$$du/[g(u)-u] = dx/x.$$

After integration, we replace
$$u = y/x$$
back in the result, and isolate, if possible, y(x).

■ Equations of the form: a·(dy/dx)+ b·y = f(x) -- Integrating factors

The expression
$$a \cdot (dy/dx) + b \cdot y = f(x)$$

constitutes the most general form of a first-order, linear, ordinary differential equation. The equation can be re-written as

$$dy/dx + (b/a) \cdot y = (1/a) \cdot f(x),$$

You can prove that, by multiplying both sides of this form of the equation by a function,

$$IF(x) = \exp(b \cdot x/a),$$

known as an *integrating factor*, the equation becomes:

$$\frac{d}{dx}\left(a\cdot\exp\left(\frac{b\cdot x}{a}\right)\cdot y(x)\right) = \frac{1}{a}\cdot\exp\left(\frac{b\cdot x}{a}\right)\cdot f(x).$$

This equation can be easily integrated to read:

$$y(x) = \exp\left(-\frac{b\cdot x}{a}\right)\cdot\left(\frac{1}{a}\cdot\int\exp\left(\frac{b\cdot x}{a}\right)\cdot f(x) + C\right).$$

In terms of the integrating factor, this solution will be:

$$y(x) = (1/IF(x))\cdot[(1/a)\cdot\int IF(x)\cdot f(x)\cdot dx + C].$$

Integrating factors for first-order, linear ODEs with variable coefficients

An equation with variable coefficients such as

$$K_1(x)(dy/dx) + K_2(x)y(x) = K_3(x),$$

can be reduced to the form,

$$dy/dx + g(x)y(x) = f(x),$$

by dividing the entire equation by $K_1(x)$. The latter equation can be solved by multiplying both sides of the equation by the integrating factor

$$IF(x) = \exp(\int g(x)dx).$$

After identifying the integrating factor, IF(x), the solution procedure is very similar to the case of a first-order, constant-coefficient ODEs, i.e.,

$$y(x) = (1/FI(x))\cdot[\int FI(x)\cdot f(x)\cdot dx + C].$$

Exact differential equations

An expression of the form,

$$F(x,y)\cdot dx + G(x,y)\cdot dy = 0,$$

Is said to be an exact differential equation in two dimensions, if the components $F(x,y)$ and $G(x,y)$ satisfy the conditions

$$\partial F/\partial y = \partial G/\partial x.$$

In such case, it is possible to find a function $u(x,y)$, such that

$$F(x,y) = \partial u/\partial x, \quad G(x,y) = \partial u/\partial y.$$

The equation $u(x,y) = C$, where C is a constant, will represent a solution to the exact differential equation:

$$F(x,y) \cdot dx + G(x,y) \cdot dy = 0.$$

Solutions of homogeneous linear equations of any order with constant coefficients

Consider the linear, constant-coefficient, homogeneous ODE of order n:

$$d^{(n)}y/dx^{(n)} + b_{n-1} \cdot (dy^{(n-1)}/dx^{(n-1)}) + \ldots + b_2 \cdot (d^2y/dx^2) + b_1 \cdot (dy/dx) + b_0 \cdot y = 0.$$

where the coefficients $b_0, b_1, \ldots, b_{n-1}$, are constant. We can use the operator $D^{(k)} = d^{(k)}/dx^{(k)}$, to re-write the equation as

$$D^{(n)}y + b_{n-1} \cdot D^{(n-1)}y + \ldots + b_2 \cdot D^2 y + b_1 \cdot Dy + b_0 \cdot y = f(x).$$

Treating the operators $D^{(k)}$, $(k = n, n-1, \ldots, 1)$, as algebraic terms, the equation is re-written as

$$[D^{(n)} + b_{n-1} \cdot D^{(n-1)} + \ldots + b_2 \cdot D^2 + b_1 \cdot D + b_0] \cdot y = 0.$$

The idea is that the linear combination of the operators, shown above in square brackets, is applied to the function $y(x)$, in a similar manner as algebraic terms would be multiplied to it.

Associated with the latter expression is a polynomial known as the *characteristic equation* of the ODE, and written as

$$\lambda^n + b_{n-1} \cdot \lambda^{n-1} + \ldots + b_2 \cdot \lambda^2 + b_1 \cdot \lambda + b_0 = 0.$$

Suppose that the characteristic equation has n independent roots, then the general solution of the linear, constant-coefficient, homogeneous ODE of order n given earlier is

$$y = C_1 \cdot e^{\lambda_1 x} + C_2 \cdot e^{\lambda_2 x} + \ldots + C_{n-1} \cdot e^{\lambda_{n-1} x} + C_n \cdot e^{\lambda_n x}.$$

If out of the n roots there is one that has multiplicity m, then the m terms corresponding to this root λ in the solution, will be

$$C_{(1)} \cdot e^{\lambda x} + C_{(2)} \cdot x \cdot e^{\lambda x} + C_{(1)} \cdot x^2 \cdot e^{\lambda x} + \ldots + C_{(1)} \cdot x^{m-1} \cdot e^{\lambda x}.$$

Example 1 — Determine the general solution to the homogeneous equation

$$d^3y/dx^3 - 4 \cdot (d^2y/dx^2) - 11 \cdot (dy/dx) + 30 \cdot y = 0.$$

In terms of the D operator, this ODE can be written as

$$[D^3 - 4 \cdot D^2 - 11 \cdot D + 30]y = 0.$$

The characteristic equation corresponding to this ODE is

$$\lambda^3 - 4 \cdot \lambda^2 - 11 \cdot \lambda + 30 = 0.$$

To obtain solutions to this equation in SCILAB use:

```
-->lam = poly(0,'lam')
 lam  = lam

-->p = lam^3-4*lam^2-11*lam+30
 p   =
                     2     3
     30 - 11lam - 4lam + lam

-->roots(p)
 ans  =
 !   2. !
 ! - 3. !
 !   5. !
```

Thus, a general solution to the ODE under consideration is

$$y = C_1 \cdot e^{2x} + C_2 \cdot e^{-3x} + C_3 \cdot e^{5x}.$$

Example 2 – Determine the general solution to the homogeneous ODE:

$$d^4y/dx^4 - 7 \cdot (d^3y/dx^3) + 18 \cdot (d^2y/dx^2) - 20 \cdot (dy/dx) + 8 \cdot y = 0.$$

In terms of the D operator, this ODE can be written as:

$$[D^4 - 7 \cdot D^3 + 18 \cdot D^2 - 20 \cdot D + 8]y = 0.$$

Thus, the characteristic equation is

$$\lambda^4 - 7 \cdot \lambda^3 + 18 \cdot \lambda^2 - 20 \cdot \lambda + 8 = 0.$$

To obtain the solution of this equation using SCILAB try the following commands:

```
-->p = lam^4-7*lam^3+18*lam^2-20*lam+8
 p  =
                   2       3      4
     8 - 20lam + 18lam - 7lam + lam

-->roots(p)
 ans  =

 !   1. !
 !   2. !
 !   2. !
 !   2. !
```

Since root $\lambda = 2$ has multiplicity of 3, the solution becomes:

$$y(x) = C_1 e^x + e^{2x}(C_2 + C_3 x + C_4 x^2).$$

Obtaining the particular solution for a second-order, linear ODE with constant coefficients

Thus, how do we come up with a particular solution y_p, to complete the solution to a non-homogeneous equation, $y = y_h + y_p$, given the solution to the homogeneous equation y_h? In this section we present a general method to obtain y_p for second-order, linear ODEs with constant coefficients. The reason why we choose second-order equations is not only because they are the simpler equations to solve (not including first-order equations, which were discussed in great detail in an earlier section), but also because they are useful to model a number of real-life situations. Typical systems modeled by second-order ODEs are the damped and undamped oscillatory behavior in spring-mass and electric circuit systems.

The general expression for a second-order, linear, non-homogeneous ODE with constant coefficients is

$$d^2y/dx^2 + b_1 \cdot (dy/dx) + b_0 \cdot y = h(x).$$

The first step is to obtain the solution to the homogeneous equation

$$d^2y/dx^2 + b_1 \cdot (dy/dx) + b_0 \cdot y = 0,$$

by using the solutions to the characteristic equation

$$\lambda^2 + b_1 \cdot \lambda + b_0 = 0.$$

Consider the case in which the solutions to the characteristic equation are real numbers. The solutions to this quadratic equation can be two different values, say λ_1 and λ_2, in which case the homogeneous solution is written as

$$y_h(x) = C_1 \cdot \exp(\lambda_1 \cdot x) + C_2 \cdot \exp(\lambda_2 \cdot x),$$

or a single solution of multiplicity 2, say λ_0, in which case we write

$$y_h(x) = (C_1 + C_2 \cdot x) \exp(\lambda_0 \cdot x).$$

If the two solutions to the quadratic (characteristic) equation are complex numbers, they must be complex conjugates of each other as required by the fundamental theorem of algebra. In this case we can write

$$\lambda_1 = \alpha + \beta i, \text{ and } \lambda_2 = \alpha - \beta i,$$

where α and β are real numbers. Thus, the solution $C_1 \cdot \exp(\lambda_1 \cdot x) + C_2 \cdot \exp(\lambda_2 \cdot x)$, becomes

$$C_1 \cdot e^{(\alpha+\beta i)x} + C_2 \cdot e^{(\alpha-\beta i)x} = C_1 \cdot e^{\alpha x} \cdot e^{i\beta x} + C_2 \cdot e^{\alpha x} \cdot e^{-i\beta x} = e^{\alpha x} \cdot (C_1 \cdot \cos \beta x + i \cdot C_1 \cdot \sin \beta x + C_2 \cdot \cos \beta x - i \cdot C_2 \cdot \sin \beta x) = e^{\alpha x} \cdot [(C_1 + C_2) \cdot \cos \beta x + i \cdot (C_1 - C_2) \cdot \sin \beta x] = e^{\alpha x} \cdot (K_1 \cdot \cos \beta x + K_2 \cdot \sin \beta x),$$

where

$$K_1 = (C_1+C_2), \text{ and } K_2 = i \cdot (C_1-C_2).$$

Thus, for the case of two complex solutions to the characteristic equation, the homogeneous solution is a sinusoidal function whose amplitude grows ($\alpha>0$) or decreases ($\alpha<0$) with x:

$$y_h(x) = e^{\alpha x} \cdot (K_1 \cdot \cos \beta x + K_2 \cdot \sin \beta x).$$

If the solutions are imaginary numbers, i.e., if $\alpha = 0$ in the previous result, the homogeneous solution is a pure sinusoidal function:

$$y_h(x) = K_1 \cdot \cos \beta x + K_2 \cdot \sin \beta x.$$

To obtain the particular solution, $y_p(x)$, that will produce the overall solution of the non-homogeneous ODE, $y(x) = y_h(x) + y_p(x)$, follow this rule that refers to the sub-sequent table of functions:

■ If h(x), in the general non-homogeneous ODE, is given by one of the functions in the first column of the table shown below, choose for $y_p(x)$ a linear combination of h(x) and its linearly independent derivatives, as shown in the second column of the table.

■ If h(x) is the sum of some of the functions shown in column 1 of the table below, choose for $y_p(x)$ the sum of the functions in the corresponding lines.

■ If a term in h(x) is a solution of the homogeneous equation corresponding to the ODE under consideration, modify your choice of $y_p(x)$ by multiplying the appropriate line of column 2 by x or x^2, depending on whether the root of the characteristic equation (column 3) is simple or double.

Term in h(x)	Choice for $y_p(x)$	Root of char. eqn.
$c \cdot e^{\alpha x}$	$C_0 \cdot e^{\alpha x}$	α, real
$c \cdot x^n$ (n = 0, 1, ...)	$C_n \cdot x^n + C_{n-1} \cdot x^{n-1} + \ldots + C_1 \cdot x + C_0$	0
$c \cdot \sin \beta x$	$C_1 \cdot \sin \beta x + C_2 \cdot \sin \beta x$	$i\beta$, imaginary
$c \cdot \cos \beta x$	$C_1 \cdot \sin \beta x + C_2 \cdot \sin \beta x$	$i\beta$, imaginary

Once the particular solution is set up by following the rule above, the undetermined coefficients in $y_p(x)$ can be determined by substituting yp(x) into the ODE.

Example 1 – Obtain the general solution to the non-homogeneous, second-order, linear ODE:

$$d^2y/dx^2 - 5 \cdot (dy/dx) + 6 \cdot y = x^2.$$

The characteristic equation of the homogeneous equation is

$$\lambda^2 - 5 \cdot \lambda + 6 = 0,$$

or

$$(\lambda-3) \cdot (\lambda-2) = 0,$$

with solutions
$$\lambda = 2, \text{ and } \lambda = 3.$$
Thus, the homogeneous solution is
$$y_h(x) = K_1 \cdot e^{2x} + K_2 \cdot e^{3x}.$$

Since the right-hand side of the non-homogeneous equation is
$$h(x) = x^2,$$
from the table above we select
$$y_p(x) = C_2 x^2 + C_1 x + C_0.$$

To obtain the values of C_0, C_1, and C_2, replace the solution $y(x)$ into the ODE. The derivatives are, $dy_p/dx = 2C_2 x + C_1$, and $d^2 y_p/dx^2 = 2C_2$, which replaced into the equation produce
$$2C_2 - 5(2C_2 x + C_1) + 6(C_2 x^2 + C_1 x + C_0) = x^2,$$
or
$$6C_2 x^2 + (6C_1 - 10C_2)x + (6C_0 - 5C_1 + 2C_2) = x^2.$$

Comparing the coefficients of the terms x^2, x^1, and x^0, in both sides of the resulting equation allows us to write the following system of linear equations:
$$6C_2 = 1$$
$$6C_1 - 10C_2 = 0$$
$$6C_0 - 5C_1 + 2C_2 = 0$$

A solution, using SCILAB, produces:

```
-->A = [0,0,6;0,6,-10;6,-5,2],  b = [1;0;0]
 A  =

!    0.     0.     6.  !
!    0.     6.   - 10. !
!    6.   - 5.     2.  !


 b  =

!    1.  !
!    0.  !
!    0.  !

-->C = A\b
 C  =

!    .1759259  !
!    .2777778  !
!    .1666667  !
```

The solution is:
$$C_0 = 0.1759259, C_1 = 0.2777778, \text{ and } C_2 = 0.1666667$$
Thus,
$$y_p(x) = 0.1666667 x^2 + 0.2777778 x + 0.1759259,$$

and the general equation to the non-homogeneous equation becomes:

$$y(x) = y_h(x) + y_p(x) = K_1 \cdot e^{2x} + K_2 \cdot e^{3x} + 0.1666667x^2 + 0.2777778x + 0.1759259.$$

Applications of ODEs I : analysis of damped and undamped free oscillations

Consider the mass-spring system shown in the figure below. The mass is removed from its equilibrium position ($x = 0$) and released at a position $x = x_0$ at $t=0$. At the moment of its release the body was moving with a speed $v = v_0$. The diagram shows the body of mass m being acted upon by the restoring force of the spring $F_s = -k \cdot x$, and by a viscous damping force $F_v = -\beta \cdot v = -\beta \cdot (dx/dt)$.

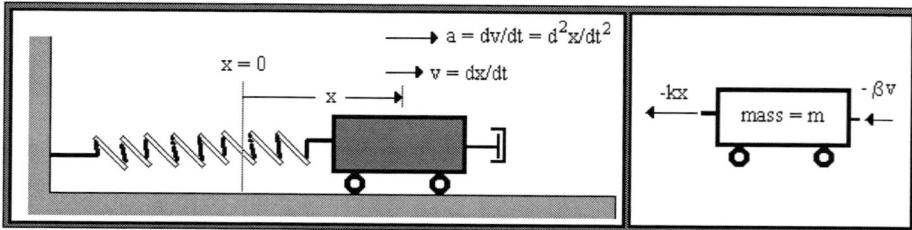

Newton's second law, when applied in the x-direction to the mass m is written as:

$$-kx - \beta (dx/dt) = m (d^2x/dt^2),$$

which results in the second-order, linear, ordinary differential equation:

$$d^2x/dt^2 + (\beta/m) \cdot (dx/dt) + (k/m) \cdot x = 0.$$

Undamped motion

Let us first consider the case in which the motion is undamped, i.e., b = 0. The equation in this case reduces to

$$d^2x/dt^2 + (k/m) \cdot x = 0.$$

The corresponding characteristic equation is

$$\lambda^2 + (k/m) = 0,$$

with solutions,

$$\lambda = \pm i \cdot \sqrt{(k/m)} = \pm i \cdot \omega_0.$$

This result suggest a solution of the form

$$x(t) = C_1 \cos \omega_o t + C_2 \sin \omega_o t.$$

Alternatively, by taking

$$C_1 = A \cos \phi, \text{ and } C_2 = -A \sin \phi,$$

the solution can be written as

$$x(t) = A \cdot \cos(\omega_o t + \phi).$$

The quantity

$$\omega_o = \sqrt{(k/m)}$$

is known as the *natural angular frequency* of the harmonic motion that results when no viscous damping is present. The frequency of the oscillation can be calculated from

$$f = 2\pi/\omega_o = 1/T,$$

where T is the period of the oscillation (i.e. the time that the mass takes to return to a pre-defined position in the motion). The quantity ϕ is known as the angular phase of the oscillation, and A is known as the amplitude.

The velocity of the motion is given by

$$v = dx/dt = -\omega_o \cdot A \sin(\omega_o t + \phi),$$

and its acceleration, is

$$a = dv/dt = -\omega_o^2 \cdot A \cos(\omega_o t + \phi),$$

The initial conditions, $x(0) = x_o$, $v(0) = v_o$, can be used to evaluate the constants A and f, as follows:

$$x_o = x(0) = A \cos \phi,$$

and

$$v_o = v(0) = -\omega_o \cdot A \sin \phi.$$

Thus,

$$\tan \phi = -v_o/(\omega_o x_o), \text{ or } \phi = \tan^{-1}(-v_o/(\omega_o x_o)),$$

and

$$A = [x_o^2 + (v_o/\omega_o)^2]^{1/2}.$$

Damped motion

If damping occurs $\beta \neq 0$), the characteristic equation becomes

$$\lambda^2 + (\beta/m) \cdot \lambda + \omega_o^2 = 0,$$

whose solutions are

$$\lambda = -(\beta/(2 \cdot m)) \pm \sqrt{([\beta/(2 \cdot m)]^2 - \omega_o^2)} = -\alpha \pm \sqrt{(\alpha^2 - \omega_o^2)},$$

where

$$\alpha = \beta/(2 \cdot m).$$

The nature of the solution will depend on the relative size of the coefficients α and ω_0, as follows:

- If $\alpha < \omega_0$, then $\sqrt{(\alpha^2 - \omega_0^2)} = i \cdot \omega_1$, where

$$\omega_1 = \sqrt{(\omega_0^2 - \alpha^2)}$$

is real, and the solutions of the characteristic equation are

$$\lambda_1 = -\alpha + i \cdot \omega_1, \text{ and } \lambda_2 = -\alpha - i \cdot \omega_1.$$

The solution to the ODE therefore, is written as

$$x(t) = e^{-\alpha t}(C_1 \cos \omega_1 t + C_2 \sin \omega_1 t) = A_0 \cdot e^{-\alpha t} \cdot \cos(\omega_1 t + \phi_1).$$

The parameter

$$\omega_1 = \sqrt{(\omega_0^2 - \alpha^2)} = \sqrt{[(k/m)^2 - (\beta/(2m))^2]} = \sqrt{(4k^2 - \beta^2)}/(2m),$$

represents the damped angular frequency of the oscillation, and ϕ_1 represents the corresponding angular phase. A_0 is the amplitude of the oscillation at $t = 0$. If we define a variable amplitude,

$$A(t) = A_0 \cdot e^{-\alpha t},$$

then the solution to the ODE, also known as the signal, can be written as

$$x(t) = A(t) \cdot \cos(\omega_1 t + \phi_1).$$

Please notice that this solution is very similar to the case of an undamped oscillation, except for the fact that in a damped oscillation the amplitude decreases with time. The amplitude decreases, or decays, with time because the parameter $\alpha = \beta/(2m)$ is positive. Therefore, the function $\exp(-\alpha t)$ decreases with time.

- If $\alpha = \omega_0$, then the characteristic equation produces the solution $\lambda = -\alpha$, with multiplicity 2, in which case the solution becomes

$$x(t) = e^{-\alpha t}(C_1 + C_2 \cdot t).$$

This solution represents a linear function of t subjected to a decay factor $\exp(-\alpha t)$.

- If $\alpha > \omega_0$, then $\sqrt{(\alpha^2 - \omega_0^2)} = K$ is real, and $K < \alpha$, the solutions of the characteristic equation become

$$\lambda_1 = -\alpha + K = -c_1, \text{ and } \lambda_2 = -\alpha - K = -c_2,$$

both negative. Therefore, the resulting signal can be written as:

$$x(t) = C_1 \cdot \exp(-c_1 t) + C_2 \cdot \exp(-c_2 t).$$

Notice that the last two cases, namely, $\alpha = \omega_0$ and $\alpha > \omega_0$, produce signals that decay with time. These cases correspond to harmonic motions that are said to be over-damped, i.e., the viscous damping is large enough to quickly damp out any oscillation after the body of mass m is released.

Initial conditions for damped oscillatory motion

The expression for the position of a damped oscillatory motion is given by

$$x(t) = A_0 \cdot e^{-\alpha t} \cdot \cos(\omega_1 t + \phi_1),$$

while the velocity, $v(t) = dx/dt$, is given by

$$v(t) = -A_0 \, e^{-\alpha t} (\alpha \cos(\omega_1 t + \phi_1) + \omega_1 \sin(\omega_1 t + \phi_1)).$$

Given the initial conditions $x(t_0) = x_0$ and $v(t_0) = v_0$, we can form a system of two non-linear equations in the unknowns A_0 and ϕ_1, namely,

$$f_1(A_0, \phi_1) = A_0 \cdot e^{-\alpha t_0} \cdot \cos(\omega_1 t_0 + \phi_1) - x_0,$$

$$f_2(A_0, \phi_1) = -A_0 \, e^{-\alpha t_0}(\alpha \cos(\omega_1 t_0 + \phi_1) + \omega_1 \sin(\omega_1 t_0 + \phi_1)) - v_0.$$

With appropriate values of the parameters α, ω_1, t_0, x_0, and v_0, we can use SCILAB function *fsolve* to obtain the values of A_0 and ϕ_1, as illustrated in an upcoming example.

Before presenting the example, however, we will write out the expression for the acceleration so that we can use it in producing the graphics of the example:

$$a(t) = A_0 \, e^{-\alpha t}(\alpha^2 \cos(\omega_1 t + \phi_1) + 2\alpha \omega_1 \sin(\omega_1 t + \phi_1) - \omega_1^2 \cos(\omega_1 t + \phi_1)).$$

Example 1 – Damped oscillatory motion: Plot position, velocity, and acceleration corresponding to the following parameters: $m = 1$ kg, $\beta = 0.1$ N·s/m, $k = 0.5$ N/m. To determine the constants A_0 and ϕ_1, use initial conditions, $x_0 = 1.5$ m, and $v_0 = -5.0$ m/s. With these values,

$$\omega_0 = (k/m)^{1/2} = (0.5\text{N}/1\text{kg·m})^{1/2} = (0.5 \, s^{-2})^{1/2} = 0.7071 \, s^{-1} = 0.7071 \text{ rad/s},$$

and

$$\alpha = \beta/(2m) = 0.1 \text{ N·s}/(2 \times 1 \text{ kg·m}) = 0.05 \, s^{-1} = 0.05 \text{ rad/s}.$$

Since, $\alpha < \omega_0$, the resulting signal is that of a damped oscillation with

$$\omega_1 = \sqrt{(\omega_0^2 - \alpha^2)} = \sqrt{(0.7071^2 - 0.05^2)} = 0.7053 \text{ rad/s}.$$

To solve for the constants A_0 and ϕ_1 with SCILAB, we first define the set of non-linear equations to be solved. In the function thus defined A is represented by $s(1)$ and ϕ_1 is represented by $s(2)$:

```
-->deff('[FF]=f(s)',['f1=s(1)*exp(-a*t0)*cos(wI*t0+s(2))-x0';...
-->'f2 = -s(1)*exp(-a*t0)*(a*cos(wI*t0+s(2))+wI*sin(wI*t0+s(2)))-v0';...
-->'FF = [f1;f2]'])
```

Next, we enter the known values, and select a first guess for the solution *s*:

```
-->w0 = 0.7071; a = 0.05; wI = 0.7053; x0 = 1.5; v0 = -5.0; t0 = 0;

-->s0 = [5;%pi/3]
 s0  =

!   5.        !
!   1.0471976 !
```

The solution for $s(1) = A_0$ and $s(2) = \phi_1$ is obtained by using:

```
-->fsolve(s0,f)
 ans =

!   7.1421364 !
!   1.3591997 !
```

Thus, $A_0 = 7.1221364$ and $\phi_1 = 1.3591997$, and the position x(t) is given by

$$x(t) = A_o \exp(-0.05t) \cos(0.7053t - \phi_1).$$

Expressions for the position x(t), velocity v(t), and acceleration a(t) for this motion can be entered into SCILAB by defining the following functions:

```
-->A0 = 7.1421364; phi1 = 1.3591997;

-->deff('[xs]=x(t)','xs = A0.*exp(-a.*t).*cos(wI.*t+phi1)')

-->deff('[vs]=v(t)',...
-->'vs =-A0.*exp(-a.*t).*(a.*cos(wI.*t+phi1)+wI.*sin(wI.*t+phi1))')

-->deff('[acc]=aa(t)',...
-->'acc=A0.*exp(-a.*t).*(a^2.*cos(wI.*t+phi1)+...
-->2.*a.*wI.*sin(wI.*t+phi1)-wI^2.*cos(wI.*t+phi1))')
```

To plot the signals x(t), v(t), and a(t) in the t-interval (0,30) use the following SCILAB commands:

```
-->tt = [0:0.1:30]; xx = x(tt); vv = v(tt); -->aaa = aa(tt);

-->plot2d([tt',tt',tt'],[xx',vv',aaa'],[2,3,4],'111',...
-->'position@velocity@acceleration',[0 -10 30 10])

-->xtitle('Damped oscillatory motion', 't', 'x,v,a')
```

The results are shown in the following graph:

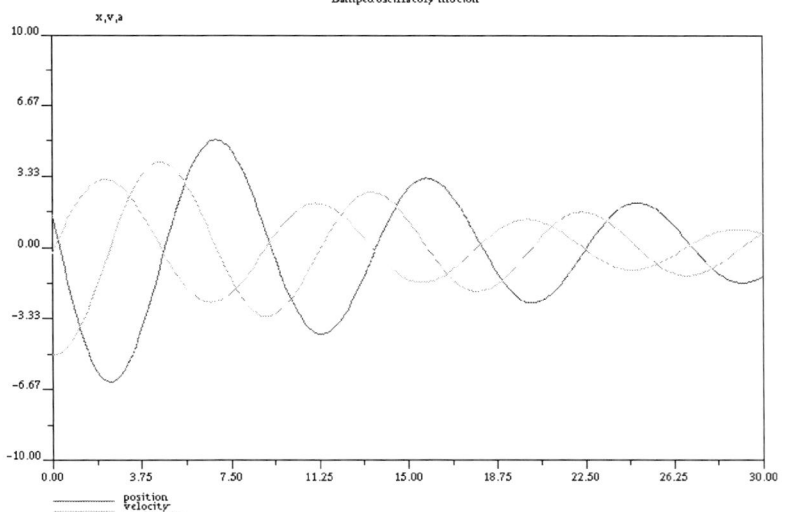

Notice the oscillatory nature of the three functions, as well as their amplitudes' decay with time as expected.

Creating phase portraits of oscillatory motion

A phase portrait for oscillatory, or any kind of, motion is a plot involving the dependent variable and one of its derivatives, or two derivatives of the dependent variable. For example, a plot of velocity, v(t), versus position, x(t), represents a phase portrait. Other phase portraits would be a(t) vs. x(t), and a(t) vs. v(t).

Example 1. Plot the time-dependent plots and phase portraits for the signal obtained in Example 1 in the previous section. To plot these phase portraits we generate data on position, velocity, and acceleration as function of time t in the interval [0,90], as follows:

```
-->tt = [0:0.1:90]; xx = x(tt); vv = v(tt); aaa = aa(tt);
```

The phase portraits are generated as follows:

```
-->xset('window',1);plot(xx',vv')
-->xtitle('v-vs-x phase portrait','x','v')
```

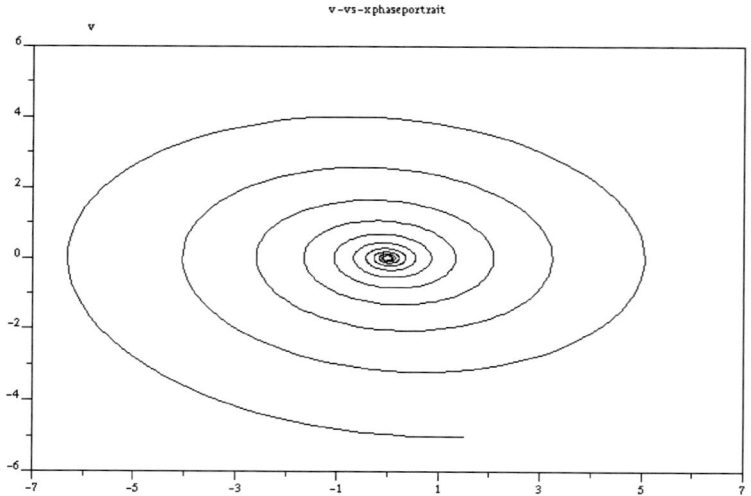

```
-->xset('window',2);plot(xx',aaa')
-->xtitle('a-vs-x phase portrait','x','a')
```

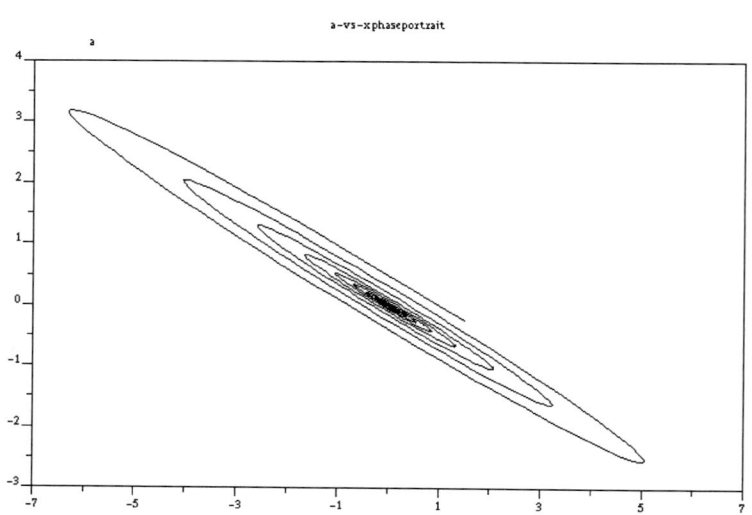

```
-->xset('window',3);plot(vv',aaa')
-->xtitle('a-vs-v phase portrait','v','a')
```

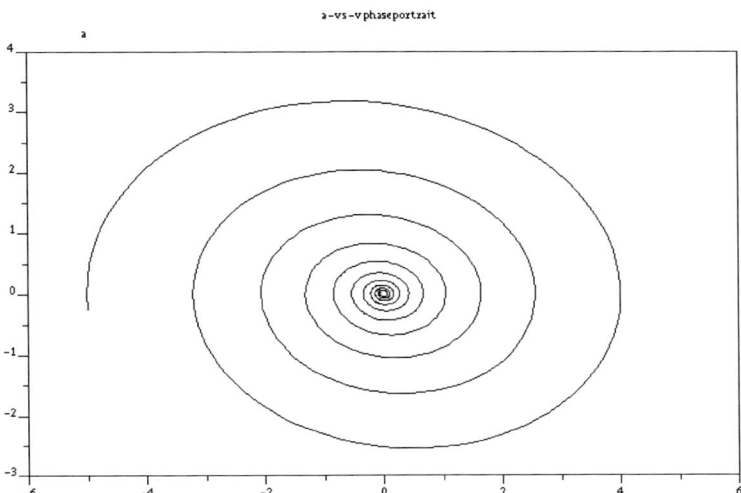

The three phase portraits show orbits spiraling inwards towards the center of the picture, i.e., towards (0,0). This is because the amplitude of the variables included in the phase portrait decreases at about the same rate with time.

Applications of ODEs II : analysis of damped and undamped forced oscillations

Earlier we presented the analysis of damped and undamped free oscillations, meaning that, once the particle subjected to oscillatory motion is released, all forces acting on it (the restoring force of the spring, ad the damping force from the dashpot) are internal to the system. If the particle is continuously subjcted to an external force (a excitation), then the type of oscillations thus generated are termed *forced oscillations*. Of interest are excitations that are themselves oscillatory. The simplest case will be an external force,

$$F_e(t) = F_o \cos \omega t.$$

The differential equation for the mass-spring-dashpot system, including the excitation $(t_F$, is now written as:

$$d^2x/dt^2 + (\beta/m) \cdot (dx/dt) + (k/m) \cdot x = (F_o/m) \cdot \cos \omega t.$$

Let's assume that the values of the parameters m, b, and k are such that the solution of the homogeneous equation is

$$x_h(t) = A_o \cdot e^{-\alpha t} \cdot \cos(\omega_o t + \phi).$$

Also, because the term $\cos \omega t$ shows up in the right-hand side term, the table for selecting the particular solution (shown earlier in this chapter), suggest that we try

$$x_p(t) = C_1 \cos \omega t + C_2 \sin \omega t.$$

Because this particular solution must satisfy the governing ODE, we can write

$$d^2x_p/dt^2 + (\beta/m)\cdot(dx_p/dt) + (k/m)\cdot x_p = (F_o/m)\cdot \cos \omega t.$$

The values of C_1 and C_2, using $\omega_0^2 = k/m$, are:

$$C_1 = \frac{F_o m(\omega_0^2 - \omega^2)}{\omega^2 \beta^2 + m^2(\omega_0^2 - \omega^2)^2}.$$

$$C_2 = \frac{F_o \omega \beta}{\omega^2 \beta^2 + m^2(\omega_0^2 - \omega^2)^2}.$$

The particular solution can be written now as

$$x_p(t) = F_o \cdot \frac{m(\omega_0^2 - \omega^2)\cdot \cos(\omega \cdot t) + \omega \beta \cdot \sin(\omega \cdot t)}{\omega^2 \beta^2 + m^2(\omega_0^2 - \omega^2)^2}.$$

Suppose that we want to write this solution as

$$x_p(t) = A_p \cos(\omega t + \phi_p) = A_p \cos \omega t \cos \phi_p - A_p \sin \omega t \sin \phi_p,$$

by comparing the last two expressions we find that

$$A_p \cos \phi_p = F_o m(\omega_0^2 - \omega^2)/[\omega^2\beta^2 + m^2(\omega_0^2 - \omega^2)^2],$$

and

$$A_p \sin \phi_p = -F_o \omega \beta /[\omega^2\beta^2 + m^2(\omega_0^2 - \omega^2)^2],$$

from which,

$$A_p^2 = F_o^2/[\omega^2\beta^2 + m^2(\omega_0^2 - \omega^2)^2],$$

and

$$\tan \phi_p = -\omega\beta/(m(\omega_0^2 - \omega^2)).$$

Thus, the particular solution can be written as:

$$x_p(t) = \frac{F_o}{\sqrt{\omega^2 \beta^2 + m^2(\omega_0^2 - \omega^2)^2}} \cdot \cos(\omega \cdot t + \phi_p).$$

To analyze the behavior of this particular solution, first we study the case in which no damping is present, i.e., $\beta = 0$. In such case, $\phi_p = 0$, and the particular solution becomes

$$x_p(t) = \frac{F_0}{m(\omega_0^2 - \omega^2)} \cdot \cos\omega \cdot t = \frac{F_0/(m \cdot \omega_0)}{1 - (\omega/\omega_0)^2} \cdot \cos\omega \cdot t = A_p(\omega) \cdot \cos\omega \cdot t.$$

For this case, the amplitude of the oscillation, $A_p(\omega)$, becomes infinity as $\omega \to \omega_0$. This condition is known as *resonance*. Thus resonant conditions will occur if the exciting force has the same frequency as the natural frequency of the system. In practice, the amplitude of the undamped oscillations grows without bound until the system is severely damaged or destroyed. This is important for analyzing building response to earthquakes. Every building has a natural frequency of vibration. If a building is subjected for a long period of time to an earthquake with a frequency similar or equal to its natural frequency, the building may suffer severe damages as consequence of the earthquake.

If damping is present, then the amplitude of the oscillation is given by

$$A_p(\omega) = \frac{F_0}{\sqrt{\omega^2 \beta^2 + m^2(\omega_0^2 - \omega^2)^2}},$$

which has a maximum

$$A_p(\omega) = \frac{2mF_0}{\beta\sqrt{4m^2\omega^2 - \beta^2}},$$

when

$$\beta^2 = 2m^2(\omega_0^2 - \omega^2).$$

Since the general solution of the damped equation,

$$x_h(t) = A_o \cdot e^{-\alpha t} \cdot \cos(\omega_b t + \phi),$$

decreases with time, it will eventually become negligible when compared to the particular solution. Thus, it is said that the general solution represents the *transient (temporary) response* of the system to the exciting force, $F(t)$. The particular solution, which turns out to be a sinusoidal wave, represents *the steady-state response* of the system.

The following is a graph showing the amplitude $A_p(\omega)$, as function of the angular frequency, w, for a particular set of values of the parameters, namely, $_0F= 25$ N, k = 100 N/m, m = 1.0 kg, which gives w_0 = 3.162277 rad/s. The graph is obtained using SCILAB as shown below. First, we define the function for $A_p(\omega)$, and the constant parameters:

```
-->deff('[AA]=Ap(om)','AA=F0./sqrt(om.^2.*b.^2+m.^2.*(w0.^2-om.^2).^2)')

-->F0 = 25; k = 10; m = 1.0; w0 = sqrt(k/m)
 w0  = 3.1622777
```

Next, we define a vector *bb* containing 5 different values of the damping parameter β, and a vector *om* containing values of ω in the range (0,6). The lengths of vector *bb* and *om* are the values *n* and *m*, respectively:

```
-->bb = [1.0, 5.0, 10.0, 50.0, 100.0]; om = [0:0.1:6];

-->n = length(bb); m = length(om);
```

The next step is to create a matrix *Amp* (Amplitudes) with *m* rows and *n* columns whose elements will contain the values $Amp_{ij} = Ap(om_i, bb_j)$. The following commands show how to load matrix *Amp*:

```
->Amp = zeros(m,n);

-->for j = 1:n
-->    b = bb(j); Amp(:,j) = Ap(om');
-->end;
```

To produce the plot showing curves of $A_p(\omega)$ for different values of β is produced by using:

```
-->plot2d([om',om',om',om',om'],...
-->[Amp(:,1),Amp(:,2),Amp(:,3),Amp(:,4),Amp(:,5)],...
-->[1:1:5],'111','b=1@b=5@b=10@b=50@b=100',[0 0 6 1.8])

-->xtitle('Amplitude of forced oscillation','w','A(w)')
```

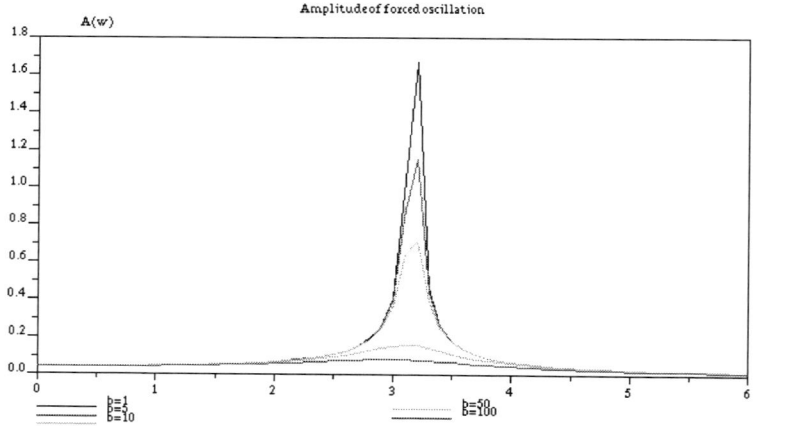

The plot shows that as the value of β decreases the amplitude reaches a maximum near the value of $\omega = \omega_0$. If there were no damping, i.e., $\beta \to 0$, then $A_p(\omega) \to \infty$ at that point, indicating the condition of resonance

Applications of ODEs III: Oscillations in electric circuits

Electric circuits involving resistors, capacitors, and inductors are often times characterized by an oscillatory behavior represented by electric current through the circuit. Consider a simple series RLC circuit as shown in the figure below.

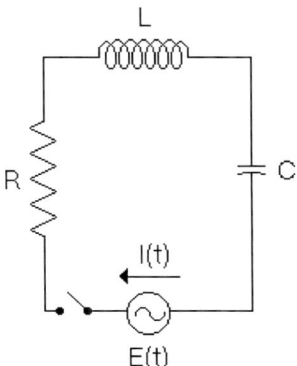

In the figure, $E(t)$ stands for the time-dependent voltage (volts), $I(t)$ is the electric current through the circuit once the switch is set to ON (amperes), R is the equivalent resistance of the circuit (ohms), L is the equivalent inductance of the circuit (henrys), and C is the equivalent capacitance (farads). The electric current $I(t)$, is the rate of change of electric charge with respect to time, i.e., $I(t) = dq/dt$, where q = electric charge (coulombs), and t is time (sec). The properties of resistors, capacitors, and inductors are such that if V represents the voltage across one of those components the following relationships hold:

- Resistors, $V_R = R \cdot I = R \cdot (dq/dt)$
- Capacitors, $V_C = q/C$
- Inductors, $V_L = L \cdot (dI/dt) = L \cdot (d^2q/dt^2)$

To put together a differential equation for this circuit we use Kirchoff's law of voltages around the series circuit: $V_R + V_L + V_C = E(t)$, i.e.,

$$R \cdot (dq/dt) + L \cdot (d^2q/dt^2) + q/C = E(t).$$

Alternatively, we can take the derivative of this equation with respect to t and write the equation in terms of the current, $I = dq/dt$, as follows:

$$R \cdot (dI/dt) + L \cdot (d^2I/dt^2) + (1/C) \cdot I = dE/dt.$$

Thus, we can either solve the equation in terms of the electric charge, $q(t)$, re-written as:

$$(d^2q/dt^2) + (R/L)\cdot(dq/dt) + q/(LC) = E(t)/L,$$

or, in terms of the electric current, I(t), re-written as:

$$(d^2I/dt^2) + (R/L)\cdot(dI/dt) + I/(LC) = (1/L)(dE/dt).$$

To simplify the solution we introduce the constants $\omega_0^2 = 1/(LC)$ and $\beta = R/(2L)$, and solve the equation in terms of the electric charge $q(t)$, i.e.,

$$(d^2q/dt^2) + 2\cdot\beta\cdot(dq/dt) + \omega_0^2\cdot q = E(t)/L.$$

Solution to the homogeneous equation

Consider first, the homogeneous case, i.e. $E(t) = 0$, which is the situation that would occur is the capacitor is charged and the voltage source is by-passed. The resulting governing equation is

$$(d^2q/dt^2) + 2\cdot\beta\cdot(dq/dt) + \omega_0^2\cdot q = 0,$$

which is the same as the case of free oscillations with damping for a spring-mass-dashpot system.

If the constant value

$$\omega_1 = \sqrt{\omega_0^2 - \beta^2}$$

is real, the solution is a damped oscillation, i.e.,

$$q(t) = Q_0 e^{-\beta t}\cos(\omega_1 t + \phi).$$

If ω_1 is not real, then the solution is a combination of exponential functions, i.e.,

$$q(t) = C_1 e^{-\alpha_1 t} + C_2 e^{-\alpha_2 t}$$

Since the governing equation for $q(t)$ in an RLC circuit is the same as the governing equation for the position of a particle in a mass-spring-dashpot system, we can borrow many of the results obtained in the previous two sections to analyze RLC circuits. Some applications are presented in the exercise section.

Finite differences and numerical solutions

To solve differential equations numerically we can replace the derivatives in the equation with finite difference approximations on a discretized domain. This results in a number of algebraic equations that can be solved one at a time (explicit methods) or simultaneously (implicit methods) to obtain values of the dependent function y_i corresponding to values of the independent function x_i in the discretized domain.

Finite differences

A finite difference is a technique by which derivatives of functions are approximated by differences in the values of the function between a given value of the independent variable, say x_0, and a small increment (x_0+h). For example, from the definition of derivative,

$$df/dx = \lim_{h \to 0} (f(x+h)-f(x))/h,$$

we can approximate the value of df/dx by using the finite difference approximation

$$(f(x+h)-f(x))/h$$

with a small value of h.

The following table shows approximations to the derivative of the function

$$f(x) = \exp(-x) \sin(x^2/2),$$

at $x = 2$, using finite differences. The actual value of the derivative is -0.23569874791. The third column in the table shows the error in evaluating the derivative, i.e., the difference between the numerical derivative $\Delta f/\Delta x$ and the actual value.

h	$\Delta f/\Delta x$	error
0.1	-0.244160077	0.00846132909
0.01	-0.236684829	0.00098608109
0.001	-0.235798686	0.00009993809
0.0001	-0.235708734	0.00000998609
0.00001	-0.235699726	0.00000097809
0.000001	-0.235698825	0.00000007709
0.0000001	-0.235698734	0.00000001391
0.00000001	-0.235698724	0.00000002391
0.000000001	-0.235698752	0.00000000409

This exercise illustrates the fact that, as $h \to 0$, the value of the finite difference approximation, $(f(x+h)-f(x))/h$, approaches that of the derivative, df/dx, at the point of interest.

A plot of the error as a function of h also reveals the fact that the error is proportional to the value of the x-increment h. The following plots, using different ranges of h, are produced with SCILAB out of the data in the table.

```
-->h = [1e-1,1e-2,1e-3,1e-4,1e-5,1e-6,1e-7,1e-8,1e-9];

-->er = [0.00846132909,0.00098608109,0.00009993809,0.00000998609,...
-->      0.00000097809,0.00000007709,0.00000001391,0.00000002391,...
-->      0.00000000409];

-->xset('mark',-9,2)
-->plot2d(h,er,1,'011',' ',[0 0 0.1 0.01])
-->plot2d(h,er,-9,'011',' ',[0 0 0.1 0.01])
-->xtitle('error vs. x-increment','h','error')
```

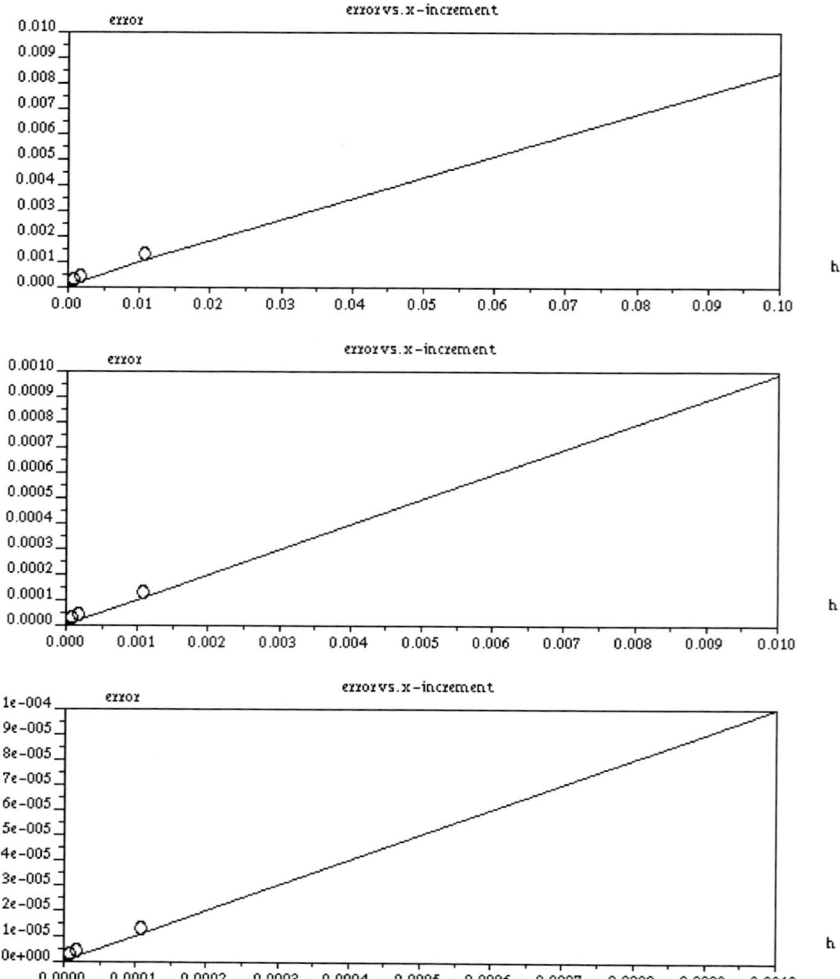

The graphs seem indicate that the error varies linearly with the increment h in the independent variable. It is very common to indicate this dependency by saying that "the error is of order h", or $error = O(h)$. The magnitude of the error can be estimated by using Taylor series expansions of the function $f(x+h)$.

Finite difference formulas based on Taylor series expansions

The Taylor series expansion of the function $f(x)$ about the point $x = x_0$ is given by the formula

$$f(x) = \sum_{n=0}^{\infty} \frac{f^{(n)}(x_0)}{n!} \cdot (x - x_0)^n.$$

Where $f^{(n)}(x_0) = (d^n f/dx^n)|_{x=x_0}$, and $f^{(0)}(x_0) = f(x_0)$.

If we let $x = x_0 + h$, then $x - x_0 = h$, and the series can be written as

$$f(x_0 + h) = \sum_{n=0}^{\infty} \frac{f^{(n)}(x_0)}{n!} \cdot h^n = f(x_0) + \frac{f'(x_0)}{1!} \cdot h + \frac{f''(x_0)}{2!} \cdot h^2 + O(h^3),$$

Where the expression $O(h^3)$ represents the remaining terms of the series and indicates that the leading term is of order h^3. Because h is a small quantity, we can write $1 > h$, and $h > h^2 > h^3 > h^4 > \ldots$. Therefore, the remaining of the series represented by $O(h^3)$ provides the order of the error incurred in neglecting this part of the series expansion when calculating $f(x_0+h)$.

From the Taylor series expansion shown above we can obtain an expression for the derivative $f'(x_0)$ as

$$f'(x_0) = \frac{f(x_0 + h) - f(x_0)}{h} + \frac{f''(x_0)}{2!} \cdot h + O(h^2) = \frac{f(x_0 + h) - f(x_0)}{h} + O(h).$$

In practical applications of finite differences, we will replace the first-order derivative df/dx at $x = x_0$, with the expression $(f(x_0+h)-f(x_0))/h$, selecting an appropriate value for h, and indicating that the error introduced in the calculation is of order h, i.e. error $= O(h)$.

Forward, backward and centered finite difference approximations to the first derivative

The approximation

$$df/dx = (f(x_0+h)-f(x_0))/h$$

is called a _forward difference formula_ because the derivative is based on the value $x = x_0$ and it involves the function $f(x)$ evaluated at $x = x_0+h$, i.e., at a point located forward from x_0 by an increment h.

If we include the values of $f(x)$ at $x = x_0 - h$, and $x = x_0$, the approximation is written as

$$df/dx = (f(x_0)-f(x_0-h))/h$$

and is called a _backward difference formula_. The order of the error is still $O(h)$.

A centered difference formula for df/dx will include the points $(x_0-h, f(x_0-h))$ and $(x_0+h, f(x_0+h))$. To find the expression for the formula as well as the order of the error we use the Taylor series expansion of $f(x)$ once more. First we write the equation corresponding to a forward expansion:

$$f(x_0+h) = f(x_0)+f'(x_0)\cdot h+1/2\cdot f''(x_0)\cdot h^2+1/6\cdot f^{(3)}(x_0)\cdot h^3 + O(h^4).$$

Next, we write the equation for a backward expansion:

$$f(x_0-h) = f(x_0)-f'(x_0)\cdot h+1/2\cdot f''(x_0)\cdot h^2-1/6\cdot f^{(3)}(x_0)\cdot h^3 + O(h^4).$$

Subtracting these two equations results in

$$f(x_0+h) - f(x_0-h) = 2\cdot f'(x_0)\cdot h+1/3\cdot f^{(3)}(x_0)\cdot h^3+O(h^5).$$

Notice that the even terms in h, i.e., h^2, h^4, ..., vanish. Therefore, the order of the remaining terms in this last expression is $O(h^5)$. Solving for $f'(x_0)$ from the last result produces the following *centered difference formula for the first derivative*:

$$\frac{df}{dx}\Big|_{x=x_0} = \frac{f(x_0+h)-f(x_0-h)}{2\cdot h} + \frac{1}{3}\cdot f^{(3)}(x)\cdot h^2 + O(h^4),$$

or,

$$\frac{df}{dx} = \frac{f(x_0+h)-f(x_0-h)}{2\cdot h} + O(h^2).$$

This result indicates that the centered difference formula has an error of the order $O(h^2)$, while the forward and backward difference formulas had an error of the order $O(h)$. Since $h^2<h$, the error introduced in using the centered difference formula to approximate a first derivative will be smaller than if the forward or backward difference formulas are used.

Forward, backward and centered finite difference approximations to the second derivative

To obtain a *centered finite difference formula for the second derivative*, we'll start by using the equations for the forward and backward Taylor series expansions from the previous section but including terms up to $O(h^5)$, i.e.,

$$f(x_0+h) = f(x_0)+f'(x_0)\cdot h+1/2\cdot f''(x_0)\cdot h^2+1/6\cdot f^{(3)}(x_0)\cdot h^3 + 1/24\cdot f^{(4)}(x_0)\cdot h^4 + O(h^5).$$

and

$$f(x_0-h) = f(x_0)-f'(x_0)\cdot h+1/2\cdot f''(x_0)\cdot h^2-1/6\cdot f^{(3)}(x_0)\cdot h^3 + 1/24\cdot f^{(4)}(x_0)\cdot h^4 - O(h^4).$$

Next, add the two equations and solve for $f''(x_0)$:

$$d^2f/dx^2 = [f(x_0+h)-2\cdot f(x_0)+f(x_0-h)]/h^2 + O(h^2).$$

Forward and backward finite difference formulas for the second derivatives are given, respectively, by

$$d^2f/dx^2 = [f(x_0+2\cdot h)-2\cdot f(x_0+h)+f(x0)]/h^2 + O(h),$$

and

$$d^2f/dx^2 = [f(x_0) -2\cdot f(x_0-h)+f(x_0-2\cdot h)]/h^2 + O(h).$$

Solution of a first-order ODE using finite differences - Euler forward method

Consider the ordinary differential equation,

$$dy/dx = g(x,y),$$

subject to the boundary condition,

$$y(x_1) = y_1.$$

To solve this differential equation numerically, we need to use one of the formulas for finite differences presented earlier. Suppose that we use the forward difference approximation for dy/dx, i.e.,

$$dy/dx = (y(x+h)-y(x))/h.$$

Then, the differential equation is transformed into the following difference equation:

$$(y(x+h)-y(x))/h = g(x,y),$$

from which,

$$y(x+h) = y(x)+h\cdot g(x,y).$$

This result is known as _Euler's forward method_ for numerical solution of first-order ODEs.

Since we know the boundary condition (x_1,y_1) we can start by solving for y at $x_2 = x_1+h$, then we solve for y at $x_3 = x_2+h$, and so on. In this way, we generate a series of points (x_1, y_1), (x_2, y_2), ..., (x_n, y_n), which will represent the numerical solution to the original ODE. The upper limit of the independent variable x_n is either given or selected arbitrarily during the solution.

The term "*discretizing the domain of the independent variable*" refers to obtaining a series of values of the independent variable, namely x_i, $i = 1,2,..., n$, that will be used in the solution. Suppose that the range of the independent variable (a,b) is known, and that we use a constant value $h = \Delta x$ to divide the range into n equal intervals. By making $x_1 = a$, and $x_n = b$, then we find that the values of x_i, $i = 2,3, ... n$, are given by

$$x_i = x_1 +(i-1)\cdot \Delta x = a+(i-1)\cdot \Delta x,$$

and that for $i = n$, $x_n = x_1 + (n-1) \cdot \Delta x$. This latter result can be used to find n given Δx,

$$n = (x_n - x_1)/\Delta x + 1 = (b-a)/\Delta x + 1,$$

or, to find Δx given n,

$$\Delta x = (x_n - x_1)/(n-1) = (b-a)/(n-1).$$

The recurrent equation for solving for y is given by

$$y_{i+1} = y_i + \Delta x \cdot g(x_i, y_i),$$

for $i = 1, 2, \ldots, n-1$. Because the method solves $y_{i+1} = f(x_i, y_i, \Delta x)$, i.e., one value of the dependent variable at a time, the method is said to be an *explicit method*.

The following example illustrates the application of the Euler first-order method to the solution of the differential equation $dy/dx = g(x,y) = x + y$ using SCILAB. First, we define function $g(x,y)$:

```
-->deff('[Df]=g(x,y)','Df=x+y')
```

We solve the equation in the range of values of x from $x_0 = 0$ to $x_n = 2.0$ with an increment $Dx = 0.1$. The initial condition is $y_0 = 1.0$ for $x_0 = 0$:

```
-->x0 = 0; y0 = 1; Dx = 0.1; xn = 2.0;
```

The following commands generate a vector of values of x, a vector y of the same length of x, initialized with zeros, and determines the value of n as the length of vector y (or x):

```
-->x=[x0:Dx:xn]; y = zeros(x); n = length(y);
```

The following *for..end* loop takes care of calculating the values of y_i for $i = 2, 3, \ldots, n$:

```
-->for j = 1:n-1
-->    y(j+1) = y(j) + Dx*g(x(j),y(j));
-->end;
```

To produce a plot of the results we determine the minimum and maximum values of y:

```
-->ymin = min(y), ymax = max(y)
 ymin  =

    0.
 ymax  =

    3.7274999
```

The plot is generated by using:

```
-->plot2d(x,y,1,'011',' ',[0 0 2 4])
-->plot2d(x,y,-9,'011',' ',[0 0 2 4])
-->xtitle('Euler solution dy/dx = x + y, Dx = 0.1','x','y(x)')
```

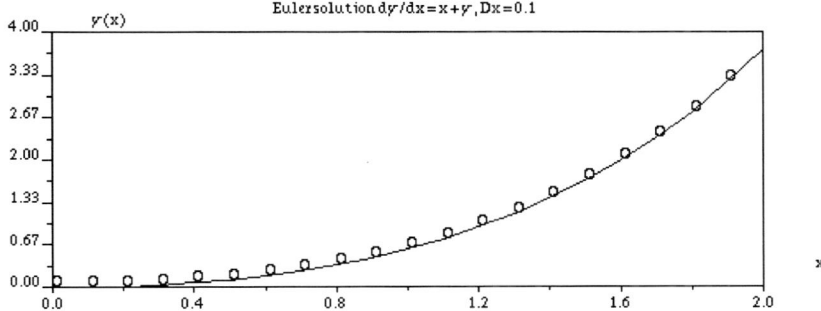

A function to implement Euler's first-order method

The following function, *Euler1*, implements the calculation steps outlined in the previous example. The function detects if there is overflowing introduced in the solution and stops the calculation at that point providing the current results.

```
function [x,y] = Euler1(x0,y0,xn,Dx,g)

//Euler 1st order method solving ODE
//   dy/dx = g(x,y), with initial
//conditions y=y0 at x = x0.  The
//solution is obtained for x = [x0:Dx:xn]
//and returned in y

ymaxAllowed = 1e+100;

x = [x0:Dx:xn]; y = zeros(x); n = length(y); y(1) = y0;

for j = 1:n-1
        y(j+1) = y(j) + Dx*g(x(j),y(j));
        if y(j+1) > ymaxAllowed then
             disp('Euler 1 - WARNING: underflow or overflow');
             disp('Solution sought in the following range:');
             disp([x0 Dx xn]);
             disp('Solution evaluated in the following range:');
             disp([x0 Dx x(j)]);
                n = j; x = x(1,1:n); y = y(1,1:n);
             break;
        end;
end;

//End function Euler1
```

Next, we use function *Euler1* to solve the differential equation from the previous example, namely, *dy/dx = g(x,y) = x+y*, for different values of the x increment Δx = 0.5, 0.2, 0.1, and 0.05, with the same initial conditions and range of values of x as before:

```
-->getf('Euler1')
```

```
-->deff('[Df]=g(x,y)','Df = x+y')
-->[x1,y1]=Euler1(0,1,2,0.5,g);
-->[x2,y2]=Euler1(0,1,2,0.2,g);
-->[x3,y3]=Euler1(0,1,2,0.1,g);
-->[x4,y4]=Euler1(0,1,2,0.05,g);
```

The exact solution for this equation is $y(x) = -x - 1 + 2e^x$. Set of values of the exact solution are calculated as follows:

```
-->xx = [0:0.1:2]; yy = -xx-1+2.*exp(xx);
```

To plot the exact and numerical solutions we first determine the minimum and maximum values of y:

```
-->ymax = max([y1 y2 y3 y4 y5 yy])
 ymax  = 11.778112

-->ymin = min([y1 y2 y3 y4 y5 yy])
 ymin  = 1.
```

The plot of the solutions is produced through the use of the following calls to function plot2d:

```
-->plot2d(xx,yy,1,'011',' ',[0 0 2 12])
-->plot2d(x1,y1,-1,'011',' ',[0 0 2 12])
-->plot2d(x2,y2,-2,'011',' ',[0 0 2 12])
-->plot2d(x3,y3,-3,'011',' ',[0 0 2 12])
-->plot2d(x4,y4,-4,'011',' ',[0 0 2 12])
-->xtitle('Euler 1st order - dy/dx = x+y','x','y(x)')
```

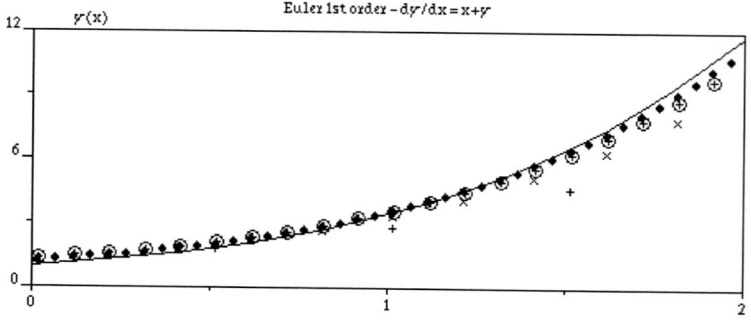

A second example of application of function Euler1 is shown next for the differential equation $dy/dx = xy + 1$, with initial condition $x_0 = 0$, $y_0 = 1$, in the range $0 < x < 2$, with Δx = 0.5, 0.2, 0.1, 0.05, and 0.01. The SCILAB commands used are exactly the same as before except for the definition of function g(x,y) and the title of the plot. The function $g(x,y) = xy+1$ is defined as:

```
-->deff('[Df]=g(x,y)','Df=x*y+1')
Warning :redefining function: g
```

Numerical solutions to the differential equation for the different values of are obtained from:

```
-->[x1,y1]=Euler1(0,1,2,0.5,g);

-->[x2,y2]=Euler1(0,1,2,0.2,g);

-->[x3,y3]=Euler1(0,1,2,0.1,g);

-->[x4,y4]=Euler1(0,1,2,0.05,g);

-->[x5,y5]=Euler1(0,1,2,0.01,g);
```

Next, we determine the minimum and maximum values of y:

```
-->ymin = min([y1 y2 y3 y4 y5 yy])
 ymin  = 1.

-->ymax = max([y1 y2 y3 y4 y5 yy])
 ymax  = 15.872217
```

We define a plot rectangle as:

```
-->rect = [0 0 2 16]
 rect =

!   0.    0.    2.    16. !
```

The plot of the numerical solution is accomplished through:

```
-->plot2d(x1,y1,-1,'011',' ',rect)
-->plot2d(x2,y2,-2,'011',' ',rect)
-->plot2d(x3,y3,-3,'011',' ',rect)
-->plot2d(x4,y4,-4,'011',' ',rect)
-->xtitle('Euler 1st order - dy/dx = x*y+1','x','y(x)')
```

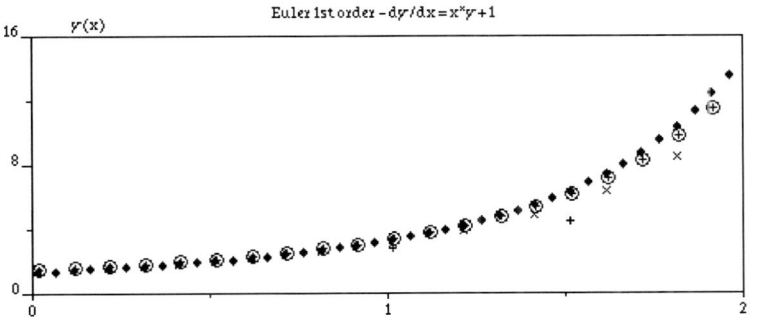

The following example solves the differential equation $dy/dx = g(x,y) = x + sin(xy)$ in the interval $0 < x < 6.5$, with initial conditions $x_0 = 0$, $y_0 = 1$, for $\Delta x = 0.5, 0.2, 0.1, 0.05,$ and 0.01. The steps are the same as in the two previous example:

```
-->deff('[Df]=g(x,y)','Df=x+sin(x*y)')
Warning :redefining function: g

-->[x1,y1]=Euler1(0,1,6.5,0.5,g);

-->[x2,y2]=Euler1(0,1,6.5,0.2,g);

-->[x3,y3]=Euler1(0,1,6.5,0.1,g);

-->[x4,y4]=Euler1(0,1,6.5,0.05,g);

-->ymin = min([y1 y2 y3 y4 y5 yy])
 ymin  =   1.

-->ymax = max([y1 y2 y3 y4 y5 yy])
 ymax  = 22.628614

-->rect = [0 0 7 25]
 rect  =
!   0.    0.    7.    25. !

-->plot2d(x1,y1,-1,'011',' ',rect)
-->plot2d(x2,y2,-2,'011',' ',rect)
-->plot2d(x3,y3,-3,'011',' ',rect)
-->plot2d(x4,y4,-9,'011',' ',rect)
-->xtitle('Euler 1st order - dy/dx = x+sin(x*y)','x','y(x)')
```

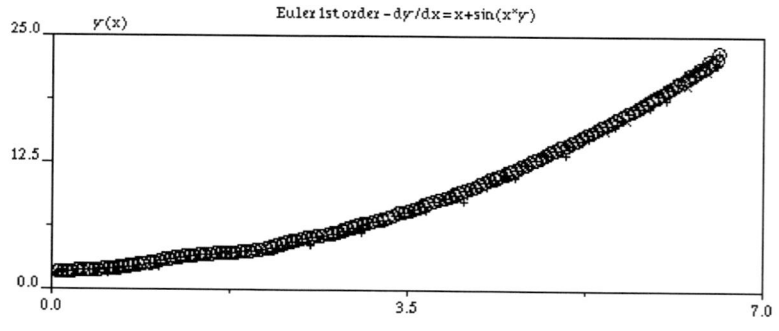

Finite difference formulas using indexed variables

In the presentation of the Eler forward method, above, we demonstrated how you can get, from the general formula for the first derivative,

$$dy/dx = [y(x+h)-y(x)]/h,$$

the recurrence formula for the explicit solution, namely,

$$y_{i+1} = y_i + \Delta x \cdot g(x_i, y_i),$$

for $i = 1, 2, \ldots, n-1$. This suggest re-writing the formula for the derivative as,

$$dy/dx = (y_{i+1} - y_i)/\Delta x + O(\Delta x).$$

Using this sub-index notation, we can summarize the forward, centered, and backward approximations for the first and second derivatives as shown below:

First Derivative
FORWARD: $\quad dy/dx = (y_{i+1} - y_i)/\Delta x + O(\Delta x).$

CENTERED: $\quad dy/dx = (y_{i+1} - y_{i-1})/(2 \Delta x) + O(\Delta x^2).$

BACKWARD: $\quad dy/dx = (y_i - y_{i-1})/\Delta x + O(\Delta x).$

Second Derivative
FORWARD: $\quad d^2y/dx^2 = (y_{i+2} - 2 \cdot y_{i+1} + y_i)/(\Delta x^2) + O(\Delta x).$

CENTERED: $\quad d^2y/dx^2 = (y_{i+1} - 2 \cdot y_i + y_{i-1})/(\Delta x^2) + O(\Delta x^2).$

BACKWARD: $\quad d^2y/dx^2 = (y_i - 2 \cdot y_{i-1} + y_{i-2})/(\Delta x^2) + O(\Delta x).$

Solution of a first-order ODE using finite differences - an implicit method

Consider again the ordinary differential equation $dy/dx = g(x,y)$, subject to the boundary condition, $y(x_1) = y_1$. This time, however, we use the centered difference approximation for dy/dx, i.e.

$$dy/dx = (y(x+h) - y(x-h))/(2^*h).$$

With this approximation the ODE becomes,

$$(y(x+h) - y(x-h))/(2^*h) = g(x, y).$$

In terms of sub-indexed variables, this latter equation can be written as:

$$y_{i-1} + 2\Delta x \cdot g(x_i, y_i) - y_{i+1} = 0, \quad (i = 2, 3, \ldots, n-1)$$

where the substitutions $y(x) = y_i$, $y(x+h) = y_{i+1}$, $y(x-h) = y_{i-1}$, and $h = \Delta x$, have been used.

If the function $g(x,y)$ is linear in y, then the equations described above consist of a set of $(n-2)$ equations. For example, if $n = 5$, we have 3 equations:

$$y_1 + 2\Delta x \cdot g(x_2, y_2) - y_3 = 0$$
$$y_2 + 2\Delta x \cdot g(x_3, y_3) - y_4 = 0$$
$$y_3 + 2\Delta x \cdot g(x_4, y_4) - y_5 = 0$$

Since y_1 is known (it is the initial condition), there are still 4 unknowns y_2, y_3, y_4, and y_5. We need to find a fourth equation to obtain a solution. We could use, for example, the forward difference equation applied to $i = 1$, i.e.,

$$(y_2 - y_1)/\Delta x = g(x_1, y_1),$$

or

$$y_2 - \Delta x \cdot g(x_1, y_1) - y_1 = 0.$$

The values of x_i, and n (or Δx), can be obtained as in the Euler forward (explicit) solution.

Example 1 -- Solve the ODE

$$dy/dx = y \sin(x),$$

with initial condition $y(0) = 1$, in the interval $0 < x < 5$. Use $\Delta x = 0.5$, or $n = (5-0)/0.5 + 1 = 11$.

Exact solution: the exact is $y(x) = \exp(-\cos(x))/(\cosh(1)-\sinh(1))$.

Numerical solution: Using a centered difference formula for dy/dx, i.e.,

$$dy/dx = (y_{i+1} - y_{i-1})/(2\Delta x),$$

into the ODE, we get $(y_{i+1} - y_{i-1})/(2\Delta x) = y_i \sin(x_i)$, which results in the $(n-2)$ implicit equations:

$$y_{i-1} + 2\Delta x \cdot \sin(x_i) \cdot y_i - y_{i+1} = 0, \quad (i = 2, 3, \ldots, n-1).$$

We already know that

$$y_1 = 1$$

(initial condition), thus we have $(n-1)$ unknowns left. We still need to come up with an additional equation, which could be obtained by using a forward difference formula for $i=1$, i.e.,

$$dy/dx|_{x=1} = (y_2 - y_1)/\Delta x = -y_1 \sin(x_1),$$

or

$$(1 + \Delta x \sin(x_1)) \cdot y_1 - y_2 = 0.$$

These equations can be written in the form of a matrix equation, for example, for n = 5:

$$\begin{bmatrix} 1 & 0 & 0 & 0 & 0 \\ 1+\Delta x \cdot \sin(x_1) & -1 & 0 & 0 & 0 \\ 1 & 2 \cdot \Delta x \cdot \sin(x_2) & -1 & 0 & 0 \\ 0 & 1 & 2 \cdot \Delta x \cdot \sin(x_3) & -1 & 0 \\ 0 & 0 & 1 & 2 \cdot \Delta x \cdot \sin(x_4) & -1 \end{bmatrix} \cdot \begin{bmatrix} y_1 \\ y_2 \\ y_3 \\ y_4 \\ y_5 \end{bmatrix} = \begin{bmatrix} y0 \\ 0 \\ 0 \\ 0 \\ 0 \end{bmatrix}$$

where y0 represents the initial condition for y. Note: The data requires n = 11. The example for n = 5 is presented above to provide a sense of the algorithm to fill out the matrix of data]. The matricial equation can be written as A·y = b. Matrix A and column vector b can be defined using SCILAB, as indicated below, and the solution found by using left-division. First, we enter the basic data for the problem:

```
-->x0=0;xn=5;Dx=0.5;y0=1;x=[x0:Dx:xn];n=(xn-x0)/Dx+1
 n  = 11.
```

Next, we fill the main diagonal, and the two diagonals below the main diagonal in matrix A using:

```
-->A=zeros(n,n); A(1,1) = 1; for j =2:n, A(j,j)=-1; end;

-->A(2,1)  =  1+Dx*sin(x(1));   for  j  =  3:n,   A(j,j-1)=2*Dx*sin(x(j-1));   end;
//second diagonal

-->for j = 3:n, A(j,j-2) = 1; end;         //Third diagonal
```

The right-hand side vector is defined as:

```
-->b = zeros(n,1); b(1) = 1;               //Right-hand side vector
```

The implicit solution is obtained from:

```
-->y = A\b;                                 //Solving for y
```

To compare the implicit solution we calculate also the explicit solution obtained through the Euler first-order solution:

```
-->deff('[z]=ff(x,y)','z=y*sin(x)')
-->getf('Euler1')
-->[xx,yy]=Euler1(x0,y0,xn,Dx,ff);
```

To produce data reproducing the exact solution we use:

```
-->deff('[y]=fE(x)','y=exp(-cos(x))/(cosh(1)-sinh(1))')
-->xE = [0:0.05:5]; yE = fE(xE);
```

The following commands will generate the plot showing the exact, implicit, and explicit solution in the same set of axes:

```
-->plot2d(xE',yE',1,'011','  ',[0 0 5 8])
-->plot2d(x',y,-1,'011','  ',[0 0 5 8])
```

```
-->plot2d(xx',yy',-9,'011',' ',[0 0 5 8])
-->xtitle('+ Implicit    o   Explicit','x','y')
```

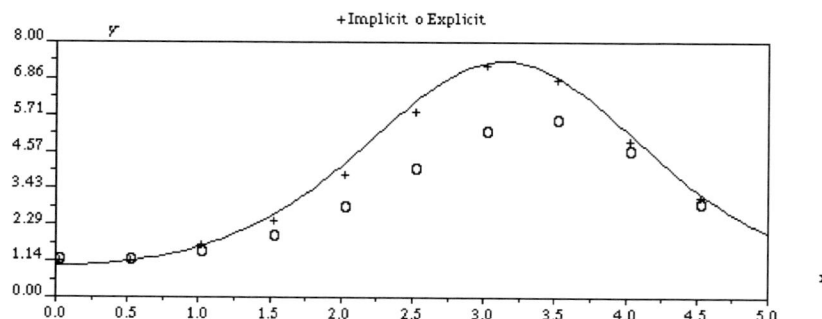

Explicit versus implicit methods

The idea behind the _explicit method_ is to be able to obtain values such as

$$y_{i+1} = f(x_i, y_i), \quad y_{i+2} = f(x_i, x_{i+1}, y_i, y_{i+1}), \text{ etc.}$$

In other words, your solution proceeds by solving explicitly for a new unknown value in the solution array, given all previous values in the array. On the other hand, _implicit methods_ imply the simultaneous solution of n linear algebraic equations that provide, at once, the elements of the solution array. With this distinction in mind between explicit and implicit methods, we outline explicit and implicit solutions for second-order, linear ODEs.

Outline of explicit solution for a second-order ODE

For example, to solve the ODE

$$d^2y/dx^2 + y = 0,$$

in the x-interval (0,20) subject to $y(0) = 1$, $dy/dx = 1$ at $y = 0$. Use $\Delta x = 0.1$.

First, we discretize the differential equation using the finite difference approximation

$$d^2y/dx^2 = (y_{i+2} - 2 \cdot y_{i+1} + y_i)/(\Delta x^2),$$

which results in

$$(y_{i+2} - 2 \cdot y_{i+1} + y_i)/(\Delta x^2) + y_i = 0.$$

An explicit solution can be obtained from the recurrence equation:

$$y_{i+2} = 2 \cdot y_{i+1} - (1+\Delta x^2) \cdot y_i, \quad i = 1, 2, \ldots, n-2;.$$

This equation is based on the two previous values of y_i, therefore, to get started we need the values $y = y_1$, and $y = y_2$. The value y_1 is provided in the initial condition $y(0) = 1$, i.e.,

$$y_1 = 1.$$

The value of y_2 can be obtained from the second initial condition $dy/dx = 1$, by replacing the derivative with the finite difference approximation:

$$dy/dx = (y_2 - y_1)/\Delta x,$$

which results in

$$(y_2 - y_1)/\Delta x = 1,$$

or

$$y_2 = y_1 + \Delta x.$$

The x-domain is discretized in a similar fashion as in the previous examples for first derivatives, i.e., by making $x_1 = a$, and $x_n = b$, and computing the values of x_i, $i = 2, 3, \ldots n$, with

$$x_i = x_1 + (i-1) \cdot \Delta x = a + (i-1) \cdot \Delta x,$$

where,

$$n = (x_n - x_1)/\Delta x + 1 = (b-a)/\Delta x + 1.$$

The implementation of the solution for this example is left as an exercise for the reader.

Outline of the implicit solution for a second-order ODE

We use the same problem from the previous section: solve the ODE

$$d^2y/dx^2 + y = 0,$$

in the x-interval (0,20) subject to $y(0) = 1$, $dy/dx = 1$ at $x = 0$. Use $\Delta x = 0.1$.

We discretize the differential equation using the finite difference approximation

$$d^2y/dx^2 = (y_{i+2} - 2 \cdot y_{i+1} + y_i)/(\Delta x^2),$$

which results in

$$(y_{i+1} - 2 \cdot y_i + y_{i-1})/(\Delta x^2) + y_i = 0.$$

From this result we get the following implicit equations:

$$y_{i-1} - (2-\Delta x^2) \cdot y_i + y_{i+1} = 0,$$

for $i = 2, 3, \ldots, n-1$. There are a total of $(n-2)$ equations. Since we have n unknowns, i.e. $y_1, y_2, \ldots, y_n$, we need two more equations to solve a system of linear equations. The remaining equations are provided by the two initial conditions:

From the initial condition, $y(0) = 1$, we can write $y_1 = 1$. For the second initial condition, $dy/dx = 1$, at $x = 0$, we will use a forward difference, i.e.,

$$dy/dx = (y_2 - y_1)/\Delta x,$$

or

$$y_2 - y_1 = \Delta x.$$

The x-domain is discretized in a similar fashion as in the previous examples. The n equations resulting from discretizing the domain can be written as a matrix equation similar to that of Example 1. Solution to the matrix equation can be accomplished, for example, through the use of left-division for matrices. The implementation of the solution for this example is left as an exercise for the reader.

SCILAB provides a number of functions for the numerical solution of differential equations. These functions are designed to operate on single differential equations (i.e., similar to the examples presented so far), as well as on systems of differential equations. Therefore, before presenting the SCILAB functions for solving ordinary differential equations, we present some concepts related to systems of such equations.

Systems of ordinary differential equations

To introduce the idea of systems of differential equations we will limit the coverage of the subject to first-order, linear equations with constant coefficients. A system of ordinary differential equations consists of a set of two or more equations with an equal number of unknown functions, $y_1(x)$, $y_2(x)$, etc. As an example consider the following *homogeneous* system:

$$\frac{dy_1}{dx} + 3y_1 - 2y_2 = 0, \quad \frac{dy_2}{dx} - y_1 + y_2 = 0.$$

In a homogeneous system the right-hand sides of the equations are zero. The following example represents a *non-homogeneous* system of ordinary differential equations:

$$\frac{dy_1}{dx} + 2y_1 - 5y_2 = \sin(x), \quad \frac{dy_2}{dx} - 4y_1 + 3y_2 = e^x.$$

Systems of ordinary differential equations using matrices

A homogeneous system of ODEs can be written as a single matrix differential equation by using vector functions and a matrix of coefficients as illustrated in the following example. First, we re-write the homogeneous system presented above to read:

$$\frac{dy_1}{dx} = -3y_1 + 2y_2,$$

$$\frac{dy_2}{dx} = y_1 - y_2.$$

Then, we define the vector function $\mathbf{f}(x) = [y_1(x)\ y_2(x)]^T$, and the matrix $\mathbf{A} = [-3\ 2;\ 1\ -1]$, and write the differential equation:

$$\frac{d}{dx}\mathbf{f}(x) = \mathbf{A}\ \mathbf{f}(x).$$

This result is equivalent to writting:

$$\frac{d}{dx}\begin{bmatrix} y_1(x) \\ y_2(x) \end{bmatrix} = \begin{bmatrix} -3 & 2 \\ 1 & -1 \end{bmatrix} \cdot \begin{bmatrix} y_1(x) \\ y_2(x) \end{bmatrix}.$$

The non-homogeneous system presented earlier can be re-written as

$$\frac{dy_1}{dx} = -2y_1 + 5y_2 - \sin(x),$$

$$\frac{dy_2}{dx} = 4y_1 - 3y_2 + e^x.$$

For this system we will use the same vector function $\mathbf{f}(x)$ defined earlier, but change the matrix $\mathbf{A}$ to $\mathbf{A} = [-2\ 5;\ 4\ -3]$. We also need to define a new vector function $\mathbf{g}(x) = [-\sin(x)\ \exp(x)]^T$. With these definitions, we can re-write the non-homogeneous system as:

$$\frac{d}{dx}\mathbf{f}(x) = \mathbf{A}\ \mathbf{f}(x) + \mathbf{g}(x),$$

or

$$\frac{d}{dx}\begin{bmatrix} y_1(x) \\ y_2(x) \end{bmatrix} = \begin{bmatrix} -2 & 5 \\ 4 & -3 \end{bmatrix} \cdot \begin{bmatrix} y_1(x) \\ y_2(x) \end{bmatrix} + \begin{bmatrix} -\sin(x) \\ \exp(x) \end{bmatrix}.$$

Systems of linear homogeneous ODEs - solution using matrices

Consider the system of linear nonhomogeneous ODEs with constant coefficients given by:

$$dy_1/dx = y_1 + y_3,\ dy_2/dx = y_1 + y_2 - y_3,\ dy_3/dx = 5y_1 + y_2 + y_3.$$

In matricial form, this can be written as:

$$\frac{d}{dx}\begin{bmatrix} y_1(x) \\ y_2(x) \\ y_3(x) \end{bmatrix} = \begin{bmatrix} 1 & 0 & 1 \\ 1 & 1 & -1 \\ 5 & 1 & 1 \end{bmatrix} \cdot \begin{bmatrix} y_1(x) \\ y_2(x) \\ y_3(x) \end{bmatrix}.$$

or,

$$\frac{d}{dx}\mathbf{f}(x) = \mathbf{A}\,\mathbf{f}(x).$$

We can use the eigenvalues and eigenvectors of matrix **A** to obtain the solution to the system of homogeneous equations by following this procedure:

1. Determine eigenvalues of the nxn matrix **A**. Call these eigenvalues $\lambda_1, \lambda_2, ..., \lambda_n$.

2. Determine the eigenvectors of the nxn matrix **A**. Call these eigenvectors

$$x_1 = [x_{11}, x_{12}, ..., x_{1,n}],\ x_2 = [x_{21}, x_{22}, ..., x_{2,n}],\ ....\ x_n = [x_{n,1}, x_{n,2}, ..., x_{n,n}].$$

3. The general solutions to the system are put together as follows:

$$y_1(x) = x_{11} B_1 \exp(\lambda_1 x) + x_{21} B_2 \exp(\lambda_2 x) + .. x_{1,n} B_n \exp(\lambda_n x),$$

$$y_2(x) = x_{21} B_1 \exp(\lambda_1 x) + x_{22} B_2 \exp(\lambda_2 x) + .. x_{2,n} B_n \exp(\lambda_n x),$$

$$\cdot$$
$$\cdot$$
$$\cdot$$

$$y_n(x) = x_{n,1} B_1 \exp(\lambda_1 x) + x_{n,2} B_2 \exp(\lambda_2 x) + .. x_{n,n} B_n \exp(\lambda_n x).$$

i.e.,

$$y_k(x) = \sum_{j=1}^{n} x_{k,j} B_j\, e^{(\lambda_j x)},\ k = 1,2,..., n$$

These general solutions include n unknown constants, $B_1, B_2, ..., B_n$. We will need n initial conditions to solve for the n constants to uniquely determine the solution to the system.

For the system under consideration, the solution steps can be translated into SCILAB instructions as shown below. To obtain eigenvalues and eigenvectors we use the user-defined function *eigenvectors* defined in Chapter 5.

```
-->A = [1,0,1;1,1,-1;5,1,1]
 A =

!   1.    0.     1. !
!   1.    1.   - 1. !
!   5.    1.     1. !

-->getf('eigenvectors')

-->[x,lambda] = eigenvectors(A)
 lambda =

!   3.1149075  - .8608059    .7458983 !
```

x =

```
!   .4170021  -  .3827458  -  .1983289 !
! - .2198294     .5884340     .9788391 !
!   .8819208     .7122156     .0503957 !
```

The solutions are, therefore,

$$y_1(x) = 0.4170021 B_1 e^{3.1149x} - 0.3827458 B_2 e^{-0.8608059x} - 0.198328 B_3 e^{0.7458983x},$$
$$y_2(x) = -0.219829 B_1 e^{3.1149x} + 0.5884340 B_2 e^{-0.8608059x} + 0.9788391 B_3 e^{0.7458983x},$$
$$y_3(x) = 0.8819208 B_1 e^{3.1149x} + 0.7122156 B_2 e^{-0.8608059x} + 0.0503957 B_3 e^{0.7458983x}.$$

Substituting the following initial conditions $y_1(0) = 1$, $y_2(0) = 2$, and $y_3(0) = 3$, produce a system of linear equations:

$$0.4170021 B_1 - 0.3827458 B_2 - 0.198328 B_3 = 1$$
$$-0.219829 B_1 + 0.5884340 B_2 + 0.9788391 B_3 = 2$$
$$0.8819208 B_1 + 0.7122156 B_2 + 0.0503957 B_3 = 3$$

which can be solved using left-division as follows:

```
-->AA=x;bb=[1;2;3]
 bb  =

!   1. !
!   2. !
!   3. !

-->B=AA\bb
 B  =

!   3.5181246 !
! -  .3600066 !
!   3.049763  !
```

The results are $B_1 = 3.5181246$, $B_2 = -0.3600066$, and $B_3 = 3.049763$.

To determine the coefficients in the solutions we can use:

```
-->C=AA.*[B B B]

 C  =

!   1.4670652 - 1.3465474 -  .6977459 !
!    .0791400 -  .2118401 -  .3523886 !
!   2.6896495   2.1720889    .153695  !
```

Thus, the solutions are:

$$y_1(x) = 1.4670652 e^{3.1149x} - 1.3465474 e^{-0.8608059x} - 0.6977459 e^{0.7458983x},$$
$$y_1(x) = 0.0791400 e^{3.1149x} - 0.2118401 e^{-0.8608059x} - 0.3523886 e^{0.7458983x},$$
$$y_1(x) = 2.6896495 e^{3.1149x} + 2.1720889 e^{-0.8608059x} + 0.153695 e^{0.7458983x}.$$

These solutions can be shown graphically by defining the following three functions:

```
-->deff('[y]=y1(x)',['y=0';'for j=1:3';'y=y+C(1,j)*exp(lambda(j)*x)';'end'])
-->deff('[y]=y2(x)',['y=0';'for j=1:3';'y=y+C(2,j)*exp(lambda(j)*x)';'end'])
-->deff('[y]=y3(x)',['y=0';'for
j=1:3';'y=y+C(3,j)*exp(lambda(j)*x)';'end'])
```

A plot of the solution is shown next:

```
-->xx=[0:0.1:1];yy1=real(y1(xx));yy2=real(y2(xx));yy3=real(y3(xx));
-->xset('window',1);xset('mark',[-1 -2 -3],1);
-->plot2d([xx' xx' xx'],[yy1' yy2' yy3'],[-1,-2,-3],'011',' ',[0 -20 1 80])
-->plot2d([xx' xx' xx'],[yy1' yy2' yy3'],[1,2,3],'011',' ',[0 -20 1 80])
```

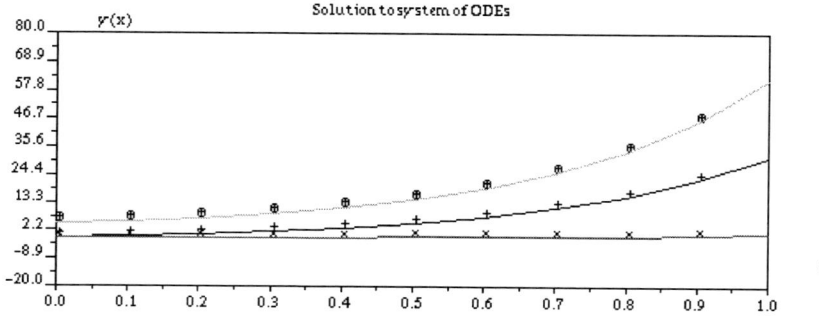

The solution to the non-homogeneous system $\frac{d}{dx} \mathbf{f}(x) = \mathbf{A}\,\mathbf{f}(x)$, can be accomplished in a straightforward manner by using the equation,

$$\mathbf{f}(x) = \exp(\mathbf{A}x)\mathbf{b},$$

where **b** is a vector containing the initial conditions, i.e.,

$$\mathbf{b} = [y_1(0)\ y_2(0)\ldots y_n(0)]^T.$$

and the expression $exp(At)$ is a matrix defined as:

$$\exp(\mathbf{A}t) = \mathbf{I} + \mathbf{A}t + \frac{1}{2!}\mathbf{A}^2 t^2 + \ldots = \mathbf{I} + \sum_{k=1}^{\infty} \frac{1}{k!}\mathbf{A}^k t^k,$$

where $\mathbf{I}$ is the identity matrix, $A^2 = \mathbf{AA}$, $A^3 = A^2\mathbf{A}$, ... To evaluate the expression $exp(Ax)$, SCILAB provides function $expm$.

The solution to the linear system under consideration, using the equation $f(x) = exp(\mathbf{A}x)\mathbf{b}$, can be obtained as follows using SCILAB (matrix A is the same matrix of coefficients of the ODE system defined earlier):

```
-->deff('[y] = fm(t)','y=real(expm(A*t)*bb)')
```

A plot of the solution using this matrix approach is produced with the following SCILAB statements:

```
-->xx=[0:0.1:1]; n = length(xx)
 n  = 11.

-->ym=[];for j=1:n, ym=[ym fm(xx(j))]; end;

-->plot2d([xx',xx',xx'],[ym(1,:)',ym(2,:)',ym(3,:)'],[1,2,3])

-->xtitle('Solution to system of ODEs','x','y(x)')
```

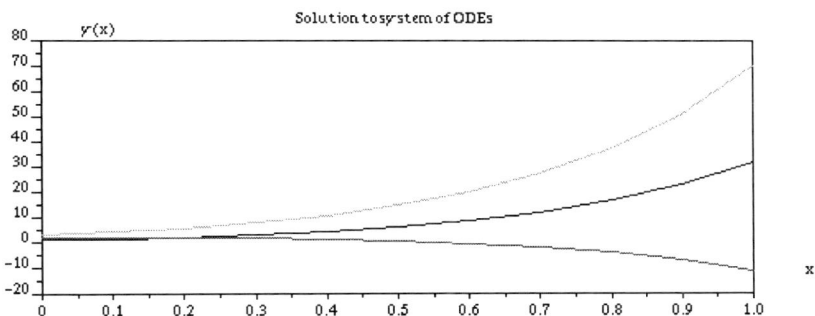

Systems of linear nonhomogeneous ODEs - solution using matrices

Consider the system of linear nonhomogeneous ordinary differential equations with constant coefficients given by

$$\frac{dy_1}{dx} = y_1 + y_3 + e^x, \quad \frac{dy_2}{dx} = y_2 - y_3 + \sin(x), \text{ and } \frac{dy_3}{dx} = 5y_1 + y_2 + y_3 + \cos(x)$$

This system can be written as a matricial differential equation as:

$$\begin{bmatrix} \frac{\partial}{\partial x} y1(x) \\ \frac{\partial}{\partial x} y2(x) \\ \frac{\partial}{\partial x} y3(x) \end{bmatrix} = \begin{bmatrix} 1 & 0 & 1 \\ 0 & 1 & -1 \\ 5 & 1 & 1 \end{bmatrix} \begin{bmatrix} y1(x) \\ y2(x) \\ y3(x) \end{bmatrix} + \begin{bmatrix} e^x \\ \sin(x) \\ \cos(x) \end{bmatrix}$$

In general, a nonhomogeneous system can be written in matricial form as

$$\frac{d}{dx} \mathbf{f}(x) = \mathbf{A}\ \mathbf{f}(x) + \mathbf{g}(x).$$

For the case under consideration, we have:

$$A := \begin{bmatrix} 1 & 0 & 1 \\ 0 & 1 & -1 \\ 5 & 1 & 1 \end{bmatrix}$$

$$g := \begin{bmatrix} e^x \\ \sin(x) \\ \cos(x) \end{bmatrix}$$

A solution to the system of ODEs is given by

$$\mathbf{f}(x) = \Phi(x)\mathbf{C} + \Phi(x) \int \Phi(x)^{(-1)} \mathbf{g}(x)\, dx,$$

where $\Phi(x) = \exp(Ax)$ is known as a *fundamental matrix* of the system, $\Phi(x)^{(-1)}$ is the inverse matrix of $\Phi(x)$, and $\mathbf{C}$ is a vector of constants, i.e., $\mathbf{C} = [C_1\ C_2 \ldots C_n]$.

Unlike the homogeneous case, the presence of the integral in the solution $\mathbf{f}(x)$ complicates the calculation or programming of the solution using SCILAB. The reader is referred to symbolic packages such as *Maple* or *Mathematica* to obtain such solutions. Numerical solutions, however, are possible with SCILAB, as will be demonstrated in subsequent sections of this book.

Converting second-order linear equations to a system of equations

A second-order linear ODE of the form $\frac{d^2 y}{dx^2} + \frac{b\,dy}{dx} + c\,y = r(x)$, can be transformed into a linear system of equations by introducing the relationship $u(x) = \frac{dy}{dx}$, so that $\frac{d^2 y}{dx^2} = \frac{du}{dx}$, thus, the equation reduces to $\frac{du}{dx} + b\,u + c\,y = r(x)$, or $\frac{du}{dx} = -b\,u - c\,y + r(x)$. The resulting system of equations is:

$$\frac{du}{dx} = -b\,u - c\,y + r(x),$$

$$\frac{dy}{dx} = u.$$

Which can be written in matricial form as $df/dx = A\,f(x) + g(x)$, with

$$f(x) = \begin{bmatrix} u \\ y \end{bmatrix},\ A = \begin{bmatrix} -b & -c \\ 1 & 0 \end{bmatrix},\ g(x) = \begin{bmatrix} r(x) \\ 0 \end{bmatrix}.$$

For example, the solution to the second order differential equation

$$\frac{d^2 y}{dx^2} + \frac{5\,dy}{dx} - 3\,y = x,$$

can be obtained by solving the equivalent first-order linear system:

$$\frac{du}{dx} = -5\,u + 3\,y + x,$$

$$\frac{dy}{dx} = u.$$

The procedure outlined above to transform a second order linear equation can be used to convert a linear equation of order n into a system of first-order linear equations. For example, if the original ODE is written as:

$$\frac{d^n y}{dx^n} + a_{n-1}\frac{d^{(n-1)} y}{dx^{(n-1)}} + \ldots + a_2\frac{d^2 y}{dx^2} + \frac{a_1\,dy}{dx} + a_0 y = r(x),$$

we can re-write it as

$$\frac{d^n y}{dx^n} = -a_{n-1}\frac{d^{(n-1)} y}{dx^{(n-1)}} - \ldots - a_2\frac{d^2 y}{dx^2} - \frac{a_1\,dy}{dx} - a_0 y + r(x),$$

and transform it into a system of n first-order linear equations given by:

$$\frac{du_{n-1}}{dx} = -a_{n-1}\,u_{n-1} - a_{n-2}\,u_{n-2} - \ldots - a_2\,u_2 - a_1\,u_1 - a_0 y + r(x),$$

$$\frac{du_{n-2}}{dx} = u_{n-1}, \quad \frac{du_{n-3}}{dx} = u_{n-2}, \quad \ldots, \quad \frac{du_1}{dx} = u_2, \quad \frac{dy}{dx} = u_1,$$

or, in matricial form,

$$\mathbf{f}(x) = \begin{bmatrix} u_{n-1} \\ u_{n-2} \\ \vdots \\ u_2 \\ u_1 \\ y \end{bmatrix}, \quad A = \begin{bmatrix} -a_{n-1} & -a_{n-2} & -a_{n-3} & \cdots & -a_1 & -a_0 \\ 1 & 0 & 0 & \cdots & 0 & 0 \\ 0 & 1 & 0 & \cdots & 0 & 0 \\ 0 & 0 & 1 & \cdots & 0 & 0 \\ \vdots & \vdots & \vdots & \ddots & \vdots & \vdots \\ 0 & 0 & 0 & \cdots & 1 & 0 \end{bmatrix}, \quad \mathbf{g}(x) = \begin{bmatrix} r(x) \\ 0 \\ \vdots \\ 0 \\ 0 \\ 0 \end{bmatrix}$$

For example, to transform the following fourth-order ($n=4$) linear ODE

$$\frac{d^4 y}{dx^4} + \frac{3 d^3 y}{dx^3} - \frac{2 d^2 y}{dx^2} + \frac{5 dy}{dx} + y = 0,$$

subjected to $y = 1$, $\frac{dy}{dx} = -1$, $\frac{d^2 y}{dx^2} = 0$, $\frac{d^3 y}{dx^3} = -1$, at $x = 0$, into a first-order linear system, we would write:

$du_3/dx = -3u_3(x) + 2u_2(x) - 5u_1(x) - y(x) + x^2/2$, $du_2/dx = u_3(x)$, $du_1/dx = u_2(x)$, and $dy/dx = u_1(x)$,

or

$$\frac{d}{dx}\begin{bmatrix} u_3(x) \\ u_2(x) \\ u_1(x) \\ y(x) \end{bmatrix} = \begin{bmatrix} -3 & 2 & -5 & -1 \\ 1 & 0 & 0 & 0 \\ 0 & 1 & 0 & 0 \\ 0 & 0 & 1 & 0 \end{bmatrix} \cdot \begin{bmatrix} u_3(x) \\ u_2(x) \\ u_1(x) \\ y(x) \end{bmatrix} + \begin{bmatrix} x^2/2 \\ 0 \\ 0 \\ 0 \end{bmatrix}.$$

with $\mathbf{v}(x) = [u_3(x); u_2(x); u_1(x); y(x)]^T$, $A = [-3,2,-5,-1;1,0,0,0;0,1,0,0;0,0,1,0]$; and $\mathbf{g}(x) = [x^2/;0; 0; 0]^T$, the system of differential equations is written as $d\mathbf{v}/dx = A\mathbf{v} + \mathbf{g}(x)$. The initial conditions are $y(0) = 1$, $u_1(0) = dy/dx = -1$, $u_2(0) = du_1/dx = d^2y/dx^2 = 0$, $u_3(0) = du_2/dx = d^2u_1/dx^2 = d^3y/dx^3 = -1$, or $\mathbf{u}_0 = [-1;0;-1;1]$.

SCILAB functions for the numerical solutions of initial value problems (IVP)

SCILAB provides function *ode* for the solution of initial value problems, i.e., those subject to initial, rather than boundary, conditions.

Function *ode*

The simplest call to function *ode* is

$$y=ode(y0,x0,x,f)$$

where the point *(x0,y0)* represents the initial conditions for the differential equation

$$dy/dx = f(x,y),$$

and *x* is a vector of values of the independent variable.

The function *f* can be a single function *f(x,y)* or a vector of functions,

$$f(x,y) = \begin{bmatrix} f_1(x,y) \\ f_2(x,y) \\ \vdots \\ f_n(x,y) \end{bmatrix} = \begin{bmatrix} f_1(x,y_1,y_2,\cdots,y_n) \\ f_2(x,y_1,y_2,\cdots,y_n) \\ \vdots \\ f_n(x,y_1,y_2,\cdots,y_n) \end{bmatrix}.$$

In the latter case, *y* is also a vector representing the variables $y = [y_1\ y_2\ \ldots\ y_n]^T$.

The first example shows the solution to the differential equation *dy/dx = xy*, in the range *0<x<2*, with initial conditions *y(0) = 1*.

```
-->deff('[z]=f(x,y)','z=x.*y')

-->x0 = 0; y0 = 1; Dx = 0.1; xn = 2; x = [x0:Dx:xn];

-->y = ode(y0,x0,x,f);

-->plot(x,y,'x','y','ode solution to dy/dx = x*y')
```

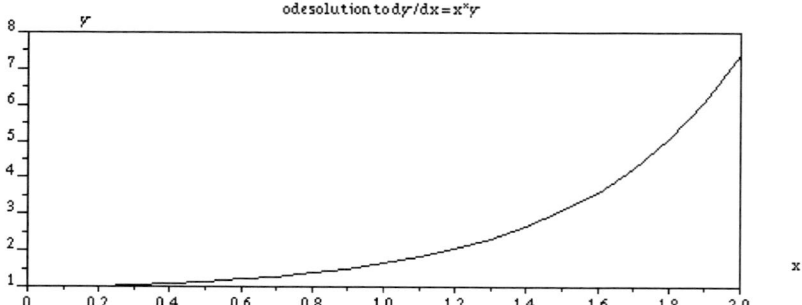

In the second example, we solve the differential equation $du/dt = u\,\sin(t)$, in the range $0<t<10$, with initial condition $u(0) = 5$.

```
-->deff('[w]=g(t,u)','w=u.*sin(t)')

-->t0=0;Dt=0.1;tn=1;u0=5;t=[t0:Dt:tn];

-->u = ode(u0,t0,t,g);

-->plot(t,u,'t','u','ode solution to du/dt = u*sin(t)')
```

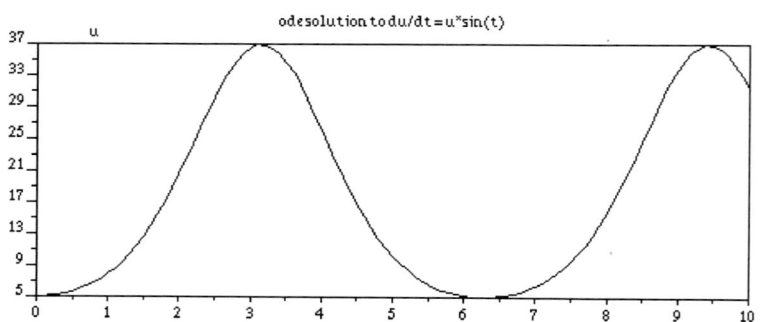

The next example uses a system of two differential equations, namely,

$$dy_1/dx = y_2 + x$$
$$dy_2/dx = -y_1$$

with initial conditions $y_1 = 1$, $y_2 = 2$, for $x_0 = 0$.

```
-->deff('[w]=f(x,y)',['y1=y(2)+x','y2=-y(1)','w = [y1;y2]'])

-->x0 = 0; Dx = 0.1; xn = 2; y0 = [1;2];

-->x = [x0:Dx:xn]; y = ode(y0,x0,x,f);
```

```
-->min(y),max(y)
 ans   = - 2.8322936
 ans   =   2.999147

-->plot2d([x',x'],[y(1,:)', y(2,:)'],[1,-1],'111','y1@y2',[0 -3 2 4])

-->xtitle('ode solution for two functions','x','y')
```

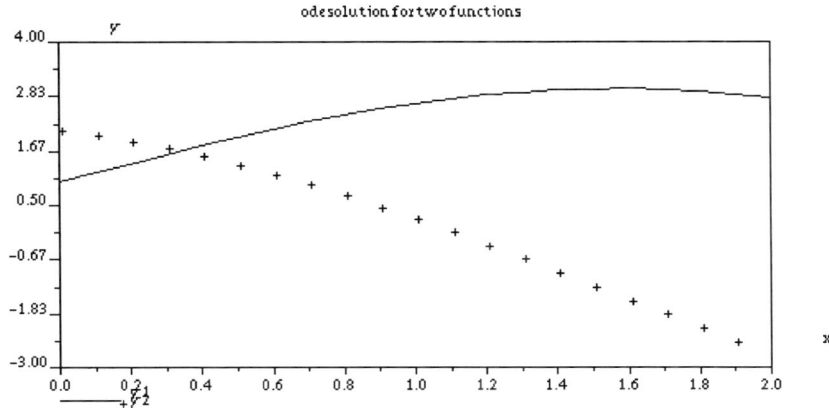

Numerical methods used in function *ode*

Function *ode* uses as default the numerical method known as the Adams method. In general, Adams methods for solving the differential equation $dy/dx = f(x,y)$ basically consist in obtaining $y_{k+1} = y(x_{k+1})$ through the fitting of a polynomial that interpolates $f(x,y)$ at selected points (x_j, y_j) of the solution. The *k*-th order Adams-Bashforth method is an explicit method that uses the current point (x_n, y_n) and *k-1* points for the solution. The *k*-th order Adams-Moulton method is an implicit method using points x_{n+1}, y_{n+1}, (x_n, y_n) and *k-2* previously calculated points. Adams methods are also known as *predictor-corrector* methods because their solution involves an initial *predictor* step, which is then modified in a *corrector* step that improves the solution.

Function *ode* can be called with an additional argument that specifies the numerical method to be used for a solution. This argument becomes the first argument in the call to function *ode*. The function call, if such optional argument is used, is

$$[y] = ode([type], y0, t0, t, f)$$

where *type* is one of the following character strings: *"adams"*, *"stiff"*, *"rk"*, *"rkf"*, *"fix"*, *"discrete"*, or *"roots"*. The meaning of each of these options is presented next:

"adams":   Default value. Uses the Adams predictor-corrector method for the solution.

"stiff":   This option invokes the use of a Backward Differentiation Formula (BDF) for the solution of stiff ordinary differential equations.

"rk":   Invokes an adaptive, 4-th order, Runge-Kutta method.

"rkf": Invokes a Fehlberg's Runge-Kutta method of order 4 and 5 (RKF45).

"fix": Same solver as "rkf", a simpler user interface.

"root": ODE solver with root finding capabilities.

"discrete": Discrete time simulation.

The type options "root" and "discrete" do not represent different methods for solving ordinary differential equations. Instead, they represent enhanced abilities for function code for root finding and combining discrete and continuous systems. The applications of these options will be presented later.

Adams-Bashforth methods

These methods involve explicit functions for y_i in terms of k points in the solution. The equations describing the Adams-Bashforth methods of orders 1 through 5 are shown below. In these equations the term f_n represents $f(x_n, y_n)$ and Δx is the increment in the independent variable x:

$y_{n+1} = y_n + \Delta x \cdot f_n$ (same as Euler 1st order method)
$y_{n+1} = y_n + (\Delta x /2)(3f_n - f_{n-1})$
$y_{n+1} = y_n + (\Delta x /12)(23f_n - 16f_{n-1} + 5f_{n-2})$
$y_{n+1} = y_n + (\Delta x /24)(55f_n - 59f_{n-1} + 37f_{n-2} - 9f_{n-3})$
$y_{n+1} = y_n + (\Delta x /720)(1901f_n - 2774f_{n-1} + 2616f_{n-2} - 1274f_{n-3} + 251f_{n-4})$

Adams-Moulton methods

The following equations represent the Adams-Moulton methods of orders 1 through 5. These are implicit methods, in which the term $f_{n+1} = f(x_{n+1}, y_{n+1})$:

$y_{n+1} = y_n + \Delta x \cdot f_{n+1}$
$y_{n+1} = y_n + (\Delta x /2)(f_{n+1} - f_n)$
$y_{n+1} = y_n + (\Delta x /12)(f_{n+1} + 8f_n - f_{n-1})$
$y_{n+1} = y_n + (\Delta x /24)(9f_{n+1} + 19f_n - 5f_{n-1} + f_{n-2})$
$y_{n+1} = y_n + (\Delta x /720)(251f_{n+1} + 646f_n - 264f_{n-1} + 106f_{n-2} - 19f_{n-3} + 251)$

Adams-Bashforth-Moulton methods

The Adams-Bashforth-Moulton predictor-corrector method uses one of the Adams-Bashforth formulas to produce a first approximation for the solution (a predictor value), followed by an evaluation of the function $f(x_{n+1}, y_{n+1}) = f_{n+1}$, which is used in an Adams-Moulton formula to produce a better approximation to the solution (a corrector value). Depending on the order of the formula used for the predictor part of the algorithm, we need one or more values of the solution to get the algorithm started. The Runge-Kutta method, described below, can be used to generate those few initial data values necessary to get the Adams-Bashforth-Moulton procedure started.

Runge-Kutta methods

The general approach for the Runge-Kutta methods consists of the following equations

$$k_1 = \Delta x \, f(x_n, y_n)$$
$$k_2 = \Delta x \, f(x_n + \alpha h, y_n + \beta k_1)$$
$$y_{n+1} = y_n + \alpha k_1 + \beta k_2$$

where the values of the parameters α and β are selected from Taylor series expansions representing different orders of the approximation. For example, for an error of order ^{3}, the Runge-Kutta method is given by

$$k_1 = \Delta x \, f(x_n, y_n)$$
$$k_2 = \Delta x \, f(x_n + h, y_n + k_1)$$
$$y_{n+1} = y_n + (k_1 + k_2)/2.$$

A fourth-order Runge-Kutta method is given by the formulas

$$k_1 = \Delta x \, f(x_n, y_n)$$
$$k_2 = \Delta x \, f(x_n + \Delta x /2, y_n + k_1/2)$$
$$k_3 = \Delta x \, f(x_n + \Delta x /2, y_n + k_2/2)$$
$$k_4 = \Delta x \, f(x_n + \Delta x, y_n + k_3)$$
$$y_{n+1} = y_n + (k_1 + 2k_2 + 2k_3 + k_4)/6.$$

A fourth-fifth order Runge-Kutta method produces a fourth order and a fifth order estimate (y_{n+1}, z_{n+1}) of the function through the following algorithm:

$$k_1 = \Delta x \cdot f(x_n, y_n)$$

$$k_2 = \Delta x \cdot f(x_n + \frac{\Delta x}{4}, y_n + \frac{k_1}{4})$$

$$k_3 = \Delta x \cdot f(x_n + \frac{3\Delta x}{8}, y_n + \frac{3k_1}{32} + \frac{9k_2}{32})$$

$$k_4 = \Delta x \cdot f(x_n + \frac{12\Delta x}{13}, y_n + \frac{1932k_1}{2197} - \frac{7200k_2}{2197} + \frac{7296k_3}{2197})$$

$$k_5 = \Delta x \cdot f(x_n + \Delta x, y_n + \frac{439k_1}{216} - 8k_2 + \frac{3680k_3}{513} - \frac{845k_4}{4104})$$

$$k_6 = \Delta x \cdot f(x_n + \frac{\Delta x}{2}, y_n - \frac{8k_1}{27} + 2k_2 - \frac{3544k_3}{2565} + \frac{1859k_4}{4104} - \frac{11k_5}{40})$$

$$y_{n+1} = y_n + \frac{25}{216}k_1 + \frac{1408}{2565}k_3 + \frac{2197}{4104}k_4 - \frac{1}{5}k_5$$

$$z_{n+1} = y_n + \frac{16}{135}k_1 + \frac{6656}{12825}k_3 + \frac{28561}{56430}k_4 - \frac{9}{50}k_5 + \frac{2}{55}k_6$$

Examples of function ode with different numerical methods

In this first example we solve the differential equation $dy/dx = (x+1)e^{-0.01y}$ in the range $0<x<5$, with initial condition $y(0) = 0$ using different methods within function ode:

```
-->deff('[z]=f(x,y)','z = (x+1).*exp(-0.01.*y)')

-->x0=0;Dx=0.1;xn=5.0;y0=0;x=[x0:Dx:xn];

-->y1 = ode('adams',y0,x0,x,f);

-->y2 = ode('rk',y0,x0,x,f);

-->y3 = ode('rkf',y0,x0,x,f);

-->min([y1 y2 y3]),max([y1 y2 y3])
 ans   = 0.
 ans   = 16.126815

-->plot2d([x',x',x'],[y1',y2',y3'],[-1,-2,-3],'111',...
-->'Adams method@Runge-Kutta 4th order@Runge-Kutta 4-5th order',...
-->[0 0 5 20])

-->xtitle('dy/dx = (x+1)*exp(-0.01*y)','x','y')
```

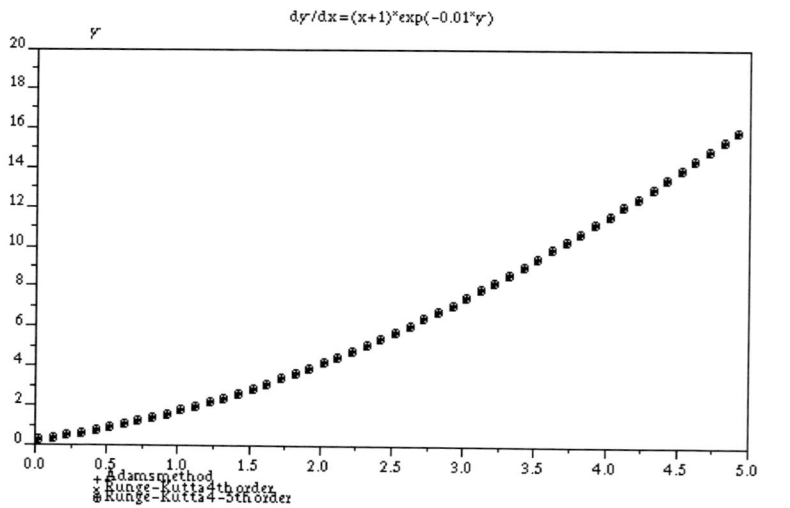

In the following example we solve the system of equations

$$dy_1/dx = -y_1,\ dy_2/dx = y_2$$

in the range $0<x<5$, with initial conditions $y_1(0) = -1$, $y_2(0) = 1$:

```
-->deff('[z]=f(x,y)',['z1=-y(1)','z2=y(2)','z=[z1;z2]'])
-->x0=0;Dx=0.1;xn=5.0;y0=[-1;1];x=[x0:Dx:xn];
-->y1 = ode('adams',y0,x0,x,f);
-->y2 = ode('rk',y0,x0,x,f);
-->y3 = ode('rkf',y0,x0,x,f);

-->min(y1), max(y1)
 ans  =   - 1.
 ans  =     148.4132

-->plot2d([x',x',x'],[y1(1,:)',y2(1,:)',y3(1,:)'],[-1,-2,-3],'111',...
-->'Adams method@Runge-Kutta 4th order@Runge-Kutta 4-5th order',...
-->[0 -1 5 0])

-->xtitle('System of equations - y(1)','x','y')
```

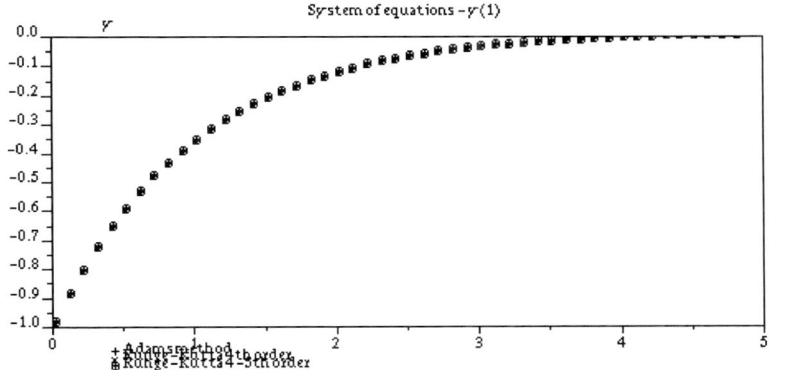

```
-->plot2d([x',x',x'],[y1(2,:)',y2(2,:)',y3(2,:)'],[-1,-2,-3],'111',...
-->'Adams method@Runge-Kutta 4th order@Runge-Kutta 4-5th order',...
-->[0 -1 5 150])
```

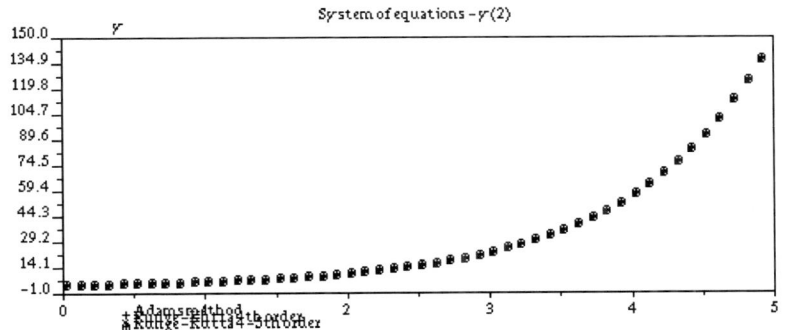

Stiff ordinary differential equations

There are a number of definitions of a stiff matrix (see, for example, Hoffman, J.D., 1992, "Numerical Methods for Engineers and Scientists," McGraw-Hill, Inc., New York) based on their requirements for stability or on the presence of a rapidly decaying transient. The concept of *stability* in the numerical solution of an ordinary differential equation involves the analysis of the error inherent in the numerical method. If a small error introduced in the first step of the numerical solution remains constant or decays as solution steps accumulate, the solution is said to be *stable*. If, on the other hand, a small error involved in the first step of the solution increases without bound as the solution steps accumulate the solution is said to be *unstable*.

Thus, based on the numerical solution of an ordinary differential equation, *stiff* equation is defined as one which requires a step size so small for stability that round-off errors (inherent in computer calculations) become significant. Alternatively, a *stiff* equation is one that contains some transient component that decays rapidly compared to the main transient component.

As an example, consider the ordinary differential equation $dy/dx = f(x,y) = -1000(y-x)+2001$, whose exact solution is $y(x) = -\exp(-1000x)+x+2$. The solution is composed of two parts $y_1(x) = -\exp(-1000x)$, and $y_2(x) = x+2$, which vary at significantly different rates as x varies. The first component, $y_1(x)$, goes quickly to zero, while the second component $y_2(x)$, produces a simple linear solution. Component $y_1(x)$ is only significant for very small values of x. The following two graphs illustrate the behavior of the solution $y(x)$ for small and relatively large values of x.

```
-->deff('[y]=f(x)','y=-exp(-1000.*x)+x+2')

-->plot(xs,ys,'x','y','solution for small values of x')
```

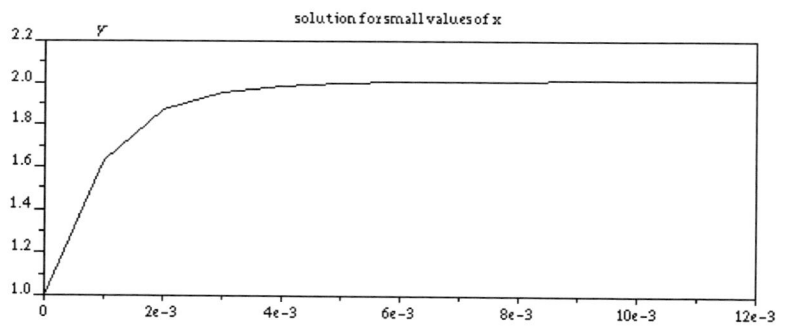

```
-->xl=[0:0.001:1]; yl=f(xl);

-->plot(xl,yl,'x','y','solution for larger values of x')
```

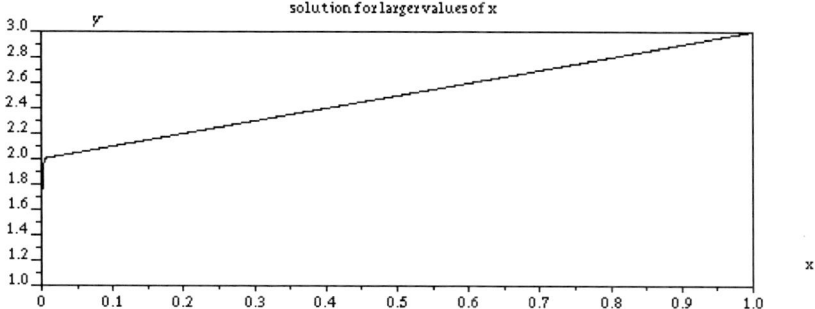

To determine the effect that the increment in the independent variable Δx, has on the solution, we attempt solutions using function *Euler1* that implements Euler's first-order method using values of Δx = 0.0005, 0.0010, 0.0020, 0.0025. We then plot the solution to compare the results for different values of Δx.

```
-->deff('[dydx]=g(x,y)','dydx=-1000.*(y-x)+2001')
-->getf('Euler1')
-->Dx=0.0005;x0=0;xn=0.01;y0=1;[x1,y1]=Euler1(x0,y0,xn,Dx,g);
-->Dx=0.0010;x0=0;xn=0.01;y0=1;[x2,y2]=Euler1(x0,y0,xn,Dx,g);
-->Dx=0.0020;x0=0;xn=0.01;y0=1;[x3,y3]=Euler1(x0,y0,xn,Dx,g);
-->Dx=0.0025;x0=0;xn=0.01;y0=1;[x4,y4]=Euler1(x0,y0,xn,Dx,g);

-->min([y1 y2 y3 y4]), max([y1 y2 y3 y4])
 ans  = - 3.0525
 ans  =   5.3825

-->rect = [0 -4 0.01 6];
-->plot2d(x1,y1,-1,'011',' ',rect)
-->plot2d(x2,y2,-2,'011',' ',rect)
-->plot2d(x3,y3,-3,'011',' ',rect)
-->plot2d(x4,y4,-4,'011',' ',rect)
-->plot2d(x1,y1,1,'011',' ',rect)
-->plot2d(x2,y2,2,'011',' ',rect)
-->plot2d(x3,y3,3,'011',' ',rect)
-->plot2d(x4,y4,4,'011',' ',rect)
-->plot(xl,yl,'x','y','solution for larger values of x')
-->xtitle('Stiff equation numerical solution Euler 1st order','x','y')
```

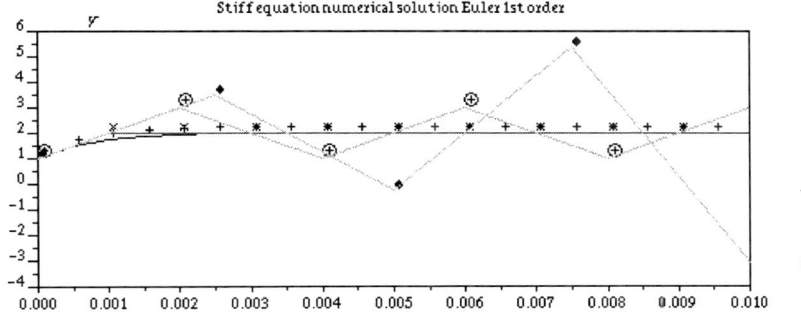

The points indicated by the crosses and asterisks correspond to the values Δx = 0.0005 and 0.0010. The values indicated by the crosses enclosed in circles correspond to Δx = 0.0020, and the dark diamond marks correspond to Δx = 0.0025. The result indicates that Δx must be of size 0.0010 or smaller to ensure stability. This is a characteristic of a stiff ordinary differential equation since a very small step Δx is required for stability.

Function *ode* allows the use of the argument 'stiff' to change the numerical method for the solution to a Backward Differentiation Formula (BDF) for its solution. The following SCILAB commands demonstrate the use of function *ode* with the argument 'stiff' for the solution of the differential equation under consideration. The graph thus produced shows that the solutions are stable for the four values of Δx used.

```
-->deff('[dydx]=g(x,y)','dydx=-1000.*(y-x)+2001')

-->Dx=0.0005;x0=0;xn=0.01;y0=1;x1=[x0:Dx:xn];y1=ode('stiff',y0,x0,x1,g);

-->Dx=0.0010;x0=0;xn=0.01;y0=1;x2=[x0:Dx:xn];y2=ode('stiff',y0,x0,x2,g);

-->Dx=0.0020;x0=0;xn=0.01;y0=1;x3=[x0:Dx:xn];y3=ode('stiff',y0,x0,x3,g);

-->Dx=0.0025;x0=0;xn=0.01;y0=1;x4=[x0:Dx:xn];y4=ode('stiff',y0,x0,x4,g);

-->min([y1 y2 y3 y4]), max([y1 y2 y3 y4])
 ans  = 1.
 ans  = 2.0099544

-->rect = [0 0 0.01 2.5];

-->plot2d(x1,y1,-1,'011',' ',rect)
-->plot2d(x2,y2,-2,'011',' ',rect)
-->plot2d(x3,y3,-3,'011',' ',rect)
-->plot2d(x4,y4,-4,'011',' ',rect)

-->xtitle('Stiff equation - ode function with option stiff','x','y')
```

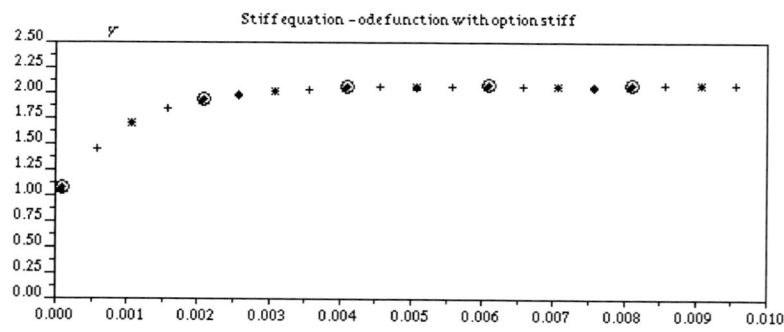

Function *ode* with root finding option

Function *ode* can be invoked with the first argument *'root'* if the solution of the ordinary differential equation $dy/dx = f(x,y)$ is subject to the constraint $g(x,y) = 0$. The solution is calculated for a range of values of x (a vector) and stopped when the constraint $g(x,y)=0$ is satisfied. For example, suppose that we are solving the differential equation $dy/dx = f(x,y) = x \sin(y)$, with initial conditions $y(0) = 1$, subjected to the constraint $g(x,y) = x + y - 5 = 0$, in the range $0 < x < 10$. We will obtain the solution by using:

```
-->deff('[dydx]=f(x,y)','dydx = x*sin(y)')

-->deff('[w]=g(x,y)','w = x+y-5')

-->y0=1;x0=0;x=[0:0.1:10];

-->[y,rd]=ode('root',y0,x0,x,f,1,g);
```

We can check that the solution was stopped before reaching the maximum value of x by checking the lengths of the vectors x and y:

```
-->length(x), length(y)
 ans  =   101.

 ans  =   23.
```

Vector *rd* contains information on the point where the calculation was stopped.

```
-->rd
 rd  =

!   2.1889184    1. !
```

To plot the results of the recent call to function *ode* we create a new vector of x values, xx:

```
-->xx = x(1:23);

-->plot(xx,y,'x','y','ode function with root option')
```

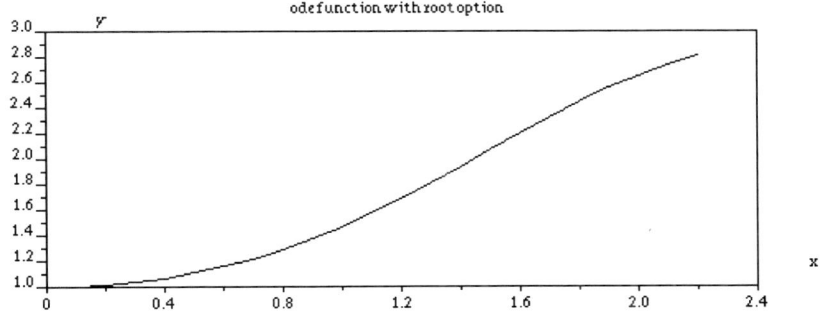

The following plot shows the truncated solution altogether with the solution for the full x range (0,10):

```
-->yf = ode(y0,x0,x,f);

-->plot(x,yf,'x','y','ode function solution')

-->plot2d(xx,y,-9,'011',' ',[0 1 10 3.4])
```

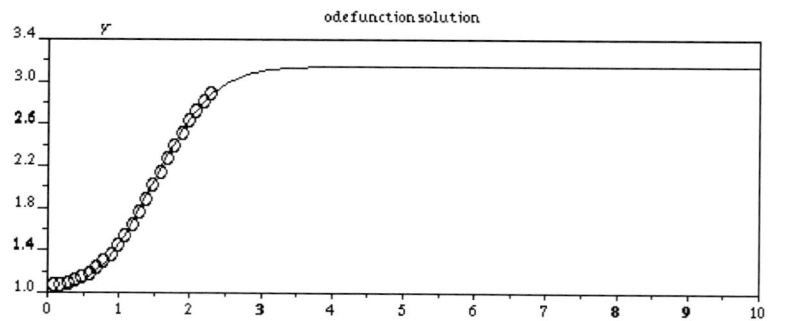

Discrete solutions with function ode

Function ode provides the option "discrete" for the solution of a differential equation $dy/dx = f(x,y)$ based on a set of discrete (integer) indices kvect, that starts with k0. The initial condition is $y(k0) = y0$. The simplest call to the function is

$$[y] = ode('discrete', y0, k0, kvect, f).$$

When using this option, the solution is calculated recursively by using $y_{k+1} = f(k, y_k)$, for $k = 1, 2, \ldots$

As an example, we solve the differential equation $dy/dx = 2x$, in a discrete domain $k = 1, 2, \ldots, 20$, with $y(1) = 2.5$:

```
-->deff('[dydx]=f(x,y)','dydx=x.^2-1')

-->k0 = 1; kvect = [1:1:20];  y0 = 2.5;

-->y = ode('discrete',y0,k0,kvect,f);
```

The following plot shows the results of y as function of k:

```
-->plot(kvect,y,'k','y','ode function with option discrete')
```

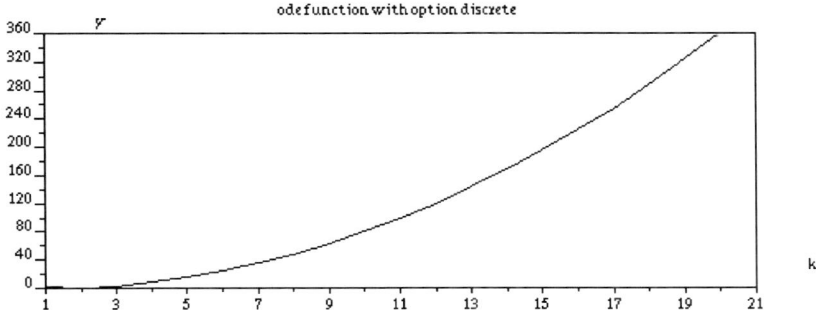

Changing ODE numerical solution parameters with odeoptions

Function *ode* uses a number of parameters which can be redefined through the use of the function *odeoptions()*. When this command is used, SCILAB generates an input form where the parameters of the numerical methods for ordinary differential equations can be modified. Application of the function *odeoptions()* can be used to modify the global variable *%ODEOPTIONS*. This variable is a vector containing the following information:

$$[itask, tcrit, h0, hmax, hmin, jactyp, mxstep, maxordn, maxords, ixpr, ml, mu]$$

where the different elements are described as follows:

itask - identifies the task required from the numerical method. Possible values of *task* are:

1 : normal computation at specified times
2 : computation at mesh points (given in first row of output of *ode*)
3 : calculate one step at one internal mesh point and return
4 : normal computation without overshooting *tcrit* (see below)
5 : one step, without passing *tcrit* (see below), and return

tcrit - this value applies when *itask* = 4 or 5, representing a critical value of the independent variable *t*.

h0 - represents the first step in the independent variable tried in the numerical solutions when adaptive methods are used.

hmax - maximum step size

hmin - minimum step size

jactype - Jacobian type. This option can be used when additional derivatives (a Jacobian) are provided for the solution. Possible values of this option are:

0 : functional iterations, no Jacobian used ("adams" or "stiff" only)
1 : user-supplied full Jacobian

2 : internally generated full Jacobian
3 : internally generated diagonal Jacobian ("adams" or "stiff" only)
4 : user-supplied banded Jacobian (see *ml* and *mu* below)
5 : internally generated banded Jacobian (see *ml* and *mu* below)

mxstep - Maximum number of iterations allowed.

maxordn - Maximum non-stiff order allowed for the numerical method (maximum allowed is 12).

maxords - Maximum stiff order allowed, at most 5-th order.

ixpr - print level, either 0 or 1.

ml,mu - see description below:

> If *jactype* = 4 or 5, *ml* and *mu* are the lower and upper half-bandwidths of the banded Jacobian. The band includes those terms of the Jacobian J_{ij}, with i-ml <= j <= ny-1.

> If *jactype* = 4 the Jacobian function must return a matrix J which has $(ml+mu+1)$ rows and *ny* columns (where *ny* is the number of elements of *y* in $dy/dt = f(t,y)$), such that the first column of J is made of *mu* zeros followed by $\partial f_1/\partial y_1$, $\partial f_2/\partial y_1$, $\partial f_3/\partial y_1$, ... (1+ml possibly non-zero entries). Column 2 of J is made of *mu-1* zeros followed by $\partial f_1/\partial x_2$, $\partial f_2/\partial x_2$, etc

The default value of the global variable %ODEOPTIONS is [1,0,0,%inf,0,2,500,12,5,0,-1,-1], i.e., *itask* = 1, *tcrit* = 0, *h0* = 0, *hmax* = , *hmin* = 0, *jactype* = 2, *mxstep* = 500, *maxordn* = 12, *maxords* = 5, *ixpr* = 0, *ml* = -1, *mu* = -1.

Applications of numerical solutions to IVPs

This section presents the solution to initial value problems (IVPs) some of which are obtained from the physical sciences, e.g., mechanical systems, electric circuits, etc.

Systems of ODEs from mechanical systems

Systems of ODEs can obtained from the analysis of two linked particles in oscillatory motion or from the analysis of electric circuits. For example, the figure below shows two particles P_1, and P_2, linked by three springs. The figure at the top represents the system in their state of equilibrium, while the one at the bottom shows the system at any generic point at time t>0.

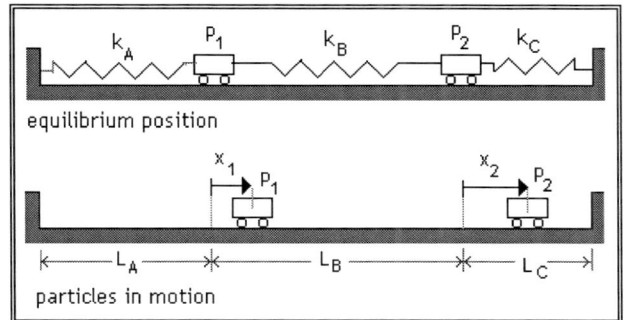

equilibrium position

particles in motion

The displacement of particle P_1 with respect to its equilibrium position is given by $x_1(t)$, while that of particle P_2 is given by $x_2(t)$. The magnitude of the force applied by a spring on an attached particle is given by Hooke's law,

$$F = -k(L - L_0),$$

where k is the spring constant, L is the stretched length of the spring, and L_0 is the unstretched length of the spring. The force that spring A, with constant k_A, applies on particle P_1 is given by

$$F_A = k_A(L_A + x_1 - L_A) = k_A x_1,$$

while that applied by spring B on particle P_1 is

$$F_B = k_B(L_A + L_B + L_C - L_A + x_1 - L_C - x_2 - L_B) = k_B(x_1 - x_2)$$

For the position illustrated in the Figure above, both forces will act in the negative direction of x_1, thus, writting Newton's second law for particle P_1 of mass m_1 results in:

$$-F_A - F_B = m_1 a_1, \quad \text{or} \quad -k_A x_1 - k_B(x_1 - x_2) = m_1 \frac{d^2 z_1}{dt^2}$$

Similarly, for particle P_2, of mass m_2, with the magnitude of the force applied by spring C given by

$$F_C = |k_C(L_C - x_2 - L_C)| = k_C x_2,$$

we can write

$$F_B - F_C = m_2 a_2, \quad \text{or} \quad k_B(x_1 - x_2) - k_C x_2 = m_2 \frac{d^2 x_2}{dt^2}$$

The resulting system of equations can be written as:

$$\frac{d^2 x_1}{dt^2} = -\frac{k_A + k_B}{m_1} x_1 + \frac{k_B}{m_1} x_2, \quad \text{and} \quad \frac{d^2 x_2}{dt^2} = \frac{k_B}{m_2} x_1 - \frac{k_B + k_C}{m_2} x_2.$$

These two second-order equations can generate a system of four first order equations if we define $x_3 = dx_1/dt$, and $x_4 = dx_2/dt$. The resulting system is:

$$dx_1/dt = x_3$$

$$dx_2/dt = x_4$$

$$dx_3/dt = -(k_A+k_B)x_1/m_1 + k_B x_2/m_1$$

$$dx_4/dt = k_B x_1/m_2 - (k_B+k_C)x_2/m_2$$

or, using vectors, $dx/dt = f(t,x)$, where $x = [x_1\ x_2\ x_3\ x_4]^T$, and

$$f(t,x) = \begin{bmatrix} x_3 \\ x_4 \\ -\dfrac{k_A + k_B}{m_1} x_1 + \dfrac{k_B}{m_1} x_2 \\ \dfrac{k_B}{m_2} x_1 - \dfrac{k_B + k_C}{m_2} x_2 \end{bmatrix}.$$

Suppose we use the following values k_A = 20 N/m, k_B = 40 N/m, k_C = 50 N/m, m_1 = 2 kg, m_2 = 5 kg, and given the initial conditions x_1 = 0.5 m, x_2 = 0.2 m, $x_3 = dx_1/dt$ = -0.1 m/s, $x_4 = dx_2/dt$ = 0.1 m/s, at t = 0, we will solve the system of equations in the interval 0 < t < 100 s, using a time increment of Δt = 0.1. This is the SCILAB solution:

First, we define the function f from $dy/dt = f(t,y)$ and enter the values of the parameters:

```
-->deff('[ff]=f(t,x)','ff=[x(3);x(4);-(kA+kB).*x(1)/m1+kB.*x(2)/m1; ...
-->kB.*x(1)/m2-(kB+kC).*x(2)/m2]')

-->kA = 20; kB = 40; kC = 50; m1 = 2; m2 = 5;
```

Next, we calculate the parameters for the solution and the solution itself:

```
-->t0=0;Dt=0.1;tn=10;x0=[0.5;0.2;-0.1;0.1];t=[t0:Dt:tn];

-->x = ode(x0,t0,t,f);
```

To produce a plot of the positions $x_1(t)$ and $x_2(t)$ we use:

```
-->plot2d([t',t'],[x(1,:)',x(2,:)'],[1,9],'111','x1@x2 ',[0 -1 10 1])
-->xtitle('Two particle oscillation','t(s)','x1(m) & x2(m)')
```

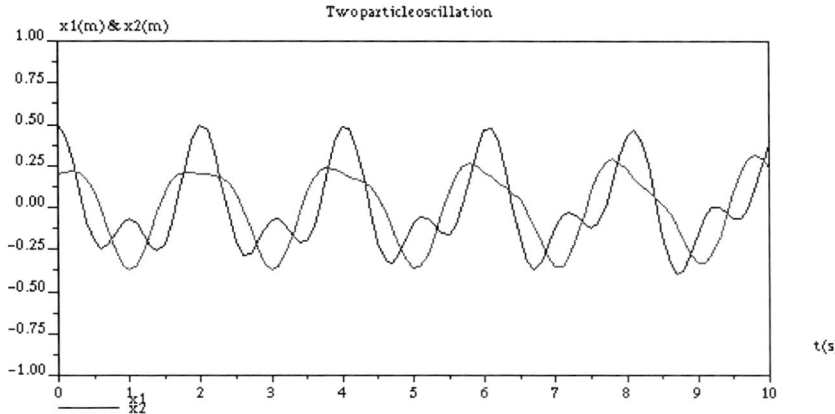

The corresponding velocities $v_1(t)$ and $v_2(t)$, are plotted by using:

```
-->plot2d([t',t'],[x(3,:)',x(4,:)'],[1,9],'111','v1@v2 ',[0 -2.5 10 2.5])
-->xtitle('Two particle oscillation','t(s)','v1(m/s) & v2(m/s)')
```

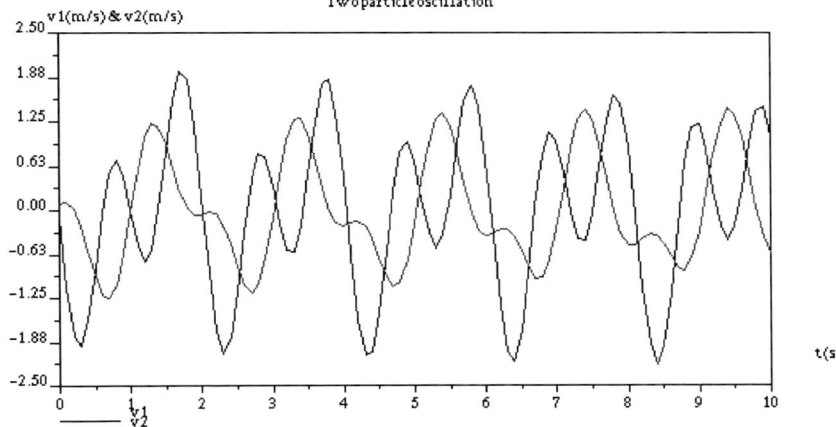

System of ODEs from Electric Circuits

A second application of systems of ordinary differential equations can be obtained from electric circuits. Consider the circuit shown in the figure below. The circuit consists of two loops each with a capacitor, an inductor, and a voltage source. The two loops share the resistor R. The electrical current circulating in the left-hand side loop is referred to as $I_1(t)$ and it is assumed to be positive in the counterclockwise direction. A similar electric current, $I_2(t)$, circulates in the right-hand side loop. The voltages $E_1(t)$ and $E_2(t)$ are positive in the sense indicated by the arrow. The equations for the voltage across individual components are:

- Resistor, $V_R = RI$
- Capacitor, $V_C = \dfrac{q}{C}$
- Inductor, $V_L = \dfrac{L\,dI}{dt}$

where V = voltage (volts), R = resistance (ohms), I = electric current (amperes), q = electric charge (coulombs), C = capacitance (farads), L = inductance (henrys), t = time (seconds). By definition, $I = \dfrac{dq}{dt}$.

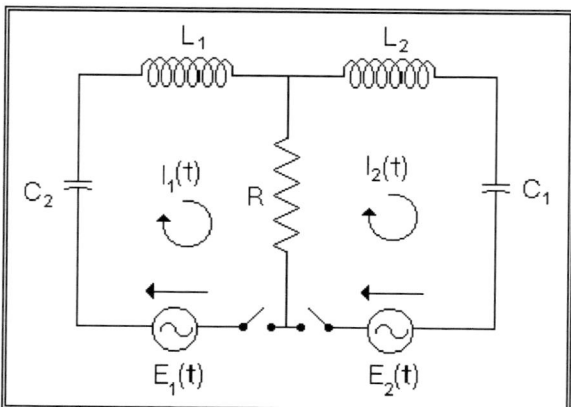

For the purpose of writing the governing equations we use Kirchoff law of conservation of voltage in a closed loop in a circuit with voltages across resistors, capacitors, and inductors decreasing in the direction of circulation of the current. Thus, for loops number 1 and 2, we would write, respectively:

$$E_1 - \frac{q_1}{C_1} - \frac{L_1\,dI_1(t)}{dt} - R(I_1 - I_2) = 0,$$

and

$$E_2 - R(I_2 - I_1) - \frac{L_2 \, dI_2}{dt} - \frac{q_2}{C_2} = 0.$$

Introducing the definition of the electric currents in the equations, $I_1 = \frac{dq_1}{dt}$, and $I_2 = \frac{dq_2}{dt}$, and rearranging terms we get a system of four first-order differential equations:

$$\frac{dI_1}{dt} = -\frac{RI_1}{L_1} + \frac{RI_2}{L_1} - \frac{q_1}{L_1 C_1} + \frac{E_1}{L_1}, \quad \frac{dq_1}{dt} = I_1, \quad \frac{dI_2}{dt} = \frac{RI_1}{L_2} - \frac{RI_2}{L_2} - \frac{q_2}{L_2 C_2} + \frac{E_2}{L_2}, \quad \frac{dq_2}{dt} = I_2.$$

These four equations can be transformed into a system of differential equations $dy/dt = f(t,y)$, with $y = [y_1 \; y_2 \; y_3 \; y_4]^T = [q_1 \; q_2 \; I_1 \; I_2]^T$, and

$$f(t,y) = \begin{bmatrix} y_3 \\ y_4 \\ -\frac{Ry_3}{L_1} + \frac{Ry_4}{L_1} - \frac{y_1}{L_1 C_1} + \frac{E_1}{L_1} \\ \frac{Ry_3}{L_2} - \frac{Ry_4}{L_2} - \frac{y_2}{L_2 C_2} + \frac{E_2}{L_2} \end{bmatrix}.$$

Suppose that we use the values $R = 1800$ ohms, $L_1 = 500$ henrys, $L_2 = 800$ henrys, $C_1 = 0.005$ farads, $C_2 = 0.010$ farads, $E_1 = E_2 = 0$, with initial conditions $q_1 = 100$ coulombs, $q_2 = I_1 = I_2 = 0$, the following two example illustrate how to produce the solution for the charges $q_1(t)$, $q_2(t)$, and the currents $I_1(t)$, $I_2(t)$.

The first example uses constant voltages E_1 and E_2. First we define the system function $f(t,y)$ and the parameters of the circuit:

```
-->deff('[dydt]=f(t,y)','dydt = [y(3);y(4);...
-->-R*y(3)/L1+R*y(4)/L1-y(1)/(L1*C1)+E1/L1;...
--> R*y(3)/L2-R*y(4)/L2-y(2)/(L2*C2)+E2/L2]')

-->R=1800;L1=500;L2=800;C1=0.005;C2=0.010;E1=0;E2=0;
```

Next, we define the parameters of the solution and calculate the solution using function ode:

```
-->t0 = 0; Dt = 0.1; tn = 10; t = [t0:Dt:tn];y0 = [100;0;0;0];
-->y = ode(y0,t0,t,f);
```

To produce plots of electric charge we use:

```
-->min([y(1,:) y(2,:)]),  max([y(1,:) y(2,:)])
 ans  = - 117.01482, ans  =    100.
-->plot2d([t',t'],[y(1,:)',y(2,:)'],[1,9],'111','q1@q2',[0 -120 100 120])
-->xtitle('Electric charge ODE solution','t(s)','q1,q2(coulomb)')
```

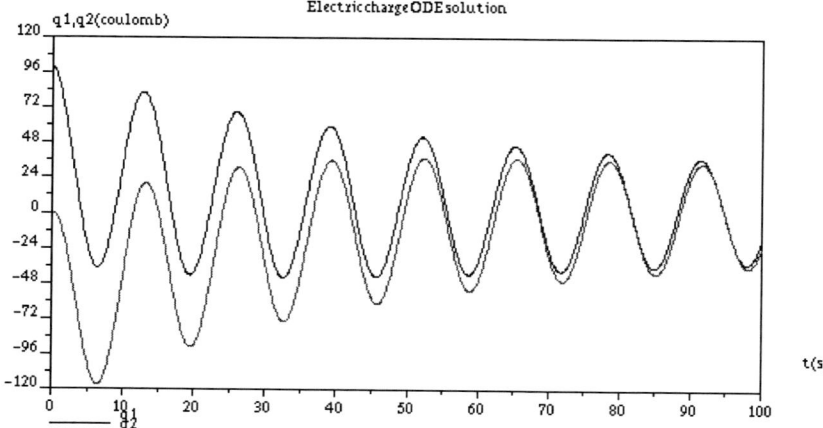

A plot of electric current follows:

```
-->min([y(3,:) y(4,:)]), max([y(3,:) y(4,:)])
 ans  = - 32.655809
 ans  =   31.88677

-->plot2d([t',t'],[y(3,:)',y(4,:)'],[1,9],'111','I1@I2',[0 -40 100 40])
-->xtitle('Electric current ODE solution','t(s)','I1,I2(ampere)')
```

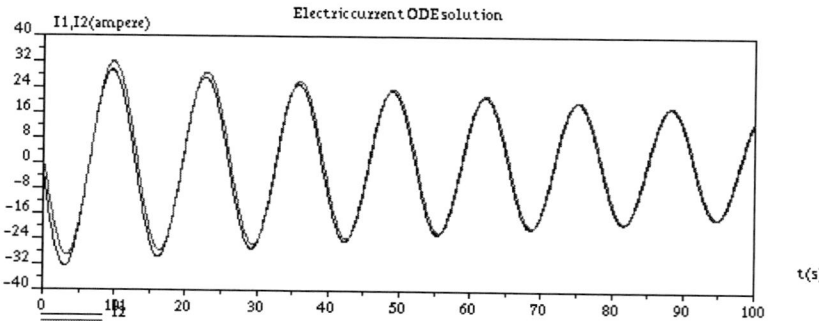

In the following example we introduce sinusoidal driving voltages $E_1(t)$ and $E_2(t)$:

```
-->deff('[EE1]=E1(t)','EE1=12*cos(120*%pi*t)')

-->deff('[EE2]=E2(t)','EE2= 6*cos( 60*%pi*t)')
```

Next, we redefine the function f(t,y) to include $E_1(t)$ and $E_2(t)$:

```
-->deff('[dydt]=f(t,y)','dydt = [y(3);y(4);...
--->-R*y(3)/L1+R*y(4)/L1-y(1)/(L1*C1)+E1(t)/L1;...
--> R*y(3)/L2-R*y(4)/L2-y(2)/(L2*C2)+E2(t)/L2]')
```

The parameters for the solution will be now:

```
-->t0 = 0; Dt = 0.1; tn = 50; t = [t0:Dt:tn];
```

Because the system function f(t,y) is now complicated by the presence of time-dependent voltages E1(t) and E2(t), function ode will take a few minutes to complete the solution.

```
-->y = ode(y0,t0,t,f);
```

To produce a plot of electric charges use:

```
-->min([y(1,:) y(2,:)]), max([y(1,:) y(2,:)])
 ans  = - 154.45894
 ans  =   200.

-->plot2d([t',t'],[y(1,:)',y(2,:)'],[1,9],'111','q1@q2',[0 -200 50 200])

-->xtitle('Electric charge ODE solution - CASE 2','t(s)','q1,q2(coulomb)')
```

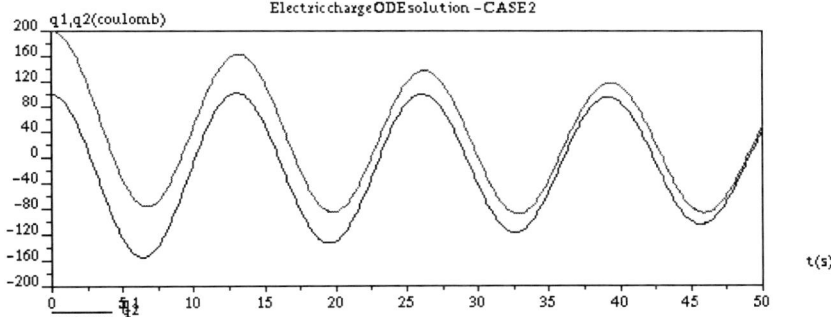

For a plot of the electric currents use:

```
-->min([y(3,:) y(4,:)]), max([y(3,:) y(4,:)])
 ans  = - 65.0047
 ans  =   61.126823


-->plot2d([t',t'],[y(3,:)',y(4,:)'],[1,9],'111','I1@I2',[0 -70 50 70])
-->xtitle('Electric current ODE solution - CASE 2','t(s)','I1,I2(ampere)')
```

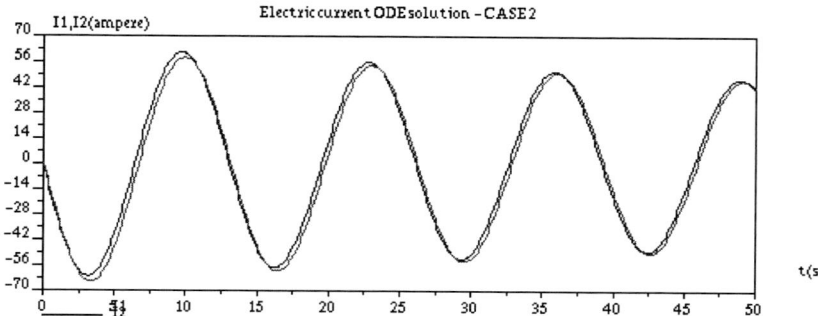

Solving a fourth-order equation

Consider the fourth-order linear equation presented in an earlier section

$$\frac{d^4 y}{dx^4} + \frac{3 d^3 y}{dx^3} - \frac{2 d^2 y}{dx^2} + \frac{5 dy}{dx} + y = 0,$$

subjected to $y = 1$, $\frac{dy}{dx} = -1$, $\frac{d^2 y}{dx^2} = 0$, $\frac{d^3 y}{dx^3} = -1$, at $x = 0$. To solve this equation we transform the fourth-order equation into a first-order system of linear equations:

$$du_3/dx = -3u_3(x)+2u_2(x)-5u_1(x)-y(x)+x^2/2,$$
$$du_2/dx = u_3(x),$$
$$du_1/dx = u_2(x),$$
$$dy/dx = u_1(x),$$

or

$$\frac{d}{dx}\begin{bmatrix} u_3(x) \\ u_2(x) \\ u_1(x) \\ y(x) \end{bmatrix} = \begin{bmatrix} -3 & 2 & -5 & -1 \\ 1 & 0 & 0 & 0 \\ 0 & 1 & 0 & 0 \\ 0 & 0 & 1 & 0 \end{bmatrix} \cdot \begin{bmatrix} u_3(x) \\ u_2(x) \\ u_1(x) \\ y(x) \end{bmatrix} + \begin{bmatrix} x^2/2 \\ 0 \\ 0 \\ 0 \end{bmatrix}.$$

With

$$v(x) = \begin{bmatrix} u_3(x) \\ u_2(x) \\ u_1(x) \\ y(x) \end{bmatrix}, \quad A = \begin{bmatrix} -3 & 2 & -5 & -1 \\ 1 & 0 & 0 & 0 \\ 0 & 1 & 0 & 0 \\ 0 & 0 & 1 & 0 \end{bmatrix}, \quad g(x) = \begin{bmatrix} x^2/2 \\ 0 \\ 0 \\ 0 \end{bmatrix},$$

the system of differential equations is written as

$$dv/dx = Av + g(x).$$

The initial conditions are $y(0) = 1$, $u_1(0) = dy/dx = -1$, $u_2(0) = du_1/dx = d^2y/dx^2 = 0$, $u_3(0) = du_2/dx = d^2u_1/dx^2 = d^3y/dx^3 = -1$,

$$u(0) = \begin{bmatrix} -1 \\ 0 \\ -1 \\ 1 \end{bmatrix}.$$

To implement the solution using SCILAB we first define the function f(x,v) and the parameters for the solution

```
-->deff('[dvdx]=f(x,v)','dvdx=A*[v(1);v(2);v(3);v(4)]+[x^2;0;0;0]')
-->A = [-3,2,-5,-1;1,0,0,0;0,1,0,0;0,0,1,0];

-->v0 = [-1;0;-1;1];t0=0;Dt=0.1;tn=10;t=[t0:Dt:tn];
```

The numerical solution to the system of differential equations is obtained through:

```
-->v = ode(v0,t0,t,f);
```

To produce a plot of the solution y(t) we use:

```
-->min(v(4,:)),max(v(4,:))
 ans  =  - 3.903516
 ans  =    137.7293

-->plot(t,v(4,:),'t','y(t)','Solution to 4th order equation')
```

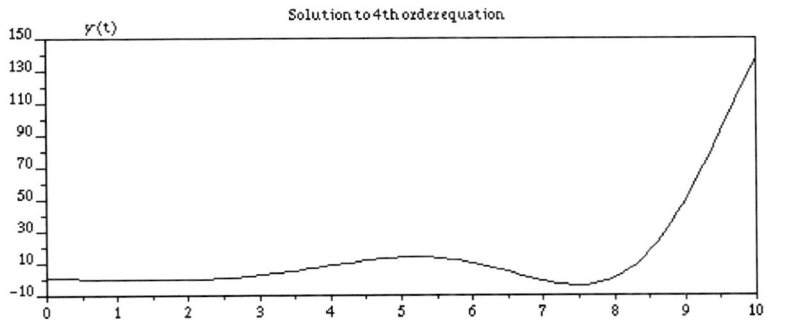

The Van der Pol equation

The Van der Pol equation results from the analysis of the Van der Pol oscillator circuit shown in the figure below.

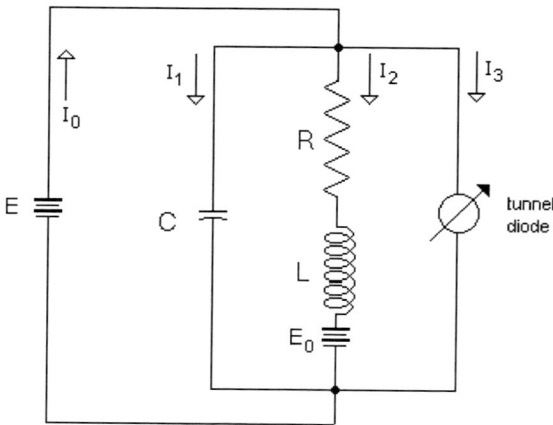

Application of Kirchoff's laws to this circuit results in the following equations:

$$C(dE/dt) = I_1, \quad RI_2 + L(dI_2/dt) = E + E_0, \quad I_3 = f(E), \quad I_0 = I_1 + I_2 + I_3$$

This set of four equations can be reduced to two differential equations

$$C(dE/dt) = I_0 - I_2 - f(E)$$
$$L(dI_2/dt) = E + E_0 - RI_2$$

If we eliminate the resistor from the circuit ($R=0$), the two differential equations can be combined into a single second order differential equation

$$C(d^2E/dt^2) + f'(E)(dE/dt) + (E+E_0)/L = dI_0/dt.$$

The function $f(E)$ represents the response of the tunnel diode to the voltage E and can be taken to be the third-order polynomial

$$f(E) = K E(E^2/3 - (E_1+E_2)E/2 + E_1 E_2).$$

Tuning the voltage source E so that $E_0 = -(E_1+E_2)/2$, we can write

$$f(E) = K E(E^2/3 + E_0 E/2 + E_1 E_2).$$

If we define $E = (E_2-E_1)y/2 + (E_1+E_2)/2 = (E_2-E_1)y/2 + E_0$, and scale the time so that $\tau = t(LC)^{1/2}$, we can transform the governing equation into the Van der Pol equation

$$d^2y/d\tau^2 + \kappa(y^2-1)(dy/d\tau) + y = 0,$$

where $\kappa = K((E_2-E_1)/2)^2 (L/C)^{1/2}$ and $dl_0/dt = 0$.

The Van der Pol equation, being a second-order equation, can be transformed into a set of two first-order equations, by using $dy/d\tau = u_1(\tau)$, and $y = u_2(\tau)$. The system of equations is

$$du_1/d\tau = -\kappa(u_2^2-1)u_1 - u_2$$
$$du_2/d\tau = u_1$$

or,

$$du/dt = f(\tau,u),$$

with

$$u(\tau) = \begin{bmatrix} u_1(\tau) \\ u_2(\tau) \end{bmatrix}, \quad f(\tau,u) = \begin{bmatrix} -\kappa(u_2^2-1)u_1 - u_2 \\ u_1 \end{bmatrix}.$$

The Van der Pol equation is solved next using SCILAB's function ode. The initial conditions used are $u_1(\tau) = du_2/d\tau = dy/d\tau = 2$, $u_2(\tau) = y = 1$ at $\tau = 0$. The solution is obtained for the range $0 < \tau < 100$, and for values of $\kappa = 0.01$ and $\kappa = 4.0$. First, we define the function $f(\tau,u)$:

```
-->deff('[ff]=f(t,u)','ff=[-k*(u(2)^2-1)*u(1)-u(2);u(1)]')
-->u0=[1;2];t0=0;Dt=0.1;tn=100.0;t=[t0:Dt:tn];
```

The solution for k = 0.01 is found first:

```
-->k=0.01;u1=ode(u0,t0,t,f);
```

To produce plots of the function we determine the maximum and minimum values of u:

```
-->min(u1),max(u1)
 ans  =  - 2.2268766
 ans  =    2.231914
```

First, we plot the signals $u_2(\tau) = y$, and $u_1(\tau) = dy/d\tau$ against τ.

```
-->plot2d([t' t'],[u1(2,:)' u1(1,:)'],[1,-1],'111','y@dy/dt',[0 -3 100 3])
-->xtitle('Van der Pol equation - k = 0.01','t','y,dy/dt')
```

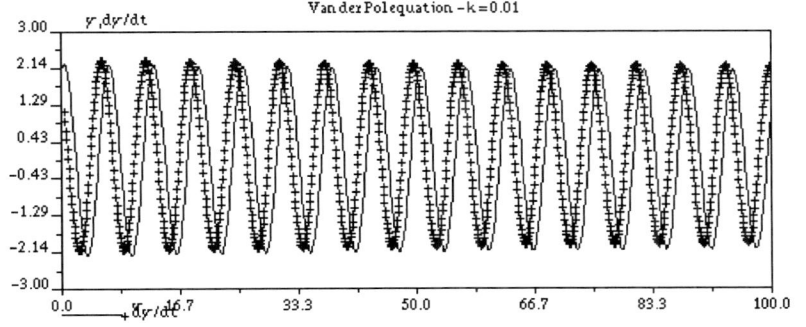

The phase portrait $dy/d\tau$ vs. y is shown next:

```
-->plot(u1(1,:),u1(2,:),'y','dy/dt','Van der Pol equation - k = 0.01')
```

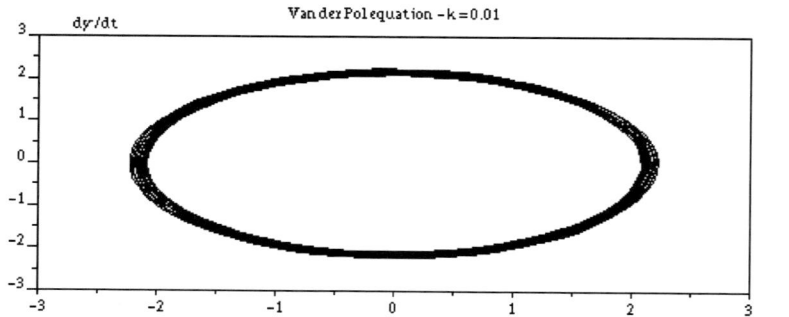

The solution to the Van der Pol equation for $\kappa = 4$, and the corresponding plots are obtained with the following SCILAB commands:

```
-->k=4.00;u2=ode(u0,t0,t,f);
```

```
-->plot(t,u2(2,:),'t','y','Van der Pol equation - k = 4')   //Signal y vs. t
```

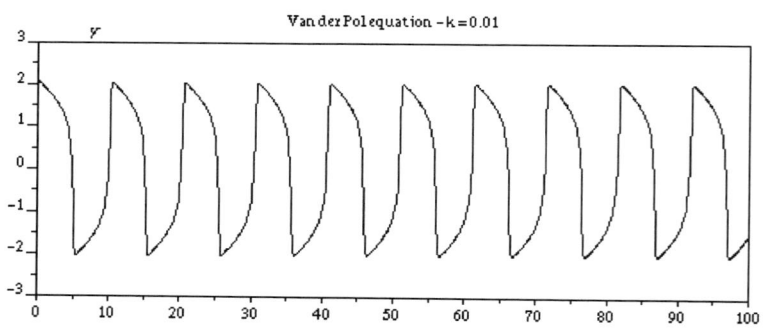

```
-->plot(u2(1,:),u2(2,:),'y','dy/dt','Van der Pol equation - k = 4')   //Phase
portrait
```

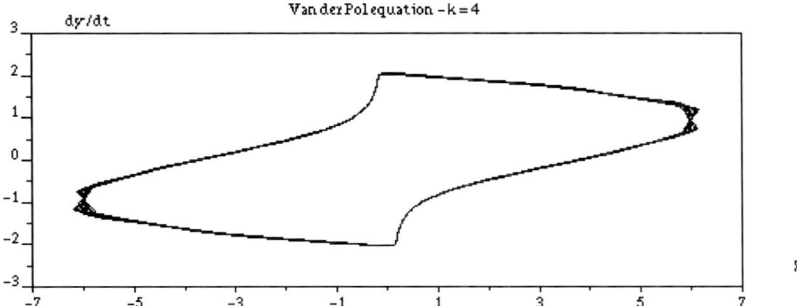

The Rössler flow

In the analysis of chaotic dynamical systems, a three-dimensional flow is described by a set of three ordinary differential equations involving three variables $x(t)$, $y(t)$, and $z(t)$. The Rössler flow is given by the equations (see Bergé et al., 1984, "Order within Chaos - Towards a deterministic approach to turbulence," John Wiley & Sons, New York):

$$dx/dt = -y - z$$
$$dy/dt = x + ay$$
$$dz/dt = b + xz - cz$$

To solve this system using SCILAB function ode we re-write the system as

$$du/dt = f(t,u)$$

with

$$u(t) = \begin{bmatrix} u_1(t) \\ u_2(t) \\ u_3(t) \end{bmatrix} = \begin{bmatrix} x(t) \\ y(t) \\ z(t) \end{bmatrix}, \quad g(t,x) = \begin{bmatrix} -u_2 - u_3 \\ u_1 + au_2 \\ b + u_1 u_3 - cu_3 \end{bmatrix}.$$

In the following exercise we solve for the Rössler flow using $a = b = 0.2$, $c = 5.7$, in the interval $0 < t < 200$, with initial conditions $x(0) = y(0) = z(0) = 1$. We use a time increment $\Delta t = 0.1$. The solution starts by defining the function $f(t,u)$ and the parameters of the flow and of the solution:

```
-->deff('[w]=f(t,u)','w=[-u(2)-u(3);u(1)+a*u(2);b+u(1)*u(3)-c*u(3)]')
-->a=0.2; b=0.2; c=5.7; t0=0; Dt=0.1; tn=200; t=[t0:Dt:tn]; u0=[1;1;1];
```

The solution is stored in variable u from:
```
-->u=ode(u0,t0,t,f);
```

The following are plots of the signals $x(t)$, $y(t)$, and $z(t)$ resulting from the solution:

```
-->plot(t,u(1,:),'t','x','Rossler flow')
```

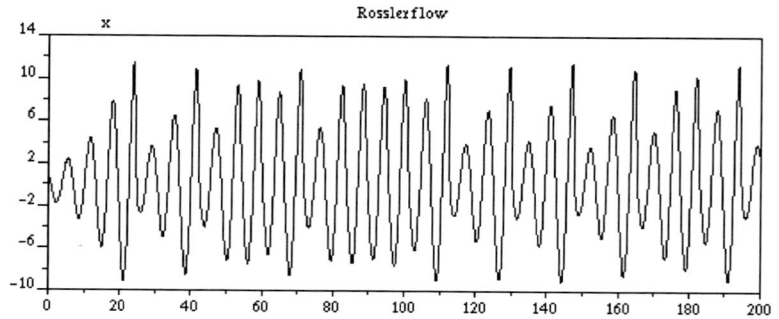

```
-->plot(t,u(2,:),'t','y','Rossler flow')
```

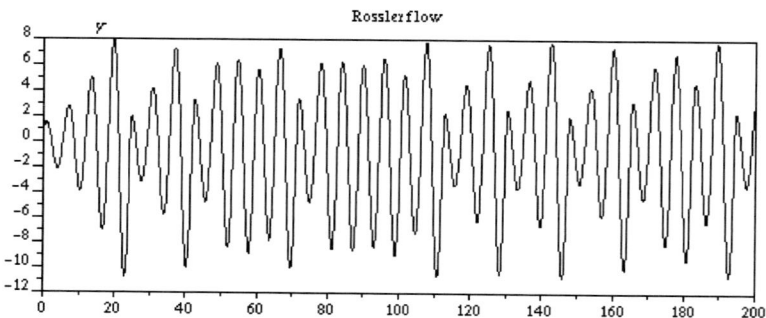

```
-->plot(t,u(3,:),'t','z','Rossler flow')
```

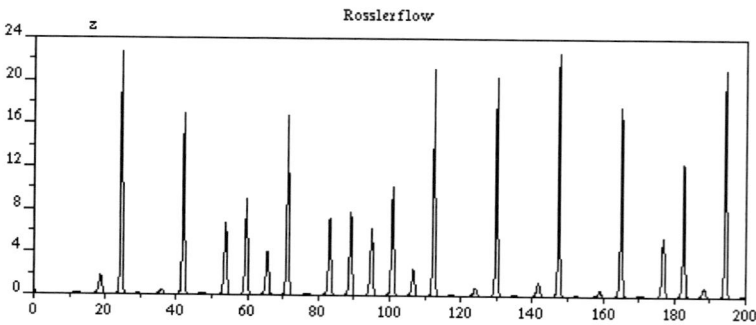

The behavior of the signals is, in general, aperiodic or chaotic. Phase portraits of signals may provide additional information regarding strange attractors resulting from the solution. A phase portrait of signal y vs. x follows:

```
-->plot(u(1,:),u(2,:),'x','y','Rossler flow')
```

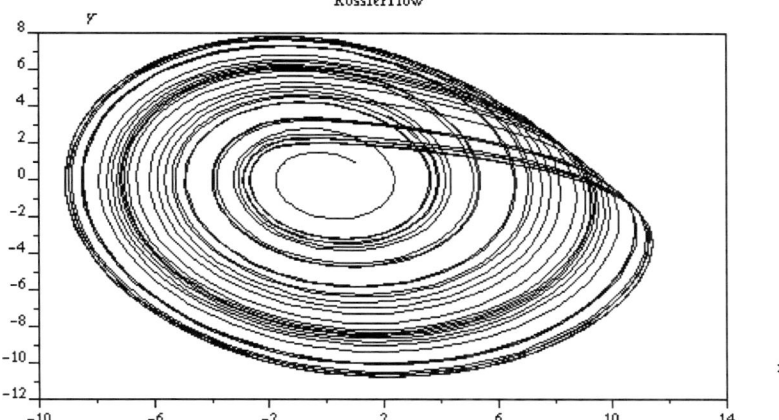

A phase portrait of the rate of change in x, dx/dt, vs. x, is obtained next. First, we determine the length of vector $x = u(1,:)$, and use function *mtlb_diff* (see Chapter ...) to estimate the derivative dx/dt. The next step is to produce a vector xx consisting of the data in $u(1,:)$ but reduced by one to make it of the same length as dx. The phase portrait is shown below:

```
-->n=length(u(1,:))
 n  = 2001.
-->dx = mtlb_diff(u(1,:))/Dt;
-->xx=u(1,1:n-1);
-->plot(xx,dx,'x','dx/dt','Rossler Flow')
```

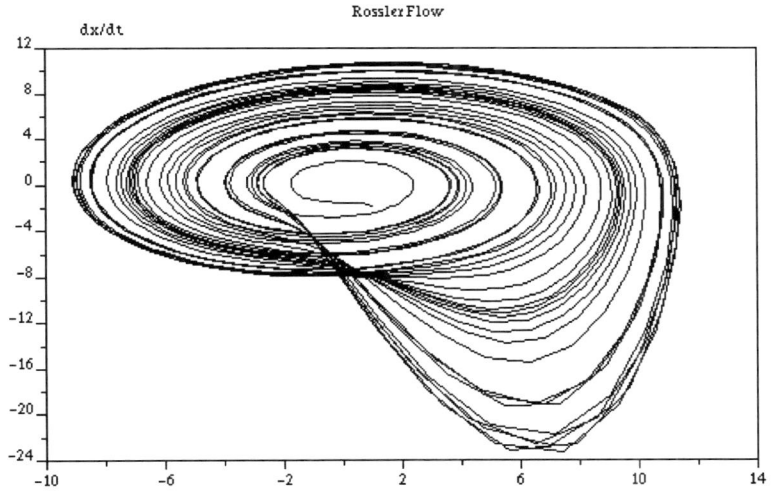

Solutions to boundary value problems (BVPs)

Boundary value problems consist of ordinary differential equations with conditions provided at different values of the independent variable. Unlike initial boundary problems, which can be solved using the same numerical solution after transforming the differential equation into a system of first-order differential equations with appropriate initial conditions, boundary value problems are not suitable for solution through a single numerical method. In this section, we explore some approaches to the solution of boundary value problems.

The shooting method

The simplest type of boundary value problems consists of a second order differential equation, $d^2y/dx^2 = g(x,y,dy/dx)$ subject to the boundary conditions $y(x_0) = y_0$ and $y(x_1) = y_1$. The figure below illustrate three possible solutions to the initial value problem represented by the same differential equation, namely, $d^2y/dx^2 = g(x,y,dy/dx)$, subject to the initial condition $y(x_0) = y_0$, and different initial derivative conditions. There is one value of dy/dx at $x = x_0$ that produces the solution that satisfies the second boundary condition $y(x_1) = y_1$. The solution to the boundary value problem will be curve (II) in the figure.

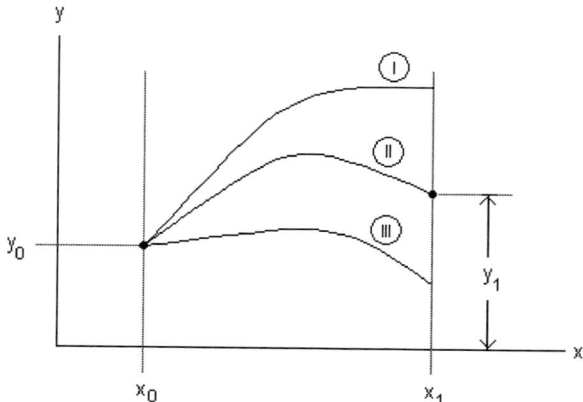

The so-called "shooting" method consists in solving the initial value problem $d^2y/dx^2 = g(x,y,dy/dx)$, subject to the initial condition $y(x_0) = y_0$, $dy/dx|_{x = x0} = y'(x_0) = y_0'$, for different values of y_0', and obtaining the corresponding boundary values $y_1 = y(x_1)$. As a result we get a set of data values $\{[(y_0')_1,(y_1)_1], [(y_0')_2,(y_1)_2], ..., [(y_0')_n,(y_1)_n]\}$ from which we can interpolate the value of y_0' corresponding to the given value of y_1. The solution to the boundary value problem, thus, becomes the solution to a number of initial value problems followed by an interpolation. Once the proper value of y_0' is determined, the initial value problem is solved one last time.

A function to implement the shooting method

The following SCILAB user-defined function *shooting*, produces the solution to a second-order boundary value problem given the boundary conditions $y(x_0) = y_0$ and $y(x_1) = y_1$. The second-order differential equation $d^2y/dx^2 = g(x,y,dy/dx)$ is transformed into a first-order system of two ordinary differential equations of the form $du/dx = f(x,u)$, with $u_1 = y(x)$, $u_2 = du_1/dx = dy/dx$, and

$$u = \begin{bmatrix} u_1 \\ u_2 \end{bmatrix}, \quad f(x,u) = \begin{bmatrix} u_2 \\ g(x,u_1,u_2) \end{bmatrix}.$$

The general call to the function is

$$[u, table, y0p] = shooting(yb, yp, x, f)$$

The boundary conditions are passed on to the function as a vector $yb = [y_0\ y_1]$. The solution is obtained on a range represented by vector x. We also need to provide a vector of values of the derivative y_0', referred to as yp. The function returns the values of u as a $2 \times n$ matrix, where the first row is the function $y(x)$ and the second row is the derivative dy/dx corresponding to the values of x. The function *shooting* also returns variable *table* which is a table of values of y_0' and the corresponding values of $y(x_1)$ that were used to interpolate the initial condition for the derivative at $x = x_0$ for the final solution. The first row in the table are the values of y_0', while the second row in the table are the values of $y(x_1)$. In addition to matrices u and *table*, function *shooting* returns also the derivative boundary condition $y0p = dy/dx|_{x=x_0}$, interpolated from the shooting method.

A listing of the function is shown next:

```
function [y,xyTable,yderiv] = shooting(yb,yp,x,f)

//Shooting method for a second order
//boundary value problem
//yb = [y0 y1] -> boundary conditions
//x = a vector showing the range of x
//f = function defining ODE, i.e.,
//    dy/dx = f(x,y), y = [y(1);y(2)].
//yp = vector with range of dy/dx at x=x0
//xyTable = table for interpolating derivatives
//yderiv  = derivative boundary condition

n  = length(yp);
m  = length(x);
y1 = zeros(yp);

for j = 1:n
        y0     = [yb(1);yp(j)];
        yy     = ode(y0,x(1),x,f);
        y1(j)  = yy(1,m);
end;

xyTable = [y1;yp];
yderiv  = interpln(xyTable,yb(2));
y0      = [yb(1);yderiv];
y       = ode(y0,x(1),x,f);
```

Consider the case of the second order boundary value problem defined by the ordinary differential equation

$$d^2y/dx^2 + dy/dx + y = \sin(3x),$$

subject to the boundary conditions $y(0) = 1$, $y(5) = -1$. We re-cast the ODE into the following first-order system,

$$du/dx = f(x,u),$$

with

$$u_1 = y(x), \quad u_2 = du_1/dx = dy/dx,$$

$$u(x) = \begin{bmatrix} u_1(x) \\ u_2(x) \end{bmatrix}, \quad f(x,u) = \begin{bmatrix} u_2 \\ \sin(3x) - u_1 - u_2 \end{bmatrix}.$$

The boundary conditions are now $u_1(0) = 1$, $u_1(5) = -1$. The solution to this boundary value problem with SCILAB is accomplished as follows:

```
-->deff('[w]=f(x,u)','w=[u(2);sin(3*x)-u(1)-u(2)]')

-->yb=[1,-1];x0=0;Dx=0.1;xn=5;x=[x0:Dx:xn];yp=[-10:1:10];

-->[u,tabl,y0p]=shooting(yb,yp,x,f);
```

The plot of the solution is produced by using:

```
-->plot(x,u(1,:),'x','y','shooting method solution 2nd order BVP')
```

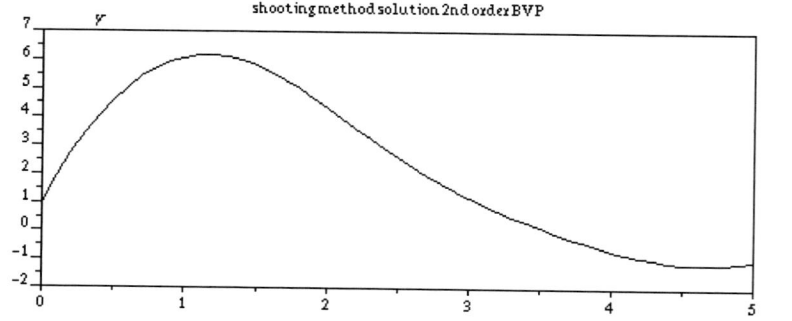

To illustrate the shooting method applied to th second-order boundary value problem presented above, we produce numerical solutions to the corresponding second-order ordinary differential equation using initial conditions $y(0) = 1$ and different derivative boundary conditions to produce the following graph. The solution to the boundary value problem with boundary conditions $y(0) = 1$ and $y(5) = -1$ is discontinuous curve in the graph.

```
-->yp0 = [3,6,9,12,15];     //Different values of dy/dx at x = 0

-->um = zeros(5,m);         //Calculate different solutions

-->for k =1:5
-->    y0 = [1;yp0(k)];
-->    uu = ode(y0,x0,x,f);
-->    um(k,:) = uu(1,:);
-->end;

-->plot2d([x',x',x',x',x'],[um(1,:)',um(2,:)',um(3,:)',um(4,:)',um(5,:)'],...
-->[1,2,3,4,5],'111','y0p=3@y0p=6@y0p=9@y0p=12@y0p=15',...
-->[0 -5 5 10])

-->plot2d(x',u(1,:)',-1,'011',' ',[0 -5 5 10])

-->xtitle('Boundary value solution - shooting method','x','y')
```

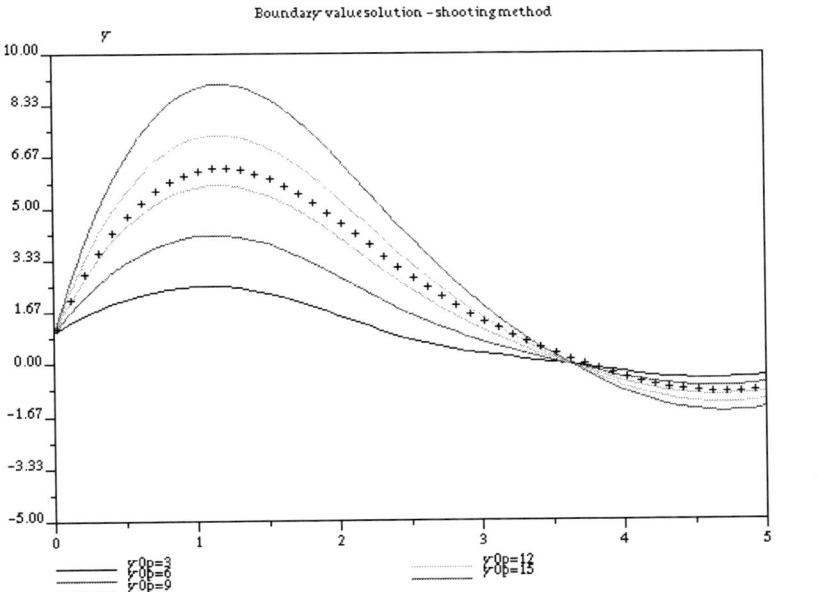

Outline of the implicit solution for a second-order BVP

In this section we present the outline for an implicit, finite-difference based solution to the second order boundary value problem

$$d^2y/dx^2 + y = 0,$$

in the x-interval $(0,5)$ subject to $y(0) = 1$, and $y(5) = 0$. Use $\Delta x = 0.1$.

We discretize the differential equation using the finite difference approximation

$$d^2y/dx^2 = (y_{i+2} - 2 y_{i+1} + y_i)/(\Delta x^2),$$

which results in

$$(y_{i+1} - 2^* y_i + y_{i-1})/(\Delta x^2) + y_i = 0.$$

From this result we get the following implicit equations:

$$y_{i-1} - (2 - \Delta x^2) \cdot y_i + y_{i+1} = 0,$$

for $i = 2, 3, \ldots, n-1$. There are a total of $(n-2)$ equations, corresponding to the $(n-2)$ unknowns $y_2, y_3, \ldots, y_{n-2}, y_{n-1}$ [$y_1 = y(0)$ and $y_n = y(5)$]. Therefore, the resulting set of linear algebraic equations has a unique solution. The implementation of the solution for this example is left as an exercise for the reader.

Function *bvode* for the solution of boundary value problems

SCILAB provides function *bvode* for the numerical solution of boundary value problems. The function works on a general boundary value problem, which, as indicated earlier, requires a lot of detailed information in its set up. The problem solved through function *bvode* consists of the boundary value problem:

$$\frac{d^{m*}y}{dx^{m*}} = f(x,u), \quad \text{with} \quad u = \begin{bmatrix} u_1 \\ u_2 \\ u_3 \\ \vdots \\ u_{m*} \end{bmatrix} = \begin{bmatrix} y \\ dy/dx \\ d^2y/dx^2 \\ \vdots \\ d^{m*-1}y/dx^{m*-1} \end{bmatrix} = \begin{bmatrix} y \\ du_1/dx \\ du_2/dx \\ \vdots \\ du_{m*-1}/dx \end{bmatrix}.$$

For example, the second-order differential equation

$$d^2y/dx^2 + 5(dy/dx) + y = \cos(x),$$

is re-written as

$$d^2y/dx^2 = \cos(x) - y - 5(dy/dx),$$

or, with $u_1 = y(x)$, $u_2 = dy/dx$, as

$$d^2y/dx^2 = f(x,u) = \cos(x) - u_1 - 5u_2.$$

External SCILAB functions used with bvode

Using SCILAB, the function f(x,u) can be defined, for example, as

```
deff('[ff] = f(x,u)','ff=cos(x)-u(1)-5*u(2)')
```

The general boundary value problem $d^{m^*}y/dx^{m^*} = f(x,u)$ is solved in the interval $[xL, xR]$, with the boundary conditions provided through a function $g(i,u) = 0$, so that $g(i,u) = u_i - bc_j$, with $u_i = d^{i-1}y/dx^{i-1}$, and bc_j being the corresponding boundary condition at point $= \zeta_j$. The values of ζ_j, $j = 1, 2, ..., m^*$, are provided in vector ζ (zeta), and they are either xL or xR, i.e., the location of the boundaries for the problem.

For example, if the equation is of order $2 m(^*=2)$, and the boundary conditions are $y(xL) = y_0$ and $y(xR) = y_1$, we will write the vector zeta as $\zeta = [xL, xR]$, or $\zeta_1 = xL$, $\zeta_2 = xR$, and $g(1,u) = u_1 - y_0$, $g(2,u) = u_2 - y_1$. The latter results are equivalent to $u_1(\zeta_1) = y(xL) = y_0$ and $u_2(xR) = y(xR) = y_1$.

As a second example, assume that the equation to be solved is of order $3 m(^*=3)$ subject to boundary conditions $y(xL) = y_0$, $dy/dx|_{x=xL} = y_0'$, and $y(xR) = y_1$. The vector zeta is written as $\zeta = [xL, xL, xR]$, and the function $g(i,u)$ given by $g(1,u) = u_1 - y_0$, $g(2,u) = u_2 - y_0'$, $g(3,u) = u_1 - y_1$. If instead, the boundary conditions are $y(xL) = y_0$, and $y(xR) = y_1$, $dy/dx|_{x=xR} = y_1'$, the vector zeta is written as $\zeta = [xL, xR, xR]$, and function $g(i,u)$ given by $g(1,u) = u_1 - y_0$, $g(2,u) = u_1 - y_1$, $g(3,u) = u_2 - y_1'$. Another possibility is that two of the boundary conditions are derivatives, e.g., $y(xL) = y_0$, $dy/dx|_{x=xL} = y_0'$, and $dy/dx|_{x=xR} = y_1'$. In this case we would have $\zeta = [xL, xL, xR]$, and $g(1,u) = u_1 - y_0$, $g(2,u) = u_2 - y_0'$, $g(3,u) = u_2 - y_1'$. Thus, there is a one-to-one relationship between the elements of vector zeta and values of function $g(i,u)$ representing boundary conditions of the problem.

Function *bvode* requires that we pass also derivatives of the functions $f(x,u)$ and $g(x,u)$. Let's refer to the functions that calculate those derivatives as $df(x,u)$ and $dg(i,u)$. Function df represents a vector $[df_1, df_2, ..., df_m]$ with $df_i = df(x,u)/du_i$, while function dg represents a vector whose elements are $dg_{ij} = dg_i/du_j$ for a fixed value of i. Referring to the second-order boundary value problem described earlier, namely $d^2y/dx^2 = f(x,u) = cos(x) - u_1 - 5u_2$, subject to the boundary condition $y(1) = 0.5$ and $y'(2) = -1.5$, we would define the zeta vector as $\zeta = [1,2]$, with $g_1 = g(1,u) = u_1 - 0.5$, and $g_2 = g(2,u) = u_2 + 1.5$. The derivative functions would be $df_1 = \partial f/\partial u_1 = -1$, $df_2 = \partial f/\partial u_2 = -5$, $dg_{11} = \partial g_1/\partial u_1 = 1.0$, $dg_{12} = \partial g_1/\partial u_2 = 0.0$, $dg_{21} = \partial g_2/\partial u_1 = 0$, $dg_{22} = \partial g_2/\partial u_2 = 1.0$. Using SCILAB, we will define the functions $f(x,u)$, $g(i,u)$, $df(x,u)$, $dg(i,u)$ as follows:

```
deff('[ff]  = f(x,u) ','ff=cos(x)-u(1)-5*u(2)');
deff('[dff] = df(x,u)','dff = [-1,-5]');
deff('[gg]  = g(i,u) ',['gg=[u(1)-1,u(2)+1]','gg=gg(i)']);
deff('[dgg] = dg(i,u)',['dgg = [1,0;0,1]';'dgg=dgg(i,:)']);
```

Notice that functions $f(x,u)$ and $g(x,u)$ return a single value, while functions $df(x,u)$ and $dg(x,u)$ return vectors.

The user may also define a function that provides initial guesses of the solution. The general call for this function is [u0,du0] = guess(x)

where x is a vector, e.g., $x = [xL:Dx:xR]$, with Dx = increment in x. Function *guess* provides initial guesses for the solution $u0 = [(u_1)_0; (u_2)_0; ...;(u_m)_0]$ and for the derivative of the solution, $du0 = [(du_1/dx)_0, (du_2/dx)_0, ..., (du_m/dx)_0]$. Typically, this function is not used in the solution, i.e., no initial guesses of the solution and its derivative are provided, and the function *guess* can simply be defined as

```
deff('[u0,du0] = guess(x)', ['u0= 0', 'du0 =0'])
```

General call to function *bvode*

The general call to the function *bvode* is as follows:

[u] = =bvode(x,n,m,xL,xR,zeta,ipar,ltol,tol,fixpnt,f,df,g,dg,guess)

where x is a vector of values of the independent variable, $x = [xL:DX:xR]$; *n* is the number of differential equations to be solved ($n = 1$ for the case under consideration); *m* is a vector whose elements indicate the order each of the equations being solved ($m=[m^*]$ in this case); *xL* and *xR* are the extremes of the interval where the solution is sought; *zeta* is the vector specifying the location of the boundary conditions (examples of how to put together vector *zeta* were presented earlier); *ipar* is a vector of 11 solution parameters whose components are described below; *ltol* and *tol* are vectors specifying the number of the component of *f* and the tolerance for the solution of those components; *fixpnt* indicates the number of fixed points in the interval [xL, xR] other than the extremes (typically, *fixpnt* = 0); *f*, *df*, *g*, *dg*, and *guess* are external SCILAB functions described earlier.

Description of elements of vector *ipar*

Next, we describe the elements of vector *ipar*, showing typical values for the solution of simple boundary value problems. For a more detailed description of these parameters, use

```
--> help bvode
```

- *ipar(1)* determines whether the boundary value problem is linear (*ipar(1)* = 0) or non-linear (*ipar(1)* = 1).

- *ipar(2)* determines the number of collocation points per subinterval. Typically *ipar(2)* = 0.

- *ipar(3)* = number of subintervals in the initial mesh. Typically *ipar(3)* = 0, in which case the number of subintervals is set to 5.

- *ipar(4)* = number of solution and derivative tolerances, with $0 < ipar(4) \leq m^*$.

- *ipar(5), ipar(6)* = dimensions of workspaces (vectors). Select a relatively large number for those parameters, say 10000 or 15000.

- *ipar(7)* determines the type of output produced by the function *bvode*. With *ipar(7) = -1*, *bvode* produces a full diagnostic printout, with *ipar(7) = 0* bvode produces selected printout, and with *ipar(7) = 1* bvode produces no printout.

- *ipar(8)* controls the type of mesh used in the solution. *ipar(8) = 0* bvode generates a uniform initial mesh.

- *ipar(9)* is used to indicate whether or not initial guesses for the solution are provided. For example, if *ipar(9) = 0*, bvode understands that no initial guess for the solution is provided.

- *ipar(10)* offers options for breaking out of function *bvode* in case convergence problems are detected. For regular problems use *ipar(10) = 0*.

- *ipar(11)* = number of fixed points in the mesh other than *xL* and *xR*. This number is the same as the dimension of *fixpnt*. Typically, *ipar(11) = 0*.

For the solution of the second-order boundary value problem described earlier in this section, the vector *ipar* can be put together as:

```
ipar=0*ones(1,11)
ipar(3)=1;ipar(4)=2;ipar(5)=10000;ipar(6)=2000;ipar(7)=1
```

Application of function *bvode* to a second order boundary value problem

The problem to be solved is the one that has been described above, namely,

$$d^2y/dx^2 = f(x,u) = cos(x) - u_1 - 5u_2,$$

subject to the boundary conditions

$$y(1) = 0.5 \text{ and } y'(2) = -1.5.$$

The parameters *n* and *m* in the call to function *bvode* for this problem are *n = 1* and *m = [2]*. Also, *fixpnt = 0*. Functions *f, df, g, dg,* and *guess* for this problem were defined earlier. We also defined the vectors *zeta* and *ipar*. The boundaries are located at *xL = 1* and *xR = 2*. Using an x-increment *Dx = 0.1*, we can define the solution points as *x = [xL:Dx:xR]*. There is a couple of arguments, namely, *ltol* and *tol* that need to be defined. Vector *ltol* indicates the indices of *u* for which a tolerance for convergence will be defined. For this case we can take *ltol = [1,2]* to define convergence tolerance for both the first and second components of *u*. The tolerances are relatively small numbers, say *tol = [1e-10, 1e-10]*.

Having defined all the arguments for function *bvode* we put all the steps leading to the function call together in the following SCILAB script:

```
//Script for 2nd order boundary value problem solution with bvode
    deff('[ff]   = f(x,u) ','ff=cos(x)-u(1)-5*u(2)');
    deff('[dff]  = df(x,u)','dff = [-1,-5]');
    deff('[gg]   = g(i,u) ',['gg=[u(1)-1,u(2)+1]','gg=gg(i)']);
    deff('[dgg]  = dg(i,u)',['dgg = [1,0;0,1]';'dgg=dgg(i,:)']);
    deff('[u0,du0] = guess(x)' , ['u0= 0', 'du0 =0']);
```

```
n=1;m=[2];fixpnt=0;xL=0;xR=2;Dx=0.1;
x = [xL:Dx:xR];
zeta=[xL,xR];

ipar=zeros(1,11);
ipar(3)=1;ipar(4)=2;ipar(5)=10000;ipar(6)=2000;ipar(7)=1;

ltol=[1,2];
tol=[1.e-5,1.e-5];

u=bvode(x,n,m,xL,xR,zeta,ipar,ltol,tol,fixpnt,f,df,g,dg,guess);

xset('window',1)
plot(x,u(1,:),'x','y(x)','BVODE 2nd order solution')

xset('window',2)
plot(x,u(2,:),'x','dy/dx','BVODE 2nd order solution')
```

Placing this script in file *bvp2* within the SCILAB working directory, it can be executed through:

```
-->exec('bvp2')
```

The resulting plot shows the solution for *y(x)* and *dy/dx* versus *x*:

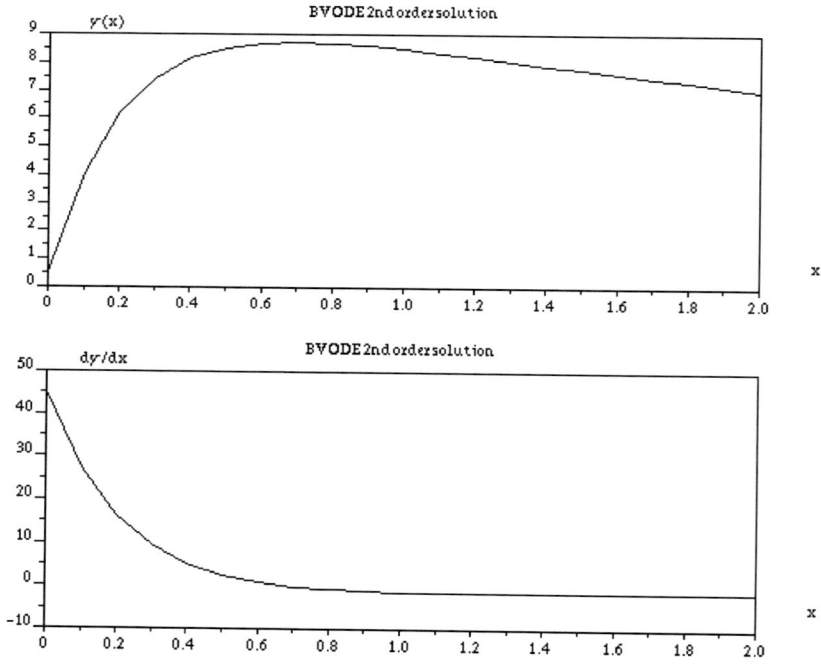

Function *bvode* applied to a third-order boundary value problem

Consider the third-order ordinary differential equation

$$x^2(d^3y/dx^3) + (1-x)(d^2y/dx^2) - 3(dy/dx) + y = x+1$$

subject to the boundary conditions $y(0) = 2.5$, $y(10) = 4.5$, $dy/dx|_{x=10} = -1$. To solve this problem using function *bvode* we first re-cast the differential equation as

$$d^3y/dx^3 = f(x,u) = (x+1-(1-x)u_3 - 3u_2 + u_1)/x^2$$

with $u_1 = y(x)$, $u_2 = dy/dx$, $u_3 = d^2y/dx^2$, and $u = [u_1;u_2;u_3]$. The boundary condition functions will be $g_1 = g(1,u) = u_1 - 2.5$, $g_2 = g(2,u) = u_1 - 4.5$, and $g_3 = g(3,u) = u_2 + 1$. The derivative functions will be $df = [1/x^2, -3/x^2, (1-x)]$, and $dg = [1,0,0;1,0,0;0,1,0]$. The zeta vector is $zeta = [0,10,10]$. Also, $n = 1$, $m = [3]$, $fixpnt = 0$.

The following script solves the boundary value problem and produces graphs of the function $y(x)$ and its first two derivatives:

```
//Script for 3rd order boundary value problem solution with bvode
deff('[ff]   = f(x,u) ','ff=(x+1-(1-x)*u(3)-3*u(2)+u(1))/x^2');
deff('[dff]  = df(x,u)','dff = [1/x^2,-3/x^2,(1-x)/x^2]');
deff('[gg]   = g(i,u) ',['gg=[u(1)-2.5,u(1)-4.5,u(2)+1]','gg=gg(i)']);
deff('[dgg]  = dg(i,u)',['dgg = [1,0,0;1,0,0;0,1,0]';'dgg=dgg(i,:)']);
deff('[u0,du0] = guess(x)' , ['u0= 0', 'du0 =0']);
n=1;m=[3];fixpnt=0;xL=0;xR=10;Dx=0.1;
x = [xL:Dx:xR];
zeta=[xL,xR,xR];
ipar=zeros(1,11);
ipar(3)=1;ipar(4)=3;ipar(5)=50000;ipar(6)=50000;ipar(7)=1;
ltol=[1,2,3];
tol=[1.e-5,1.e-5,1e-5];
u=bvode(x,n,m,xL,xR,zeta,ipar,ltol,tol,fixpnt,f,df,g,dg,guess);
xset('window',1);plot(x,u(1,:),'x','y(x)','BVODE 3rd order solution')
xset('window',2);plot(x,u(2,:),'x','dy/dx','BVODE 3rd order solution')
xset('window',3);plot(x,u(3,:),'x','d2y/dx2','BVODE 3rd order solution')
```

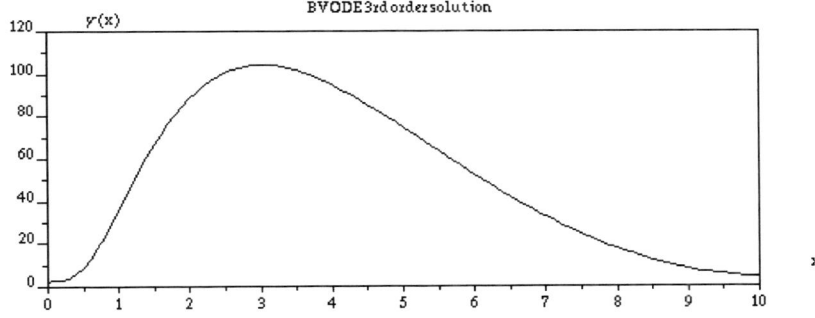

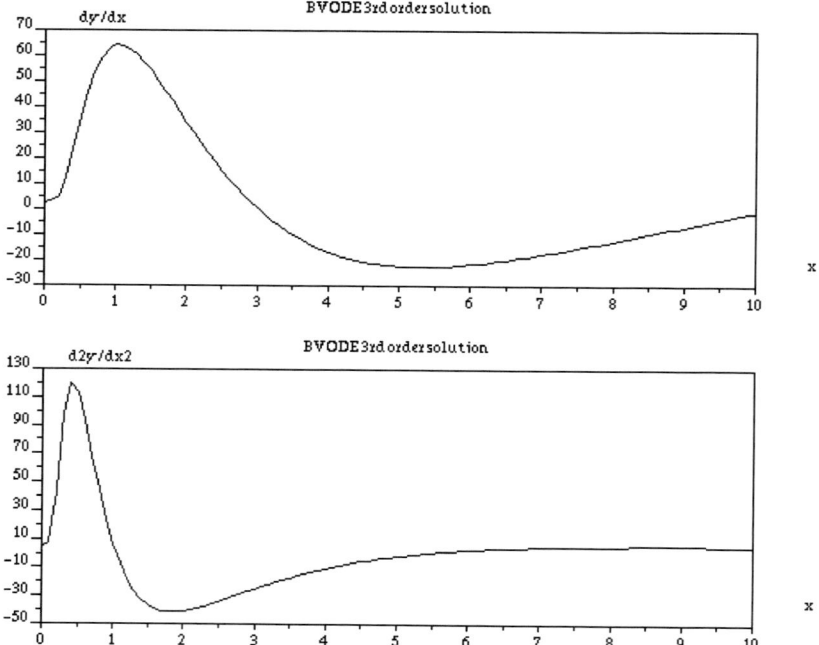

Application of *bvode* to a third-order problem with one interior fixed point

The following example solves the same third-order boundary value problem as before, except that now the boundary conditions are located at three different locations $y(0) = 2.5$, $y(5) = 4.5$, $y(10) = -1$. To account for boundary conditions at three different locations, it is necessary to change a few of the parameters in the script, including introducing $M = 5$, and using *fixpnt* = [5], zeta=[xL,xM,xR], ltol=[1], and tol=[1.e-5]. Also, the option *ipar(11)=1* is introduced.

```
//Script for 3rd order boundary value problem solution with bvode
//Case of three different boundary points
    deff('[ff]     = f(x,u) ','ff=(x+1-(1-x)*u(3)-3*u(2)+u(1))/x^2');
    deff('[dff]    = df(x,u)','dff  = [1/x^2,-3/x^2,(1-x)/x^2]');
    deff('[gg]     = g(i,u) ',['gg=[u(1)-2.5,u(1)-4.5,u(1)+1]','gg=gg(i)']);
    deff('[dgg]    = dg(i,u)',['dgg  = [1,0,0;1,0,0;1,0,0]';'dgg=dgg(i,:)']);
    deff('[u0,du0] = guess(x)' , ['u0= 0', 'du0 =0']);
    n=1;m=[3];fixpnt=[5];xL=0;xR=10;Dx=0.1;xM = 5;
    x = [xL:Dx:xR];
    zeta=[xL,xM,xR];
    ipar=zeros(1,11);
    ipar(3)=1;ipar(4)=1;ipar(5)=50000;ipar(6)=50000;ipar(7)=1;ipar(11)=1;
    ltol=[1];
    tol=[1.e-5];
```

```
u=bvode(x,n,m,xL,xR,zeta,ipar,ltol,tol,fixpnt,f,df,g,dg,guess);
xset('window',1)
plot(x,u(1,:),'x','y(x)','BVODE 3rd order solution')
xset('window',2)
plot(x,u(2,:),'x','dy/dx','BVODE 3rd order solution')
xset('window',3)
plot(x,u(3,:),'x','d2y/dx2','BVODE 3rd order solution')
```

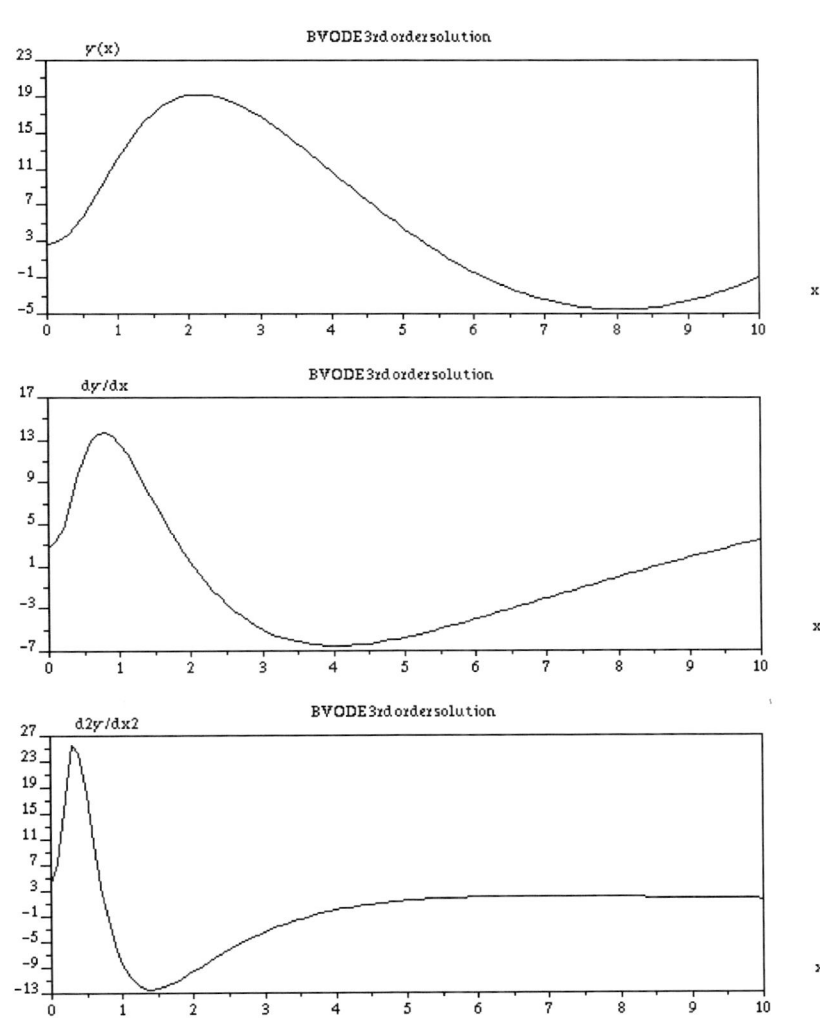

Application of *bvode* to a fourth-order problem with two interior fixed points

Consider the fourth-order ordinary differential equation

$$x^3(d^4y/dx^4) + 6x^2(d^3y/dx^3) + 6x(d^2y/dx^2) = (x+1)^{1/2},$$

subject to the boundary conditions $y(1) = 1$, $dy/dx|_{x=1.2} = -2$, $d^2y/dx^2|_{x=1.7} = -0.5$, $d^3y/dx^3|_{x=7} = -0.1$. With $u_1 = y$, $u_2 = dy/dx$, $u_3 = d^2y/dx^2$, $u_4 = d^3y/dx^3$, and $u_5 = d^4y/dx^4$, the fourth-order system is written as

$$d^5y/dx^5 = f(x,u) = (1-6x^2u_4 - 6xu_3)/x^3 + (x+1)^{1/2}.$$

The boundary conditions will be described by

$$g_1 = g(1,u) = u_1 - 1,\ g_2 = g(2,u) = u_2 + 2,\ g_3 = g(3,u) = u_3 + 0.5,\ g_4 = g(4,u) = u_3 + 0.1.$$

The derivatives of functions f and g are given by

$$df_1 = 0,\ df_2 = 0,\ df_3 = -6/x^2,\ df_4 = -6/x,$$

and

$$dg = \begin{bmatrix} 1 & 0 & 0 & 0 \\ 0 & 1 & 0 & 0 \\ 0 & 0 & 1 & 0 \\ 0 & 0 & 0 & 1 \end{bmatrix}.$$

The parameters *fixptn* and *ipar(11)* are redefined as *fixptn* = [1.2,1.7] and *ipar(11)* = 2. Since we have four possible derivatives to deal with in the boundary conditions we want to redefine *ltol* and *tol* as *ltol* = [1,2,3,4] and *tol*=[1e-5, 1e-5, 1e-5, 1e-5], respectively. The value of *ipar(4)* is changed to *ipar(4)* = 4. The value of *m* is changed to *m* = [4].

The following SCILAB script produces the solution for the problem just described.

```
//Script for 4th order boundary value problem solution with bvode
//Problem includes 2 interior points
    deff('[ff]   = f(x,u) ','ff=(1-6*x**2*u(4)-6*x*u(3))/x**3+sqrt(x+1)');
    deff('[dff]  = df(x,u)','dff = [0,0,-6/x**2,-6/x]');
    deff('[gg]   = g(i,u) ',['gg=[u(1)-1,u(2)+2,u(3)+0.5,u(4)+0.1]', 'gg=gg(i)']);
    deff('[dgg]  = dg(i,u)',['dgg = [1,0,0,0;0,1,0,0;0,0,1,0;0,0,0,1]';...
        'dgg=dgg(i,:)']);
    deff('[u0,du0] = guess(x)' , ['u0= 0', 'du0 =0']);
    n=1;m=[4];fixpnt=[1.3,1.7];xL=1;xR=2;Dx=0.1;x = [xL:Dx:xR];
    zeta=[1,1.3,1.7,2];
    ipar=zeros(1,11);
    ipar(3)=1;ipar(4)=4;ipar(5)=20000;ipar(6)=20000;ipar(7)=1
    ipar(11)=2;
    ltol=[1,2,3,4]
    tol=[1.e-11,1.e-11,1.e-11,1.e-11]
    u=bvode(x,n,m,xL,xR,zeta,ipar,ltol,tol,fixpnt,f,df,g,dg,guess);
    xset('window',1); plot(x,u(1,:),'x','y(x)','BVODE 4th order solution')
    xset('window',2); plot(x,u(2,:),'x','dy/dx','BVODE 4th order solution')
```

```
xset('window',3); plot(x,u(3,:),'x','d2y/dx2','BVODE 4th order solution')
```

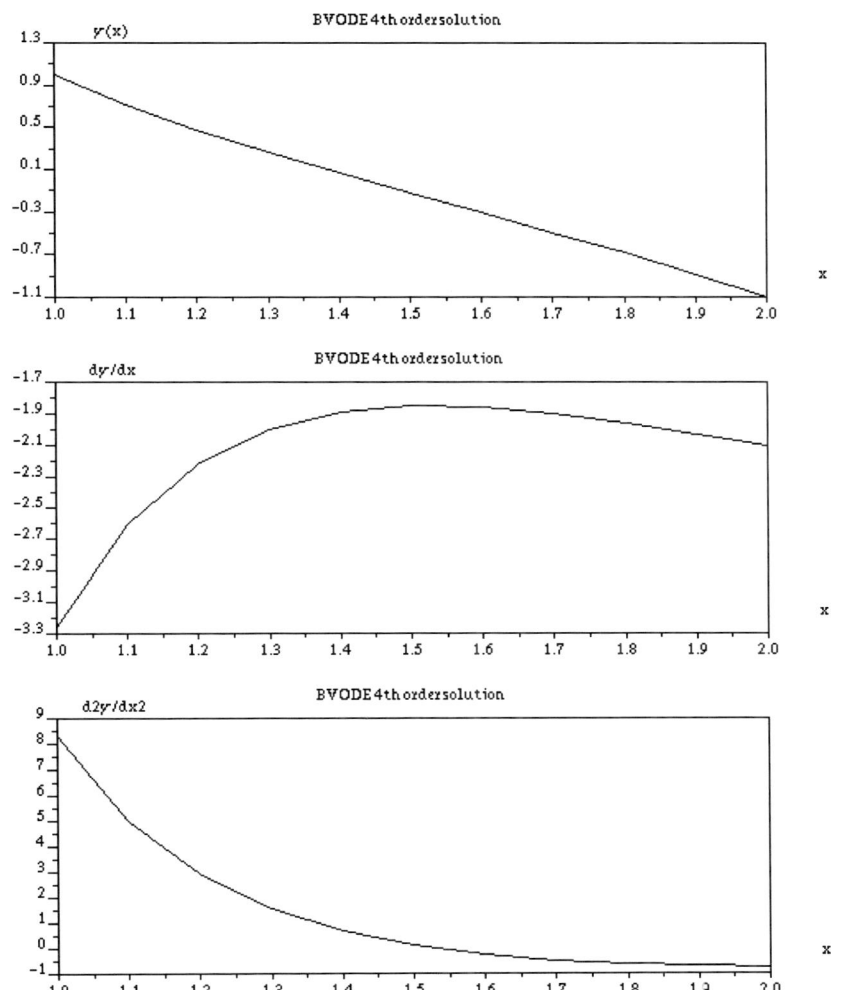

Boundary value problems with eigenvalues

Consider the boundary value problem

$$\frac{d^2y}{dx^2} + \lambda y = 0,$$

subject to $y(0) = 0$ and $y(L) = 0$, where λ is an unknown value. Assuming that $\lambda > 0$, the solution is a sinusoidal wave, i.e.,

$$y(x) = C_1 \sin(\sqrt{\lambda}x) + C_2 \cos(\sqrt{\lambda}x).$$

Replacing the boundary condition $y(0) = 0$ produces $0 = C_2$, thus, the solution reduces to

$$y(x) = C_1 \sin(\sqrt{\lambda}x).$$

The second boundary condition, namely $y(L) = 0$, produces the *eigenvalue* equation

$$0 = C_1 \sin(\sqrt{\lambda}L).$$

Since, in general, we want the constant C_1 to be different from zero, the equation is satisfied if

$$\sin(\sqrt{\lambda}L) = 0,$$

i.e., if $\sqrt{\lambda}L = \pi, 2\pi, \ldots$ Thus, the problem has an infinite number of eigenvalues $\lambda_n = n^2\pi^2/L^2$, $n = 1, 2, \ldots$ Associated with each eigenvalue is the eigenfunction $\sin(n\pi x/L)$. The most general solution to the original boundary value problem is a linear combination of the eigenfunctions, i.e.,

$$y(x) = \sum_{n=1}^{\infty} C_n \cdot \sin\left(\frac{n^2\pi^2 x}{L^2}\right).$$

Notice that the ordinary differential equation that defines the boundary value problem has a solution only for specific values of the constant λ.

Numerical solution to a boundary value problem with eigenvalues

Using finite difference approximations for the derivatives, it is sometimes possible to find a few eigenvalues of a boundary value problem such as the one described above. Using, for example, a centered finite difference formula for the derivative d^2y/dx^2, i.e.,

$$\frac{d^2y}{dx^2} \approx \frac{y_{i+1} - 2y_i + y_{i-1}}{(\Delta x)^2},$$

into the differential equation

$$\frac{d^2y}{dx^2} + \lambda y = 0,$$

produces the following difference equation

$$\frac{y_{i-1} - 2y_i + y_{i+1}}{(\Delta x)^2} = -\lambda \cdot y_i,$$

for $i=2,3,..,n-1$. Implied in the latter result is the fact that the range of values of x, i.e., $0 < x < L$, is divided into $n-1$ increments of size $\Delta x = L/(n-1)$. Thus, $y_i = y(x_i)$, where $x_i = i \cdot \Delta x$. Also, $y_1 = y(0) = 0$, and $y_n = y(L) = 0$.

The problem involves $n-2$ unknowns $y_2, y_3,..., y_{n-1}$, in $n-2$ equations. For example, for $L = 1$, $n = 5$, $\Delta x = 1/(5-1) = 0.25$, $1/(\Delta x)^2 = 16$. The general equation becomes

$$16 \cdot y_{i-1} - 32 y_i + 16 y_{i+1} = -\lambda \cdot y_i,$$

for $i=2,3,4$. We have, therefore, the following three equations:

$$16y_1 - 32y_2 + 16y_3 = -\lambda y_2,$$
$$16y_2 - 32y_3 + 16y_4 = -\lambda y_3,$$
$$16y_3 - 32y_4 + 16y_5 = -\lambda y_4.$$

With $y_1 = y_5 = 0$, the three equations result in

$$-32y_2 + 16y_3 = -\lambda y_2,$$
$$16y_2 - 32y_3 + 16y_4 = -\lambda y_3,$$
$$16y_3 - 32y_4 = -\lambda y_4.$$

The resulting system of equations can be written in matricial form as

$$\begin{bmatrix} 32 & -16 & 0 \\ -16 & 32 & -16 \\ 0 & -16 & 32 \end{bmatrix} \cdot \begin{bmatrix} y_2 \\ y_3 \\ y_4 \end{bmatrix} = \lambda \cdot \begin{bmatrix} y_2 \\ y_3 \\ y_4 \end{bmatrix},$$

or, with

$$\mathbf{A} = \begin{bmatrix} 32 & -16 & 0 \\ -16 & 32 & -16 \\ 0 & -16 & 32 \end{bmatrix}, \quad \mathbf{y} = \begin{bmatrix} y_2 \\ y_3 \\ y_4 \end{bmatrix},$$

as,
$$Ay = \lambda y.$$

This is the classical eigenvalue problem which can be solved using SCILAB function *spec* or the user-defined function *eigenvectors* developed in Chapter 5.

A function for calculating eigenvalues for a boundary value problem

The following function, *BVPeigen1*, programs the solution to the boundary value problem described earlier, namely,

$$\frac{d^2y}{dx^2} + \lambda y = 0,$$

subject to y(0) = 0 and y(L) = 0, where λ is an unknown value. The function call is

[x,y,lam] = BVPeigen1(L,n)

where x is a vector containing the values, xy is a matrix whose columns are the eigenvectors of the eigenvalue problem developed earlier (these eigenvectors are computed using function *eigenvectors*, developed in Chapter 5), and *lam* is a vector containing the *n* eigenvalues of the problem. The arguments of the function are the domain length *L* and the number of points in the solution *n*. The function also plots the eigenvectors for the first five eigenvalues found. These eigenvectors represent eigenfunctions $y_i(x)$. A listing of the function follows:

```
function [x,y,lam] = BVPeigen1(L,n)

Dx = L/(n-1);
x=[0:Dx:L];
a = 1/Dx^2;
k  = n-2;

A = zeros(k,k);
for j = 1:k
    A(j,j) = 2*a;
end;
for j = 1:k-1
    A(j,j+1) = -a;
    A(j+1,j) = -a;
end;

getf('eigenvectors');

[yy,lam]=eigenvectors(A);
//disp('yy');disp(yy);

y = [zeros(1,k);yy;zeros(1,k)];
//disp('y');disp(y);

xmin=min(x);xmax=max(x);ymin=min(y);ymax=max(y);
rect = [xmin ymin xmax ymax];
xset('window',1);xset('mark',[-1:-1:-10],1);
```

```
if k>=5 then
    m = 5;
else
    m = k;
end

for j = 1:m
    plot2d(x',y(:,j), j,'011',' ',rect);
    //plot2d(x',y(:,j),-j,'011',' ',rect);
end;
xtitle('Eigenfunctions for D2y+lam*y=0','x','y')
```

For example, for L = 1 and n = 5, the following solution is obtained:

```
-->getf('BVPeigen1')

-->[x,y,lam]=BVPeigen1(1,5)
 lam  = !   9.372583     32.     54.627417 !


 y    =

 !  0.            0.            0.         !
 !   .5         - .7071068      .5         !
 !   .7071068    3.140E-16    - .7071068 !
 !   .5           .7071068      .5         !
 !  0.            0.            0.         !
 x    =

 !  0.    .25    .5    .75    1. !
```

Notice that the first eigenvalue found is $\lambda_1 = 9.372583$, close to the theoretical value of $\pi^2 = 9.8696$. A plot of the eigenfunctions follows.

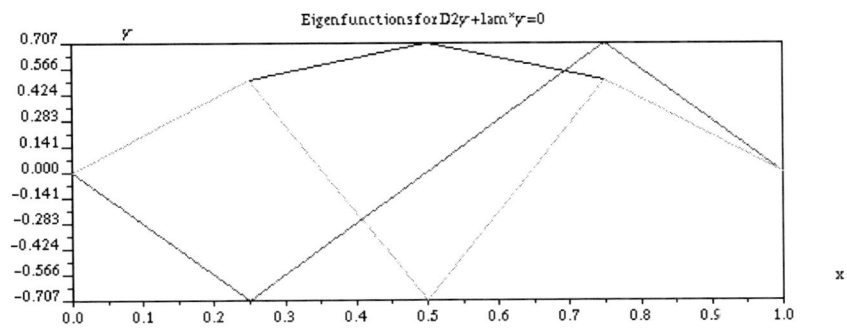

To see the eigenfunctions in a more continuous fashion, we call function BVPeigen1 using n = 50:

```
-->[x,y,lam]=BVPeigen1(1,50);
```

The first eigenvalue for $n=50$ is 9.866224 closer to the theoretical value of $\pi^2 = 9.8696$ than the first eigenvalue found earlier for $n=5$. The plot of the eigenfunctions for $n=50$ is shown below.

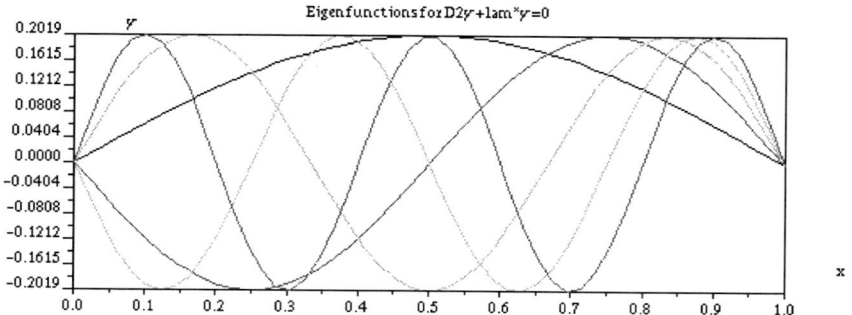

Notice that if the equation under consideration $d^2y/dx^2 + \lambda y = 0$, represents the equation of a vibrating string, the eigenfunctions represent what are referred to as the different modes of vibration of the string. The eigenvalues represent the different natural angular frequencies of vibration of the string.

Exercises

[1]. Determine the general solution to the following linear ordinary differential equations using the corresponding characteristic equation:

(a) $d^3y/dx^3 + 4(dy/dx) + 5y = 0$.
(b) $d^2y/dx^2 + 2(dy/dx) + y = 0$.
(c) $d^4y/dx^4 + d^2y/dx^2 + dy/dx + 3y = 0$
(d) $d^2y/dx^2 - 3y = 0$

[2]. Obtain the particular solution to the following second order equations:

(a) $d^2y/dx^2 + 3(dy/dx) + y = 2e^{-x}$
(b) $d^2y/dx^2 + 2y = 2x^2 + x$
(c) $d^2y/dx^2 + dy/dx = \sin(2x)$
(d) $d^2y/dx^2 + y = \cos x$

[3]. Plot the time variation of position, velocity, and acceleration of a damped mechanical oscillator for the following parameters:

(a) $m = 2$ kg, $\beta = 0.01$ Ns/m, $k = 2$ N/m, $x_0 = 0.2$ m, $v_0 = 1.2$ m/s
(b) $m = 4$ kg, $\beta = 0.10$ Ns/m, $k = 2$ N/m, $x_0 = 0.2$ m, $v_0 = 1.2$ m/s
(c) $m = 1$ kg, $\beta = 0.02$ Ns/m, $k = 2$ N/m, $x_0 = 0.2$ m, $v_0 = 1.2$ m/s
(d) $m = 0.5$ kg, $\beta = 0.25$ Ns/m, $k = 2$ N/m, $x_0 = 0.2$ m, $v_0 = 1.2$ m/s

[4]. Plot v-vs-x, a-vs-x, and a-vs-v phase portraits of the motions described in problem [3].

[5]. The mechanical oscillators described in problem [3] are subjected, respectively, to the driving forces shown below. In each case, plot the time variation of position, velocity, and acceleration of the resulting motions. Also, plot the v-vs-x, a-vs-x, and a-vs-v phase portraits of the motions.

(a) $F_0 = 2.5$ N, $\omega = 0.5$ rad/s
(b) $F_0 = 10$ N, $\omega = 0.05$ rad/s
(c) $F_0 = 0.5$ N, $\omega = 1.5$ rad/s
(d) $F_0 = 4$ N, $\omega = 0.25$ rad/s

[6]. For the following functions approximate the derivative df/dx at $x = a$ with $(f(a+h)-f(a))/h$ using values of $h = 0.1, 0.01, 0.001, 0.0001, 0.00001$. Plot the error involved in the numerical estimate of the derivative against the value of h.

(a) $f(x) = \sin(2x)$, $x = \pi$
(b) $f(x) = (x^2+3x)/(x+1)$, $x = 2$
(c) $f(x) = 1/(1+x^2)$, $x = -1$
(d) $f(x) = \tan(x)$, $x = \pi/4$

[7]. Repeat problem [4] but using a centered difference, i.e $(f(a+h)-f(a-h))/(2h)$.

[8]. Repeat problem [4] for the second derivative d^2f/dx^2 using the forward difference approximation $(f(a+2h)-2f(a+h)+f(h))/h^2$.

[9]. Repeat problem [4] for the second derivative d^2f/dx^2 using the centered difference approximation $(f(a-h)-2f(a)+f(a+h))/h^2$.

[10]. Given the ODE,

$$dy/dx = y \cdot \sin(x),$$

and the boundary condition,

$$y(0) = 1,$$

write a SCILAB function that uses the Euler method to obtain a numerical solution to this ODE in the interval $0 < x < 2.5$. Use $\Delta x = 0.25, 0.1,$ and 0.05. The exact solution is given by

$$y = 2/(\cos x + 1).$$

Plot the numerical solution against the exact solution for comparison.

[11]. Write a SCILAB function to produce an implicit solution for the first-order ODE from problem [10]. The exact solution is $y(x) = 1/x$.

[12]. Write a SCILAB function to complete the explicit solution for the second-order ODE $d^2y/dx^2 + y = 0$. An outline of the solution is presented elsewhere in this chapter. The exact solution is $y(x) = \sin x + \cos x$.

[13]. Write a SCILAB function to complete the implicit solution for the second-order ODE from problem [12]. The exact solution is $y(x) = \sin x + \cos x$.

[14]. Use SCILAB function ode to solve the following ordinary differential equations numerically. Plot the numerical results for the different values Δx.

(a) $dy/dx = xy + \sin(x)$, $y(0) = 1$, $a = 0$, $b = 1$, $\Delta x = 0.2, 0.1, 0.05, 0.01$
(b) $dy/dx = \sin(x)\cos(y)$, $y(0) = 0$, $a = 0$, $b = \pi$, $\Delta x = \pi/10, \pi/20, p/50, \pi/100$
(c) $dy/dx = \exp(xy)$, $y(0) = 1$, $a = 0$, $b = 10$, $\Delta x = 1, 0.5, 0.2, 0.1$
(d) $dy/dx = x^2 - \sin(x)$, $y(0) = 2$, $a = 0$, $b = 5$, $\Delta x = 0.5, 0.25, 0.1, 0.05$

[15]. Solve the following systems of differential equations using matrices. Plot the solutions against x.

(a) $dy_1/dx = 2y_1 - y_2$, $dy_2/dx = 2(y_2-y_1)$, $y_1(0) = 1$, $y_2(0) = -1$
(b) $dy_1/dx = -5y_1 + y_2 + x^2$, $dy_2/dx = -y_1-y_2 - 5x$, $y_1(0) = 0$, $y_2(0) = 2$
(c) $dy_1/dx = 2y_1 - y_2$, $dy_2/dx = 2y_2-y_1$, $dy_3/dx = y_3-y_1$, $y_1(0) = 1$, $y_2(0) = -1$, $y_3(0) = 2$
(d) $dy_1/dx = 2y_1 - y_2 + y_3 + x$, $dy_2/dx = -y_1 + 2y_2 - 2x$, $dy_3/dx = y_3-y_1$, $y_1(0) = 1$, $y_2(0) = -1$, $y_3(0) = 2$

[16]. Solve the systems of differential equations of problem [15] using SCILAB function ode. Plot the solutions against x.

[17]. Convert the following linear differential equations into systems of first-order ODEs and solve for y(x) using SCILAB function ode. Plot the solution y(x):

(a) $d^2y/dx^2 + dy/dx + 2y = x$, $y(0) = 1$, $dy/dx = -1$ at $x = 0$.
(b) $d^3y/dx^3 - 5(dy/dx) + y = 0$, $y(0) = 0$, $dy/dx = -1$ and $d^2y/dx^2 = 1$ for $x = 0$
(c) $d^3y/dx^3 - (d^2y/dx^2) + y = x$, $y(0) = 0$, $dy/dx = -1$ and $d^2y/dx^2 = 1$ for $x = 0$
(d) $d^2y/dx^2 + 2y = \sin(x)$, $y(0) = 1$, $dy/dx = -1$ at $x = 0$.

[18]. The figure below shows two particles P_1 and P_2, of mass m_1 and m_2, respectively, linked by three springs (k_A, k_B, k_C). The figure at the top represents the system in their state of equilibrium, while the one at the bottom shows the system at any generic point at time 0. The displacement of particle P_1 with respect to its equilibrium position is given by $x_1(t)$ while that of particle P_2 is given by $x_2(t)$. The corresponding velocities are $v_1 = dx_1/dt$ and $v_2 = dx_2/dt$. The magnitude of the forces applied by the springs on the particles are given by Hooke's law, $F = k(L-L_0)$, where L is the stretched length of the spring, L_0 is the unstretched length of the spring, and k is the spring constant. The particles are also provided by dashpots that produce a viscous damping force whose magnitude is given by $F = \beta v$, where b is a damping constant and v is the speed of the particle, i.e. $F = \beta (dx/dt)$, where x = position of the particle.

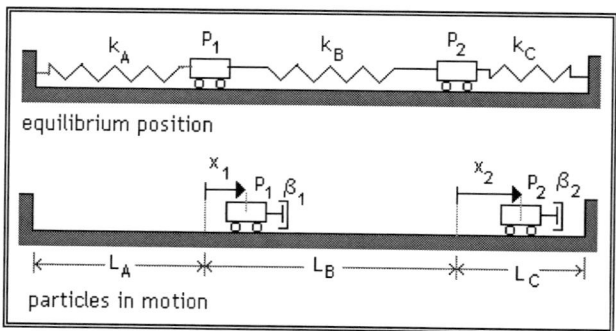

(a) Write down the differential equations describing the motion of the two linked particles including spring and damping forces as shown in the figure above.

(b) Solve for $x_1(t)$ and $x_2(t)$ if $m_1 = 10$ kg, $m_2 = 20$ kg, $k_A = 80$ N/m, $k_B = 120$ N/m, $k_C = 100$ N/m, $\beta_1 = 1$ N·s/m, $\beta_2 = 5$ N·s/m. The initial conditions are given by $x_1(0) = 0.5$ m, $x_2(0) = 0.25$ m, $v_1(0) = 0$, $v_2(0) = 1.0$ m/s. Plot the signals and the velocity versus time for $0 < t < 5$ s.

(c) Solve for $x_1(t)$ and $x_2(t)$ if $m_1 = 10$ kg, $m_2 = 20$ kg, $k_A = 80$ N/m, $k_B = 120$ N/m, $k_C = 100$ N/m, $\beta_1 = 0$, for values of $\beta_2 = 0, 0.1, 0.5, 1$, and 5 N·s/m. The initial conditions are given by $x_1(0) = 0.5$ m, $x_2(0) = 0.25$ m, $v_1(0) = 0$, $v_2(0) = 1.0$ m/s. Plot the signals and the velocity versus time for $0 < t < 5$ s for the different values of β_2.

(d) Write the differential equations for $x_1(t)$ and $x_2(t)$ if an external force $F_1 = F_0 \sin(\omega_0 t + \phi_0)$ is applied to particle P_1 in addition to the spring and damping forces.

(e) Using the conditions of part (a) of this problem solve for $x_1(t)$ and $x_2(t)$ for the case in which particle P_1 is subject to the external force $F_1 = F_0 \sin(\omega_0 t + \phi_0)$ with $F_0 = 20$ N, $\omega_0 = 2.5$ rad/s, and $\phi_0 = 1.5$ rad. Plot the signals, velocity, and acceleration versus time for $0 < t < 5$ s for the different values of β_2.

[19]. Consider the following two-loop electric circuit with R_1 = 2500 ohms, R_2 = 1500 ohms, R_2 = 1000 ohms, L_1 = 500 henrys, L_2 = 800 henrys, C_1 = 0.00006 farads, and C_2 = 0.001 farads.

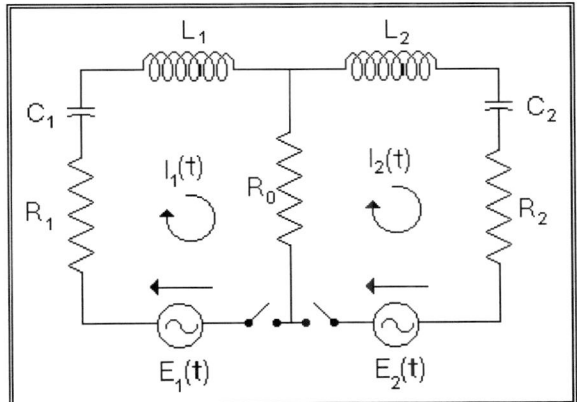

(a) Write down the system of differential equations describing the electric charges $q_1(t)$ and $q_2(t)$ in the capacitors C_1 and C_2, respectively, and the electric currents $I_1(t)$ and $I_2(t)$ in the loops when the switches are turned on.

(b) For $q_1(0) = 0$, $q_2(0) = 0$, $I_1(0) = 0$, $I_2(0) = 0$, $E_1(t) = 0$, $E_2(t) = 120 \cos(30t)$ volts, determine the electric currents $I_1(t)$ and $I_2(t)$. Plot the results for $0 < t < 120$ s.

(c) For $q_1(0) = 0$, $q_2(0) = 0$, $I_1(0) = 0.2$ amperes, $I_2(0) = 0.1$ amperes, $E_1(t) = 6$ volts, $E_2(t) = 12$ volts, determine the electric currents $I_1(t)$ and $I_2(t)$. Plot the results for $0 < t < 120$ s.

(d) For $q_1(0) = 50$ coulombs, $q_2(0) = 100$ coulombs, $I_1(0) = 0$, $I_2(0) = 0.12$ amperes, $E_1(t) = 6 \sin(10t)$ volts, $E_2(t) = 12 \cos(30t)$, determine the electric currents $I_1(t)$ and $I_2(t)$. Plot the results for $0 < t < 120$ s.

(e) For $q_1(0) = 0$, $q_2(0) = 0$, $I_1(0) = 0$, $I_2(0) = 0$, $E_1(t) = E_2(t) = 120 \cos(120t)$, determine the electric currents $I_1(t)$ and $I_2(t)$. Plot the results for $0 < t < 120$ s.

[20]. The Zeeman's equations can be used to model the fluctuations on the length of the heart's fibers as the heart pumps blood through the blood vessels of a human body:

$$dx/dt = k(-y - x^3/3 + rx)$$
$$dy/dt = x/k,$$

where x is a measure of the fiber length fluctuation y is a measure of the electrical stimulus that produces the fiber fluctuations, and k and r are constants. Solve the Zeeman's equation for the following parameters:

(a) $k = 0.5$, $p = 1$, $x(0) = 0$, $y(0) = -1$
(b) $k = 0.5$, $p = 5$, $x(0) = 0$, $y(0) = -1$
(c) $k = 0.5$, $p = 10$, $x(0) = 0$, $y(0) = -1$
(d) $k = 0.5$, $p = 20$, $x(0) = 0$, $y(0) = -1$

Plot the signals x vs. t, y vs. t, and the phase portrait x vs. y.

[21]. The Lorenz equations are used to simulate the convection of a layer of fluid of infinite horizontal extent heated from below. The model is a simplified version of the heating of the atmosphere. The equations are obtained by expanding the terms for temperature and pressure involved in the problem with their Fourier series expansion and simplifying the expansion to the first three modes represented by the variables y, and z. The resulting system of equations is

$$dx/dt = \sigma(-x+y)$$
$$dy/dt = rx - y - xz$$
$$dz/dt = xy - bz$$

where σ, r, and b are constants that result from combining physical parameters of the problem. (For a detailed derivation refer to Berge, P., Y. Pomeau, and C. Vidal, 1984 Order within Chaos - Towards a deterministic approach to turbulence," John Wiley & Sons, New York).

Solve the Lorenz equations for the following combination of parameters:

(a) $\sigma = 10$, $r = 25$, $b = 2.666$, $x_0 = 1$, $y_0 = 1$, $z_0 = 1$
(b) $\sigma = 10$, $r = 75$, $b = 2.666$, $x_0 = 1$, $y_0 = 1$, $z_0 = 1$
(c) $\sigma = 10$, $r = 25$, $b = 2.666$, $x_0 = 1$, $y_0 = 1$, $z_0 = 1$
(d) $\sigma = 10$, $r = 25$, $b = 2.666$, $x_0 = 1$, $y_0 = 1$, $z_0 = 1$

Plot the signals x-vs-t, y-vs-t, z-vs-t, as well as the phase portraits x-vs-y, x-vs-z, and y-vs-z.

[22]. The governing equation for a pendulum of length L is the second-order ODE,

$$d^2\theta/dt^2 + (g/L)\theta = 0,$$

where g is the acceleration of gravity, and θ is the angle measured from the vertical position of the string. Solve the pendulum equation for the following conditions:

(a) $L = 1.2$ m, $g = 9.806$ m/s^2, $\theta_0 = \pi/3$, $(d\theta/dt)_0 = -1$
(b) $L = 3$ ft, $g = 32.2$ ft/s^2, $\theta_0 = \pi/6$, $(d\theta/dt)_0 = 1$
(c) $L = 2.0$ m, $g = 9.806$ m/s^2, $\theta_0 = \pi/2$, $(d\theta/dt)_0 = -0.5$
(d) $L = 6$ ft, $g = 32.2$ ft/s^2, $\theta_0 = 3\pi/4$, $(d\theta/dt)_0 = -0.5$

Plot the signals θ-vs-t, and $(d\theta/dt)$-vs-t. Also, plot the phase portrait $d\theta/dt$-vs-θ.

[23]. Repeat the solutions of problem [22] if the pendulum is subjected to a periodic excitation so that the governing equation becomes

$$d^2\theta/dt^2 + (g/L)\,\theta = (F_0/(mL))\cos(\omega t + \phi).$$

The values to use for each of the cases in problem [22] are as follows:

(a) $F_0 = 2.5$ N, $m = 0.2$ kg, $\omega = \pi/2$ rad/s, $\phi = \pi/3$
(b) $F_0 = 0.5$ N, $m = 0.8$ kg, $\omega = 1.0$ rad/s, $\phi = 0$
(c) $F_0 = 1.5$ N, $m = 1.2$ kg, $\omega = 0.1$ rad/s, $\phi = 2\pi/3$
(d) $F_0 = 3.0$ N, $m = 0.1$ kg, $\omega = 0.05$ rad/s, $\phi = -\pi/3$

[24]. Solve the following boundary value problem using the shooting method.

(a) $d^2y/dx^2 + 3(dy/dx) + 2y = \sin(2x)$, $y(0) = 1$, $y(1) = 0$
(b) $d^2y/dx^2 - 3y = 1 + x$, $y(0) = -1$, $dy/dx|_{x=1} = -0.5$
(c) $d^2y/dx^2 + dy/dx = \ln(x)$, $dy/dx|_{x=0} = 0$, $y(1) = 1$
(d) $d^2y/dx^2 - dy/dx - y = 2\sin(x)$, $y(1) = -2$, $y(2) = 3$

[25]. Solve the boundary value ODEs of problem [24] by using an implicit solution with finite differences.

[26]. Solve the boundary value ODEs of problem [24] by using function bvode.

[27]. Solve the following boundary value ODEs using function bvode:

(a) $d^3y/dx^3 + y = 1 + x^2$, $y(0) = 1$, $y(1) = 2$, $y(3) = -1$
(b) $d^3y/dx^3 + d^2y/dx^2 = x$, $y(0) = 1$, $dy/dx|_{x=1} = -1$, $y(2) = 0$
(c) $d^2y/dx^2 - dy/dx = e^{-x/2}$, $dy/dx|_{x=0} = -1$, $y(1) = 2$
(d) $d^3y/dx^3 + dy/dx = -1 + x$, $y(0) = 1$, $dy/dx|_{x=2} = -1$, $d^2y/dx^2|_{x=2} = 1$

[28]. Determine the first n eigenvalues of the problem $d^2y/dx^2 + \lambda y = 0$, subject to $y(0) = 0$, $y(L) = 0$, for the following combinations of values of n and L:

(a) $n = 10$, $L = 10$ (b) $n = 20$, $L = 5$
(c) $n = 15$, $L = 1$ (d) $n = 30$, $L = 100$

[29]. For the differential equation

$$x^2(d^2y/dx^2) + x(dy/dx)' + (1+\lambda)y = 0, \quad y(1) = y(2) = 0,$$

use centered-difference approximations for the derivatives to perform an implicit numerical solution. Obtain the first 10 eigenvalues of the problem. Plot the corresponding eigenfunctions.

[30]. Solve the following system of equations

$$dx/dt = -y(x^2+y^2),$$

$$dy/dt = x(x^2+y^2),$$

for the initial conditions $x(0) = 2$, $y(0) = 1$. Plot the signals x-vs-t and y-vs-t, as well as the phase portraits x-vs-y, (dx/dt)-vs-x, (dy/dt)-vs-y, and (dy/dt)-vs-(dx/dt).

[31]. The following system of equations is known as a set of coupled logistic equations and can be used to model the behavior of two linked populations $x_1(t)$ and $x_2(t)$:

$$dx_1/dt = kx_1(1 - (x_1+x_2)/N),$$

$$dx_2/dt = kx_2(1 - (x_1+x_2)/N).$$

Solve the system for the following combination of parameters and initial conditions:

(a) $k = 1$, $N = 1$, $(x_1)_0 = 1$, $(x_2)_0 = 1$
(c) $k = 2.5$, $N = 10$, $(x_1)_0 = -2$, $(x_2)_0 = 0$

(b) $k = 0.5$, $N = 5$, $(x_1)_0 = 0$, $(x_2)_0 = -1$
(d) $k = 12$, $N = 25$, $(x_1)_0 = 1$, $(x_2)_0 = 1$

[32]. The governing equation for gradually varied flow in an open channel is given by

$$\frac{dy}{dx} = \frac{S_0 - S_f}{1 - F^2},$$

where S_0 is the slope of the channel bed, i.e., the rate of change of bed elevation z, with distance, x, along the channel bed $S_0 = -dz/dx$, S_f is the slope of the energy head, i.e., the rate of change of the total energy head, H (energy per unit weight), with $x S_f = -dH/dx$), and F is a dimensionless quantity known as the Froude number. The energy head, is the sum of the bed elevation z, the water depth y, and the velocity head (kinetic energy per unit weight) $V^2/(2g)$, i.e.,

$$H = z + y + V^2/2g,$$

where V is the flow velocity in the cross section (V = Q/A, Q = flow discharge, A = cross-sectional area). The energy slope is calculated by using Manning's equation with

$$S_f = \left(\frac{nQ}{C_u}\right)^2 \frac{P^{4/3}}{A^{10/3}},$$

where n is the Manning coefficient (a measure of the channel bed roughness C_u is a constant that depends on the system of units used $C_u = 1.0$ for the S.I., $C_u = 1.486$ for the English system), and P is the wetted perimeter of the cross-section (part of the channel cross-sectional perimeter in contact with the water).

The Froude number squared is calculated from

$$F^2 = \frac{Q^2 T}{g A^3},$$

where T is the top-width of the cross-section (i.e., the length of the free surface at the cross section).

For a trapezoidal section of bottom width b, side slope z, and depth y, the area, wetted perimeter, and top width are given by

$$A = (b+zy)y$$
$$P = b + 2y(1+z^2)^{1/2}$$
$$T = b + 2zy$$

For a trapezoidal cross-section open channel with $b = 2.5$ ft, $z = 1$, $S_0 = 0.00001$, $g = 32.2$ ft/s^2, $C_u = 1.486$, $n = 0.012$, $Q = 5.0$ ft^3/s, and with initial conditions $y = 2.5$ ft at $x = 10000$ ft, plot the solution $y(x)$ between $x = 0$ and $x = 10000$ ft.

Notes on problem [32]:
(1). A plot of the solution y-vs-x is called the water surface profile or a backwater curve. Backwater curves are created whenever there is a so-called *control point* in the channel. For example, the depth of 2.5 ft at position $x = 10000$ ft, used as initial conditions in this problem, could be created by a small sill placed across the channel at that position.

(2). At points where the energy slope S_f is the same as the bed slope, S_0, i.e., $S_f = S_0$, then $dy/dx = 0$. At those points the flow is said to have reached uniform conditions (uniform flow) and the constant depth thus achieved is referred to as the *normal depth*, y_n. You can check that for the conditions of the present problem $y_n = 2.311973$ ft by solving for y from the Manning's equation $S_f(y) = S_0$).

(3). At a point where the Froude number is equal to 1, the flow is said to be critical. The corresponding depth is referred to as the critical depth y_c. You can check that for the conditions of the present problem $y_c = 0.4673298$ ft by solving for y from the equation defining the Froude number squared, i.e. $F^2(y) = 1$.

Appendix A - REFERENCES

Abramowitz, M. and I.A. Stegun (editors), 1965, "*Handbook of Mathematical Functions with Formulas, Graphs, and Mathematical Tables*," Dover Publications, Inc., New York.

Arora, J.S., 1985, "*Introduction to Optimum Design*," Class notes, The University of Iowa, Iowa City, Iowa.

Asian Institute of Technology, 1969, "*Hydraulic Laboratory Manual*," AIT - Bangkok, Thailand.

Berge, P., Y. Pomeau, and C. Vidal, 1984, "*Order within chaos - Towards a deterministic approach to turbulence*," John Wiley & Sons, New York.

Bras, R.L. and I. Rodriguez-Iturbe, 1985, "*Random Functions and Hydrology*," Addison-Wesley Publishing Company, Reading, Massachussetts.

Brogan, W.L., 1974, "*Modern Control Theory*," QPI series, Quantum Publisher Incorporated, New York.

Browne, M., 1999, "*Schaum's Outline of Theory and Problems of Physics for Engineering and Science*," Schaum's outlines, McGraw-Hill, New York.

Farlow, Stanley J., 1982, "*Partial Differential Equations for Scientists and Engineers*," Dover Publications Inc., New York.

Friedman, B., 1956 (reissued 1990), "*Principles and Techniques of Applied Mathematics*," Dover Publications Inc., New York.

Gomez, C. (editor), 1999, "*Engineering and Scientific Computing with Scilab*," Birkhäuser, Boston.

Gullberg, J., 1997, "*Mathematics - From the Birth of Numbers*," W. W. Norton & Company, New York.

Harman, T.L., J. Dabney, and N. Richert, 2000, "*Advanced Engineering Mathematics with MATLAB® - Second edition*," Brooks/Cole - Thompson Learning, Australia.

Harris, J.W., and H. Stocker, 1998, "*Handbook of Mathematics and Computational Science*," Springer, New York.

Hsu, H.P., 1984, "*Applied Fourier Analysis*," Harcourt Brace Jovanovich College Outline Series, Harcourt Brace Jovanovich, Publishers, San Diego.

Journel, A.G., 1989, "*Fundamentals of Geostatistics in Five Lessons*," Short Course Presented at the 28th International Geological Congress, Washington, D.C., American Geophysical Union, Washington, D.C.

Julien, P.Y., 1998, "*Erosion and Sedimentation*," Cambridge University Press, Cambridge CB2 2RU, U.K.

Keener, J.P., 1988, *Principles of Applied Mathematics - Transformation and Approximation*," Addison-Wesley Publishing Company, Redwood City, California.

Kitanidis, P.K., 1997, *"Introduction to Geostatistics - Applications in Hydrogeology*," Cambridge University Press, Cambridge CB2 2RU, U.K.

Koch, G.S., Jr., and R. F. Link, 1971, *Statistical Analysis of Geological Data - Volumes I and II*," Dover Publications, Inc., New York.

Korn, G.A. and T.M. Korn, 1968, *Mathematical Handbook for Scientists and Engineers*," Dover Publications, Inc., New York.

Kottegoda, N. T., and R. Rosso, 1997, *Probability, Statistics, and Reliability for Civil and Environmental Engineers*," The Mc-Graw Hill Companies, Inc., New York.

Kreysig, E., 1983, *Advanced Engineering Mathematics - Fifth Edition*," John Wiley & Sons, New York.

Lindfield, G. and J. Penny, 2000, *Numerical Methods Using Matlab®*," Prentice Hall, Upper Saddle River, New Jersey.

Magrab, E.B., S. Azarm, B. Balachandran, J. Duncan, K. Herold, and G. Walsh, 2000, *An Engineer's Guide to MATLAB®*, Prentice Hall, Upper Saddle River, N.J., U.S.A.

McCuen, R.H., 1989, *"Hydrologic Analysis and Design - second edition*," Prentice Hall, Upper Saddle River, New Jersey.

Middleton, G.V., 2000, *Data Analysis in the Earth Sciences Using Matlab®*," Prentice Hall, Upper Saddle River, New Jersey.

Montgomery, D.C., G.C. Runger, and N.F. Hubele, 1998, *Engineering Statistics*," John Wiley & Sons, Inc.

Newland, D.E., 1993, *An Introduction to Random Vibrations, Spectral & Wavelet Analysis - Third Edition*," Longman Scientific and Technical, New York.

Nicols, G., 1995, "*Introduction to Nonlinear Science*," Cambridge University Press, Cambridge CB2 2RU, U.K.

Parker, T.S. and L.O. Chua, , *Practical Numerical Algorithms for Chaotic Systems*," 1989, Springer-Verlag, New York.

Peitgen, H-O. and D. Saupe (editors), 1988, *The Science of Fractal Images*," Springer-Verlag, New York.

Peitgen, H-O., H. Jürgens, and D. Saupe, 1992, *Chaos and Fractals - New Frontiers of Science*," Springer-Verlag, New York.

Press, W.H., B.P. Flannery, S.A. Teukolsky, and W.T. Vetterling, 1989, *Numerical Recipes - The Art of Scientific Computing (FORTRAN version)*," Cambridge University Press, Cambridge CB2 2RU, U.K.

Raghunath, H.M., 1985, *Hydrology - Principles, Analysis and Design*," Wiley Eastern Limited, New Delhi, India.

Recktenwald, G., 2000, *Numerical Methods with Matlab - Implementation and Application*," Prentice Hall, Upper Saddle River, N.J., U.S.A.

Rothenberg, R.I., 1991, *Probability and Statistics*," Harcourt Brace Jovanovich College Outline Series, Harcourt Brace Jovanovich, Publishers, San Diego, CA.

Sagan, H., 1961, *Boundary and Eigenvalue Problems in Mathematical Physics*," Dover Publications, Inc., New York.

Spanos, A., 1999, *Probability Theory and Statistical Inference - Econometric Modeling with Observational Data*," Cambridge University Press, Cambridge CB2 2RU, U.K.

Spiegel, M. R., 1971 (second printing, 1999), *Schaum's Outline of Theory and Problems of Advanced Mathematics for Engineers and Scientists*," Schaum's Outline Series, McGraw-Hill, New York.

Tanis, E.A., 1987, *Statistics II - Estimation and Tests of Hypotheses*," Harcourt Brace Jovanovich College Outline Series, Harcourt Brace Jovanovich, Publishers, Fort Worth, TX.

Tinker, M. and R. Lambourne, 2000, *Further Mathematics for the Physical Sciences*," John Wiley & Sons, LTD., Chichester, U.K.

Tolstov, G.P., 1962, *Fourier Series*," (Translated from the Russian by R. A. Silverman), Dover Publications, New York.

Tveito, A. and R. Winther, 1998, *Introduction to Partial Differential Equations - A Computational Approach*," Texts in Applied Mathematics 29, Springer, New York.

Urroz, G., 2000, *Science and Engineering Mathematics with the HP 49 G - Volumes I & II*", www.greatunpublished.com, Charleston, S.C.

Urroz, G., 2001, *Applied Engineering Mathematics with Maple*", www.greatunpublished.com, Charleston, S.C.

Winnick, J., , *Chemical Engineering Thermodynamics - An Introduction to Thermodynamics for Undergraduate Engineering Students*," John Wiley & Sons, Inc., New York.

Appendix B – INDEX

"

"File" menu, 4
"Functions" menu, 4

%

%e, 2
%eps, 2
%f, 2
%i, 2
%inf, 2
%pi, 2
%t, 2

A

Abort, 4
amplitude, 473
analytical complex function, 338
angular phase, 473
ans, 30
anti-symmetric matrix, 133
Apropos, 3
augmented matrix, 170

B

backward substitution, 169
Backwater curves, 564

C

capacitance, 484
Cartesian coordinates, 77
Cartesian representation of complex numbers, 248
*Cauchy-Riemann differentiability cond*itions, 338
center of mass, 95, 344
Change Directory, 4
characteristic equation, 261, 467
characteristic polynomial of a matrix, 190
cntl-N, 7
cntl-P, 7
colon (:) operator, 5
colormap, 37
command history, 7
Command Input, 7
Comments, 2

comparison operators, 14
complex conjugates, 470
concatenation, 6, 24
condition number of a matrix, 162
conditional constructs, 15
conservation of energy, 458
correlation coefficient, 236
Cramer's rule, 167
critical depth, 564
cross product, 81
cubic equations, 254

D

Debugging, 19
Define User Function, 4
definite integral, 335
del operator, 413
Demos, 4
density plot, 61
determinant of a matrix, 87, 163
diagonal matrix, 114
Dimensional analysis, 221
dimensional homogeneity, 221
Dirac's delta function, 228
directed segment, 79
direction cosines, 225
discretizing the domain, 490
dot vector product, 81

E

eigenvalue equation, 190
eigenvalues, 190
eigenvectors, 190
Einstein's summation convention, 117
electric current, 484
electrical circuit, 216
elements of a matrix, 114
energy line, 296
energy slope, 564
entropy, 455
error bars, 36
Euler formula, 248
Exec, 4
Exit, 4

F

facets, 67

factorial, 31
For loop, 15
forward elimination, 169
Frobenius norm, 20, 160
Froude number, 564
full matrix, 199
full pivoting, 179

G

Gaussian elimination, 169
Gauss-Jordan elimination, 188
Gauss-Seidel method, 214
Get Current Directory, 4
Getf, 4
global variable, 18
gradually varied flow, 563
graphics animation, 54
graphics window, 42
grayscale plot, 61

H

half-life, 456
harmonic functions, 338
harmonic motion, 473
heat transfer, 458
Help menu, 3
Histograms, 51
History, 4
hydraulic grade line, 296

I

identity matrix, 114
imaginary part, 248
imaginary unit, 248
inductance, 484
integrating factor, 466
internal vector product, 81
Interupt, 4
inverse matrix, 126

J

Jacobi iterative method, 214
Jacobian, 277

K

kinematic viscosity, 299
Kronecker's delta function, 115

L

labeled output, 29
Laurent series, 391
line integral, 340
linear equation systems, 143
linear systems, 6
Load, 4
local variable, 18
logical operators, 14
logistic equations, 563
Lorenz equations, 561
LU matrix decomposition, 152

M

main diagonal of a matrix, 114
Manning's coefficient, 308
Manning's equation, 308
mapping, 337
Matrices, 6
matrix *decomposition*, 152
mean value, 31
median, 31
moment of a force, 103
Moody diagram, 298
multiple linear fitting, 232

N

natural angular frequency, 473
natural logarithm, 297
non-singular matrix, 162
normal depth, 564
normal stress, 226
normal unit vector, 225

O

on-line functions, 17
orbits, 480
Orthogonal matrices, 156
Output, 7

P

parametric surface, 67
partial pivoting, 178
Pause mode, 4
pendulum equation, 562
permutation matrix, 179
phase portrait, 477
piezometric head, 296
pivot, 178
pixmap, 53

planar motion, 105
polar coordinates 77
polar representation of complex numbers, 248
Polynomial fitting, 234
polynomial long division, 390
polynomials, 91
position vector, 94
Principal stresses, 230
Projectile motion, 289
projection of a vector, 80
Pseudo-code, 255
pump rating curve, 304

Q

quadratic equations, 254

R

random numbers, 446
rational expression, 396
real part, 248
relative acceleration, 105
relative position vector, 99
relative velocity, 105
remainder, 400
resistance, 484
resonance, 481
Restart, 4
resultant, 97
Resume, 4
Reynolds number, 297
right-hand rule for vector product, 81
rigid body, 105
row vector, 113
Run bash command, 4

S

Save, 4
Scalars, 3
SCILAB graphic functions, 74
script file, 7
shear stress, 226
Show Commands, 4
Show Variables, 4
singular matrix, 162
Singular Value Decomposition, 156
singular values, 156
singular vectors, 156
Sparse matrices, 199

spline interpolation, 335
square matrix, 114
standard deviation, 31
steady-state response, 482
Stress at a point in a solid, 225
stress tensor, 227
String functions, 25
strings, 6
Structural mechanics, 218
sum of square errors, 236, 445
sum of squared totals, 236
superheated steam, 455
suspended sediment concentration, 384
SVD, 156
symmetric matrix, 133
Systeme Internationale, 308

T

tensor, 115
Thomas algorithm, 210
Topic, 3
TRACE, 168
trace of matrix, 168
transient response, 482
transpose of a matrix, 115
tridiagonal matrix, 115
tri-diagonal matrix, 209

U

unit vector, 80

V

vector field, 62
vector product, 81
vector triple product, 82
Vectors, 5
viscous damping force, 472
voltage, 484

W

wetted perimeter, 310
While loop, 15

Z

Zeeman's equations, 561

ABOUT THE AUTHOR

Gilberto E. Urroz is an Associate Professor of Civil and Environmental Engineering and a researcher at the Utah Water Research Laboratory, both at Utah State University, in Logan, Utah. He has been a teacher of engineering disciplines for more than 15 years both in his native Nicaragua and in the United States. His teaching experience includes courses on introductory physics, engineering mechanics, probability and statistics for engineers, computer programming, fluid mechanics, hydraulics, and numerical methods. His research interests include mathematical and numerical modeling of fluid systems, hydraulic structures, and erosion control applications. Dr. Urroz is an expert on the HP 48 G and HP 49 G series calculator, and on specialized mathematical software such as Maple and SCILAB. He has written several books on applications of these computing devices and software to disciplines such as engineering mechanics, hydraulics, and science and engineering mathematics.

ABOUT GREATUNPUBLISHED.COM

greatunpublished.com is a website that exists to serve writers and readers, and remove some of the commercial barriers between them. When you purchase a greatunpublished.com title, whether you receive it in electronic form or in a paperback volume or as a signed copy of the author's manuscript, you can be assured that the author is receiving a majority of the post-production revenue. Writers who join greatunpublished.com support the site and its marketing efforts with a per-title fee, and a portion of the site's share of profits are channeled into literacy programs.

So by purchasing this title from greatunpublished.com, you are helping to revolutionize the publishing industry for the benefit of writers and readers.
And for this we thank you.

181499